Cities
of Tomorrow

Cities
of Tomorrow

An Intellectual History
of Urban Planning and Design in the
Twentieth Century

PETER HALL

BLACKWELL
Oxford UK & Cambridge USA

Copyright © Peter Hall 1988

First published 1988
Reprinted 1989
First published in paperback 1990
Reprinted 1990, 1991, 1992, 1993, 1994

Blackwell Publishers
108 Cowley Road, Oxford OX4 1JF, UK

238 Main Street
Cambridge, Massachusetts 02142, USA

British Library Cataloguing in Publication Data
A CIP catalogue record for this book is available from the British Library.

Library of Congress Cataloging in Publication Data
Hall, Peter Geoffrey.
    Cities of tomorrow: an intellectual history of urban planning
    and design in the twentieth century / Peter Hall.
    p. cm.
    Bibliography, p.
    Includes index.
    1. City Planning—History—20th century. I. Title.
    HT166.H349 1988
    307.1'2'0904—dc19
    ISBN 0–631–17567–9 (pbk)

Typeset in 10 on 12 pt Baskerville by Photographics, Honiton, Devon
Printed in Great Britain by Hartnolls Ltd, Bodmin, Cornwall

This book is printed on acid-free paper

For Berkeley

Contents

List of Figures

Preface

Anyone who writes a history of planning should probably start the preface in self-defence: surely planners should plan, not retreat into reminiscence. Simply, I wrote this because I found the subject intriguing. As elsewhere in human affairs, we too often fail to realize that our ideas and actions have been thought and done by others, long ago; we should be conscious of our roots. I rest my plea.

Unfashionably, I had no grant, hence no benefactor to thank; nor an assistant, hence no one to blame but me. And, since I also typed it, I should first thank the anonymous authors of WordStar and WordPerfect; Chuck Peddle for his legendary Sirius I; and the unknown cottage-fabricators of the Taiwanese clone that – following the iron laws of peripheral Fordism – latterly replaced it in my study. Rosa Husain deftly typed the references and turned them into footnotes, thereby initiating herself into the pleasures and the terrors of WordPerfect's macros.

But, as ever, I want to thank the librarians. Those who argue for the law of declining public services, and we are all occasionally goaded into joining them, must never use the great reference libraries of the world. I have been privileged to spend much pleasurable time in three of them while researching this book: the British Library Reference Division (alias the British Museum Reading Room), the British Library of Political and Economic Science (the LSE Library) and the Library of the University of California, Berkeley. My tribute to the devoted staff in all three. And, though perhaps invidious, a special thanks to Elizabeth Byrne for her transformation of Berkeley's Environmental Design Library into the splendid place it is today.

Small bits of the text had previous incarnations: the start of chapter 4, as an article in *New Society* (republished in *Town and Country Planning*, then in an anthology *Founders of the Welfare State*, edited by Paul Barker); morsels throughout, in Tony Sutcliffe's *Metropolis 1890–1940*; a section in chapter 9, published many years ago in *Man in the City of the Future*, edited by Richard Eells and Clarence Walton. I think I wrote them right first time; so no apology for self-plagiarism. And chapter 12 contains a brief piece of autobiography, that I judged necessary to tell the tale properly; hence the apparent immodesty.

My publisher, John Davey, showed great forbearance. I hope that he finds the result worth while. Elizabeth Lake did a splendid job on the pictures.   Very special thanks go to the two colleagues and good friends who acted guinea pig by reading the first draft: Lyn Davies in Reading and Roger Montgomery in Berkeley. I cannot hope to have satisfied them, but I do plead in defence that I have taken very careful note of their comments. And thanks also to Carmen Hass-Klau, for her nick-of-time detection of certain howlers in the German history.

Lastly thanks, as ever, to Magda for impeccable logistical support services; and more besides.

Peter Hall
Berkeley and London.

Acknowledgements

The author and publishers wish to thank the following who have kindly given permission to quote from the following: John Murray (Publishers) Ltd., for 'Slough' from John Betjeman *Collected Poems*.

The author and publishers are also grateful to the following for their kind permission to reproduce illustrations: Aerofilms Ltd. 3.12; © 1988 The Art Institute of Chicago, All Rights Reserved, 6.1 (Portrait of Daniel Henry Burnham), 6.2, 6.3 (D. H. Burnham and E. H. Bennett *Plan of Chicago*, 1908, plate 85 *Plan of a complete system of street circulation* . . . and plate 132 *View looking west of the proposed Civic Center Plaza* . . . by Jules Guerin, on permanent loan to the Art Institute of Chicago from the City of Chicago); Australian Overseas Information Service, Canberra 6.7, 6.8; BBC Hulton Picture Library 10.1, Bodleian Library, Oxford 2.5, 2.6 (R. W. DeForest & L. Veiller *The Tenement House Problem*, 1903, 247554.d.2, p. 10, opp. p. 14), 3.9 (R. Unwin *Nothing Gained by Overcrowding!*, 1912, 2479116.d.4(6), p. 9, fig. 111), 3.10 (Ministry of Health *Type Plans and Elevations*, H.M.S.O. 1920, 2279.c.10.(10), plate 9), 4.8 (R. Unwin *Town Planning in Practice*, 1920, 2479116.d.5, p. 172, plate 116), 7.8 (J. H. Forshaw & P. Abercrombie *County of London Plan*, 1943, G.54.c.17.40.3, frontispiece); Bodleian Library and Hodder & Stoughton Ltd. 3.7 (R. Reiss *The Home I Want*, 1919, 24755.e.77, jacket illustration); Chicago Historical Society 12.1, 12.3, 12.4 (photograph by Jun Fujita); Columbia University Libraries, Rare Book and Manuscript Library, Columbia University 4.21; Cornell University Libraries, Department of Manuscripts and University Archives, Cornell University 4.16; Country Life 6.6; Country Life Books 6/4; © DACS 1988 7.3; Armand Dayot *Louis XIV, Illustrations d'apres de Peintures, Sculptures, Gravures, Objets, etc., du temps* (Flammarion, 1909) 7.2; First Garden City Heritage Museum, Letchworth 4.4, 10.2; Peter Hall, Harry Gracey, Roy Drewett & Ray Thomas *The Containment of Urban England*, 1973, by permission of Unwin Hyman Limited 5.8; The Hampstead

Garden Suburb Archives Trust 4.7; David Hoffman 12.6, 12.7; Holiday Inn 9.8; Fried. Krupp GmbH, Historical Archive 4.12; Osbert Lancaster *Here of all Places* (1959) by permission of John Murray Publishers Ltd. 3.11; Landesbildstelle Berlin 2.4, 6.9; Liverpool Daily Post & Echo Ltd. 11.1; London Borough of Ealing, Central Library, Local History Library 3.3, 4.6; London Docklands Development Corporation 11.5; London Transport Museum 3.4, 3.5, 3.6; Mary Lutyens 6.5; Mansell Collection 2.2, 2.3; Moorland-Spingarn Research Center, Howard University 12.5; Sophie Mumford 5.2; Museum of the City of New York 9.1; Museum of London 2.1; National Library of Scotland (photographs: Antonia Reeve) 5.1, 5.4, 5.5; J. C. Nichols Company 9.4; N.Y. Daily News 9.2; Popperfoto 7.1; Joseph Rowntree Memorial Trust 4.5; St. Louis Post-Dispatch 7.11; St. Louis Public Library 7.10; Madhu Sarin 7.4, 7.5; Scottish Tourist Board 5.3; Tennessee Valley Authority 5.7; Town and Country Planning Association 3.8, 4.1, 4.9, 4.10, 4.11, 8.2; John F. C. Turner 8.1; University of Illinois at Chicago, The University Library 2.7, 2.8, 2.9 (Jane Addams Memorial Collection) 12.2 (Chicago Woman's Aid Society Records); Venturi, Rauch and Scott Brown 9.7; The Frank Lloyd Wright Memorial Foundation, Copyright © The Frank Lloyd Wright Foundation 1958 9.5. All other photographs were kindly supplied by the author.

Cities of Imagination

Then I asked: "does a firm perswasion that a thing is so, make it so?"
He replied: "All Poets believe that it does, & in ages of imagination this firm perswasion removed mountains; but many are not capable of a firm perswasion of any thing."

William Blake
The Marriage of Heaven and Hell (*c.* 1790–3)

Chr.: Sir, said *Christian*, I am a Man that am come from the City of *Destruction*, and am going to the *Mount Zion*, and I was told by the man that stands by the Gate at the head of this way; that if I called here, you would shew me excellent things, such as would be an help to me in my Journey.

John Bunyan
The Pilgrim's Progress (1678)

For we must consider that we shall be a city upon a hill. The eyes of all people are upon us, so that if we deal falsely with our God in this work we have undertaken, and so cause Him to withdraw His present help from us, we shall be made a story and a byword through the world.

John Winthrop
A Model of Christian Charity (1630)

. . . on a huge hill,
Cragg'd, and steep, Truth stands, and hee that will
Reach her, about must, and about must goe;
And what the hills suddennes resists, winne so . . .

John Donne
Satyre III (1594–5)

I

Cities of Imagination

Alternative Visions of the Good City,
1880–1987

'Practical men, who believe themselves to be quite exempt from any intellectual influences, are usually the slaves of some defunct economist': thus Keynes, in a celebrated passage at the end of the *General Theory*. 'Madmen in authority', he wrote, 'who hear voices in the air, are distilling their frenzy from some academic scribbler of a few years back.'[1] For economists, he might as aptly have substituted planners. Much if not most of what has happened – for good or for ill – to the world's cities, in the years since World War Two, can be traced back to the ideas of a few visionaries who lived and wrote long ago, often almost ignored and largely rejected by their contemporaries. They have had their posthumous vindication in the world of practical affairs; even, some might say, their revenge on it.

This book is about them, their visions, and the effect of these on the everyday work of building cities. Their names will repeatedly recur, as in some Pantheon of the planning movement: Howard, Unwin, Parker, Osborn; Geddes, Mumford, Stein, MacKaye, Chase; Burnham, Lutyens; Corbusier; Wells, Webber; Wright, Turner, Alexander; Friedmann, Castells, Harvey. The central argument can be succinctly summarized: most of them were visionaries, but for many of them their visions long lay fallow, because the time was not ripe. The visions themselves were often utopian, even millenarian: they resembled nothing so much as secular versions of the seventeenth-century Puritans' Celestial City set on Mount Zion, now brought down to earth and made ready for an age that demanded rewards there also. When at last the visions were discovered and resuscitated, their implementation came often in very different places, in very different circumstances, and often through very different mechanisms, from those

[1] Keynes, 1936, 383.

their inventors had originally envisaged. Transplanted as they were in time and space and socio-political environment, it is small wonder that the results were often bizarre, sometimes catastrophic. To appreciate this, it is thus important first to strip away the layers of historical topsoil that have buried and obscured the original ideas; second to understand the nature of their transplantation.

The Anarchist Roots of the Planning Movement

Specifically, the book will argue that in this process of belatedly translating ideal into reality, there occurred a rather monstrous perversion of history. The really striking point is that many, though by no means all, of the early visions of the planning movement stemmed from the anarchist movement, which flourished in the last decades of the nineteenth century and the first years of the twentieth. That is true of Howard, of Geddes and of the Regional Planning Association of America, as well as of many derivatives on the mainland of Europe. (To be sure, it was very definitely untrue of Le Corbusier, who was an authoritarian centralist, and of most members of the City Beautiful movement, who were faithful servants of finance capitalism or totalitarian dictators.) The vision of these anarchist pioneers was not merely of an alternative built form, but of an alternative society, neither capitalistic nor bureaucratic-socialistic: a society based on voluntary co-operation among men and women, working and living in small self-governing commonwealths. Not merely in physical form, but also in spirit, they were thus secular versions of Winthrop's Puritan colony of Massachusetts: the city upon a hill. When however the time at last came for their ideals to be translated into bricks and mortar, the irony was that – more often than not – this happened through the agency of state bureaucracies, which they would have hated. How this came about, how far it was responsible for the subsequent disillusionment with the idea of planning, will be a central question that the book must address.

Neither the idea, nor its treatment here, is new or novel. The anarchist roots of planning have been well dissected by a number of writers, notably Colin Ward in Britain and Clyde Weaver in the United States.[2] I owe a great personal debt to them, both through their writings and through conversations with them. And this account will rely, for much of the essential background, on secondary sources; the history of planning now has an extremely rich literature, which I have plundered freely. So this book is to be judged as a work of synthesis, rather than of original research. There is however an important exception: I have tried to allow the key figures, the sources of the main ideas, to tell them in their own words.

[2] Ward, 1976; Friedmann and Weaver, 1979; Weaver, 1984a.

A Warning: Some Boulders in the Trail

The job will not always be easy. Visionaries are apt to speak in strange tongues, difficult to interpret; a striking common feature of many – though mercifully not all – of the great founding figures of planning is their incoherence. Their primitive disciples, all too anxious to undertake the task, may create a gospel at variance with the original texts. The ideas may derive from those of others and in turn feed back into their sources, creating a tangled skein that is difficult to disentangle. The cultural and social world they inhabited, which provided the essential material for their perceptions, has long since vanished and is difficult to reconstruct: the past *is* a foreign country, with a different language, different social mores, and a different view of the human condition.

I have tried, as far as possible, to let the founders tell their own tales. Since some of them tell theirs discursively or obscurely or both, I have wielded a heavy, but I hope a judicious, axe: I have eliminated verbiage, removed parentheses, elided thoughts that seemed to require it, thus to try to do for them what they might have wished for themselves.

If all that is hard enough, even harder is the job of understanding how, eventually, the ideas came to be rediscovered and rehabilitated and sometimes perverted. For here, large questions of historical interpretation enter in. A now powerful, even dominant, school argues that planning, in all its manifestations, is a response of the capitalist system – and in particular of the capitalist state – to the problem of organizing production and especially to the dilemma of continuing crises. According to this interpretation, the idea of planning will be embraced – and the visions of the pioneers will be adopted – precisely when the system needs them, neither sooner nor later. Of course, the primitive simplicity of this reciprocating mechanism is concealed by a complex mass of historical pulleys and belts: Marxist historians, too, allow that time and chance happeneth – within limits – to us all. But the limits are real: finally, it is the technological-economic motor that drives the socio-economic system and, through it, the responses of the political safety-valve.

Anyone purporting to write history at all – and especially in a field such as this, where so many sophisticated Marxian intelligences have laboured – must take a stand on such para-theological questions of interpretation. I might as well take mine now: historical actors do perform in response to the world they find themselves in, and in particular to the problems that they confront in that world. That, surely, is a statement of the blindingly obvious; ideas do not suddenly emerge, by some kind of immaculate conception, without benefit of worldly agency. But equally, human beings – especially the most intelligent and most original among them – are almost infinitely quirksy and creative and surprising; therefore, the real interest in history, beyond the staggeringly self-evident, lies in the complexity and variability of the human reaction. Thus, in this book, the Marxian basis of historical events is taken almost as a given; what can make history worth writing, and what can make some history worth reading, is the understanding of all the multifarious ways in which the general stimulus is related to the particular response.

Another personal statement had better be made now. Because of the vastness of the subject, I have had to be highly selective. The choice of major themes, each of which forms the subject matter of one chapter, is necessarily personal and judgemental. And I have deliberately made no attempt to conceal my prejudices: for me, however unrealistic or incoherent, the anarchist fathers had a magnificent vision of the possibilities of urban civilization, which deserves to be remembered and celebrated; Le Corbusier, the Rasputin of this tale, in contrast represents the counter-tradition of authoritarian planning, the evil consequences of which are ever with us. The reader may well disagree with these judgements, at least with the intemperance with which they are sometimes put; I would plead that I did not write the book with cosy consensus in mind.

There is another problem, of a more pedestrian technical kind. It is that many historical events stubbornly refuse to follow a neat chronological sequence. Particularly is this true of the history of ideas: the products of human intelligence derive from others, branch out, fuse, lie dormant or are awakened in exceedingly complex ways, which seldom permit of any neat linear description. Worse, they do not readily submit to any schematic ordering either. So the analyst who seeks to write an account around a series of main themes will find that they criss-cross in a thoroughly disorderly and confusing way. He will constantly be reminded of the advice from the stage Irishman in that old and overworked tale: to get to there, he shouldn't start from here at all. The solution perforce adopted here is to tell each story separately and in parallel: each theme, each idea, is traced through, sometimes down six or seven decades. That will mean constantly going back in history, so that quite often things will come out backwards-forwards. It will also mean that quite often, the order in which you read the chapters does not much matter. That is not quite true; I have given much thought to putting them in the least confusing sequence, that is, the most logical in terms of the evolution and interaction of ideas. But a warning is due: often, it will not quite work out.

And this problem is compounded by another. In practice, the planning of cities merges almost imperceptibly into the problems of cities, and those into the economics and sociology and politics of cities, and those in turn into the entire socio-economic-political-cultural life of the time; there is no end, no boundary, to the relationships, yet one – however arbitrary – must be set. The answer here is to tell just so much about the world as is necessary to explain the phenomenon of planning; to seat it firmly, Marxian-fashion, on its socio-economic base, thus to begin the really interesting part of the historian's task.

Even that decision leaves remaining boundary disputes. The first concerns the meaning of that highly elastic phrase, city (or town) planning. Almost everyone since Patrick Geddes would agree that it has to include the planning of the region around the city; many, again following the lead of Geddes and of the Regional Planning Association of America, would extend that to embrace the natural region, such as a river basin or a unit with a particular regional culture. And virtually all planners would say that their subject includes not merely the planning of one such region, but the relationships between them: for instance, the centrally important topic of the relationship between the spreading Megalopolis and the depopulating countryside. But where, then, does the subject stop? It immediately embraces regional economic planning, which is logically inseparable from national economic planning, and thus from the general question of economic development; again, the spreading circles threaten to embrace the whole world of discourse. There has to be a more-or-less arbitrary boundary line; I shall draw it to include general discussions of national urban and regional policies, but to exclude questions of pure economic planning.

The secondary boundary problem is when to start. This is, or was, supposed to be a history of planning in the twentieth century. But, since the subject matter originated in reaction to the nineteenth-century city, it is clearly necessary to start there: specifically, in the England of the 1880s. But the ideas that circulated then can be traced back, at least to the 1880s and 1840s, perhaps to the 1500s. As usual, history is a seamless web, a Gordian knot, requiring some more-or-less arbitrary unpickings in order to get started.

There is yet a third boundary problem: a geographical one. This is supposed to be a global history, yet – given the all-too-evident confines of space and of the author's competence – it must fail in the endeavour. The resulting account is glaringly Anglo-Americocentric. That can be justified, or at least excused: as will soon be seen, so many of the key ideas of twentieth-century western planning were conceived and nurtured in a remarkably small and cosy club based in London and New York. But this emphasis means that the book deals all too shortly with other important planning traditions, in France, in Spain and Latin America, in the Russian Empire and the Soviet Union, in China. Those must provide matter for other books by other hands.

Finally, this is a book about ideas and their impacts. So the ideas are central and front of stage; the impacts on the ground are clearly crucial too, but they will be treated as expressions – sometimes, to be sure, almost unrecognizably distorted – of the ideas. This helps explain two of the book's major idiosyncrasies. First, since the ideas tended to come early, it is heavily biased toward the first forty years of the century. Secondly and associatedly, many key showpieces of actual planning on the ground get treated cursorily, or even not at all. Books, like other noxious substances, should carry warnings, and the message here should read: Do not attempt to read this as a textbook of planning history; it may be dangerous to your health, especially in preparing for student examinations.

All of this, inevitably, is by way of apologia. The critics may have their field day with the book's obvious omissions and confusions; meanwhile – to ward off some of their strictures, and to guard potential buyers against rash expenditure and consequent disgruntlement – I need now to set down the main lines of argument in slightly more detail, so as to provide some guide through the coming thickets.

A Guide Through the Maze

The book says, first and by way of preliminary, that twentieth-century city planning, as an intellectual and professional movement, essentially represents a reaction to the evils of the nineteenth-century city. That is one of those statements that are numbingly unoriginal, but also desperately important: many of the key ideas, and key precepts, cannot be properly understood save in that context. Secondly, and centrally, it says that there are just a few key ideas in twentieth-century planning, which re-echo and recycle and reconnect. Each in turn stems from one key individual, or at most a small handful of such: the true founding fathers of modern city planning. (There were, alas, almost no founding mothers; of the consequences, the reader must judge.) These sometimes reinforce each other, often come into conflict: as with Blake's visions of Christ, one man's is another's greatest enemy.

Chapter 2 argues the point about the nineteenth-century origins of twentieth-century planning. It tries to show that the concerns of the pioneers arose, objectively enough, from the plight of the millions of poor trapped in the Victorian slums; that, less worthily but quite understandably, those who heeded their message may also have been obsessed with the barely suppressed reality of violence and the threat of insurrection. Though the problem, and some of the resulting concern, were replicated in every great western city, they were most evident and certainly most felt in the London of the mid-1880s, an urban society racked by huge social tensions and political ferment; hence the chapter's main focus.

Chapter 3 goes on to suggest a central irony: even as the first tentative experiments were made in creating a new planned social order, so the market began to dissolve the worst evils of the slum city through the process of mass suburbanization, though only at the expense – arguably and certainly not as self-evidently – of creating others. Again, for several decades London led the world in this process, though to do so it imported American transportation technologies and entrepreneurship. So, here too, the Anglo-American focus must remain; but with a prolonged sideways glance, to ask why Paris and Berlin were so slow to follow suit.

The first and overwhelmingly the most important response to the Victorian city was the garden-city concept of Ebenezer Howard, a gentleman amateur (there being, by definition, no professionals then), of great vision and equal persistence, who conceived it between 1880 and 1898. It proposed to solve, or at least to ameliorate, the problem of the Victorian city by exporting a goodly proportion of its people and its jobs to new, self-contained, constellations of new towns built in open countryside, far from the slums and the smoke – and, most importantly, from the overblown land values – of the giant city. As Chapter 4 will show, it reverberated around much of the world, in the process acquiring some strange guises that made it sometimes well-nigh unrecognizable. These manifestations ranged all the way form pure dormitory suburbs, which ironically represented the complete antithesis of all Howard stood for, to utopian schemes for the depopulation of great cities and the recolonization of the countryside. Some of these variants, as well as the purer Howardian vision, were executed by his lieutenants, who thereby acquired their own special niche in the pantheon of planning, second only to his: Raymond Unwin, Barry Parker and Frederic Osborn in Britain, Henri Sellier in France, Ernst May and Martin Wagner in Germany, Clarence Stein and Henry Wright in the United States. Others were conceived independently, like the Spanish Arturo Soria's vision of the Linear City, or Frank Lloyd Wright's decentralized Broadacre City. Each, and the interrelations of all, will demand a special place in the story.

The second response followed logically, if not quite chronologically, from this: it is the vision of the regional city. It takes Howard's central theme much further, conceptually and geographically; it says that the answer to the sordid congestion of the giant city is a vast programme of regional planning, within which each subregional part would be harmoniously developed on the basis of its own natural resources, with total respect for the principles of ecological balance and resource renewal. Cities, in this scheme, become subordinate to the region; old cities and new towns alike will grow just as necessary parts of the regional scheme, no more, no less. This vision was developed just after 1900 by the Scots biologist Patrick Geddes and interpreted during the 1920s by the founder-members of the Regional Planning Association of America: Lewis Mumford, Clarence Stein and Henry Wright aforesaid, Stuart Chase, Benton MacKaye. To this group were related others, principally American: the Southern Regionalists led by Howard Odum, New Deal planners like Rexford Tugwell, even – indirectly – Frank Lloyd Wright. This rich and visionary tradition, the tragedy of which was that it promised so much and in practice delivered so little, is the subject matter of chapter 5.

The third strand is in stark contrast, even conflict, with these first two: it is the monumental tradition of city planning, which goes back to Vitruvius, if not beyond, and which had been powerfully revived in the mid-nineteenth century in the hands of such master planners as Georges-Eugène Haussmann in Paris or Ildefonso Cerda in Barcelona. In the twentieth century, as shown in chapter 6, it reappeared fitfully in some odd and ill-assorted places: as the handmaiden of civic pride allied to commercial boosterism in America, as the expression of imperial majesty in British India and Africa and of new-won independence in Australia, as the agent of totalitarian megalomania in Hitler's Germany and Stalin's Russia (and, less ambitiously but more effectively, in Mussolini's Italy and Franco's Spain). When and where it was allowed to finish the job – sometimes belatedly, sometimes never – it did the job expected of it: symbolic, expressive of pomp and power and prestige, finally innocent of – even hostile to – all wider social purpose.

There was yet another tradition that half-relates, confusingly, to both the garden-city and the monumental-city strains. It is the vision of the Swiss-born French architect-planner Le Corbusier, who argued that the evil of the modern city was its density of development and that the remedy, perversely, was to increase that density. Le Corbusier's solution, whereby an all-powerful master planner would demolish the entire existing city and replace it by a city of high-rise towers in a park, is discussed in chapter 7. In its pure full-blooded form it never found favour – perhaps understand-ably – with any real-life city administration, either in his lifetime or after it. But parts of it did, and the effects were at least as immense as those of Howard's rival vision: one entire new city on the plains of northern India, rivalling in formal scale and sweep Lutyens's definitive neo-classical monument of the Raj at New Delhi; more significant still, in human impact, hundreds of partial bull-dozings and rebuildings in older cities from Detroit to Warsaw, Stockholm to Milan.

There is another major line of planning thought, or planning ideology – the two merge imperceptibly and confusingly – that demands separate attention. But again, like the last, it proves to weave in and out of several other major strains, informing and colouring them. It argues that the built forms of cities should, as generally they now do not, come from the hands of their own citizens; that we should reject the tradition whereby large organizations, private or public, build for people, and instead embrace the notion that people should build for themselves. We can find this notion powerfully present in the anarchist thinking that contributed so much to

Howard's vision of the garden city in the 1890s, and in particular to Geddesian notions of piecemeal urban rehabilitation between 1885 and 1920. It forms a powerful central ingredient of Frank Lloyd Wright's thinking in the 1930s, and in particular of his Broadacre City. It resurfaces to provide a major, even a dominant, ideology of planning in third-world cities through the work of John Turner – himself drawing directly from anarchist thinking – in Latin America during the 1960s. And it provides a crucial element in the intellectual evolution of the British-American architectural theorist, Christopher Alexander, in that and the following decade. Finally, it culminates in the community-design movement which in the 1970s and 1980s swept the United States and above all Britain, there achieving the ultimate accolade of royal patronage. This long and sometimes strange tale is the burden of chapter 8.

There was yet another tradition, though it is harder to fix in philosophical terms and it is less firmly associated with one dominant prophet. It is the vision of a city of infinite mobility through advances in transportation technology, above all the private automobile, that is treated in chapter 9. This is a tradition that runs from H.G. Wells's remarkable turn-of-the-century prediction of the mass suburbanization of southern England, through the visions embodied in transportation plans like that for Los Angeles in 1939 and almost every other place between 1955 and 1965, to Melvin Webber's depiction of the nonplace urban realm in 1963–4. Frank Lloyd Wright's vision of Broadacre City is closely akin to it, as it is to so many other of the major traditions; so is the vision of the Soviet deurbanists of the 1920s; so, in its way, very early on, was Soria's concept of the linear city and all its countless subsequent derivatives. Of all the great traditions, this surely is the one that most melds and interrelates with almost all the others; for Howard, Le Corbusier, the regionalists all had their own private versions of this particular gospel.

Most of these ideas, though bereft of all possibility of realization when first conceived, were essentially the product of activists, of the doers of this world. Sooner or later, more often sooner, their creators abandoned talk or writing for action; if you seek their monuments, you must look around you. But it is important for any history of the planning movement also to grasp and to emphasize that since the 1950s, as planning has become more and more a craft learned through formal education, so it has progressively acquired a more abstract and a more formal body of pure theory. Some of this theory, so its own jargon goes, is theory *in* planning: an understanding of the practical techniques and methodologies, that planners always needed even if they once picked them up on the job. But the other, the theory *of* planning, is a horse of a different colour: under this rubric, planners try to understand the very nature of the activity they practise, including the reasons for its existence. And it is here that – as they have a habit of doing – theory has followed theory, paradigm has replaced paradigm, in increasingly fast, often bewildering, sometimes acerbic, fashion. Even to seek to make partial sense of this story runs the immediate and obvious risk of joining the whole process, of getting locked into the very syndrome one seeks to understand. How well chapter 10 avoids that pitfall, the reader must decide.

While academia was going its way, the world was going another. Stemming indirectly from the community design movement described in chapter 8, there came a belief that much of what has been done in the name of planning had been irrelevant at the higher and more abstract strategic level, pernicious at the ground level where the results emerge for all to see. This was because, in half a century or more of bureaucratic practice, planning had degenerated into a negative regulatory machine, designed to stifle all initative, all creativity. Here was yet another historic irony: left-wing thought returned to the anarchistic, voluntaristic, small-scale, bottom-up roots of planning; right-wing think-tanks began to call for an entrepreneurial style of development; and the two almost seemed in danger of embracing back-of-stage. Hence the moves, in several countries, for simplified planning regimes and for streamlined agencies that could cut through red tape and generate a vigorous, independent, entrepreneurial culture, without too many hang-ups or hiccups. During the 1980s this belief, never far below the surface in North America, quite suddenly emerged in countries long thought immune, like Great Britain. Tracing these connections, often subtle and very indirect, will be a central concern of chapter 11.

Meanwhile, amidst all the resulting plethora of agencies and initiatives, cities were continuing to go their ways. And what began disturbingly to suggest itself, from the mid-1960s onwards, was that instead of getting better, some parts of some cities – and definitely some people in those parts of those cities – were getting worse, at least in a relative sense, possibly also in an absolute one. Further, it might be that these people were simply transmitting their plight from one generation to another, becoming steadily less capable of catching up as the mainstream economy and society pulled away from them. These suggestions were indignantly, even vehemently, attacked; but they would not go away, because the phenomenon glaringly remained. This debate, and the phenomena that triggered it, are analysed in chapter 12.

So there is an odd and disturbing symmetry about this book: after one hundred years of debate on how to plan the city, after repeated attempts – however mistaken or distorted – to put ideas into practice, we find we are almost back where we started. The theorists have swung sharply back to planning's anarchist origins; the city itself is again seen as a place of decay, poverty, social malaise, civil unrest and possibly even insurrection. That does not mean, of course, that we have got nowhere at all: the city of the 1980s is a vastly different, and by any reasonable measure a very much superior, place compared with the city of the 1880s. But it does mean that certain trends seem to reassert themselves; perhaps because, in truth, they never went away.

The City of
Dreadful Night

... the great cities of the earth ... have become ... loathsome centres of fornication and covetousness – the smoke of their sin going up into the face of heaven like the furnace of Sodom; and the pollution of it rotting and raging the bones and the souls of the peasant people round them, as if they were each a volcano whose ashes broke out in blains upon man and upon beast.

John Ruskin
Letters to the Clergy on the Lord's Prayer and the Church (1880)

'What people do you mean?' Hyacinth allowed himself to inquire.

'Oh, the upper class, the people who've got all the things.'

'We don't call them the *people*,' observed Hyacinth, reflecting the next instant that his remark was a little primitive.

'I suppose you call them the wretches, the scoundrels!' Rose Muniment suggested, laughing merrily.

'All the things, but not all the brains,' her brother said.

'No indeed, aren't they stupid?' exclaimed her ladyship. 'All the same, I don't think they'd all go abroad.'

'Go abroad?'

'I mean like the French nobles who emigrated so much. They'd stay at home and fight; they'd make more of a fight. I think they'd fight very hard.'

Henry James
The Princess Casamassima (1886)

2

The City of
Dreadful Night

Reactions to the Nineteenth-Century Slum City:
London, Paris, Berlin, New York,
1880–1900

In 1880 James Thomson, a poet whose Victorian industriousness never quite compensated for monumental lack of talent, published a collection of doggerel named after its initial offering: an overlong, sub-Dantesque excursion into the underworld. The verse was soon forgotten but the title, *The City of Dreadful Night*, was not. That, perhaps, was because the dreadfulness of the Victorian city, whether by night or by day, soon became one of the major themes of the decade. Thomson's opening lines,

> The City is of Night, perchance of Death,
> But certainly of Night; for never there
> Can come the lucid morning's fragrant breath
> After the dewy morning's cold grey air[1]

might well have described contemporary London, Liverpool or Manchester. Perhaps W. T. Stead, the sensationalist muck-raking editor of the London evening *Pall Mall Gazette*, consciously or unconsciously recalled the verse when, in an editorial in October 1883, he commented that 'The grim Florentine might have added to the horrors of his vision of hell by a sojourn in a London slum.'

Stead's leader was headed 'IS IT NOT TIME?' In the stentorian tones for which he was already celebrated, he harangued his radical middle-class audience: 'The horrors of the slums', he wrote, represented 'the one great domestic problem which the religion, the humanity, and the statesmanship of England are imperatively summoned to solve.' With a journalist's acute

---

[1] Thomson 1880, 3.

FIGURE 2.1 *Little Collingwood Street, Bethnal Green, ca. 1900.*
The Victorian 'respectable poor', probably Booth's Class C, in their cruel habitations.

sense of timing, and a special talent for recognising the cause of the hour, he had seized upon a pamphlet just published by a Congregationalist clergyman, Andrew Mearns. As shrewdly promoted by Stead, *The Bitter Cry of Outcast London* provided a sensation. It had 'immediate and cataclysmic' effect:[2] it provoked immediate demands for an official inquiry not only from the *Pall Mall Gazette* but from much more conservative papers like *The Times* and *Punch*, and eventually from Queen Victoria herself, leading directly to the appointment of the Royal Commission on the Housing of the Working Classes in 1884.[3] It proved one of the most influential writings in the whole history of British social reform; Stead later claimed that through its triggering effect on the appointment of the Royal Commission, it was responsible for the birth of modern social legislation.[4]

The Bitter Cry

It was not the first such attempt to shake the smug self-confidence of late Victorian society; but it proved the pin that pricked the bubble. That was because of Mearns's uncanny ability to take his readers inside the slum. Even after a century, the descriptions make the flesh creep and the stomach turn; they have an almost televisual quality. Only extended quotations will convey their impact:

> Few who read these pages have any conception of what these pestilential human rookeries are, where tens of thousands are crowded together amidst horrors which call to mind what we have heard of the middle passage of the slave ship. To get to them you have to penetrate courts reeking with poisonous and malodorous gases arising from accumulations of sewage and refuse scattered in all directions and often flowing beneath your feet; courts, many of them which the sun never penetrates, which are never visited by a breath of fresh air, and which rarely know the virtues of a drop of cleansing water. You have to ascend rotten staircases, which threaten to give way beneath every step, and which, in some cases, have already broken down, leaving gaps that imperil the limbs and lives of the unwary. You have to grope your way along dark and filthy passages swarming with vermin. Then, if you are not driven back by the intolerable stench, you may gain admittance to the dens in which these thousands of beings who belong, as much as you, to the race for whom Christ died, herd together.[5]

Now, Mearns brings his bourgeois visitor into the horrific interior of the slum:

> Walls and ceiling are black with the accretions of filth which have gathered upon them through long years of neglect. It is exuding through cracks in the

---

[2] Wohl, 1977, 206.   [3] Wohl, 1970, 31–3; Wohl, 1977, 200, 206.
[4] Wohl, 1970, 33.   [5] Mearns, 1883, 4.

boards overhead; it is running down the walls; it is everywhere. What goes by the name of a window is half of it stuffed with rags or covered by boards to keep out wind and rain; the rest is so begrimed and obscured that scarcely can light enter or anything be seen outside.[6]

Furniture might include 'a broken chair, the tottering remains of an old bedstead, or the mere fragment of a table; but more commonly you will find rude substitutes for these things in the shape of rough boards resting upon bricks, an old hamper or box turned upside down, or more frequently still, nothing but rubbish and rags.'[7]

That set the scene for the human horrors within.

Every room in these rotten and reeking tenements houses a family, often two. In one cellar a sanitary inspector reports finding a father, mother, three children, and four pigs! In another a missionary found a man ill with small-pox, his wife just recovering from her eighth confinement, and the children running about half naked and covered with filth. Here are seven people living in one underground kitchen, and a little child lying dead in the same room. Elsewhere is a poor widow, her three children, and a child who has been dead thirteen days. Her husband, who was a cab driver, had shortly before committed suicide.[8]

In another room lived a widow and her six children, including one daughter of twenty-nine, another of twenty-one, and a son of twenty-seven. Another contained father, mother and six children, two of them ill with scarlet fever. In another nine brothers and sisters, from twenty-nine years of age downwards, lived, ate and slept together. In yet another was 'a mother who turns her children into the street in the early evening because she lets the room for immoral purposes until long after midnight, when the poor little wretches creep back again if they have not found some miserable shelter elsewhere.'

The inevitable result was what shocked Mearns's audience as much as the physical horror:

Ask if the men and women living together in these rookeries are married, and your simplicity will cause a smile. Nobody knows. Nobody cares. Nobody expects that they are. In exceptional cases only could your question be answered in the affirmative. Incest is common; and no form of vice and sensuality causes surprise or attracts attention. ... The only check upon communism in this regard is jealousy and not virtue. The vilest practices are looked upon with the most matter-of-fact indifference. ... In one street are 35 houses, 32 of which are known to be brothels. In another district are 43 of these houses, and 428 fallen women and girls, many of them not more than 12 years of age.[9]

For the Victorian middle class, this was perhaps the most shocking feature of all.

[6] Ibid.   [7] Ibid.   [8] Ibid. 5   [9] Ibid. 7

What was certain, Mearns argued, was that for people so literally destitute, crime did pay. Lingering around Leicester Square were 'several well-known members of the notorious band of "forty thieves", who, often in conspiracy with abandoned women, go out after dark to rob people in Oxford Street, Regent Street, and other thoroughfares.' The arithmetic of crime was inexorable: 'A child seven years old is easily known to make 10s.6d. a week by thieving, but what can he earn by such work as match-box making, for which 2¼d. a gross is paid . . .? Before he can gain as much as the young thief he must make 56 gross of match-boxes a week, or 1,296 a day. It is needless to say that this is impossible . . .'[10]

At the root of the problem was the fact that the people of the slum were overwhelmingly, grindingly poor. Women trouser-finishers worked seventeen hours, from 5.00 in the morning to 10.00 at night, for one shilling; for shirt-finishing, the rate was half that. Illness and drink compounded their plight:

> Who can imagine the suffering that lies behind a case like the following? A poor woman in an advanced stage of consumption, reduced almost to a skeleton, lives in a single room with a drunken husband and five children. When visited she was eating a few green peas. The children were gone to gather some sticks wherewith a fire might be made to boil four potatoes which were lying on the table, and which would constitute the family dinner for the day. . . . In a room in Wych Street, on the third floor, over a marine store dealer's, there was, a short time ago, an inquest as to the death of a little baby. A man, his wife and three children were living in that room. The infant was the second child who had died, poisoned by the foul atmosphere; and this dead baby was cut open in the one room where its parents and brothers lived, ate and slept, *because the parish had no mortuary and no room in which post mortems could be performed*! No wonder that the jurymen who went to view the body sickened at the frightful exhalations.[11]

For Mearns,

> The child-misery that one beholds is the most heart-rending and appalling element in these discoveries; and of these not the least is the misery inherited from the vice of drunken and dissolute parents, and manifest in the stunted, misshapen, and often loathsome objects that we constantly meet in these localities. . . .
>
> Here is one of three years old picking up some dirty pieces of bread and eating them. We go in at a doorway and find a little girl twelve years old. 'Where is your mother?' 'In the madhouse.' 'How long has she been there?' 'Fifteen months.' 'Who looks after you?' The child, who is sitting at an old table making match-boxes, replies, 'I look after my little brothers and sisters as well as I can.'[12]

When Mearns came to 'what it is proposed to do', he was in no doubt: 'We shall be pointed to the fact that without State interference nothing

[10] Ibid. 9   [11] Ibid. 11–12   [12] Ibid. 13

effectual can be performed upon any large scale. And *it is* a fact.'[13] The root of the problem was simple economics. The people were overcrowded because they were poor, and because they were poor they could not afford the obvious remedy: to move out where house room was cheaper:

> These wretched people must live somewhere. They cannot afford to go out by train or tram into the suburbs; and how, with their poor emaciated, starved bodies, can they be expected – in addition to working twelve hours or more, for a shilling, or less – to walk three or four miles each way to take and fetch?[14]

The British Royal Commission of 1885

This evoked a sympathetic chord. Though some commentators, like the Marquess of Salisbury, thought in terms of charitable trusts and others, like Joseph Chamberlain, thought in terms of local authority action, there was a general willingness to see concerted intervention.[15] Even *The Times*, with evident disapproval, observed that 'it can hardly be doubted by any one who watches the tendencies of the time that *laissez-faire* is practically abandoned and that every piece of state interference will pave the way for another.'[16] And even Salisbury, in a crucially important speech of November 1884, raised the question of state intervention.[17] The appointment of a prestigious Royal Commission, chaired by Sir Charles Wentworth Dilke and including among its members the Prince of Wales, Lord Salisbury and Cardinal Manning, followed. But, while the Commission's report of 1885 abundantly confirmed the nature of the problem, it could reach no unanimous conclusion as to remedy. It concluded definitively,

> First, though there was great improvement . . . in the condition of the houses of the poor compared with that of 30 years ago, yet the evils of overcrowding, especially in London, were still a public scandal, and were becoming in certain localities more serious than they ever were; second, that there was much legislation designed to meet these evils, yet the existing laws were not put into force, some of them having remained a dead letter from the date when they first found place in the statute book.[18]

Abundant evidence confirmed that in London, one family to a room was typical, and that family might number up to eight souls. This was exacerbated by the custom, in the capital, of dividing up houses into one-room tenements, which must then share one water supply and one closet. And, because the front door was seldom shut, at night the staircases and passages might fill up with the ironically titled ''appy dossers': the completely

---

[13] Ibid. 14   [14] Ibid. 15   [15] Tarn, 1973, 111–12.   [16] cit. Wohl, 1977, 234.
[17] Ibid. 238.   [18] G. B. R. C. Housing, 1885, I. 4.

FIGURE 2.2 *The Royal Commission on the Housing of the Working Classes in session, 1884.*
Shaftesbury, centre right, gives evidence on the life styles of the poor; the Prince of
Wales, leaning forward centre left, appears aghast.

homeless.[19] Within the rooms, the widespread practice of home work –
often noxious, such as rag-picking, sack-making, matchbox-making and
rabbit-pulling – made bad conditions worse.[20] In the provincial cities,
though there were big variations, overall the same problem of overcrowding
did not exist as in London.[21]

For some, like the veteran social reformer Lord Shaftesbury, the one-
room system was 'physically and morally beyond all description':

> I was saying that we dare not tell all we know, and I should be very sorry
> to go into details of things that I do not know; but I will give an instance
> of the evil consequences of the one-room system, and this not an instance of
> the worst kind. This case only happened last year, but it is of frequent
> occurrence. A friend of mine, who is at the head of a large school, going
> down one of the back courts saw two children of tender years, 10 or 11 years
> old, endeavouring to have sexual connection on the pathway. He ran and
> seized the lad and pulled him off, and the only remark of the lad was, 'Why
> do you take hold of me?' There are a dozen of them at it down there.' You
> must perceive that this could not arise from sexual tendencies, and that it
> must have been bred by imitation of what they saw.[22]

But others disagreed; and the Royal Commission concluded that the
'standard of morality . . . is higher than might have been expected.'[23]

That perhaps was some small comfort. The remarkable fact was that the
average tenement dweller had far less space than that mandated by the
Victorian state for those incarcerated in prisons or workhouses. Predictably,
mortality levels – especially for children – remained alarmingly high. Those
who survived, the Commission calculated, lost an average of twenty days'
work a year because they 'get depressed and weary.' And all this was
compounded by the fact that 'the warmest apologist for the poorest classes
would not assert the general prevalence of cleanly habits among them.'[24]

The root causes, just as Mearns had shown, were stark poverty
and consequent inability to move out. Unskilled London workers like
costermongers and hawkers earned a mere 10s. to 12s. a week; dockers
averaged only 8s. to 9s.; the average Clerkenwell labourer might bring
home 16s. Nearly one half of London families, 46 per cent, had to pay
over one quarter of these meagre earnings for rent; and, while rents were
rising, wages were not.[25] And poverty was compounded by the casual
nature of so much low-paid work, including that of their home-working
wives; so that 'an enormous proportion of the dwellers in the overcrowded
quarters are necessarily compelled to live close to their work, no matter
what the price charged or what the condition of the dwelling they inhabit.'[26]
Middlemen rack-renters, who managed houses on short end-leases, blatantly

[19] G. B. R. C. Housing 1885, I. 7–9.   [20] Ibid. I. 11.   [21] Ibid. I. 8.   [22] Ibid. II. 2.
[23] Ibid. I. 13.   [24] Ibid. I. 14–15.   [25] Ibid. I. 17.   [26] Ibid. I. 18.

exploited the housing shortage for all they were worth. And demolitions – for new streets like Charing Cross Road and Shaftesbury Avenue, since London in the 1880s was undergoing a mini-Haussmannization, or for the new Board Schools that followed the 1870 Education Act – had worsened the problem.[27]

Underlying all this was an incompetent and often corrupt local government system, unable or unwilling to use the powers it had. Outside London, the historic Public Health Act of 1875 had provided the basis for a more effective local government system;[28] but in the capital, an archaic and chaotic pattern still ruled. Only two vestries or district boards, out of thirty-eight in all London, had taken any vigorous action. There were hardly any inspectors: Mile End, a poor area, had one to 105,000 people. And those were hardly competent: in one London parish, the assistant inspector was 'formerly something in the jewellery trade', said the vestry clerk, who added 'I don't know that any special training is required. If a man was endowed with good common sense I think that would be about as good a training as he could have.'[29]

So the Royal Commission's main recommendations, rather than adding new powers, focused on how to ensure that local authorities used existing ones. These embraced the so-called Torrens Act (The Artisans' and Labourers' Dwellings Act, 1868), which allowed local authorities to build new dwellings for the labouring classes, and the Cross Act (The Artisans' and Labourers' Dwellings Improvement Act, 1875) which allowed them to clear large areas of unfit housing and to rehouse the inhabitants, both of which were very largely dead letters. They did, however, say that these local authorities should be able to borrow money from the Treasury at the lowest possible rate of interest that would not bring actual loss to the national exchequer. And, in London, they proposed that the vestries and joint boards should surrender their powers under the housing acts to the Metropolitan Board of Trade.[30] The Housing of the Working Classes Act, 1885, which immediately followed, implemented these recommendations. It also extended Lord Shaftesbury's ancient 1851 Lodging Houses Act, redefining these to include separate dwellings and cottages for the working classes: a powerful suggestion that the Victorian parliament would at last countenance municipal socialism in housing.[31] The problem remained that local authorities would not move; to which, the Royal Commission could only suggest that it was time that the depressed working classes of the cities should begin to show an interest in their plight.[32]

[27] Ibid. I. 19–21.   [28] Ashworth, 1954, 73.   [29] R. C. Housing, 1885, I. 22, 33.
[30] Ibid. I. 40–1.   [31] Wohl, 1977, 248.   [32] Gauldie, 1974, 289.

Depression, Violence and the Threat of Insurrection

Perhaps, indeed, they would. For the 1884 Reform Act had extended the franchise to a large part of the urban male working class. And this class was just then suffering the effects of a major depression in trade and industry, comparable in its impact with those that followed in the 1930s and 1980s. There was indeed an ominous foretaste of what was to come: the problem, a Royal Commission concluded in 1886, was in part a matter not of the trade cycle, but of a structural weakness in British industry compared with its major international competitors, above all Germany. The Germans were about as good at production as the British; and in the arts of winning and keeping markets they were gaining ground.[33] The Commissioners warned that Britain was taking less trouble 'to discover new markets for our produce, and to maintain a hold upon those which we already possess . . . There is also evidence that in respect of certain classes of products the reputation of our workmanship does not stand so high as it formerly stood.'[34] They rejected suggestions that ascribed the cause to 'legislative restrictions on the employment of labour and to the action of the working classes themselves by strikes and similar movements' or 'to the action of trades unions or similar combinations.'[35]

Whatever the causes, there was no doubt about the effects. During the mid-1880s, throughout the cities and above all throughout London, there was a spirit of cataclysmic, even violent, change in the air. The questions of the hour, Beatrice Webb later wrote, were 'on the one hand, the meaning of the poverty of masses of men; and, on the other, the practicability and desirability of political and industrial democracy as a set-off to, perhaps as a means of redressing, the grievances of a majority of the people.'[36] But these discussions were for the intelligentsia: 'it was, in truth, no section of the manual workers that was secreting . . . 'the poison of socialism' . . . Born and bred in chronic destitution and enfeebling disease, the denizens of the slums had sunk into a brutalized apathy. . . .' The ferment, in her recollection forty years later, was within one section of the Victorian governing class; it consisted in 'a new consciousness of sin' which 'was a collective or class consciousness; a growing uneasiness, amounting to conviction, that the industrial organism, which had yielded rent, interest and profit on a stupendous scale, had failed to provide a decent livelihood and tolerable conditions for a majority of the inhabitants of Great Britain.'[7] Later historians might doubt that; the predominant emotion, one asserted, was not guilt, but fear. The poor 'were generally pictured as coarse, brutish,

[33] G. B. R. C. Depression, 1886, xx.   [34] Ibid.   [35] Ibid., xx, xxi.
[36] Webb, 1926, 149.   [37] Ibid. 154-5.

drunken, and immoral; through years of neglect and complacency they had become an ominous threat to civilization.'[38]

The reactions often took a heady form. Those apostles of gradualism, the Fabians, whom Beatrice Webb soon joined, produced an early manifesto bearing the clear imprint of George Bernard Shaw, and ending with the stark propositions:

> That the established Government has no more right to call itself the State than the smoke of London has to call itself the weather.
>
> That we had rather face a Civil War than such another century of suffering as the present one has been.[39]

H. M. Hyndman, leader of the Social Democratic Foundation, wrote in the same year that 'Even among the useless men and women who dub themselves 'society', an undercurrent of uneasiness may be detected. The dread word 'Revolution' is sometimes spoken aloud in jest, and more often whispered in all seriousness.'[40] Hyndman doubted that the ferment was restricted to the middle class; for

> . . . books, pamphlets and fly-leaves are finding their way into workshop and attic, which deal with the whole problem from top to bottom. Theories drawn from Dr. Karl Marx's great work on Capital, or from the programme of the Social democrats of Germany and the Collectivists of France, are put forward in cheap and readable form.[41]

But Hyndman also drew attention to a phenomenon that few could fail to notice: 'Among the ugliest growths of modern society are the numerous gangs of organized roughs . . . who parade our great cities, and too often, not content with mauling one another, maltreat the peaceful wayfarer.'[42] In London alone, he claimed, according to the police there were 300,000 members of the 'dangerous classes'.[43] No one, Hyndman argued, 'had taken the trouble to analyze the manner in which these people were fostered into their present brutality.'[44]

Some did not even think it worth the trouble. During 1886 and 1887, the respectable citizens of Liverpool began to complain that they were being terrorized by gangs; 'the district from Athol Street to Luton Street' was 'infested by these scoundrels', wrote an indignant correspondent to the local paper in February 1887. The same month the most notorious among them, the High Rip Gang, went on a wild rampage through the streets of Liverpool, indiscriminately attacking men, women and children with knives and slingshot, and stealing from pawnshops. On 20 May the gang, described as 'four rough-looking young men . . . labourers, entered as being imperfectly educated', appeared at the Liverpool Assizes on eight charges of malicious

---

[38] Stedman Jones, 1971, 285.   [39] Fabian Society, 1884b, 2.   [40] Hyndman, 1884, 3.
[41] Ibid. 28.   [42] Ibid. 25.   [43] Ibid. 32.   [44] Ibid. 25.

wounding with intent to do grievous bodily harm, and robbery with violence. The trial judge, Mr Justice John Charles Frederick Sigismund Day, was a mutton-chop-whiskered sexagenarian with a profound distrust of modern penological theories, whose fixed conviction about violent criminals was that they needed a particularly short sharp shock; or, as his son quaintly put it, 'that the only appeal to their reason was through their epidermis.'[45]

Pronouncing that 'with all his experience he has never heard such outrageous conduct narrated as he had this day heard', he ordered the most draconian sentences ever recorded in the courts of Victorian England: as well as terms of hard labour, each of the four was to receive three separate floggings of twenty lashes each. Thus fortified by his one-man attack on the city's crime problem, Mr Day returned to the fray at the November Assizes, where – among seven floggings ordered on one day – he sentenced two men to twenty lashes each for stealing a halfpenny and a plug of tobacco. The respectable citizens, his son later claimed, were eternally in Mr Day's debt, though 'members of philanthropical societies, and some others, denounced the 'flogging judge' as a well-meaning brute, and regarded his method of dealing with criminals as medieval and mistaken.'[46] In any case, there is no evidence at all that Day's reign of terror had any effect at all on violent crime in Liverpool. The odd fact is, that despite the fears of the citizens, it seems clear that crime in late Victorian England was following a long secular downward trend, albeit punctuated by periodic outbursts of violence such as in the mid-1880s.[47]

The real terror among the middle classes, notwithstanding Beatrice Webb's scepticism, was that the working class would rise in insurrection. And nowhere was this fear greater than in the seat of government. In February 1886, their worst fears were realized. For weeks, unemployed workers and socialist intellectuals had been holding meetings in Trafalgar Square. On Monday, 8 February, a huge meeting, including 'a considerable proportion, larger than usual, of the roughest element'[48], was met by a force of over 600 police officers. Fearing an attack on Buckingham Palace, they moved into the Mall; the mob, numbering between 3,000 and 5,000 people, instead went on the rampage past the clubs of Pall Mall, into the streets of St James's and Mayfair, breaking windows and looting shops. An official inquiry condemned the Metropolitan Police for inadequate crowd control, and the Commissioner was forced to resign.[49]

The new Commissioner, Sir Charles Warren, was made of sterner stuff. During the autumn of 1887 tension again rose, with huge crowds gathering daily in Hyde Park and Trafalgar Square to hear speeches. Repeated

[45] *Liverpool Echo*, 20 May 1887; Day, 1916, 120. [46] Ibid. 121; *Liverpool Daily Post*, 25 Nov 1887. [47] Jones, 1982, 119–20, 123, 143. [48] G. B. Committee Disturbances, 1886, v. [49] Ibid., *passim*.

clashes with the police took place. *The Times*, which habitually referred to the 'so-called unemployed', called for firm action:

> We trust that if these men, or any other of their class, attempt to carry out their threats as they did last year, they will get their deserts, in the form not of a convenient term of imprisonment for a few months, but of hard penal servitude. . . . The only question worth asking is which of the two parties is the stronger – the would-be smashers of windows and wreckers of tradesmen's shops or the guardians of the public peace.[50]

Thus the stage was set. On Sunday, 23 October, a huge crowd gathered in the square, raising the red flag, to hear speeches demanding Sir Charles' dismissal. Just before 3.00 in the afternoon, headed by the red flag, the mob suddenly moved down Whitehall and invaded Westminster Abbey during the service. The resulting scenes resembled the final act of Brecht's *Dreigroschenoper*, which perhaps they inspired. According to *The Times*, 'a large number of boys, youths, and men, many of them of a very dirty appearance' entered as the organ played a voluntary. They mixed with the congregation, 'the more manly [of whom] quietly exercised their influence to restrain the most shameless. . . . The roughs shouted bitter words about 'capitalists', seeming to suppose that all those who were in the Abbey at worship were 'capitalists.' Canon Rowsell tried to argue with them. 'The mob listened quietly.' Just outside, Hyndman spoke: 'he looked forward to the time when the Socialistic flag and motto of "Each for all and all for each" should be placed above that abbey, and they should be inside, preaching the doctrine of revolution.'[51]

The demonstrators then returned to the square, where 'from every side of Nelson's column meetings were being addressed', with a huge crowd spilling out across the square and into neighbouring places. The police panicked and had to call in the army to control the crowds; in the mêlée, over 100 people were injured; later, two of the crowd died. Massive and mutual recriminations followed. One indignant correspondent wrote to *The Times* that the meetings were 'an advertisement to all anarchists, here and elsewhere, to flock to the only great capital in the world where they would be tolerated.'[52] Hyndman wrote with a different view: 'Men and women will not starve any longer. That I, for one, know. The present agitation is quite spontaneous and unorganized.' The editorial view was predictable: 'This capital itself is menaced by riotous mobs, avowing their determination to profit by the example of the party of disorder in Ireland and to extort the concession of their demands by terrorism.'[53] Stead's *Pall Mall Gazette* in contrast accused Warren of trying to establish 'police rule': in the Abbey, the interruptions during the service had been the result of overcrowding, and the unemployed had left in perfectly orderly fashion. At Bow Street,

[50] *The Times*, 15 Oct 1887.   [51] *The Times*, 24 Oct 1887.
[52] *The Times*, 27 Oct 1887.   [53] *The Times*, 24 Oct 1887.

sundry persons were charged; some were jailed, others fined or bound over. Later, R. Cunninghame Graeme, MP, and the Socialist leader John Burns were convicted at the Old Bailey and imprisoned for six weeks; they became popular heroes.[54]

The Booth Survey: The Problem Quantified

Out of the mayhem of these months came at least some rational response. Charles Booth, the Liverpool shipowner, had been inspired by *The Bitter Cry* to go into the East End of London in order to embark on what became the first modern social survey. Aided by an army of able young assistants, including Beatrice Potter, later Webb – who here enjoyed her initiation into academic research – he presented his first results before the Royal Statistical Society in May 1887, and a second paper a year later. According to Booth, the poor of East London numbered some 314,000, or over 35 per cent of the city's population; extending that percentage pro rata, that meant 1,000,000 Londoners in poverty. They could be divided, he said, into four subgroups.

The first, Class A, included a mere 11,000 in the East End, perhaps 50,000 in all London: 1.25 per cent of the population. It 'consists of some (so-called) labourers, loafers, semi-criminals, a proportion of the street sellers, street performers and others.' It included many young people: 'young men who take naturally to loafing; girls who take almost as naturally to the streets'; they led 'a savage life, with vicissitudes of extreme hardship and occasional excess. Their food is of the coarsest description, and their only luxury is drink.'[55] Booth was sanguine that this group was so small: 'The hordes of barbarians of whom we have heard who, coming forth from their slums, will some day overwhelm modern civilisation, do not exist. The barbarians are a very small and decreasing percentage.'[56] But it still represented an irreducible problem: 'They render no useful service and create no wealth; they oftener destroy it. They degrade whatever they touch, and as individuals are almost incapable of improvement. . . . It is much to be hoped that this class may become less hereditary in its character.'[57]

These, then, were the classic Victorian Undeserving Poor: the raw material of the mob, the perpetual nightmare of the respectable classes, albeit much smaller than Hyndman and others had claimed. The second group, Class B, were, however, much more of a problem. For one thing, they were a much bigger group: 100,000 in the East End, perhaps 300,000 in London as a whole, over 11 per cent of the city's population. Booth

[54] Ensor, 1936, 180–1.   [55] Booth, 1887, 334–5.
[56] Booth, 1888, 305.   [57] Booth, 1887, 334–5.

FIGURE 2.3 *Charles Booth.*
The shipowner-turned-sociologist, presumably intent on the results of his survey;
perhaps it was the young Beatrice Potter who was reporting.

described them as being 'in chronic want': 'These people, *as a class*,' he
wrote, 'are shiftless, hand-to-mouth, pleasure loving, and always poor; to
work when they like and play when they like is their ideal.'[58] Their problem
was the casual nature of their earnings. They included relatively large
numbers of widows, unmarried women, young persons and children. Booth
felt that the solution to the problem of poverty was 'the entire removal of
this class out of the daily struggle for existence.' since 'they are a constant
burthen to the State. . . . Their presence in our cities creates a costly and
often unavailing struggle to raise the standard of life and health.'[59]

Immediately above them came Class C, numbering some 74,000 people
in the East End or 250,000 in London as a whole: over 8 per cent of the

[58] Ibid. 329.   [59] Booth, 1888, 299.

total. They formed 'a pitiable class, consisting largely of struggling, suffering, hopeless people ... the victims of competition, and on them falls with particular severity the weight of recurrent depressions of trade.'[60] Their basic problem was the irregular nature of their earnings. And finally Class D, those who suffered from regular but low earnings, included about 129,000 East Enders or 14.5 per cent of the city's population; say 400,000 in London as a whole. They 'live hard lives very patiently', and the hope for their improvement could come only through their children, since 'for the class as a whole the probability of improvement is remote.'[61]

One group who read these early Booth results with particular interest was the Fabian Society, in which the patient fact-grubbing of Sidney Webb was now married to the acid pen of Bernard Shaw. The definitive Fabian classic, *Facts for Socialists*, first published in 1887, was repeatedly reprinted, selling 70,000 copies within eight years; two years later came a sequel, *Facts for Londoners*. 'In London', the researchers found, 'one person in every five will die in the workhouse, hospital, or lunatic asylum.'[62]

> Of the 1,000,000 Londoners estimated by Mr. Booth to be in poverty ... practically none are housed as well as a provident man provides for his horse. These 200,000 families, earning not more than a guinea a week ... and that often irregularly, pay from 3s. to 7s. per week for filthy slum tenements of which a large proportion are absolutely 'unfit for habitation', even according to the lax standards of existing sanitary officers. London needs the rebuilding of at least 400,000 rooms to house its poorest citizens.[63]

The results were predictable: while the average age of death among the nobility, gentry, and professional class of England and Wales was fifty-five, among the artisan classes of Lambeth it was twenty-nine; the infantile death rate in Bethnal Green was double that in Belgravia.[64]

The heart of the problem, as contemporaries saw it, was housing. 'The housing problem was central to the social problem of London in the 1880s'; 'from 1883 onwards the quarterly journals and the press were full of warnings of the necessity of immediate reform to ward off the impending revolutionary threat.'[65] There was but one remedy, in the Fabian view: 'The re-housing of London's poor can only be adequately dealt with by London's collective power.'[66] Between the first and second editions of the *Facts* pamphlet, that statement had become much more realistic and practicable; for, following the recommendation of the Royal Commission on Housing, the Local Government Act of 1888 had transferred the responsibilities of the Metropolitan Board of Works to a new democratically elected body, the London County Council. And, in 1890, yet another

[60] Booth, 1887, 332.   [61] Ibid. 332.
[62] Fabian Society, 1889, 7; cf. Fabian Society, 1887, 15.
[63] Fabian Society, 1889, 25.   [64] Fabian Society, 1887, 14.
[65] Stedman Jones, 1971, 217, 290.   [66] Fabian Society, 1889, 28.

Housing of the Working Classes Act did what the 1885 Act had failed to do: in Part III, it provided for the redevelopment of large areas, with compulsory purchase if needs be, for the purpose of building working-class lodging houses, defined to include 'separate houses or cottages for the working classes, whether containing one or several tenements.'[67]

Though the Act was actually contradictory on its attitude to local authority ownership and management of housing – Part I discouraged it, Part III allowed if it did not encourage it – the new LCC seized on the opportunity it presented, by immediately establishing a Housing of the Working Classes Committee.[68] In 1894 borrowing powers were extended to the relevant section of the Act; in 1900 local authorities, including the LCC and the new London boroughs which had replaced the vestries by a London Government Act the previous year, were enabled to buy land outside their own boundaries to implement this section of the 1890 Act.[69]

The Slum City in Europe

London, rather than any provincial British city, was the stage on which most of this drama was played out. But that was because – as the Royal Commission recognized in 1885 – the housing problem was so much worse there; and that, in large measure, was a simple measure of London's size. With its 5.6 million people at the start of the 1890s, no other British urban area could compete with it; housing densities, land rents, transportation problems, competition for space were all bound to be so much more acute there.

Even on the international scale, against the Paris region's 4.1 million and Greater Berlin's 1.6 million, London was unchallengeably the greatest city in Europe and even the world.[70] But these other cities, being relatively smaller and denser, had their own competitive horror stories to offer. In Paris the historic city's 2.45 million people, in 1891, lived at a density twice that of the LCC area. Bertillon concluded at that date that 14 per cent of the Paris poor, 330,000, lived in overcrowded dwellings; the poor were even worse housed than in London. Sellier calculated in 1911 that the total was still 216,000, with another 85,000 in the suburbs, living at two or more per room.[71] There, too, legislation – in 1894, 1906 and 1912 – had allowed the construction of low-cost housing for the working classes, and the last provided for local authorities to establish offices to build and manage such housing, backed by state money. Yet down to 1914, only 10,000 such dwellings had been built in the Paris region, an

---

[67] Wohl, 1977, 252.   [68] Tarn, 1973, 122; Gauldie, 1974, 294–5.
[69] Tarn, 1973, 124, 127.   [70] Mitchell, 1975, 76–8.
[71] Sellier, 1927, 1–2; Bastié, 1964, 190.

FIGURE 2.4 *Berlin Mietskasernen.*
In Berlin, a model housing design brings congestion and misery.

unimpressive total compared with the LCC achievement.[72] The stark fact
was that neither the city nor the state had the money for slum clearance:
other huge public works – building schools and the Sorbonne in the 1880s
and 1890s, building the Métro in the decade 1900–10 – took priority.[73]

Berlin, where the population was growing at almost American speed –
a near-doubling in twenty years, from 1.9 million in 1890 to 3.7 million
in 1910 – was, like Paris, an extraordinarily compact, and therefore
congested, city: its growth was accommodated in densely packed five-storey
'rental barracks' around courtyards as narrow as 15 feet wide, the minimum
necessary to bring in fire-fighting equipment. This kind of development,
apparently first developed by Frederick the Great to house soldiers' families,
became universal as a result of the city plan of Police-President James
Hobrecht, in 1858; apparently designed to achieve social integration, with
rich and poor in the same block, it simply produced miserable congestion,
and the pattern even spread to new suburban development after a change
in regulations there in the 1890s;[74] speculation, guided by the plan and

[72] Bastié, 1964, 192; Sutcliffe, 1970, 258; Evenson, 1979, 218.
[73] Morizet, 1932, 332; Bastié, 1964, 196; Sutcliffe, 1970, 327–8.
[74] Voigt, 1901, 126, 129; Hegemann, 1930, 170; Peltz-Dreckmann, 1978, 21;
Niethammer, 1981, 146–7.

fuelled by an exceptionally favourable mortgage system, did the rest.[75]

The result, according to the calculations of the British planning pioneer T. C. Horsfall in 1903, was that while in London in 1891 the average number of inhabitants to a building was 7.6, in Berlin it was 52.6;[76] as late as 1916, no less than 79 per cent of all dwellings had only one or two heatable rooms.[77] And Berliners paid much more to rent their apartments than did their equivalents in Hamburg or Munich – the poor, ironically, paying the highest proportions of their wages.[78] Further, though Germany was faster to electrify its tram systems than Britain, in Berlin the private tram companies did not serve as a means of outward movement in the same way as the LCC, and underground railway development was held up by legal wrangles.[79] Patrick Abercrombie, the British planner, visiting Berlin just before World War One, was intrigued by the contrast with London: 'Berlin is the most compact city in Europe; as she grows she does not straggle out with small roads and peddling suburban houses, but slowly pushes her wide town streets and colossal tenement blocks over the open country, turning it at one stroke into full-blown city.'[80]

There was an interesting reaction to growth and overcrowding in the European capitals: both in London and in Berlin, fears began to develop that the city population was in some way biologically unfit. Around 1900, recruitment for the South African War exposed the fact that out of 11,000 young men in Manchester, 8,000 were rejected and only 1,000 were fit for regular service. Later, in World War One, the Verney Commission reasserted that the physique of the urban part of Britain tended to deteriorate, and was maintained only by recruitment from the countryside.[81] Similarly, in Berlin, only 42 per cent of Berliners were found fit for army service in 1913, against 66 per cent of those from rural areas.[82]

From this soon followed the argument that city people – and eventually, the whole population – would fail to reproduce itself, an argument first used by Georg Hansen in his book *Die drei Bevölkerungsstufen* in the 1890s, and developed by Oswald Spengler in his classic *The Decline of the West*, in 1918: 'Now the giant city sucks the country dry, insatiably and incessantly demanding and devouring fresh streams of men, till it wearies and dies in the midst of an almost uninhabited waste of country.'[83] But in both countries, there were wider fears. Charles Masterman, the Liberal MP, suggested in his book *The Heart of the Empire* (1901) that the Londoner was unstable:

> The England of the past was an England of reserved, silent men, dispersed in small towns, villages and country houses. . . . The problem of the coming

[75] Hegemann, 1930, 302, 317; Grote, 1974, 14; Hecker, 1974, 274.

[76] Horsfall, 1904, 2–3.   [77] Eberstadt, 1917, 181.   [78] Ibid. 189, 197.

[79] Ibid. 431–3.   [80] Abercrombie, 1914, 219.   [81] Bauer, 1934, 21; Purdom, 1921, 111.

[82] Eberstadt, 1917, 214.   [83] Spengler, 1934, II. 102.

years is just the problem of . . . a characteristic *physical* type of town dweller: stunted, narrow-chested, easily wearied; yet voluble, excitable, with little ballast or endurance – seeking stimulus in drink, in betting, in any unaccustomed conflicts at home and abroad.[84]

Similarly, in Germany in the 1920s *die Angst vor der Stadt* was a fear of social decomposition, suggested by evidence of suicide, alcoholism and venereal disease, 'excessive rationality' and lack of political stability.[85]

New York: The Tumour in the Tenements

Overall, Andrew Lees concludes in his monumental study of nineteenth-century urban attitudes, fear and dislike of the city were very much an Anglo-German phenomenon: 'Few Americans displayed the vitriolic dislike of urban living as such that permeated much of the German literature'; yet 'many men and women articulated a keen awareness of the moral blemishes that disfigured the face of the American as well as the European city.'[86] Such fears were openly, even obsessively, expressed in the New York of the 1890s. There, a traditional Jeffersonian concern, that the city was 'pestilential to the morals, the health and the liberties of men', a cancer or tumour on the body social and the body politic, was fuelled by industrialization and immigration: New York became the greatest city of immigrants in the world, with 'half as many Italians as Naples, as many Germans as Hamburg, twice as many Irish as Dublin and two and a half times as many Jews as Warsaw'.[87]

The intellectuals were unanimous on the result. Henry James wrote that 'New York was both squalid and gilded, to be fled rather than enjoyed'.[88] Many came to accept the judgement of Josiah Strong, in 1885, that to the city was traceable every danger that threatened American democracy: poverty and crime, socialism and corruption, immigration and Catholicism.[89] Alan Forman, in the *American Magazine* in 1885, wrote of 'a seething mass of humanity, so ignorant, so vicious, so depraved that they hardly seem to belong to our species', so that it was 'almost a matter for congratulation that the death rate among the inhabitants of these tenements is something over fifty-seven per cent.'[90] In 1892, no less authoritative a journal than the *New York Times* complained about the invasion of 'the physical, moral and mental wrecks' from Europe, 'of a kind which we are better without.'[91] Even the *American Journal of Sociology*, in 1897, was forced to concede the power of the 'popular belief' that 'large cities are great centers of social corruption and . . . degeneration.'[92] F. J. Kingsbury in 1895 was moved

[84] Masterman, 1901, 7–8.   [85] Peltz-Dreckmann, 1978, 62–3; Lees, 1979, 65–6.
[86] Lees, 1985, 164.   [87] Schlesinger, 1933, 73.   [88] White and White, 1962, 17, 75, 218.
[89] Gelfand, 1975, 18.   [90] Ford, 1936, 174.   [91] Lubove, 1962b, 53–4.
[92] Boyer, 1978, 129.

to comment that 'one would think after reading all this about the evils of cities from the time of Cain to the last New York election that nothing short of the treatment applied to Sodom and Gomorrah will meet the necessities of the case.'[93]

The man who above all gave expression to these feelings was Jacob Riis: a rural-born Dane who emigrated to New York in 1870, at the age of twenty-one, and became a journalist seven years later. His *How the Other Half Lives*, published in 1890, created a sensation uncannily similar to the impact of *The Bitter Cry* on London seven years earlier.[94] It too was a brilliant piece of journalism. Its descriptions of tenement slum life skilfully combined two contemorary fears: the city as a kind of parasite on the body of the nation, and the immigrant as corrupter of American racial purity and social harmony. These new immigrants, 'beaten men from beaten races; representing the worst failures in the struggle for existence',[95] became a threat to order and to the very future of the Republic, recalling the earlier New York City riots of 1863:

> The sea of a mighty population, held in galling fetters, heaves uneasily in the tenements. Once already our city, to which have come the duties and responsibilities of metropolitan greatness before it was able to fairly measure its task, has felt the swell of its relentless flood. If it rise once more, no human power may avail to check it.[96]

But now the tenements had spread,

> Crowding out all the lower wards, wherever business leaves a foot of ground unclaimed; strung along both rivers, like ball and chain that is tied to the foot of every street, and filling up Harlem with their restless, pent-up multitudes, they hold within their clutch the wealth and business of New York, hold them at their mercy in the day of mob-rule and wrath. The bullet-proof shelters, the stacks of hand-grenades, and the Gatling guns of the sub-Treasury are tacit admissions of the fact and of the quality of the mercy expected. The tenements today are New York, harboring three-fifths of its population.[97]

A Tenement House Commission of 1894 estimated that nearly three in five of the city's population lived in tenement houses, so grossly over-built that on average nearly four-fifths of the ground was covered in buildings.[8] In these tenement districts, two factors combined to create an acute human problem. First, the incomers were desperately poor and – because of language and cultural barriers – hopelessly immobile. The American planner and housing expert, Charles Abrams, who had the rare authority of having grown up in a tenement, later explained: 'the landlord cannot

---

[93] cit. Cook, 1973, 11. [94] Lubove, 1962b, 55–7. [95] cit. ibid. 54.
[96] Riis, 1890, 296. [97] Ibid. 19–20. [98] Ford, 1936, 187–8.

be blamed; the builder cannot be blamed. They built to meet a market. The market was determined by what the tenant could pay. What the tenant could pay was determined by the wages he received.'[99]

If the poor immigrant had not had such an apartment, he would have had nothing. And poor families crowded into them because they were within walking distance of jobs. Nearly 75 per cent of the Russian Jews were packed into three city wards and especially into one, the 10th, which contained a majority from (or with parents from) Russia and Russian Poland. By 1893, with more than 700 people to the acre, this ward was well over 30 per cent more crowded than the most congested part of any European city; part of the adjacent 11th Ward, with nearly 1,000 to the acre, was even more congested than the worst district of Bombay, and so was almost certainly the most crowded urban neighbourhood in the world – though, ironically, in the mid-1980s some parts of Hong Kong well exceed it.[100]

Secondly, they crowded into tenements that, as in Berlin, perversely resulted from a so-called improved housing design: developed in a competition in 1879, the notorious dumb-bell tenement allowed twenty-four families to be crowded on to a lot 25 feet wide and 100 feet deep, with ten out of fourteen rooms on each floor having access only to an almost lightless (and airless) lightwell.[101] Not infrequently, two families crowded into each of these wretched apartments; in 1908, a census of East Side families suggested that half slept at three or four people to a room, nearly a quarter at five or more to a room; they depended on a few communal taps, and fixed baths were non-existent.[102] Thus an ordinary street block could house 4,000 people, and in 1900 some 42,700 Manhattan tenements housed more than 1.5 million people, at an average of nearly thirty-four to each building.[103]

The reaction of respectable society – meaning older-established, White Anglo-Protestant Society – was up to a point identical to that in London. Two successive Tenement House Commissions, in 1894 and 1900, confirmed the evils of tenement-house living; the first achieved little, but the second was followed – after a huge political battle – by legislation in 1901, 'the most significant regulatory act in America's history of housing', which outlawed the construction of further dumb-bells and compelled the modification of existing ones.[104] Its secretary, Lawrence Veiller, was a young man in his twenties, who had fought vested interests to get it set up.[105] His own view was that many of the city's problems stemmed from the too sudden transition from European peasant to American urbanite,

[99] Abrams, 1939, 72–3.   [100] Ibid. 187; Scott, 1969, 10.
[101] DeForest and Veiller, 1903, I. 101; Lubove, 1962b, 30–1.   [102] Howe, 1976. 27.
[103] Glaab and Brown, 1976, 152.   [104] Ford, 1936, 205.
[105] Lubove, 1962b, 82–3, 90–3, 125–7, 132–9.

which he would propose to remedy via mass rural resettlement. But meanwhile, for those trapped in the city, urgent and drastic action was needed to redress the worst evils of tenement life: more light, more air, new bathrooms, better fire protection.[106]

As Veiller described these evils, they were 'almost beyond belief':[107] in one block measuring a mere 200 by 400 feet were crowded thirty-nine tenement houses with 605 separate units, housing 2,781 people, with a mere 264 water-closets, and with not one bath among them; 441 rooms had no ventilation whatsoever, another 635 got theirs solely from narrow air shafts.[108] The 1894 Commission's recommendations, which sought to prevent overbuilding, had been largely circumvented, Veiller wrote:

> Unrestrained greed has gradually drawn together the dimensions of these tenements, until they have become so narrowed that the family life has become dissolved, and the members have been thrust out and scattered. The father is in the saloon; the youth team in procession up and down the lighted streets past concert halls and licensed dens of infamy; the boys rove in hordes in the alley, the girls in the rear yards. . . . The redemption of the tenement classes lies partly in the restoration of the family, the most conservative unit in civilization, to its proper share of space, natural light and air, and the cultivation of the domestic arts, one of which is personal cleanliness.[109]

The Commissioners concluded:

> The tenement districts of New York are places in which thousands of people are living in the smallest place in which it is possible for human beings to exist – crowded together in dark, ill-ventilated rooms, in many of which the sunlight never enters and in most of which fresh air is unknown. They are centres [sic] of disease, poverty, vice, and crime, where it is a marvel, not that some children grow up to be thieves, drunkards and prostitutes, but that so many should ever grow up to be decent and self-respecting.[110]

So there was a huge problem; on that, the Commission was at one with the British Royal Commission of 1885. But, when it came to solutions, Veiller and his commissioners sharply diverged from the British – and indeed the European – road. They looked at the London model of public housing, and decisively rejected it. 'No good purpose could be thereby served,' they concluded: at most, municipal housing would 'better the living conditions of a favored few' and 'would furnish no better demonstration than private benevolence has furnished in the past and can be relied upon to furnish in the future'; there would be no way to determine 'where should the wage line be drawn between those for whom they should and those for whom they should not provide.'[111] Besides, they felt, public housing would

[106] Ibid. 131–4. [107] DeForest and Veiller, 1903, I. 112. [108] Ibid. I. 112–13. [109] Ibid. I. 435. [110] Ibid. I. 10. [111] Ibid. I. 44.

FIGURES 2.5 AND 2.6 *New York Dumbbells (Old Law Tenements)*. As in Berlin, so in New York, another 'improved' housing design perversely brings no light, no air, but instead monumental overcrowding.

mean a ponderous bureaucracy, political patronage, the discouragement of private capital. So it was to be resisted: physical regulation of the private developer was to provide the answer. The 1901 Act, meticulously divided into more than 100 detailed sections, codified space standards, fire protection, plumbing provision.[112] Perhaps, in the conditions of the time and the place, that was a realistic judgement; though soon, other housing reformers – Edith Elmer Wood, Frederick Ackerman – were beginning to take issue with it. Whatever the case, in comparison with Europe, it was to set the cause of public housing back for decades, as Catherine Bauer was to bemoan in the 1930s.[113]

The reasons have intrigued historians. For they entailed a divorce in America between the infant arts of planned housing and planned cities. Early American planning, as will emerge in chapter 6, was dominated by the City Beautiful movement, and that was planning without social purpose – or even with a regressive one: the zoning movement, which profoundly influenced the subsequent course of American suburban development, was, if anything, socially exclusionary in its purpose and its impact. Regional plans, like the celebrated New York Regional Plan of

112 Friedman, 1968, 33–5, 76.   113 Lubove, 1962b, 178–9, 182–3.

1931, were largely concerned with better housing for those that could afford to pay. Thus, 'housing, proclaimed as a major concern at the beginning of each of three milestones in the evolution of planning in the United States, in each case becomes joined with other issues; in each case solutions emerge either unrelated to housing or in fact aggravating those very housing conditions that had seemed to beget the effort.'[114]

Peter Marcuse's explanation is that of the three reasons why housing emerged as an issue – externalities like fire and disease dangers, concern for social order, and the protection of real estate values – the first two faded after 1910, as public health and fire control improved and as the immigrants were assimilated; thence, planning depended only on 'the alliance of real estate interests with middle-income home-owning voters', who had no interest whatsoever in programmes for rehousing the poor. And this provided a sharp contrast with Europe, where a strong working-class consciousness allied with an interventionist bureaucracy.[115]

What did emerge, in its place, was something odd and distinctly American: a voluntary movement dedicated to saving the immigrant from his (and, especially, her) own errors and excesses, socializing him into American folkways, and adjusting him to city life. The oddity lies partly in the fact that the idea was borrowed from Europe, and specifically from London's East End. There, a host of social endeavours had developed during the 1870s and 1880s to bring Christian morality and clean habits to the people of the slums. Jane Addams, on her first visit to England at the age of twenty-two, was profoundly affected by the publication of *The Bitter Cry of Outcast London*. On a second trip, in June 1888, she just as providentially heard of Toynbee Hall, Canon Samuel Barnett's Christian settlement in St Jude's in East London, the 'worst parish in London'. The next year, she embarked on establishing a similar settlement in Chicago. Located at the middle of four poor immigrant communities – Italian, German, Jewish, Bohemian – Hull House was staffed by idealistic, college-educated young people, almost all female and highly religious. The kind of young woman who earlier would have become a missionary or tried to save a drunken husband, a newspaper reporter wrote, would now go into the settlement house.[116] Some observers, as a result, found the atmosphere insufferable: Thorstein Veblen wrote of 'punctilios of upper-class propriety', Sinclair Lewis of 'cultural comfort-stations . . . upholding a standard of tight-smiling prissiness.'[117] Their clientele, too, were chiefly female: a male immigrant later recalled that 'we went there for an occasional shower, that was all.'[118] They dispensed continuing education for early school-leavers, summer camps to take children back to nature or playgrounds for those

---

[114] Marcuse, 1980, 38.   [115] Ibid. 40–9.   [116] Davis, 1967, 37.
[117] Ibid. 17.   [118] Ibid. 88.

FIGURE 2.7 *Jane Addams.*
The face of compassion and do-goodism, ready to battle for the bodies and souls
of Chicago's slumdwellers.

who stayed behind, an old people's club (designed to break down their
prejudice against the immigrants), a boarding club for girls, a programme
to save 'fallen women', and a day nursery. They also pursued social inquiries
consciously modelled on the Booth survey, and worked for reform of the
labour laws.[119] Finally, they campaigned against the gin-palace:

> These coarse and illicit merrymakings remind one of the unrestrained jollities
> of Restoration London, and they are indeed their direct descendants,
> properly commercialized, still confusing joy with lust, and gaiety with debauch-
> ery.[120]

Years later, after a decade of prohibition had brought mayhem to the
streets of Chicago, she still warmly supported it, suggesting that the answer
was to disarm the gangsters.[121]

It seems touching. Visitors from Britain – the Warden of Toynbee Hall,
John Burns – were puzzled at the evident lack of any municipal intervention:

[119] Addams, 1910, 41–2, 69, 85–9, 98–9, 121, 105–8, 129–31, 136, 146, 169, 198–230;
Davis, 1967, 45, 58–9, 61–2, 85.
[120] Addams, 1965, 87. [121] Addams, 1929, 54–5.

FIGURE 2.8 AND 2.9 *Chicago tenement life, ca. 1900.*
The immigrant mothers and their children await the reformer from Hull House.

the condition of the houses, where immigrants followed rural folkways in the middle of the city – slaughtering sheep and baking bread in basements – would have made them quite illegal in London, they exclaimed.[122] But the Hull House programme was only an especially idealistic, and exceptionally well-publicized, variant of what was happening in every American city before World War One: there were six such centres in the United States in 1891, more than 100 by 1900, more than 400 by 1910.[123] The objective was to integrate the immigrant into the city, first by individual moral example, secondly – if that should fail – through moral coercion and even, so some supporters believed, segregation or repatriation of 'the tramp, the drunkard, the pauper, the imbecile'.[124] But, thirdly, these were to be accompanied by a systematic upgrading of the urban environment, through parks and playgrounds and eventually through a wider system of city parks which – so argued the father of American landscape architecture, Frederick Law Olmsted – would exert a 'harmonizing and refining influence . . . favorable to courtesy, self-control and temperance'.[125] Some supporters went further, arguing for neighbourhood revival as a way of restoring the quality of urban life, though Jane Addams herself would have none of such 'geographical salvation'.[126] And from this grew the notion that the city itself could engender civic loyalty, thus guaranteeing a harmonious moral order; the city's physical appearance would symbolize its moral purity. This became the central tenet of the City Beautiful movement.[127] Whether it made an adequate substitute for planned public housing, no one apparently thought to ask those most directly affected. In practical terms, Jane Addams followed the Lawrence Veiller prescription: she played a key role in launching Robert Hunter's inquiry into Chicago tenement housing, the exact equivalent of the New York report, which revealed equally horrifying conditions and resulted in a tenement-house ordinance of 1902.[128]

An International Problem

The remedies then were different. But the problem, and the perception of it, were similar on both sides of the Atlantic. The problem was the giant city itself. The perception of it was the source of multiple social evil, possible biological decline and potential political insurrection. From 1880 to 1900, perhaps 1914, middle-class society – the decision-makers, the leader-writers, the pamphleteers, the activists – was running scared. Much of this fear was grotesquely exaggerated, some of it deliberately so by practised

[122] Addams, 1910, 295–5.   [123] Davis, 1967, 11–12.   [124] Ibid 92; Boyer, 1978, 191.
[125] Boyer, 1978, 239.   [126] Davis, 1967, 76.
[127] Boyer, 1978, 252.   [128] Hunter, 1901, *passim*; Davis, 1967, 67.

self-publicists. But the underlying reality was horrific enough, and it stemmed from poverty. The rich might, through revolution, have given to the poor; it would not have done anyone much good, for there was all too little to go around. That poverty had been endemic since the beginnings of society, but in the countryside it could be more or less hidden; once concentrated in the city, it was revealed. The poor who crowded from Wessex or East Anglia into London, from Italy and Poland into New York, were actually better off than they had been on the land; or at least, they thought they were, and they were in the best position to know.

The difference then lay in the fact of concentration, whereby some thousands of the rich and some millions of the middle classes were brought into close contact with millions of the poor and very poor. In this sense industrialization and urbanization, as the Marxists always say, did create a new set of social relationships and a new set of social perceptions. But that, as I argued in chapter 1, just states the obvious. Until 1883–5 in London and Liverpool, until 1900–1 in New York and Chicago, the urban bourgeoisie remained blissfully unaware of the horrific fate of their proletarian counterparts next door. After that, there could be no doubt. Veiller and Hunter described that fate all too graphically. Here is Veiller, interviewing a housewife from the tenements:

The Secretary	What is the chief trouble with the tenement house in your experience?
Mrs. Miller	– Well, there doesn't seem to be any 'chief' about it. It seems to be about all trouble. In the first place, the way the tenements are run. Then the air shaft is the chief and greatest nuisance.
The Secretary	– What is the trouble with the air shaft?
Mrs. Miller	– It is a place of foul odors rather than air. For light, you get light on the top floor, but no place else, and the noises – I do not think it has a very good influence on the people.
The Secretary	– In what way?
Mrs. Miller	– Well, it is not very nice to be waked up in the middle of the night and hear someone yell out 'Oh, that is down on the first floor. He has got delirium tremens again.' Two houses kept awake by that man yelling. Boys and girls hear it and tease the children about it next day.[129]

And here Hunter, describing life in the frame-house tenements of Chicago:

To cook and wash for seven, to nurse a crying baby broken out with heat, and to care for a delirious husband, to arrange a possible sleeping-place for seven, to do all these things in two rooms which open upon an alley, tremulous with heated odors and swarming with flies from the garbage and manure boxes, was something to tax the patience and strength of a Titan.[130]

---

[129] DeForest and Veiller, 1903, I. 404.
[130] Hunter, 1901, 63.

The problem, then, was well-nigh universal. The question for historians must be why, given the similarity of the underlying economic structures and the resulting social relationships in the leading industrial countries around 1900, the subsequent urban outcomes should be so different. That is a question that will recur in the following chapters.

The City of
By-Pass Variegated

And the newness of everything! The raw, mean look! Do you know the look of these new towns that have suddenly swelled up like balloons in the last few years, Hayes, Slough, Dagenham and so forth? The kind of chilliness, the bright red brick everywhere, the temporary-looking shopfronts, full of cut-price chocolates and radio parts.

George Orwell
Coming up for Air (1939)

Come, friendly bombs, and fall on Slough
It isn't fit for humans now,
There isn't grass to graze a cow
Swarm over, Death!

Come, bombs and blow to smithereens
Those air-conditioned, bright canteens,
Tinned fruit, tinned meat, tinned milk, tinned beans
Tinned minds, tinned breath.

Mess up the mess they call a town –
A house for ninety-seven down
And once a week for half-a-crown
For twenty years . . .

John Betjeman
'Slough' (*Continual Dew*) (1937)

3
The City of
By-Pass Variegated

The Mass Transit Suburb:
London, Paris, Berlin, New York,
1900–1940

Almost precisely in 1900, as a reaction to the horrors of the nineteenth-century slum city, the clock of planning history started ticking. But, paradoxically, as it did so, another much older and bigger timepiece started to drown it out. The very problem, that the infant planning movement sought to address, almost instantly began to change its shape. Most of the philosophical founders of the planning movement continued to be obsessed with the evils of the congested Victorian slum city – which indeed remained real enough, at least down to World War Two, even to the 1960s. But all the time, the giant city was changing, partly through the reaction of legislators and local reformers to these evils, partly through market forces. The city dispersed and deconcentrated. New homes, new factories were built at its suburban periphery. New transportation technologies – the electric tram, the electric commuter train, the underground railway, the motor bus – allowed this suburbanization process to take place. New agencies – building societies, public and non-profit housing agencies – exploited the opportunities thus offered. Cheap labour and cheap materials reduced the real costs of new housing, especially in the late 1920s and early 1930s. Better, more subtle planning and development regulations curbed the congestion and also some of the tedium of the nineteenth-century cities. The result was an extraordinary and quite sudden improvement in the housing standards of a wide spectrum of the population. But the results were often visually unimpressive and sometimes woeful – not, maybe, to those most immediately affected, but certainly to those who styled themselves expert guardians of the public taste.

And all this took place even while the pioneers were writing, campaigning, exerting influence on the body politic. The resulting dilemma is an unresolvable dilemma for the writer (and the reader) of planning history: it is never clear which came first, the suburbanizing chicken or the philosophical egg. But after all, it does not matter: the story only makes sense if both lines are understood together. So, though it is a logical impossibility, this and the following chapters – above all the next – need to be read simultaneously.

The process of suburbanization, especially the market-led variety, was far more pervasive and more evident in London and New York than in Paris or Berlin or other European capitals. And in certain key aspects – the role of public transport, the importance of cheap long-term mortgages, the relationship between private and large-scale public developments – London remained the most interesting, the most vital, the most evidently problematic of all the great cities in these years. So the story had better focus on it.

The London County Council Starts to Build

Right at the start of the new century, the British Census of 1901 showed just how acute remained London's problems of congestion and overcrowding. Some 45 per cent families in one inner London borough (Finsbury) still lived in one or two rooms, while in a whole ring of neighbouring boroughs[1] the proportion exceeded one-third.[2] That year, Charles Booth published yet another paper, extolling the virtues of 'improved means of locomotion as a first step towards the cure of the housing difficulties of London'. What was needed, Booth argued, was 'a large and really complete scheme of railways underground and overhead, as well as a net-work of tram lines on the surface; providing adequately for short as well as for long journeys. A system extending well outside the present metropolitan boundaries into the outskirts of London, wherever the population has gone, or may go.'[3] True, Booth – never a believer in government action, save in dire necessity – saw this as a means to free the private builder to provide the cure. But the more collectivist mind of the LCC's Progressive Party had already moved in the same direction. Though the Royal Commission of 1885 had recommended rehousing the working classes in the centre, during the 1890s that idea was speedily abandoned.[4]

The Progressive – that is, Fabian-influenced – majority dominated the LCC's Housing Committee from the start in 1890;[5] in 1898 it recommended that the Council itself build on a large scale on vacant land using Part III of the 1890 Act, and the full Council – after much agitation and a big debate – endorsed the policy. Finding that they were precluded from building outside their own constricted inner-London boundaries – even then, almost entirely built up – the LCC pressured Parliament for an

---

[1] Stepney, Shoreditch, St Pancras, St Marylebone, Holborn.   [2] Wohl, 1977, 310.
[3] Booth, 1901, 15–16.   [4] Stedman Jones, 1971, 329.   [5] Wohl, 1977, 251.

FIGURE 3.1 *Old Oak Estate, built ca. 1913.*
The LCC Architect's Department out-Unwins Unwin: Germanic vernacular, curves
and gable ends according to Sitte.

amendment in 1900, allowing them to build estates of 'working class tenements' on green-field sites at the edge of the County and even beyond it, which they immediately used to start work on four such estates. And, even though that same year the Moderate (Conservative) Party took control, keeping it until 1914, the LCC maintained a big house-building programme. Between 1900 and 1914, they provided some 17,000 rooms in rehousing schemes on slum-clearance sites within their own boundaries, and another 11,000 in peripheral and out-county estates.

In 1899, even before they got parliamentary powers, they moved to buy the Totterdown Fields site at Tooting in south London.[6] The means to its development was the electrification of the tramway, which the LCC had acquired from private interests a few years earlier. In May 1903, when the Prince of Wales opened the line from Westminster and Blackfriars Bridges to Totterdown Street, he was also able to visit the first cottages, just occupied. A second peripheral estate, at Norbury outside the LCC area, was slightly more problematic; the LCC trams terminated at the boundary half a mile short. A third, White Hart Lane at Tottenham in north London, 2 miles from the county line, was a bigger challenge still: the LCC had

[6] Tarn, 1973, 137.

hoped for a tube line as part of the construction mania of the mid-Edwardian years, but it failed to come to pass.[7]

At the fourth site, Old Oak in west London, they were luckier; the estate was planned around an extension of the Central London Railway, which, begun in 1913, was delayed by World War One and opened only in 1920.[8] The whole estate, minuscule though it may be, is thus a classic example of a satellite settlement planned around a transit line from the city; it anticipates by more than a decade what Bruno Taut was to do at Onkel Toms Hütte in Berlin in the 1920s and, much later, Sven Markelius was to achieve at Vällingby and Farsta in Stockholm in the period 1955–65.

It fell short in one respect, for the LCC: they were not in charge of the underground fares, as on the trams they were. From the outset, they saw the trams as 'instruments of social policy':[9] early-morning cheap workmen's fares would ensure that rent and fare combined would be less than central-London rentals. 'The advantages of air-space and pleasant surroundings can, therefore, be secured at practically no extra cost and even, in the majority of instances, with some reduction of necessary expenses': so they argued in 1913.[10] Thus,

> [Though] the Council has not been free to abandon the policy of central housing or rehousing . . . the policy laid down by Parliament has often led to the retention in central districts of many working-class families who might have been accommodated in the suburbs at less cost to the community and at greater advantages to themselves.[11]

By 1914, the trams were carrying 260,000 passengers a day, against 560,000 on the cheap early-morning workmen's trains.[12] About this time, Charles Masterman described the effect in south London, where the LCC routes were especially dense: 'Family after family are evacuating the blocks and crowded tenements for little four-roomed cottages, at Hither Green and Tooting. The unaccustomed sign 'To Let' can be seen in almost every street.'[13]

So the LCC prescription worked – for some. What Masterman, for all his acuteness of observation, may not have noticed was that the migration was socially selective. It was the better-off skilled artisan who got a bargain from the move: the LCC cottages gave his family more and better-designed space for their money, but they still cost more than the rent of a miserable room near the centre, and in them, subletting was specifically and stringently barred. So those earning £1 a week or less – the casual labourer, the carman, the market porter, the docker – who had only 7s. left for rent after buying food, were still trapped in the slums; and, during this first full

[7] Barker and Robbins, 1974, 78–84, 91, 98.   [8] Ibid. 243.   [9] Ibid. 96.
[10] London County Council, 1913, 113.   [11] Ibid. 115.   [12] Wohl, 290–3.
[13] cit. Barker and Robbins, 1974, 99.

decade of LCC building from 1901 to 1911, overcrowding in London actually worsened.[14]

But for those who could escape, the effect must have been dramatic. Both the early peripheral estates, and the more numerous inner-city slum-clearance schemes, represent some of the earliest examples in Britain of large-scale town planning, and both kinds achieved an extraordinarily high level of architecture and civic design. The credit for that belongs to the new LCC Architect's Department, to whom came a group of young and talented architects steeped in the traditions of William Morris, Norman Shaw and the Arts and Crafts movement. This is the first, but not the last, point in this story when chronology and organization run awry: this early LCC style was in many ways identical, in spirit and in practical outcome, to that practised in the same years by Raymond Unwin and Barry Parker at New Earswick Garden Village outside York, at Letchworth Garden City and at Hampstead Garden Suburb, which forms a main focus of chapter 4.

Where it differed, at least in the earliest examples, was a result not of philosophy, but of legal constraint. Working outside existing cities, and sometimes able to pressure traditionalist local authorities, Unwin and Parker were able to set aside the rigid local by-laws which, ironically, had been created thirty or forty years earlier to guarantee minimum standards of light and air for working-class housing, but which did so at the expense of uniform and dull gridiron layouts. The LCC architects were seldom so lucky. In their earliest scheme of all, completed in 1900 – the Boundary Street estate in Shoreditch, a central-area rehousing scheme on the site of the Jago, a notorious nineteenth-century slum – they had been able to achieve a remarkable effect with five-storey walk-up blocks, designed by various hands like large pavilions around a leafy central circus: a kind of palace for the poor, still impressive even after nearly ninety years, and even in an appalling state of local authority run-down. But, in their earliest edge-of-town and out-of-town schemes – 1,261 houses at Totterdown Fields (1903–9), 881 houses at White Hart Lane (1904–13) and 472 houses at Norbury (1906–10) – they were stuck with the grid and had to do the best they could with it: by varying the length and setting back some of the terrace rows, by constantly imaginative treatment of the façades, and – at Tottenham – by incorporating a private donation of open space to create a remarkable central quadrangle of houses around a park.[15]

Only after 1910 did they begin to break loose. On the small site for 304 houses at Old Oak in Hammersmith, where they had a free hand, they were able for the first time to build on curving streets to create an

[14] Wohl, 1977, 266, 303.
[15] London County Council, 1913, 71–6; Tarn, 1973, 138–140; Wohl, 1977, 256, 364.

Unwinesque townscape of cosy corners, overhanging gable ends, and gateways that provide glimpses into half-hidden interior courts. The whole effect is cunningly conceived around the underground station, and set against the vast green expanse of Wormwood Scrubs, which – like the Heath at Hampstead Garden Suburb – forms a permanent green belt, separating the new satellite from the dense terraces of North Kensington a mile away. Here as in the other estates, the LCC planners laboured under extraordinary constraints: costs were as low as £50 a room, densities as high as thirty houses or 130 people to the acre (which, Abercrombie and Forshaw would argue thirty years later, required a high-rise solution), grim prison walls loomed just around the corner. Yet here they created a magic world that, even today, somewhat down at heel and graffiti-ridden, has the capacity to astonish. Then, in a second stage (1919–21) at Norbury, they brought off a *tour de force* in the Unwin–Parker tradition, almost outclassing the masters: they exploited a small hill to create a brilliant courtyard of terrace houses, rising above the by-law streets like a walled German medieval market town.

The First Town-Planning Schemes

Meanwhile, compared with the LCC, the other great urban authorities of England were doing relatively little. And many shared Booth's view that better urban transit, coupled with private housebuilding, offered the main route to the eventual solution of the problem: the infant art of town planning should concentrate on providing a better framework, within which the developer could work. That logic led to the Liberal Government's Housing, Town Planning, etc. Bill, which, bitterly fought through parliament – the second reading deferred no less than nineteen times, axed at the end of the 1907–8 session, reintroduced, and with no less than 360 House of Lords amendments – was passed into law in 1909.[16] Introducing it, John Burns – now, as President of the Local Government Board, retaining some echoes of the oratory that had once swayed Trafalgar Square – intoned:

> The object of this Bill is to provide a domestic condition for the people in which their physical health, their morals, their character, and their whole social condition can be improved. . . . The Bill aims in broad outlines at, and hopes to secure, the home healthy, the house beautiful, the town pleasant, the city dignified, and the suburb salubrious.[17]

The principal means to the 'home healthy' would be more extensive slum-clearance and rebuilding powers for the local authorities: 'On its housing

---

[16] Gauldie, 1974, 305; Brown, 1977, 144, 150.   [17] Burns, 1908, 949.

FIGURE 3.2 *Norbury Estate, ca. 1921.*
Another LCC exercise in Unwinesque vernacular, around a hillside courtyard.

side the Bill seeks to abolish, reconstruct, and prevent the slum. It asks –
at least, I do for it – the House of Commons to do something to effect the
ghettos of meanness and the Alsatias of squalor that can be found in many
parts of the United Kingdom.'[18] To that end, the bill reformed the 1890
legislation, giving local authorities unambiguous powers to retain the houses
they built under slum-clearance schemes, thus paving the way for the post-
World War One public housing drive; it also allowed the Local Government
Board to prod recalcitrant authorities into action.[19] But the most important
section dealt with the new town planning powers which, Burns explained,
'seek to diminish what have been called bye-law streets, with little law and
much monotony. It hopes to get rid of the regulation roads that are so
regular that they lack that line of beauty that Hogarth said was a curve.'[20]

The model was the small group of schemes that had already managed
to escape from the tyranny of the by-laws: 'They have only to take a motor
car or any other vehicle, and go to places like Balham, Millbank, Boundary
St., Tooting, Ealing, Hampstead and Northfield to see how modified
schemes of town planning, accompanied by schemes of transit, tram, train
and tube are progressing.'[21]

The objective, accepting that London's population would continue to
grow outwards, was to plan for it by gaining agreement between the public
and the private sector: 'to get them to turn together towards one outlook
with one scheme, instead of mutually fighting each other to each other's
detriment':[22]

> Let us take Bournville for the poor and Bournemouth for the rich. Let us
> take Chelsea for the classes and Tooting for the masses. What do you find?
> You find in those four instances that your public-spirited corporations and
> your public-spirited landowners have been at work, and . . . you will find
> very much done without damage to anybody of what we hope to make
> universal by this Bill.[23]

The press were unimpressed by the oratory. But eventually, on
3 December 1909, the Bill was passed. Its most important provision was
to allow and encourage local authorities to make town planning schemes
for large areas liable to be developed for new housing. The earliest schemes
approved by the Local Government Board were three linked areas on
the west side of Birmingham, Edgbaston, Harborne and Quinton, a total
of 2,320 acres; a scheme for east Birmingham soon followed, with the firm
intention eventually to cover the entire periphery of the city. George
Cadbury in 1915 commended them for their role in reducing 'the great
stirrings of social unrest, which are such a striking manifestation in these
days', since 'undoubtedly at the present time a large factor in the Labour

---

[18] Ibid.   [19] Gauldie, 1974, 305–6.   [20] Ibid.
[21] Ibid. 954.   [22] Ibid. 955.   [23] Ibid. 956.

Unrest is the desire of the masses of the working classes to obtain the means to live a proper life for both themselves and their families.'[24] But another prominent Birmingham industrialist and social reformer, J. S. Nettlefold, who had originally conceived of the schemes in imitation of best German planning practice, doubted that they would have any effect of the kind: 'Neither of the two Birmingham schemes are in the least degree likely to help those people who so badly need assistance, if only for the sake of their children.'[25]

For Nettlefold, the London scheme that was approved at about the same time, at Ruislip–Northwood, was much superior. It was very much larger, covering some 6,000 acres as against 4,000 in the two Birmingham schemes; it set out roads, building lines, open spaces, shopping, factory and residential areas. With a maximum density of twelve houses to the acre, it included many areas with less. At its heart was a design – commended by Burns in the debate – by A. and J. Soutar for the Ruislip Manor Company, the winner in a competition assessed by Raymond Unwin and Sir Aston Webb.[26]

Today, in a short tour of west London, the earnest student of planning history can take in three early classics: the LCC's Old Oak estate of 1912–14, the Ealing Tenants' nearby co-operative garden suburb of 1906–10, and Ruislip–Northwood. The comparison is not to Ruislip–Northwood's advantage. Speculative builders, even enlightened ones, could hardly compete with the early LCC Architect's Department at its best, or with Unwin and Parker's small gem at Ealing. What additionally disappoints is the quality of the Ruislip layout. The core is the Ruislip Manor scheme, and in turn the core of that is a formal main axis which climbs gradually, through a series of traffic circles, to form the main shopping parade passing under the Metropolitan Railway line that provides a *raison d'être* of the whole development, thence to the summit of a pronounced hill, which looks down the far side to the northern boundary of the scheme, an extensive green belt reserved mainly for recreation.

By the standards of by-law planning, of course, it is a notable advance: there is a coherence of a rather formal kind, the open space is generous and flexibly disposed (a green wedge, for instance, runs alongside the railway, right in to the edge of the shopping centre), some pieces of the road pattern are interesting. But, surprisingly, there are also long unbroken lines of almost straight street, of unequalled by-law tedium; Burns, one feels, orated in vain. And, coupled with the uninspired neo-Georgian of the shopping parade – a style to be repeated countless times, all over suburban London, in the 1920s and 1930s – the effect is one of rather crushing

---

[24] Cadbury, 1915, 14, 136.   [25] Nettlefold, 1914, 123.
[26] Ibid. 124–8; Aldridge, 1915, 537.

FIGURE 3.3 *Ealing Tenants' meeting, ca. 1906.*
Howard's Freedom and Co-operation in full flight in one of the first Garden Suburbs, but the flavour is decidedly middle-class.

formalism: a City Beautiful that isn't very beautiful. It provides an inauspicious start for the golden age of the English suburb.

New York Discovers Zoning

The Americans had already done much better than that. Their classic nineteenth-century and early twentieth-century suburbs, all planned around commuter railroad stations – Llewellyn Park in New Jersey, Lake Forest and Riverside outside Chicago, Forest Hills Gardens in New York – all had a conspicuously high standard of design; Riverside, as we shall see in chapter 4, was almost certainly one of the models for Ebenezer Howard's Garden City. And, as American cities rapidly extended their basic municipal services outwards, the citizens of these suburbs were the main beneficiaries:

> They owned the flush toilets and bathtubs that flowed with ample supplies of municipal water; they were the bicyclists who benefited from the fresh

asphalt pavements; and they also rode the lengthy streetcar lines to suburban neighborhoods for a price equal to that paid by inner-city commuters for shorter journeys.[27]

The problem was that down to 1900 there were not many of them.

That was especially true in New York and Chicago, which were already too big for effective streetcar access; here, the future would depend on subway or commuter lines. New York opened its first subway segment in 1904,[28] and the sysem began to spread in the following years. But, as the Tenement House Commission had reported in 1900, while 'undoubtedly better transit facilities will enable some of the more ambitious and better paid tenement dwellers to provide themselves with separate houses in the outlying districts . . . it is evident that the bulk of the laboring classes will continue to live in tenement houses'; they could not afford to move.[29] Nevertheless, one indirect effect of Veiller's work was the Commission on Congestion of Population, established through the efforts of settlement house leaders in 1907, which reported in 1911 in favour of decentralization through transit.

But – as the Commission had recognized in its own exhibition on congestion three years earlier, and as civic leaders appreciated – better transit was a double-edged sword: it could also spell even worse congestion in the city's core, by bringing more workers in and raising land values. This was the paradox, and it could be resolved only through a complementary measure: restrictions on the height and massing of buildings.[30]

The Commission's executive secretary was Benjamin C. Marsh, a lawyer and social reformer, who visited Europe at the start of its work in 1907–8 and published an early tome on city planning in 1909, the year of the first National Conference on City Planning in Washington. Both Marsh and a fellow-visitor, a New York lawyer called Edward M. Bassett, were most struck by the success of the Germans in zoning land uses and building heights in their cities. Marsh in particular singled out Frankfurt, under its Bürgermeister Franz Adickes, as the model for American cities to follow;[31] Marsh was also impressed by the results of zoning in Düsseldorf and by Werner Hegemann's work in Berlin.[32]

So zoning came to New York from Germany. Perhaps that is an over-simplification: mundanely, American land-use zoning seems to have originated in an attempt to control the spread of Chinese laundries in California, first in the city of Modesto and then in San Francisco, in the 1880s; and from 1909 onwards Los Angeles developed comprehensive

[27] Teaford, 1984, 280.   [28] Cheape, 1980, 90–2.   [29] DeForest and Veiller, 1900, 6.
[30] Ford, 1936, 226–7; Makielski, 1966, 10; Klein and Kantor, 1976, 427–8.
[31] Williams, 1916, 81; Williams, 1922, 212–14; Mullin, 1977, 1.
[32] Bassett, 1939, 116.

land-use zoning.[33] But it was the German model of combined land-use and height zoning that was imported to New York City in its 1916 zoning ordinance, which – so contemporaries believed – was the most significant development in the early history of American city planning.[34]

The main agents were Bassett, who regarded it as his great life achievement, and his fellow New York reform politician George McAneny. Their moment of opportunity came in 1911, when Fifth Avenue garment retailers, worried by the spread of the manufacturing workshops that served them, formed a quasi-official commission to pressure the city into action. It brought speedy results: in 1913, the city's Board of Estimate voted to create a Committee on City Planning, empowered to appoint an advisory Commission on Heights of Buildings. The Commission's report, in December the same year, predictably argued for a system of zoning based on the concept of police power: the notion, anciently developed in American out of English law, that the state had the right to regulate the private use of property so as to guarantee 'the health, safety, morals, comfort, convenience, and welfare of the community'.[35] A charter amendment to permit zoning followed early in 1914, and a Zoning Commission set to work to prepare the actual ordinance. Skilfully marshalling popular support and disarming opposition, it reported in 1916 in favour of four types of land use zone, two of which – residential and business – would be subject to height restrictions.[36]

As more than one observer pointed out, both then and subsequently, New York embraced zoning so enthusiastically because it was good for business. The Fifth Avenue merchants were concerned that floods of immigrant garment workers on the noontime streets would destroy the exclusive character of their businesses and would thus threaten their property values; they appealed to 'every financial interest' and to 'every man who owns a home or rents an apartment'; the Commission on Heights of Buildings confirmed that zoning secured 'greater safety and security in investment'.[37] The very year of the New York ordinance, John Nolen could agree with an English writer that American city planning essentially aimed at civic improvements that did not interfere with vested interests.[38] And, as the zoning movement rapidly spread from New York across the nation, this was its image.

It was indeed an odd kind of planning. For the relationship between zoning and planning was an indirect and tortuous one. True, the movement spread rapidly in the 1920s: in 1921 Herbert Hoover, as Secretary of Commerce, created an Advisory Committee on Zoning that included Bassett and Veiller; it resulted in a Standard State Zoning Enabling Act of 1923,

[33] Williams, 1922, 267; Bassett, 1936, 13; Walker, 1950, 55–6; Toll, 1969, 29; Marcuse, 1980, 32–3.   [34] Williams, 1922, 272.

[35] Bassett, 1936, 27–8; Makielski, 1966, 21; Toll, 1969, 17.   [36] Makielski, 1966, 33.

[37] Scott, 1969, 154–5; Toll, 1969, 158–9, 186; Glaab and Brown, 1976, 266.

[38] Nolen, 1916b, 22.

which was widely adopted. In 1927 it was followed by a Standard City Planning Enabling Act, which was adopted by many States to give legal authority to city master plans,[39] by 1929 more than 650 municipalities had planning commissions and 754 communities had adopted zoning ordinances.[40] And a series of landmark legal judgements, culminating in the historic 1926 case before the United States Supreme Court, *Village of Euclid, Ohio, et al. v. Ambler Realty Company*, established the validity of zoning as a legitimate expression of the general police power.[41] But city planning was commonly done on an advisory, non-mandatory basis; in 1937, out of 1,178 Commissions, no less than 904 had no financial appropriation at all.[42] In practice, despite the assertions of Bassett and others, planning and zoning were largely divorced from each other. Cincinnati, where the pioneer work of Alfred Bettman had achieved some real powers for the Planning Commission and where zoning was an arm of planning, was unusual.[43] As Bassett explained to his readers in 1936, though zoning was logically part of the city plan, commonly planning and zoning commissions had to be legally separate.[44]

In any case, the real point was why American cities so enthusiastically embraced the concept of zoning. The sordid reason was self-interest. As in New York, 'zoning became primarily a static process of attempting to set and preserve the character of certain neighborhoods, in order to preserve property values in these areas, while imposing only nominal restrictions on those areas holding a promise of speculative profit.'[45] In *Euclid* v. *Ambler*, the great planner-lawyer Alfred Bettman — whose brief, submitted late in the hearing, may well have proved crucial — argued that the 'public welfare' served by zoning was the enhancement of the community's property values.[46] The point, significantly, was whether land should be zoned industrial or residential; the Court gave the respectable residents of Euclid, a middle-class dormitory village next door to Cleveland, a guarantee that their investments would not be threatened. Bassett, the father of the New York scheme, later wrote that one of the major purposes of zoning was to prevent the 'premature depreciation of settled localities'.[47] Or, as a later commentator put it:

> The basic purpose of zoning was to keep Them where They belonged – Out. If They had already gotten in, then its purpose was to confine Them to limited areas. The exact identity of Them varied a bit around the country. Blacks, Latinos and poor people qualified. Catholics, Jews, and Orientals were targets in many places. The elderly also qualified, if they were candidates for public housing.[48]

---

[39] Hubbard and Hubbard, 1929, 21; Toll, 1969, 201.

[40] Hubbard and Hubbard, 1929, 3.   [41] Walker, 1950, 67–77.

[42] Ibid. 77; Bassett, 1938, 67; Foster, 1981, 137.   [43] Bassett, 1938, 75; Toll, 1969, 203.

[44] Bassett, 1936, 35.   [45] Walker, 1950, 60.   [46] Fluck, 1983, 333.

[47] Bassett, 1936, 25.   [48] Popper, 1981, 54.

A standard text of the late 1920s, indeed, could openly promote zoning on the basis that it stabilized property values: in every city with well-established zoning, the authors reported, 'property values are reported stabilized and in many instances substantially increased', a fact that had been quickly recognized by financial institutions everywhere.[49] *'Zoning and plat control'*, they emphasized, *'divide honors in being reported the most profitable results of city planning.'*[50] As they proudly proclaimed in a chapter heading, 'IT PAYS TO PLAN'.[51] Far from realizing greater social justice for the poor locked in the tenements of New York and Chicago, the planning-and-zoning system of the 1920s was designed precisely to keep them out of the desirable new suburbs that were being built along the streetcar tracks and the subway lines.

London: The Tube Brings Suburban Sprawl

Something like that was happening around London and other great British cities – but with an important difference. There, too, the age of mass suburbanization began after World War One. The key, in London and Birmingham as in New York or Chicago, was of course transport: the developments, at any rate in London and the big provincial cities, were well outside walk-to-work range. That meant municipal trams and then buses in places like Birmingham, Liverpool and Manchester, and underground railways and commuter railways as well in London. Above all, the growth of speculative housing around London – which roughly trebled the capital's area in twenty years – depended on rail transit. Unlike that in provincial England, this system was provided by private enterprise: specifically, the Underground group, which had absorbed the London General Omnibus Company in 1912, and the main-line railway companies, of which two – the Southern, and the London and North Eastern – developed major commuter networks.

A significant part of this system was created by American capital and enterprise. But that was not surprising. Americans had been quick to see the commercial potential of land development following new rail or streetcar lines, and some of the earliest textbook examples of the planned railway suburb – Llewellyn Park at West Orange, New Jersey (1853), Chestnut Hill in Philadelphia (1854), Lake Forest, Illinois (1856) and Riverside, Illinois (1869) – all anticipate the first classic British essay in the genre, Bedford Park in west London (1876).[52] From here it was a short step to the notion that an entrepreneur would deliberately lay out rail- or streetcar

---

[49] Hubbard and Hubbard, 1929, 188–9.   [50] Ibid. 188–9, 283.   [51] Ibid. 281.
[52] Stern and Massingdale, 1981, 23–4; Stern, 1986, ch. 4.

FIGURE 3.4   *Charles Tyson Yerkes.*
'Not a safe man' by Chicago standards, but the builder of three of London's tubes;
he died before he could reap his speculative rewards, but his legacy lives on.

lines in order to develop suburbs around them, as illustrated by the careers
of F. M. 'Borax' Smith in the San Francisco area or Henry E. Huntingdon
in Los Angeles.[53] But the most colourful, if perhaps the least savoury,
example was provided – first in Chicago, then in London – by the career
of Charles Tyson Yerkes (1837–1905).

  Yerkes was disarmingly open about his operations: 'The secret of my
success is to buy old junk, fix it up a little, and unload it on other fellows.'[54]
Contemporaries called him 'a buccaneer from a Pennsylvania penitentiary'
(he had been gaoled for early fraud) and 'not a safe man'.[55] He developed

[53] Jackson, K., 1985, 119–22.   [54] cit. Powers, 1961, 344.   [55] Ibid. 348, 353.

the street-railway system of Chicago and connected it into a network via the downtown Loop, controlling over 400 miles of street railway.[56] When the time came in 1897 to extend his franchises, he paid 1 million dollars to buy the State Legislature and then the City Council; successful in the first, he was unsuccessful in the second and nearly provoked a riot, after which he felt it provident to leave the city.[57]

London was a natural port of call. For there – as Theodore Dreiser recounts in his last novel, a thinly disguised fiction – he immediately realized that the Circle underground line was a ready-made downtown loop which could be exploited through new lines, then projected to start.[58] When Chicago heard of all this, Dreiser wrote, there were 'snarls of rage' that 'such a ruthless trickster, so recently ejected from that city' should now descend on London.[59] But descend he did; by 1901 Yerkes had acquired a large part of the London network, existing and new, and had welded it into a new company, the Underground Electric Railways of London Limited, and was engaged in a titanic struggle with another American tycoon, J. Pierpont Morgan, for the right to build new tubes in London.[60] The key to the operation is revealed by the fictional Yerkes: 'maybe you can find out something about the land values that are likely to be made by what we do, and whether it might be worth while to buy in advance in any direction, as we have done here in Lakeview and other places.[61] The gains would not come directly from the new lines, however: expensive to construct, these barely reached the built-up edge of London. They would come from tramway feeder lines, developed by separate companies, with syndicates to buy and sell land on the American pattern; UERL already controlled one tramway net, in west London.[62] Unfortunately for him, in 1905, while the new tube lines were actually under construction, Yerkes died.

But at least some of his legacy was to live after him – though stripped of the colourful financial aspects. Londoners are unconsciously reminded of it every time they hear that Americanism, 'Pass down the *cars*, please'. But it went deeper. The year after Yerkes's death his successor as Chairman of UERL, George Gibb, brought in a young statistical assistant called Frank Pick. The year after that, the company in deep financial trouble, UERL's directors bowed to the wishes of their American controlling interests and appointed to the post of general manager a thirty-two-year-old British émigré to the United States, then manager of the Public Services Corporation of New Jersey, Albert Stanley. Stanley (later Lord Ashfield) and Pick, men of very different, but complementary, personalities, were to form arguably

---

[56] Barker and Robbins, 1974, 61–2. [57] Malone, 1936, 610–11.
[58] Dreiser, 1947, 35–6, 200. [59] Ibid. 125. [60] Barker and Robbins, 1974, ch. 4.
[61] Dreiser, 1947, 23. [62] Jackson, 1973, 73; Barker and Robbins, 1974, 63.

FIGURE 3.5   *Frank Pick.*

the greatest management team ever known in the history of urban public transport; from 1933, on formation of London Transport, Ashfield would become chairman, Pick vice-chairman and chief executive officer.[63] In 1912, when UERL took over the London General Omnibus Company, Pick, now the company's commercial manager, began to develop feeder buses from the tube termini, on the model of Yerkes's original tramways plan. Within six months, with a new slogan 'Where the Railway Ends the Motor Bus begins', he more than doubled the number of routes, and extended the service area five times.[64]

---

[63] Menzler, 1951, 104–5, 110–11; Barker and Robbins, 1974, 140, 142.
[64] Barman, 1979, 66, 70.

FIGURE 3.6 *Albert Stanley, Lord Ashfield.*
Frank Pick and Albert Stanley, the greatest management team in the history of
London Transport, and – through their creation of the interwar suburbs – the true
creators of modern London.

But that was just the provisional start. After World War One, Pick began
systematically to analyse the gaps in existing rail services and the possibilities
of providing new ones. Successive governments, apparently impressed by
the notion that public works would relieve unemployment, provided public
money at zero or minimal rates of interest.[65] The results were presented
in a number of papers that Pick – that most academic-minded of managers –
gave to learned and professional societies from 1927 onwards: a tube line,
running at average speed of 25 miles an hour, would give an urban area

[65] Ibid. 78, 88, 147–8; Jackson, 1973, 220.

of 12-mile radius; by wide spacing of outer stations and by closing inner ones (as Pick did on the Piccadilly Line in 1932–4) this could be edged out to perhaps 15 miles, but hardly anyone would pay the equivalent of more than a 6*d*. fare, so by the late 1930s – when the last tube extensions were being built – the whole system had reached a limit.[66]

The development, thus triggered, took two forms, both presaged by the pioneering prewar schemes: first, an explosion of speculative building, above all around London, partly within the framework of town planning schemes, partly running ahead of them; second, a great extension of local-authority housing estates, especially around the great cities, generally in the form of dependent satellite towns linked to the parent city by tram, bus or rail. Both came to be condemned for failures in planning; but while in the first place the condemnation was muted and partial, in the second it was well-nigh universal, providing in the process the fuel that powered the movement for a more effective town and country planning system.

The Legacy of Tudor Walters

Down to World War One, local authorities had provided a negligible share of new housing in Britain: a total of 18,000 houses under the 1890 Act, the great majority of them in London; between 1910 and 1914, indeed, demolitions had outrun completions.[67] And, though there was a deepening crisis in the supply of working-class housing, there was no agreement as to the solution; some, like Nettlefold in Birmingham, thought that the framework of the 1909 Act would serve to release the energies of the private builders; others that co-partnership schemes provided the answer.[68] During the war, the problem actually worsened; rent strikes in Glasgow and in the new munitions-factory areas led to the hasty imposition of rent control.[69] At its end, the government faced a dilemma; it wanted to lift rent control, but it dare not unless the supply of new housing increased, and that could come only through local authority intervention.[70] In his highly influential book *The Home I Want* (1918), the housing reformer Captain Reiss could assert that it was 'generally agreed, even by those who believe in private

---

[66] Pick, 1927, 165; Pick, 1936, 215–16; Pick, 1938, Q. 3083–4, 3090–5.
[67] Gauldie, 1974, 306.   [68] Daunton, 1983, 289–92.   [69] Castells, 1983, 27–37.
[70] Bowley, 1945, 9.

FIGURE 3.7   *Homes fit for Heroes.*
The Lloyd George quotation that never was; the actual slogan, though less memorable, decided the Khaki election of 1918.

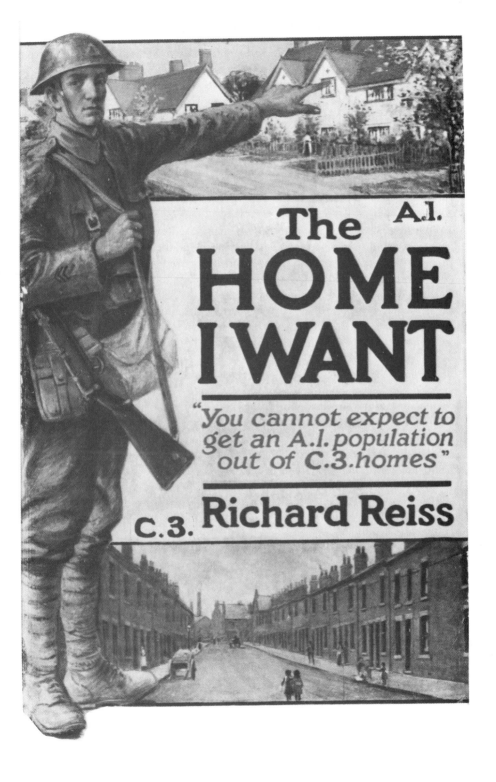

The **A.I.**

HOME
I WANT

"You cannot expect to get an A.I. population out of C.3. homes"

C.3. Richard Reiss

enterprise, that no other policy can be adopted immediately after the war' than local-authority building. 'It has been a bitter reproach to us that thousands of the men who have gone out to fight for 'Home and Country' have had no home worthy of that name and but little for which to thank their country.'[71]

All this was to change. Almost overnight, the housing of the working classes – the term was still openly used, then and for long after – came to be a public responsibility. The result, between the two world wars, was more than a million local authority dwellings, most of them single-family cottage houses, with their own gardens, in the form of satellites at the peripheries of the cities. Sometimes, as with the developments by Manchester at Wythenshawe, Liverpool at Speke, or London at Becontree, these amounted almost to new towns – albeit lacking sufficient industry to make them anything like self-contained. But they were the largest planned developments in England at that time, dwarfing the then garden cities: Becontree reached the 116,000 mark in 1939, Wythenshawe at the end of the 1930s was one-third of the way to the same target.

They represent the supreme achievement, though some would say the supreme failure, of Raymond Unwin. Here, not for the last time, we go out of historical sequence. Unwin's considerable early reputation came from his designs for the first Garden City at Letchworth and for Hampstead Garden Suburb, to be chronicled in chapter 4. In 1915, at considerable financial sacrifice, he had joined the Local Government Board as Town Planning Inspector in order to influence housing reform. Two years later, his opportunity came: he was appointed a member of the Committee on Housing chaired by Sir John Tudor Walters, which reported a month before the war's end, in October 1918.

That report proved one of the most potent influences on the development of the twentieth-century British city. It essentially argued four propositions. First, that though public utility societies, formed by groups of large employers, 'should be made an important auxiliary to the work of the local authorities', the latter alone – subsidized, of course, by government – could complete the task of building some 500,000 houses in a short time, 100,000 a year; speculative builders, the report dismissively declared, 'present a rather more difficult problem, but they most certainly have their place.' Second, that the local authorities must chiefly build on cheap undeveloped land on the outskirts of cities, carefully phasing their plans in with tramway development so that they did not have to pay enhanced value:

> With respect to the large towns, it is most desirable that, in order to avoid further overcrowding in the built-up areas, the new schemes should be provided in the outskirts, and the first step in this direction is to speed up the town-planning schemes coupled with foresight in tramway extension and other means of transit.[72]

[71] Reiss, 1918, 7. [72] G. B. Local Government Board, 1918, 5.

FIGURE 3.8 *Raymond Unwin.*
Heavily influenced by William Morris and John Ruskin; the creator, with Barry Parker, of the Garden City-Garden Suburb architectural vernacular.

Thirdly, it argued that on such sites, it was both possible and desirable to build at maximum densities of twelve single-family houses to the acre, each with its own garden, securing economies in land use by skilful design – of which they gave numerous examples. Fourthly, that to ensure good quality of design the plans should be produced by architects and must be approved by local commissioners of the Local Government Board and its Scottish equivalent.[73]

The report represented Unwin's personal triumph. All his basic ideas, carried through from his pamphlet *Nothing Gained by Overcrowding!* (1912),

[73] Ibid. 4–7, 13–17, 77.

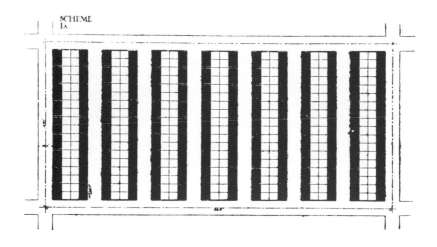

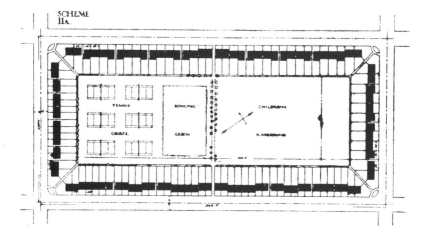

FIGURE 3.9   *Nothing Gained by Overcrowding!*
Unwin's enormously influential 1912 pamphlet dealt the death blow to the bye-law street and ushered in the age of the council estate and the cottage home.

were here: the minimum distance of 70 feet between houses to guarantee winter sunshine, the use of short terraces, the garden for every family, the use of spare backland as recreational space, the emphasis on culs-de-sac for safe children's play. Partly these recommendations stemmed from the remarkable experiment of employing a separate Women's Housing Sub-Committee, of whose recommendations Unwin seems to have taken just so much as he wished – rejecting, for instance, their recommendation that every house must have a separate parlour.[74]

The report was radical enough; what was remarkable was its immediate endorsement. But the fact was that the government was running scared. The day after the Armistice, Lloyd George announced what came to be known as the Carpon Election, promising, in one of those celebrated statements that are always misquoted, 'habitations fit for the heroes who have won the war'.[75] The next February, back in office at a conference with Ministers, the Prime Minister recounted an anecdote:

> A well-to-do man went to remonstrate with the miners. One of them, a fairly educated man and a Scotsman, said 'Do you know the place I live in?' He lives in one of those houses that are back-to-back, with all the sewage brought right through the living-room, and he has all his children living in that place. He said 'Supposing your children lived in these conditions, what would happen to you? The well-to-do man said frankly, 'I should be a Bolshevik.'[76]

Neville Chamberlain responded: 'I agree that our housing problem has got into such a condition that it is a threat to the stability of the State.'[77] The next month, in Cabinet, Lloyd George returned to what was evidently an obsession:

> In a short time we might have three-quarters of Europe converted to Bolshevism. . . . Great Britain would hold out, but only if people were given a sense of confidence. . . . We had promised them reform time and time again, but little had been done. . . . Even if it cost a hundred million pounds, what was that compared with the stability of the State?[78]

A month after, the Parliamentary Secretary to the Local Government Board repeated that 'the money we are going to spend on housing is an insurance against Bolshevism and Revolution.'[79] And this was to be embodied not merely in the fact that a house was built, but also in its design: 'The new houses built by the state – each with its own garden, surrounded by trees and hedges, and equipped internally with the amenities of a middle-class home – was to provide visible proof of the irrelevance of revolution.'[80]

The insurance policy was duly taken out, in the form of the Addison Act, named after Christopher Addison, Minister of Reconstruction, and then of Health: officially, the Housing and Town Planning Act, 1919. It imposed a duty on each local authority to survey housing needs – not just for slum clearance, but generally – and to make and carry out plans. It also guaranteed a state subsidy, independent of costs, to take account of the tenant's ability to pay; the costs were not to be passed on.[81] It also

[74] G. B. Ministry of Reconstruction, 1918a; Swenarton, 1981, 98.
[75] Swenarton, 1981, 79.   [76] cit. Johnson, 1968, 370.   [77] Ibid. 371.
[78] Swenarton, 1981, 78.   [79] Ibid. 79.   [80] Swenarton, 1981, 87.
[81] Bowley, 1945, 16–18.

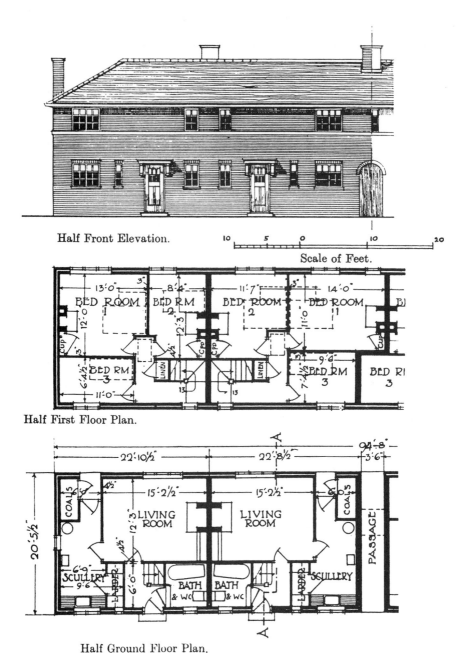

Half Front Elevation.

Scale of Feet.

Half First Floor Plan.

Half Ground Floor Plan.

FIGURE 3.10   *Cottage Homes for the People.*
Basic Unwin plans from the Ministry of Health Manual of 1920, following the
Tudor Walters report; they would be repeated in their thousands across the face
of England, but the Garden City purists felt betrayed.

made plan preparation mandatory for all urban areas with 20,000 and more people.

The same year, the Ministry of Health – a brand-new Ministry, formed out of the old Local Government Board, and responsible for the new housing programme – issued an immensely influential Housing Manual which bore Unwin's stamp all over it; its central argument, that urban densities of twelve houses per acre could be justified on cost grounds, derived directly from *Nothing Gained by Overcrowding!*. It also carried over from the Tudor Walters report other key arguments, such as the minimum distance of 70 feet between houses; it 'became an unwritten, unexplained, but universally accepted code of practice.'[82] But it also repeated another argument, which Unwin had used in a lecture at the University of Manchester in 1912 and which had recurred in the Tudor Walters report: that the resulting developments should take the form of semi-autonomous 'satellites' rather than full-fledged garden cities. Unwin, in other words, here made his definitive and immensely influential break with the pure garden-city gospel.

Here, it came to be challenged by another Ministry initiative of 1919: a committee, comprising Chamberlain as chairman, George Pepler (Unwin's chief of planning at the Ministry) and Captain Reiss, to report on the problem of unhealthy areas. Its interim report on London, published in March 1920, argued that the capital still suffered from an intolerable housing problem: 184,000 people in the LCC area lived in unhealthy areas, 549,000 in all under unsatisfactory conditons. There were two main remedies: to build up, or to move out. The first was 'quite unsuitable for a working-class population who are dependent on their own services for domestic services and the care of their children', as well as putting occupants 'at the mercy of any undesirable tenant'; the testimony of Medical Officers of Health and of social workers made it clear that 'the self-contained house is what appeals to working people.'[83] So the long-term solution must be garden cities, some based on existing country towns, of 30,000–50,000 people, surrounded by green belts. But, to achieve them, the problem was how to co-ordinate housing and industrial movement: 'The only way to escape from the vicious circle is by the investment of the State . . . of a considerable amount of capital . . . the return upon which must be delayed for a considerable period.'[84] And for this, a first essential was an integrated plan for the development of the whole built-up area of London.[85] The year after, in its final report, the Committee repeated and underlined this last recommendation; it also asked for government loans to get the garden cities started.[86]

[82] Edwards, 1981, 106; G. B. Ministry of Health, 1920a.
[83] G. B. Ministry of Health, 1920b, 3.   [84] Ibid. 3.   [85] Ibid. 4.
[86] G. B. Ministry of Health, 1921, 4–5.

It was crying for the moon. By 1921, following a sustained campaign by the Beaverbrook and Northcliffe presses against government waste, Christopher Addison – architect of the whole programme, first as Minister of Reconstruction, then of Health – had been sacrificed by Lloyd George in order to salvage his precarious coalition government.[87] His successor at Health, Sir Alfred Mond, slashed the programme. The era of reconstruction, of Homes fit for Heroes, was over. To be fair, housing subsidies came back, and with them large-scale local-authority housebuilding: through the 1923 Act, significantly passed when Chamberlain had replaced Mond at Health, and the Labour Government's Wheatley Act of 1924 which represented a partial return to the 1919 programme. Betwen 1919 and 1933–4, local authorities in Britain built 763,000 houses, some 31 per cent of the total completions.[88]

They built them, however, according to the latter-day Unwin prescription, in the form of peripheral satellites rather than full-fledged garden cities. The LCC housed 19,000 at Watling in north-west London, 30,000 at Downham in south-east London, 40,000 at St Helier around the new Morden tube station, and no less than 116,000 in the huge satellite at Becontree, the largest planned residential suburb in the world, and bigger than many English provincial towns.[89] They provided an immense improvement in housing standards, though ironically for the artisan, the small tradesman and the clerk rather than for the really poor, who could not afford the combined burden of rent and fares.[90] Architecturally, they were debased sub-Unwin, following the Housing Manual with little imagination and no inspiration. They are plain dull: a sudden and sad decline from the standards set a few years earlier at Old Oak.

In terms of detailed planning, they aped the worst faults of the speculative builder. The White Hart Lane extension, the Wormholt estate in Hammersmith and St Helier are all cut in half by huge arterial roads, which were actually built at the same time as an integral part of the plan (though, truth to tell, Unwin and Parker got in the same tangle at the northern edge of Hampstead Garden Suburb); no one, apparently, then anticipated what traffic would do to the local environment. Local jobs were few, and public transport links to jobs poor; by the late 1930s overcrowding on the Morden tube (which served both Watling and St Helier) was the subject of parliamentary questions, and the comedian Max Miller was making questionable jokes about it;[91] until the District Line was extended there in 1932, commuters from Becontree faced a 75-minute journey to Charing Cross.[92] None of the estates, even the biggest, had any kind of

[87] Minney, 1958, 176, 185; Gauldie, 1974, 309.   [88] Bowley, 1945, 59.
[89] Young, 1934, 98; Jackson, 1973, 291, 302, 309; Burnett, 1978, 231.
[90] Young, 1934, 118–20; Burnett, 1978, 233.   [91] Jackson, 1973, 271.
[92] Young, 1934, 140.

planned green belt around it, though Becontree had a partial and very narrow park girdle. Becontree was well planted with trees, though, as the sociologist Terence Young reported in his pioneer survey of 1934, 'the children have made their existence insecure'; the world was not innocent of vandalism, even then.[93]

Thus the new estates were not always popular with their occupants; at Becontree, the most distant, more than 30,000 left over a ten-year period and more than 10,000 in one year, 1928–9, alone;[94] at Watling in north-west London, surveyed by the young Ruth Glass at the end of the 1930s, some had returned to the slums because they could not afford rent and fares.[95] And some, doubtless, yearned for the bustle of the city:

> One afternoon in the autumn of 1937, early in the history of the Watling Estate, a woman banged loudly at the door of her neighbour. When it was opened she cried out: 'What has happened?' 'Why,' said her neighbour, 'what should have happened; what is the matter?' 'Everything is so terribly quiet,' said the first woman, still frightened to death.[96]

Nor was the prospect of an LCC estate popular with locals: at Becontree there were the usual press stories about people who pulled off their front doors for firewood;[97] at an inquiry in the 1930s, an impassioned exchange took place:

Mrs. Bastard: You haved [sic] ruined my home! (turning to LCC officers) Do any of you gentlemen live near an LCC estate?
                  receiving no answer
                  No, I don't suppose you do.
                  (*addressing the Minister's Inspector*):
                  Do you live near an estate?
The Inspector: They have just bought some land near my house.
Mrs. Bastard: Do you like it?
The Inspector: No.[98]

The Building of Suburbia

This reaction came, of course, from someone on the other side of the great housing divide which by then had sprung up across England, though nowhere more starkly than in the Home Counties around London. On that other side, a new industry had effectively been created, catering for a new market. Before World War One, the overwhelming majority of the entire population had rented their homes. After it, a number of factors conspired to persuade millions of the new middle class to buy. Huge changes in the

[93] Ibid. 98.   [94] Ibid. 210.   [95] Durant, 1939, 17–18.   [96] Ibid. 1.
[97] Young, 1934, 23.   [98] Jackson, 1973, 161.

structure of the economy were creating a new white-collar class, whose numbers rose from 20 to 30 per cent of the workforce between 1911 and 1951.[99] Real incomes for a large section of the population – especially this new white-collar group and the skilled blue-collar workers, whose jobs were disproportionately in and around London – were rising sharply. The Building Societies attracted huge funds, especially in the depression of the 1930s when industrial shares became unattractive. By various devices – insurance guarantees, the development of a 'builder's pool' whereby the developer took the risk – the proportion loaned could be raised as high as 95 per cent; at Bexley in the 1930s, keys to the cheapest houses could be had for a £5 deposit, and if this were lacking the estate agent or builder would lend it. Interest payments reached a low point of 4½ per cent in the mid-1930s.[100]

On the supply side, larger established builders like Costain, Crouch, Laing, Taylor Woodrow, Wates and Wimpey competed with a host of small firms existing on precarious profit margins and cash flows, which often went under, but kept prices keen.[101] And, in the depths of an agricultural depression, land was cheap; a plot could be had for as little as £20.[102] So families with modest incomes – skilled manual workers earning as little as £3. 10s. (£3.50) a week – could now afford to buy.[103] In the 1930s £1 a week would buy the standard three-bedroomed semi-detached, while those earning £300–£500 a year – teachers, bank officials, executive class civil servants – could afford bigger houses, perhaps detached.[104]

These circumstances powerfully conditioned the resulting product. 'To be saleable, a speculative house had to be emphatically middle-class, but if it had to be middle-class it also had to be cheap.' That meant romantic-looking, conservative in style, cheap to build, yet a status symbol.[105] Novean Homes advertised for 'families of good breeding who wish to acquire a house to be proud of at a cost of less than £1 a week'.[106] 'Every house different' and 'No pair of houses alike' were favourite slogans.[107] Because the Royal Institute of British Architects banned speculative architectural practice in 1920, the vast majority of these houses – nearly 3 million of them, between the two world wars – were designed by unqualified assistants or from pattern books or magazines. Only in the 1930s did the bigger firms begin to use architects.[108]

In the 1920s, at any rate, they were also designed without benefit of much planning. Though local authorities everywhere scrambled to follow

---

[99] Burnett, 1978, 247.

[100] Jackson, 1973, 193, 196; Boddy, 1980, 13–15; Carr, 1982, 244.

[101] Jackson, 1973, 110; Burnett, 1978, 257.   [102] Carr, 1982, 247.

[103] Jackson, 1973, 190–1.   [104] Barnett, 1978, 248.   [105] Edwards, 1981, 127–8.

[106] Burnett, 1978, 249–50.   [107] Ibid. 264.   [108] Ibid. 253; Edwards, 1981, 133.

the lead of Birmingham and Ruislip–Northwood by schemes under the 1909 and then the 1919 and 1932 Acts, the builders were as often as not ahead of them; and in any case, there was a lack of positive direction from the Ministry of Health and a lack of qualified local planners.[109] Councils, frightened of claims for compensation if they refused permission under the then legislation, would gratefully accept gifts of open space from developers in return for an agreement to build denser and cheaper.[110] Many areas must have resembled Edgware, where in 1927, the Chairman of the Ratepayers' Association said that the town-planning scheme appeared to be framed by land-development exploiters: 'Aesthetic purposes can nowhere be seen in the plans.'[111] Thus, the amount of planning depended on what you could pay.

> A carefully-designed development would be marked by a variety of house-styles, winding roads, closes and crescents, generous gardens, tree-plantings and grassed verges. But often the speculative suburb lacked any overall plan, being developed road by road by numerous builders until the land ran out. . . . The result of such activity was sometimes a long sprawl of monotonously similar semi-detached houses along a busy arterial road, backed by a waste of derelict agricultural land, remote from amenities such as shops, schools and stations.[112]

Since the frontage was the dearest aspect and also the basis of cost, long narrow plots between 25 and 35 feet wide were the rule, producing parallel rows on identical plots. At the bottom end of the market, speed of building was of the essence; a rural landscape could be transformed into a new estate within a month. So trees were uprooted and natural features ignored; roads were laid out in aimless serpentine fashion or simply followed old field paths, giving an impression that managed to be simultaneously restless and monotonous.[113] The result was a segregated landscape of suburbia, in which the kind and density of the housing immediately suggested the social status of those within it. And the 1932 Act actually encouraged this, by giving councils the opportunity to lay down variations in density, all the way down to one house per 5, 10 or 25 acres, invariably without liability to pay compensation.[114]

Usually, the starting-point was either a concentration of shops and flats in Mock Tudor or Debased Classical, around the railway or tube station; a giant cinema might be another prominent feature, Thence, building proceeded in ribbons, following feeder bus services along the new arterial by-pass roads – designed, ironically, to reduce traffic congestion, and financed under unemployment-relief programmes in two bursts, in the early

---

[109] Jackson, 1973, 321.   [110] Carr, 1982, 254.   [111] Jackson, 1973, 255.
[112] Burnett, 1978, 249.   [113] Jackson, 1973, 126–7; Burnett, 1978, 256; Carr, 1982, 247.
[114] Burnett, 1978, 249; Sheail, 1981, 77; Carr, 1982, 255.

FIGURE 3.11   *By-Pass Variegated.*
Osbert Lancaster's merciless rendering of the genre; complete with leaded windows,
lace curtains, crazy paving and the Wall's Ice Cream Tricycle.

1920s and the mid-1930s – without benefit, until an Act of 1935, of any
limitation on frontage development. The result pattern was immortalized
by the cartoonist Osbert Lancaster, as By-Pass Variegated:

> ... here are some quaint gables culled from *Art Nouveau* surmounting a façade
> that is plainly modernistic in inspiration; there the twisted beams and leaded
> panes of Stockbrokers' Tudor are happily contrasted with bright green tiles
> of obviously Pseudish origin; next door some terra-cotta plaques, Pont Street
> Dutch in character, enliven a white wood Wimbledon Transitional porch,
> making it a splendid foil to a red-brick garage that is vaguely Romanesque
> in feeling.[115]

Rustic names like Meadowside, Woodsview and Fieldsend all too soon
became misnomers; the Southern Railway, with three successive stations

---

[115] Lancaster, 1959, 152.

called Park – Raynes, Motspur and Worcester – narrowly avoided the appellation being awarded to yet a fourth, Stoneleigh.[116]

The result was universally derided and condemned. The fact was that the prosecutors were all upper-middle class and the offenders were mostly lower-middle cass: in a typical such suburb, Bexley, which gained 18,000 houses and 52,000 people in the 1930s, the 1951 Census showed that the overwhelming majority came from Social Class III, the skilled manual and junior non-manual grades.[117] Moving as they did from by-law terraces without bathrooms or inside lavatories, they were enjoying a quantum leap in their quality of life, and 'whatever their place in the hierarchy of snobbery, all suburbs showed the same characteristic of one-family houses in gardens and in an environment more or less removed from the dirt, noise and congestion of the city.'[118]

But suburbia did more for them. Uniform and monotonous as they might seem from the outside, for their new occupants each house embodied tiny variations, built in or bought in, which gave it individuality: a stained-glass window, a porch, a kitchen fitting, even a garden gnome. The house itself was designed to express individuality: hence the bay window and the corner door, the great variation in very minor detail, the general lack of collective space around the house, all consciously designed to be as unlike 'council housing' as possible.[119]

But architects did not like it. Repeatedly, in their journals, at their congresses, during the 1930s they railed about the suburbs. The suburbs' chief fault seems to have been that they conspicuously diverged from either of the then main standards of good taste: the neo-Georgian as still taught in leading schools like Liverpool, or the uncompromisingly modern embraced by the young members of CIAM.[120] Instead, their cosy imitation-vernacular derived from a much older architectural tradition pioneered by John Nash at Blaise Hamlet and Park Village West, and subsequently developed to a high art by such late Victorians as Philip Webb, Norman Shaw and Raymond Unwin. Perhaps significantly, the first two had opposed the whole idea of a closed architectural profession, and Parker was trained as an interior decorator.[121] But of course, the result was a pastiche; and often an unsuccessful one. Osbert Lancaster put it all better, that is to say more savagely, than any of the professionals:

> If an architect of enormous energy, painstaking ingenuity and great structural knowledge, had devoted years of his life to the study of how best to achieve the maximum of inconvenience, in the shape and arrangement under one roof of a stated number of rooms, and had the assistance of a corps of research workers ransacking architectural history for the least attractive materials and

[116] Jackson, 1973, 128, 170.   [117] Carr, 1982, 238, 241.
[118] Burnett, 1978, 249; Jackson, 1973, 146.   [119] Oliver, 1981, 115–17.
[120] Ibid. 41, 50, 67–9.   [121] Creese, 1966, 255; Oliver, 1981, 64.

building devices known in the past, it is just possible, though highly unlikely, that he might have evolved a style as crazy as that with which the speculative builder, with no expenditure of mental energy at all, has enriched the landscape on either side of our great arterial roads. . . . Notice the skill with which the houses are disposed, that insures that the largest possible area of countryside is ruined with the minimum of expense; see how carefully each householder is provided with a clear view into the most private offices of his next-door neighbour and with what studied disregard of the sun's aspect the principal rooms are planned.[122]

The Architects' Revenge

Whether it was sour grapes or not, the architects were angry; they wanted revenge. They were not the only ones; though they led the attack. Their metaphors were sometimes military, sometimes clinical. Clough Williams-Ellis, in *England and the Octopus* (1928), wrote of ribbon development as 'the disfiguring little buildings [that] grow up and multiply like nettles along a drain, like lice upon a tape-worm'; bungalows 'constitute England's most disfiguring disease, having, from sporadic beginnings, now become our premier epidemic.'[123] By 1933 he was declaring that

> I would certainly sooner go back for another year in wartime Ypres than spend a twelvemonth in post-war Slough. Should that sound like an over-statement I should explain that it is merely the prudent desire of one who desires to remain happily alive, and who would therefore assuredly choose an eighty per cent risk of being shot, gassed or blown up in heroic company to the certainty of cutting his own throat in surroundings of humiliating squalor.[124]

Slough, as also for Betjeman, became the symbol of all that was wrong. Yet Betjeman loved some suburbia, as witness his television labour of love on Metro-land: 'A verge in front of your house and grass and a tree for the dog. Variety created in each façade of the houses – in the colouring of the trees. In fact, the country had come to the suburbs. Roses are blooming in Metro-land just as they do in the brochures.'[125] These, like Surrey, were the *good* suburbs, inhabited by lovable Betjemanesque characters like Pam the great big mountainous sports girl, or Miss J. Hunter Dunn sitting the evening long in the car park in the full Surrey twilight; but Slough, like Ruislip Gardens – from which Metro station,

> With a thousand Ta's and Pardon's
> Daintily alights Elaine,

[122] Lancaster, 1959, 152.   [123] Williams-Ellis, 1928, 141.
[124] Williams-Ellis, 1933, 105.   [125] Betjeman, 1978, 225.

FIGURE 3.12 *The Great West Road.*
1930s By-Pass Variegated *en masse* from the air, clustered around Osterley tube station (foreground), one of Charles Holden's brilliant designs for Frank Pick.

were quite other places, occupied exclusively by lower-middle-class despoilers of the countryside.

Abercrombie, who had taken the lead in founding the Council for the Preservation (later Protection) of Rural England in 1926, took a more sanguine view of the bungalow disease: 'Seriously, is not the damage largely skin deep? . . . will many of what you rightly call Blasphemous Bungalows, blaspheme for long? And is not much of England virgin country, *intacta?*'.[126] He was more concerned about ribbon growth: 'These strips of the countryside are . . . being colonised with no more rationale of social grouping, or economies of estate development or aesthetics of rural design than existed during the industrial revolution of last century.'[127] But he too was convinced that 'this rural England of ours is at this moment menaced with a more sudden and more thorough change than ever before', too rapid to permit automatic adjustment.[128] He wrote wistfully of the Chinese practitioner of *Feng Shui,*

> whose job it is to study and expound the shapes which the spiritual forces of nature have produced and to prescribe the ways in which all buildings, roads, bridges, canals and railways must conform to them, is placed in a position of extreme power; and we ourselves can hardly hope to be able similarly to explode some flaring upstart bungalow or 'Satanic Mill' or conflagrate the perpetuation of certain countryside-blasting advertisements in their own spirit.[129]

But, he thought, they certainly showed the right way.

In 1938 Williams-Ellis was back on the attack with *Britain and the Beast,* an edited volume of essays by such leading figures of the day as Keynes, E. M. Forster, C. E. M. Joad, G. M. Trevelyan and many others. In it, Joad presented the 'People's Claim' to the countryside. 'To thousands, nature, newly discovered, has been a will-o'-the-wisp', as those lured into the countryside find that it has disappeared: 'In fifty years' time there will, in southern England, be neither town nor country, but only a single dispersed suburb, sprawling unendingly from Watford to the coast.' To guard against this, 'the extension of the towns must be stopped, building must be restricted to sharply defined areas, and such re-housing of the population as may be necessary must be carried on within these areas.'[130]

Thomas Sharp, perhaps the most prolific writer on planning problems in the early 1930s, took – here as elsewhere – a harder line. For him, the evil started with Ebenezer Howard's vision of Town-Country, which in practice had produced a degenerate mixture:

> From dreary towns the broad, mechanical, noisy main roads run out between ribbons of tawdry houses, disorderly refreshment shacks and vile, untidy garages. The old trees and hedgerows that bordered them a few years ago have given place to concrete posts and avenues of telegraph poles, to hoardings and enamel advertisement signs. Over great areas there is no longer any country bordering the main roads; there is only a negative semi-suburbia.[131]

And, if the present ideals continued to hold sway, under the influence of new technologies – radio, television, the car – things could only get worse.

---

[126] Williams-Ellis, 1928, 181.   [127] Abercrombie, 1926, 20.   [128] Ibid. 56.
[129] Ibid. 52.   [130] Joad, 1938, 81–2.   [131] Sharp, 1932, 4.

Tradition has broken down. Taste is utterly debased. There is no enlightened guidance or correction from authority. . . . Rural influences neutralize the town. Urban influences neutralize the country. In a few years all will be neutrality. The strong, masculine virility of the town; the softer beauty, the richness, the fruitfulness of that mother of men, the countryside, will be debased into one sterile, hermaphrodite beastliness.[132]

The root of this sterilization process, it emerged, was fantasy about the countryside:

For a hundred years we have behaved like film-struck servant girls blinded to the filth around us by romantic dreams of worlds as yet and ever likely to be unrealised. More than anything it is this pitiful attitude of escape which has brought the English town from its beauty and hopefulness of a hundred and fifty years ago to its shapeless and shameful meanness of today.[133]

The remedy will be through 'great new blocks of flats which will house a considerable part of the population of the future town' – and indeed of the countryside, where old country houses can be demolished to make way for them.[134] Thus Sharp joined the Corbusian camp, distancing himself decisively from the garden-city tradition.

What he shared with them, and with commentators generally at this time, was a terror of what Anthony King has called the democratization of the countryside: the lower-middle-class and working-class invasion of an area that had hitherto been the preserve of an aristocratic and upper-middle-class elite.[135] Joad, in his essay in 1938, expressed it revealingly:

And then there are the hordes of hikers cackling insanely in the woods, or singing raucous songs as they walk arm in arm at midnight down the quiet village street. There are people, wherever there is water, upon sea shores or upon river banks, lying in every attitude of undressed and inelegant squalor, grilling themselves, for all the world as if they were steaks, in the sun. There are tents in meadows and girls in pyjamas dancing beside them to the strains of the gramophone, while stinking disorderly dumps of tins, bags, and cartons bear witness to the tide of invasion for weeks after it has ebbed; there are fat girls in shorts, youths in gaudy ties and plus-fours, and a roadhouse round every corner and a café on top of every hill for their accommodation.[136]

This clash of attitudes was neatly expressed when Brighton proposed that, in order to preserve the South Downs from building, it would lease land as a motor racing track. There was immediate expression of outrage from the Society of Sussex Downsmen, *The Times*, the West and East Sussex Councils and a House of Lords Committee. Lord Buxton, in the Second Reading debate, said: 'I say frankly it is not so much the actual track to

---

[132] Ibid. 11.   [133] Sharp, 1936, 98.   [134] Ibid. 107; 1939, 119.
[135] King, 1980, 462.   [136] Joad, 1938, 72–3.

which I object. It is more the fact of there being that track, which will bring immense numbers of people to the Downs, to the destruction of the amenities.' To which the Committee chairman, Lord Redesdale, was forced to point out: 'By all means exclude the public from the Downs, but then you must not say you are preserving the Downs for the Public. At least be honest and say you are preserving the Downs for the Society of Sussex Downsmen and the actual inhabitants of the Downs.'[137]

In all the furore over the English countryside at this time, therefore, there were a few dissenting voices. One significant one was that of the young Evelyn Sharp, secretary of the Town and Country Planning Advisory Committee of the Ministry of Health, who was writing of the need to

> remember that the countryside is not the preserve of the wealthy and leisured classes. The country rightly prides itself on the fact that since the War there has been an unparalleled building development, a development which every Government has done its utmost to stimulate, and whose effect has been to create new and better social conditions for a very large number of persons . . . persons of very limited means.[138]

Any serious attempt to reverse the policy, she argued, would 'undoubtedly run counter to the wishes of a large section of the community.'[139] There, indeed, spoke the future Permanent Secretary.

By that time, indeed, Interim Development Orders covered some 19.5 million acres or 50 per cent of the entire country – the half, moreover, where large-scale development was occurring. In Surrey, one of the counties most affected by London's growth, almost all landowners were voluntarily accepting restrictions on development, thus avoiding death and estate duties.[140] The then Permanent Secretary of the Ministry of Health commented that 'nobody who goes about the country today can fail to observe that the tide of sporadic, unregulated development that threatened to engulf the south after the war, is being stemmed, and that planning is beginning to leave a visible mark on the English countryside.'[141] The 1932 Act, with its provisions for voluntary agreements and for extreme low-density zoning, was thus beginning to bite. But not everyone would agree – certainly not Professor Joad.

By 1938, the Williams-Ellises and the Joads had a new and a powerful supporter. On every one of his public appearances in the 1920s and 1930s, Frank Pick bemoaned the opportunity that was being lost by the failure to plan. In 1927,

> There was much planning, but no plan. . . . The needs of the moment are met sometimes exceedingly well but without reference to the whole. . . . Unfortunately for London it has so far never had a directing head. . . . It is

---

[137] Sheail, 1981, 107. [138] Ibid. 89. [139] Ibid. [140] Ibid. 16, 76. [141] Ibid. 1981, 128.

at that low stage of animal development in which the brain is rudimentary and ganglia scattered throughout the organism stimulate such activity as serves to keep the creature alive.

In 1936, 'such developments ... are almost analogous to a cancerous growth'; in 1938, the risk was of 'an amorphous mass of building' in which 'London's country would suffer from a confluent pox.'[142]

His voice, joined to the chorus, proved irresistible. Neville Chamberlain, on becoming Prime Minister at the end of 1937, almost immediately set up a Royal Commission on the Geographical Distribution of the Industrial Population, chaired by Sir Anderson Montague-Barlow. Next year, in his evidence to the Barlow Commission, Pick had arrived at the argument that if London grew beyond the magic 12 to 15-mile limit set by the economics of the tube, it 'must cease to be intrinsically London ... a unitary conception.'[143] So, he argued, London's growth should be contained: 'It would be possible to go on layering first industry and then residences, and then industry and then residences, and building indefinitely, but that would not be London. It would be putting rings of industrial towns around London, and that would not be London.'[144] For this reason, he favoured both a green belt at least 1 mile wide around London, and controls on new industry at the edge of London.[145]

Perhaps Pick's enthusiasm for planning was not entirely disinterested; he wanted controls on London's physical growth, but not on further expansion of jobs, which suited London Transport's book; his prophetic fear, that the growth of the car would lead to low-density sprawl, was also the view of a public-transport advocate.[146] But, in all he wrote, there emerges a consistent, almost cartoon-like, vision of a giant organically planned conurbation, in which a single integrated public transport system would provide the nerve-structure for the body, and land-use planning would guide the healthy growth of the organism. Pick was in no doubt, in the 1930s, that the latter was lacking: 'What goes by the name is idle and useless so far.'[147] He was in a better position than anyone to know. And the Barlow Commissioners accepted what he said.

[142] Pick, 1927, 162; 1936, 213; 1938, para. 8.   [143] Pick, 1938, Q. 3099, 3101.
[144] Ibid., Q. 3107.   [145] Ibid., Q. 2999–3001, 3120–1.
[146] Pick, 1936, 213; 1938, Q. 2989.   [147] Pick, 1936, 210.

The City
in the Garden

Forget six counties overhung with smoke,
Forget the snorting steam and piston stroke,
Forget the spreading of the hideous town;
Think rather of the pack-horse on the down,
And dream of London, small and white and clean,
The clear Thames bordered by its gardens green.

William Morris,
The Earthly paradise (1868)

Let every dawn of morning be to you as the beginning of life, and every
setting sun be to you as its close:- then let every one of these short lives leave
its sure record of some kindly thing done for others – some goodly strength
or knowledge gained for yourselves; so, from day to day, and strength to
strength, you shall build up indeed, by Art, by Thought, and by Just Will,
an Ecclesia of England, of which it shall not be said, 'See what manner of
stones are here', but, 'See what manner of men'.

John Ruskin,
Lectures on Art (1870)

(found in Raymond Unwin's favourite quotations)

4
The City
in the Garden

The Garden City Solution:
London, Paris, Berlin, New York,
1900–1940

It is invidious, but it needs saying: despite doughty competition, Ebenezer Howard (1850–1928) is the most important single character in this entire tale. So it is important to get him right; even though almost everyone has got him wrong. His many self-appointed critics have, at one time or another, been wrong about almost everything he stood for. They called him a 'planner', a term of derogation, whereas he earned his living as a shorthand writer. They said that he advocated low-density prairie planning; in fact, his garden city would have had densities like inner London's, which – so later planners once came to believe – needed high-rise towers to make them work. They confused this garden city with the garden suburb found at Hampstead and in numerous imitations – though, it must be confessed, one of his principal lieutenants, Raymond Unwin, was originally to blame for that. They still think that he wanted to consign people to small towns isolated in the deep countryside, while he actually proposed the planning of conurbations with hundreds of thousands, perhaps millions, of people. They accuse him of wanting to move people round like pawns on a chessboard, whereas in fact he dreamed of voluntary self-governing communities. Most mistakenly of all, they see him as a physical planner, ignoring the fact that his garden cities were merely the vehicles for a progressive reconstruction of capitalist society into an infinity of co-operative commonwealths.

They cannot claim that he made it difficult for them. In his seventy-eight years he wrote only one book, and a slim one at that. First published in 1898 under the title *To-morrow: A Peaceful Path to Real Reform*, it was reissued in 1902 with the title *Garden Cities of To-morrow*. This was perhaps catchier, but it diverted people from the truly radical character of the message, demoting him from social visionary into physical planner.

FIGURE 4.1 *Ebenezer Howard.*
The great man reduced to modest humility (or stupefaction) by an unknown orator.
The audience seems to share his reaction. Probably photographed at Welwyn
Garden City.

The Sources of Howard's Ideas

Better to appreciate Howard's contribution, he must be set against the
background of his time. He developed his ideas in the London of the 1880s
and 1890s, the age of radical ferment described in chapter 2. An eclectic
thinker, he borrowed freely from the ideas that were circulating at the
time.[1] But there were other, earlier influences. Born in the City of London
in 1850 – a fact commemorated by a plaque at the edge of the huge
Barbican redevelopment, which almost certainly he would not have liked
at all – he grew up in small country towns in southern and eastern England:

[1] Osborn, 1950, 228–9.

Sudbury, Ipswich, Cheshunt. At twenty-one he emigrated to America and became a pioneer in Nebraska. He proved a disaster as a farmer, and from 1872 to 1876 was in Chicago, beginning the career as a shorthand writer which he was to follow all his life.

We know little about these years, but they must have been important to him. As a farmer on the frontier he had personal experience of the Homestead Act of 1862, which opened up the prairies and the plains to pioneers free of charge, thus establishing an economy and a society of prosperous farms and small towns, and an educational system devoted to technical improvement in agriculture and the mechanical arts. Then, as a resident of Chicago, he saw the city's great rebuilding after the fire of 1871. Still, in these pre-skyscraper days, it was universally known as the Garden City: the almost certain source of Howard's better-known title. He must have seen the new garden suburb of Riverside, designed by the great landscape architect Frederick Law Olmsted, arising on the Des Plaines river 9 miles outside the city.[2]

Back in Britain, he began in earnest to think and to read. Later, in the book, he was adamant that he had thought out the central ideas himself but that he had then found other writers who supplied the details. But there were certainly plenty of precursors. Edward Gibbon Wakefield, fifty years earlier, had developed the idea of planned colonization for the poor. The scheme he had promoted, Colonel Light's celebrated scheme for Adelaide in South Australia, provided the idea that once a city had reached a certain size, a second city, separated from it by a green belt, should be started: the origin of the notion of Social City, as Howard acknowledged. James Silk Buckingham's plan for a model town gave him most of the main features for his diagram of Garden City: the central place, the radial avenues, and the peripheral industries. Pioneer industrial villages in the countryside, like Lever's Port Sunlight near Liverpool and Cadbury's Bournville outside Birmingham, provided both a physical model and a practical illustration of successful industrial decentralization from the congested city.

The economist Alfred Marshall, in an article of 1884, had suggested the idea that there were 'large classes of the population of London whose removal into the country would in the long run be economically advantageous – that it would benefit alike those who moved and those who remained behind.'[3] His reasoning had been that new technologies would permit this dispersal – an idea taken up by the anarchist Peter Kropotkin in his *Fields, Factories and Workshops* of 1898, which certainly influenced Howard. And Marshall even suggested the mechanism:

> The general plan would be for a committee, whether specially formed for the purpose or not, to interest themselves in the formation of a colony in some

[2] Osborn, 1950, 226–7; Stern 1986, 133–4.   [3] Marshall, 1884, 224.

place well beyond the range of London smoke. After seeing their way to buying or building suitable cottages there, they would enter into communication with some of the employees of low-waged labour.[4]

Charles Booth, wrestling with the problem of his Class B poor, 'the crux of the social problem', had a paternalistic version of the same answer: to withdraw them from the labour force by the formation of labour colonies, 'an extension of the Poor Law', outside London:

> My idea is that these people should be allowed to live as families in industrial groups, planted wherever land and building materials were cheap; being well housed, well fed, and well warmed; and taught, trained, and employed from morning to night on work, indoors or out, for themselves or on Government account; in the building of their own dwellings, in the cultivation of the land, in the making of clothes, or in the making of furniture. That in exchange for the work done the Government should supply materials and whatever else was needed.[5]

Booth admitted that this solution was draconian: 'The life offered would not be attractive' and 'the difficulty lies solely in inducing or driving these people to accept a regulated life.'[6] His (non-related) namesake, General William Booth of The Salvation Army, was similarly advocating the colonization of the destitute into agricultural small-holding colonies with small-scale industries, within reasonable distance of London but far enough from any town or village to escape the influence of the public house, 'that upas tree of civilisation':[7] a feature Howard endorsed in his book and then imposed on bone-dry Letchworth, where the Skittles Inn offered rustic pastimes and wholesome conversation over lemonade and ginger beer.

Canon Barnett's Toynbee Commission of 1892 had followed the same tradition in calling for 'industrial regiments' for the 'demoralised residuum', providing 'compulsory work under human discipline'; a solution later embraced by the Fabian Society.[8] But Howard, following Marshall, did not see his garden cities as colonies for the undeserving poor. On the contrary: they were to be founded, and managed, by the stratum immediately above – Charles Booth's Class C – who were thereby to be freed from the thraldom of the urban slum. His solution was not paternalistic – at least, apart from some residual undertones; rather, it belonged firmly in the anarchistic tradition.

Howard's intellectual debts did not end there. From Herbert Spencer he borrowed the idea of land nationalization, and then from a forgotten predecessor, Thomas Spence, he discovered a superior variant: purchase of farmland by a community, at agricultural values, so that the increased values, which would follow from the construction of a town, would automatically pass back to the community coffers. Every single one of his

---

[4] Ibid. 229. [5] Booth, 1892, 167. [6] Ibid. 166. [7] Booth, 1890, 128.
[8] Stedman Jones, 1971, 305–6, 334.

ideas can in fact be found earlier, often several times over: Ledoux, Owen, Pemberton, Buckingham and Kropotkin all had towns of limited populations with surrounding agricultural green belts; More, Saint-Simon, Fourier all had cities as elements in a regional complex;[9] Marshall and Kropotkin saw the impact of technological development on industrial location, and Kropotkin and Edward Bellamy also appreciated that it would come to favour small-scale workshops. But Howard, attracted as he was to Bellamy's best-selling science-fiction *Looking Backward* (1888), rejected his centralized socialist management and his insistence on the subordination of the individual to the group, which he saw as authoritarian.[10]

More widely, Howard could not fail to be influenced by the Back to the Land movement, which – fuelled by urban growth and urban squalor, agricultural depression, nostalgia, quasi-religious motives, and anti-Victorian conventions – flourished among the intelligentsia between 1880 and 1914: a genuine alternative movement, similar in many respects to such movements in the 1960s and 1970s.[11] At least twenty-eight such nineteenth-century communities can be traced, all but five or six of which were rural; their inhabitants included utopian socialists, agrarian socialists, sectarians and anarchists. Few survived for long, though sometimes their settlements do, transmogrified: Heronsgate, established by the Chartists in Hertfordshire after the failure of their political demands in 1848, is today a smart stockbroker community next to the M25 motorway.[12] Behind these manifestations lay a much wider movement, well represented by such writers as Morris and Ruskin, which aimed to reject the grosser trappings of industrialization and to return to a simpler life based on craft and community. So, as Howard wrote, the idea of community-building was everywhere in the air.

The Garden City and the Social City

The ingredients, then, were far from original. What Howard could claim – and did, in a chapter heading, claim – was that his was a unique combination of proposals. He started with the famous diagram of the Three Magnets. Today it has archaic charm, particularly in the coloured version of the first edition. But it packs on to one page a set of complex arguments that would take far more space to say in modern jargon. The Victorian slum city, to be sure, was in many ways an horrific place; but it offered economic and social opportunities, lights and crowds. The late-Victorian

---

[9] Batchelor, 1969, 198.   [10] Meyerson, 1961, 186; Fishman, 1977, 36.
[11] Marsh, 1982, 1–7.   [12] Darley, 1975, 10; Hardy, 1979, 215, 238.

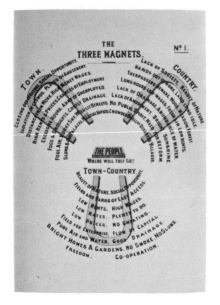

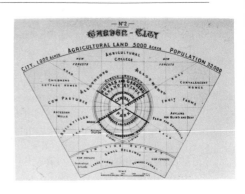

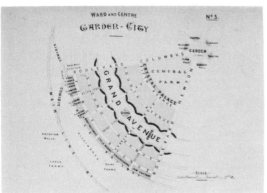

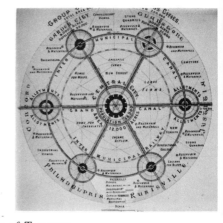

FIGURE 4.2   *Garden Cities of To-morrow.*
Key diagrams from the first 1898 edition, entitled *To-morrow,* of Howard's classic.
The fourth, showing his vision of the polycentric Social City, was never afterwards
reproduced in this complete form.

countryside, now too often seen in a sentimental glow, was in fact equally
unprepossessing: though it promised fresh air and nature, it was racked by
agricultural depression and it offered neither sufficient work and wages,
nor adequate social life. But it was possible to square the circle, by
combining the best of town and country in a new kind of settlement, Town-
Country.

To achieve this, a group of people – necessarily, including several with commercial competence and creditability – should establish a limited-dividend company, borrowing money to establish a garden city in the countryside, far enough from the city to ensure that the land was bought at rock-bottom, depressed-agricultural, land values. They should get agreement from leading industrialists to move their factories there; their workers would move too, and would build their own houses. The garden city would have a fixed limit – Howard suggested 32,000 people, living on 1,000 acres of land, about one and a half times the historical medieval city of London. It would be surrounded by a much larger area of permanent green belt, also owned by the company – Howard proposed 5,000 acres – containing not merely farms, but also all kinds of urban institutions, like reformatories and convalescent homes, that could benefit from a rural location.

As more and more people moved out, the garden city would reach its planned limit; then, another would be started a short distance away. Thus, over time, there would develop a vast planned agglomeration, extending almost without limit; within it, each garden city would offer a wide range of jobs and services, but each would also be connected to the others by a rapid transit system (for, as Howard called it, an Inter-Municipal Railway), thus giving all the economic and social opportunities of the giant city. Howard called this polycentric vision Social City. Because the diagram was truncated in the second and in all subsequent editions, most readers have failed to understand that this, not the individual garden city, was the physical realization of town-country: the third magnet.

But it was more than just a physical blueprint. The final words under the third magnet, FREEDOM, CO-OPERATION, are not just rhetoric; they are the heart of the plan. As Lewis Mumford so rightly says in his introduction to the book (1946), Howard was much less interested in physical forms than in social processes.[13] The key was that the citizens would own the land in perpetuity. There was another coloured diagram in the first edition that was subsequently omitted, with dire consequences to the understanding of Howard's message: entitled The Vanishing Point of Landlord's Rent, it illustrates how, as urban land values built up in garden city, these would flow back to the community. The citizens would pay a modest rate-rent for their houses or factories or farms, sufficient to repay the interest on the money originally borrowed, to provide a sinking fund to repay the capital, and then – progressively, as the money was paid back – to provide abundant funds for the creation of a local welfare state, all without need for local or central taxation, and directly responsible to the local citizens. In particular, it would be able 'to found pensions with

---

13 Mumford, 1946, 37.

liberty for our aged poor, now imprisoned in workhouses; to banish despair and awaken hope in the breasts of those that have fallen; to silence the harsh voice of anger, and awaken the soft notes of brotherliness and goodwill.'[14]

Howard could thus argue that his was a third socio-economic system, superior both to Victorian capitalism and to bureaucratic centralized socialism. Its keynote would be local management and self-government. Services would be provided by the municipality, or by private contractors, as proved more efficient. Others would come from the people themselves, in a series of what Howard called pro-municipal experiments. In particular, people would build their own homes with capital provided through building societies, friendly societies, co-operative societies, or trade unions. And this activity would in turn drive the economy; forty years before John Maynard Keynes or Franklin Delano Roosevelt, Howard had arrived at the solution that society could spend its way out of a recession.

It would do so, however, without large-scale central state intervention. Howard's plan was to be realized through thousands of small-scale enterprises: every man and woman a craftsman, an entrepreneur. It would call, he said

> for the very highest talents of engineers of all kinds, of architects, artists, medical men, experts in sanitation, landscape gardeners, agricultural experts, surveyors, builders, manufacturers, merchants and financiers, organizers of trades unions, friendly and co-operative societies, as well as the very simplest forms of unskilled labour, together with all those forms of lesser skill and talent which lie between.[15]

It is a peculiarly American vision: the homesteading spirit, brought back home to industrial England. But it is homesteading harnessed to new technology, to create a new socio-economic order: a remarkable vision, not least for its startling modernity, even a near-century later.

Letchworth and Hampstead: Unwin and Parker

Howard was thus a dreamer of great dreams, but he was much more: he was quintessentially a doer. The modern reader, going back to his book, is surprised that so much of it consists of pages of calculations about finance; Howard was writing not for utopian simple-lifers, but for hard-nosed Victorian businessmen who wanted to be sure they would get their

---

[14] Howard, 1898, 141.   [15] Ibid. 140.

FIGURE 4.3 *New Earswick.*
A classic Unwin-Parker design around an enclosed green space, intended to recapture the communal quality of the medieval quadrangle.

money back. One of the many brilliant features of the plan was that it could be achieved incrementally, by a series of separate local initiatives which would progressively reinforce each other. So, eight months after the book was published, Howard took the lead in setting up a Garden City Association to discuss his ideas, and 'ultimately to formulate a practical scheme on the lines of the project with such modifications as may seem desirable'; he took care to make it politically bipartisan and to include manufacturers, merchants and financiers as well as co-operators, artists and ministers.[16] A year later, in 1900, it resolved to form the First Garden City, Limited, with capital of £50,000 and a 5-per-cent dividend; two years after that, the Garden City Pioneer Company was registered with a capital of £20,000, in order to survey potential sites.[17]

The directors of the Pioneer Company laid down criteria closely following Howard's: a site of between 4,000 and 6,000 acres, with good rail connections, a satisfactory water supply and good drainage. The favourite site, Chartley Castle east of Stafford, was rejected as too far from London. Letchworth, 34 miles from London in an area of severely depressed agriculture and low land prices, met the criteria and – after delicate secret negotiations with fifteen owners – the 3,818-acre site was bought for £155,587. The First Garden City Company was registered on 1 September 1903, with a £300,000 capital, of which £80,000 was to be raised immediately, and a 5-per-cent dividend.[18]

Progress was slow. It took a year even to raise £148,000 towards the purchase price. The first profits came in 1912. In the first two years, only 1,000 people came. Industry proved difficult to attract; it was a major breakthrough when the printing and binding works of J. M. Dent, a major publisher, was attracted.[19] So the first inhabitants were the idealist, artistic middle-class, who gave Letchworth a permanent reputation for crankiness that it later ill deserved: 'Here was a whole colony of eccentrics making an exhibition of themselves rather too near our sacred borders. We wished they would remove their mad city a little nearer Arlesley.'[20] Arlesley was the local mental institution. That was doubtless overdone, but there were grounds for suspicion. At The Cloisters, a residential college where residents slept on hammocks separated by canvas screens arranged in a horseshoe around a marble fountain, they grew wheat according to what were thought to be Kropotkinesque principles, each grain getting individual attention; the result was mainly weeds and thistles.[21]

Soon, though, the original middle-class eccentrics had been overwhelmed by the blue-collar workers who were to provide the *raison d'être* for the

---

[16] Macfadyen, 1933, 37.   [17] Ibid. 37–9; Simpson, 1985, 14.
[18] Culpin, 1913, 16; Simpson, 1985, 14–17.
[19] Jackson, F., 1985, 71; Simpson, 1985, 20, 35.   [20] Macfadyen, 1933, 47.
[21] Marsh, 1982, 238–9.

garden city's existence. But ironically, far from participating in the co-operative spirit of the enterprise, they embraced trades unionism and socialism.[22] Many, in a development that had its own special irony, joined in-commuters from neighbouring Hitchin in the giant Spirella factory, 'to make corsets which Letchworth women obviously never wear, but which their husbands sell at great profit to the less enlightened women in other towns.'[23]

What survived from all this was however the essence of the Howard vision. The town began to pay dividends after a decade; it continued' to grow, more slowly than the promoters hoped, to reach 15,000 – less than half its planned target – in 1938; after World War Two, aided by government-subsidized decentralization schemes, it was at last completed, on a slightly smaller scale than originally planned. Ironically, at that point it became the victim of land speculation, from which it was rescued by an Act of Parliament in 1962 that put its management in the hands of a special corporation.[24] Above all, it found its perfect physical realization in the hands of Raymond Unwin (1863–1940) and Barry Parker (1867–1947). Almost too perfect, in fact; Unwin-Parker architecture clothed the Howard skeleton so memorably that, ever after, people could hardly distinguish one from the other.

To understand what Unwin and Parker so memorably achieved, here and at Hampstead and in other places, they need to be set in a context of place, time and culture. Unwin was born in 1863, Parker in 1867, within a dozen miles of Sheffield in northern England; they were half-cousins, and Unwin married Parker's sister. Neither was formally trained as an architect; Unwin started as an engineer, Parker was an interior decorator. They grew up in an intense ferment of ideas, deriving in large measure from William Morris, which were to influence all their subsequent work. They believed that creativity came from an imaginative understanding of the past; that the Middle Ages provided an historic standard; that old buildings grew out of the ground they stood on; that the village was an organic embodiment of the small, personally related community; that the architect and planner were guardians of social and aesthetic life, maintaining and enhancing the traditional values of the community for future generations.[25]

Unwin early became a socialist in the William Morris tradition, joining the Sheffield group started by Edward Carpenter, a founder of the Fabian Society; here Kropotkin lectured on the union of craft and intellectual work.[26] Before 1900, he was working on the design of cottages for mining villages in his local area.[27] From this stemmed his book *Cottage Homes and*

[22] Simpson, 1985, 34.   [23] Macfadyen, 1933, 51; Marsh, 1982, 234.
[24] Miller, 1983, 172–4.
[25] Creese, 1966, 169–70; Miller, 1981, 74; Jackson, F., 1985, 41, 168.
[26] Jackson, F., 1985, 17.   [27] Creese, 1966, 184–5.

FIGURE 4.4 *Letchworth.*
The medieval village green motif as interpreted by Parker and Unwin in the first garden city.

Common Sense (1902), an impassioned plea for better working-class housing: 'It does not seem to be realized that hundreds of thousands of women spend the bulk of their lives with nothing better to look on than the ghastly prospect offered by these back yards, the squalid ugliness of which is unrelieved by a scrap of fresh green to speak of spring, or a falling leaf to tell of autumn.' Yet, 'if, instead of being wasted in stuffy yards and dirty back streets, the space which is available for a number of houses were kept together, it would make quite a respectable square or garden'; cottages, each correctly orientated to give a sunny aspect to the chief room, would be planned around 'quadrangles opening one into the other' after the manner of Oxford and Cambridge colleges.[28]

Already, that year, Parker and Unwin were working on their first major commission: the garden village of New Earswick for the Rowntree chocolate family, to be developed, not as a charity but as an independent trust, close to their factory on the northern edge of York. It contains in embryo many of the features that were to be worked out on a much larger canvas at Letchworth and then at Hampstead. The village is separated from the

[28] Unwin, 1902, 4.

FIGURE 4.5 *Barry Parker.*
Unwin's partner and co-designer at New Earswick, Letchworth and Hampstead;
later the sole author of the plan for Manchester's Wythenshawe, truly England's
third Garden City.

factory, and from the city, by a narrow, but quite distinct, green belt, part
natural, part in playing-fields. The cottages are disposed in terraces and
grouped either around communal greens, or along pedestrian ways – thus
anticipating the Radburn layout by more than a quarter-century – and,
later in the design process, culs-de-sac. A village green and a folk hall are
prominent central features. Everywhere, natural features – trees, a small
brook – are integrated into the design. It has in supreme measure what
Parker and Unwin themselves called 'the first essential in the form and
design of any decorative object . . . reposefulness';[29] the visitor, arriving in
whatever psychological state, immediately receives a quite extraordinary
impression of calm, of an informal but natural order of things, which is

[29] Parker and Unwin, 1901, 5.

all-pervasive. Beautifully preserved, sympathetically restored to Unwin and Parker's original intentions, New Earswick is a small gem, dazzling to the eye at the age of more than eighty. In one respect only it failed: the standards of design were so high that the lowest-paid could not afford it. That, indeed, was to prove a recurrent defect.

At Letchworth they had a larger and more complex problem. For one thing, industry had to be integrated in with the housing. The fact that a railway line bisected the site determined that here the industry must be. As against New Earswick's modest village hall and row of shops, a whole town centre had to be planned. Writing later in his great textbook of planning, Unwin exhaustively analysed the town plans of the past, concluding that both formal and informal approaches had their merits. Though it was never in doubt that his tastes lay toward the informal, Letchworth also has more formal elements in the form of radial avenues, *ronds-points* and above all the big central Town Square dominated by the major municipal buildings. It does not work out right. The best of the informal housing layouts are as good as New Earswick, some – planned around huge village-green-like spaces – maybe even better. And the Spirella Factory is a joy, designed – perhaps to try and avoid the associations – in a very free Viennese *Jugendstil*. But the town centre is a terrible mess, with streets that seem to lead nowhere in particular, lined (well after Unwin and Parker departed) by an amorphous mixture of the worst interwar commercial neo-Georgian and even worse sixties tatty, all gone slightly to seed.

Significantly, Unwin confessed that when designing it all he had not yet read Camillo Sitte's book *Die Städtebau nach der künstlerischen Grundsätzen*, published over a decade previously, with its stress on the informal qualities of medieval cities.[30] It was a lesson Unwin was not to forget; *Town Planning in Practice*, published in 1909 – a mere half-decade after Letchworth – is memorable above all for the brilliant line drawings of old English and French and German towns and villages, from which he developed his understanding of the relationships of buildings and spaces. Or, rather *their* understanding: together, Unwin and Parker raised the art of civic design to a level of pure genius, after which almost everything else was pedestrian anticlimax. They werĕ specific that their job was above all to promote beauty or amenity, terms which for them were interchangeable: 'above all, we shall need to infuse the spirit of the artist into our work.'[31] But, as well, their thoughts were always imaginatively with the people who would live in the buildings, walk or play in the spaces they created. And this went down to minute particulars: good architecture and planning, for them, was the multiplication of right details:

[30] Unwin, 1920, 225.   [31] Ibid. 9.

The children, too, must not be forgotten in the open spaces. The *kinderbank*, or low seat to suit their short legs, should always be provided, and where possible spaces of turf be supplied with swings or seesaws, with ponds for sailing boats, and with sand pits where these can be kept sufficiently clean.[32]

They wanted, too, to pursue social ends. 'Both in town and site planning it is important to prevent the complete separation of different classes of people which is such a feature of the modern English town.'[33] But, in Edwardian England, there were limits. Both at Letchworth and at Hampstead, areas are shown for 'cottages', away from the grander middle-class houses: close enough, but not too close.

Hampstead was a turning-point, both for the English garden-city movement in general and for Unwin in particular. For it was self-confessedly not a garden city, but a garden suburb; it had no industry, and was openly dependent on commuting from an adjacent tube station, which opened just as it was being planned. In fairness, and for the historical record, it must be said that it was not the only or even the first in this genre. Ealing Tenants Limited, the first London housing co-operative, had been founded in 1901 and had bought their 32-acre Brentham Estate site off The Mount Avenue in 1902, even before Letchworth; they had hired Unwin and Parker to design a model garden village by 1906, a year before the Hampstead commission.[34] It was a garden village suburb, little different in scale from New Earswick, distinguished by the high quality of its design, its inimitable feeling of easeful domesticity, its central social club – a notion borrowed from New Eastwick, and indeed from the first garden suburb at nearby Bedford Park thirty years previously – and its proto-green-belt, formed by the meadows of the adjacent River Brent.

Ealing is interesting for more than design, though. It represents the way that garden cities and garden suburbs were supposed to be built: Howard's freedom and co-operation in action. Unwin had commended co-operative housing in a pamphlet of 1901, arguing that this way groups of prospective owners could get housing at low cost on land bought at farm value: Howard's argument again. But additionally, 'the houses could be grouped together and so arranged that each would obtain a sunny aspect and an open outlook; and portions of the land could be reserved for ever from being built on to secure these views'; and common rooms could be provided for music and general recreation, and also for meals. Groups of houses, he suggested, could be developed around quadrangles, each with a common room; the quintessence of that medieval spirit of community, that Unwin so earnestly wanted to recapture.[35] Unwin sat on the executive

[32] Ibid. 287.   [33] Ibid. 294.
[34] Jackson, F., 1985, 73; Co-Partnership Tenants, 1906, 70–1; Abercrombie, 1910a, 119.   [35] Parker and Unwin, 1901, 96–7, 106; Hayden, 1984, 126, 129.

FIGURE 4.6 *Ealing Garden Suburb.*
Construction in progress, Denison Road, ca. 1907.

committee of the Co-Partnership Tenants Housing Company; he and Parker developed not only Ealing, but also suburbs outside Leicester, Cardiff, and Stoke-on-Trent.[36] The 1909 Housing and Town Planning Act allowed such 'Public Utility Societies' to borrow public money at low rates of interest, and by 1918 there were more than 100 of them.[37]

But Hampstead was an altogether bigger affair. Its begetter was Dame Henrietta Barnett, redoubtable wife of the Warden of Toynbee Hall. They had a weekend house at Hampstead, and heard in 1896 of a plan to build a new tube station next door. (The line soon became part of the empire of Charles Tyson Yerkes). In true English middle-class fashion she resolved to campaign to buy up land to extend Hampstead Heath and frustrate the real-estate ambitions of the promoters. After a five-year campaign involving the dispatch of 13,000 letters, the 80-acre Heath extension was bought up by the LCC for £43,241; the tube station, stopped in mid-construction, became one of the London underground's several ghost stations. In the middle of it all, someone suggested the idea of a garden suburb; it took

[36] Jackson, F., 1985, 73, 109–10.   [37] Reiss, 1918, 85–6.

FIGURE 4.7   *Henrietta Barnett.*
The Dame takes charge: plan of Hampstead Garden Suburb
in her hand, moral fervour and reforming zeal in her eyes.

another 243-acre purchase from the Eton College Estate, using £112,000
invested from the appeal, in 1907. A trust was already set up to provide
8000 houses; Unwin and Parker were appointed architects.

From the first, the suburb had high social purposes: as a contemporary
put it, it would be a place 'where the poor shall teach the rich, and the
rich, let us hope, shall help the poor to help themselves'; the first plan
included barns for the storage of coster barrows.[38] But soon, land values
and rents began to rise, and – like Letchworth, or Bedford Park before
that – the suburb began to acquire a reputation, which Dame Henrietta
was at pains to refute: it was untrue that the inhabitants were 'all eccentric,
sandalled, corsetless "cranks"':

[38] Jackson, 1973, 78.

We are just ordinary men and women. . . . Some of us keep servants, some don't; some of us have motors, others use 'Shanks' pony'; some read, some paint, some make music, but we all work, we all wash ('no house, however small, without a bathroom' – vide advertisement) – and we all garden . . . relieved from the oppression of wealth, and able to meet each other on the simpler and deeper grounds of common interests and shared aspirations.[39]

Of the three separate house-building organizations that provided the great bulk of the houses, two were co-partnerships.[40] But the objective, 'day-to-day coexistence which would sooner heal the estrangement of the classes',[41] was frustrated by the suburb's own success; today, even the tiny artisans' cottages are well and truly gentrified.

What does survive is the physical quality. In some ways it is curiously transitional. Unwin was by now heavily influenced by Sitte and by his own German wanderings; restrictive local by-laws were overcome by using special parliamentary powers.[42] So Unwin was free to demonstrate on the ground what a few years later, in his enormously influential pamphlet *Nothing Gained by Overcrowding!*, he demonstrated on paper: that a proper planning scheme could give everyone much more space, without using more land. The key to this trick was to cut the land needed for roads from 40 per cent (as in the typical by-law scheme) to 17 per cent, thus raising the land available for gardens and open space from 17 to no less than 55 per cent of the total area.[43] This new freedom is used at Hampstead to produce a typically informal layout, with irregular curving streets, culs-de-sac and great variety of housing types; Unwin aimed, even at this early date, to design traffic out, and even today it notably proceeds with respectful sedateness.[44] And the design consciously, even winsomely, recalls German medieval models: there is a town wall against the Heath extension, with gatehouses; next to the shopping parade on the Finchley Road, Unwin places a huge gateway that looks as if it has been bodily airlifted out of old Nuremberg.

But in the central Town Square, placed by desire of the Dame on the suburb's highest point,[45] and in the adjacent streets, Unwin defers completely to Lutyens, the designer of the two big churches and the adjacent Institute. The result is an anomalous, heavily formal exercise in the City Beautiful tradition: approaching through the main gateway from the Heath, the expectant visitor expects to find a pastiche of Rothenburg-ob-der Tauber, with narrow streets leading to the kind of market place Unwin delighted to draw, but instead gets a processional way that looks suspiciously like a dummy run for the approach to the Viceroy's Palace at New Delhi (chapter 6). And the whole concept, vast in scale, is curiously dead; hardly

[39] Barnett, 1918, 205.   [40] Abercrombie, 1910a, 32.   [41] Creese, 1966, 227.
[42] Jackson, 1973, 79.   [43] Unwin, 1912, 6.   [44] Creese, 1966, 239.   [45] Ibid. 223.

· PROPOSED SHOPS · HAMPSTEAD GARDEN SUBURB ·

BARRY PARKER · AND ·
RAYMOND UNWIN ARCHITECTS

FIGURE 4.8 *Hampstead Garden Suburb.*
Old Nuremberg (or is it Rothenburg?) comes to the Finchley Road; the product,
most likely, of Unwin's last summer sketching holiday.

anyone ever goes there, and the square looks as if it is waiting for an
Imperial Durbar that will never now take place. Perhaps, though, as Creese
said, the intention was not to entertain the inhabitants, or offer them
recreation or shopping, but to impress them; and it presumably did that.[46]
But Unwin had blessed it; and at Letchworth, he too had formal moments.

But Hampstead thoroughly confused the faithful. From the start, as
Abercrombie pointed out in 1910, the Garden City Association had as
objectives, as well as the 'building of new towns in country districts on well
thought out principles', also 'the creation of Garden Suburbs, on similar
principles, for the immediate relief of existing towns' as well as 'the building
of Garden Villages . . . for properly housing the working classes near their
work.[47] The question would increasingly be whether the good was not the
enemy of the best. Hampstead in Unwin and Parker's hands was allowable,
even commendable; so, presumably, were most of the dozen or so schemes
co-ordinated by Co-Partnership Tenants between 1901 and World War
One;[48] the problem was that of 'quite a number of schemes which take the
title "Garden City" promiscuously, without having any claim whatever to
use the name, their objects being as foreign as possible to the conceptions
of the founders of ther movement.'[49] After the war, C. B. Purdom, the new

[46] Ibid. 234.   [47] Abercrombie, 1910a, 20.   [48] Culpin, 1913, *passim.*   [49] Ibid. 5.

FIGURE 4.9 *Sunday lunch in Welwyn Garden City.*
Howard's ideal personified; the working man and his wife come into their patrimony.

FIGURE 4.10 *The Mall, Welwyn Garden City.*
Louis de Soissons brings classical formality and Georgian good taste to the Second
Garden City.

editor of the Association's magazine, complained: 'There is hardly a district
in which the local council does not claim to be building one, and
unscrupulous builders everywhere display the name on their advertisements
... The thing itself is nowhere to be seen at the present date, but in
Hertfordshire, at Letchworth and Welwyn Garden City.'[50]

In 1919, the Association – by now renamed the Garden Cities and Town
Planning Association – adopted a carefully restrictive definition of the
'thing itself'; the following year, embarrassed by the sixty-nine-year-old
Howard's purchase of a huge tract of land at Welwyn without consultation
or the money to pay for it, they bailed him out and started the second
garden city there.[51] Designed by Louis de Soissons in the neo-Georgian
style that by then had swept the Unwin–Parker neo-vernacular off the
stage – Unwin himself had turned coat – it is much more formal than
either Letchworth or Hampstead, especially in its huge Lutyens-like central
mall, almost a mile long: a kind of Garden City Beautiful. But the
architecture shows how very good neo-Georgian can be in the right hands,

[50] Purdom, 1921, 33.　　[51] Ibid. 34; Osborn, 1970, 9–10.

and it has been beautifully cared for; a cheat, perhaps, because unlike
Letchworth it soon became popular with middle-class commuters. The fact,
heretical though it may be to say out loud, is that it is actually much more
appealing than Letchworth.

The Garden City Movement Between the Wars

Meanwhile, in 1918 and 1919 the movement had faced a double crisis. In
1912 Unwin had already committed what for some was the great apostasy:
in a lecture at Manchester University, he had commended the building of
'satellite towns' next to cities, garden suburbs depending on the city for
employment. In 1918, placed in a position of unequalled power as key
member of the Tudor Walters Committee, he wrote that into the official
prescription for the postwar public-housing programme, which received
legislative blessing in the Addison Act the next year; the consequences have
been detailed in chapter 3. The result was that of the million or so publicly
subsidized dwellings built by local authorities between the wars, none –
with the exception of a handful at Letchworth and Welwyn – was built in
the form of true garden cities. This was a severe blow to the Association,
which was campaigning simultaneously for a vastly expanded public housing
programme and for garden cities. Howard himself had no faith at all in
the capacity of the state to do the job, and perhaps no ideological relish
for the idea either: as he told his faithful lieutenant Frederic Osborn (1885–
1978) in 1919, 'My dear boy, if you wait for the Government to do it you
will be as old as Methuselah before you start.'[52]

So Howard got Welwyn by his own unconventional methods, the country
got satellite towns, and the cause of large-scale new town building in Britain
was set back thirty years. Perhaps it was inevitable: the political objections
to the large-scale removal of urban slum-dwellers into the countryside,
coupled with the threat of massive boundary extensions, would have been
huge, as the LCC's troubles in planning its satellite estates, and Manchester's
at Wythenshawe, amply demonstrated.

Partly the problem was one of failure of imagination. Some of the so-
called satellites – above all the LCC's at Becontree, in Essex – were huge,
many times Howard's planned target of 30,000, and equal to a medium-
sized English town. And they were distant from their parent urban authority.
But they lacked the necessary industry to make them self-contained –
though, after 1928, Becontree had the windfall of the Ford Dagenham
plant – and they even lacked decent public-transport links. And, too often,
they were design failures too. The housing was worthy enough, and it

[52] Osborn, 1970, 8; cf. Hebbert, 1981, 180.

FIGURE 4.11 *Frederic Osborn.*
First Howard's lieutenant, then his successor as indefatigable campaigner-in-chief
for garden cities; in his Welwyn garden, aged 80, the next polemic ready for the
printer.

conformed to Unwin's pattern books; it, and the layouts within which it
was embodied, were just plain dull.

The provincial satellites were partial exceptions. And Wythenshawe,
designed by Barry Parker for Manchester in 1930, really is a rather
outstanding one. Its early history was tortuous. Abercrombie, appointed as
consultant, had recommended that the city buy the 4,500-acre estate; it
purchased half of it in 1926. There had followed a huge battle by
Manchester to incorporate the area, won in Parliament in 1931; it was
unsuccessful in getting an order to buy the rest of the land. Meanwhile, in
1927 the City had commissioned Parker to produce a plan. On a huge site
of 5,500 acres he was given a free hand to design a virtual new town. By
1938, with over 7,000 corporation and some 700 private houses, it was
already bigger than either Letchworth or Welwyn and was still only one-
third of the way to its planned target of 107,000.[53] Parker himself described
it, in 1945, as 'now the most perfect example of a garden city'.[54] It is, to

[53] Macfadyen, 1933, 115–21; G. B. R.C. Geographical Distribution, 1938, *passim.*
[54] Creese, 1966, 255.

be sure, an imperfect one. The population target was three times that recommended by Howard, though close to that of the larger post-World War Two new towns. Though the land was purchased at near-agricultural values, it was separated from the city only by a half-mile-wide, 1,000–acre green belt along the River Mersey. Though a large industrial area was planned – like Letchworth, alongside a railway that bisects the site – it could not provide jobs for all the working inhabitants; a subsidized express bus service to the city was necessary.

Its achievement lay in introducing three American planning principles, borrowed directly by Parker from the New York region, which he had visited in 1925.[55] The first of these was the neighbourhood unit principle, the origins of which need to be discussed later in this chapter. The second was the principle of the Radburn layout, which Clarence Stein and Henry Wright had developed in their plan for the garden city of the same name in 1928, also to be described later in this chapter, which they had discussed with him as early as 1924.[56] The third was the principle of the parkway, which Parker had observed in the New York region, but which he now used in a completely original way.

The original New York parkways – the Bronx River Parkway of 1914, and the examples developed by Robert Moses as part of his recreational parks plans of the 1920s – were limited-access highways designed for private-car traffic only, and deliberately landscaped to provide a recreational experience.[57] Parker's genius at Wythenshawe was to combine these with another, older American parkway tradition, conceived by Frederick Law Olmsted and widely used by planners in the City Beautiful tradition at the start of the century: the idea of parkways as access roads to residential areas, linked to civic parks[58] – an idea that had been tentatively employed in Britain, by Soissons at Welwyn and by the landscape architect T. H. Mawson around Stanley Park, Blackpool, in the 1920s – to provide the main element of the circulation plan for an entire garden city.[59] Thereby he planned to avoid one of the principal planning defects of the 1930s, so evident around London, of ribbon development along new arterial roads. At Wythenshawe, he explained,

> such roads . . . will lie in strips of parkland and they will not be development roads. They have been planned to skirt existing parks, future recreation grounds, school playing fields, existing woodlands, coppices and spinnies, the proposed golf course, the banks of streams and everything which will enhance their charm and will widen them out into great expanses of unbuilt upon country.[60]

These roads, he argued, should in American terminology properly be called 'freeways', not 'parkways', because they were not restricted to recreation

[55] Ibid. 261.   [56] Ibid. 266.   [57] Caro, 1974, 10–11; Jackson, K. 1985, 166–7.
[58] Gregg, 1986, 38, 41–2.   [59] Mawson, 1984, 195.   [60] Parker, 1932, 40.

and would be used by all kinds of traffic. (Indeed, they were akin to the notion of segregated arterial roads as the highest level in a hierarchical system of traffic planning, as enunciated by Alker Tripp in 1938 and then borrowed by Abercrombie and Forshaw as a major element in their County of London Plan in 1943.) But eventually, once finished, Parker's main north–south artery was called the Princess Parkway. Its fate was ironic: originally planned with junctions to the local street system at grade, thirty years later it was upgraded into a motorway by the transport planners. Approached from the city through a mass of concrete spaghetti, it is now a freeway in the Angeleno sense of that word, with a vengeance. The other planned parkway, unaccountably, was abandoned half-way, the park strip wandering on shorn of its original point.

Manchester in fact has not dealt kindly with its masterpiece. The shopping centre, completed very belatedly, is 1960s–tawdry; some of the postwar flats are monstrosities. A second and third generation of incomers have not treated the place as kindly as the original arrivals; there is all too much evidence, for those who would like to believe that civilized surroundings will engender civilized behaviour, of graffiti and vandalism and petty crime. The place looks down at heel in that distinctively English way, as if the city has given up on it; though in that respect, it is no different from the rest of Manchester. But despite its best efforts, it could not obliterate Parker entirely. The huge green space of Wythenshawe Park, right in the centre, almost turns the green-belt concept inside-out; this is a green heart city. The housing, which deftly embodies Georgian motifs into the vernacular of Letchworth, is cunningly grouped round a multitude of small green spaces. For all its latter-day shabbiness, it fully deserves the appellation of third garden city.

Meanwhile the faithful soldiered on. Chamberlain, always the friend of garden cities while in office, got government subsidy written in to legislation in 1921, 1925 and – in the fact of Treasury opposition – in 1932.[61] But it did not do much good. By the 1930s the Permanent Secretary of the Ministry of Health, Sir Arthur Robinson, was openly confessing,

> Beginning as a supporter of garden cities, properly so called, I have in the course of time changed my views on them – they are fine in theory but in practice they do not seem to work. What is properly called a satellite town is a much better method of approach. . . . But the satellite town is just what several of the large housing schemes of local authorities are producing, and the line of progress is to encourage it.[62]

And, once Chamberlain had managed to create the Barlow Commission, Unwin, giving evidence to it in 1938, could argue that Howard's great

---

[61] Macfadyen, 1933, 104; Sheail, 1981, 125–6.
[62] Sheail, 1981, 126.

contribution had been the garden suburb, not the garden city; satellite development would be sufficient to guard against the continued sprawl of London.[63]

In vain, Osborn railed at the consequences: 'To build cottage estates on the outskirts gives people good immediate surroundings, but imposes on them an intolerable burden of journeys, costing money, energy and leisure. It also cuts off London as a whole from playing fields and open country.'[64] The only way out of this, he was arguing in 1938, was to establish a London Regional Planning Commission with powers to establish executive boards to build new towns or expand existing ones', and to decentralize industry and business within an enlarged region.[65] Against that view, of course, it could be argued that London was special; for the much smaller provincial cities, satellites – like Manchester's Wythenshawe or Liverpool's Speke – were perfectly acceptable. But Osborn would have none of that: 'the fate of London may give cause to those responsible for the great towns and town-conglomerations of the North and Midlands. . . . what Londoners can be got to stand today, England will be asked to stand tomorrow.'[66] The establishment of the Barlow Commission – one of the first acts of Neville Chamberlain on becoming Prime Minister – at last gave him his chance; he did not miss it. As he confessed shamelessly to Lewis Mumford, he redrafted for Abercrombie some of the key paragraphs of the 1940 majority report and of Abercrombie's own minority report, which recommended sweeping controls on industrial location and which finally – in 1945 – was embodied into legislation.[67] After years in the political wilderness, the friends of the garden city were at last about to come into their own.

The Garden City in Europe

Over the water on the European mainland, the garden-city notion soon became just as thoroughly diluted or, as the faithful would say, traduced. One problem was that several countries each had a home-grown garden-city advocate, who could – and sometimes did – claim that he thought of the idea independently. Insofar as these claims can ever be settled, all did; but in any case, their notions are subtly, but importantly, different from Howard's.

The first in time was undoubtedly the Spanish engineer Arturo Soria y Mata (1844–1920), who conceived of his idea of *La Ciudad Lineal* in a magazine article of 1882 and developed it into a detailed proposal of 1892. Its essence was that a tramway, or light rail, system running out from a big city could give extraordinary linear accessibility, which would permit

[63] G.B. R.C. Geographical Distribution, 1938, Q. 7221.   [64] Osborn, 1937, 51.
[65] Osborn, 1938, 100–2.   [66] Osborn, 1934, 5–6.   [67] Hughes, 1971, 271.

the development of a planned linear garden city: 'A Cada Familia, Una Casa, En Cada Casa, Una Huerta y un Jardin' as an advertisement put it.[68] But the linear city was never more than a commuter suburb, developed as a commercial speculation. Started in 1894 and completed in 1904, the first section of the planned 48-kilometre (30-mile) city ran for 5 kilometres (3 miles) circumferentially between two major radial highways east of Madrid; on either side of a main axis 40 metres wide, carrying the tramway (originally worked by horses, and not electrified until 1909), villas were laid out on superblocks measuring approximately 200 metres in depth and with 80- or 100-metre frontages.[69] That was all that got built, and in 1934 the Compania Madrilena de Urbanizacion gave up the ghost.[70] After World War Two the stupendous growth of the city almost buried the linear city; travellers from the airport pass under it without noticing. Those curious enough to divert will find it still quite recognizably there, with the trams replaced by the metro; they thoughtfully named a station for Arturo Soria. Some of the original villas, too, are still standing; but one by one, they are being replaced by apartment blocks, and soon the linear city will be a memory. Soria had grander dreams of linear cities across Europe, which in 1928, after his death, inspired a Association Internationale des Cités Linéaires master-minded by the influential French planner Georges Benôit-Lévy; echoes of his scheme can be found in the Russian deurbanists of the 1920s and in Corbusier's thinking of the 1930s, where we shall encounter them later.

The French Howard was Tony Garner (1869–1948), an architect from Lyon, who seems to have conceived his *Cité industrielle* in 1898, the year of publication of *To-morrow*, though he waited until 1918 to publish it; it is possible, though unlikely, that he had read it. Its intellectual provenance is the French regional thinking of Le Play and of the French school of geography, with its anti-metropolitan stress on the development of vigorous provincial craft culture; it is anarchist in its emphasis on common property and its rejection of such symbols of bourgeois repression as police stations, law courts, gaols or churches, and its large central building where 3,000 citizens could meet together.[71] All the odder, then, that Garnier makes his city depend economically on a single huge metallurgical plant (though questions of economics get short shrift), and that the physical plan is dominated by strong axial boulevards and housing on rectangular grids; rather, as Reyner Banham put it, like Camillio Sitte with the serpentinings taken out.[72]

If Garnier is not quite of one piece, his German equivalent is even weirder. Theodor Fritsch published his *Die Stadt der Zukunft* two years before

---

[68] Soria y Pug, 1968, 35, 43, Fig. 7.   [69] Ibid. Figs. 2–10.
[70] Ibid. 1968, 44–9, 52.   [71] Wiebenson, 1969, 16–19; Veronesi, 1948, 56.
[72] Banham, 1960, 36–8.

Howard, in 1896; he had an obsession that Howard had stolen his ideas, though it seems clear that Howard had developed his independently before that.[73] True, in purely physical terms there are similarities between Garden City and City of the Future: the circular form, the division between land uses, the open land at the centre and the surrounding green belt, the low-rise housing, the peripheral industry, the communal landownership. But these recur in other ideal plans, including Buckingham's, which Howard specifically acknowledged. And Fritsch's city, 'eine Mischung von Grossstadt und Gartenstadt', lacks the specific function of urban decentralization which is central to Howard's thinking; it apparently would have been much bigger, with up to 1 million people.[74] Most important, the underlying ideology is totally different: Fritsch, a rabid propagandist of racism, plans a city where each individual immediately knows his place in a rigid, segregated social order.[75] Overall, any resemblance between Fritsch and Howard is one of surface appearance; and, as already seen, Howard was not in the least concerned about that.

Before long, it was Howard's ideas which – to the chagrin of Fritsch – were carried across the water to influence thinking on the European mainland; but there, almost immediately, they got misunderstood. One of the earliest foreign interpretations of Howard's ideas, *Le Cité-Jardin* by Georges Benoît-Lévy, managed to make an elementary confusion between garden city and garden suburb, from which French planners never afterwards extricated themselves.[76] Or, perhaps, they thought that the pure Howard gospel would not work for the incurably urban French. Henri Sellier, who as director of the Office Public des Habitations à Bon Marché du Département de la Seine planned sixteen *cités-jardins* around Paris between 1916 and 1939, certainly understood that his interpretation was not pure Howard, but Unwin's Hampstead variant; he took his architects to visit Unwin in England, in 1919, and used the Unwin text as a basis for design.[77]

What they shared was some key aspects of the Unwin prescription, albeit translated into French terms: small size, between 1,000 and 5,500 units; land bought outside the city at low agricultural prices; densities that were low for Paris, 95–150 persons to the hectare (40–60 to the acre), and plenty of open space. Then, rising land and housing costs, plus population pressure, brought modifications: more and more blocks of five-storey flats were included; densities rose to 200 or 260 to the hectare (80–105 per acre), though still with generous open space and social services.[78] Visited

---

[73] Bergmann, 1970, 145–7; Hartmann, 1976, 33.
[74] Reiner, 1963, 36–8; Peltz-Dreckmann, 1978, 45.
[75] Peltz-Dreckmann, 1978, 45–7.
[76] Benoît-Lévy, 1904; Batchelor, 1969, 199.
[77] Read, 1978, 349–50; Swenarton, 1985, 54.
[78] Read, 1978, 350–1; Evenson, 1979, 223–6.

today, a typical example like Suresnes – 6 miles from the centre of Paris, a mere mile from the Bois de Boulogne – looks like nothing so much as an LCC inner-London apartment-block scheme of the same period: Unwin's, certainly, is not the first name that springs to mind. And in the 1930s, as the proportion of apartment blocks rose even higher and the architects joined the modern movement, the divergence was complete.

In Germany, they did better. In 1902 a salesman visiting England, Heinrich Krebs, brought back Howard's book, got it translated, ran a conference and started a German equivalent of the Garden City Association. There was an enthusiastic response: German industrialists, almost unbelievably, thought that the garden-city movement helped explain good British industrial labour relations.[79] That, to be sure, was some kind of obsession with German industrialists.

Before World War One its outstanding expression was the garden village of Margarethenhöhe at the edge of Essen in the Ruhrgebiet, developed by the Krupp family in 1912 as the latest in a long line of such industrial housing estates that went back as early as 1863. Small, with only 5,300 people at the end of the 1930s, it is physically a transplanted New Earswick. Its architect, Georg Metzendorf, faithfully followed the Unwin–Parker tradition to create a magic little town, separated from the city by a wooded mini-green belt, its entrance gateway, its central market square, its medieval-looking inn, its narrow, curving streets from which all through traffic is excluded. Thus, ironically, it out-Unwins Unwin; it really does look like a twentieth-century Rothenburg. Perhaps it took a German architect, working in a German environment, to achieve what Unwin so zealously strived for. Whether it served Krupp's purposes is another question altogether; apparently, by herding his workers together in their own town, it made them even more class-conscious.[80]

The *Gartenstadtbewegung*, however, aimed higher: they wanted a German Letchworth, as their leader Hans Kampffmeyer said in 1908.[81] They never quite got it, though they got near. The garden city at Hellerau, 8 kilometres (5 miles) outside Dresden, was – like Margarethenhöhe – essentially a garden suburb at the end of a tram line. But, like Letchworth in its heady early years, it – and the movement in general – was heavily imbued with principles of the Life Reform Movement: not merely housing, but eating, clothing and lifestyle generally were to be simplified and stripped of nineteenth-century dross. Hellerau contained the Deutsche Werkstätte für Handbaukunst, and even a Society for Applied Rhythmics.

The latter-day pilgrim, visiting it, goes into a time warp. It stands isolated from the city, in open heathland that provides a natural green belt

[79] Kampffmeyer, 1908, 599.   [80] Peltz-Dreckmann, 1978, 50.
[81] Kampffmeyer, 1908, 595.

FIGURE 4.12 *Margarethenhöhe.*
Georg Metzendorf's brilliant exercise in the Sitte tradition, for the Krupp family,
outside Essen: the essence of German industrial paternalism.

against the city, but also today serves as a Red Army training ground,
punctuating the arcadian peace with eerie explosions. Yet, perhaps because
there have been no resources to do much with it, in its slightly down-at-
heel way it manages ineffably to project its original spirit. Heinrich
Tressenow's terrace and semi-detached houses, utterly faithful to the
Unwin–Parker tradition, wear their years lightly. There is even a Radburn-
style pedestrian layout, anticipating Radburn itself by two decades. It leads
to the *Werkstätte*, now a People's Owned Enterprise. The market square,
reminiscent of Margarethenhöhe – which, surely, Tressenow must have
visited – manages to achieve what Unwin and Parker should have done at
Letchworth and Hampstead, but unaccountably never did. It is an
anomalous small gem.

It represents what could be called the left-wing side of the German
garden-city movement; but there was always another side too, and over
time it became more and more insistent. It stemmed from the fear of the
giant city; it spoke of biological decline of the race in the great cities, and

of the need to recolonize the declining countryside, especially on the borders of German settlement against Slav Europe. Already, ominously, in the middle of World War One, the word *Lebensraum* was in use; it entailed the removal of population that was harmful to the 'national character'.[82] In the 1920s, these themes were to become a potent element of Nazi thinking.

But that, still, was in the realm of intellectual speculation. In the real world, immediately after World War One, the reality was similar to that in Britain: a fear of revolution. And perhaps in Germany it had sounder foundation. In Frankfurt, as elsewhere, a Workers' and Soldiers' Council dominated politics for a year after the 1918 armistice. When the Social Democrats finally acheived power in the city, their strategy under mayor Ludwig Landmann (1924–33) was to restore social peace through an implicit compact between capital and labour: a theme that was to recur in the creation of the *Wohlfahrtsgesellschaft* after World War Two. Frankfurt's central business district was to be preserved and enhanced as Germany's leading financial centre; the banks of the Main were to be developed for high-technology industry. But, to satisfy the demands of labour, the city would also embark on an active housing policy.

Landmann attracted the architect-planner Ernst May (1886–1970), who had acquired a considerable reputation with his plans for the city of Breslau (Wrocław). Thanks to the far-sighted policies of Frankfurt's famous pre-war mayor, Franz Adickes, the city had acquired enormous landholdings, at rock-bottom agricultural prices, in the open countryside around.[83] Thus, on arrival in 1925, May had all he needed to develop a startlingly innovative development plan.

May, like Sellier in Paris, was heavily influenced by the garden city movement; he had worked with Unwin, in 1910, on both Letchworth and Hampstead; he maintained close contact with him. His original notion was a pure garden-city one, with new towns 20–30 km (15–20 miles) distant, separated from the city by a wide green belt. It proved impossible to realize politically; May fell back on a compromise, the development of satellite cities (*Trabantenstädte*), separated from the city by only a narrow green belt, or 'people's park', dependent on it for jobs and for all but immediate local shopping needs, and therefore linked to it by public transportation.[84] But these were to be developed by the city, as public housing; the comparison is with the British housing programme after the 1919 Act (chapter 3), not with the early British garden cities and garden suburbs.

In another important respect May broke away completely from his master Unwin, and indeed from the British tradition of the 1920s: his satellites were to be designed uncompromisingly as modern architecture, in the form

[82] Bergmann, 1970, 169–71.   [83] Yago, 1984, 87–8, 94, 98–9.
[84] Fehl, 1983, 188–90.

of long terraces of flat-roofed houses with roof gardens, on which people could breakfast, sunbathe, raise plants. But that difference is skin-deep: in his insistence on single-family homes with gardens, carefully aligned in relation to the light of the sun, May proved an apt pupil of his master Unwin.

The entire programme was not large: 15,000 houses, though it did constitute the great bulk of all housing built in the city in that period, 1925–33. The individual schemes, for all their fame then and subsequently, were minuscule, and many of them were disposed unmemorably on small plots around the city; only a few, strung out along the valley of the river Nidda north-west of the city, represent the classic satellites, and even these are surprisingly small: 1,441 dwellings at Praunheim, 1,220 at Römerstadt.[85] What made them memorable was the disposition of the houses in long rows alongside the river, the placing of schools and *Kindergarten* on the lower land, and the use of the valley as a natural green belt in which are concentrated all kinds of uses: allotments, sports grounds, commercial garden plots, gardening schools for young people, even perhaps a fairground.[86] But the project was never completed as planned; the money ran out, and the community halls – an echo, perhaps, of Unwin – were never completed.

After the war, Frankfurt dealt brutally with its miniature masterpiece: two urban motorways now slice across the valley, one cuts Römerstadt in half, the satellites are totally swallowed up in a much larger and completely amorphous satellite town called – with appropriate impersonality – Nordweststadt. But still, with the eye of imagination and the eye of faith, one can get a feeling for what it might have been, what it was, and what it still remarkably is. It is almost totally gentrified, with only 11 per cent of the blue-collar workers for which it was designed; but it is beautifully maintained. After more than half a century the vegetation is mature, making of it the garden city that May imagined. In the summer sunlight the hard clean lines of the long cream-coloured terraces are masked, almost submerged, by the trees and flowers; across the valley, the blue industrial haze achieves the serendiptious effect of making the city's new high-rise townscape appear almost like a magical world.

What has vanished is the spirit. And that, now, is hard even to imagine. May differed on many things with the other great planner of the Weimar time, Berlin's Martin Wagner (1885–1957); but both shared a belief in a new social partnership between capital and labour, and in a reintegration of working and living. This they also had in common with Howard and Unwin; but there was an absolutely crucial difference. The May–Wagner variant was a collective one, diverging sharply from the anarchist-co-

---

[85] Gallion and Eisner, 1963, 104.   [86] Fehl, 1983, 191.

operative sources of the Howard–Unwin tradition: in May's own words, it aimed at 'the collective ordering of the elements of living'.[87] For May, a well-planned residential environment could complement the pursuit of efficiency in the workplace, and – to quote May again – 'the uniform box-shapes of the roof gardens symbolize the idea of collective living in a uniform style, like the similarly shaped honeycombs of the beehive, symbolizing the uniform living conditions of their inhabitants.'[88]

It all sounds too perfectly like raw material for a Marxist Ph.D. thesis: the capitalist state co-opting the local state in a plot to secure the reproduction of the labour force. In any event, both Howard and Unwin would have hated it; no wonder, perhaps, that Unwin made himself thoroughly unpopular by holding out against modern architecture to the end. And no wonder either, perhaps, that after Frankfurt May went on to design model cities in the Soviet Union – none of which, ironically, ever got built as planned, for by then the spirit of Stalin had descended on the Soviet City.

Wagner, like May, was co-ordinating a major housing and planning programme, albeit on a much larger scale. His big difference with May concerned the role and thus the character and the location of the new estates. Wagner did not believe at all in satellites; his ideal was the *Siedlung* – the concept and the term was first developed by the coal and iron barons of the Ruhrgebiet – wherein houses were grouped around a factory, but with no independent – or even semi-independent – existence from the rest of the city.[89] The ideal is Siemensstadt, developed by the giant electrical company around their complex of works in the north-west sector of the city between 1929 and 1931. It is a *Grosssiedlung*, a complex of housing areas, planned and executed on a lavish scale; every name in German architecture of the 1920s has his piece of it; it is a place of reverent pilgrimage, and pieces are being restored by the Federal Government as historic monuments. The pilgrims arrive at the U-Bahn station Siemensdamm, a busy urban boulevard a mere 20 minutes from the centre of West Berlin; this announces itself from the start as an urban development. Yet, a couple of minutes away, they are in another world: the masters – Scharoun, Bartning, Häring, Gropius and others – have placed their four- and five-storey apartment blocks in a huge garden, that – as with the two-storey rows of Römerstadt – has grown over the decades so as to seem almost to envelop them.[90]

The overwhelming impression, just as much as in any English garden city, is that of peacefulness. Any sceptic from Britain or the United States, who believes that collective apartment schemes mean slum living, any indeed who believes that an apartment garden city is a contradiction in

[87] Ibid. 186.   [88] Ibid. 190.
[89] Uhlig, 1977, 56.   [90] Rave and Knöfel, 1968, 193.

FIGURE 4.13 *Römerstadt.*

FIGURE 4.14 *Siemensstadt.*

FIGURE 4.15 *Onkel Toms Hütte.*
The garden suburb reinterpreted by the masters of the modern movement, May in Frankfurt, Gropius and Taut in Berlin: functionalism, even in four-storey apartments, can prove liveable too.

terms, should see Siemensstadt and think again. The reflections have to be these: first, uncompromisingly modern apartment blocks, so long as kept moderately low and strongly horizontal, can be as reposeful – that special Unwin–Parker quality – as uncompromisingly modern houses, or as traditional ones. Second, the quality of the surrounding garden space is crucial. And third, maintenance is all: Siemensstadt works, as does Römerstadt, because it is in good heart.

The same goes, outstandingly, for the two other great developments of the Wagner years in Berlin: the *Grosssiedlungen* Onkel-Toms-Hütte at Zehlendorf in the south-west sector of the city, and Britz, in the south. Both were developed by Gehag, the great housing agency formed in 1924 through the merger of several building societies with trades union funds and the Berlin Social Housing Society, which was responsible for so much publicly subsidized housing in Berlin at that time and in the Federal Republic after World War Two: a living illustration of the kind of agency Howard wanted to build his garden city, but never got on the scale needed.[91] (Ironically, its postwar successor was racked by scandal in the 1980s.) Both were and are pure garden suburbs, at the then periphery of the city, developed on extensions of the U-Bahn system.

[91] Lane, 1968, 104.

Onkel-Toms-Hütte, built between 1926 and 1931, calls itself a forest settlement (*Waldsiedlung*) and indeed the first impression is of the huge canopy of tall trees that extends, with almost military uniformity, across the whole site. Under its cover are two- and three-storey houses, the bulk of them by Bruno Taut and Hugo Häring, uncompromisingly in 1920s modern idiom, washed in pastel shades, developed in rows along long gently curving or shorter straight streets.[92] Again – especially to those hardened by experience of British council estates – the astonishing feature is the level of upkeep: the houses, still owned by the housing association, convey the unreal impression that they are almost brand-new. Britz (1925–31), designed by Bruno Taut and Martin Wagner, is more formal: its two- and three-storey terraces of houses are grouped around the celebrated *Hufeisensiedlung*, where the four-storey block wraps itself in a huge horseshoe round a lake.[93] In the streets around, the houses – again impeccably maintained – show an unexpected counterpoint: Bruno Taut's are respectably conservative, Martin Wagner's Disneyland-fantastic. An underground station stands at each end of the settlement, which on its east side faces out on to the huge open space of the Köningsheide – now, alas, brutally bisected by *Die Mauer*.

Both these developments are splendid; both, ironically, represent the very antithesis of the garden city idea. It might be argued that May in Frankfurt, like Parker in Manchester, was dealing with a spatial scale different in kind from that of London, which provided Howard's model urban problem; both were quintessentially medium-sized provincial cities, with between half and three-quarters of a million people, and so a satellite solution might seem more workable and more appropriate. But the same could hardly be said of the Greater Berlin of the mid-1920s, already – with some 4 million people – the second greatest single urban mass in Europe. The fact was that by this time, racked by lack of funds and by political realities, the planners of the Weimar Republic no longer thought that the self-containment of the garden city was worth fighting for.[94]

Garden Cities for America

Across the Atlantic Ocean, too, the garden-city tradition never quite developed as Howard had hoped. It was not, however, for want of trying. During the 1920s, the Regional Planning Association of America not only acted as guardians of the sacred treasures; rather in the manner of a reforming church, they actually extended and purified the gospel, writing the holy texts that Howard might have delivered if appropriate disciples

[92] Rave and Knöfel, 1968, 146.   [93] Rave and Knöfel, 1968, 79.   [94] Hartmann, 1976,   44.

had been at his sleeve. But their god was a twin god, Howard–Geddes, and their creed embraced the planning of entire regions; so they deserve a goodly part of a chapter to themselves, which they will get in chapter 5. Here, we need to talk of their contributions to the garden city without benefit of that context; difficult, illogical even, but, in the interests of coherence, necessary.

The architects in this small and distinguished group were Clarence Stein (1882–1975) and Henry Wright (1878–1936). Their unique contribution to the garden city lay in the handling of traffic and pedestrian circulation through the so-called Radburn layout, which they developed for the garden city of the same name in 1928. But to appreciate it fully, they need to be related to another figure, oddly not associated with the RPAA group at all: Clarence Perry (1872–1944).

Perry was a very early example of a breed that was to become commoner, the sociologist-planner. He worked as a community planner for the New York-based Russell Sage Foundation from 1913 until his retirement in 1937. Even before this, he had become interested in a movement – clearly derivative from the approach of Jane Addams in Chicago – to develop local schools into community centres through the involvement of parents. He was also profoundly influenced by the writings of the American sociologist Charles Horton Cooley, who had stressed the importance of the 'primary group', 'characterized by intimate face-to-face association and cooperation', which he held to be 'fundamental in forming the social nature and ideals of the individual' and which was especially important in the dense, highly fragmented life of the modern city.[95]

That was a theme taken up by leaders of the settlement house movement, who had argued that the time had come for 'a great renewal of confidence in the vitality of the neighborhood as a political and moral unit', especially in those 'disorganized neighborhoods . . . which have lost their responsible leadership', whereby 'under-average mothers in relatively resourceless neighborhoods . . . can be trained and held to their task' and 'the loss of productive power' could be corrected by 'the vocational extension of our public school system'.[96] Socialization of the immigrant, and of the immigrant's children, was clearly the object here.[97] But it was more than that; as a resident in the model garden suburb of Forest Hills Gardens, developed by the Russell Sage Foundation from 1911 – itself a railroad suburb, some 9 miles from Manhattan, where Grosvenor Atterbury's plan is clearly derivative from Chicago's Riverside and London's Bedford Park – Perry learnt just how much good design could contribute to the development of a neighbourhood spirit.[98] It derives in spirit from Unwin and Parker's

[95] Cooley, 1909, 23, 408–9.   [96] Woods, 1914, 17–18, 20–1.   [97] Lubove, 1962b, 205.
[98] Perry, 1929, 90–3; 1939, 205–9, 217; Mumford, 1954, 260; Lubove, 1962b, 207.

FIGURE 4.16   *Clarence Stein.*
Compaigner for new towns in America, and builder of three brilliant designs; he
gave the Radburn layout to the planner's vocabulary.

quasi-Teutonic at Hampstead, and from the real thing at Margarethenhöhe
and Hellerau; but it goes beyond any of them, to create a kitsch-like quality
that anticipates Hollywood. Yet, like all the best suburban dream
environments before it, from Nash's Blaise Hamlet onwards, the point is
that it works: in the presence of this superb theatrical set, disbelief is
immediately suspended.

But theatre is put to serious purpose. Life in Forest Hills Gardens gave
to Perry the concept of the neighbourhood unit, which he first developed
at a meeting of the American Sociological Association and the National
Community Center Association in Washington, DC, on 16 December 1923,
and subsequently developed in greater detail in his monograph of 1929 for
the Regional Plan of New York, which was financed by Russell Sage and
in which Perry played a principal role as a social planner.[99] Its size would

[99] Perry, 1939, 214; Lubove, 1962b, 207.

FIGURE 4.17 AND 4.18 *Forest Hills Gardens.*
The New York commuter garden suburb where Clarence Perry discovered the principle of the neighbourhood unit.

be set by the catchment area of the local elementary school, and so would depend on population density; its central features would be this local school and an associated playground, reachable on foot within half a mile; local shops, which, by being placed at the corners of several neighbourhoods, could be within a quarter-mile; and a central point or common place for the encouragement of community institutions:

> The square itself will be an appropriate location for a flagpole, a memorial monument, a bandstand, or an ornamental fountain. In the common life of the neighborhood it will function as the place of local celebrations. Here, on Independence Day, the Flag will be raised, the Declaration of Independence will be recited, and the citizenry urged to patriotic deeds by eloquent orators.[100]

The inspiration is unmistakable: it is a latter-day reinterpretation of Jane Addams's desire to integrate the new immigrant, now become the immigrant's American-born children, as they move out from the city slums to their new suburban homes. The *raison d'être* then was socio-cultural; but, Perry already argued at the end of the 1920s, 'the automobile menace' had made the definition of such neighbourhood units imperative, proving thus 'a blessing in disguise'.[101] The arterial streets, wide enough to carry all through traffic, would thus provide logical boundaries; the internal street network would be designed to facilitate internal circulation but to discourage through traffic.[102]

In the celebrated diagram in the 1929 report, one element only is missing: a clear indication of how, precisely, the unwanted traffic was to be kept out. Perry himself knew this to be the only real defect of the Forest Hills Gardens plan.[103] But already, a few miles nearer Manhattan along the same commuter rail line, Stein and Wright were tentatively showing the way. In 1924 Alexander Bing, a successful developer, had been inspired by Stein to launch the City Housing Corporation in order to build an American garden city. As a first trial, from 1924 to 1928, they took Sunnyside Gardens, a still-undeveloped 77-acre inner-city site only 5 miles from Manhattan, planning it on the basis of big traffic-free superblocks to create vast interior garden spaces – albeit frustrated by the same kind of rigid restrictions against which Unwin had fought in England.[104] Lewis Mumford, who was one of the first residents, long after testified to the quality of life, both physical and social, there[105]; but it was no garden city.

Thus apprenticed, they moved on to the real thing. In the borough of Fairlawn in New Jersey, 15 miles from Manhattan – a place with no zoning ordinance and no roads plan – the City Housing Corporation bought 2 square miles, on which Stein and Wright planned three neighbourhoods.[106]

[100] Perry, 1939, 65.   [101] Perry, 1929, 31.   [102] Ibid. 34–5.   [103] Perry, 1939, 211.
[104] Stein, 1958, 21.   [105] Mumford, 1982, 411–21.
[106] Stein, 1958, 39–41; Schaffer, 1982, 147.

The trick was to take the Sunnyside superblock, release it from the rigid New York City grid, and to combine it with cluster housing so that noat merely through traffic, but all traffic, was excluded. As one of the consultants on the design put it, 'we abolished the backyard and made it the front yard . . . we are building houses that have no backs, but have no fronts'[107] – a feature Wright had noticed in Irish peasant houses.[108]

There seems to be some kind of general law in planning history that the first time is the best. Certainly that was true of New Earswick and Letchworth; certainly it is so here. Radburn is the best Radburn layout. The hierarchical arrangement of roads – here used for the first time, though almost immediately copied by Parker at Wythenshawe – is very natural and easy. The houses, modest enough in themselves, cluster cosily alongside the short culs-de-sac from the distributor roads – a motif borrowed directly from Unwin and Parker at Hampstead and the later part of New Earswick, as Stein freely acknowledged;[109] obscured by the rich New Jersey summer vegetation, they look almost as if they grow out of the ground. The central open space, with its serpentine pedestrian and bicycle paths diving under rusticated overbridges, has an informal naturalness. It looks and feels right.

The feeling was bought at a cost. Though a Radburn Association controlled and managed the space, the houses were sold, and – despite the hopes of social mix – by 1934 three in five family heads were at least middle executives; there were no blue-collar workers at all. Even worse, the realtors kept out Jews and blacks.[110] From the start, the site was too small to allow for a proper green belt. The Depression stopped further development, keeping the population pegged at 1500: far too low to support the elaborate range of community programmes and services originally envisaged. Even to maintain the communal part of the development, the Association depended on CHC and Carnegie grants. It proved difficult to attract industry; so, to keep up cash flow, the CHC was forced to abandon all hope of creating a true garden city, advertising it as a pure commuter suburb. Many owners were forced to sell; finally the CHC too, overwhelmed by land-carrying costs, went down in a sea of acrimony and legal actions.[111] Finally, Stein reflected more than twenty years after, the Radburn experience showed that a private corporation had at best a gambler's chance to build a new community.[112]

There were, nonetheless, two other Radburns, on both of which Stein served as consultant; Chatham Village (1932) in Pittsburgh, a pioneer venture in low-rent housing only 2 miles from the Golden Triangle; and

---

[107] cit. Schaffer, 1982, 156.   [108] Stein, 1958, 48.   [109] Ibid. 44.
[110] Schaffer, 1982, 173–4, 177.
[111] Stein, 1958, 39, 41, 68–9; Schaffer, 1982, 149–50, 160, 186–7.
[112] Stein, 1958, 69.

FIGURE 4.19 *Radburn.*

Baldwin Hills Village (1941) in Los Angeles. Both were financial successes. At Baldwin Hills, the planners significantly modified the layout, substituting collective vehicle courts for the culs-de-sac, and throwing some of the three linked central open spaces – vast enough, to be sure – into private enclosed space, thus saving maintenance costs.[113] But the shopping centre and three child-care centres disappeared in budget cuts, and a second phase was never started; worst irony of all, though the project was at first racially integrated, after a decade many white families left complaining of problem families; in the 1970s a rescue group converted the development from rental housing to condominiums, banned children under eighteen, and – final ignominy – renamed it the Village Green.[114] Today, though Baldwin Hills still has an extraordinary physical quality, its nearness to a low-income public-housing project gives unease to its predominantly older residents; after nightfall motor-bike patrols guard the estate, making mockery of the very qualities it was designed to protect.

The Stein–Wright Radburn cities are unquestionably the most important American contributions to the garden-city tradition. True, on strict criteria,

[113] Ibid. 189–90, 193, 198.
[114] Hayden, 1984, 10–11; Moore, Becker and Campbell, 1984, 282.

FIGURE 4.20   *Greenbelt.*
The first Radburn layouts applied to entire neighbourhoods; in Greenbelt, as earlier
in Weimar Germany, functional architecture is successfully married to the garden
city-garden suburb tradition.

like their European counterparts they fail to quality; all three are now long
since submerged in the general sprawl of suburbia, and to seek them out
on the ground demands a good map and some degree of determination.
But as garden suburbs, they mark perhaps the most significant advance in
design beyond the standards set by Unwin and Parker. They are not,
however, the only examples of new towns in America. Most of the others
are one-off examples associated with particular initiatives, like the new
town of Norris in Tennessee, developed as part of the TVA exercise in
regional development, which will be briefly discussed in the appropriate
place (chapter 5). But the greenbelt cities, developed by Rexford Guy
Tugwell's Resettlement Administration in the early years of Franklin Delano
Roosevelt's New Deal (1935–8), deserve separate and special attention.

There are curious historical parallels between their origin, and that of
Howard's idea: both were conceived in the depths of a major depression;
in both, destitute ex-farm workers were crowded in poverty-stricken cities,
which could offer them no work. By 1933, there was an embarrassing
shanty-town of the unemployed right in the heart of Washington. FDR's
original notion was a back-to-the-land movement; Tugwell (1891–1979),

a Columbia University economist who had become one of the most innovative members of his brains trust, persuaded him that this path led nowhere. His idea was 'to go just outside centers of population, pick up cheap land, build a whole community, and entice people into them. Then go back into the cities and tear down whole slums and make parks of them.'[115] He used a threat of resignation to force Roosevelt, in April 1935, to create the Resettlement Administration, which neatly bracketed the land and the poverty problem; under the Emergency Relief Appropriation Acts of 1934, this was given the power of eminent domain (compulsory purchase of land).[116]

'Just outside the cities' was the critical phrase: intended essentially to be self-contained, the greenbelt cities would also have to offer the possibility of commuting to the city, so a suburban fringe location was essential; this also represented the existing trend of population.[117] Tugwell hoped for 3,000 of them; but of the first list of twenty-five, the programme was allocated funds only to start eight; Congress whittled this to five, of which two (in New Jersey, and outside St Louis) were blocked by legal action. So the eventual programme consisted of just three towns: Greenbelt, Maryland, outside Washington; Greenhills, Ohio, outside Cincinnati; and Greendale, Wisconsin, outside Milwaukee.[118] Persuaded out of a prejudice against architects, Tugwell – working at speed against a deadline – hired separate teams for each town: so Greenbelt and Greendale have Radburn-style superblocks, Greendale has conventional streets and traditional architecture. But all have very low densities of between 4 and 8 units per acre.[119] And the largest of the three – Greenbelt, designed with advice from Stein and from fellow-RPAA architect Tracy Augur – is a classic adaptation of the Radburn layout: the houses, built in five superblocks forming a huge horseshoe around a central open space, all have direct pedestrian access to parks, shops and community facilities.[120] The architecture is more uncompromisingly modern-movement than at Radburn, and the overall effect is curiously reminiscent of the best German schemes of the 1920s: an exclave of Frankfurt, or Berlin, in the middle of the Maryland countryside.

All too soon, the programme was at an end. As a leading New Deal planner, Tugwell was an obvious target for conservative Congressmen, the media, the building and real-estate industries and the banks, to whom he 'Tugwelltowns' represented the start of a socialist takeover; they complained about 'shifting people around from where they are to where Dr Tugwell thinks they ought to be.'[121] The United States Court of Appeals, in May

---

[115] Myhra, 1974, 178–81; 1983, 231; Jackson, 1985, 195.
[116] MacFarland, 1966, 221; Arnold, 1971, 24–6; Myhra, 1974, 181; Weaver, 1984, 228. [117] Conkin, 1959, 307; Arnold, 1971, 26, 201.
[118] Conkin, 1959, 308; Glaab and Brown, 1976, 277.
[119] Myhra, 1974, 183–5; 1983, 241. [120] Arnold, 1983, 199. [121] Arnold, 1971, 31, 197, 209.

FIGURE 4.21 *Rexford Guy Tugwell.*
Creator of the experimental greenbelt communities of the mid-1930s: bitterly attacked in Congress as socialistic, and indeed a model for Britain's postwar government-funded new towns.

1936, held that the provisions of the 1934 Emergency Relief Appropriation Acts were invalid; and, though the ruling applied only to the proposed town at Greenbrook, New Jersey, few doubted that this was the end of the road.[122] Construction was virtually complete by mid-1938, when the three towns were transferred to the Federal Republic Housing Agency; in the 1950s, they were sold off.[123] At Greenbelt, by far the largest of the three, the original core of the development went to a cooperative housing association which has managed to maintain it intact; extensively (and expensively) rehabilitated with Federal loan money between 1979 and 1983, it is now on the National Register of Historic Places. But the rest of the huge site has been cut through by major highways and developed piecemeal by different developers, with no continuity of style at all.[124]

In purely quantitative terms, therefore, the greenbelt towns were almost a non-event: 'providing an attractive environment for only 2267 families

[122] Myhra, 1974, 185.   [123] Conkin, 1959, 322–5.   [124] Arnold, 1983, 201–2, 204.

can hardly be called that significant.'[125] And, as experiments in planning, they were – like so much that FDR did – curiously circumspect: blacks were excluded; the rents, though moderate, excluded the poorest; unit costs were high; local jobs were lacking, public transportation links with the parent cities were often poor; the houses and parking areas and shops are now all too small-scale to meet the needs of affluent Americans.[126]

They are less important in fact for what they did, than for what they symbolized: complete federal control over development, bypassing local government altogether; thus complete discretion to Tugwell in choice of sites; compulsory purchase of the land; control over construction by the same agency; even, because the land was federal, no right to local authorities to levy property taxes. Doing what successive interwar British governments never dared do, they in fact provided a model for the postwar new towns.[127] No wonder that almost everyone was against them.

They provide, therefore, something of an exception in the first forty years of the garden-city movement. Though private initiative built two true garden cities (Letchworth, Welwyn), and though sometimes municipalities built satellite towns (Wythenshawe, Römerstadt), nowhere else did government move in to produce the real thing. There is a slight irony in that it all happened in the United States, which is almost the last country anyone would expect it to happen. And there, it is hardly surprising that it failed.

New Towns for Britain: The State Takes Over

It is hardly surprising either that after World War Two Europe again seized the lead; or that, this time around, the state took control. But even then, it was touch and go. In Britain, Lewis Silkin, the incoming Labour Minister, conscious of possible reluctance among colleagues to launch such a programme, appointed a committee in October 1945 to tell him how they should be built. At its head he put John Reith, the ex-Director-General of the BBC: an intense, driven man who had managed to offend almost everyone in British public life and who had, in consequence, become virtually unemployable. Osborn was a member; the others were L. J. Cadbury of Birmingham and Monica Felton of the LCC, both known new-town advocates.

Unsurprisingly, given this composition, within a mere three months the committee emerged with interim recommendations: new towns should be in the size range 20,000–60,000, just as the Town and Country Planning

---

[125] Glaab and Brown, 1976, 278.
[126] Stein, 1958, 130; Arnold, 1971, 143–4, 153; Wilson, 1974, 159–60; Arnold, 1983, 202.
[127] MacFarland, 1966, 219–23.

Association (which had now dropped garden cities from their name) had always said; they should generally be built by public corporations, one for each town, financed directly by the Exchequer. In certain cases, one or more local authorities might do the job; and, though housing associations probably lacked both legal authority and competence, specially constituted 'authorised associations', promoted for this specific purpose, would be appropriate. So the committee paid its lip service to Ebenezer Howard; but the public corporation was 'our primary choice of agency'.[128] Thus, ironically, at one stroke they resolved the perennial problem of how to fund the new towns, but also destroyed the essence of Howard's plan, which was to fund the creation of self-governing local welfare states. Top-down planning triumphed over bottom-up; Britain would have the shell of Howard's garden-city vision without the substance.

At any rate, Osborn was not to be as old as Methuselah before the government started on new towns; he was sixty-one when, on 1 August 1946 (even before the Reith Committee's final report was out), the New Towns Act received the royal assent; on 11 November the first, Stevenage, was already designated.[129] Between then and 1950, the Labour Government designated thirteen new towns in Britain: eight for the London area, two for Scotland, two in north-east England, one in Wales and one in the English midlands. That emphasis, again, underlines that in the 1940s as in the 1890s the core of the British urban problem was still seen to lie in London; though new towns were actively considered for Manchester, Liverpool and a number of other cities, and though sites for Manchester at Mobberley and Congleton in Cheshire were seriously considered, both ran into objections.[130]

Four of the eight London new towns were in one county, Hertfordshire; and three of them form a group, running along the Great North Road and the parallel main railway line north of London. Stevenage, the first to be designated, was soon joined by Welwyn Garden City, which was given the dignity of a development corporation shared with next-door Hatfield, where there was an urgent need to tidy up some messy development around a big aircraft factory. And, though Letchworth remained fiercely independent, it forms effectively part of the group; so that here, uniquely, the student can see Howard's vision of the Social City on the ground. Each garden city is surrounded by its own green belt, so that each appears as a separate urban community against a background of agricultural land. But all four are tied together by the modern equivalent of Howard's inter-municipal railway: the electrified commuter line that also joins them to central

---

[128] G.B. Ministry of Town and Country Planning, 1946, 11.   [129] Cullingworth, 1979, 29–30.
[130] Cullingworth, 1979, 95–101, 112.

London, and the motorway completed in the mid-1980s. Passing from one to another in a few minutes, you go from the roar of the motorway into a serene, green world; none of the new towns is any longer new, and the vegetation long ago lushly enveloped them, softening some of the over-simple lines of the budget-conscious housing. There are detailed quibbles in plenty, to be sure; but it looks and feels very much like that final chapter of *To-Morrow*.

It had, however, come about by a route of which Howard would probably have disapproved. In the land of its birth, the garden city was now nationalized and bureaucratized, as the coal-mines and the railways were shortly to be. That is unsurprising, in a way; the Attlee Government was committed to that particular variety of Socialism; Reith, who was convinced that his BBC was God's own design for broadcasting, could be relied on to repeat a similar prescription for new towns or indeed any other new institution. And there was wisdom in it too: if London's persistent housing problem was as bad after half-a-century as Abercrombie's Greater London Plan was just then saying, and if the evident mistakes of the interwar years were not to be repeated, then some very tough and resilient machinery must be provided, capable of rolling roughshod over local special interests if needs be. Almost immediately, the unholy row that broke out over the Stevenage designation was to underline the point. The angry residents renamed their railway station Silkingrad, deflated the Minister's tyres when he came to plead his case, and fought him up to the High Court. Later, after 1951, when the incoming Conservative Government resisted further designations, the resulting strains and stresses caused them within a decade to reverse that decision.[131]

The Marxist commentators can of course again have their field day: once again, the capitalist state was managing the system to make it acceptable; new towns had become an essential part of that welfare-state management, designed to guarantee the reproduction of the skilled labour force for the high-technology industries that so enthusiastically moved there. Yet as usual, all this misses the rich complexity of the decision process. There was a new, fresh, radical Labour Government, swept into power not by the machinations of the capitalist machine, but by the votes of the armed forces. It was determined to make a fresh start. New towns were an important part of its ideology; Attlee himself had written in favour of the national planning of towns and countryside.[132] The garden-city propaganda machine had swung into action, led by Osborn; and Osborn, unlike his erstwhile mentor, had campaigned for a quarter-century in favour of state new towns. Of course, they might all be mere puppets, agents of the system; but difficult, for anyone who knew him, thus to view Osborn.

---

[131] Ibid. 27–31, 127, 165; Collings, 1987, 14–19.   [132] Wilde, 1937, 24.

What is certain is that in the process, a great deal was gained and something got lost. The new towns got built, and in the imperfect world of politics that was something of a miracle: eight of them around London, almost as Abercrombie had prescribed, and roughly according to a timetable laid down. True, they were criticized at first, often by people who had no sympathy from the start: their architecture was boring; they had no urban feel; the people moving into them, deprived of the crowds of London and often suffering from belated building of shops and other services, suffered from 'new town blues'. (This last was a distinct sociological curiosity; the phenomenon was discovered not in a new town at all, but in one of the LCC's inadequately planned and hastily built satellite estates,[133] yet the media either did not know or did not want to know the difference.) True, too, the new towns absorbed a mere 400,000, a mere fraction of the population growth in the belt around London in the 1950s and 1960s; Abercrombie's sums had failed to allow for the baby boom. All that said, the new towns were built as planned, according to the latter-day Reithian version of the Howard gospel; and, so far as anyone can judge, they did what their supporters always expected of them. They are still rather good places to work and to live, and the best thing that can be said about them is that in the 1980s, forty years after they were started, they are almost non-newsworthy: the media notice them only on the rare occasions when (like the *Guardian* in August 1986) they want to write about a place without problems.

---

[133] Jefferys, 1965, 207–55.

The City
in the Region

Thus they went along towards the Gate, now you must note that the City stood upon a mighty hill, but the Pilgrims went up that hill with ease, because they had these two men to lead them up by the arms; also they had left their *Mortal* Garments behind them in the River; for though they went in with them, they came out without them. They therefore went up here with much agility and speed though the foundation upon which the City was framed was higher than the Clouds. They therefore went up through the Regions of the Air, sweetly talking as they went, being comforted, because they had safely got over the River, and had such glorious Companions, to attend them.

John Bunyan
The Pilgrim's Progress (1678)

And as the moon rose higher the inessential houses began to melt away until gradually I became aware of the old island here that flowered once for Dutch sailors' eyes – a fresh, green breast of the new world. Its vanished trees, the trees that made way for Gatsby's house, had once pandered in whispers to the last and greatest of all human dreams; for a transitory enchanted moment man must have held his breath in the presence of this continent, compelled into the aesthetic contemplation he neither understood nor desired, face to face for the last time in human history with something commensurate to his capacity for wonder.

And as I sat there brooding on the old, unknown world, I thought of Gatsby's wonder when he first picked out the green light at the end of Daisy's dock. He had come a long way to this blue lawn, and his dream must have seemed so close that he could hardly fail to grasp it. He did not know that it was already behind him, somewhere back in that vast obscurity beyond the city, where the dark fields of the republic rolled on under the night.

F. Scott Fitzgerald
The Great Gatsby (1926)

5
The City
in the Region

The Birth of Regional Planning:
Edinburgh, New York, London,
1900–1940

If the garden city was English out of America, then the regional city was undoubtedly American out of France via Scotland. Regional planning began with Patrick Geddes (1854–1932), an unclassifiable polymath who officially taught biology (more probably, anything but biology) at the University of Dundee, gave India's rulers idiosyncratic advice on how to run their cities and tried to encapsulate the meaning of life on folded scraps of paper. From his contracts with French geographers at the turn of the century, Geddes had absorbed their creed of anarchistic communism based on free confederations of autonomous regions. Through his meeting in the 1920s with Lewis Mumford (1895–), a sociologist-journalist who could make his thoughts coherent in a way he never could, this philosophy passed to a small, but brilliant and dedicated, group of planners in New York City, whence – through Mumford's immensely powerful writings – it fused with Howard's closely related ideas, and spread out across America and the world; exercising enormous influence, in particular, on Franklin Delano Roosevelt's New Deal, in the 1930s, and on the planning of the capitals of Europe, in the 1940s and 1950s. But, ironically, in this process – just as with Howard – the truly radical quality of the message got muffled and more than half lost; nowhere on the ground today do we see the true and remarkable vision of the Regional Planning Association of America, distilled via Geddes from Proudhon, Bakunin, Reclus and Kropotkin.

Geddes and the Anarchist Tradition

The tale must start with Geddes: a hard thing to do, since he always went round in increasing circles. A secretary, who (like all secretaries) was in the best position to judge, once said: 'Geddes must be accepted . . . as a

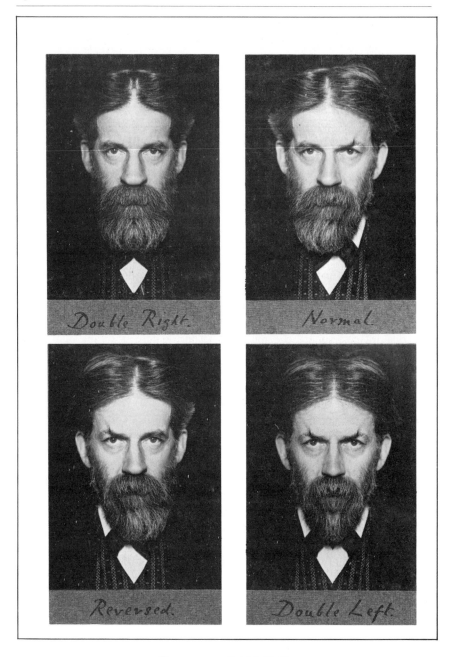

FIGURE 5.1 *Patrick Geddes.*
The indefatigable folder of paper and drawer of diagrams here conducts an incomprehensible experiment on himself.

FIGURE 5.2 *Lewis Mumford.*
His only meeting with Geddes was a disaster, but at last the professor had found
his scribe; the Regional Planning Association of America would bring the master's
message to the world.

good Catholic accepts grief, with an open heart and no reserves, *if* he is
to benefit those whom his presence scourges.'[1] He was the archetypal comic
professor: 'he had never mastered the art of making himself audible, either
on the platform or in closer quarters'; he was 'always forgetting engagements,
or making two or three for the same time'; his were 'the unformed theses,
the unwritten books, mostly remained unformed and unwritten';[2] he was,
Abercrombie related, 'a most unsettling person, talking, talking, talking . . .
about anything and everything.'[3] His fateful meeting with Mumford, in
New York in 1923, was a disaster: he wanted to turn the twenty-eight-
year-old rising star into an assistant; when he demurred, they seldom even
corresponded again.[4] But Geddes, without knowing it, had found the author
for his gospel.

Geddes in turn had borrowed his key ideas from France: 'the central

[1] Mumford, 1982, 319.   [2] Ibid. 321, 326, 331.
[3] Defries, 1927, 323.   [4] Mumford, 1982, 322.

and vital tradition of Scottish culture', he argued, 'has always been wedded with that of France.'[5] He took his central concepts from the founding fathers of French geography, Élisée Reclus (1830–1905) and Paul Vidal de la Blache (1845–1918), and from the early French sociologist Frederic Le Play (1806–82), whose new academic disciplines acquired respectability in France some years before they did in Britain or the United States.[6] From them he got his idea of the natural region, as exemplified by his famous valley section. And it is significant that like them, he preferred to study the region in its purest form, far from the shadow of the giant metropolis:

> Coming to concrete Civic Survey, where shall we begin? . . . London may naturally claim pre-eminence. Yet even at best, does not this vastest of world cities present a less or more foggy labyrinth, from which surrounding regions with their smaller cities can be but dimly described. . . . For our more general and comparative survey, then, simpler beginnings are preferable . . . the clear outlook, the more panoramic view of a definite geographic region such, for instance, as lies beneath us upon a mountain holiday. . . . Such a river system is, as one geographer has pointed out, the essential unit for the student of cities and civilisations. Hence this simple geographical method must be pled [sic] for as fundamental to any really orderly and comparative treatment of our subject.[7]

Planning must start, for Geddes, with a survey of the resources of such a natural region, of the human responses to it, and of the resulting complexities of the cultural landscape: in all his teaching, his most persistent emphasis was on the survey method.[8] This also he derived from Vidal and his followers, whose 'regional monographs' were attempts to do just that.[9] In the famous Outlook Tower, that craggy monument that still stands at the end of the Royal Mile in Edinburgh, he created a model for what he wanted to see everywhere: a local survey centre, in which people of all kinds could come to understand the relationship of Le Play's trilogy of Place–Work–Folk.[10] The student of cities, he asserted, must go first to the study of such natural regions: 'Such a survey of a series of our own river basins . . . will be found the soundest of introductions to the study of cities . . . it is useful for the student constantly to recover the elemental and naturalist-like point of view even in the greatest cities.'[11]

It sounds deceptively simple; but, as the great British planner Patrick Abercrombie once said, civic survey in actuality 'is a sinister and complicated business', the more so since it must widen to embrace the region and finally the world. Yet Abercrombie, who if anyone should have known, believed

---

[5] Defries, 1927, 251.   [6] Weaver, 1984a, 42, 47–8; Andrews, 1986, 179.
[7] Geddes, 1905, 105.   [8] Mairet, 1957, 216.   [9] Weaver, 1984a, 47.
[10] Mairet, 1957, 216.   [11] Geddes, 1905, 106.

FIGURE 5.3 *The Outlook Tower.*
From its castellated top, complete with camera obscura, Geddes ranged the rooftops
of Edinburgh and taught the lesson of Survey before Plan.

that in Britain in the early 1920s 'the errors of our national reconstruction can be attributed to the neglect of this teaching of Geddes.'[12]

For this great work, Geddes constantly argued, the planner's ordinary maps were useless: you must ideally start with the great globe which Reclus

[12] Defries, 1927, 323–4.

proposed, but which never got built; failing that, you must draw cross-sections 'of that general slope from mountains to sea which we find everywhere in the world [which] we can readily adapt to any scale, and to any proportions, of our particular and characteristic range, of hills and slopes and plain.' Only such a 'Valley Section, as we commonly call it, makes vivid to us the range of climate, with its corresponding vegetation and animal life . . . the essential sectional outline of a geographer's "region", ready to be studied.' Examined closely, it 'finds place for all the nature-occupations'. 'Hunter and shepherd, poor peasant and rich; these are our most familiar occupational types, and manifestly successive as we descend in altitude, and also come down the course of social history.'[13] In turn,

> These variously occupied folk each come to develop their own little hamlet or village, with its characteristic type of family, and folk-ways, even institutions; not simply of home-building, though each with its germ of appropriate architectural style. In this way their villages are ranged, from fishing port to forest and mountain pass, from gardens and fields below to mine and quarry usually above.[14]

And, at the centre of this region, lay the 'Valley in the Town', where 'we must excavate the layers of our city downwards, into its earliest past – the dim yet heroic cities over and upon which it has been built; and thence we must read them upwards, visualizing them as we go.'[15]

Much of that, in outline, has become familiar, even trite; every freshman planner knows that the aphorism, Survey before Plan, comes from Geddes. And it derives from a kind of traditional regional geography, which – vulgarized in a thousand staple school texts – has long since been derided and swept away. But that misses its truly radical point. For Vidal and his followers, as for Geddes, regional study gave understanding of an 'active, experienced environment' which 'was the motor force of human development; the almost sensual reciprocity between men and women and their surroundings was the seat of comprehensible liberty and the mainspring of cultural evolution', which were being attacked and eroded by the centralized nation-state and by large-scale machine industry.[16] So the deliberately archaic quality of the regional survey, the emphasis on traditional occupations and on historic links, was no mere quirk: like Geddes's attempts to recapture past civic life through masques and pageants,[17] it was a quite conscious celebration of what, for him, was the highest achievement of European culture.

But this, quasi-mystical though it might be, had a very radical purpose. For Geddes, as for Vidal, the region was more than an object of survey; it was to provide the basis for the total reconstruction of social and political life. Here, again, Geddes was indebted to geography and in particular to

---

[13] Geddes, 1925c, 289–90, 325.   [14] Geddes, 1925d, 415.   [15] Ibid. 396.
[16] Weaver, 1984a, 47.   [17] Boardman, 1978, 234–40.

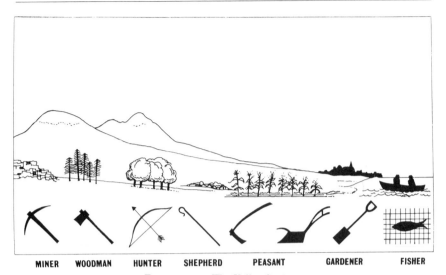

MINER   WOODMAN   HUNTER   SHEPHERD   PEASANT   GARDENER   FISHER

FIGURE 5.4   *The Valley Section.*
The essence of Geddes' regional scheme, from a paper of 1905: Folk-Work-Place
in perfect harmony, the city in the centre of things.

the French tradition. Elisée Reclus (1830–1905) and Peter Kropotkin
(1842–1921) were both geographers; but both were also anarchists.
Kropotkin, who was exiled from his native Russia, was expelled from both
France and Switzerland and lived for thirty years as a refugee in Brighton;[18]
Reclus had indeed been expelled from France for fighting on the Communard
side in 1871, and lived in exile.[19] Both based their ideas on Pierre-Joseph
Proudhon (1809–65), the French anarchist best known for his declaration
'Property is Theft.' Ironically, Proudhon's writings had been dedicated to
proving the exact opposite: his argument was that individual property
ownership was the essential guarantee of a free society, so long as no one
owned too much. Such a society, he believed, could alone provide the basis
for a decentralized, non-hierarchical system of federal government:[20] an
idea shared by the Russian anarchist Michael Bakunin (1814–76), whose
defeat and expulsion by Karl Marx in the First International Conference
at The Hague in 1872 was one of the decisive events in the history of
Socialism.[21]

   Reclus and Kropotkin were the inheritors of this tradition; and both met
Geddes more than once during the 1880s and 1890s. Reclus's most
important works, two huge multi-volume studies on the earth and its
peoples,[22] argued that the naturally collectivist small-scale societies of

---

[18] Woodcock, 1962, 181–96.   [19] Mairet, 1957, 89; Stoddart, 1986, 131–3.
[20] Edwards, 1969, 33, 107.   [21] Lehning, 1973, 71, 169, 236.
[22] Reclus, 1878–94; Reclus, 1905–8.

primitive peoples, living in harmony with their environments, had been destroyed or distorted by colonialism. But Kropotkin was even more significant; for he developed the anarchist philosophy and translated it into the conditions of the early twentieth century, and through him it had incalculable influence on both Howard and Geddes. His creed was 'Anarchist Communism, Communism without government – the Communism of the Free';[23] society must rebuild itself on the basis of co-operation among free individuals, such as can be found naturally even in animal societies; this, he thought, represented the logical tendency toward which human societies were moving.[24]

More than this, Kropotkin developed a remarkable historical thesis: that in the twelfth century, there had occurred a 'communalist' revolution in Europe, which had saved its culture from suppression by theocratic and despotic monarchies. This revolution expressed itself both in the local village community, and in thousands of urban fraternities and guilds. In the late-medieval city, each section or parish was the province of an individual self-governing guild; the city itself was the union of these districts, streets, parishes and guilds, and was itself a free state.[25] And, he argued,

> In those cities, under the shelter of their liberties acquired under the impulse of free agreement and free initiative, a whole new civilization grew up and attained such expansion, that the like has not been seen up till now. . . . Never, with the exception of that other glorious period of ancient Greece – free cities again – had society made such a stride forwards. Never in two or three centuries, had man undergone so profound a change nor so extended his power over the forces of nature.[26]

These achievements had been swept away by the centralized state in the sixteenth century, which represented the triumph of what Kropotkin called the Roman-imperial-authoritarian tradition. But now, he believed, this was in turn again challenged by its opposite, the popular-federalist-libertarian movement.

The reason, he thought, was the technological imperative: new sources of power, hydraulic and especially electric, meant that a big central unit of power was no longer needed; industries that depended chiefly on skilled labour had no economies of scale; observably, the newer industries tended to be small in scale. Thus, big industrial concentrations represented pure historical inertia:

> There is absolutely no reason why these and like anomalies should persist. The industries must be scattered all over the world; and the scattering of industries amidst the civilized nations will be necessarily followed by a further scattering of factories over the territories of each nation.[27]

---

[23] Kropotkin, 1906, 28.   [24] Ibid. 90; 1927, 96.
[25] Kropotkin, 1920, 14–17.   [26] Ibid. 18–19.   [27] Kropotkin, 1913, 357.

This scattering of industries over the country – so as to bring the factory amidst the fields, to make agriculture derive all those profits which it always finds in being combined with industry . . . and to produce a combination of industrial with agricultural work – is surely the next step. . . . This step is imposed by the very necessity of *producing for the producers themselves*; it is imposed by the necessity for each healthy man and woman to spend a part of their lives in manual work in the free air.[28]

This was one of the most crucial insights that Geddes borrowed from Kropotkin; already in 1899, presumably just after reading the first edition of *Fields, Factories and Workshops*, he had christened the new age of industrial decentralization the 'neotechnic' era;[29] the following year, in a display at the great Paris Exposition, he was using the terms palaeotechnic and neotechnic.[30] As he later wrote, 'we may distinguish the earlier and ruder elements of the Industrial Age as Palaeotechnic, the newer and still often incipient elements disengaging themselves from these as Neotechnic.'[31] Only in this new era – here he directly followed Kropotkin – would we 'apply our constructive skill, our vital energies, towards the public conservation instead of the private dissipation of resources, and towards the evolution instead of the destruction of the lives of others.'[32]

From Reclus and Kropotkin, and beyond them from Proudhon, Geddes also took his position that society had to be reconstructed not by sweeping governmental measures like the abolition of private property, but through the efforts of millions of individuals; the 'neotechnic order' meant 'the creation, city by city, region by region, of a Eutopia'. After World War One he believed that the League of Nations should be a league of cities – and not of the capitals, which were the centres of the war-machines, but of the great provincial cities which, regaining their former independence, would then voluntarily federate on a Swiss model.[33] This idea prompted a characteristic outpouring, which demands extended quotation – though, in Geddesian terms, it is a mere fragment:

The natural eugenic centre is in every home; its young go out to make new homes; these make the village, the town, the city small or great; so the would-be Eugenist has to work at all these towards their betterment. Federate homes into co-operative and helpful neighbourhoods. Unite these grouped homes into renewed and socialized quarters – parishes, as they should be – and in time you have a better nation, a better world. . . . Each region and city can learn to manage its own affairs – build its own houses, provide its own scientists artists and teachers. These developing regions are already in business together; can't they make friends and organize a federation as far as need be . . . May not this be the time prophesied by Isaiah? . . . 'When it shall come,

[28] Ibid. 361.   [29] Mairet, 1957, 94.   [30] Kitchen, 1975, 188–9.
[31] Geddes, 1912, 177.   [32] Ibid. 183.
[33] Defries, 1927, 268; Boardman, 1944, 382–3.

then I will gather all nations and all tongues and they shall come' and 'there
shall be a new heaven and a new earth . . . and the former shall not be
remembered . . . they shall build houses and inhabit them . . . and I will
direct their work in truth.'[34]

When his bemused questioner tried to get him to explain himself, he replied
that a flower expressed itself by flowering, not by being labelled.[35]

Indeed there was more to come; much more. There were the themes
first developed by Geddes's equally discursive collaborator, Victor Branford:
the role of the church and the university in practical relationship to the
civic community;[36] the union of eugenics and civics with town planning
and social welfare in a system of civic education[37]; 'the increase, within
the civic domain, of woman's influence and that of her friends and allies,
the artist, the poet and the educationalist', so to meet 'the need to provide
the women [sic] of the people with this cultural environment, necessary . . .
for her full dignity as a spiritual power.'[38] Repetitively, circuitously, too
often obscurely, the ideas pour out: the raw material for a score of still
unwritten dissertations. But there is one further concept, central to Geddes's
thesis of regional planning as part of social reconstruction.

In 1915 Geddes published his book *Cities in Evolution*. It is the most
coherent exposition of his views, save for the articles collected in the
American magazine *Survey* a decade later (which, based on his lectures in
1923, it took two years to render into sense).[39] In it, he drew attention to
the fact that the new neotechnic technologies – electric power, the internal
combustion engine – were already causing the great cities to disperse and
thus to conglomerate: 'Some name, then, for these city-regions, these town
aggregates, is wanted. Constellations we cannot call them; conglomerations
is, alas! nearer the mark, at present, but it may sound unappreciative;
what of 'conurbations'?[40]

In Britain he identified Clyde-Forth, Tyne-Wear-Tees, 'Lancaston', the
West Riding and 'South Riding', 'Midlandton', 'Waleston' and Greater
London; among the great European 'World-Cities', Paris, the French
Riviera, Berlin and the Ruhr; in the United States Pittsburgh, Chicago
and New York-Boston.[41] Presaging Gottmann's celebrated study of *Megalopolis* half a century later, he wrote: 'the expectation is not absurd that the
not so distant future will see practically one vast City-line along the Atlantic
Coast for five hundred miles; and stretching back at many points; with a
total of, it may well be well-nigh as many millions of people.'[42]

The problem was that these spreading cities were still the outcome of
the bad old palaeotechnic order, which he saw 'as dissipating resources

[34] Defries, 1927, 218–19, 230–1.   [35] Ibid. 231.   [36] Branford, 1914, 294–6, 323.
[37] Ibid. 283.   [38] Branford and Geddes, 1919, 250–1.   [39] Boardman, 1944, 412.
[40] Geddes, 1915, 34.   [41] Ibid. 41, 47, 48–9.   [42] Ibid.

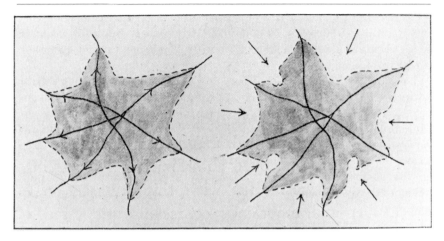

FIG. 20.—Town→Country : Country→Town.

FIGURE 5.5   *The Process of Conurbation, right and wrong.*
Diagram from Geddes' *Cities in Evolution* (1915) showing urban sprawl and its
remedy.

and energies, as depressing life, under the rule of machine and mammon,
and as working out accordingly its specific results, in unemployment and
misemployment, in disease and folly, in vice and apathy, in indolence and
crime'.[43] The first step, since 'the children, the women, the workers of the
town can come but rarely to the country', was that 'we must therefore
bring the country to them', 'make the field gain on the street, not merely
the street gain on the field';[44] 'towns must now cease to spread like
expanding ink-stains and grease-spots', but must grow botanically, 'with
green leaves set in alternation with its golden rays';[45] the people of the city
would thus grow up amidst the sights and smells of the country.

All this was no more than Howard had said, in one sense; but Geddes
was saying it at the level of the entire city region, and that constituted its
unique novelty.

> Regional Survey and their [*sic*] applications – Rural Development, Town
> Planning, City Design . . . are destined to become master-thoughts and
> practical ambitions for the opening generation, not less fully than have been
> Business, Politics, and War to the past, and to our passing one. . . . Already,
> for thinking geographers here and there, for artists and engineers, for town
> planners also, the neotechnic order is not only becoming conscious, but
> generalised, as comprehensively geotechnic; and its arts and sciences are
> coming to be valued less as intellectual pleasures, attainments, distinctions,
> and more in the measure in which they can be organised into the geographical
> service, the regional regeneration of Country and Town.[46]

[43] Ibid. 86.   [44] Ibid. 96.   [45] Ibid. 97.   [46] Ibid. 400.

To say that geography is an essential basis of planning did not sound very radical in the 1980s, or indeed for thirty years before that; but in 1915, when for most people town planning still equalled the City Beautiful, it was revolutionary.

The trouble was that, revolutionary as it was, it was also quintessentially incoherent; that quotation gives the all-too-characteristic flavour of the 402 pages, as of the many thousands of others that Geddes wrote. That is why Mumford, and his fellow-members of the Regional Planning Association of America, were such critically important torchbearers. 'Geddes', Mumford wrote, 'gave me the frame for my thinking: my task has been to put flesh on his abstract skeleton.'[47] In the preface of his greatest and most influential work, *The Culture of Cities* (1938), he was at pains to acknowledge that debt.

The Regional Planning Association of America

In his autobiography, Mumford recalls how the RPAA came into being. Already, in a very early paper of 1917, when he was only twenty-two, he had written a piece, 'Garden Civilizations in preparing for a new Epoch', apparently unpublished, on industrial decentralization and garden cities. In the autumn of 1922 he met Clarence Stein, an architect. The RPAA arose from a chance association of Mumford, Stein, Benton MacKaye (whose proposal for an Appalachian Trail Stein had published in the *Journal of the American Institute of Architects* in 1921) and Charles Harris Whitaker. Other founder members of the group, at its inception around March, 1923, included the economist Stuart Chase, the architects Frederick Lee Ackerman and Henry Wright, and the developer Alexander Bing; Catherine Bauer was appointed Executive Director and Research Assistant to Stein.[48] It was a small and diverse group, never exceeding twenty in number, mainly but not exclusively New York-based, with 'no prima donnas'; its core members seem to have been Mumford, Stein, Wright, Ackerman and MacKaye.[49] In June 1923, during Geddes's visit to New York, it adopted a fivefold programme which included the creation of garden cities within a regional plan; development of relationships with British planners, especially Geddes; development of regional projects and plans to further the Appalachian Trail; collaboration with the AIA's committee on Community Planning to propagate regionalism; and surveys of key areas, notably the Tennessee Valley basin.[50]

---

[47] Boardman, 1978, 345.
[48] Dal Co, 1979, 231; Mumford, 1982, 337-9; Goist, 1983, 260.
[49] Lubove, 1967, 17; Mumford, 1982, 339-40.   [50] Dal Co, 1979, 232.

FIGURE 5.6 *The RPAA Manifesto.*
Edited by Lewis Mumford, this collective issue was the definitive statement of the philosophy of the small New York group, which proved one of the most important documents of planning's history.

Two years later came the RPAA's first major opportunity: *Survey*, a magazine with an influential circulation among liberal intellectuals and a special link with the social work movement, invited it to produce a special number for the New York meeting of the International Town Planning and Garden Cities Association. Conceived by MacKaye, it was commissioned and edited by Mumford.[51] Out of print for half a century until reprinted by Carl Sussman in his book *Planning the Fourth Migration*, it remains – apart from *The Culture of Cities* – the group's definitive manifesto, and constitutes one of the most important documents of this history.

It opens as only Mumford could:

> This is the Regional Plan number of Survey Graphic. It owes its underlying idea to a long-bearded Scot whose curiosity would not let him rest until from his Outlook Tower in Edinburgh he had seen clear through the pother of civilization to the land which sustained it and, in spite of human fumbling, nurtured it.
>
> This number has been produced by a group of insurgents who, as architects and planners, builders and rebuilders, have tried to remold cities in conventional ways and, finding the task a labor of Sisyphus, have pinned their faith boldly to the new concept of the Region.[52]

He had his audience in his hand: Geddes's message would at last be understood. The opening article, 'The Fourth Migration', also came from Mumford. He wrote of two Americas: 'the America of the settlement', the coasts and the plains devloped by 1850, and

> the America of the migrations; the first migration that cleared the land west of the Alleghenies and opened the continent, the work of the land pioneer; the second migration, that worked over this fabric a new pattern of factories, railroads and dingy industrial towns, the bequest of the industrial pioneer; and finally ... the America of the third migration, the flow of men and materials into our financial centers, the cities where buildings and profits leap upwards in riotous pyramids.[53]

But now, 'we are again in another period of flow', a fourth migration, based on 'the technological revolution that has taken place during the last thirty years – a revolution that has made the existing layout of cities and the existing distribution of population out of square with our new opportunities.' The automobile and the trunk road had opened up markets and sources of supply. 'The tendency of the automobile ... is within limits to disperse population rather than to concentrate it; and any projects which may be put forward for concentrating people in Greater-City areas blindly run against the opportunities the automobile opens out'; the telephone, the radio and the parcel post had the same effect; so did electric power.[54] The

---

[51] Mumford, 1982, 344–5.   [52] Anon, 1925, 129.   [53] Mumford, 1925, 130.
[54] Mumford, 1925a, 130, 132–3.

difference, as against the first three migrations, was that this time we had the capacity to guide the movement. 'Fortunately for us, the fourth migration is only beginning: we may either permit it to crystallize in a formation quite as bad as that of our earlier migrations, or we may turn it to better account by leading it into new channels.'[55]

Clarence Stein, in the following article, takes up Mumford's theme: unknown to almost everyone living and working in them, the new technologies were making New York, Chicago, Philadelphia, Boston and the rest into 'Dinosaur Cities', which were breaking down under the weight of congestion, inefficiency and escalating social cost, and finally complete physical collapse. The result was that these cities were fast becoming the least logical places to locate industry. In a remarkable prophecy – this, remember, was 1925 – Stein wrote:

> When the local overhead cannot be shifted, and when smaller centers are, in spite of their poorer financial and business facilities, able to make their industrial advantages felt, the great city's industries will have to migrate or declare bankruptcy. We are still in the day of postponement; but the day of reckoning will come; and it behooves us to anticipate it.[56]

In turn the group's economist, Stuart Chase, developed the argument further: much of the American economy consisted in carrying 'coals to Newcastle', moving goods across the continent that had no need to be moved at all. He asks:

> Now what, specifically, is the matter? Where does the energy, particularly transport energy, go to waste, and how would planned communities reduce this waste so that the wayfaring man instead of falling behind, or making unheard-off efforts to keep where he is, can begin to make ground against the cost of living?[57]

This marks an important shift in the argument: it is necessary not merely to go with the flow of technological change, as Mumford and Stein had argued, but to intervene in order to correct the grosser inefficiencies of the system. A 'national plan' would involve 'regions delimited on the basis of natural geographic entities'; 'a maximum of foodstuffs, textiles and housing materials grown and manufactured in the home region'; 'a minimum of interregional exchanges based only on such products as the home region cannot economically produce'; plus regional power plants, short hauls by truck and 'a decentralized distribution of population':[58]

> The regional planning of communities would wipe out uneconomic national marketing, wipe out city congestion and terminal wastes, balance the power load, take the bulk of coal off the railroads, eliminate the duplication of milk and other deliveries, short circuit such uneconomic practices as hauling

[55] Ibid. 133.   [56] Stein, 1925, 138.   [57] Chase, 1925, 144.   [58] Ibid.

Pacific apples to New York customers by encouraging local orchards, develop local forest areas and check the haulage of western timber to eastern mills, locate cotton mills near cotton fields, shoe factories near hide producing areas, steel mills within striking distance of ore beds, food manufacturing plants in small giant power units, near farming belts. Gone the necessity for the skyscraper, the subway and the lonely country-side![59]

It was again prophetic: the argument for conservation, half a century before the Club of Rome. But it involved a plan, and a consequent interference with private business, that was frankly socialist; well did Chase say, a few years later, 'We were mildly socialist, though not at all communist; liberal but willing to abandon large areas of the free market in favor of a planned economy. So we were not doctrinaire socialists. We were open-minded; kind of Fabian Socialists.'[60]

That emerges clearly enough as the group moves into proposals. Mumford now returns specifically to that choice for the coming neotechnic era: society can have already overgrown cities getting bigger and bigger, 'in Professor Geddes's sardonic phrase, more and more of worse and worse'.[61] Or it can have regional planning.

Regional planning asks not how wide an area can be brought under the aegis of the metropolis, but how the population and civic facilities can be distributed so as to promote and stimulate a vivid, creative life throughout a whole region – a region being any geographic area that possesses a certain unity of climate, soil vegetation, industry and culture. The regionalist attempts to plan such an area so that all its sites and resources, from forest to city, from highland to water level, may be soundly developed, and so that the population will be distributed so as to utilize, rather than to nullify or destroy, its natural advantages. It sees people, industry and the land as a single unit. Instead of trying, by one desperate dodge or another, to make life a little more tolerable in the congested centers, it attempts to determine what sort of equipment will be needed in the new centers.[62]

Here it is, at last: what Geddes was struggling, through all those torrents of words, to say. But it is Geddesian, too, in its purpose: neotechnic technology can be the means not merely to greater mechanical efficiency, but also to

a fuller quality of life, at every point in the region. No form of industry and no type of city are tolerable that take the joy out of life. Communities in which courtship is furtive, in which babies are an unwelcome handicap, in which education, lacking the touch of nature and of real occupations, harden into a blank routine, in which people achieve adventure only on wheels and happiness only by having their minds 'taken off' their everyday lives –

[59] Ibid., 146.   [60] Sussman, 1976, 23.   [61] Mumford, 1925b, 151.   [62] Ibid.

communities like these do not sufficiently justify our modern advances in science and invention.[63]

This is where Howard comes in. For if regional planning provides the framework, the garden city provides the 'civic objective':[64] 'not as a temporary haven of refuge but as a permanent seat of life and culture, urban in its advantages, permanently rural in its situation'. But it meant 'a change in aim as well as a change of place':

> our garden cities represent fuller development of the more humane arts and sciences – biology and medicine and psychiatry and education and architecture . . . all that is good in our modern mechanical developments, but also all that was left out in this one-sided existence, all the things that fifth century Athens or thirteenth century Florence, for all their physical crudity, possessed.[65]

Kropotkin, again. But it is more than Kropotkin, more even than Geddes: there is another strain, which is specifically American.

> Regional planning is the New Conservation – the conservation of human values hand in hand with natural resources . . . Permanent agriculture instead of land-skinning, permanent forestry instead of timber mining, permanent human communities, dedicated to life, liberty and the pursuit of happiness, instead of camps and squatter-settlements, and to stable buildings, instead of the scantling and falsework of our 'go-ahead' communities – all this is embodied in regional planning.[66]

That American theme is taken up by Benton MacKaye in his article 'The New Exploration'. At one level it is pure Geddes: long transects through valley sections at different scales, from the Berkshires of upstate Massachusetts down to Boston and the ocean, down the little Somerset Valley along the Upper Deerfield river. And the plan for the Somerset Valley is intended to achieve just that ecological balance, that Vidal and his followers found in those long-settled regions of France. The difference is that it is planned: it is based on '*forest culture* against *forest mining*', for this alone 'will keep Somerset Valley in a truly settled state.'[67] America, this relatively new-settled land, must learn the same time scales, the same unconscious capacity for natural regeneration through good husbandry, that European peasants had passed on from generation to generation through centuries. This emphasis goes back to several different strands of nineteenth-century American thinking: to the concept of 'structure, process and stage' of the early Harvard physical geographers, Nathaniel S. Shaler and William M. Davis; to the views of an even earlier geographer, George Perkins Marsh, on ecology and resource planning; to David Thoreau's emphasis on the return to living amidst nature, and on natural balance.[68]

[63] Ibid. [64] Ibid. [65] Ibid. 152. [66] Ibid.
[67] MacKaye, 1925, 157. [68] Lubove, 1963, 91–6.

And in addition, there was a newer skein of intellectual movements in the universities of the depressed rural South. There were the conservative southern agrarians at Vanderbilt University in Nashville, Tennessee, with their rejection of northern industrialism and their model of the rural medieval or early New England economy.[69] And, in sharp ideological contrast, there were the southern regionalists around Howard Odum, with their emphasis on decentralization of wealth and power, and on balanced regeneration of the region's rich legacy of badly exploited natural resources, who were just then beginning to develop their thinking at the University of North Carolina, but whose major work would come in the 1930s.[70]

These developing – though sometimes inconsistent – strains come together in MacKaye's complete statement of his own brand of RPAA philosophy, *The New Exploration*.[71] Here, he developed the notion of two contrasting Americas: the indigenous, 'a compound of the primeval and the colonial', and the metropolitan, 'a compound of the urban and the world-wide industrial'. The job of the regional planner was painstakingly to reconstruct and conserve the environments of that older indigenous America, the primeval wilderness, the early village communities of New England, and 'the real city, the complement of the real village'.[72]

But this would be difficult:

> The contest in the country will be between Metropolitan America and Indigenous America. These now stand vis-à-vis, not only psychologically, but also physically and geographically. The metropolitan world ... is a mechanized molten framework of industry which flows ... mightiest in the valleys and weakest on the mountain ridges. The strategy of the indigenous world is just the other way. It is still mighty within the primeval environment, as along the ridgeways of the Appalachian barrier ... strong also in such regions as up country, where, although the farms and villages are depleted, the resources both physical and psychologic are still there, and are yet open to restoration and renewed development.[73]

The problem, then, 'concerns the remolding of the Metropolitan America in its contact with the Indigenous America.' For indigenous America was Mumford's America of the settlement; metropolitan America, his America of the migrations.[74] And Mumford's fourth migration was a 'backflow', 'a relocation of the populations and industries resulting from the second and third migrations', which had become a flood from a broken reservoir.[75] The question for regional planning then was 'What manner of embankments ... can we construct downstream to hold our deluge in check?'[76]

---

[69] Ciucci, 1979, 341–2.   [70] Odum, 1936; Odum and Moore, 1938; Kantor, 1973c, 284–5; Friedmann and Weaver, 1979, 35–40.
[71] MacKaye, 1928.   [72] Ibid. 64.   [73] Ibid. 73.   [74] Ibid. 75–6.
[75] Ibid. 170.   [76] Ibid. 178.

MacKaye's answer was a typical RPAA strategem: it was to harness the new technology, but thereby to control its impact on the natural environment. The metropolitan environment would be extended by 'motor ways'; between these, the hill areas would be kept as a primeval (or 'near-primeval) 'wilderness area', 'serving the double purpose of a public forest and a public playground', through which a system of open ways, 'equipped for actual use as a zone of primeval sojourn and outdoor living', would serve as 'a series of breaks in the metropolitan deluge; it would divide – or tend to divide – the flood waters of metropolitism into separate 'basins' and thereby seek to avert their complete and total confluence.'[77] Additionally, 'as an adjunct of the motor way system' would run an *intertown*: 'a series of open ways, or zones, straddling the motor road between successive towns and villages' and free of all inappropriate structures and land uses.[78] This was the very opposite of 'Roadtown', 'the embodiment of the metropolitan flood'.[79] It would not be bereft of buildings – 'Fear not, we have no notion of sounding a civic curfew' – but these buildings would not be 'chucked together', they would be 'assembled' through good planning.[80] And, developing the idea two years later, he came up with the notion of the Townless Highway: a limited access road around Boston, with service stations at intervals, but with no other access. No wonder that, nearly forty years after, Lewis Mumford credited MacKaye with the invention of the modern motorway; not quite true, as chapter 9 will show, but fair testimony to the remarkable prescience of the RPAA founders.[81]

How in practice this would look can be seen from the maps and charts prepared by Henry Wright for the New York State Commission of Housing and Regional Planning: Epoch I (1840–80), of 'State-Wide Activity and Intercourse' is followed by 'Epoch II' (1880–1920), in which population concentrates along mainline transportation. But in 'Epoch III' we see 'the possible state of the future in which each part serves its logical function in support of wholesome activity and good living.' A magnified close-up, 'an ideal section', proves to be Geddes's familiar diagram applied to the land fronting on to Lake Erie: forests and storage reservoirs in the highlands, dairy farms in the bordering upland, two parallel motorways flanking the highway and railroad on the fertile plain, cities and towns neatly disposed like beads on a string.[82]

Not much of this, in the America of the 1920s, was practical policy; even the constitutionality of zoning was in doubt until the historical Supreme Court decision of 1926.[83] True, as Governor of New York, Franklin D. Roosevelt bought at least Stuart Chase's prescription, for – by manipulating dairy-health regulations – he protected New York dairy

[77] Ibid. 179–80. [78] Ibid. 182. [79] Ibid. 186. [80] Ibid. 186–7.
[81] MacKaye, 1930; Mumford, 1964; Guttenberg, 1978.
[82] Smith, 1925, 159–60. [83] Fluck, 1986.

farmers against out-of-state competition.[84] And, through the agency of Alexander Bing, the RPAA did manage to float the two experimental communities at Sunnyside Gardens in New York City and at Radburn in New Jersey (chapter 4). But mostly, the RPAA was in the business of marketing long-term dreams.

The RPAA versus the Regional Plan of New York

In their one major clash over policy, they found an unlikely adversary. Thomas Adams (1871–1940) had been one of the founding fathers of British town planning: first general manager of Letchworth Garden City, first planning inspector, founder-member and first president of the Town Planning Institute.[85] And, arrived in North America, fully four years before foundation of the RPAA he had emphasized 'the importance of one of the most modern aspects of town planning, namely, the direction and control of the growth taking place within the rural and semi-rural districts where the new industries are being established', arguing that 'no city planning scheme can be satisfactory which is not prepared with due regard to the regional development surrounding the city.'[86] So when Charles Dyer Norton – former Chairman of the Commercial Club of Chicago and thus commissioner of the Burnham plan, now treasurer of the Russell Sage Foundation – approached him to direct an ambitious survey and plan for the whole New York region, it was a challenge he could hardly refuse. Confirmed after Norton's death by his successor Frederic Delano, he was appointed Director of Plans and Surveys in July 1923.[87]

There was however another respect in which he was the perfect candidate; for this was to be a businessmen's plan, the core movers of which were ex-Chicago business leaders, that would cost them a total of over $1 million over a decade,[88] and Adams, in his fifties, 'his philosophical mould long set', was a businessman's planner. He believed that the plan must represent the art of the possible: 'the Regional Plan was to be no revolutionary prescription' but a set of mild controls on market abuses to aid efficiency, plus some uncontroversial good things like new roads, parks and beaches.[89] This, needless to say, was a recipe for headlong conflict with the idealists of the infant RPAA.

It was not the geographical scope of the plan that was wrong. For Norton had called for a wide compass: 'From the City Hall a circle must be swung which will include the Atlantic Highlands and Princeton; the lovely Jersey

---

[84] Roosevelt, 1932, 484.   [85] Simpson, 1985, 191.   [86] Scott, 1969, 178–9.
[87] Hays, 1965, 7–11; Simpson, 1985, 136.
[88] Kantor, 1973, 36–7; Wilson, 1974, 136.   [89] Simpson, 1985, 135–6.

hills back of Morristown and Tuxedo; the incomparable Hudson so far as Newburg; the Westchester lakes and ridges, as far as Bridgeport and beyond, and all of Long Island.'[90] The resulting area – over 5,000 square miles, with nearly 9 million people – was a far bigger canvas than any plan before had covered.[91] Nor was it the survey methodology: Adams assembled an unrivalled team, whose detailed volumes constitute some of the uncontested classics of planning literature, with conclusions that echo those of Mumford, Chase and Stein. Here is Robert Murray Haig on the urban economy,[92] showing that many activities were already moving out because they had less need of a central location, and arguing for zoning controls to take account of negative externalities: 'Zoning finds its economic justification in that it is a useful device for ensuring an approximately just distribution of costs, of forcing each individual to bear his own expenses.'[93] Here is the volume on population and land values, arguing that the problem was the excessive concentration of transportation facilities which in turn encouraged excessive concentration of economic activities, hence further congestion, hence economic waste.[94] Here is the volume on zoning and land use, arguing that high land values in New York are the direct result of the permitted height and bulk.[95] And here is Perry's volume on neighbourhood units, with its recognition that the automobile was naturally creating the cellular city.[96]

It was none of this: it was the philosophy, which Adams shared with his committee. It was the belief that in practice, the form of the region was fixed and that only incremental, marginal change was possible. It expressed itself in a hundred ways: in the acceptance of the existing highway plan, with merely 'by-passes or belt lines . . . to permit free circulation between the major subdivisions of the Region'; in the costly investment in yet more radial commuter rail links into Manhattan;[97] in the advocacy – though his name was nowhere mentioned – of the Corbusian principle of widely spaced skyscrapers in a park;[98] above all, in the suggestion that 'what is needed in connection with the problems of concentrated industrial and business growth in a region is not decentralization but a reorientation of centralization on the basis of making all its centers and sub-centers healthy, efficient and free from congestion',[99] and the resulting suggestion that 'recentralization'

[90] Scott, 1969, 177.
[91] Regional Plan of New York, I, 1927, xii; Kantor, 1973a, 39.
[92] Regional Plan of New York, I, 1927, 23–8.
[93] Ibid. 44.
[94] Regional Plan of New York, II, 1929, 25–6.
[95] Regional Plan of New York, VI, 1931, 102–3.
[96] Regional Plan of New York, VII, 1931, 30.
[97] Regional Plan of New York, III, 1927, 126–32.
[98] Regional Plan of New York, VI, 1931, 103–5.
[99] Regional Plan of New York, II, 1929, 31.

of business and industry into sub-centres within the region could relieve
congestion;[100] in the associated rejection of the garden city as a general
solution, 'except for the very small part of industry and population that
could be made to move to new centers';[101] in the rejection of any wider
unit of government to plan for the entire region.[102] Above all, it was in
the passive assumption that the region would continue to grow, from
14.5 million people to perhaps 21 million by 1965, coupled with the lack
of any firm proposals as to where the extra people were to go;[103] the basic
aim was 'to decentralize and decongest New York enough for it to continue
functioning in traditional ways.'[104]

Predictably, it provoked a bitter response. In a celebrated review,
Mumford condemned the plan in almost every last particular. Its spatial
frame, wide as it might seem, was too narrow; it accepted growth as
inevitable, ignoring the potential of planning to influence it; it failed to
consider alternatives; it continued to allow overbuilding of central areas;
it condemned the last remaining piece of open space near to Manhattan,
the Hackensack Meadows of New Jersey, to be built over; it dismissed
garden cities as utopian; it condoned the filling in of suburban areas;
through its rejection of the principle of public housing, it condemned the
poor to live in poor housing; it favoured yet more subsidy for the commuter
lines into Manhattan, thus helping create more of the very congestion it
condemned; its highway and rapid transit proposals were an alternative to
a community-building project, not a means toward it. Its central fault was
that it appeared to support everything: concentration and dispersal, planning
control versus speculation, subsidization versus the market. But, despite
appearances to the contrary, it really meant a drift to yet more
centralization.[105] Mumford concluded:

> In sum: the 'Plan for New York and its Environs' is a badly conceived
> pudding into which a great many ingredients, some sound, more dubious,
> have been poured and mixed: the cooks tried to satisfy every appetite and
> taste, and the guiding thought in selecting the pudding-dish was that it
> should 'sell' one pudding to the diners, specially to those who paid the cooks.
> The mixture as a whole is indigestible and tasteless: but here and there is a
> raisin or a large piece of citron that can be extracted and eaten with relish.
> In the long run, let us hope, this is how the pudding will be remembered.[106]

Adams, clearly irritated, decided to sting Mumford by calling Geddes in
aid:

[100] Ibid.; Hays, 1965, 20; Scott, 1969, 262.
[101] Regional Plan of New York, VI, 1931, 125.
[102] Regional Plan of New York, II, 1929, 197.   [103] Ibid. 35.
[104] Wilson, 1974, 137; cf. Simpson, 1981, 35.
[105] Sussman, 1976, 227–47.   [106] Ibid. 259.

This is the main point on which Mr Mumford and I, as well as Mr Mumford and Geddes, differ – that is whether we stand still and talk ideals or move forward and get as much realization of our ideals as possible in a necessarily imperfect society, capable only of imperfect solutions to its problems.[107]

The paradox was that Adams, too, continued to believe that New York was too big and that 'from an economic, and perhaps from a health standpoint we should get as many people and industries out of their central areas and into garden cities as is possible.'[108] But the very success of garden cities, he argued, was lessening the need for them as a solution: the solution 'is not to be found in an indiscriminate process of decentralization, but both in well-planned decentralization in Garden Cities and equally well-planned diffusion in urban regions.'[109]

There, they parted ways; Adams tried to set up a continuing dialogue, but Mumford – though remaining personally amiable – became ever more savage in his criticism.[110] The New York plan went ahead, through the medium of a Regional Plan Association under business elite leadership, and Planning Commissions for each area: it was particularly successful in its highway, bridge and tunnel proposals, mainly because that master-builder Robert Moses was in charge.[111] Meanwhile, Mumford's alternative prescription – state-aided new cities and the extensive rebuilding of blighted areas – remained on paper.[112]

New Deal Planning

This might seem a strange outcome; for in 1933 Franklin Delano Roosevelt was inaugurated as President and the New Deal began. And Roosevelt was heavily committed in principle to a programme along pure RPAA lines. In 1931, he had floated the idea of a mass return to the land, by providing a house and a few acres and money and tools; he was also borrowing RPAA ideas when he argued that electric power and the truck were aiding decentralization of industry to small communities and rural areas, while electricity, radio, cinema and parcel post were bringing an urban quality of life to the countryside; he specifically proposed a State Commission on Rural Homes, to establish a plan based on 'cooperative planning for the common good'.[113] A few months later, he had called for 'a definite plan by which industry itself will seek to move certain firms . . . out of the congested centers where unemployment is greatest into the smaller communities, closer to the primary food supply'.[114] And in 1932, just

[107] Ibid. 263.   [108] Adams, 1930, 142–3.   [109] Ibid. 146.   [110] Simpson, 1985, 155.
[111] Hays, 1965, 25–31, 36–40; Sawers, 1984, 234.   [112] Sussman, 1976, 250.
[113] Roosevelt, 1938, 505, 508–9, 510–11, 514.   [114] Ibid. 518.

before election, he asked 'if out of this regional planning we are not going to be in a position to take the bull by the horns in the immediate future and adopt some kind of experimental work based on a distribution of population.'[115] His uncle Frederic Delano had guided the New York Regional Plan, and had given him, he said in 1931, an abiding interest in the question; the day might not be far distant, he said, when planning would become part of the national policy of the country.[116]

He was a good as his word: following Rexford Tugwell, who in turn was advised by Stuart Chase, he pushed a Public Works Bill through Congress in June 1933, providing $25 million to resettle people on the land, thus giving people the chance 'to secure through the good earth the permanent jobs they have lost in the overcrowded, industrial cities and towns';[117] but the people would not go.[118] The response was the greenbelt-towns programme of the Resettlement Administration, in 1935, already described in chapter 4: a glorious failure, with hardly anything to show on the ground.

Beyond that, New Deal policy on regional planning mainly meant a prodigious multiplication of paper. The National Resources Planning Board and its variously named predecessor organizations, which survived exactly a decade (1933–43), have been described as 'the most nearly comprehensive national planning organization this country has ever known';[119] when first created in 1933 as the National Planning Board, they numbered three of the most distinguished names on the roll of American planning, Frederic Delano, Charles E. Merriam and Wesley C. Mitchell; in all they produced some 370 printed and major mimeographed reports, totalling 43,000 pages.[120] Yet for all that, it is hard work to find anything out there on the ground. The 1935 report of the National Resources Committee (as it was then known), *Regional Factors in National Planning*, recommended regrouping the field districts of the various Federal agencies in a limited number – say ten or twelve – major regional centres; the resulting regional planning commissions would have no regional executive, so that they would require 'a conduit running to an established executive', a National Planning Agency.[121] But there is no record of the outcome. And their 1937 report, *Our Cities: Their Role in the National Economy*, though it drew attention to the problems of blight, speculation, social disruption, crime and urban public finance that were even then wracking American cities, failed in its recommendations to take explicit note of the regional dimensions; on the critical question of centralization versus decentralization it sat firmly on

[115] Roosevelt, 1932, 506.   [116] Lepawsky, 1976, 22.   [117] Gelfand, 1975, 25.
[118] Ibid. 25–6; Schaffer, 1982, 222.   [119] Clawson, 1981, xvi.
[120] Karl, 1963, 76; Clawson, 1981, 7.
[121] U.S. National Resources Committee, 1935, IX; Clawson, 1981, 168.

the fence, stating that 'the most effective environment for the urban dweller and for the effective use of human and material resources is more likely to be found between these two extremes'; the aim, it concluded vaguely enough, was 'to loosen up the central areas of congestion to create a more decentralized urban pattern', a statement to which both Adams and Mumford would doubtless have acceded.[122] Both FDR and Congress proved massively uninterested, and the report fell into a political limbo.[123]

The TVA

To the mountain of paper, of course, there was one shining counterweight on the ground: the Tennessee Valley Authority, undeniably the greatest achievement of New Deal planning, and – at least in legend – the realization of the most radical ideas of both the RPAA and the Southern regionalists. Addressing the last RPAA conference in 1932, Roosevelt described the TVA idea as an example of regional planning; but this, like so much of his language, was 'a phrase so loose and imprecise that it could fit almost any program, and yet so elusive that it involved few specific commitments.'[124] In fact, it brought together several strands: to improve navigation at Muscle Shoals in Alabama (a pet Corps of Engineers project since the previous century), to develop power there, to provide an armaments-production facility there and to control floods; Roosevelt's achievement was to pull all this together with notions of rural planning and regional development, and to drop arms production.[125] Yet all these concerns proved tangential in the actual negotiations that led to passage of the Act; and the directors in consequence had little notion of what the planning sections mandated or allowed.[126] FDR certainly did not offer them any guidance, perhaps because he did not know either.[127]

Geography ensured also that TVA was bound to make an odd example of regional river-basin planning. The river was 650 miles long, its basin the size of Britain, the region diverse in climate, resources, racial composition and cultural patterns.[128] What it had in common was poverty: the eastern Appalachian half was possibly the poorest part of the poorest region in the United States, with thousands of families subsisting on cash incomes of less than $100 a year.[129] They were to be lifted out of their condition by a set of multi-purpose dams – themselves a challenge to the conventional engineering wisdom – around which a series of programmes would develop

[122] U.S. National Resources Planning Board, 1937, VIII–XI, 84;
Clawson, 1981, 162–4.   [123] Gelfand, 1975, 97.
[124] Conkin, 1983, 26.   [125] Ibid. 20.   [126] Ibid. 26–7.   [127] Tugwell, 1950, 47.
[128] Lowitt, 1983, 35; Conkin, 1983, 26.   [129] Morgan, 1974, 157; Lowitt, 1983, 37.

the region's natural resources. At least, that was the theory implicit in the passage of the Act and in the early policy of the TVA Board.[130]

Soon, however, it blew apart. To the TVA board, Roosevelt appointed three members who would make a totally, explosively incompatible mixture. In the chairman's seat he put A. E. Morgan, President of Antioch College: a utopian, ascetic, almost mystical visionary, who – though neither a socialist nor a Christian – had much in common with the early utopian communitarians.[131] He saw the job as his life's opportunity to realize his personal vision of a new physical and cultural environment: a vision he believed FDR to share.[132] As second member, and as the expert on public power development, he put David Lilienthal: an immensely ambitious, driving young man with the reputation of stealing any show he joined.[133] And as third he chose Harcourt A. Morgan, no relation of the chairman: President of the University of Tennessee, representative of the conservative agrarian interests at Vanderbilt, obsessed with the idea of rural extension services and in particular with a scheme for a phosphate fertilizer programme, he readily made common cause with Lilienthal. Within five months they were condemning the 'variety' – later to become 'vagaries' – in the chairman's grand design.[134] Within two years, the chairman was openly criticizing his colleagues in the public prints: a major tactical error, as it proved.[135]

Soon, Lilienthal and Harcourt Morgan outvoted the chair and divided responsibilities: Lilienthal got power development, H. A. Morgan agricultural extension work. From now on, these were to be TVA's work: A. E. Morgan's vision of a regional planning authority – for many, the true TVA mission – simply got buried.[136] The agriculturalists were sworn enemies of the Land Planning Division, whom they pejoratively called 'the geographers'; they fought over powers to acquire public lands around reservoirs, which were progressively whittled down to the absolute minimum.[137] Their opponents described the agriculturalists as 'fanatical', identifying less with the Authority than with local interests.[138] Finally, after two years of agonizing indecision – during which both A. E. Morgan and Lilienthal suffered nervous breakdowns – in 1938 FDR dismissed A. E. Morgan for 'insubordination and contumacy'; he was later exonerated by a Congressional Committee.[139] Thus, despite Lilienthal's insistence in the much read popular official account that policies were based on 'principles of unity',[140] they had evidently long since ceased to be based on anything but violent dissension.

[130] Neuse, 1983, 491–3; Ruttan, 1983, 151.
[131] McCraw, 1970, 11; McCraw, 1971, 38–9.
[132] Morgan, 1974, 54–55, 155.   [133] Ibid. 22.   [134] Morgan, 1974, 55.
[135] McCraw, 1970, 95, 107.   [136] Selznick, 1949, 91–2, 149.
[137] Ibid. 152, 186–205.   [138] Ibid. 211–2.
[139] McCraw, 1970, 108; Lowitt, 1983, 45.   [140] Lilienthal, 1944, 51.

Yet to the outside world at the time, TVA was a triumphant example of 'grassroots democracy'. Lilienthal's argument was that it was 'a policy, fixed by law, that the federal regional agency work co-operatively with and through local and state agencies.'[141] The reality seems to have been that this was a 'protective ideology', allowing TVA to appear as the champion of local institutions and interests; in order to justify its autonomy, and head off possible opposition from powerful local groups and individuals, it delegated the agricultural programme to an organized constituency, the land-grant colleges, thus compromising much of its role as a conservation agency. (Selznick's study of TVA acidly commented that 'the way to get democratic administration is to begin by organizing a central government strong enough to eliminate those conditions which make much of our life grossly undemocratic.'[142]

In one way, however, TVA went against the ideology of the rural fundamentalists at Vanderbilt University. They, recall, had shared with RPAA the notion that movement from the land should be slowed and even reversed; and FDR had appeared to side with them. Yet in practice, under the Lilienthal–H. A. Morgan alliance, the TVA became more and more a power generating authority, devoted to creation of a big industrial–urban base: as Tugwell put it, 'from 1936 on the TVA should have been called the Tennessee Valley Power Production and Flood Control Corporation.'[143] By 1944, it was already the second-largest producer of power in the United States, generating half as much as the entire national production of 1941.[144] The reason was ironic: it was the huge increase in power demand arising from the establishment of the Atomic Energy Authority's plutonium production plant at Oak Ridge, as basis for production of the Atomic Bomb.[145] The one element that Roosevelt had removed from the TVA prescription, munitions production, was now driving the economic development of the Valley.

The dams and the reservoirs must have looked good to the pilgrim tourist, rather like all those dams on the Volga and the Dnieper, over which left-wing visitors enthused at the end of the 1930s. But of regional planning – especially that radical variant espoused by the RPAA – there was an imperceptible residue: community development, health and educational services got a minuscule sliver of the total budget;[146] the new town of Norris next to the great Tennessee dam, though planned by an RPAA member (Tracy Augur) and extolled by Benton MacKaye as a first step in regional community development, was most accurately described

[141] Ibid. 153.   [142] Tugwell, 1950, 54.
[143] Ibid. 50; Ruttan, 1983, 151–2.   [144] Lilienthal, 1944, 17.
[145] Hewlett and Anderson, 1962, 77, 105–8, 116–22, 130; Allardice and Trapnell, 1974, 15–17.   [146] Ruttan, 1983, 157–8.

FIGURE 5.7 *Norris, Tennessee.*
Tracy Augur's small gem for the Tennessee Valley Authority: one of the few manifestations of its original regional planning ideals which it so soon lost.

by TVA's Planning Director as a 'rural village'.[147] A. E. Morgan's idealistic hopes for Norris – a town where rich and poor would live together, and where the inhabitants would combine agriculture and craft industries – was never fulfilled. Built in a hurry, the tiny town – a mere 1,500 people – is almost buried in dense woods; so informal is its layout, that its origins might never be guesssed.[148] It is an interesting footnote to garden city history, but in terms of the RPAA's grand vision it represents a ridiculous mouse. The fact was that America – even New Deal America – was not politically ready for that vision.[149]

The Vision Realized: London

Thus, by one of the many ironies in this history, the real impact of Mumford, Stein, Chase, and MacKaye was not to be on their own unsympathetic country, but on Europe's capitals. And there London was to provide the exemplar. Throughout the 1920s and 1930s, British and American planners continued a vigorous two-way transatlantic traffic. Thomas Adams crossed the ocean almost every year, sometimes three or

[147] Johnson, 1984, 35.   [148] Schaffer, 1984, *passim.*
[149] Schaffer, 1982, 224–5, 230.

four times a year, between 1911 and 1938; Stein and Wright met Howard and Unwin in England in 1923; Geddes met the RPAA in 1923, Unwin and Howard in 1925.[150] So, throughout these doldrum years, a small group of planners was already applying American ideas in a variety of British contexts.

One of the most successful, ironically, was the RPAA's *bête noir*. During his years on the New York Regional Plan, Thomas Adams continued as a partner in the planning practice of Adams, Thompson and Fry, who between 1924 and 1932 produced eight out of twelve exercises in the emerging field of advisory regional plans for the area around London. To these plans Adams brought many American concepts: parkways in West Middlesex and the Mole Valley, green girdles and green wedges to limit urban sprawl.[151] But the philosophy, as in New York, was planning as the art of the possible: planning should remain an advisory function, it should not try to achieve more than marginal changes, and it must work within the limits of existing powers.

The remaining four plans carry an equally significant name: they come from the partnership of Davidge, Abercrombie and Archibald. Leslie Patrick Abercrombie (1879–1957), ninth child of a Manchester businessman, oddly owned his career to gutter journalism; starting his career as an architect, he converted to town planning through a research fellowship established at the University of Liverpool by the soap magnate William Hesketh Lever, founder of Port Sunlight, with the proceeds of a successful libel action against a newspaper. He proved so apt that in 1914, when the first Professor of Civic Design at Liverpool, Stanley Adshead, moved to a new chair in London, Abercrombie was his logical successor.[152] Through his editorship of the *Town Planning Review*, he early acquired unrivalled knowledge of what was happening in the world of planning. Even before World War One he won a prize for a town plan for Dublin, which, setting the city in its regional context, demonstrated his debt to Geddes.[153] After it, his growing reputation led him to a pioneer exercise in regional planning for the Doncaster area, in 1920–2, and thus in 1925 to a plan for east Kent: a new coalfield, set in the garden of England, in which Abercrombie boldly set out to demonstrate a Geddesian thesis that in the neotechnic age, even palaeotechnic industry could be absorbed into the landscape. He proposed eight small new towns, each in a fold in the rolling chalk landscape, set within a continuous green belt:[154] a prophetic echo, down to the precise number, of his strategy eighteen years later for Greater London. That report, widely reviewed though in practical terms a failure,

[150] Simpson, 1985, 193; Dal Co, 1979, 233.
[151] Simpson, 1985, 174–5, 181, 193.   [152] Dix, 1978, 329–30.
[153] Ibid. 332.   [154] Ibid. 337; Dix, 1981, 106–9.

set him on a career in regional planning that would lead him on to the heights of the Greater London Plan.

The failure in implementation, though, was indicative: here as elsewhere, regional plans were advisory; they depended on co-operation among many different small district planning authorities, often not forthcoming. Particularly this applied to limiting suburban sprawl, which just then (chapter 3) was becoming a very vexed question in southern England. Abercrombie in east Kent thought that even with existing powers, local authorities could buy up the land to build new towns; the North Middlesex Joint Committee also advocated satellite towns.[155] But nothing got done in either place. Otherwise, both Adams's and Abercrombie's plans sought to achieve control by rural – that is, very-low-density – zoning; on the efficacy of that, opinions differed. Even so, according to one calculation the twelve plans together set aside enough land to house 16 million people at the then prevailing densities.[156]

The fact was that these plans, impressive as they might look on paper, were little more than ameliorative exercises. Indeed, they were probably less effective than Adams's New York plan for the simple reason that in England, organized business had less clout. The more radical concept of regional planning, represented by the RPAA, could come only if by legislation the British government gave comprehensive powers to plan a whole region, including the ability to stop urban sprawl; and of this, as seen in chapter 3, there was no trace down to 1939. This is well illustrated by the sad story of Raymond Unwin's Committee.

In 1927 Neville Chamberlain used his position as Minister of Health to give a boost to regional planning by the creation of a Greater London Regional Planning Committee, covering some 1,800 square miles within a 25-mile radius of central London, and with forty-five members from local authorities; Raymond Unwin was made technical adviser. Its interim report of 1929 proposed a complete reversal of the then planning system: instead of planning authorities trying to reserve pieces of land for open space, they should allocate certain areas for building, on the assumption that all the remainder be left open: towns against a background of open space. This would require an overall Joint Regional Planning authority with executive powers over larger regional matters, including reservations for building. Local authorities, it thought, should be able to deny development without compensation, but with payment from a pool of values among landowners – a proposal, originating from Unwin, that the then Minister found impracticable.[157]

[155] Abercrombie, 1926, 39–40; Cherry, 1974, 91.
[156] Beaufoy, 1933, 201, 204, 212; Simpson, 1985, 176, 180–1.
[157] Greater London Regional Plan Committee, 1929, 4–7; Jackson, F., 1985, 147.

Meanwhile, in a major address in 1930 Unwin had spelt out his concept of regional planning:

> Regional Planning schemes should be made effective . . . without depriving the local authorities within the region of their freedom to make Town Planning Schemes for their areas. . . . The main purpose of the plan is to secure the best distribution of the dwellings, the work and the play places of the people. The method shall be to lay out this distribution in a convenient pattern on a protected background of open land.'[158]

> If development were guided into reasonably self-contained nuclei, forming attractive urban groups of different sizes, spaced out on an adequate background of open land, there would be ample space in the Region for any increase in population which may reasonably be expected, still leaving the greater part of the area as open land.[159]

But at present, 'all land is potentially building land'; anybody could build anywhere, so that sporadic building and ribbon development would continue.[160]

So nothing happened; and by 1933, when the committee's final report emerged, it had effectively been put into cold storage by government spending cuts.[161] The report came back to the same theme: there should be a narrow green girdle around the existing built-up area of Greater London, to provide space for playing fields and open spaces; through this could run an orbital parkway; outside that, 'every effort should be made by full powers in the Town and Country Planning Act to define the areas . . . which may be allowed to building development, and thus secure the background of open lands from which public open spaces may be obtained as and when needed.'[162] New industrial areas should be planned in self-contained satellites within 12 miles of central London, and in Garden Cities between 12 and 25 miles distant. And both industrialists and developers, the report argued, could benefit from such a clear plan; the problem, again, was to compensate those whose land would not be developed, and this would require legislation.[163]

It did not happen. The Town and Country Planning Bill, before Parliament in 1931, fell victim to the election; it was revived and passed in 1932, but in a weakened form. Unwin, embittered, decided that the possibility of good legislation had been put back for years;[164] in a sense he was right, since it took until 1947 to get the powers his committee had thought vital. He went to America, preferring to spend his last years telling students at Columbia how to plan.

[158] Unwin, 1930, 186.   [159] Ibid. 189.   [160] Ibid. 186.
[161] G. B. R.C. Geographical Distribution, 1938, paras. 68–70.
[162] Greater London Regional Plan Committee, 1933, 83.
[163] Ibid. 95–9, 101–2.   [164] Jackson, F., 1985, 154.

One thing he had, however, achieved: there was at least a clear vision of a future planned region. Not all of it was new: as with Howard's ideas, curious students can find individual elements of the plan in George Pepler's 'green girdle' and associated parkway, of 1911, or Austin Crow's plan for ten 'cities of health' at a distance of 14 miles from London, the same year.[165] And, of course, Howard's diagram of Social City provides the theoretical basis for almost all subsequent schemes.[166] But it is more fully worked out than any of these; and the link between it and the 1944 Abercrombie plan is clear. Unwin had, in a sense, atoned for his great apostasy of 1918–19, when he had steered the course of English urban development away from garden cities and towards suburban satellites: a trend that, much later, even Osborn said he could probably have not avoided, given the state of opinion at that time.[167]

But in the eleven years since Unwin's final report and the Abercrombie plan, as seen in chapter 4, a lot of water had flowed under Thames bridges. Neville Chamberlain, on becoming Prime Minister, had almost as a first step created the Barlow Commission. Patrick Abercrombie, appointed to it, had been carefully steered by Frederic Osborn to his minority report and his dissentient memorandum with their demands for a national planning framework, for stringent general powers over industrial location, and for powers to make regional plans stick;[168] Reith had come and gone as first Minister of Planning. And Abercrombie had collaborated with Forshaw, the London County Council's Chief Architect, on the County of London Plan.

For purists like Mumford or Osborn, Abercrombie could never be forgiven for selling the pass, in the County Plan, on the vital question of density and decentralization:

> I was too confident about Abercrombie [Osborn wrote to Mumford]. I kick myself that I didn't sit on his doorstep at County Hall as I did on Barlow's doorstep during the sittings of the Commission. But I could not have believed that any planner could state in full detail the case for Decentralization, and then produce a Plan that doesn't do the main thing necessary – permit the majority of people to have decent family homes.

So London, 'led by middle-class Labour Councillors right out of touch with popular opinion but ... terrified of a drop in rateable value or of a loss of their slum electorate', would experience what Osborn called 'token' decentralization, or just over a million people.[169]

Osborn, of course, was less than fair; Abercrombie, working with LCC officials, must have been acutely sensible that here above all, planning was

---

[165] Pepler, 1911, 614–5; Crow, 1911, 411–12.   [166] Hall, 1973, II. 52–5.
[167] Hughes, 1971, 62.   [168] Ibid. 271–2; Dix, 1978, 345–6.
[169] Hughes, 1971, 40.

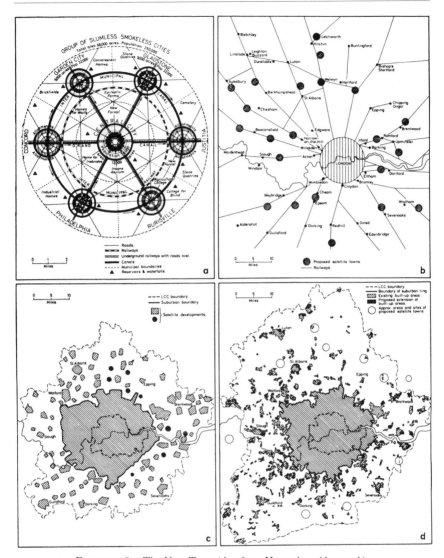

FIGURE 5.8   *The New Town idea from Howard to Abercrombie.*
The notion of a host of satellite cities around a metropolis, from Howard (1898),
through Purdom (1921) and Unwin (1929–33), to Abercrombie's definitive Greater
London Plan of 1944.

the art of the possible. And, viewed as half of the single regional plan
which the two volumes represent, the County Plan has striking qualities
that should have commended itself to the most pure-minded RPAA member.
There is, first, its insistence on Geddesian survey methods to tease out the

elusive community structure of London, that metropolis of villages. Then, there is its brilliant combination of Perry's neighbourhood unit principle with Stein and Wright's roads hierarchy – as interpreted by a Scotland Yard traffic policeman, Alker Tripp (1883–1954), in two influential books[170] – to create a new spatial order for London: in it, fast traffic highways not only solve the traffic congestion problem, but also give definition and shape to the reconstructed communities they separate, by flowing through green strips which additionally bring much-needed open space to London. Georgian and Victorian London's major problems – congestion, obsolescence, incoherence, lack of greenery – are tackled simultaneously, in a solution that imposes order on the world's least orderly great city; but in a way so natural that no one would notice.[171]

Specifically, the County Plan used the new road system to create a cellular London: the new order was to be implicitly organic.[172] Abercrombie's debt to Geddes is clear here, though there was also an important strain that came from Perry via Wesley Dougill, Abercrombie's inspired assistant and ex-Liverpool colleague, an enthusiastic advocate of the neighbourhood unit principle for London, who died as the plan was nearing completion.[173] The important point is that in going from the County Plan to the Greater London Plan, Abercrombie retains this same organic structure. There is first the basis in concentric rings, of decreasing intensity of population and activity: Inner (slightly larger than the County, with central London forming an innermost ring), Outer or suburban, Green Belt, Outer Country. Then, again, there is the way in which each of these is neatly defined by a ring road, part of the hierarchical system that produces the cells: the innermost A ring encloses the central area, the arterial B ring effectively defines the edge of inner London, the C ring runs through the suburbs and the arterial D ring encloses them, the parkway E ring is the central feature of the green belt and helps define the start of the outermost ring.[174]

And again, there is the use of open space as a structuring element. Here, Abercrombie pays his debts to Unwin:

> Sir Raymond Unwin first posed the alternative solutions to London's outward spread: either a continuous zone of free-entry for universal building at varying degrees of density (some of them, in high-class [sic] districts, quite low), its continuity broken at intervals by areas of green (as public open space) and, in practice, by patches of farmland left over from the builder's demand: or a continuous green background of open country in which are embedded at suitable places compact spots of red, representing building. We have

[170] Tripp, 1938, 1943.
[171] Forshaw and Abercrombie, 1943, 3–10; Hart, 1976, 54–87.
[172] Ibid. 58–9, 78–9.
[173] Forshaw and Abercrombie, 1943, v; Perry, 1939, 79–80.
[174] Abercrombie, 1945, 7–10.

unhesitatingly adopted the second alternative, which he advocated, for the two outer rings.[175]

There would be 'a gigantic Green Belt around built-up London', with special stress on outdoor recreation; but there should also be 'lesser girdles for the separate communities, old and new; this local girdle need not be wide, if beyond it is open agricultural country.' Finally, green wedges would run inward from the Green Belt into the heart of built-up London.[176]

Of the total of 1,033,000 people to find new homes as a result of reconstruction and redevelopment in inner London, all but 125,000 would move beyond the Green Belt: 644,000 would go to the Outer Country ring (383,000 to new towns, 261,000 to extensions of existing ones), nearly 164,000 just beyond this ring but within 50 miles of London, 100,000 farther still. There would be eight new towns, of maximum population 60,000 people, between roughly 20 and 35 miles from the centre of London.[177] The point was that out here, the organic structure would be retained; but it would now be turned inside out. Instead of highways and narrow park strips defining the communities, the basic element would now be the green background, against which the individual communities – each, like those in London, consisting of smaller cells or neighbourhoods – would appear as islands of urban development.

It was the vision of the RPAA, at last realized. Mumford himself, in a letter to Osborn, called it 'the best single document on planning, in every respect, that had come out since Howard's book itself; in fact it may almost be treated as the mature form of the organism whereof *Garden Cities of Tomorrow* was the embryo.'[178] 'The original job of making the ideal credible has been performed', he continued, 'and the main task now is to master the political methods that will most effectively translate it into a reality. We have not yet reached that stage here. . . . And I fear the results of our immaturity here once the post-war building boom . . . gets under way.'[179]

The 'political methods' were learned soon enough. The new Minister for Town Planning, Lewis Silkin, quickly told the planning authorities that the Abercrombie plan would serve as the interim development guide for the region.[180] Even before this, as told in chapter 4, he had accepted the principle of the new towns and had appointed John Reith to head a committee to tell him how to build them. With equal dispatch the committee gave him the answer: establish bureaucracies, in the form of development corporations, to bypass the complexities and foot-draggings and compromises of local democracy. In a strictly instrumental sense, it proved right: the New Towns Act received the Royal Assent in the summer of 1946, all the eight Abercrombie new towns were designated by 1949 (though not always

[175] Ibid. 11.   [176] Ibid.   [177] Ibid. 14.   [178] Hughes, 1971, 141.
[179] Ibid.   [180] Hart, 1976, 55.

in the places he proposed), and were well on the way to completion by the mid-1960s. The machinery for the other major element of the plan, the expansions of existing towns, took longer to establish and even longer to get into motion: the relevant Town Development Act was passed in 1952, the first notable results did not appear until the 1960s.

But they too finally appeared as major elements of the Abercrombie landscape. Even though during the 1950s and 1960s implementation almost became overwhelmed under unexpected population growth and continued industrial development in and around London – necessitating three further and much bigger new towns, started in the second half of the 1960s – an odd fact is that the basic Abercrombie principles proved remarkably resilient to stresses and strains. Odd, because as the American commentator Donald Foley noticed, the Abercrombie plan's most striking feature was its fixed, unitary quality, which 'stresses the primacy of striving toward a positively-stated future spatial form as a physical environmental goal product. The plan is characteristically presented for a hypothetical future point or period of time.'[181]

Yet, as Foley also noticed, it soon came to be absorbed into a political and economic process within central government that represented the very opposite: an adaptive approach, evolutionary rather than deterministic, that recognizes the importance of political and economic decisions in the planning process.[182] And, in this very different context, it worked: it proved capable of being bent without breaking. Details soon had to be changed: Abercrombie's new town at Ongar was dropped, while one in the Pitsea–Laindon area appeared; White Waltham, west of London, was abandoned and replaced by Bracknell near by;[183] later, after a change of government, the whole policy came in question, and was nearly truncated prematurely.[184] Somehow, it survived; and the London region is one of the few places in the world where it is possible to see the Howard–Geddes–Mumford vision of the world made actual.

But finally, doubts remain. One is that the policy did survive precisely because, in a complex and also conservative society, it served – imperfectly, to be sure – as a consensus among very different, indeed conflicting, political views. Liberal–socialist idealists could join forces with the conservative squirearchy to support a plan that simultaneously preserved the English countryside (and the traditional English rural way of life), and also provided model communities that would consciously seek to erode traditional English class barriers. This fragile alliance did survive, at least until the late 1970s when it fell victim to demographic and economic stagnation; but the result was far from the original vision of the founders,

[181] Foley, 1963, 56.   [182] Ibid. 173.
[183] Cullingworth, 1979, 53, 82–6, 89–93.   [184] Ibid. 147.

which in the process almost became obscured. The inhabitants of Stevenage and Bracknell are certainly part of the neotechnic economy, but they do not, as Kropotkin had supposed, spend part of their days in the fields.

Nor did the Abercrombie plan show any sign of challenging the autonomy of one of the most centralized and monolithic bureaucracies to be found in any western democracy: on the contrary, the processes of implementation actually strengthened it, and the quality of civilization in Basildon or Crawley does not yet recall the glories of fifth-century Athens or fifteenth-century Florence. Nor, though the planning system did preserve the countryside, did it produce anything like the integrated regional development of which Chase and MacKaye dreamed. The people of the Berkshire and Hertfordshire countryside eat vegetables flown in the holds of 747s from all over the world and brought to them via London wholesale markets, and the grubbed-up hedgerows and industrialized farm buildings bear witness to the fact that for the British farmer it is the account book that rules.

Of course, much does remain of the vision of the pioneers: the new towns are self-evidently good places to live and above all to grow up in; they do exist in harmony with their surrounding countryside and the sheer mindless ugliness of the worst of the old sprawl has been eliminated. But it is not quite as rich and worthy and high-minded as they hoped: a good life, but not a new civilization. Perhaps the place was wrong; the English, those archetypally cosy people of low expectations, were the last people to achieve it. Or, as with Gatsby's dream, it was already out there behind them, never to be realized.

The City of Monuments

Make no little plans. They have no magic to stir men's blood and probably themselves will not be realized. Make big plans; aim high in hope and work, remembering that a noble, logical diagram once recorded will never die, but long after we are gone will be a living thing, asserting itself with ever-growing insistency. Remember that our sons and grandsons are going to do things that would stagger us. Let your watchword be order and your beacon beauty.

Daniel Burnham
Unknown address of 1907, q. C. Moore, *Daniel H. Burnham: Architect,
Planner of Cities* (1921)

Why always the biggest? I do this to restore to each individual German his self-respect.

Adolf Hitler
Speech to Construction Workers (1939)

6

The City of Monuments

The City Beautiful Movement:
Chicago, New Delhi, Berlin, Moscow,
1900–1945

The City Beautiful movement had its nineteenth-century origins on the boulevards and promenades of the great European capitals: Haussmann's reconstruction of Paris under Napoleon III, and the contemporaneous construction of the Vienna Ringstrasse, were its classic models. Yet its twentieth-century manifestations came mainly in other places and cultures: in the great commercial cities of middle and western America, where civic leaders built to overcome collective inferiority complexes and boost business; and in the newly designated capitals of far-flung pieces of Empire, where British civil servants commissioned plans that would express imperial dominance and racial exclusiveness. Then, ironically, the city beautiful came back full circle to its geographical and spiritual point of origin: in Europe, culminating in the 1930s, totalitarian dictators sought to impose megalomaniac visions of glory on their capitals. Despite the superficially very different contexts, there are strange similarities in the outcomes, with implications that perhaps should be disquieting.

Burnham and the City Beautiful Movement in America

Each of the great planning movements in this account has its prophet, and this one is no exception. He was Daniel Hudson Burnham (1846–1912), partner in the architectural practice of Burnham and Root in Chicago, designer of several of the classic early skyscrapers in that city during the 1880s and 1890s, and chief of construction for the World's Columbian Exposition, one of the definitive World Fairs of all time, held there in 1893. The money that flowed from the lucrative architectural work, allowing him to take planning commissions at little or no fee, was one impulse that turned the young architect into the middle-aged city planner. The other

FIGURE 6.1   *Daniel Burnham.*
The maker of no small plans, in a suitably large and magisterial pose.

was the experience of designing the magical White City on the shores of Lake Michigan: if it proved thus possible to create an instant city of beauty, to last a mere summer long, it should surely be feasible to do the same thing for a real-life work-soiled American commercial city, to longer-lasting effect.

The notion struck a responsive chord; for, as seen in chapter 2, the 1890s were a period of intense introversion in urban America. For many among the civic-minded bourgeoisie, faced with increasing ethnic and cultural heterogeneity and escalating threat of disorder, the problem appeared to be the very preservation of the urban social fabric. Henry Morgenthau, banker and real-estate figure, put it plainly enough at a conference of 1909: the planner's first aim was to eliminate the breeding places of 'disease, moral depravity, discontent, and socialism'.[1] And

---

[1] cit. Boyer, 1978, 269.

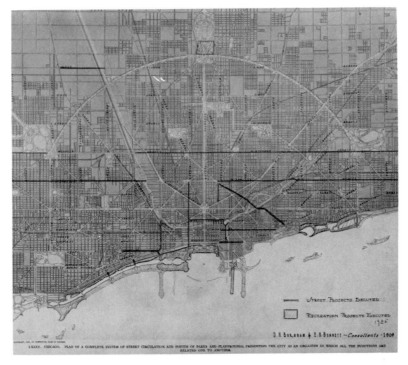

FIGURE 6.2   *The Chicago Plan of 1909.*
A compete scheme of classical civic order is laid down on the Illinois grid. And
amazingly, spurred by civic boosterism, by 1925 much of it is complete.

nowhere was this truer than of Chicago, the scene of ugly riots in the 1880s
that ended in the execution of the ringleaders in an atmosphere of near-
insurrectionary tension.

The Chicago Plan of 1909 was indeed Burnham's greatest achievement.
But he came back to his own city via some triumphs and some failures in
other places. The first, which was nearly all triumph, was the long-fought
battle for the reconstruction of The Mall in Washington, DC, which began
in 1901. In his plan of 1791 L'Enfant, following George Washington's
original ideas, had intended it as a great park, 400 feet broad and more
than a mile long, from the Capitol to the Potomac – then lapping as far
east as the front of the White House. But the plan was never completed;
the strip remained as common pasture ground, invaded by commercial
land uses; and in the 1870s, final indignity, a railroad was built across it.

For many, both in and out of Congress, the disfigured Mall came to stand as a symbol of all that was wrong with America's cities.[2]

In 1901, prompted by the architect Charles Moore, Senator James McMillan of Michigan, Chairman of the Committee on the District of Columbia, successfully proposed a resolution permitting it to study the park system, including appointment of experts. Soon after, Burnham became head of a three-man commission, the other members being Frederick Law Olmsted, Junior, and the New York architect Charles McKim; later a sculptor, Augustus St Gaudens, joined them. Burnham insisted that they all went to Europe to study the finest urban models, ignoring the obvious irony that many of these had been created by the very tyrannies against which Americans had revolted. Later, he insisted that the report contained enough purple passages for it to get plenty of notice from the press as well as from his architectural peers.[3]

The result was the original L'Enfant concept, writ large, with a Mall doubled to 800 feet in width, nearly doubled in length to take in the reclaimed floodplain of the Potomac, and intersected by two major cross-park strips. It got much praise but also, inevitably, some opposition, that for a time almost seemed to kill it. Eventually the whole scheme was completed, just as Burnham had intended it, with the dedication of the Lincoln Memorial in 1922.[4] It was an exercise in pure Beaux Arts design. Behind it, appalling slums continued to proliferate.[5]

But Washington, as everyone would insist, was special: a city apart from other American cities, in which the ceremonial and symbolic aspects must loom large. Burnham now moved on to bolder enterprises still: attempts to bring a missing civic order to the great industrial and port cities of the United States. He started in an unpropitious enough environment: Cleveland, the Ohio lake-front city, a place of rampant uncontrolled industrialism, racked by pollution, labour unrest and violence. Burnham was appointed head of a commission in 1902; it reported the next year. It predictably recommended a new civic centre in which half a dozen major civic buildings would be grouped in a set of linked public parks, alongside the lake-front and on a broad mall at right angles to it, which together would form an impressive open space in front of the city's relocated main railway station: a clear echo of the Washington plan, which had also included a resited Union Station. It demanded the clearance of over 100 acres of dense, miserable slums including the city's red-light district. The city leadership applauded the plan and set vigorously to work on it; only the station, which depended on agreement among competing railroads, failed to see the light of day. No one apparently gave any thought at all

[2] Hines, 1974, 140–1.   [3] Ibid. 150–1.
[4] Moore, 1921, *passim*; Hines, 1974, 140–55, 354–5; Gutheim, 1977, 133–4.
[5] Green, 1963, 132–46; Scully, 1969, 74–5, 140.

to the fate of the slum dwellers; the market, presumably, would take care of them.[6]

But Cleveland was essentially Washington by Lake Erie; ambitious as it was, it was still a pure city-centre plan. For San Francisco, in 1905, Burnham proposed something far grander. Here, a new civic centre complex – strategically located at the junction of Market Street, the city's main commercial street, and Van Ness Avenue – was to be the focus of a set of radiating boulevards, from which in turn subsidiary radials would take off at invervals; thus the city's regular grid would be brought into 'miraculous formal equilibrium' by another logic of angular abutments and natural irregularities used as sites for boulevards and formal buildings.[7] One of these would form a continuous park strip leading to the Golden Gate Park on the west side of the city. There would be a formal architectural treatment on the Twin Peaks which dominate the city's south-west side, with an Athenaeum and a monumental statue facing out over the Pacific Ocean.

Ironically, despite the extraordinary accident of the earthquake and fire, which uniquely gave the city a virtually clean slate on which to implement the plan, commercial pressures doomed it; only fragments, including the oddly dispiriting civic centre put in a different place than Burnham intended, form a partial memorial. Today, many San Franciscans are profoundly relieved that Burnham's grand boulevards and ronds-points have not drowned out the gridiron streets that climb up and down the hills, and the Victorian gingerbread houses that line them, which help give the city its unique charm.[8]

Chicago, then, is the definitive Burnham plan: the big one that amazingly, despite apparently insuperable odds, got for the most part carried out. Its basic concept was grand enough, even if singularly vague as to instrumentalities: it was 'to restore to the city a lost visual and aesthetic harmony, thereby creating the physical prerequisite for the emergence of a harmonious social order';[9] the chaotic city, that had arisen through too-rapid growth and too-rich mixture of nationalities, would be given order by cutting new thoroughfares, removing slums, and extending parks.[10] Its very confusion of social objectives and purely aesthetic means was, apparently, the quality that endeared it to the upper and middle classes who backed the Progressive Movement.[11]

Introducing the plan, Burnham was confident about the standard of comparison: it was the great European cities. 'The task which Haussmann accomplished for Paris corresponds with the work which must be done for

[6] Hines, 1974, 159–68.   [7] Manieri-Elia, 1979, 89.
[8] Hubbard and Hubbard, 1929, 264; Burnham, 1905, *passim*; Hines, 1974, 182–95.
[9] Boyer, 1978, 272.   [10] Ibid.   [11] Peterson, 1976, 429–30.

Chicago.'[12] But, since the backers were the businessmen first of the Commercial Club, then of the Merchants' Club, there was a gloss to the argument: Napoleon III's City Beautiful had proved a good investment.[13] 'The changes brought about by him made that city famous, and as a result most of the idle people of great means in the world habitually linger there, and I am told that the Parisians annually gain in profits from visitors more than the Emperor spent in making the changes.'[14] So too in Chicago:

> We have been running away to Cairo, Athens, The Riviera, Paris, and Vienna, because life at home is not as pleasant as in these fashionable centers. Thus a constant drain upon the resources of the town has been going on. No one has estimated the number of millions of money made in Chicago and expended elsewhere, but the sum must be a large one. What would be the effect upon our retail business at home if this money were circulated here? ... What would be the effect upon our prosperity if the town were so delightful that most of the men who grow independent financially in the Mississippi Valley, or west of it, were to come to Chicago to live? Should we not without delay do something competent to beautify and make our city attractive for ourselves, and especially for these desirable visitors?'[15]

He even went on to argue that Pericles' 'investment' in ancient Athens was still paying off in tourist revenue. Burnham, who certainly understood the Chicago ethos only too well, may have had tongue in cheek; he knew how to make a sales pitch when he had to. All this was by way of preliminary to the exposition of the actual plan, which had a huge price tag attached. The Lake Front was to be reclaimed and turned into a park, with a parkway running through it. One of the streets running at right angles from this park, Congress Street, was to become the principal axis of the new Chicago, with a park strip 300 feet wide. A mile inland, where this axis intersects Hubbard Street, two wide diagonal avenues would radiate from a huge domed civic centre: the focus of the whole plan, and ironically one of the few features that never got built. The banks of the Chicago river, which here run parallel to the lake between it and Hubbard, were to be straightened, reclaimed and lined with new streets and buildings. Large public buildings were to be placed at prominent positions in the park strip. There was to be 'a stately white Museum, resting on the Grand Terrace called the Lake Front, and dominating all the elements of it; the lawns, the fountains, the monuments, all of which should be placed so as to have some reference to that particular building. No structure in the world has ever had a nobler setting than this would be.'[16] There was to be a 7½-mile Shore drive, reached from the land by seven viaducts, and a lagoon 30,000 feet in length. In describing it, Burnham waxed lyrical:

---

[12] Burnham, 1909, 18.   [13] McCarthy, 1970, 229–31.   [14] Ibid. 102.
[15] Burnham, 1909, 102–3.   [16] Ibid. 105.

Both shores of the Lagoon should be ornamented with trees and shrubs adapted to our climate, and especially with those that blossom – the apple, the pear, the peach, the horse-chestnut, the wild-chestnut, the catalpa, the crab, the lilac, syringas, acacias, dogwood. The days of May and June should be a festival-time upon the water. In the spring and summer, and in the autumn, when floating upon the Lagoon, one should be conscious of the presence of flowers. On the banks should be sweet-briar, heliotrope, mignonette, and wild sweet grasses – the plants that fill the air with fragrance.[17]

And he concludes with his vision of the future Chicago:

Before us spreads a plantation of majestic trees, shadowing lawns and roadways, upon the margin of the Lake. In contrast with it, the shining Lagoon stretches away to the north. Behind this the soft banks of the shore, and trains glancing in and out through waving willows. Behind all, the wall of a stately terrace, covered with clinging vines and crowned with statues, and upholding quiet lawns, surrounding lovely homes.

The Lake has been singing to us many years, until we have become responsive. We see the broad water, ruffled by the gentle breeze; upon its breast the glint of oars, the gleam of rosy sails, the outlines of swift gliding launches. We see racing shells go by, urged onward by bronzed athletes. We hear the rippling of waves, commingled with youthful laughter, the music swelling over the Lagoon dies away under the low branches of the trees. A crescent moon swims in the western sky, shining faintly upon us in the deepening twilight.

We float by lawns, where villas, swan-like, rest upon their terraces, and where white balustrades and wood-nymphs are just visible in the gloaming. The evening comes, with myriad colored lights twinkling through air perfumed with water-lilies, and Nature enfolds us, like happy children.[18]

It is an extraordinary, poetic picture; one of the very few in the history of planning. And the haunting pastel washes by Jules Guerin, which show the great city from the air, with radiating boulevards marching away into the vast prairies of Illinois at last light, are like no other urban visions that have ever been: the muted flat colours, the luminosity of reflected light on wet pavements, these faintly recall Whistler, but Whistler never achieved such panoramic sweep.

It was also, of course, superb public relations. But, finally, for whom? Burnham's answer brings us brutally back to earth: 'Not for rich people solely or principally, for they can take care of themselves', but rather for the mass of the people; yet 'do not these latter depend upon the circulation among them of plenty of ready money, and can this be brought about without the presence of large numbers of well-to-do people?'[19] That is, with a vengeance, trickle-down urban development; implicit in it, never spelt

[17] Ibid. 109.   [18] Ibid. 110–11.   [19] Ibid. 111.

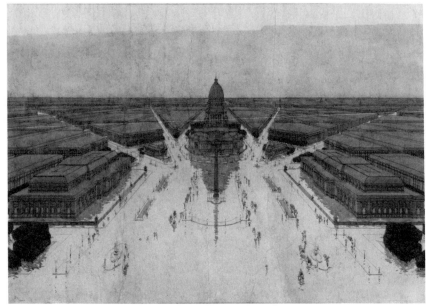

FIGURE 6.3   *Chicago Civic Center.*
Jules Guerin's haunting pastel vision of a magnificiently Haussmannized Chicago:
formal, symmetrically ordered, but devoid of broader social objective or content.
Ironically, this central element was the part that never got completed.

out, is a notion of an urban economy led by what Thorstein Veblen was
just then castigating as conspicuous consumption, on the part of a European-
style leisure class.

It is also too easy to deride this; and plenty of critics, from traditional
left-liberals to Marxists in need of an easy case study, have had a field
day. Already in 1922, when the plan was in course of implementation –
co-ordinated through an Executive Committee of the Plan Commission,
which was dominated by Commercial Club members, at a cost of over
$300 million[20] – Lewis Mumford was castigating the Burnham approach
as 'municipal cosmetic'; later he was to compare the results with planning
exercises of totalitarian regimes.[21] Everyone attacked it for ignoring housing,
schools, and sanitation. Burnham might have claimed in defence that he
did say at one point that Chicago might have to go the London route of
subsidized housing, but, to put it at its mildest, it was clearly not his
central concern.[22] Of the three objectives of planning that Abercrombie

[20] McCarthy, 1970, 248; Hines, 1974, 340.
[21] Lubove, 1962, 219; Boyer, 1978, 289.
[22] Hines, 1974, 333; Schlereth, 1983, 89.

was to lay down in his slim textbook of 1933,[23] beauty clearly stood supreme for Burnham, commercial convenience was significant, but health, in its widest sense, came almost nowhere.

More subtly, the plan – like those for San Francisco and Cleveland before it – could be called centrocentrist: it was based on a business core with no conscious provision for business expansion in the rest of the city.[24] As Mel Scott put it, 'the Chicago of the Burnham plan is a city of the past that America never knew', an aristocratic city for merchant princes.[25] In that respect, it was like many other urban development strategies to come. But even there, it contained a basic contradiction: as Herbert Croly pointed out at the time in the New York *Architectural Record*, posited as it was on formal qualities, it accorded ill with the realities of downtown real-estate development, which demanded overbuilding and congestion.[26]

That proved its downfall in its native land. At the First National Conference on City Planning and Congestion in 1909, some planners and their business supporters came to see that utopia would demand more than some were willing to pay. The City Beautiful rapidly gave way to the City Functional, to be achieved by zoning – a topic to which the Burnham Plan had devoted scant attention.[27]

Burnham died in 1912 at the height of his fame, which by then had spread far afield: Europe was returning his compliment. He had urged Chicagoans that 'as a people we must, if we can, do for ourselves what elsewhere has been done by a single ruler.'[28] But in Berlin, the Kaiser – so wrote the Berlin correspondent of the *Chicago Record-Herald* – had already appointed a commission to prepare a similar plan, only regretting that Berlin was too solidly built up and lacked Chicago's lake frontage.[29] The initiative seems to have died a death; but it was to be revived, with a vengeance, a quarter-century later.

The City Beautiful under the British Raj

But before the City Beautiful came back to its European homeland, it first spread out over the world. Its most spectacular manifestations, between 1910 and 1935, came in the last flowering of the British Raj. And this was no accident: seeking to establish what were often new and precarious holds on conquered territory, anxious therefore to build visible symbols of authority and domination, concerned also to house their servants in the style of life to which they were accustomed, the British India Office and

[23] Abercrombie, 1933, 104–9.   [24] Schlereth, 1983, 89.   [25] Scott, 1969, 108.
[26] Kantor, 1973b, 171.   [27] Walker, 1950, 273; Klein and Kantor, 1976, 430–1.
[28] Burnham, 1909, 111.   [29] Hines, 1974, 344.

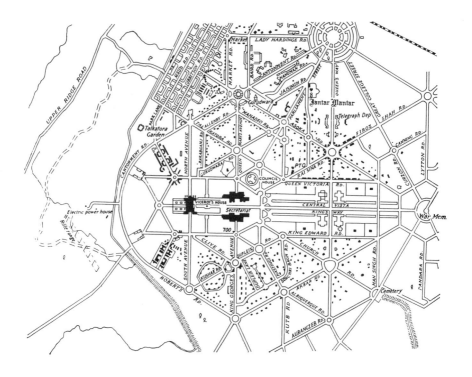

FIGURE 6.4 *New Delhi.*
The Lutyens-Baker plan: symbolic of the awesome power of the Raj, and completely
unrelated to the organic life of the indigenous city next door.

Colonial Office found themselves employing consultants to create instant
capital cities in far corners of the globe.

Many, constrained by an anxious Treasury in the Depression years, were
decidedly modest exercises; no pomp, straitened circumstance. But one,
appropriately, was not: it was the jewel in the crown. At his Coronation
Durbar in 1911, George V made the momentous announcement that the
capital of British India would be transferred from Calcutta to Delhi: a site
suitable for its central position, easy access and healthy climate, it also had
political significance as the historic capital, important symbolically in a
country already torn by Hindu–Muslim conflict. So the new capital would
be the concern of a great monumental exercise by a people lacking the
taste for monumentality: 'an Anglo-Indian Rome . . . one size larger than
life'.[30] Ironically, taking twenty years to finish, it was then to fill that role
for a mere sixteen years.

[30] Hussey, 1953, 237, 240.

FIGURE 6.5 *Planning New Delhi.*
Captain Stanley, Edwin Lutyens, Herbert Baker and an unidentified elephant wallah practice the Geddesian principle of Survey before Plan.

The architect-planners chosen for this historic mission were in many ways an odd pair. Herbert Baker (1862–1946) had early established a claim as the architect of imperialism, having progressed from the Pretoria railway station to the government buildings for the new Union of South Africa; his architectural ideas were 'nationalist and Imperialist, symbolic and ceremonial'.[31] The Indian Viceroy, Hardinge, wanted him for New Delhi but – after pressure from London – chose Edwin Lutyens (1869–1944), then best known as a country-house architect; Lutyens, realizing that he could not do all the work himself, then asked for Baker as collaborator.[32] At his first encounter with Lutyens, Baker appreciated the 'wilful masterfulness which early success had developed in him'.[33] But Baker relished the challenge, writing to Lutyens:

> It is really a great event in the history of the world and of architecture, – that rulers should have the strength and sense to do the right thing. It would only be possible now under a despotism – some day perhaps democracies will follow. . . . It must not be Indian, nor English, nor Roman, but it must be Imperial. In 2000 years there must be an Imperial Lutyens tradition in Indian architecture . . . Hurrah for despotism![34]

There was, however, a third senior partner in the design team: the Viceroy himself. The first question on which he proved decisive was that of a site. Delhi in 1911 consisted of two cities: the densely packed 'native city', where 233,000 people lived on just over $1\frac{1}{2}$ square miles, and the British 'civil lines' a safe sanitary distance away to the north-west; there was also a near-by military 'cantonment', vacant since 1861 but reserved for army use, the scene of the historic Durbar.[35] A powerful interest wanted the new capital here for reasons of tradition and sentiment.[36] But the Viceroy saw that it offered no room for the new 10-square-mile city and 15-square-mile cantonment, and took appropriately Viceregal action:

> I then mounted and asked Hailey . . . Commissioner of Delhi, to accompany me to choose a new site, and we galloped over the plain to a hill some distance away. From the top of the hill there was a magnificent view . . . I said at once to Hailey, 'This is the site for Government House', and he readily agreed.[37]

Splendid, but historically somewhat simplified. The architecture-planning committee in fact had recommended this site to the south of the Indian city, known as Raisina, in June 1912; Hardinge, who had originally favoured a site on top of the ridge to the west, dominating the city, seems

[31] Stamp, 1982, 34.
[32] Baker, 1944, 57–63; Irving, 1981, 278–9; Lutyens, 1982, 35.
[33] Baker, 1944, 64.   [34] Hussey, 1953, 247.   [35] King, 1976, 228–30.
[36] Baker, 1944, 65.   [37] Hardinge, 1948, 72.

to have given his agreement in November. Meanwhile Lutyens and Baker, who only received their formal appointments in January 1913, had taken the result for granted and had begun design work, taking the crucial decision to put the Viceroy's House and Secretariat Building at the same level on the flat hilltop; the Viceroy, at first evidently affronted by the disrespect to His Majesty, was persuaded.[38]

The critical decisions on the plan of the new city came very quickly in February–March 1913; the choice of the southern site was ratified on 7 March, the plan outlines were confirmed on 20 March. From the acropolis on the heights of Raisina, the main axis would run east to the ancient capital of Indrapat, symbolizing 'the keystone of the rule over the Empire of India', as the committee's report had it; two other major radials would also fan out from it, in classic City Beautiful fashion; a cross-radial, joining the new Anglican Cathedral on the south and the railway station on the north, would intersect them.[39] The resulting final plan reflects Lutyens's passion for formal geometry: the Secretariat and the War Memorial Arch both have seven radiating routes, the great railway station circle no less than ten; virtually all main roads make thirty or sixty-degree angles with the routes connecting these three foci, and all major buildings are at centers or angles or mid-sides of hexagons. As Baker came to realize years after, there are uncanny similarities with L'Enfant's plan for Washington.[40]

The buildings sometimes match up to the roads, more often not. The big ones are very grand indeed. In Lutyens's Viceregal House, the staff quarters for the top officials are virtually palaces in themselves; at the close of British rule, there were more than 2,000 servants in all.[41] Beside it is Baker's Secretariat building: nearly a quarter-mile long, designed to impress, 'a majestic stage set for the spectacle of the Indian Civil Service, the tiny corps who were governors over a quarter of the human race . . . known in common parlance as the "heaven-born".[42] Between them is a hump in the road that represented the parting of the ways between Baker and Lutyens, and in doing so shook the British Empire to its foundations.

Very early, as already seen, the two architects had agreed that the Viceregal House and Secretariat should share the same level. But for Lutyens, it was central and crucial to the whole plan that the main east–west radial should rise at a constant gradient to Raisina, so that the Viceroy's House should be continuously visible between the wings of the Secretariat. Nevertheless, in March 1913 – tired, ill (almost certainly with dysentery) and anxious to return to England – he signed a minute agreeing to a final gradient that would obscure the view. Baker thought he understood

[38] Baker, 1944, 65; Hussey, 1953, 261–2; Irving, 1981, 46, 51, 67–8.
[39] Irving, 1981, 67–8, 71, 73.   [40] Ibid. 79, 84.
[41] Ibid. 227.   [42] Ibid. 280.

the consequences; Lutyens ever after claimed that he was deluded by perspective drawings, exhibited at the Royal Academy in May 1914, which were drawn from an imaginary point 30 feet above the ground.[43] Discovering his error in 1916 when construction was well advanced, Lutyens pressed for a change; the committee refused him on the ground that it would cost £2,000. Lutyens, increasingly obsessed by the idea that he was victim of a trick, appealed to everyone: to the Viceroy, who was unsympathetic, then to King George V on no less than two occasions; one feels that he would have appealed to God (in Hindu, Muslim and Christian versions) if appropriate channels had been open. In vain, Baker wrote to ask why he wouldn't play cricket; Lutyens later said that he had met his Bakerloo.[44]

They were not the only problems. The Viceroy found Baker's plans 'admirable' and within the stated cost limits; not so Lutyens, whose plans, 'though beautiful, were made absolutely regardless of cost.'[45] The Public Works Department, furious at being displaced by outside architects, wanted an Indian style of architecture; Hardinge too, as he stressed in a letter to Lutyens just before his formal appointment, believed that for political reasons there must be a strong Indian motif. And Lutyens, though insisting on his formal classical plan, came round to their view.[46] But Lutyens was not an easy person: once, asked what he thought an asinine question by a Royal Commission, he allegedly answered 'The answer is in the plural and they bounce.' Later, Baker reflected that their natures were too different: Lutyens was the abstract geometrician, devoid of human concerns; Baker cared more for 'national and human sentiment'. 'What more might we have achieved with unity of counsel!', he bewailed.[47]

And, perhaps, with more money. Most of the huge axial boulevards contain no such seeds of controversy; they are lined with one-storey bungalows.[48] Within the hexagonal grids, houses were allocated according to a bewilderingly complicated formula of race, occupational rank and socio-economic status:

> From the Viceroy, via the Commander-in-Chief, Members of the Executive Council, senior gazetted officers, gazetted officers, down to superintendents, peons, sweepers and *dhobis*, a carefully stratified spatial order was integrated, both in terms of physical distance and spatial provision, to the social structure of the city.[49]

This feat, to conceive intellectually of an elaborate social structure and then to render it literally in concrete on the ground, was a triumph of highly abstract planning; it had nothing to do with the traditional structure

[43] Hussey, 1953, 286–7, 323; Lutyens, 1980, 126; Irving, 1981, 143–50.
[44] Hussey, 1953, 355–6, 363–6, 410–12.   [45] Hardinge, 1948, 96.
[46] Hussey, 1953, 260, 265, 268, 300; Lutyens, 1982, 37–8.
[47] Baker, 1944, 68–9.   [48] Ibid. 79.   [49] King, 1976, 246.

FIGURE 6.6   *New Delhi: Lutyens' 'Bakerloo'.*
Obscuring the view of the Secretariat and the Viceroy's palace, the kink in the
great processional way caused a fatal rift between Lutyens and Baker and nearly
shook the Empire.

of 'Civil Lines' in India, which had evolved in a very British fashion, that
is to say informally.[50]

And, as so often in post-colonial cities, it all goes on to this day:
architectural styles and housing standards are still colonial, the by-laws are
obsolete, the subsidy structure favours the upper-income groups, there are
almost unbelievable disparities between the standards of the rich and the
poor;[51] so pervasive are the ways of the past that, when Anthony King
visited the Connaught Circus shopping centre in 1970, the music shop was
still adorned with pictures of Harry Roy, Geraldo, Evelyn Laye and Albert
Sandler.[52] The ways of the Raj indeed die hard.

And not merely in India. In South and East Africa, where the British
came late and did not stay long, they produced a number of instant mini-
capitals: Salisbury (later Harare), Lusaka, Nairobi, Kampala. In all,
consultants produced plans based on the fiction that these cities were
completely white with, perhaps, a separate Indian bazaar area at a respectful
distance; Africans were either assumed not to exist, since they were officially
supposed to be farmers, or were herded into squatter reservations with the

[50] Ibid. 264.   [51] Bose, 1973, 184–5.   [52] King, 1976, 259.

aid of mass deportations and pass systems.[53] In Nairobi between 1932 and 1947, the city spent a total of £1,000–2,000 a year, between 1 and 2 per cent of revenue, for 20,000 Africans.[54]

The basis was hygienic: the government medical service, invariably of military origin, had a virtual stranglehold over the planning system. Since the British settlers fell like ninepins to tropical diseases, they' had to take themselves to the hills, segregate themselves as best they could, and live bungalow-style at exceedingly low densities, even when that meant – as it invariably did – high infrastructure costs and long journeys.[55] Typically, as in Nairobi, the Europeans would get the best – that is, the highest – areas, the Indians the next best, the Africans anything that was left.[56] Here, the Feetham Committee in 1927 recommended strict control over 'ingress of natives' to control 'idle, vicious, or criminal' elements.[57] A town plan was produced in 1926 by F. Walter Jameson (popularly known as Jacaranda Jim), of Kimberley, and Herbert Baker; another came from a further South African consultancy in 1948. Both, unsurprisingly, accepted and reinforced the existing racial divisions;[58] the latter observing that it must note the fact that the government had disowned segregation between whites and Asians, then commented that many people wanted it, and proceeded to take refuge in 'the principles of planning which take their measure on the human and technical needs', which presumably meant back-door segregation. The Africans were dismissed on the ground that though they were the most numerous they were also the most transitory; the plan did not even show African housing areas.[59]

In Lusaka, the official plan embodied the same division between the spacious European quarters and the primitive African areas, which mostly lacked the most elementary services.[60] It had come in 1931 from Professor Stanley Adshead, who had bluntly stated the view that 'it would be a mistake to treat the Africans as if they were Europeans ... it would be foolish to offer them those bodily comforts which they had never known and which generations and generations of habit have made necessary to the white man';[61] as in Kampala, the plan – despite emerging contrary evidence – took refuge in the myth that the African was migratory.[62] Within the European area, there were to be three classes of housing (though the Professor noted that it would be objectionable to call them that); even in official correspondence, the top class, next to the offices on top of the ridge, came to be known as Snob's Hill.[63] Over the next twenty years,

---

[53] Van Zwaneberg, 1975, 261, 267, 270–1.   [54] Ibid. 268.
[55] Southall, 1966, 486; King, 1976, 125; King, 1981b, 211–15.
[56] Hallinan and Morgan, 1967, 106.
[57] Hake, 1977, 44.   [58] Ibid. 56–7.   [59] Thornton White, 1948, 21 and maps.
[60] Davies, 1969, 10–12.   [61] Kay, 1967, 114.   [62] Collins, 1980, 232.   [63] Ibid. 119.

Adshead's already low densities were thinned out still further; his grandest concept – a 400-foot-wide Independence Avenue, along the ridge – became a relatively minor link between three far-flung garden suburbs.[64]

Common to all these plans was the land use and settlement structure. There would be a central government-office node and a near-by commercial-office area; the central shopping area would be adjacent to both. All these would be designed around a formal geometrical road layout, with broad avenues meeting at traffic circles. They would be surrounded by very low-density European residential areas, within which individual bungalow-style houses hid themselves in huge private grounds; a style known in Lusaka, and elsewhere, as 'garden city', which usage might make the recently dead Ebenezer Howard return to complain. The African compound, revealing title, was relatively very small and was clearly segregated on one side of the city, separated as far as possible from the European areas by a physical barrier such as a railway track. There might be an older shopping area in or near the African area, the assumption being that shopping too would be racially segregated. In general, the interesting basic assumption was that apart from a necessary quota of house servants, the Africans did not exist.

There were however key differences as against New Delhi, and they were not just a matter of money. The consultants' plans for the African capitals, though they imposed a degree of formal organization on the European centre and suburbs, never aimed at Lutyens's geometrical complexities. Nor, though the Government house was always given a prominent and dignified position, was there anything like the elaboration of the great structures of Raisina; there were, presumably, fewer people who needed impressing, and perhaps it was assumed that they could be impressed more easily. Nor, despite the three-caste system in Lusaka, did their plans reflect an elaborate occupational and social hierarchy – presumably because running Kenya or Northern Rhodesia did not require such elaborate distinctions.

Here, as elsewhere, the end of the Raj brought its own ironies: the rulers of the newly independent states, finding themselves faced with the same problems of squatter settlement as the old colonial officials, reacted identically. In Lusaka, where a Cabinet Minister referred to '90,000 uninvited guests', the local newspaper in 1970 indignantly argued that 'if the people living in these terrible areas used more initiative instead of sponging from a city to which they are contributing nothing, they need not suffer in any way by being moved away from their hovels.' So occasional bulldozings took place, and even pass laws were suggested.[65] In Nairobi, the government in 1969 began systematic demolition and the mayor, Isaac

[64] Collins, 1969, 17–19.   [65] van Velsen, 1975, 295–6, 307.

Lugonzo, argued that the government should stop people without means of support moving into the city.[66]

In both places, of course, the policies were determined by an African elite who had moved into the houses vacated by the colonials: 'You forget the smell of the dust after only a few days', said one, a civil servant in Nairobi: 'There is a bigger gap between my father and myself than between myself and the average European.'[67] In such ex-European areas, Mabogunje reported in 1978, the officials knew the old building standards by heart, even when they could not find the original colonial documents.[68] To give them due credit, they changed their policies later: to upgrading in Nairobi, to upgrading and self-build in Lusaka.[69] Meanwhile even New Delhi had spawned numberless informal settlements, some packed into the very spaces that Lutyens had provided so generously along his ceremonial streets.[70]

Canberra: City Beautiful Exceptional

So, transmuted to a colonial or ex-colonial context, the City Beautiful turned out to have a few blemishes. There was however one outstanding exception, though perhaps that was because for a long time most of it remained on paper: Canberra. Its early history verged on the tragi-farcical. The new Commonwealth of Australia Government, established on New Year's Day 1901, immediately started to fulfil its remit to find a new capital within New South Wales outside a 100-mile radius of Sydney. In 1908 it chose Canberra and the site was set aside as Australian Capital Territory; in 1911 it organized an international competition to plan the city. But it was so mean about the prize (a paltry £1,750) that both the British and the American institutes of architects effectively boycotted it: obvious names like Abercrombie, Burnham, Olmsted were missing. 137 architects, presumably including a quota of starving students, competed; Walter Burley Griffin (1876–1937), an American who had worked in Frank Lloyd Wright's office, entered with his wife Marion Mahoney and won. The government then appointed a board to report on the design; it pronounced it impracticable and promptly designed its own, which it started to implement. This was so terrible that public opinion, hitherto lukewarm, swung behind Griffin; in England, Abercrombie said of it that

[66] Hake, 1977, 99, 123.   [67] cit. ibid. 74.   [68] Mabogunje, 1978, 64.
[69] Hake, 1977, 164–70; Martin, 1982, 259–61.   [70] Payne, 1977, 138–9.

FIGURE 6.7   Canberra.
Walter Burley Griffin's prizewinning plan of 1912; ignored, circumvented, finally –
three quarters of a century afterwards – nearing completion.

COMMONWEALTH OF AVSTRALIA
FEDERAL CAPITAL COMPETITION

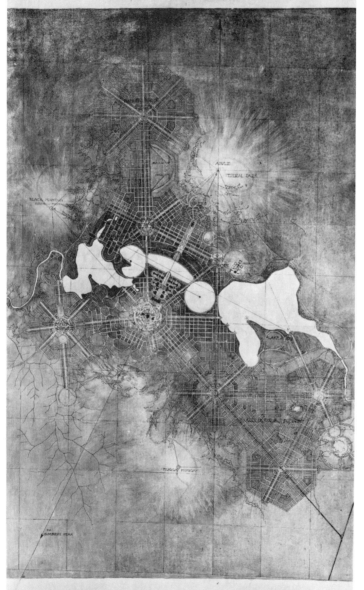

CITY AND ENVIRONS ·

SCALE

'It is the work of an amateur who has yet to learn the elementary principles.'[71]

There was a change of government; in 1913 Griffin was appointed Federal Capital Director of Design and Construction. For seven years he nearly went mad as his attempts were systematically sabotaged: plans went astray, his own drawings disappeared from his desk to resurface only thirty years later. In 1920 he gave up and his post was abolished. Numerous attempts were made in Parliament to scrap the plan, until finally it was fixed; but nothing was done to implement it. The suburbs began to grow in typical Australian fashion, that is to say sprawlingly, without plan. Finally, in 1955 a Senate Committee of Enquiry recommended a new central authority for planning, construction and development. In 1957 William Holford came from England to recommend plan modifications; the next year John Overall was appointed National Capital Development Region Director.[72] Almost unbelievably, after forty-five years Griffin's plan began to take shape; in the mid-1980s, it is nearing completion.

But the buildings are not his; only their disposition. The aboriginal name, Kamberra, means a meeting place: the site, as Griffin's introduction to the plan put it, 'may be considered as an irregular amphitheatre', on which he proposed to stage a great drama of government. Today's tourist map, which is oriented upside-down, is perversely correct: that is how, for Griffin, his audience would see it. From the mountains on the north east, which would form the rear galleries, the land fell gently to form the auditorium; the spectators, facing south-westwards with the sun behind them, would look down to the lowest point of the basin, which would be flooded to become the arena; behind that, the land rose in steps, to form a stage on which would be placed in rising order the symbolically important buildings of the Commonwealth: the Court of Justice, the Parliament House, finally – on the highest internal hill within the basin – the Capitol Building.

To accent the drama, stage and arena would form a triangle, with the Capitol Hill as the rear apex and – both these on the audience's side of the water – the military establishments and market centre to their front left, the national university and municipal centre to front right. (Here, though the plan's command of theatrical metaphor at this point fails it, drinks and ice creams would be available; this would be the commercial centre.) These two would be joined to the apex by broad highways crossing the lake. Bisecting the triangle, on the audience's side, would be a huge central processional aisle leading towards them. And, behind the stage, the nearer hills and the far-distant blue-mountain ridges would form 'the back scene of the theatrical whole'.[73]

Remarkably, it has all come out like that, with a few more changes of

71 Boyd, 1960, 13; Manieri-Elia, 1979, 112.
72 Boyd, 1960, 14–15.   73 Commonwealth of Australia, 1913, 3.

FIGURE 6.8 *Walter Burley Griffin.*
The Chicago landscape architect who worked with Frank Lloyd Wright before winning the Canberra competition.

cast. The play has been rewritten to give a bigger role to the Parliament, which in 1988, Australia's bicentennial, has been moved up to a new home on Capitol Hill. An elegantly monumental art gallery and national library have joined the courts of justice at front of stage. Visually, that right edge of the triangle has become the dominant feature: it leads the eye back from the municipal-commercial centre, past a traffic circle, via a broad highway across Lake Burley Griffin and so up to the new Parliament House, low-slung and half-buried into the hill; low-key government, this. On the lake itself, strong decorative vertical features – the carillon clock at extreme left, the huge Captain Cook memorial water jet close to the central axis, the telecom tower at extreme right – define and frame the stage. The heavily neo-classical Anzac Parade, a post-World War One war memorial and hence a very early feature, forms the central processional aisle to the auditorium. Most notably, because the actual building came so late, the architecture is of the 1970s and 1980s: in style it is international-modern-respectful. It lacks some of the zest of Niemeyer's Brasilia (of which more in chapter 7); it also lacks its monumental excesses. It is all exceedingly grand, dignified, elegant, yet (that Parker–Unwin word) reposeful; it will soon rank with Washington as one of the world's great monumental capitals, an eloquent testimony to the wisdom of making haste slowly.

Most remarkably, Griffin made some of his most innovative leaps in designing the residential suburbs. He was, remember, not a true-blue City Beautiful planner: he admired the work of the Garden City movement, and of Geddes.[74] A decade before Perry, he anticipated the neighbourhood unit. He wrote that

> the segregated sections, formed and separated by the general traffic lines, furnish not only suitable individual home sites, but comprise social units for that larger family – the neighbourhood group, with one handy district school or more for the children, and with local playground, game fields, church, club and social amenities accessible without crossing traffic tracks, or encountering the disturbing elements of temptations of business streets, since these family activities may best be directed internally toward the geographical centres of their groups for their special congregation.[75]

It sounds almost like a pre-Radburn Radburn. The original diagram shows the units as hexagons, a device Parker used later in his Radburn layouts at Wythenshawe.[76] And, in the neighbourhoods of the 1980s, that is how it has emerged: a morning jogger may emerge from the front door, go from path via linear park to a vast central space of playing fields, making a circuit of a mile or more without ever seeing traffic. These neighbourhoods, and the new towns that are supplementing them farther out, are strung like beads on the strings of the traffic roads which pass between and around them. So Canberra achieves the difficult feat of being one of the last Cities Beautiful, and also the world's biggest Garden City. It is even, in its way, one of the few extant realizations of Howard's polycentric social city: no small achievement for a city that for a long time never looked like growing up. Thus, unlike a number of other examples of the City Beautiful genre, it manages to be rather likeable.

The City Beautiful and the Great Dictators

The return of the City Beautiful to Europe was altogether less happy. It came in the age of the Great Dictators, and it too was theatre: bad

[74] Manieri-Elia, 1979, 113.   [75] Commonwealth of Australia, 1913, 13.   [76] Creese, 1966, 266–8.

melodrama. Mussolini's Rome was the curtain-warmer. Fascist ideology concerning the city was in many ways close to Nazi: only rural family life was truly healthy; the metropolis was the origin of most things bad, including labour unrest and Socialism. Ironically – an experience soon to be repeated in Franco's Spain – under Mussolini the cities boomed as never before; Fascism proved good for business. Mussolini's response was to pass laws – in 1928, in 1939 – to control migration; by one of those many ironies, the latter only became effective after World War Two.[77] It was also to carry through well-publicized rural land-reclamation schemes like those in the Pontine Marshes south of Rome, with five completely new towns.[78]

Within the metropolis, however, the role of planning was to be monumental: to rediscover the glories of Rome by removing most of the traces of the subsequent two millennia. Mussolini gave his instructions to the 1929 Congress of the Housing and Town Planning Federation in Rome:

> My ideas are clear. My orders are precise. Within five years, Rome must appear marvellous to all the people of the world – vast, orderly, powerful, as in the time of the empire of Augustus . . . you shall create vast spaces around the Theater of Marcellus, the Capitoline Hill, and the Pantheon. All that has grown around them in the centuries of decadence must disappear.[79]

In fact, the new plan – promulgated in 1931 – was internally contradictory: the street widenings, the focus on the Piazza Venezia as ceremonial square, would have covered up or destroyed imperial Rome rather than revealing it. But it did not matter; despite sweeping powers, despite generous injections of money, despite the *imprimatur* of Il Duce himself, life in Rome continued in the old sweet way. When the sweeping lines of the Master Plan were finally translated into detailed plans, broad boulevards and panoramic squares had mysteriously turned into building lots; old-fashioned chaos, compromise, and corruption saved Rome from the depredations of the master builder.[80]

There was the same inbuilt contradiction in Nazi as in Fascist thinking about the city. The party's theoretical wing at the end of the 1920s was strongly anti-urban, arguing that the Nordic people were quintessential farmers, never successful in founding cities and nearly destroyed by them. Its newspaper the *Völkische Beobachter* described the metropolis as 'the melting-pot of all evil . . . of prostitution, bars, illness, movies, Marxism, Jews, strippers, Negro dances, and all the disgusting offspring of so-called "modern art"'.[81] Shortly after the Nazis seized power, their policies – borrowing from Weimar ideas – emphasized *Kleinsiedlungen* at the edge of the big cities, such as Marienfelde, Falkensee and Falkenberg outside

[77] Treves, 1980, 470–86. [78] Calabi, 1984, 49–50. [79] Fried, 1973, 31.
[80] Ibid. 35–9. [81] Lane, 1968, 155.

Berlin; then the emphasis shifted to rural areas, but by that time the rival claims of rearmament were shrinking the whole programme.[82]

The definitive Nazi statement on urban policy, Gottfried Feder's *Die neue Stadt* of 1939, has odd echoes of the *Gartenstadtbewegung* in its emphasis on developing small self-sufficient rural towns of some 20,000 people which would combine the best feature of urban and rural life, both economically and socially, while minimizing the attendant disadvantages.[83] But perhaps not quite so odd; for, as seen in chapter 4, that movement in Germany did have its strongly conservative wing. And, following ideas that developed in the 1920s, these garden cities were to be built not near the major metropolitan centres, but in thinly populated agricultural districts like Mecklenburg and East Prussia: a return to the countryside, with a vengeance.

All of which seems hundreds of miles away, both literally and figuratively, from the plans that Hitler and his *Generalbauinspektor*, Albert Speer (1905–81), were hatching for the reconstruction of Berlin. But running through it all was a perverse logic: Germany's cities, and above all Berlin, were to perform a psychological, a quasi-religious, even a magical function as gathering-points for vast public ceremonies, while the productive population were removed to *Lebensraum* in the countryside.[84] Appropriately, the plans would have involved unparalleled destruction of the old medieval town centres to make way for ceremonial axes, assembly areas and halls, vast towers and sprawling administrative complexes, at a bill exceeding 100 billion marks.[85] The resulting irony was that the Nazis, having embraced the cult of rural virtue and the small medieval city and excorcitated the giant city, ended by trying to produce a totally mechanized, totally anti-human city of parade and spectacle.[86]

Berlin was, however, a very different canvas from Rome: here was no old master awaiting restoration, but a piece of nineteenth-century commercial art. And the retouching artist had very decided views: Hitler had failed to enter the Vienna Academy to study art, and was prone to repeat to Speer, again and again, 'How I wish I had been an architect.'[87] He had an amazingly detailed knowledge of earlier City Beautiful plans for Vienna and Paris; he knew the exact measurements of the Champs Élysées, and was obsessionally determined that Berlin should have an east–west axis two and a half times as long; the disposition of the buildings – huge and monumental, with wide spaces between them – recalls the Vienna Ring remembered from his youth.[88] He showed Speer two sketches from the 1920s, which already showed his dreams for a 650-foot domed building

[82] Peltz-Dreckmann, 1978, 102, 122, 144.   [83] Ibid. 194.
[84] Thies, 1978, 422–4.   [85] Ibid. 417–18.   [86] Schorske, 1963, 114.
[87] Speer, 1970, 80.   [88] Ibid. 75–7; Larsson, 1978, 42–3.

FIGURE 6.9 *Speer's Berlin.*
Speer's monumental North-South way leads via the Triumphal Arch to the gigantic
domed *Kupferhalle*: a city fit to be capital of the Thousand-Year Reich, none of it
even started.

and a 330-foot arch: 'he had been planning triumphant monumental
buildings when there was not a shred of hope that they could ever be
built.'[89] 'Why always the biggest?' he rhetorically asked an audience of
construction workers in 1939: 'I do this to restore to each individual
German his self-respect.'[90]

His obsession with the monumental was such that he ignored wider
aspects: 'He would look at the plans, but really only glance at them, and
after a few minutes would ask with palpable boredom: "Where do you
have the plans for the grand avenue?"'[91] Running between the two planned
central railroad stations, with the Great Hall – 726 feet high, 850 feet
across the dome – at its centre point, this north–south avenue was to spell
out in stone 'the political, military, and economic power of Germany'. In
the centre sat the absolute ruler of the Reich, and in his immediate
proximity, as the highest expression of his power, was the great domed hall
which was to be the dominant structure of the future Berlin.[92] Each time

[89] Speer, 1970, 70.   [90] Ibid. 69.   [91] Ibid. 79.   [92] Ibid. 138.

he saw the plans again, he would repeat: 'My only wish, Speer, is to see
these buildings. In 1950 we'll organize a world's fair.'[93]

The plans that bored him extended the City Beautiful principle to the
edges of the city, and beyond; Speer, who admired Washington and
Burnham's Columbian Exhibition, evidently took to heart Burnham's
exhortation to make no little plans.[94] Seventeen radial highways, along
which higher buildings were permitted all the way to the periphery, were
intersected by four rings, partly built on existing streets, partly new.[95]
There were to be big satellite towns to north and south; the bigger,
Südstadt, was to have 210,000 people and 100,000 industrial jobs. In it,
despite Nazi prejudice in favour of single-family homes, a new version of
the familiar Berlin *Mietskaserne* would dominate: a closed apartment block
around a big yard.[96] Here as in the centre, the plan had a very regular,
hard-lined, monumental quality, almost as if it were designed to be seen
from the air.[97] In its basic principles – if not in its surface clothing –
Speer's plan exhibited conventional enough qualities: incompatible land
uses were segregated, through traffic was excluded from residential areas,
there was plenty of air and light and space; very little, indeed, to which a
CIAM member could object.[98]

It was a costly obsession. Speer's own estimate was that the total cost
for Berlin alone would have been between 4 and 6 billion marks, perhaps
$5–8 billion in today's money.[99] Rearmament brought postponement. Work
on producing the east–west processional axis, much of which was already
in place, started in 1937 and was partly completed in 1939; almost
unbelievably, work was started on the main project in 1941.[100] Finally, all
that ever resulted from the whole grandiose vision was the creation of one
ceremonial space on the east–west axis, and the replanting of the historic
forest ring outside the city with a mixture of deciduous and coniferous
trees.[101] With a specially appropriate irony, after the war the Russians
completed the east–west axis in their sector, and named it Stalinallee.

Nazi Berlin would have been the ultimate City Beautiful. Its sources of
inspiration, even down to details – Burnham's domed civic centre, Lutyens's
domed Viceregal Palace – are only too evident.[102] It was also ultimately
impossible to build; even in the most favourable circumstances, it would
have taken a disproportionate part of the country's available resources. The
odd fact was that a far poorer capital under an equally megalomaniac
dictator, Joseph Stalin, managed to achieve in a short time much of what
Hitler only dreamed of.

[93] Ibid. 141.   [94] Helmer, 1980, 317, 326–7.
[95] Speer, 1970, 78; Larsson, 1978, 33–6.   [96] Larsson, 1978, 86–7, 94.
[97] Ibid. 95–6.   [98] Ibid. 112–13.   [99] Speer, 1970, 140.
[100] Larsson, 1978, 32–3, 53.   [101] Speer, 1970, 78; Helmer, 1980, 201.
[102] Larsson, 1978, 116.

The first decade of Soviet planning deserves a book to itself. As in so many other fields, it was a time of wild experiment, of impassioned debate between proponents of equally improbable theories. The urbanists wanted to house everyone in towers; naturally enough, Corbusier was their god and their ally, and so they will be discussed together with him in chapter 7. The deurbanists, a much wilder bunch, wanted to disperse everyone in mobile homes across the countryside, and eventually demolish Moscow; their spiritual affinity was with Frank Lloyd Wright, and we will encounter them in chapter 8. (As noted more than once, logic and chronology refuse stubbornly to keep in step.) Both groups consulted foreign experts: May, predictably, suggested satellite towns, Le Corbusier a completely new high-rise Moscow on a new site.[103] At the Central Committee session in June 1931, their debate came to an abrupt end.[104] The Full Assembly denounced foreign theories of planning, notably those of Le Corbusier and Wright, and called for a five-year Development Plan for Moscow, to be produced forthwith.[105]

Moscow certainly needed a plan. Its population, which had declined sharply in the chaotic years after 1917, had by 1926 climbed just above pre-revolutionary levels, to more than 2 million; by 1931 it probably exceeded 3 million.[106] Its physical structure, and its equipment, were simply archaic: it consisted mainly of one- or two-storey wooden buildings; the average housing space had been 89 square feet per person in 1926, and there had been a deterioration since then; in 1937, Ernest Simon could report that slums being demolished as unfit for habitation in Manchester – then one of the most slum-ridden cities in England – would provide better accommodation than 90 per cent of Moscow families had.[107] Water supplies, sewerage, electricity were all woefully short.

Perhaps understandably, after 1931 no more overseas experts were invited. The plan unveiled in July 1935 called for a limit on the city's future growth, coupled with forced modernization. The city was to be developed as a single integral unit; reconstruction was to be based on the 'unity and harmony of architectural compositions':[108] the City Beautiful had come to Moscow.

The impetus of course was national pride: in 1937, everybody Simon spoke to 'was most emphatic that the old two-storey houses must go, that Moscow be a real city with buildings worthy of the capital of the greatest country in the world.'[109] To achieve this, Moscow became a construction camp. What escaped the visitors was that all the emphasis was on the most visible and the most prestigious projects: three metro lines with their chandelier-light stations, housing along the main streets, public buildings,

---

[103] May, 1961, 181–2; Simon, 1937b, 382.   [104] Svetlichny, 1960, 214.
[105] Machler, 1932, 96; Parkins, 1953, 30–1.
[106] Harris, 1970a, 257; Simon, 1937b, 381.
[107] Simon, 1937a, 154–5.   [108] Parkins, 1953, 36.   [109] Simon, 1937a, 160.

stadiums, squares and parks.[110] Significantly, of all flats under construction in 1939, 52 per cent were along the main thoroughfares.[111] Perhaps this was because the projects of different ministries were never co-ordinated, while the housing programme fell more and more behind schedule;[112] perhaps, more likely, because the planners were trying to impress the public; most likely of all, because they were trying to please their master.

And Stalin knew what he liked. 'Henceforth, architecture had to be expressive, representational, oratorical. Every building, however modest its function, had henceforth to be a monument.'[113] He personally approved the plans for major buildings; once offered two versions, he chose both and the terrified architects followed him, producing a structure in which the left side did not match the right.[114] And Stalin, too, had his own Socialist equivalent of Hitler's giant domed hall: the 1,300-foot Palace of the Soviets, to be crowned by a gigantic statue of Lenin. Actually started, it ran into structural problems and began to sink into the ground; perhaps mercifully, it was abandoned.[115] But all over Moscow, the wedding-cake architecture still recalls Stalin's tastes and whims.

So Moscow in the 1930s was a kind of Potemkin village. Just like Burnham's Washington and Chicago, or indeed Haussmann's Paris, the new façades alongside the giant highways concealed a mass of ancient slums behind them. Even in the 1960s, the last remnants of that old wooden Moscow were still visible in the back streets. But doubtless, the façades pleased the master; and the planners slept a little better at nights for it.

The odd fact then is that there is no single easy explanation for the phenomenon of the City Beautiful. It manifested itself, over a forty-year period, in a great variety of different economic, social, political and cultural circumstances: as a handmaiden of finance capitalism, as an agent of imperialism, as an instrument of personal totalitarianism of both the right and left varieties, so long as those labels have meaning. What these manifestations had in common, with some qualifications and exceptions, was a total concentration on the monumental and on the superficial, on architecture as symbol of power; and, correspondingly, an almost complete lack of interest in the wider social purposes of planning. This is planning for display, architecture as theatre, design intended to impress. Only the audience differs: nouveaux riches in search of dissipation and titillation; cowed colonial subjects and haughty rulers of minor principalities; peasant migrants to the great city; depressed or dispossessed bourgeois families recalling past glories. All, with luck, will like the show; for many, rather like the Hollywood of the 1930s, it will take their minds off the grim reality outside. But at least the Hollywood productions did get released on schedule; and they did not bankrupt their audiences.

[110] Ling, 1943, 7; Parkins, 1953, 42, 44–5.   [111] Berton, 1977, 235.
[112] Parkins, 1953, 44–5.   [113] Kopp, 1970, 227.   [114] Berton, 1977, 228–9.
[115] Ibid. 223–4; Kopp, 1970, 223.

The City of Towers

Ye towers of Julius, London's lasting shame,
With many a foul and midnight murther fed.

Thomas Grey
The Bard (1757)

The simplest solution is flats. If people are going to live in large towns at
all they must learn to live on top of one another. But the northern working
people do not take kindly to flats; even when flats exist they are contemptuously
named 'tenements'. Almost everyone will tell you that he wants 'a house of
his own', and apparently a house in the middle of an unbroken block of
houses a hundred yards long seems to them more 'their own' than a flat
situated in mid-air.

George Orwell
The Road to Wigan Pier (1937)

. . . the solution of the housing problem in any great English city does not
lie in the provision of High Barbicans or High Paddingtons. They may be
physically and theoretically possible but they are completely alien to the
habits and tastes of the people who would be expected to live in them.

Harold Macmillan
Internal Memorandum as Minister of
Housing and Local Government (1954)

7
The City of Towers

The Corbusian Radiant City:
Paris, Chandigarh, Brasilia, London, St Louis,
1920–1970

The evil that Le Corbusier did lives after him; the good is perhaps interred with his books, which are seldom read for the simple reason that most are almost unreadable. (The pictures, it should be said, are sometimes interesting for what they reveal of their draughtsman.) But the effort should be made, because their impact on twentieth-century city planning has been almost incalculably great: obscurity is no barrier to communication, at least of a sort. Ideas, forged in the Parisian intelligentsia of the 1920s, came to be applied to the planning of working-class housing in Sheffield and St Louis, and hundreds of other cities too, in the 1950s and 1960s; the results were at best questionable, at worst catastrophic. How and why this should happen is one of the most intriguing, but also one of the most chastening, stories in the intellectual history of modern planning.

Perhaps the most important single facts about Le Corbusier (1887–1965) were that he was not French, but Swiss; and that this was not his real name. He was born Charles-Édouard Jeanneret at La Chaux-de-Fonds near Neuchâtel, and lived regularly in Paris only from the age of thirty-one. The Swiss, as the least perceptive visitor has noticed, are an obsessionally well-ordered people: their cities are models of neat self-control, with not a blade of grass or a stray hair out of place. All Corbusier's cities would be like that. The chaos of the old Paris, that Haussmann's reconstruction left intact behind the new façades, must have been anathema to the Calvinist mores of the rising young architect. He devoted his professional life to Genevaizing it, and any other city that had the impertinence to be unruly.

The third significant fact about him is that he came from a family of watchmakers. (The name, Le Corbusier, was a pseudonym adopted from a maternal grandfather when he began to write, in 1920.) He was to achieve greatest fame for his statement, first made at that time, that a

FIGURE 7.1 *Le Corbusier and Unité.*
A machine for living in, as prescribed by the Supreme Architect.

house is a machine to live in.[1] That was natural: the tradition, of crowding thousands of minute components into a planned harmony, came out of a long hereditary tradition. But people are not escapements, and society cannot be reduced to clockwork order; the attempt was an unhappy one for humanity. There is an anomaly, though: the Jura watchmakers were sturdy guardians of their local liberties, and for this were admired both by Proudhon and Kropotkin. Corbusier soon put that behind him.

If Switzerland gave him his view of the world, Paris provided both his raw material and his vision of an ideal order. Just as Howard cannot be understood save in the context of late nineteenth-century London, or Mumford save in that of the New York of the 1920s, so all Corbusier's ideas need to be seen as a reaction to the city in which he lived and worked from 1916 until shortly before his death in 1965.[2] The history of Paris has been one of constant struggle between the forces of exuberant, chaotic, often sordid everyday life and the forces of centralized, despotic order. In the 1920s and 1930s, it was clear that chaos was winning and order had been in long retreat. Behind the façades, the city was racked by slums and disease. The city authorities of the Third Republic had all but given up

[1] Fishman, 1977, 186.   [2] Ibid. 29, 101, 114, 183–4.

FIGURE 7.2 *Louis XIV commands the building of the Invalides.*
Le Corbusier's favourite vision of the Master Architect at work: 'We wish it'.
Unfortunately he never found his *Roi Soleil*.

the attempt even to complete the last of Haussmann's improvements, let alone take new initiatives like clearing the worst of the slums.[3]

Paris, the young Corbusier concluded, could be saved only by the intervention of *grands seigneurs*, men 'without remorse': Louis XIV, Napoleon, Haussmann.[4] Their 'grand openings' were for him 'a signal example of *creation*, of that spirit which is able to dominate and compel the mob'.[5] He concluded his early book *L'Urbanisme* with a picture of Louis XIV personally directing the construction of the Invalides, which he captioned: 'Homage to a great town planner – This despot conceived immense projects and realized them. Over all the country his noble works still fill us with admiration. He was capable of saying, "We wish it", or "Such is our pleasure".'[6] He searched all his life for a latter-day Roi Soleil, but never found him.

The Corbusian Ideal City

Meanwhile he had to make do with bourgeois patrons. His Plan Voisin of 1925 had nothing to do with neighbourhood units, but was the name of an aircraft manufacturer who sponsored it.[7] (This helps to explain the planes that fly, with such insouciant disregard of air-traffic control, in between these and other Corbusian skyscrapers.) Its eighteen uniform 700-foot-high towers would have entailed the demolition of most of historic Paris north of the Seine save for a few monuments, some of which would be moved; the Place Vendôme, which he liked as a symbol of order, would be kept.[8] He was apparently quite unable to understand why the plan aroused such an outcry in the city council, where he was called a barbarian.[9] He always thought that the Gothic cathedral-builders of thirteenth-century Europe, through whose efforts over a mere hundred years 'the new world opened up as a flower on the ruins', must likewise have been misunderstood in those first years 'when the cathedrals were white.'[10]

He was not deterred: 'The design of cities was too important to be left to the citizens.'[11] He developed his principles of planning most fully in *La Ville contemporaine* (1922) and *La Ville radieuse* (1933). The key was the famous paradox: we must decongest the centres of our cities by increasing their density. In addition, we must improve circulation and increase the amount of open space. The paradox could be resolved by building high on a small part of the total ground area.[12] This demanded, as Corbusier put

---

[3] Sutcliffe, 1970, 240–1, 257; Lavedan, 1975, 492–3, 497–500; Evenson, 1979, 208–16.
[4] Fishman, 1977, 210.   [5] Le Corbusier, 1929, 293.   [6] Ibid. 310.
[7] Fishman, 1977, 211.   [8] Banham, 1960, 255.   [9] Evenson, 1979, 54.
[10] Le Corbusier, 1937, 4.   [11] Fishman, 1977, 190.
[12] Le Corbusier, 1929, 178.

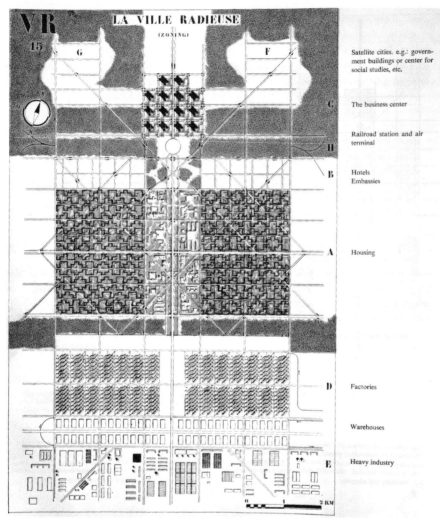

FIGURE 7.3 *La Ville Radieuse.*
The total geometrical vision: massed machines for living and working in.

it in characteristic capital letters: 'WE MUST BUILD ON A CLEAR SITE!
The city of today is dying because it is not constructed geometrically.'[13] The
needs of traffic also demanded total demolition: 'Statistics show us that
business is conducted in the centre. This means that wide avenues must

[13] Ibid. 232.

be driven through the centres of our towns. *Therefore the existing centres must come down. To save itself, every great city must rebuild its centre.*'[14] This was the first suggestion of its kind; thirty years later, it was to be taken up with a vengeance. But, as Anthony has pointed out, there is no recognition anywhere in it of the problem of garaging all these cars, or of the environmental problems that would result from their noise and emissions; they are simply ignored.[15]

The way in which the new structure was to be achieved was however not uniform across the entire city: the Contemporary City was to have a clearly differentiated spatial structure. And this was to correspond to a specific, segregated social structure: one's dwelling depended on one's job.[16] At the centre were the skyscrapers of the Plan Voisin which, Corbusier emphasized, were intended as offices for the elite *cadres*: industrialists, scientists and artists (including, presumably, architects and planners); twenty-four of these towers would provide for between 400,000 and 600,000 top people's jobs at 1,200 to the acre, with 95 per cent of the ground area left open.[17] Outside this zone, the residential areas would be of two types: six-storey luxury apartments for these same *cadres*, designed on the so-called step-back principle (in rows) with 85 per cent of ground space left open, and more modest accommodation for the workers, built around courtyards, on a uniform gridiron of streets, with 48 per cent left open.[18]

These apartments would be mass-produced for mass-living. Corbusier had no time for any kind of individual idiosyncracy; well did he call them 'cells':

> We must never, in our studies, lose sight of the perfect human 'Cell', the cell which corresponds most perfectly to our physiological and sentimental needs. We must arrive at the 'house-machine', which must be both practical and emotionally satisfying and designed for a succession of tenants. The idea of the 'old home' disappearing and with it local architecture, etc., for labour will shift about as needed, and must be ready to move, *bag and baggage.*[19]

Not only would the units all be uniform; they would all contain the same standard furniture. Possibly, he admits, 'my scheme . . . at first might seem to warrant a certain fear and dislike.' But variations in layout, and generous tree-planting, would soon overcome this.[20] And not only would the units be mass-produced; for the bourgeois elite, they would also be collectively serviced: 'though it will still always be possible to have a maid or a children's nurse of your own, a family servant if you wish', in the radiant city 'the servant problem would be solved. . . . If you desired to bring some friend back to supper round about midnight, say after the theatre, a mere

[14] Ibid. 128.   [15] Anthony, 1966, 286.   [16] Fishman, 1977, 199.
[17] Le Corbusier, 1929, 215; Fishman, 1977, 195.
[18] Le Corbusier, 1929, 215, 222–3.
[19] Ibid. 243.   [20] Ibid. 243, 250–2.

telephone call is all that is needed for you to find the table laid and waiting for you – with a servant who is not sulking.'[21] The core of the Contemporary City, clearly, was a middle-class sort of place. And, in the midst of the office centre, he created an entertainment and cultural complex to minister for their needs, where the elite would talk and dance in 'profound calm 600 feet above the ground'.[22]

The blue-collar workers and the clerks would not live like this, of course. Corbusier provided for them in garden apartments within satellite units. Here, too, there would be plenty of green space, sports facilities and entertainments – but of a different sort, appropriate for those who worked hard for eight hours a day. Unlike the Paris of the 1920s, where rich and poor tended to live in close juxtaposition, *La Ville contemporaine* would have been a completely class-segregated city.

By the time of the Radiant City, though the tenets of the Corbusian religion remained unchanged, there were important theological variations. Corbusier had lost faith in capitalists, probably because in the middle of the Great Depression they had lost the capacity to fund him. Now, he came to believe in the virtue of centralized planning, which would cover not merely city-building but every aspect of life. The way to this would come through syndicalism, but not of the anarchist kind: this would be an ordered, hierarchical system, having some close affinities to the left-wing variety of Italian Fascism. Many French syndicalists indeed joined the Vichy regime in 1940; Corbusier himself believed that 'France needs a Father. It doesn't matter who.'[23] In this system, everything would be determined by the plan, and the plan would be produced 'objectively' by experts; the people would have a say only in who was to administer it. 'The harmonious city must first be planned by experts who understand the science of urbanism. They work out their plans in total freedom from partisan pressures and special interests; once their plans are formulated, they must be implemented without oppsoition.'[24] In 1938 he designed a 'National Centre of Collective Festivals for 100,000 People', where the leader could address his people; it is like an open-air version of Hitler's Domed Hall.[25]

But the new syndicalist city is different in one vital respect: now, everyone will be equally collectivized. Now, everyone will live in giant collective apartments called *Unités*; every family will get an apartment not according to the breadwinner's job, but according to rigid space norms; no one will get anything more or less than the minimum necessary for efficient existence. And now, everyone – not just the lucky elite – will enjoy collective services. Cooking, cleaning, child care are all taken away from the family.

---

[21] Ibid. 229.   [22] cit. Fishman, 1977, 198.   [23] Ibid. 237, 239–40.
[24] Ibid. 239.   [25] Ibid. 241.

In the meantime, significantly, Corbusier had been to the Soviet Union. And, in the 1920s, an important group of Soviet architects – the urbanists – had developed ideas very close to his. They wanted to build new cities in open countryside, in which everyone would live in gigantic collective apartment blocks, with individual space reduced to the absolute minimum needed for a bed; there would be no individual or family kitchens and bathrooms. In one version, life would be regulated by the minute, from a 6.00 a.m. reveille to departure for the mine at 7.00; another urbanist envisaged a unit in which huge orchestras would induce sleep for insomniacs, drowning the snores of the others.[26] The plans by some members of this group – Ivanov, Terekhin and Smolin in Leningrad, Barshch, Vladimirov, Alexander and Vesnin in Moscow – are almost identical, down to details, to the *Unité* as developed in the Radiant City and as actually built at Marseilles in 1946.[27] But, after 1931, the Soviet regime – like the Fascist regime in Italy a few years later – rejected Corbusier's advice.

And, by the 1940s, he had modified his views again – though as usual, only in the details. His ASCORAL (Assemblé de Constructeurs pour une Rénovation Architècturale), founded during the war, argued that *les cités radio-concentriques des échanges*, the centres of education and entertainment, still designed in the old Corbusian way, should be joined together by *les cités linéaires industrielles*, which would be continuous lines of industrialization along transportation corridors.[28] He had ceased to be optimistic about the big city, believing that the population of Paris should shrink from 3 to 1 million.[29] These notions had curious echoes of the Soviet deurbanists of the 1920s, whom Corbusier had so bitterly derided. But there was a crucial difference: his were to be concentrated 'green factories' with workers living segregated, immobile lives in vertical garden cities, each having between 1,500 and 2,500 workers, of course with the inevitable collective catering.[30] He remained implacably opposed to the idea of *cités-jardins*, which he consistently confused, like most of his fellow-French planners, with garden suburbs.[31]

None of this was ever built. The remarkable fact about Corbusier is just how phenomenally unsuccessful he was in practice. He travelled all over Europe, and outside it, producing his grandiose urban visions; page after page of his book *The Radiant City* is filled with them, Algiers, Antwerp, Stockholm, Barcelona, Nemours in North Africa. All remained on paper. In World War Two, with the establishment of the puppet Pétain regime in Vichy, he thought his time at last had come. Invited to head a study

---

[26] Hamm, 1977, 62–3; Berton, 1977, 210.
[27] Kopp, 1970, 146–7, 169, 171.
[28] Le Corbusier, 1948, 48; 1959, 103, 129.
[29] Sutcliffe, 1977, 221.   [30] Le Corbusier, 1948, 54.
[31] Le Corbusier, 1937, 255, 258; 1948, 68.

commission on housing and planning, he predictably produced a scheme for an elite of town planners heading huge architectural and engineering offices, able to override all interference. At their head was to be a 'regulator', an architect-administrator who formulated the entire national plan for building. Modesty for once overcame him; he failed to name his candidate for the post.[32] In fact, he got nowhere with Vichy either. His simple-minded egomania and his total political naïvety made it difficult for him to understand his failure; at the end of the war he was a deeply disillusioned man.

The Planning of Chandigarh

Ironically, his only real planning achievement on the ground – apart from the Marseilles *Unité*, a single block that was supposed to be the start of a complex, but was never completed, plus two reverential copies in France and another in Berlin – came posthumously. The Government of India had decided for political reasons to build a new capital for the Punjab at Chandigarh. They hired a planner, Albert Mayer, who produced a worthy plan in the Unwin–Parker–Stein–Wright tradition.[33] They approved the plan, but decided to bring in a team of the most prestigious modern architects – Corbusier, his own son Jeanneret, Maxwell Fry and Jane Drew – to give expression to it. Fry describes the traumatic first meeting, for which Mayer was late:

Corbusier held the crayon and was in his element.

"*Voilà la gare*" he said "*et voici la rue commerciale*", and he drew the first road on the new plan of Chandigarh.

"*Voici la tête*", he went on, indicating with a smudge the higher ground to the left of Mayer's location, the ill effects of which I had already pointed out to him. "*Et voilà l'estomac, le cité-centre*". Then he delineated the massive sectors measuring each half by three quarters of a mile and filling out the extent of the plain between the river valleys, with extension to the south.

The plan was well advanced by the time the anxious Albert Mayer joined the group . . . not in any way was he a match for the enigmatic but determined figure of the prophet.

We sat around after lunch in a deadly silence broken by Jeanneret's saying to Mayer, "*Vous parlez français, monsieur?*" To which Mayer responded, "*Oui, musheer, je parle*", a polite but ill-fated rejoinder that cut him out of all discussion that followed.

And so we continued, with minor and marginal suggestions from us and a steady flow of exposition from Corbusier, until the plan as we now know it was completed and never again departed from.[34]

[32] Fishman, 1977, 247–8.   [33] Evenson, 1966, 13–14.   [34] Sarin, 1982, 44.

FIGURE 7.4 *Chandigarh.*
The only realized Corbusian city design: here a residential quarter, functionalist boxes for Punjabi functionaries, from the pen of the master.

FIGURE 7.5 *Chandigarh.*
The reality of the people's city behind the facades; foreground, autonomous housing; left background, tent city.

There followed arguments between the architects and the planners, followed by arguments between the architects, with Fry and Jeanneret complaining at the way Corbusier had taken complete charge, including detailed layouts and designs. Rather naïvely, they said they wanted to work within the spirit of CIAM, that is collaboratively. The outcome was significant: a division of labour, in which Corbusier got the brief for the central administrative complex.[35] But what had happened was more fundamental: a shift from a planning style to an architectural style, meaning 'a shift towards a preoccupation with visual form, symbolism, imagery and aesthetics rather than the basic problems of the Indian population. By concentrating on providing Indian architecture with forms suited to the Second Machine Age, the existing Indian situation could be more or less totally ignored.'[36]

The result was a set of rich multiple ironies. Corbusier found his patron in a post-colonial government steeped in the autocratic traditions of the British Raj. He produced for them an exercise in the City Beautiful decked in the trappings of modern architecture; a latter-day New Delhi. There was a grid of fast traffic roads, already used in plans for Marseilles and Bogotá, to cater for a level of car ownership even lower than the Paris of 1925, which was low enough. The relationship between streets and buildings is totally European, and is laid down without regard for the fierce north-Indian climate or for Indian ways of life.[37] There is a total failure to produce built forms that could aid social organization or social integration; the sections fail to function as neighbourhoods.[38] The city is heavily segregated by income and civil service rank, recalling La Ville contemporaine; there are different densities for different social groups, resulting in a planned class segregation.[39]

So the contrasts are stark: 'As one walks around the magnificent campus of the Punjab University . . . (where most of the classrooms and offices are used for only three hours a day), one can see over the high campus walls thousands of people living in slums, without any electricity or running water.'[40]

By the 1970s, 15 per cent of the population were living in squatter or semi-squatter settlements; more than half the traders were operating informally from barrows or stalls.[41] Since they conflicted with the Master Plan's concept of urban order, the authorities made repeated attempts to harass and break them up. The traders responded by a series of public events worthy of an Indian version of an old Ealing comedy. To commemorate the inauguration of a new illegal market at a time when

[35] Ibid. 45.   [36] Ibid. 47.   [37] Evenson, 1966, 92.   [38] Ibid. 95.
[39] Gupta, 1974, 363; Schmetzer, 1974, 352–3.   [40] Ibid. 368.
[41] Sarin, 1979, 137.

Sikh separatism was very sensitive, they arranged a whole series of sacred Sikh religious events. When the enforcement staff arrived, the Sikh traders announced that they would let themselves be cut to pieces before these would be stopped. Later on the traders stage-managed elaborate funeral ceremonies for the Prime Minister who had just died, thus getting huge publicity.[42]

All of which is part of the rich pageant of Indian life, and nothing to do with Corbusier. True, most of the problems were only indirectly to be laid at his door; he was by then dead, and in his last years he had been concentrating on the central monumental complex and on the general visual symbolism, the part of the plan that works best.[43] But that was just the point: at the end of the day, like Hitler dreaming his futile dreams in Berlin, what he really cared about was the monumental part. He was the last of the City Beautiful planners. The rest does not work, but in a sense that is beside the point. At least, in Chandigarh the housing was much better than what the people had known before, and probably better than they could ever have hoped for if the city had never been built. But when Corbusier's disciples finally came to apply their master's precepts in the cities of the west, it was a rather different matter.

Brasilia: The Quasi-Corbusian City

There was one other completely new Corbusian city, though he did not design it. Brazil, like many another developing country, had grown around its port city which had willy-nilly become its capital. But by the 1940s, despite partial attempts at reconstruction, Rio de Janeiro was bursting at the seams. There had long been a plan for a new Federal capital in the interior; in 1823 José Bonifácio de Andrada e Silva, 'father of his country', had suggested and named it; in 1892 a Commission had already found the site; in 1946 a new democratic commission provided for it; in 1955 another commission rediscovered the site. The same year, Jucelino Kubitschek de Oliveira, a charismatic politician, committed himself to build it during his presidential election campaign, and narrowly won.[44] There was a long Brazilian political tradition of building grandiose public works within impossibly short times; Brasilia became its apotheosis.[45] The Rio press were predictably critical: 'The limit of insanity! a dictatorship in the desert.' Kubitschek was undeterred.[46]

He went to his old friend, the architect Oscar Niemeyer. The Institute of Brazilian Architects protested; there must be a competition. Niemeyer

[42] Ibid. 152.   [43] Evenson, 1966, 39, 94.
[44] Epstein, 1973, 36, 42, 45; Evenson, 1973, 49, 108, 112–13.
[45] Ibid. 36.   [46] Evenson, 1973, 114.

was of course on the jury; it reached its decision after a mere three days' deliberation, awarding one of the biggest city-planning exercises of the twentieth century to Lúcio Costa, another pioneer of the modern architectural movement in Brazil. His entry consisted of freehand drawings on five medium-sized cards: not a single population projection, economic analysis, land-use schedule, model or mechanical drawing.[47] The jury liked its 'grandeur': 'It was apparent from the beginning that Brasilia was to be an architect's, rather than a planner's, city.'[48]

The plan was variously described as an airplane, bird or dragonfly: the body, or fuselage, was a monumental axis for the principal public buildings and offices, the wings were the residential and other areas. In the first, uniform office blocks were to line a wide central mall leading to the complex of governmental buildings. In the second, uniform apartments were to be built in Corbusian superblocks fronting a huge central traffic spine; precisely following the prescription of La Ville radieuse, everyone, from Permanent Secretary to janitor, was to live in the same blocks in the same kind of apartment.

The construction of Brasilia became a legend even in Brazil, that country of bizarre fable. An American wrote that 'It was as if the opening of the west had been delayed a hundred years and then done with bulldozers.'[49] Since at all costs the capital must be dedicated on 24 April 1960, at the end of Kubitscheck's four-year term, it was decreed that there should be non-stop 24-hour construction for one year. It all 'represented a triumph of administration in a country never noted for efficient administration; it represented adherence to a time schedule in a society where schedules are seldom met; and it represented continuous hard work for a people reputedly reluctant to work either hard or continuously.'[50] Legends abounded, all doubtless true: the truck drivers who delivered the same load of sand several times a day; typographers hired as topographers, brick-counters as accountants.[51] The last thing anyone considered was the cost. William Holford, a jury member, said that no one knew the size of the bill; the President of NOVACAP, the New Town Corporation, said that he was not bothered by accounts; Niemeyer told the British architect Max Lock that he had no idea what his Presidential Palace had cost: 'How should I know?' he disarmingly asked.[52] Well did Epstein, author of one of the two standard histories of the city, dedicate his book 'Aos trabalhadores de Brasilia, que construiram a nova capital'; 'Aos trabalhadores de Brasil, que pagaram'. ('To the workers of Brasilia, who built the new capital; To the workers of Brazil, who paid for it').[53]

[47] Epstein, 1973, 49; Evenson, 1973, 145.   [48] Evenson, 1973, 117, 142–3.
[49] Ibid. 155.   [50] Ibid. 155.   [51] Epstein, 1973, 63.
[52] Evenson, 1973, 155.   [53] Epstein, 1973, n.p.

Unbelievably, 60,000 workers got it finished. In one day 2,000 light poles were erected; overnight 722 houses were painted white. On the appointed day, the Presidential Palace, the Executive Palace, the National Congress, the Supreme Court, eleven ministries, a hotel and ninety-four apartment blocks were gleaming in the sunight on the open *campo* of central Brazil. It was of course all a shell; the buildings were unfinished inside; after the ceremony, many of the officials took planes back to Rio. But even after Kubitscheck, too much had been invested in the city to turn back; over the following decade, the whole machinery of government did move there.

And it came to work, after a fashion. As car ownership rose, the vast expressways and cloverleaves filled with traffic; since the plan did not attempt to resolve pedestrian–vehicle conflicts, streams of pedestrians cheat death daily as they weave between speeding cars on the central mall. This is a detail; the real failure was that, just as in Chandigarh, an unplanned city grew up beside the planned one. The difference was that here, it was far larger.

The Brazilian *favela*, like its equivalent in every other developing country, is a familiar feature of the urban landscape: one of the best known swarms very visibly up the hillside behind Rio's famous Copacabana beach. But Brasilia, symbol of modernity, was to have none of this; squatting was simply to be abolished there.[54] And so it was, in a sense: it was just pushed out of sight and out of mind. In the construction period, a so-called Free Town had to be created; soon, squatting created the near-by settlement of Taguantinga. After dedication, the authorities tried to destroy it, provoking an agitation; in 1961, to the dismay of the architectural profession, a law was passed permitting it to remain. By the mid-1960s, it was officially estimated that one-third of the population of the Federal District, 100,000 people, lived in 'sub-habitations'; soon, the figure was more than one-half.[55] The authorities responded to invasions by trying to lay out minimal site-and-service plots; Epstein's account of the process has a special irony.

> Actual assignment of the lots and the laying out of new streets were in the hands of two men, one of them illiterate, under the supervision of a NOVACAP foreman. None of these was formally trained in urban planning, social work or in surveying. They laid out a gridwork of streets crossing each other at right angles.[56]

Such was the end of the dream of creating a classless urban society in a country where rich and poor had always been segregated. The difference, if anything, was that in Brasilia they were more ruthlessly separated than

[54] Ibid. 57–8. [55] Ibid. 75–6, 79, 119; Cunningham, 1980, 198–9.
[56] Ibid. 121–2.

FIGURE 7.6 *Brasilia.*
The vision of a modernized, sanitized capital city, sketched by Lucio Costa on five index cards.

FIGURE 7.7 *Taguantinga, Brasilia.*
Started as a construction camp, the first of the popular settlements that represent the reality for most of the capital region's people: impossible to suppress, eventually accepted but ignored.

in any of the older cities: a *cordon sanitaire* was placed between them and the monumental, symbolic city, so that they might never spoil the view or disturb the image. Niemeyer himself, by this time, was saying that the plan had been distorted and traduced; only a Socialist regime, he felt, could have implemented it.[57] Corbusier suffered from the same feelings much of his life: it is hard to build a City Beautiful amidst the confusion of democracy and the market.

The Corbusians Come to Britain

They did little better in the developed world; though they tried. The means to the end was the influence of CIAM (Congrès International d'Architecture Moderne), 'the Jesuits of the new faith', founded in 1928 'at the invitation of the Swiss *animateur* Siegfried Giedion':[58] the Swiss connection, again, visible also five years later when Giedion took the initiative in starting the Modern Architecture Research group, MARS, in London. By 1938 Corbusier was haranguing the British faithful:

> The benefits of the new architecture must not be confined to the homes of the few who enjoy the privilege of taste or money. They must be widely diffused so as to brighten the homes, and thus the lives, of millions upon millions of workers . . . It naturally postulates the most crucial issue of our age: a great campaign for the rational re-equipment of whole countries regarded as indivisible units.[59]

He was preaching to the converted, but there were as yet not many of them. In the 1930s, despite trips abroad, most local authorities regarded flats as an unfortunate necessity, and only two schemes – one in London, one the famous Quarry Hill flats in Leeds, which originated from a visit of two councillors to Vienna – even broke the five-storey barrier.[60]

Seven years later, all was changed. There was a huge, pent-up political force. By the end of the war, a real revolution had already occurred: government in Britain had assumed responsibility for the welfare of the people in a way that would have been unthinkable in the 1930s.[61] Associated with this was an extraordinary sense that Britain must be rebuilt, that the slums must be swept away. At Plymouth, one of the worst-bombed cities, Lord Astor, the Lord Mayor, and a group of councillors received John Reith, Minister of Works; that evening, Reith witnessed an extraordinary sight:

> Two thousand people were dancing in the open air – an idea of Waldorf Astor's. Below them was spread the awful havoc lately wrought on their city;

[57] Evenson, 1973, 180.   [58] Esher, 1981, 37.   [59] cit. ibid.

[60] Ravetz, 1974, 133, 140, 144; Daunton, 1984, 140–2.

[61] Titmuss, 1950, 506.

not far away across the sea the enemy. As they danced the summer evening into night I saw a coastal forces flotilla steam out from their Devonport anchorage in single line ahead; there was business for them to do, and they would probably do it all the better for what they could see on the Hoe.[62]

Astor told him that as a result of their meeting, all opposition to the idea of planning had disappeared. In London, Abercrombie and Forshaw opened their County of London Plan with a picture that, decades later, leaps out of the page and sears the eyes: it shows a poor East End street, totally devastated, the pathetic belongings of the people loaded on to a truck. In the foreground, the children stare at the camera, as in mute accusation. Under it is a quotation from Winston Churchill.

> Most painful is the number of small houses inhabited by working folk which has been destroyed . . . We will rebuild them, more to our credit than some of them were before. London, Liverpool, Manchester, Birmingham may have much more to suffer, but they will rise from their ruins, more healthy, and, I hope, more beautiful . . . In all my life I have never been treated with so much kindness as by the people who suffered most.[63]

Abercrombie and Forshaw showed just how huge the task would be. They recognized that 'there is abundant evidence . . . that for families with children, houses are preferred to flats. They provide a private garden and yard at the same level as the main rooms of the dwelling, and fit the English temperament'.[64] But to put everyone in houses would mean that two-thirds or three-quarters of the people would have to move elsewhere. Their preference was for half houses, half flats, at 100 to the net residential acre, but even this would mean too big an overspill problem – too big, they felt, to be balanced by equivalent out-movement of jobs. So they settled on their famous inner-London density of 136 per acre, which – on the basis of the research they did – put one-third of the people in houses, and some 60 per cent in eight- and ten-storey flats; about a half of the families with two children would have to go into flats, but even this density meant an overspill of close to four in ten of all the people living in this zone in 1939. To obtain it, the old rigid 80-foot height limit on residential blocks should be replaced by a more flexible system.[65] All this, in due course, was embodied into the statutory development plan of 1951.

A whole generation was waiting for the call: the generation that had flooded from the forces into the British architectural schools, determined at last to create the brave new world. Frederic Osborn wrote to Lewis Mumford in 1952 about the cult of Corbusier at the Architectural Association school: 'the young men under his influence are completely

[62] Reith, 1949, 428.   [63] Forshaw and Abercrombie, 1943, frontispiece.
[64] Ibid. 77.   [65] Ibid. 79–83, 117–19.

FIGURE 7.8   *Bombed London East End street.*
The frontispiece from Forshaw and Abercrombie's 1943 County of London plan, which says it all.

impervious to economic or human considerations. . . . it was just as if I had, in my youth, questioned the divinity of Christ. I had the same impression of animal unreason.'[66] There was, as one chronicler wrote, 'the tradition of Newness . . . a special blend of *avant-garde* eccentricity' which 'can be continually traced through the AA. It owes something to its being an international organism just resting on English soil. . . . The AA has always been open to the incoherent, uncompromising, culturally-lateral musings of foreigners who turn up in London.'[67] Into this cultural hothouse,

> Rushing back to qualify as architects, the first post-war generation were full of enthusiasm for technology. . . . To suggest a better and special world was no arrogance – merely their inheritance. . . . Soon there were two essential sources of inspiration – Corb and Mies . . . the Ville Radieuse and the Unité d'habitation suggested a model to be applied by good hard socialist principles in good hard modernist materials.[68]

[66] Hughes, 1971, 205.   [67] Cook, 1983, 32.   [68] Ibid. 33.

Soon, as perhaps only it could, the AA was out-Corbuing Corbu. By
1954 there was Ronald Jones's Life Structure: a land-ship 2,360 m. long,
560 m. high and 200 m. wide:

> ... thermal energy tapped from a mantle of molten rock 2900 km deep will
> release man through an energy spiral to gear him on a fantastic journey on
> a nuclear earth-ship. ... Unit cities will have core, administration, elected
> government, arts and creative centres, universities, specialist colleges,
> institutes, sports and recreation stadia, stereo cinemas, hospitals, hypermarkets,
> civic shopping centres. Core areas will be linked by horizontal, vertical and
> diagonal travelators ... each metropolitan city and town will be planned to
> grow to first, second, third and fourth dimensions in response to human
> ecological need.[69]

Like so much that followed from the basement at Bedford Square, it was
good clean juvenile fantasy. The problem – as Cook details, and as the
AA's own retrospective catalogue shows – was that before many years
passed, as successive waves of students passed out into the real world, the
fantasies got turned into reality. Jones's own creation became the Hongkong
and Shanghai Bank (though its architect did not study at the AA); a high-
density housing scheme for Paddington (1956) became Parkhill in Sheffield
(1961) and Western Rise in Islington (1969); a warehouse (1957) became
the Leicester University Engineering Department (1963); housing of 1961
turned up in Milton Keynes in 1975. By that time, further flights of fantasy
were still lined up on the Bloomsbury runway: a house built of sugar-puffs
packets, or the 1971 scheme for a 'Sand Castle. A brothel for oil miners
in the Sahara ... constructed from continuous plastic tube, filled with
sand *in situ*, and wound up into a series of interconnecting vaults.'[70] By
then, 'comprehensive urbanism' had ceased to be an acceptable subject of
conversation: the winds from Europe had changed.[71] But its monuments,
from generations of AA graduates, were scattered across the face of urban
England.

The *Architectural Review* had led the attack as early as 1953 with an
editorial from J. M. Richards lambasting the early new towns for their lack
of urbanity, which was blamed on too low densities and the evil influence
of the Town and Country Planning Association.[72] In 1955 it published
'Outrage', the celebrated onslaught by Ian Nairn on the quality of British
urban design, which was uniquely influential in the general British
intelligentsia; it announced

> ... a prophecy of doom: the prophecy that if what is called development is
> allowed to multiply at the present rate, then by the end of the century Great
> Britain will consist of isolated oases of preserved monuments in a desert of
> wire, concrete roads, cosy plots and bungalows. There will be no real

[69] Ibid. 33–4.   [70] Ibid. 41.   [71] Ibid. 40.   [72] Richards, 1953, 32.

distinction between town and country . . . Upon this new Britain the REVIEW bestows a name in the hope that it will stick: SUBTOPIA.[73]

The conclusion followed inexorably: 'The more complicated our industrial system, and the greater our population, the *bigger* and *greener* should be our countryside, the *more* compact and neater should be our towns.'[74] Accordingly, two years later the editors launched Counter-Attack, a campaign against Subtopia.[75] Meanwhile, in 1955 the Royal Institute of British Architects had run an influential symposium on high flats, opened by Dame Evelyn Sharp, the Permanent Secretary of the Ministry of Housing and Local Government, who had quoted a poem on their beauty.[76]

There were plenty of allies. The farm lobby went back to the fundamentalism of the Scott Report on Rural Land Use of 1942[77] with its insistence on trying to save every possible last acre for agriculture. The sociologists weighed in with Michael Young and Peter Willmott's enormously influential *Family and Kinship in East London*, which argued that by exporting people from London to overspill estates the planners were destroying a uniquely rich pattern of working-class folk-life.[78] In vain did the agricultural economist Gerald Wibberley show that the farmland was surplus to national needs, or Peter Stone calculate the true costs of building high;[79] to no avail did F. J. Osborn tirelessly campaign against subsidies for high flats.[80] The politics were against them; the government wanted urban containment, and an end to the new towns programme, at any cost.

The Great Rebuild

All this, admittedly, was a private movement among the architects. But it had great significance, because it tweaked sympathetic political chords. In 1955 the Conservative Government, in the form of Housing Minister Duncan Sandys, launched a major slum-clearance programme that was to run for nearly two decades, and simultaneously encouraged local authorities around the major cities to designate green belts in order to contain urban growth; coupled with a birth rate which started unexpectedly to rise that very year, this soon produced an impossible land-budget arithmetic.[81] Land acquisition costs rose, especially after changes in the law in 1959. The big cities, many of which were not averse to keeping their own people rather than exporting them to new and expanded towns, read all this as a signal to build dense and build high.[82] The big builders were ready to move in,

---

[73] Nairn, 1955, 365.   [74] Ibid. 368.   [75] *Architectural Review*, 1957, *passim*.
[76] Dunleavy, 1981, 135, 165.   [77] G.B. Ministry of Works and Planning, 1943.
[78] Young and Willmott, 1957.   [79] Wibberley, 1959, Stone, 1959, 1961.
[80] Osborn, 1955.   [81] Hall et al., 1973, II. 56-9; Cooney, 1974, 160.
[82] Ibid., 161-2.

FIGURE 7.9   *The Great Rebuild in the East End.*
A 1965 picture with the job half-complete: the old two-storey terraces on the left,
LCC tower blocks and nondescript borough slabs on the right.

and sold their ability to solve the cities' housing problems fast through package deals.[83] And the government, despite a barrage of protest from Osborn at the TCPA, obligingly gave them the special subsidies they needed for the job: from 1956, three times as much for a flat in a fifteen-storey block as for a house.[84] Dutifully, the proportion of high-rise in the total public-housing programme rose year by year: units in five-storey and more blocks were about 7 per cent of the total in the late 1950s, as much as 26 per cent in the mid-1960s.[85]

In all this, there were extraordinary contradictions, even in individuals. Richard Crossman, who as Sandys's successor nearly a decade later spearheaded the Labour Government's accelerated slum-clearance and housing drive, could record in his diary that he did not like the idea of people living in huge blocks of high-rise housing, yet almost simultaneously

[83] Ibid. 168; Dunleavy, 1981, 72, 114.
[84] Dunleavy, 1981, 37; Cooney, 1974, 163.
[85] Ibid., 152.

encourage even bigger programmes of destruction and industrialized building: 'In conversation I asked why it was only 750 houses they were building at Oldham; why not rebuild the whole thing? Wouldn't that help Laing, the builders? 'Of course, it would', said Oliver [Cox], 'and it would help Oldham too'. . . . I drove back to the Ministry . . . warmed and excited.'[86]

The London County Council's immensely prestigious Architect's Department, under first Robert Matthew, then Leslie Martin, provided a model in the early years; it had an unusually free hand, because the Ministry's ordinary cost sanctions did not apply to it.[87] It first produced 'the great Corbusian slabs' which culminated at the end of the 1950s in Alton West, Roehampton, the most complete homage to – and only true realization of – *La Ville radieuse* in the world; then began 'the era of the high towers, slimmer, less oppressive, and of course more highly subsidized':[88] 384 of them, in all, completed between 1964 and 1974. After the reorganization of 1965, the new boroughs made their own distinctive contributions like Southwark's huge megastructures in north Peckham, later to become some of London's most problematic blocks.

Some few among the great British provincial cities tried to compete in prestige. Two AA graduates headed the team that developed Park Hill, the great wall of deck-access flats that juts like a fortress above the centre of Sheffield and that, it must in fairness be said, is still highly successful with its tenants. Glasgow hired Basil Spence for the Gorbals and then built huge towers up to the city's edge; here, where the tenants all had a totally un-English tradition of high-density tenement living, there were few consistent problems with the design except for those with children, unsurprising since four in five children lived above the fourth floor.[89] But there were many other places where the architect was uninspired or non-existent, and where tenants found themselves uprooted into hurriedly constructed system-built flats lacking amenities, environment, community; lacking, in fact, almost anything except a roof and four walls.

The remarkable fact was how long it took for anyone to see that it was wrong. In order to appreciate why, it is necessary to do something that for anyone born after 1960 requires an effort of imagination: to appreciate just how bad were the dense rows of smoke-blackened slums that the towers replaced. The fact that later on the bulldozers started to remove sound and savable houses may obscure the fact that most were neither. As Lionel Esher says, 'even the preservationists saw the great mass of our Victorian 'twilight areas' as expendable. Six years of war had reduced those parts of London and the great provincial cities to a sinister squalor that recalled the darkest passages of *Bleak House*.'[90] In Ravetz's words, 'For two full

[86] Crossmasn, 1975, 81.   [87] Dunleavy, 1981, 170.   [88] Esher, 1981, 129.
[89] Jephcott, 1971, 140.   [90] Esher, 1981, 45.

decades . . . any social disbenefits of clean-sweep planning and its transformation of the town passed unremarked or than by cranks, a few people with residual ideals from the 1940s, or those who lamented the passing of the old on artistic grounds.'[91] It was not the fact of clean-sweep planning that began to be criticized, but the form it took.

Accentuated by the media after the disastrous collapse of Ronan Point, an east-London system-built tower block, in a gas explosion of 1968, the criticism soon became deafening. In fact the subsidy system had been recast the previous year, and local authorities were already phasing out their high-rise blocks. Now, everything was suddenly wrong with them: they leaked, they condensed, they blew up, the lifts did not work, the children vandalized them, old ladies lived in fear. All of this had some basis: Kenneth Campbell, in charge of housing design at the LCC and GLC from 1959 to 1974, listed three failures, the lifts (too few, too small, too slow), the children (too many), the management (too little).[92]

But, in fairness to the Corbusians, some things should be said. First, though some London estates were directly inspired by the master, and some of these proved design disasters, many others up and down Britain were bought off the peg by local authorities too lazy or unimaginative to hire architects and planners of their own. It was Crossman, visiting Wigan as early as 1965, who commented on its 'enormous building programme' of 'an appalling dimness and dullness', adding that 'they have built a Wigan that in 2000 will look just as bad as the old 1880 Wigan looks in the eyes of the 1960s.'[93] Secondly, Corbusier never advocated putting people (as distinct from jobs) in high towers; his proletarian housing would have looked more like Manchester's huge Hulme Estate, the biggest urban renewal project ever carried out in Europe, which consisted of medium-rise blocks but also proved a design disaster. In fact, the architectural fashion that followed the high-rise era – high-density low-rise – had proved a failure in Glasgow immediately after World War Two[94] and would later be criticized just as severely:

> High-density low-rise in practice meant mobs of children in echoing bricky courtyards, and mobs meant vandalism. . . . They became 'hard-to-let', i.e. lettable only to the poorest and most disorderly families, who seldom had cars to occupy the now mandatory basement garages, and whose children wrecked the few they had.[95]

Ironically, this too was a Corbusian solution. All of it missed the real criticism, which was of design solutions laid down on people without regard to their preferences, ways of life, or plain idiosyncrasies; laid down, further, by architects who – as the media delighted to discover – themselves invariably lived in charming Victorian villas. (When later some actually

[91] Ravetz, 1980, 89.   [92] Esher, 1981, 129–30.   [93] Crossman, 1975, 341.
[94] Armstrong and Wilson, 1973, 74–9.   [95] Esher, 1981, 134.

lived in the places they were designing, as did Ralph Erskine's site architect Vernon Gracie in the famous Byker Wall at Newcastle, it was a matter for comment.) The main result of this failure, of which Corbusier is as fully culpable as any of his followers, was that the middle-class designers had no real feeling for the way a working-class family lived. In their world,

> Mum isn't isolated at home with the babies, she is out shopping at Harrods. The children, when small, are taken to Kensington Gardens by Nannie. At the age of eight they go to a preparatory school and at thirteen to a public school, both residential. And during the holidays they are either away in the country, or winter-sporting, sailing and so on: golden and brown in the playful wind and summer sun. At any rate they are not hanging around on the landing or playing with the dustbin lids.[96]

The rich, then, could always live well at high densities, because they had services; that is why those quotations of Corbusier were so telling. But for ordinary people, as Ward says, the suburbs have great advantages: privacy, freedom from noise, greater freedom to make a noise yourself. To get this at a high density requires expensive treatment, generally not possible in public housing. Above all, the problem is one of children: for 'unless they get a chance to play out their childhood, they are certainly going to make a nuisance of themselves when they are older.'[97] And this is especially true, as Jephcott concluded in 1971, for families with children that are less well equipped educationally, living in high-density high-rise: 'local authorities should discontinue this form of housing except for a limited range of carefully selected tenants or in cases of extreme pressure.'[98] Corbusier, of course, was blissfully unconscious of all this, because he was both middle-class and childless.[99]

Urban Renewal in America

The Americans discovered some of all this even before the British, and it is interesting to ask why. One reason is that they started earlier. Their urban-renewal programme began with the Housing Act of 1949 and the amending Act of 1954, and stems from even earlier origins: the 1937 report of the Urbanism Committee of the National Resources Planning Board, *Our Cities: their Role in the National Economy*, with its stress on urban decay caused by obsolescent land-uses, and the very influential short pamphlet of 1941 by Alvin Hansen and Guy Greer, which developed this argument and argued that federal aid would be needed to buy blighted property, the cities in return being required to draw up plans for redevelopment.[100] The

---

[96] Ward, 1976, 51.   [97] Ibid. 54.   [98] Jephcott, 1971, 131.
[99] Anthony, 1966, 286.   [100] Greer and Hansen, 1941, 3–4, 6, 8.

resulting 1949 Act represented a strange but successful coalition of conservative and radical interests: federal money could be applied to renewing outworn parts of cities, but principally residential parts; yet adequate housing tools were not provided.[101]

To understand why, it is necessary to penetrate this unlikely coalition a little deeper. Congress had passed a landmark public housing measure, the Wagner Act, as long ago as 1937. This had been the outcome of a bitter and protracted struggle between powerful interest groups. On one side were liberal housing experts like Catherine Bauer, lining up with the construction unions. On the other was the National Association of Real Estate Boards and its research arm, the Urban Land Institute. NAREB and ULI were all for federal mortgage insurance, a principle they had won when the Federal Housing Association was established in 1934. They were all against public housing. The resulting compromise established public housing as a temporary expedient for the deserving poor: the newly unemployed, who could be expected to buy their own houses as soon as the economy lifted off again. It would exclude the old poor: the predominantly black, really poor underclass. The means to discriminate lay in the finances of the act: federal funds would pay for land acquisition and development, not for running costs, which must be met from the rent. Really poor families would thus never be able to get in.[102] At the end of the 1940s, that barrier fell: welfare families began to enter the projects. But, since the financial arrangements stayed unchanged, the resulting contradictions soon after produced catastrophic consequences.[103]

The 1949 and 1954 Acts represented another triumph of the NAREB–ULI lobby. Their aim was not cheap housing, but commercial redevelopment of blighted areas at the edge of downtown, on the model successfully used by Pittsburgh in its Golden Triangle redevelopment. Though bitterly opposed to NAREB, the public-housing movement went along with the idea of urban renewal in the hope that they too could achieve their objectives.[104] In fact, though presented as a measure to secure 'the realization as soon as feasible of the goal of a decent home and a suitable living environment for every American family', urban renewal was kept separate from public housing and put in the hands of the Housing and Home Finance Agency, which promptly worked to discourage low-rent housing and to encourage commercial redevelopment; the clause in the 1949 Act, stipulating that the area should be 'predominantly residential', was progressively eroded.[105] Using the powers to tear down slums asnd offer prime land to private developers with government subsidy, cities

---

[101] Salisbury, 1964, 784–7; Lowe, 1967, 31–2; Mollenkopf, 1983, 78; Fox, 1985, 80–100.   [102] Friedman, 1968, 104–9.
[103] Meehan, 1977, 15–16, 19.   [104] Weiss, 1980, 54–9, 62.   [105] Weiss, 1980, 67.

sought 'the blight that's right', as Charles Abrams inimitably put it.[106] In city after city – Philadelphia, Pittsburgh, Hartford, Boston, San Francisco – the areas that were cleared were the low-income, black sections next to the central business district; and the promised alternative housing did not materialize because 'public housing, like the Moor in *Othello*, had done its reverence in justifying urban renewal and could now go.'[107]

The agents were 'growth coalitions', often consisting of younger business-men: bankers, developers, construction corporations, realtors, retailers. But they were not just that, because if they were they probably would have failed; they also included liberal-technocratic mayors (Lee in New Haven, Daley in Chicago) and they were supported by labour councils, construction-trade councils, good-government groups, professional planners and others, even the public-housing lobby.[108] And they also involved a small, but powerful, new group of professional urban renewal executives: Robert Moses in New York, Ed Logue in New Haven, Boston and New York, Justin Herman in San Francisco.[109] As Catherine Bauer Wurster said, 'seldom had such a diverse group of would-be angels tried to dance on the same small pin.'[110]

As a result, of course, the coalition pulled different ways; and as it did, it often pulled apart. One group, the developers and their allies, wanted large-scale redevelopment in the interests of established downtown firms – but also to attract outside business, which could bring them into conflict with local interests. They also wanted to do so, if possible, through administrative arrangements that bypassed local interests. But increasingly, through the 1950s and especially the 1960s, they fell foul of other groups: local residents conserving and defending their neighbourhoods, small businesses threatened by clearance, who could form anti-renewal coalitions.[111] That story replicated itself in city after American city.

New York was special; but, under Robert Moses (1888–1981), New York always was. In his nearly fifty years of multiple office, he became indisputably 'America's greatest builder', responsible for public works which, in terms of 1968 dollars, totalled $27 billion.[112] He built parkways, bridges, tunnels, expressways. And, when the urban renewal spigot began to flow, he built public housing. From 1949 to 1957, New York City spent $267 million on urban renewal; all other cities in the United States spent $133 million. When he resigned from the urban-renewal post, in 1960, he had built more, in terms of completed apartments, than all the rest put

[106] Abrams, 1965, 74, 118; Bellush and Hausknecht, 1967, 12; Arnold, 1973, 36; Frieden and Kaplan, 1975, 23; Kleniewski, 1984, 205.
[107] Abrams, 1965, 82; Kleniewski, 1984, 210–11.
[108] Mollenkopf, 1978, 135–6; Weiss, 1980, 68–9; Kleniewski, 1984, 212–13.
[109] Mollenkopf, 1978, 134; Hartman, 1984, 18.   [110] Mollenkopf, 1983, 5.
[111] Fainstein and Fainstein, 1983b, 255.   [112] Caro, 1974, 9–10.

together.[113] He did it, as he had done all the others before, by a unique combination of two qualities which he had learned in very early professional life: his rooted belief in top–down planning by the uncorruptible, public-spirited civil servant, as most finely represented by the British system which he so much admired; and his bitter early discovery that, in the American urban jungle at least, political connections also mattered.[114] From these two foundations he built a system of power, influence and patronage that made him almost impregnable – finally to mayors, to governors, even to Presidents:[115] 'Honest graft, endorsements, campaign contributions, Robert Moses provided the machine with everything it needed. And as a result, he bent the machine to his ends, mobilized its power and influence behind his plans.'[116]

Ironically, his last and biggest achievement, urban renewal, finally proved his undoing: 'Democracy had not solved the problem of building large-scale public works, so Moses solved it by ignoring democracy.'[117] True, as throughout his life he took care to build a broad and diverse coalition of interest groups: hospitals and universities in search of land, cultural and business promotion groups, even trades unions interested in co-operative housing, and the always supportive *New York Times*.[118] He scorned rehabilitation: 'They think we should . . . fix up with rubber bands, Scotch tape and violins.'[119]

But finally, small groups of citizens began to protest; Moses tried to ride roughshod over them, but found that he could not. Among them was a housewife and architectural journalist in West Greenwich Village, Jane Jacobs, who mobilized local opinion after she found that Moses planned to tear her neighbourhood down.[120] She won, and the experience proved the trigger that set off one of the most influential books in twentieth-century planning history. By that time, Moses was no longer in charge of renewal; and in 1968, stripped of the last of his offices at the age of seventy-nine, Robert Moses was the Master Builder no more.[121]

New Haven, the other city that first and most brilliantly exploited the new powers, provides a further classic illustration: its mayor Richard Lee came from the Catholic working class of the city, but could move easily at different levels of society including the Yale establishment; he was extremely sensitive to shifts in opinion, and was a master of public relations.[122] He formed a close team with Edward C. Logue, his Development Administrator, and Maurice Rotival, his Redevelopment Director, in which it was 'only a slight oversimplification to say that it was the Mayor's task to get the support of the major political interests in the city, the Development

[113] Lowe, 1967, 48; Caro, 1974, 12.   [114] Caro, 1974, 52–5, 70–1, 85.
[115] Ibid. 427–31.   [116] Ibid. 740.   [117] Ibid. 848.   [118] Lowe, 1967, 86–8.
[119] Ibid. 92.   [120] Ibid. 101–3.   [121] Caro, 1974, 1144.   [122] Dahl, 1961, 118–19.

Administrator's to insure the participation of developers, and the Redevelopment Director's to win the consent of the Federal agencies.'[123] Lee's coalition embraced Democrat leaders, Republican business, Yale administration and faculty, ethnic groups and trade unions; the Citizens' Action Committee, a deliberate creation by Lee, 'virtually decapitated the opposition.'[124] The result was the demolition of a major – and increasingly black – slum area to build downtown offices, aided by the use of federal highway funds to build a downtown distributor.[125]

Pittsburgh, another pioneer – even before 1949, in fact – is the same kind of story. After decades of moribund local leadership, a new business elite determined that the city must take action to prevent economic collapse. As early as 1943 it set up an Allegheny Conference on Regional Development (ACAD) to build a coalition to revitalize the downtown area. The result was an unlikely alliance between a Republican group of corporate leaders and a Democratic political boss. An Urban Renewal Authority was set up in 1946. It obtained unprecedented powers – challenged, but established as constitutional – to condemn property for city planning purposes. Renaissance I, as it came to be called, was fundamentally a private development operation, with the public sector playing a facilitatory role, and with close, overlapping membership of the main agencies: the Allegheny Conference, the Urban Renewal Authority, the Planning Commission. Over the next two decades the plans rebuilt more than a quarter of the so-called Golden Triangle, displacing at least 5,400 low-income, principally black, families, and replacing them principally by offices which have made the whole area a 9.00 to 5.00 commuter zone.[126]

San Francisco was yet another classic case. The argument for urban renewal came from organized business through the Bay Area Council, 'a private regional government', of 1944, and the Blyth–Zellerbach Committee of 1956. The San Francisco Redevelopment Agency of 1948, a year before the 1949 Act, neatly anticipated its powers; in 1958, it was reshaped under Blyth–Zellerbach impetus. Justin Herman, 'St Justin' to the downtown business group, the 'White Devil' to the low-income residents of the Western Addition and the South of Market areas next door, became its director in 1959. He stood for the sanitization of these areas, meaning the removal of their inhabitants. As one business supporter eloquently put it: 'You certainly can't expect us to erect a 50 million dollar building in an area where dirty old men will be going around exposing themselves to our secretaries.'[127]

[123] Ibid. 129.   [124] Ibid. 133.
[125] Lowe, 1967, 406, 417; Fainstein and Fainstein, 1983a, 40.
[126] Lubove, 1969, 87, 106–11, 127–31, 139–40; Lowe, 1967, 134, 140–1; Stewman and Tarr, 1982, 63–5, 74–6, 103–5.
[127] cit. Hartman, 1984, 51.

In fact, Chester Hartman argues, the 'skid row' label was a carefully cultivated image to justify renewal. Though the area south of Market Street was a zone of residential hotels overwhelmingly occupied by men, most were simply retired or disabled. They organized, and found a leader in an eighty-year-old trade unionist, George Woolf. In an epic legal fight he forced the Renewal Agency in 1970 to agree to build low-rent units. Herman, incensed, called the tenants' lawyer 'a clever, well-financed, able, ambulance-chasing lawyer'. A year later, he died of a heart attack.

Further lawsuits came and went during the following decade. While that happened, Urban Renewal funds were replaced by Community Development Block Grants, which spread funding across the city; the Renewal Agency lost its independent funding, and the Mayor's Office took greater control. But meanwhile, the office-building boom boomed ever more loudly. By the late 1980s, after three decades of confrontation, the South of Market redevelopment was nearing completion. The citizens of San Francisco, by now highly organized to protect their neighbourhoods, belatedly passed a stringent measure to restrict further office growth anywhere in their city.[128]

The astonishing feature of these coalitions in those years, in fact, is just how successful they were in pushing through policies that were clearly against the interests of voters. Boston's West End, an old-established and extremely well-knit Italian community – an urban village, in Herbert Gans's words – was a classic instance. On the advice of mortgage bankers, the clearance plans were extended to include non-blighted areas. The general population thought the whole area was a slum because the press told it so. The locals believed that it would never happen. The developers wanted the land for high-income housing, and the city went along.[129] Later, Fried found that the West Enders, particularly the traditional working class among them, had been profoundly affected by the experience, rather as if a loved one had died.[130]

But all good things come to an end. By the mid-1960s, the criticism of urban renewal had become deafening. Charles Abrams pointed out that many of the cleared areas – Washington Square South in New York City, Bunker Hill in Los Angeles, Diamond Heights in San Francisco – were, like the West End, 'no slum at all in the real estate sense': they were so because officials said so.[131] Martin Anderson calculated that to the end of 1965 renewal would evict 1 million people, most of whom paid very low rents; three-quarters of these had relocated themselves, nine in ten of them to substandard dwellings at higher rents. Overall, to March 1961 the programme had destroyed four times as many units as had been built;

[128] Fainstein et al., 1983a, 216, 226; Hartman, 1984, 185, 309–11.
[129] Gans, 1962, 4, 283–90, 318.   [130] Fried, 1963, 167–8.
[131] Abrams, 1965, 118–22.

typically, land was left vacant, since the average scheme took twelve years to complete. Nearly 40 per cent of the new construction was not for housing; and of the replacement housing units, most were privately built high-rise apartments commanding high rents.[132] Thus, though 85 per cent of all areas certified for assistance in the Act's first ten years were residential before redevelopment, only 50 per cent were so afterwards.[133] Or, as Scott Greer put it, 'At a cost of more than three billion dollars the Urban Renewal Agency (URA) has succeeded in materially reducing the supply of low-cost housing in American cities.'[134] Chester Hartman concluded that perversely, the effect of the programme had been to make the rich richer and the poor poorer.[135] Herbert Gans spelt out the absurdity of it all:

> Suppose that the government decided that jalopies were a menace to public safety and a blight on the beauty of the highways, and therefore took them away from their drivers. Suppose, then, that to replenish the supply of automobiles, it gave these drivers a hundred dollars each to buy a good used car and also made special grants to General Motors, Ford and Chrysler to lower the cost – though not necessarily the price – of Cadillacs, Lincolns and Imperials by a few hundred dollars. Absurd as this may sound, change the jalopies to slum housing, and I have described, with only slight poetic license, the first fifteen years of a federal program called urban renewal.[136]

How could this have happened? Several critics underlined the fact that the cynical explanation was not necessarily the right one: though some had profited hugely, 'there is something that one can only call civic patriotism' which 'blends nicely with financial interests.' In the growth coalition, many members had pure motives: 'mayors concerned with the central city tax base, civic leaders with a patriotic desire to "make our city center beautiful", businessmen with deep commitments to downtown real estate, and those who believe that government should innovate in the public interest' had together produced 'a program that rewards the strong and punishes the weak.'[137] The programme could only be implemented locally; and locally, most cities wanted the revival of downtown and the return of the middle class from the suburbs.[138]

Some of the worst excesses of urban renewal were later avoided, true: more areas got rebuilt for housing, there was more low-rent housing, more blacks got rehoused.[139] And clearly, since rehousing was one of the last things that the programme actually achieved in its first fifteen years of life, most of the ills of American urban renewal could not be laid at Corbusier's door. But the Corbusian and the urban-renewal prescriptions did share what Martin Anderson graphically called the Federal Bulldozer approach.

[132] Anderson, 1964, 54–67, 73, 93.   [133] Grigsby, 1863, 324.
[134] Greer, 1965, 3.   [135] Hartman, 1964, 278.   [136] Gans, 1967b, 465.
[137] Greer, 1965, 94, 122.   [138] Grigsby, 1963, 323.   [139] Sanders, 1980, 106–7, 112.

What emerges from the American critiques is that it might actually have been better to leave the poor alone: Greer quotes a local official: 'So what are we saying? The widow either has to live on $2 a month or she has to have substandard housing by those standards. There's real need for what we call secondary housing, and if we condemned it we'd wipe out the housing the people could afford.'[140] Add to this the psychic costs of breaking up old-established neighbourhoods, and the case becomes even stronger.

Counter-Attack: Jacobs and Newman

The failure of American urban renewal, and the increasing doubts about its British equivalent, help to explain the colossal impact in both countries of Jane Jacobs's *Death and Life of Great American Cities*, published in America in 1961, which rapidly became one of the most influential books in the short history of city planning. It was one of those classic cases of the right message at the right time. Jacobs hit out at both of the great orthodoxies on which city planning had based itself in its first half century of life. The garden-city movement was attacked on the ground that its 'prescription for saving the city was to do the city in', by defining 'wholesome housing in terms only of suburban physical qualities and small-town social qualities'; for good measure, it 'conceived of planning also as essentially paternalistic, if not authoritarian.'[141] The Corbusians were vilified for egotism: 'No matter how vulgarized or clumsy the design, how dreary and useless the open space, how dull the close-up view, an imitation of Le Corbusier shouts "Look what I made!" Like a great, visible ego it tells of someone's achievement.'[142]

The point, she argued, was that there was nothing wrong with high urban densities of people so long as they did not entail overcrowding in buildings: traditional inner-city neighbourhoods like New York's Brooklyn Heights, Philadelphia's Rittenhouse Square and San Francisco's North Beach were all good areas, though densely populated.[143] A good urban neighbourhood, she argued, actually needed 100 dwellings, equivalent perhaps to 200–300 people, per acre: a high density even for New York, and higher than almost anything in post-1945 London. But it could be achieved by cutting out open space:

> To say that cities need high dwelling densities and high net ground coverage, and I am saying they do, is conventionally regarded as lower than taking sides with a man-eating shark.
>
> But things have changed since the days when Ebenezer Howard looked at

[140] Greer, 1965, 46–7.   [141] Jacobs, 1962, 17, 19.   [142] Ibid. 23.   [143] Ibid. 202–5.

the slums of London and concluded that to save the people, city life must be abandoned.[144]

The Jacobs prescription amounted to keeping the inner-city neighbourhood more or less as it was before the planners had got their hands on it. It should have mixed functions and therefore land uses, to ensure that people were there for different purposes, on different time schedules, but using many facilities in common. It must have conventional streets on short blocks. It must mix blocks of different age and condition, including a significant share of old ones. And it must have a dense concentration of people, for whatever purpose they are there, including a dense concentration of residents.[145] It sounded good to her overwhelmingly middle-class readers. The irony, pointed out twenty years later, was that the result was the yuppification of the city:

> Urbanism proved as susceptible as modernism to having its egalitarian impulses subordinated to the consumer interests of the upper middle class. . . . It took over forty years to go from the first Bauhaus manifesto to the Four Seasons; it took only half that time to go from Jane Jacobs's apotheosis of her humble corner grocer to his replacement by Bonjour, Croissant and all that implies.[146]

The Dynamiting of Pruitt–Igoe

Yet, whatever the later implications, urbanism spelt doom for the Federal Bulldozer. But it took more than just that. Though by British standards America had built all too little public housing, still it had built some. And some of the biggest and most influential cities had followed a Corbusian model: St Louis, Chicago, Newark, among others. By the end of the 1970s, they were contemplating their abandonment. Many were 30- or 40-percent vacant. The classic case was Pruitt–Igoe: an award-winning 1955 project in St Louis, which achieved notoriety by being blown up seventeen years after it was built. That day, the demolition preserved for posterity on film, it became an instant symbol of all that was perceived as wrong with urban renewal, not merely in the United States but in the world at large.

When the Captain W. O. Pruitt Homes and the William L. Igoe Apartments were unveiled in 1951, the experimental high-rise design by the distinguished architect Minoru Yamasaki – a design never before used in the city of St Louis – was the subject of a laudatory article in the magazine *Architectural Forum*. The thirty-three identical blocks, containing

[144] Ibid. 218.   [145] Ibid. 152, 178, 187, 200.   [146] Muschamp, 1983, 168.

over 2,800 apartments, were completed in 1955–6. They were on a bare site open to transient traffic. To keep within cost limits, huge and arbitrary cuts were made during construction. Space inside the apartments, especially for the large families that came to occupy many of them, 'was pared to the bone and beyond to the marrow.'[147] Locks and door-knobs broke on first use, sometimes before occupancy. Window panes blew out. One lift failed on opening day. 'On the day they were completed, the buildings in Pruitt and Igoe were little more than steel and concrete warrens, poorly designed, badly equipped, inadequate in size, badly located, unventilated, and virtually impossible to maintain.'[148]

That would have been bad enough. But in addition, the tenants who came were not the ones for whom the blocks had been designed. The design, like that of most public housing down to the 1950s, was for the deserving poor. Most heads of households were to be employed males. St Louis in 1951 was a segregated city: Pruitt was all-black, but after public housing was desegregated by decision of the Supreme Court, the authority tried to integrate Igoe. To no avail: whites left, and blacks – including many welfare-dependent, female-head families – moved in. By 1965, more than two-thirds of the inhabitants were minors, 70 per cent of them under twelve; there were two and a half times as many women as men; women headed 62 per cent of the families; 38 per cent contained no employed person, and in only 45 per cent was employment the sole source of income.[149]

Rapidly, the development became a byword for disaster. Occupancy rates in Pruitt, 95 per cent in 1956, fell to 81 per cent six years later and to 72 per cent in 1965; Igoe started at less than 70 per cent and stayed at that level. The development began to deteriorate: pipes burst, there was a gas explosion. By 1966, resident poverty-programme workers recorded the scene:

> Glass, rubble and debris litter the streets, the accumulation is astonishing ... abandoned automobiles have been left in parking areas; glass is omnipresent; tin cans are strewn throughout, paper has been rained on and stuck in the cracked, hardened mud. Pruitt–Igoe from without looks like a disaster area. Broken windows are apparent in every building. Street lights

[147] Meehan, 1975, 35.   [148] Ibid. 73.   [149] Rainwater, 1970, 13.

FIGURE 7.10 AND 7.11   *Pruitt-Igoe.*
The world's most notorious high-rise housing project as it was supposed to look – and actually did look for a short while at the start – and at the moment of its demolition in 1972.

are inoperative . . . As the visitor nears the entrance to a building, the filth
and debris intensify. Abandoned rooms under the building are receptacles
for all matter of waste. Mice, roaches, and other vermin thrive in these open
areas . . .

The infamous skip-stop elevator is a revelation even for those considering
themselves prepared for anything. Paint has peeled from the elevator walls.
The stench of urine is overwhelming; ventilation in the elevators is non-
existent. . . . When the visitor emerges from the dark, stench-filled elevator
on to one of the building's gallery floors, he enters a grey concrete caricature
of an insane asylum. Institutional grey walls give way to institutional grey
floors. Rusty institutional-type screens cover windows in which no glass exists.
Radiators once used to heat these public galleries have been, in many
buildings, stripped from the walls. Incinerators, too small to accommodate
the quantity to [sic] refuse placed into them, have spilled over – trash and
garbage are heaped on the floors. Lightbulbs and fixtures are out; bare hot
wire often dangles from malfunctioning light sockets.[150]

In 1969, there was a nine-month rent strike, the longest in the history
of American public housing. At one point, twenty-eight of the thirty-four
elevators were inoperative. By 1970, the project was 65 per cent unoccupied.
In 1972, accepting the inevitable, the authority blew it up.

The question, asked by a whole series of academic observers, is how it
happened: in just a decade, a design showpiece had become one of the
worst urban slums in the United States. And there were as many
explanations as observers.

The first culprit, clearly, was the design. As Oscar Newman put it in a
celebrated analysis:

> The architect was concerned with each building as a complete, separate, and
> formal entity, exclusive of any consideration of the functional use of grounds
> or the relationship of a building to the ground area it might share with other
> buildings. It is almost as if the architect assumed the role of a sculptor and
> saw the grounds of the project as nothing more than a surface on which he
> was endeavoring to arrange a whole series of vertical elements into a
> compositionally pleasing whole.[151]

Or, as Jacobs would have said, it represented an architect's ego-trip.
Specifically, Pruitt–Igoe was designed – as were many similar Corbusian
layouts in American public housing of the early 1950s – on the basis of a
superblock of between four and twelve ordinary street blocks of the kind
Jane Jacobs commended, within which the high-rise blocks – in the Pruitt–
Igoe case, eleven-storey slabs at an average 50 units to the acre – were
freely positioned in the landscape, invariably with entry from the grounds,
not from the street.[152] This feature, plus the long high-level across decks,

[150] cit. Montgomery, 1985, 238.   [151] Newman, 1972, 59.   [152] Ibid. 56.

created the maximum possible area of what Newman, in a memorable phrase, called indefensible space: the decks, shown by the architect in his 1951 drawing as full of children, toys and (white) mothers, soon became vandalized and feared.[153]

The problem, as other observers found, was compounded by the rules of financial management imposed by Washington. Since rents must cover maintenance, and tenants could not pay the rents, the city cut maintenance. And even then tenants could not pay: in 1969, when a quarter of families were paying more than 50 per cent of their incomes for rent, they went on strike.[154] And the irony was that this non-policy of non-maintenance was being applied to apartments that had been extremely expensive to build: at $20,000 each in 1967 values, they were only a little cheaper to build than top-grade luxury apartments.[155]

The root of the problem, Newman found on deeper analysis, was the failure in architectural education to stress the need to learn how well or badly existing buildings worked, and then to improve the designs; 'the full extent of this tragedy is best appreciated when we realize that the most recognized of architects are often those who turn out the most dramatic failures.'[156] And this, in turn, was because there had been two camps in modern architecture, the 'social methodologists' and the 'style metaphysicians', but the United States had imported only the second, Corbusian, tradition.[157] This conclusion is supported by the finding that conventional low-rise developments, with similar mixes of tenants, had no such problems.[158]

But Newman was at pains to point out that design was not the only, or even the necessary, culprit. The worst deterioration occurred only after the Department of Housing and Urban Development changed its rules to admit problem families, many from rural backgrounds, into public housing, in 1965: 'In the intervening seven years, the high-rise buildings to which they were admitted have been undergoing systematic decimation';[159] not only Pruitt–Igoe, but other similar blocks (Rosen Apartments in Philadelphia, Columbus Homes in Newark) were likewise abandoned. The root cause was that very poor welfare families, with large numbers of children, with a deep fatalism about the power to influence their environment, could not cope with this kind of building, nor it with them. As one sociologist-observer, Lee Rainwater, observed, the ideals and aspirations of Pruitt–Igoeans were similar to those of other people, but they could not realize them:

> The realization of these Pruitt–Igoe ideals would produce a life hardly distinguishable from other working-class life, white or black. And it seems

[153] Ibid. 56–8.   [154] Meehan, 1979, 83; Montgomery, 1985, 232, 238.
[155] Meehan, 1975, 65; Meehan, 1979, 73–4.   [156] Newman, 1980, 322–3.
[157] Ibid. 294–5.   [158] Meehan, 1979, 86.   [159] Newman, 1972, 188.

likely that the resources necessary to maintain such a family life would require
the stability and level of income characteristic of the upper working class, a
level of income anywhere from 50 to more than 100 per cent higher than is
available to most families in Pruitt–Igoe.[160]

Middle- and upper-income families, with a proportion of families with
children that did not exceed 50 per cent, and with superintendents and at
least one parent supervising, could live comfortably in such environments,
but 'while a middle-class family will not perform too differently in one
building type versus another, the performance of a welfare family proves
to be greatly influenced by the physical environment'; for them, 'the high-
rise apartment building is to be strictly avoided.'[161] Colin Ward's statement,
exactly.

The Corbusian Legacy

The irony then was that the Corbusian city of towers was perfectly
satisfactory for the middle-class inhabitants whom he had imagined living
their gracious, elegant, cosmopolitan lives in *La Ville contemporaine*. It might
even work for the solid, tough, traditional tenement-dwellers of Glasgow,
for whom the transition from a Gorbals rear-end slum to the twentieth
floor seemed like the ascent to paradise. But, for a welfare mother born in
a Georgia shack and dumped in St Louis or Detroit with a brood of
uncontrollable children, it proved an urban disaster of the first magnitude.
The sin of Corbusier and the Corbusians thus lay not in their designs, but
in the mindless arrogance whereby they were imposed on people who could
not take them and could never, given a modicum of thought, ever have
been expected to take them.

The final irony is that, in cities all over the world, this was condemned
as the failure of 'planning'. Planning, in the common-or-garden sense,
means an orderly scheme of action to achieve stated objectives in the light
of known constraints. Planning is just what this was not.

---

[160] Rainwater, 1970, 50.   [161] Newman, 1972, 193.

The City
of Sweat Equity

Art was once the common possession of the whole people; it was the rule in the Middle Ages that the produce of handicraft was beautiful . . . today, it is prosperity that is externally ugly . . . we sit starving amidst our gold, the Midas of the ages.

William Morris
In *Forecasts of the Coming Century* (1897)

The Town Planning Movement is on this side a revolt of the peasant and the gardener, as on the other of the citizen, and these united by the geographer, from their domination by the engineer. Only when the mechanical energies of the Engineer are brought into line with all other aspects of the city, and these reunited in the service of life, can he change from blundering giant into helpful Hercules . . .

Patrick Geddes
Report on the Planning of Dacca (1917)

. . . if we are going to reform the world, and make it a better place to live in, the way to do it is not to talk about relationships of a political nature, which are inevitably dualistic, full of subjects and objects and their relationship to one another; or with programs full of things for other people to do. . . . The social values are right only if the individual values are right. The place to improve the world is first in one's heart and hands, and then work outward from there. Other people want to talk about how to expand the destiny of mankind. I just want to talk about how to fix a motorcycle. I think that what I have to say has more lasting value.

Robert M. Pirsig
Zen and the Art of Motorcycle Maintenance (1974)

8

The City
of Sweat Equity

The Autonomous Community:
Edinburgh, Indore, Lima, Berkeley, Macclesfield,
1890–1987

The reaction against the Corbusian city of towers brought the much belated triumph of the anarchist strain of planning thought, that had so heavily infused the early garden-city movement and its regional-planning derivative. So this history has not yet done with Geddes. He, more than anyone, contributed to planning theory the idea that men and women could make their own cities, thus escaping from mass industrialism to a world of craft activity, where once again things would look beautiful because they were made right. That strand is implicit in Kropotkin, explicit and central in the works of William Morris and Edward Carpenter; Unwin in turn based his philosophy on Morris and was an early member of Carpenter's Socialist group in Sheffield, where he heard Kropotkin lecture on the union of intellectual and craft work.[1]

But the main line runs through Geddes, whom Unwin met at the cheap cottages exhibition held at Letchworth in 1905.[2] It was Geddes who, as Kropotkin records in a letter of 1886 to Reclus 'now just got married, leaving his house and taking a very poor flat among the workers. Everywhere, in one form or another, one finds similar things. It is a complete reawakening. What direction will it take?'[3] Geddes himself described it, much later in his life, in a characteristic Geddesian outpouring:

> Social conscience was then stirring throughout the cities, and we had both felt it strongly – and so strengthened each other: so after a single winter of bonnie home . . . we crossed to the high James Court tenement of the Old Town opposite, with opposite view accordingly, and thus enabling us to endure, by facing and tackling of dirt and overcrowding and disorder of even more infernal slumdom than now exists in Edinburgh; and to begin such

[1] Jackson, F., 1985, 13–14, 17; Creese, 1966, 169–73.
[2] Jackson, F., 1985, 102–3. [3] Boardman, 1978, 87.

changes as might be, thus became problems as scientific, as technical, as had been those of living nature and its science for myself, or of music for my companion.[4]

They began with the basics:

> Beginning within our limited range, with flower-boxes for dull windows and colour-washing for even duller walls (than which there is no better, no simpler and no brighter beginnings for city improvements) we soon got to fuller cleanings and repairings, next even to renewals, at length to building as through Lawnmarket, Castle Hill to Ramsay Garden, of course with thanks to growing cooperation alike from students and citizens, increasingly becoming good neighbours.[5]

Their example spread:

> One by one, some denizens of the courts began to give their own time to the jobs that Geddes persuaded them to tackle with him, clearing, whitewashing, or gardening; nor could they work beside him, listening to his flow of ideas about the job in hand and the further possibilities, without capturing something of his sanguine spirit. For the first time they began to feel that something could be done to change their surroundings.[6]

James Mavor, a contemporary observer, thought that 'Geddes was really on the same track as Morris': furnishing their apartment with good Scots eighteenth-century furniture, he and his wife were providing examples for all to see 'of the surroundings of the period before the factory system had divorced the fine arts from production'; but, unlike Morris, he believed all this could be done incrementally.[7]

The result of all this a decade later was described by Israel Zangwill:

> Everywhere a litter of building operations, and we trod gingerly many a decadent staircase. Sometimes a double row of houses had already been knocked away, revealing a Close within a Close, eyeless house behind blind alley, and even so the diameter of the Court was still but a few yards ... Those sunless courts, entered by needles' eyes of apertures, congested with hellish, heaven-scaling barracks, reeking with refuse and evil odours, inhabited promiscuously by poverty and prostitution, worse than the worst slums of London itself. ... 'Do you wonder Edinburgh is renowned for medical schools?' asked the Professor grimly.[8]

Zangwill's comment is revealing: 'His own destruction was conservative in character; it was his aim to preserve the ancient note in the architecture, and to make a clean old Edinburgh of a dirty.'[9] But even conservative destruction did not come cheap: in 1896, after years in which he had earned £200 a year as part-time professor, he had acquired properties

---

[4] Ibid. 86.   [5] Ibid. 86–7.   [6] Mairet, 1957, 52.
[7] cit. Boardman, 1978, 89.   [8] cit. ibid. 146.   [9] Ibid.

worth more than £53,000. To save him from bankruptcy and his wife from nervous breakdown, that year his friends formed the Town and Gown Association, Limited, to take over most of these enterprises and put them at last on a business basis.[10] But years of recrimination followed, as Geddes accused the directors of timidity and conservatism.[11]

Geddes Goes to India

In 1914, already aged 60, Geddes sailed for India, to show his Civic Exhibition – which first saw life at the great international town planning meeting in London in 1910 – in Madras. It was a disaster: the boat carrying the exhibits was sunk by a German warship.[12] Yet, undiscouraged, in two months he travelled between two and three thousand miles, consulting on the improvement of Indian cities.[13] Here and in two subsequent visits, he developed his concept of 'conservative surgery' – or, in latter-day jargon, urban rehabilitation.[14] The resulting reports – at least twenty-four of them, perhaps thirty, some still awaiting discovery, some existing in unique copies in the India Office library in London, many of them evidently produced at extraordinary speed, a day at a time – include the best work Geddes did in his life.[15]

On that first visit, he was soon railing that

> I have a new fight before me, as with the Housing at Delhi. Here it is to be with the Sanitary Authority of the Madras Government, with its death-dealing Haussmanising [sic] and its squalid (Belfast 1858) industrial bye-laws, which it thinks, enacts and enforces as up-to-date planning . . . From the callous, contemptuous city bureaucrat at Delhi, I have now to tackle here the well-intentioned fanatic of sanitation – perhaps an even tougher proposition.[16]

He carried that battle from city to city. The fact was that even more than their brethren at home, the British in India had an obsession with drains; at the time of the Mutiny, losses from disease had been far greater than those from battle, and a Royal Commission of 1863 had pronounced:

> It is indeed impossible to separate the question of health, as it relates to troops, from the sanitary condition of the native population, especially as regards the occurrence of epidemics.

---

[10] Ibid. 146–7.   [11] Ibid. 164–6, 232–3.   [12] Ibid. 253.   [13] Ibid. 254.
[14] Mairet, 1957, 180; Boardman, 1978, 264–5.
[15] Tyrwhitt, 1947, 102–3; Geddes, 1965a, vi–vii; Geddes, 1965b, *passim*; Meller, 1981, 60–5.
[16] Mairet, 1957, 161.

The habits of the natives [it had warned] are such that, unless they are closely watched, they cover the whole neighbouring surface with filth.[17]

So for half a century the Sanitary Branch of the Home Department, and the Sanitary Commissioners, had zealously worked to extend drains and build latrines for the congested old Indian cities. Early Indian town-planning education had been largely in the hands of military engineers,[18] but, according to Geddes, they were plain wrong. At Balrampur in 1917, he wrote, 'since drains are for cities, not cities for drains, Town-Planning cannot but reverse the customary procedure for Engineering, and begin with the general problem of City Improvement, though with drainage of course as one of its many factors.'[19]

The engineer's approach led to absurdities such as provision of water-closets that cost twice as much as the value of the houses.[20] Against this belief that 'individuals and cities are only to be sanitated from behind, or from below upwards' which was 'one of the most depressing of our many modern superstitions', he suggested: 'Why not a large barrow, regularly and easily removable by hand labour: or in larger places, even a spare cart and this brightly painted, and standing on a cemented platform which can be kept comparatively dust-free in its decently screened yet accessible corner?'[21] The moral should be, he suggested, 'instead of the nineteenth century European city panacea – of 'Everything to the Sewer!' . . . the right maxim for India is the traditional rural one, of 'Everything to the Soil!'[22] The street sweepers should become gardeners, taking the waste out of the city to new suburbs, and manuring the space between the houses to create 'a verdant and fruitful garden environment'.[23]

Of course, it did not endear him to the engineers. Nor did his insistence that their road widenings and clearances were mostly unnecessary. In Lahore, he pronounced himself 'completely staggered' by the proposed demolitions in an old area, which recalled 'back-streets in Lancashire towns . . . as they were laid out by sanitarians and engineers from about 1860 onwards' until the British 1909 Planning Act had stopped that kind of thing. 'The existing roads and lanes are the past product of practical life, its movement and experience', therefore they only needed improvement.[24] For a bazaar quarter of Balrampur, similarly, he suggested clearing a few derelict houses, extending open spaces, planting trees: 'As these dilapidated and depressed old quarters reopen to one another, the old village life, with its admirable combination of private simplicity and sacred magnificence, will be seen only awaiting renewal.'[25] This was to be complemented by a new suburb of houses with gardens and patios, developed by co-operation

[17] Harrison, 1980, 171, 173.   [18] King, 1980b, 215.   [19] Geddes, 1917c, 3.
[20] Geddes, 1917b, 17.   [21] Geddes, 1917c, 37–8.   [22] Geddes, 1918, I. 73.
[23] Ibid. I. 76.   [24] Geddes, 1965a, 6–7.   [25] Geddes, 1917c, 41.

between the engineer – who would be needed to allocate sites, make roads and drains, and sink wells – and the local community; they would be developed as 'a succession of village groups, each with its own centre'.[26] Similarly, for the factory town of Indore he proposed

> antisepsis and conservative surgery – in plainer terms, cleaning up and clearing up . . . In this way the old life of the Mohallas and Bazars is substantially left to go on, upon their present lines, without any serious changes . . . By our small removals, straightenings, openings, and replannings in detail, a network of clean and decent lanes, of small streets, and open places, and even gardens, is thus formed, which is often pleasant, and I venture to say sometimes beautiful.[27]

His approach, he was at pains to stress, was both much cheaper and also brought immediate returns to dramatic reductions in sickness and in death rates: 'It cannot be too clearly affirmed . . . that it is we town planners of a later School who are careful to make streets (a) only where they are really needed, and (b) in the directions required, who are the practical men, the real utilitarians, and the economists, both of the City's purse and those of the citizens.'[28] In one of his earliest reports, for Tanjore in the Madras Presidency, he estimated that his plan would cost one-sixth the engineers' gridiron plan.[29] But he did admit that

> The conservative method, however, has its difficulties. It requires long and patient study. The work cannot be done in the office with ruler and parallels, for the plan must be sketched out on the spot, after wearying hours of perambulation – commonly among sights and odours which neither Brahmin nor Briton has generally schooled himself to endure . . . This type of work also requires maps of a higher degree of detail and accuracy than those hitherto required by law for municipal or government use. . . . Even after a good deal of experience of the game, one constantly finds oneself . . . tempted, like the impatient chess-player, to sweep a fist through the pieces which stand in the way.[30]

Yet it was essential, for the clearance policy was 'one of the most disastrous and pernicious policies in the chequered history of sanitation'; the result was to crowd the people into worse housing than they had before.[31]

Conservative surgery, he explained in his report for Lahore in 1918, as for many other places, would be complemented by the creation of proposed 'Garden Villages' around the town, to which industries would move;[32] they would attract thousands of people from the old town, 'thus the many-seated Latrines would lose their custom' and costly drainage schemes could be obviated.[33] They would be built on the co-operative-tenant principle, just

[26] Ibid. 34, 77.   [27] Geddes, 1918, I. 61.   [28] Geddes, 1965a, 15.
[29] Tyrwhitt, 1947, 41.   [30] Ibid. 44–5.   [31] Ibid. 45.
[32] Geddes, 1918, I. 40.   [33] Ibid. I. 64.

as Unwin and Parker had done at Hampstead and Ealing and other places, but here Geddes proposed an adaptation to Indian conditions: the state would provide just the land on easy terms, then 'simplifying the building itself, to a reasonable minimum to start with, yet with incentive to improvement';[34] structures would be *kucha* (temporary materials), and 'labour can often, at least partly be given by the worker himself'; the state could help by providing the materials.[35] And the whole plan, Geddes stressed, must be realized with the 'real and active participation' of the citizens; he warned against the 'Dangers of Municipal Government from above' with resultant 'detachment from public and popular feeling, and consequently, before long, from public and popular needs and usefulness'.[36]

His report on Indore, Geddes concluded significantly, was 'the fullest and most detailed of schemes, so far as the writer knows, for any City'; it 'has been the best, because fullest, opportunity of my life as a town-planner.'[37] The clue lay in the fact that

> Since City Life, like organic and individual life, exists and develops with the harmonious functioning of all its organs, and their adaptation to all its needs, the endeavour has been made to provide, and in growing measure, towards all of these, and so not only to work in, with or for each as a specialism, but also to con-specialise each towards the fuller life of the whole . . . It is but in the earlier stage of every scientific and technical education, that we analyse and see and handle things strictly apart: in the needed further phase we again see them as an interacting whole, and so re-adjust them together. It is because minds fix in the first stage, that great dis-specialised schemes – say here past Water and Drainage Schemes – so rapidly pass into failures and extravagance.[38]

He might well say all that. In 1918, he had just anticipated by exactly half a century the planning philosophy of the 1960s. The world was not quite ready. Some of the reports show signs of anguished disagreement with local officials.[39] He was not thanked for it, anywhere in the official hierarchy: Lutyens in 1914 reported that 'Hailey, Montmorency, and all from H.E. downwards' were unimpressed, in fact wildly angry,

> . . . with a certain Professor Geddes who has come out here to lecture on town planning – his exhibits were sunk by the *Emden*. He seems to have talked rot in an insulting way and I hear he is going to tackle me! A crank who don't [*sic*] know his subject. He talks a lot, gives himself away, and then loses his temper.[40]

More than ten years after his major reports, a standard manual of Indian planning practice, by one J. M. Linton Bogle (Bachelor of Engineering,

---

[34] Ibid. I. 70.   [35] Ibid.   [36] Ibid. II. 104.   [37] Ibid. II. 187, 190.
[38] Ibid. II, 187.   [39] Geddes, 1965a, 51.   [40] Hussey, 1953, 336.

Liverpool; Associate Member of the Institution of Civil Engineers, ditto of the Town Planning Institute; Chief Engineer, Lucknow Improvement Trust) was still recommending 'a well designed Street Plan' with streets as wide as 100 feet. Patrick Geddes's name, needless to say, was not mentioned.[41] Geddes, or his ghost, would have to wait awhile.

Arcadia for All at Peacehaven

Meanwhile, people who had never heard of Geddes went on building their own houses, as through the ages they always had. They were doing it all over southern England in the 1920s and 1930s, especially on the coast: on the Isle of Canvey and the Isle of Sheppey, at Peacehaven near Brighton and at Jaywick Sands near Clacton, at Shoreham Beach and Pagham Beach and a score of other places. Mostly, they were poor people using their own hands, with knock-down materials drawn from the scrapyards of industrial civilization; superannuated tramcars were a particular favourite.[42] They built very cheaply, because they had to; one, who started with a borrowed £1 note in 1932, said that she felt sorry for a latter-day generation of young couples, who did not get the chance she had.[43]

The results did not always have that happy vernacular quality that Unwin so admired, and that he tried to capture in all those drawings in *Town Planning in Practice*. They were sometimes garish, and they lacked expensive services that their builders could not afford; in the largest, the plotlands at Laindon in Essex, some three-quarters of the 8,500 houses had no sewers, half no electricity.[44] In the 1930s, they were a principal cause of the cries of woe from architects and others about the despoilation of the countryside, a story already told in chapter 3. World War Two helped these critics: the armed forces demolished a lot of them on the ground of defence against invasion. After it, the newly empowered local authority planners followed up with a whole series of legal and quasi-legal harassments: in one place they created a country park, in another a whole private-enterprise new suburb, even – at Laindon – a whole new town.[45] But they could not eliminate them entirely; England's plotlands – and their occupiers – still survive, testimony to an extraordinary era of building by the people for the people.

Some few saw and admired. One, Colin Ward, began in the early 1950s to write in the anarchist magazine *Freedom*, extolling the principles of self-build. And shortly before that, Ward had been briefly involved in a remarkable meeting of minds at the Architectural Association school in

[41] Bogle, 1929, 24, 27, 60.   [42] Hardy and Ward, 1984, *passim*.
[43] Ibid. 201.   [44] Ibid. 204.   [45] Hardy and Ward, 1984, 211–30.

London. In 1948, the AA – better known as the chief originator in Britain of megalomaniac Corbusian fantasies – acted out of character: it invited the Italian anarchist architect Giancarlo de Carlo. De Carlo had been impressed by the appalling conditions in which the Italian poor then lived: conditions, he said, 'little different from those of the slaves of the third century B.C. or from those of the plebeians in Imperial Rome'.[46] Municipal housing was no solution, for it meant 'those squalid barracks which line monotonously the perimeter of our towns'.[47] Therefore, he argued, 'the housing problem cannot be solved from above. It is a problem of *the people*, and it will not be solved, or even boldly faced, except by the concrete will and action of the people themselves.'[48]

Planning could aid this, but only so long as it were conceived 'as the manifestation of communal collaboration', whereupon 'it becomes the endeavour to liberate the true existence of man, the attempt to establish a harmonious connection between nature, industry and all human activities.'[49]

This struck a chord in one of the AA's ex-servicemen students. John Turner, unlike most of his generation, was no admirer of *La Ville radieuse*. Later he recalled that

> For some minor misdemeanor at the English public school I attended, a prefect made me read and precis a chapter of Lewis Mumford's The Culture of Cities. Mumford quoted his own teacher, Patrick Geddes, whose name stuck in my mind. Later, Geddes' work caused me to doubt the value of my professional schooling, and, when I eventually escaped into the real world, his work also guided my reschooling and reeducation.[50]

In the army, he had read *Freedom* and had been converted to anarchism. Hence, when de Carlo arrived at the AA, he was preaching to at any rate one semi-converted member of the audience. Turner went back to the Geddesian method, which 'clearly enough, was to involve himself as closely as possible with all the people involved, especially those who were suffering most from the consequences of urban dysfunctions and blight.'[51] But the possibilities for a young professional to do this 'in such a thoroughly institutionalized country as the United Kingdom seemed remote', and, when he was given the chance to work in Peru with Eduardo Neira, he jumped at it.[52]

Turner Goes to Peru

From the mid-1950s to the mid-1960s Turner worked in the Lima *barriadas*, which mushroomed from 100,000 to 400,000 people in the six years 1958–

---

[46] De Carlo, 1948, 2.   [47] Ibid.   [48] Ibid.   [49] Ibid.
[50] Turner, 1972a, 122.   [51] Ibid. 124.   [52] Ibid.

64.[53] This was a time when the orthodox view, reinforced by the publication of Oscar Lewis's influential work on the culture of poverty, was that such informal slum settlements were 'breeding-grounds for every kind of crime, vice, disease, social and family disorganization'.[54] Even in 1967, one distinguished expert, from the Massachusetts Institute of Technology, was writing of them,

> Typically, their children do not go to school, do not find work (other than the most menial and unrewarding), do not become urbane in any significant sense (other than the urbanity of big-city delinquency and crime) . . . considerable resources must be expended to maintain them even in this miserable condition of life . . . more police and firemen, more hospitals and schools, more housing and related activities.[55]

This, to be sure, represented a rather massive misunderstanding of what Lewis had actually said; like many another distinguished academic, he seems to have been quoted mainly by those who had not bothered to read him. He had written about 'a way of life, remarkably stable and persistent, passed on from generation to generation along family lines'.[56] But he had also emphasized, in an early study of Mexican peasants coming to Mexico City, that

> . . . they adapt to city life with far greater ease than do American farm families. There is little evidence of disorganization or breakdown, of culture conflict, or of irreconcilable conflicts between generations . . . Family cohesiveness and extended family ties increase in the city, fewer cases of separation and divorce occur, no cases of abandoned mothers and children, no cases of persons living alone or of unrelated families living together.[57]

And later, he was at pains to stress that the phrase, 'culture of poverty',

> is a catch one and is misused with some frequency in the current literature. . . . The culture of poverty is not just a matter of deprivation or disorganization, a term signifying the absence of something. It is a culture in the traditional anthropological sense in that it provides human beings with a design for living, with a ready-made set of solutions for human problems, and so serves a significant adaptive function. In writing about 'multiproblem' families the scientists . . . often stress their instability, their lack of order, direction and organization. Yet, as I have observed them, their behavior seems clearly patterned and reasonably predictable. I am more often struck by the inexorable repetitiousness and the iron entrenchment of their folkways.[58]

Further, he emphasized, by no means all poor people were locked into the culture of poverty; a certain rather special set of conditions had to be met, including a cash economy with high unemployment, lack of any kind

[53] Turner, 1965, 152.   [54] Ward, 1976, 89.   [55] Lerner, 1967, 24–5.
[56] Lewis, 1961, xxiv.   [57] Lewis, 1952, 39–41.   [58] Lewis, 1966, 19.

FIGURE 8.1   *San Martin de Porres, Lima, 1962.*
'The notion that the *Barriada* is a slum varies between a half-truth and an almost
total untruth.' John F. C. Turner

of organization for the poor, lack of extended kinship and a dominant value
system that suggested poverty was due to personal inadequacy.[59] Not only
this; in his study of poverty and prostitution in Puerto Rico, *La Vida*, his
central character experiences acute feelings of withdrawal when persuaded
to leave the slum for a peripheral public-housing project:

> The place is dead. It's true what the proverb says, 'May God deliver me
> from quiet places; I can defend myself in the wild ones' . . . Here even my
> saints cry! They look so sad. They think I am punishing them . . . Maybe I
> was better off in La Esmeralda. You certainly have to pay for the comforts
> you have here! Listen, I'm jittery, really nervous, because if you fail to pay
> the rent even once here, the following month you're thrown out.[60]

But, though Lewis was saying pretty well the opposite, people believed
him to be telling them what they wanted to believe: the informal housing
area was by definition a slum, therefore – again by definition – an area of

[59] Ibid. 21.   [60] Lewis, 1967, 592–4.

delinquency, breakdown and general social malaise. In the early 1960s, even as distinguished and as liberal an expert as Charles Abrams – who, having himself grown up in a slum, had fewer misconceptions than most – was doubting the value of self-help, especially in urban areas, on the grounds of difficulties of organization, delays, poor quality construction, lack of mass production, and the fact that the results generally represented safety and health hazards.[61]

Turner was the first to find what multiple sociological and anthropological research was later to prove: that the truth was almost the reverse of what the conventional wisdom was saying. In fact, the invasions that produced the *barriadas* were highly organized, orderly and peaceful; they were followed by massive investments in housing; employment, wages, literacy and educational levels were all better there than average, let alone in comparison with city slums.[62]

> The majority of the Lima Barriada population are not, by Peruvian and even by Lima standards very poor and the lives they lead in their Barriadas are a considerable improvement on their former condition, whether in the city slums from which they moved to the Barriada or in the villages from which they moved into the city slums.[63]

The notion that the *Barriada* (or its equivalents, the Brazilian *Favela*, the Mexican *Colonia Proletaria*, the Venezuelan *Rancho*) was a slum 'varies between a half-truth and an almost total untruth':[64] the owner had land, part at least or a fairly well-built dwelling, security, status and a vested interest in social development and political stability;[65] its people were 'the (very much poorer) Peruvian equivalent of the Building Society house-buyers of the suburbs of any city of the industrialized world'.[66] And these non-material aspects were particularly important; for, though the official world did not recognize it, housing was more than a material product, it also provided people with existential qualities like identity, security and opportunity, which quite transformed the quality of ordinary people's lives:[67]

> That the mass of the urban poor in cities like Lima are able to seek and find improvement through home-ownership (or *de facto* possession) when they are still very poor by modern standards is certainly the main reason for their optimism. If they were trapped in the inner cities, like so many of the North American poor, they too would be burning instead of building.[68]

What he further found was the truth that people knew best what they wanted for themselves: when they first came to the city, unmarried or just

---

[61] Abrams, 1964, 22, 172.   [62] Ward, 1976, 89.   [63] Turner, 1965, 152.
[64] Ibid.   [65] Ibid.   [66] Turner, 1968a, 357.
[67] Turner, 1972b, 151–2, 165.   [68] Turner, 1968a, 360.

married, they preferred to live in central slums, near jobs and cheap food markets; then, as children came, they looked for space and security;[69] at that point, if free to act, they preferred to live in large unfinished houses, or even large shacks, rather than in small finished ones: 'As Patrick Geddes wrote half a century ago in India: "I have to remind all concerned (1) that the essential need of a house and family is *room* and (2) that the essential improvement of a house and family is *more room*."'[70] They put the house – and community services such as markets and schools and police – first, services (save perhaps electricity) second; they knew they could get these in time.[71]

The problem was that the official world refused to recognize this. Lima's subdivision codes, dating from 1915, and minimum housing standards, dating from 1935, simply put the majority of all potential house-owners out of the market: in the legal market, people were paying a higher percentage of their incomes for worse housing than their grandfathers in the 1890s.[72] Thus 'autonomous urban settlement . . . is the product of the difference between the nature of the popular demand for dwellings and those supported by institutionalized society';[73] there was a gap between the values of the governing institutions in the society, and those that the people had developed for themselves, in response to the circumstances of their lives.[74]

In his earliest Peruvian work, in the city of Arequipa, Turner had assumed that the role of the professional was to organize the self-build process. Then he realized that the people knew perfectly well not only what to build, but how to build it: that he had been guilty of the 'liberal authoritarian view that all local autonomous organizations tended to be subversive'.[75] And, indeed, they were: to the power of the professional elite. Thus he came to his fundamental discovery that

> When dwellers control the major decisions and are free to make their own contributions in the design, construction or management of their housing, both this process and the environment produced stimulate individual and social well-being. When people have no control over nor responsibility for key decisions in the housing process, on the other hand, dwelling environments may instead become a barrier to personal fulfilment and a burden on the economy.[76]

The squatters managed to build their houses for half the amount that a contractor would charge, while creating an investment worth four or five times their annual incomes: twice the usual maximum for conventionally built housing.[77] And, on the contrary, putting people into government

[69] Mangin and Turner, 1969, 133–4.   [70] Turner, 1970, 2.   [71] Ibid. 8–9.
[72] Turner, 1972b, 149.   [73] Turner, 1969, 511.   [74] Turner, 1971, 72.
[75] Turner, 1972a, 138.   [76] Fichter, Turner and Grenell, 1972, 241.   [77] Ibid. 242.

housing projects did little to halt the cycle that developed into Lewis's culture of poverty.[78]

What then should be the role of government and of planning? Was it to walk away and leave the people well alone? Not at all, said Turner: planning should aim to provide the framework, within which people should then be left free to get on. Government should cease to be financier and builder; it should instead be promoter and coordinator. People would still need help, for they did not necessarily have the skills to build themselves;[79] it was a myth, he later stressed, that autonomous housing was cheaper because self-built, for the owner rarely contributed more than half the total labour, often very little; rather, the savings came from the fact that the owner was his own contractor.[80] For this reason, government could provide a useful function by aiding small contractors and co-operative organizations to provide materials or specialized services.[81] And government action would be essential to provide land as close as possible to possibilities of employment, to provide advance infrastructure, and to legalize the framework when the settlement was ready.[82]

Even after the settlements were built, Turner and his group recognized that problems were likely to remain; at least, some of these might be reduced during construction. The huge scale of the settlements in many Latin American cities – an estimated three-quarters of Lima's 1990 population of 6 million, against perhaps 5 per cent of 600,000 in 1940 – meant that many would be paying high costs to get to work, and perhaps for servicing their houses; and the low densities, at which many of the settlements were built, would affect this.[83] And this kind of housing required at least some minimum income, which many – even in Latin America, still more so in Africa – still lacked.[84] If lower-income people squatted at the peripheries of established settlements, then they might frustrate efforts to upgrade them.[85] And the settlers could themselves become locked into land speculation, from which, perversely, they would benefit as the value of their houses escalated: a problem that has latterly exercised many experts from the World Bank and elsewhere.[86]

Meanwhile, both academic research and professional experience had confirmed that indeed autonomous housing constituted 'slums of hope', in the phrase first used as early as 1962 by Charles Stokes.[87] By now, scores of other studies in other places had suggested that his conclusions were generally applicable. Frieden had reached the same answer for Mexico City in the mid-1960s;[88] Romanos confirmed it for Athens, Epstein for Brazilian

[78] Mangin and Turner, 1969, 136.   [79] Turner et al., 1963, 391–3.
[80] Turner, 1976, 86.   [81] Payne, 1977, 198.   [82] Ibid. 188–91, 195, 198.
[83] Turner, 1969, 523–4.   [84] Ibid. 519.   [85] Turner, 1970, 10.
[86] Dunkerley, 1983.   [87] Stokes, 1962, 189.   [88] Frieden, 1965, 89–90.

cities.[89] And Janice Perlman's celebrated study of the Rio *Favelas*, *The Myth of Marginality* (1976), found the prevailing wisdom 'completely wrong':

the favelados and suburbanos do *not* have the attitudes and behavior supposedly associated with marginal groups. Socially, they are well organized and cohesive and made wide use of the urban milieu and its institutions. Culturally, they are highly optimistic and aspire to better education for their children and to improving the condition of their houses. . . . Economically, they work hard, they consume their share of the products of others . . . and they build . . . Politically, they are neither apathetic nor radical. . . . In short, *they have the aspirations of the bourgeoisie, the perseverance of pioneers, and the values of patriots.* What they do not have is an opportunity to fulfil their aspirations.[90]

This conclusion, she suggested, was supported by many other studies. The myth persisted because it was useful: it upheld the status quo and justified any action the state might want to take, including clearance of the *favelas*.[91] In fact, the removal of one such inner-city Rio *Favela*, in the early 1970s, had caused great hardship as people were relocated in peripheral housing projects, far from work and lacking all sense of community.[92]

Backed by studies like these, by the 1980s, Turnerite policies had received the ultimate accolade of respectability: they had been embraced by the World Bank. Perhaps predictably, because he was now orthodox, an anti-Turner school of thought had by now developed. It suggested that self-build housing was in fact relatively expensive to construct, and that the apparent economy came only from uncosted do-it-yourself work; that it was most profitable to the landowners; and that the occupants could pay a high cost to establish legal tenure.[93] There was a suggestion that though the conclusions might apply to most such places, they did not extend to all: to the *bustees* of Calcutta, for instance.[94] (Ironically, at just that time, having at first tried to clear the *bustees*, Calcutta too had realized its futility and was about to start on a huge improvement programme.)[95] And of course some, taking their stand on Marxist analysis, argued that the self-builder was still a mere tool of capitalism: 'Turner's recommendations represent nothing less than the now traditional attempts of capitalist interests to palliate the housing shortage in ways that do not interfere with the effective operation of these interests.'[96]

Turner, fairly obviously just baffled by all this, took his stand on the view that housing can be a lever of social change. In any case, Gilbert and Ward's survey of people in autonomous housing in Mexico City found that – dupes of the system or not – they pronounced themselves well satisfied:

[89] Romanos, 1969, 151; Epstein, 1973, 177–8.   [90] Perlman, 1976, 242–3.
[91] Ibid. 249–50.   [92] Ibid. 230–3.   [93] Connolly, 1982, 156–63.
[94] Dwyer, 1972, 211–13.   [95] Rosser, 1972, 189–90.   [96] Burgess, 1982, 86.

... low-income groups have benefited from the process even if they have
suffered from prolonged insecurity of tenure, inadequate services, the loss of
leisure time taken up in house building and neighbourhood improvements,
and the high cost of paying for land, regularization, taxes and bribes . . . at
the end of the day, residents possess a plot which acts as a hedge against
inflation, constitutes solid equity, and can be used to generate income through
renting or sharing.[97]

Here and in Bogotá, they suggested, both the capitalist class and the low-
income group have gained; the ability of any group to control the system
is constrained by the electoral process:[98] 'structuralism is capable of
explaining both the grinding down of the working class by authoritarian
governments and the improvement of conditions for the poor. Since nothing
is precluded, nothing is explained.'[99] In fact, government planning
bureaucracies had helped the poor and also, by stabilizing the society,
helped themselves.[100]

China Goes to the Mountains and the Country

On the other side of the Third World, in these years, an even more
audacious planning experiment was taking place: perhaps, the most radical
in the whole history of twentieth-century planning. China, at the time of
the Communist revolution in 1949, was one of the world's most outstanding
examples of what later came to be called uneven development. About nine-
tenths of all the country's industrial infrastructure was concentrated in
some 100 'treaty ports' along the coast; some one-fifth in Shanghai alone.
In these foreign-controlled cities the Chinese found themselves strangers in
their own land, humiliated by the grosser trappings of colonialism: in one
Shanghai park, a notorious notice barred dogs and Chinese.[101] Small
wonder that the new Communist rulers were ideologically anti-urban:
though mostly of urban origin themselves, and dependent for support on
an urban proletariat, they had raised the flag of revolution in the countryside
and firmly believed that here lay the source of native, non-corrupt Chinese
values.[102]

There was another, harder-nosed reason why they should back rural
development: there was no option. In the first years after the revolution
people flooded from the backward and war-torn countryside into the cities,
which could not take the burden.[103] And the true reason for reversing this
flow was the need to industrialize the country.[104] The response was the

---

[97] Gilbert and Ward, 1982, 99–100.   [98] Ibid. 118.   [99] Ibid.
[100] Ibid. 120.   [101] Murphey, 1980, 27–31; 1984, 197.
[102] Ibid. 30; Kirkby, 1985, 8–9.   [103] Murphey, 1980, 43; Kirkby, 1985, 38.
[104] Kirkby, 1985, 14.

famous policy of *hsang shan xia xiang*, educated youth to the mountains and country areas: millions of graduates were shipped from the cities to help provide the leadership for rural development. It happened especially in the late 1950s, the time of the disastrous Great Leap Forward, and in the late 1960s, the period of the Cultural Revolution.[105] It involved two elements. One, not so well publicized, but almost certainly more important, was the development of large-scale industry in interior cities like Lanchow and Sinkiang, as a deliberate counterweight to the Treaty Ports. The other, which the whole world knows, was self-sufficient rural development through land reform, farm improvements and small-scale rural industry.[106]

It was heroic, and it has become the model of what has come to be called bottom-up planning.[107] The problem is that it was not what it seemed, and that it was a failure. It was never truly bottom up, because it was always directed from the centre even if – by sheer necessity – administered locally.[108] The main elements – provision for basic needs, local control of agricultural and small-scale industrial enterprises, emphasis on local self-reliance – were all secured through a national planning framework, which used tax and pricing policies to favour the rural sector.[109] And it was marked by repeated, sometimes disastrous, failures that arose from the sheer inability of the communes to manage the system, as in the Great Leap Forward.[110] The rural industries, such as the notorious backyard steel furnaces of the 1950s, proved to run at very high cost.[111] The whole structure depended on perhaps as many as 15 million urban professionals, who – disaffected, often in conflict with the peasantry – wanted nothing so much as to get back to the cities; they provided a rich source of refugees for Hong Kong, greatly aiding that city's meteoric development.[112]

Under the Deng regime of the late 1970s and early 1980s – conservative by classical Maoist standards, radical by others – it seems that the policy has been largely abandoned. Its results are meagre. The treaty ports are still by far the biggest cities of China and the key to its industrial production; small-scale rural industry employs perhaps 3 per cent of the rural workforce; the cities are still growing; in a quarter-century of Communist rule, the overall population distribution is little changed.[113] Yet, in comparison with other third-world countries, it has to be said that the number of big cities if quite small – twenty-five in all of more than 1 million people, six of more than 2 million – and the growth of the cities has been kept in line with that of the population as a whole.[114] So the great experiment achieved

[105] Kirkby, 1985, 10.   [106] Murphey, 1980, 46–7, 49–50, 60–1.
[107] Stöhr, 1981, *passim*.   [108] Wu and Ip, 1981, 155–6.   [109] Ibid. 175–7.
[110] Ibid. 162–3.   [111] Aziz, 1978, 71; Murphey, 1984, 200.
[112] Murphey, 1980, 105–7; 1984, 200.
[113] Murphey, 1980, 146; 1984, 198; Wu and Ip, 1981, 160.
[114] Aziz, 1978, 64; Murphey, 1984, 198.

something, after all. But whether it really represented the triumph of local, autonomous, bottom-up planning, as some would devoutly like to believe, is another question altogether: one on which the verdict, lacking the real documentary evidence, has still to come in.

Autonomy in the First World: Wright to Alexander·

All this had few echoes in the first world; asked to find lessons of third-world informal housing for the United States in 1968, a group of housing experts could find very few.[115] But a few people, over the years, had been thinking about it. The most notable was Frank Lloyd Wright, whom we shall logically consider as a leading exponent of the roadside city in chapter 9. But Broadacre City was more than that: it was to be a city built by its own inhabitants, using mass-produced components:[116]

> ... to start building his home he ought to be able to buy the modern, standardized privy, cheap. That civilized 'privy' is now a complete bathroom unit manufactured in factories, delivered complete to him as a single unit (his car or refrigerator is one now) ready to use when connected to the city water system and a fifteen-dollar septic tank or a forty-dollar cesspool. Well advised, he plants this first unit wherever it belongs to start his home. Other units similarly cheap and beneficial designed for living purposes may be added soon.[117]

In fact many of the strands that went into Wright's thinking, whether consciously or not, were shared with the Regional Planning Association of America: anarchism, liberation by technology, naturalism, agrarianism, the homesteading movement. Yet they, like almost everyone else, attacked him;[118] and no one in the urban establishment took heed. By one of those frequent ironies that seem to recur in the history of urbanism, the people who did implement his ideas were the Levitts, a firm of commercial builders, who just after World War Two conceived the idea of a cheap basic house of standard industrial components, which could be extended by the owner at leisure; their triumph will be detailed in chapter 9. But in American architecture and planning schools, the idea of self-build went strangely underground for another thirty years, until it reappeared at Berkeley, in the writings of Christopher Alexander.

Alexander, Viennese born, came to Britain as a child and had an extremely eclectic education in the architecture school of the University of Cambridge, from where he emigrated to America. Almost from the start, he became engaged in a personal odyssey to discover what he called 'the

---

[115] Goetze *et al.*, 1968, 354.   [116] Fishman, 1977, 130.   [117] Wright, 1945, 86.
[118] Grabow, 1977, 116–17, 121.

quality without a name' in buildings, which he described in an interview as

> a building which is like a smile on a person's face, and which has that kind of rightness about it, and which is really like that and not just saying it is like that . . . at such moments, things are completely orderly and at peace with themselves – not at all in the pretentious sense that we tend to call beautiful, but in an incredibly simple and straightforward and at the same time deep and mysterious sense.[119]

Searching for this quality, in the 1960s he developed the idea that it could be objectively determined. But he now saw that modern architects actually denied their own natures: their 'cardboard-like' architecture came out of a fear of showing emotion. True 'organic order', the 'quality without a name', could be found in traditional architecture, like the relationship of college buildings in Cambridge, or an English village street; if architects really experienced this quality, then they could not design the kinds of buildings they did.[120]

So far, it seems, he was identifying just those qualities for which Morris and then Unwin and Geddes were searching, though they did not express it that way: Unwin and Parker's best housing at New Earswick or Letchworth has this very quality. But then, about 1972, he saw that it was 'not enough to tinker with the zoning ordinances because the exact rules of the ordinances – which govern that process – are themselves produced by the process by which zoning is administered.'[121] Instead, he developed the idea that groups of people might change their own environment, partly subsidized from above: '[the] individual is not only taking care of his own needs, but also for contributing to the needs of the larger group to which he belongs.'[122] In the project People Rebuilding Berkeley, he tried to develop the idea of 'self-sustaining, self-governing' neighbourhoods.[123] It did not work, somehow getting back to traditional master planning.

Disillusioned, he then came to believe that 'in order for things to become beautiful and alive, it is necessary for people like myself to be directly involved in the act of construction rather than fiddling around on paper.'[124] It also made him feel better. So, in a self-build project at Mexicali, he actually became involved in helping the Mexicans create their own environment. The result was a set of very unusual buildings, 'a bit more funky than I would have liked', which seem to be well liked by the people who built them.[125]

Berkeley was not the only place where people were returning to ideas of self-help and community participation in the 1970s, but because of

[119] Grabow, 1983, 21. [120] Ibid. 57, 68–9, 83–6, 100.
[121] Ibid. 139. [122] Ibid. 155. [123] Ibid. 157. [124] Ibid. 222.
[125] Ibid. 170.

Alexander it was probably the most important. In England Ralph Erskine, the British-born architect who had worked for many years in Sweden, returned to Tyneside to build the remarkable Byker Wall, a redevelopment project which became one of the very few pieces of public housing that was designed in continuous dialogue with the residents. The original suspicions were broken down. 'In the end, the quantity and quality of social activity in Byker became a by-word – a local joke – but a triumph.'[126] And the result was one of the most extraordinary structures ever created in any city, let alone by a public housing authority: 'the great Wall itself, tall, austere and abstract on the cold side, bending, rising, falling, projecting, receding for a full mile and a half, has on its seemingly lower sunny side the intricate, shabby, makeshift, intensively humanized quality of a shantytown in Hong Kong.'[127] It is inhabited mainly by old people, who pay it the highest possible compliment: they say that it is like the Costa Brava.[128]

They like it; but they did not build it, and Byker categorically has the air of architectural style, even whimsy, about it. Meanwhile, in 1969 there had appeared a highly iconoclastic manifesto in the pages of the English weekly social-science journal, *New Society*. Written jointly by Reyner Banham, Paul Barker, Peter Hall and Cedric Price, it argued that

> The whole concept of planning (the town-and-country kind at least) has gone cockeyed. . . . Somehow, everything must be watched; nothing must be allowed simply to 'happen'. No house can be allowed to be commonplace in the way that things just *are* commonplace: each project must be weighed, and planned, and approved, and only then built, and only after that discovered to be commonplace after all.[129]

So the group proposed

> a precise and carefully controlled experiment in non-planning . . . to seize on a few appropriate zones of the country, which are subject to a characteristic range of pressures, and use them as launchpads for Non-Plan. At the least, one would find out what people want; at the most, one might discover the hidden style of mid-20th century Britain.[130]

The article proposed three such zones: Nottinghamshire's Sherwood Forest, the corridor up the then unbuilt M11 motorway from London to Cambridge, the Solent area on the south coast. It ended defiantly: '. . . except for a few conservation areas which we wish to preserve as living museums, physical planners have no right to set their value judgement against yours, or indeed anyone else's. If the Non-Plan experiment works really well, people should be allowed to build what they like.'[131]

---

[126] Esher, 1981, 186.   [127] Esher, 1981, 187.   [128] Ibid.
[129] Banham *et al.*, 1969, 435.   [130] Ibid. 436.   [131] Ibid. 443.

It was, of course, received in deafening silence; it took another ten years for a group at the Town and Country Planning Association, led by Colin Ward and David Lock, to try to return to the pure Howard vision with a proposal for a third garden city, to be planned – and in part built – by the people who would live in it. Frustrated after long negotiation with the new city of Milton Keynes, they finally began work on a self-build community at Lightmoor in Telford new town, which began in 1984.[132]

There was a parallel movement in the United States. In fact, Jane Jacobs can be said to have started it as early as 1961 with her plague-on-both-your-houses attack on both the Corbusians and the garden-city planners, and her appeal for a return to the density and mixed land uses of the traditional unplanned city.[133] In 1970 Richard Sennett weighed in with his *Uses of Disorder*, contrasting 'a life in which the institutions of the affluent city are used to lock men into adolescence even when physically adult' with 'the possibility that affluence and the structures of a dense, disorganized city would encourage men to become more sensitive to each other as they become fully grown.' He argued that this was 'not a utopian ideal; it is a better arrangement of social materials, which as organized today are suffocating people.'[134] In an imaginary account of the life of a young girl in such a city, he suggested how this might happen:

> She lives, perhaps, on a city square, with restaurants and stores mixed among the homes of her neighbors. When she and the other children go out to play, they do not go to clean and empty lawns; they go into the midst of people who are working, shopping, or are in the neighborhood for other reasons that have nothing to do with her. Her parents, too, are involved with their neighbors in ways that do not direclty center on her and the other children of the neighborhood. There are neighborhood meetings where disruptive issues, like a noisy bar people want controlled, have to be fought out . . . her parents are out a great deal merely to find out who their neighbors are and see what kind of accommodations can be reached where conflicts arise.[135]

The paradox, he concluded, was that 'in extricating the city from preplanned control, men will become more in control of themselves and more aware of each other'[136]

The Great War against Urban Renewal

Jacobs and Sennett were alike illustrating a general disillusionment with the results of planning from above in American cities, symbolized for many by the live television coverage of the demolition of the Pruitt–Igoe project in St Louis, described in chapter 7.[137] That disillusionment, to be sure,

---

[132] Gibson, 1985. [133] Jacobs, 1962, *passim.* [134] Sennett, 1971, 189.
[135] Ibid. 190. [136] Ibid. 198. [137] Fishman, 1980, 246.

did not take the form of a naïve desire to start reconstructing cities with hammers and nails. Rather, it expressed itself in the demand that local communities should have greater say in the shaping – and especially the reshaping – of their own neighborhoods: a demand that expressed itself forcibly in the reformulation of American urban renewal policy after 1964, and in some epic conflicts over urban reconstruction projects in the hearts of European cities in the late 1960s and early 1970s.

By 1964, with Johnson in the White House and campaigning for re-election, the criticisms of urban renewal had reached deafening levels (chapter 7). And that summer, riots broke out in the black ghetto areas of a whole series of cities, focusing the presidential mind on the political need to be seen to do something fast.[138] The Model Cities programme, centrepiece of Johnson urban policy, was designed to meet these criticisms head-on. It would attack hard-core slums; it would increase, not reduce, the supply of low-cost housing; it would help the poor; it would do so by upgrading a whole neighbourhood at a time.[139]

And it would work in a novel way: it would harness the anger and energy of the poor for constructive purposes, by involving the local community in the process of change. In each targeted area, there was to be a Community Development Agency (CDA) to get the widest possible citizen participation and local initiative.[140] True, by the time the legislation was passed by Congress in 1966, the Johnson administration had learned some bitter lessons from the experience of its earlier 'War on Poverty', enshrined in the Economic Opportunity Act of 1964, with its famous – soon notorious – requirement that the programme be administered by community action agencies 'with maximum feasible participation of the residents of the areas and the members of the groups served'. That phrase, later pilloried as 'maximum feasible misunderstanding', had become a byword for conflict between local activists and City Hall; Model Cities deftly sidestepped that, by ensuring that the CDAs would be firmly under the control of the mayors.

The original idea, put forward by Leonard Duhl and Antonia Chayes in an appendix to the 1964 report of Johnson's Task Force, suggested only three such 'demonstration' projects; the Congressional pork barrel process inexorably drove the number up, until three became sixty-six, then 150, and the jam got spread ever more thinly on the bread.[141] As the money came down from Washington, despite the stage-management, all kinds of conflict and confusion broke out. The cities resented sharing powers with community activists, or – as in some cities – being bypassed altogether.[142]

[138] Haar, 1975, 4–5.   [139] Frieden and Kaplan, 1975, 45, 52–3.
[140] Fox, 1985, 201.   [141] Frieden and Kaplan, 1975, 47–9, 215–17; Haar, 1975, 218.
[142] Frieden and Kaplan, 1975, 88–9; Haar, 1975, 175.

The guidelines from Washington were naïve and obscure, written in language that was 'more appropriate to a college classroom than a mayor's office or a residents' meeting'.[143] It proved difficult to co-ordinate the different federal agencies, partly because they resented the infant Department of Housing and Urban Development and did not want to be co-ordinated; so complex were the Washington negotiations that one task-force member was gripped by a fantasy that after death he might be reincarnated as a member.[144] The interminable federal review process, coupled with local disagreements, meant that cities spent barely half of their thin entitlement.[145] And, as the threat of riot receded, the programme lost some of its political urgency, and lacked a national, even a local, consensus;[146] Nixon tried to kill it in 1968, though it survived by the skin of its teeth.[147] Charles Haar, evaluating it after a decade of life, felt that it had not delivered on 'its own high-flown promises.[148]

The irony, Haar pointed out, was that having aimed at local participation, it had actually achieved 'the high point of technicians' dominance': the processes included 'all the buzzwords of the planning profession' – sequential, rational, co-ordination, innovation, goals and objectives, and 'the effort began to resemble a restructuring of a planning curriculum rather than an effort to guide city actions.'[149] It thus represented a failure of traditional planning, rather than the success of a new approach: extreme centralization, wrapped in the trappings of local community participation. But perhaps, truth to tell, that was the intention all along.

Small wonder that some reacted, preferring a style where the professional achieved true humility, acting merely as the agent of the people's will. That was the spirit of the first recorded exercise in community design: the Architectural Renewal Committee (ARCH) in New York's Harlem, founded in 1963 to fight a proposed Robert Moses freeway. It was also the spirit of the advocacy planning movement of the time. Both were reacting against the tradition of top–down planning, based on narrow technical performance criteria, so well represented in the urban renewal and freeway schemes of the time. They were invariably reacting against some product or other of that approach: the Cooper Square renewal scheme in New York City, the Yerba Buena scheme in San Francisco, were classic battle grounds, in which idealistic young professionals joined forces with local communities. But often, the result was a disaster: the people were incoherent, the professionals took charge, no one really knew how to achieve anything, little got produced.[150]

So, during the 1970s, the focus of community design shifted. The professionals became harder-nosed, more entrepreneurial, more single-

[143] Frieden and Kaplan, 1975, 139.   [144] Ibid. 232, 236.   [145] Ibid. 229.
[146] Ibid. 257; Haar, 1975, 254–6.   [147] Frieden and Kaplan, 1975, 203–12.
[148] Haar, 1975, 194.   [149] Ibid. 205.   [150] Comerio, 1984, 230–4.

mindedly obsessed with sticking to a job and finishing it. They also became more concerned about earning a living; now, they served small community organizations and related small businesses needing architectural services, and – subsidized by federal or state governments – able therefore to pay a fee. Nevertheless, the style was very different from anything known before: it stressed the needs of the client rather than the nature of the product, and used a variety of methods to tailor the solution to those needs. In the process, it achieved more solid results and gave both client and professional the feeling that they could succeed.[151]

Meanwhile, perhaps in reflection, the emphasis of the urban renewal programme was changing steadily: away from bulldozer clearance, toward rehabilitation and small-scale spot clearances. While Boston's notorious West End project (chapter 7) involved total clearance and an almost complete shift from low-rent to middle- or high-rent residence, the later Downtown Waterfront scheme only cleared 24 per cent of the area and achieved a net housing gain – admittedly, most in the form of luxury apartments.[152] Cynics might say that the development industry had decided that city-centre sites were more profitable and rehabilitation cheaper. But that would be less than fair: nationally, between 1964 and 1970 the residential component in renewal rose sharply.[153] So did the share of rehabilitation, in some cases dramatically: from 22 to 68 per cent in Philadelphia, from 34 to 50 per cent in Minneapolis, from 15 to 24 per cent in Baltimore.[154]

That in itself says nothing about who was doing the rehabilitation. While in some cities it came from local residents with or without city aid, in others it was done by higher-status, young urban-professional gentrifiers, most of them coming not from the suburbs but from other parts of the inner city.[155] Those displaced, according to a Department of Housing and Urban Development study, were primarily the elderly, the minorities, the renters, and the working class.[156] In many cases, the shift to rehabilitation actually gave a fillip to the gentrification process: 'sweat equity' – the term that Baltimore used to describe its 'homesteading' and 'shopsteading' programmes, where blighted structures were virtually given away to would-be renovators – may prove to be something that accumulates, like most forms of equity, in middle-class savings banks. But few of the gentrifiees reported much sense of loss or displacement; it might just be that, by giving the blighted city back to energetic yuppies, policy was achieving some kind of Pareto-optimal solution, whereby no one lost but many gained. And, in an odd way, these gentrifiers strangely resembled those indefatigable improvers of the Rio *Favelas* and the Lima *Barriadas*.

[151] Ibid. 234–40.   [152] Sanders, 1980, 109.   [153] Ibid. 110–11.
[154] Ibid. 113.   [155] Cicin-Sain, 1980, 53–4.   [156] Ibid. 71.

The War Comes to Europe

Meanwhile, at the same time in the capitals of Europe, a strange new phenomenon was visible: local community activists were beginning to do battle with their own city halls over proposals for large-scale city-centre renewal. What was new about their conflicts was that they were fighting the very idea of the bulldozer approach. Down to the mid-1960s, the prevailing ethos – shared by planner and planned alike – was that comprehensive development of large areas was a thoroughly good thing: it swept away old and outmoded buildings, it aided traffic circulation, it could above all be used to separate pedestrians from traffic. Indeed, one of the most celebrated and longest-running early controversies, over Piccadilly Circus in London, started because the objectors were *demanding* comprehensive replanning· ironically, after thirteen years of dithering, the London planning machine got back to its point of departure, piecemeal rebuilding.[157]

While all this was happening, an even bigger drama was being fought out a mile away. Covent Garden had been London's fruit and vegetable market, as well as one of its theatre centres, since the seventeenth century; but, as in other cities, it had long become an inefficient, congestion-generating anomaly, and in 1962 a New Covent Garden Market Authority took over to prepare the move to another site, which duly happened in 1974. In 1965 a consortium of local authorities began work on a redevelopment plan for the market and a much wider area around, covering no less than 96 acres and including some 3,300 residents and 1,700 firms, many of them small. Their plan, which emerged in draft in 1968 and in final form in 1971, involved a combination of conservation, especially in the historic core around the market itself, and large-scale redevelopment – partly to carry the profitable development to help pay for the scheme, partly to ease traffic flow – on the edges.[158]

Meanwhile the deputy leader of the team, a Merseysider of radical inclinations called Brian Anson, was wrestling with his conscience. At the exhibition of the plans in 1968, 3,500 people turned up and a mere 350 commented; of those, a mere eighteen were local residents, and fourteen of those were against the scheme – most of them in vituperative terms. Anson became convinced that the real beneficiaries and instigators of the plan were property developers. Expressing his doubts to local community leaders, he was abruptly removed from his post by his employers, the Greater London Council. His departure became a *cause célèbre* in the media.[159]

[157] Cherry and Penny, 1986, 176–91.   [158] Christensen, 1979, 10, 20–9.
[159] Anson, 1981, *passim*.

At the public inquiry in 1971, the plan was opposed by everyone: the local Covent Garden Community Association, the Society for the Protection of Ancient Buildings, the Georgian Group, the Victorian Society, the Civic Trust, the Town and Country Planning Association; the community group's star witness was Brian Anson.[160] 'London now had its own version of the People's Park in Berkeley . . . a conveniently accessible battleground for AA and LSE students, 'advocacy planners' and assorted activists from all over.'[161] The uproar was such that though the inquiry inspector found in favour of the plan, the Minister made huge changes that effectively invalidated it.[162] A revised plan, produced in 1976 after huge tensions between the local community group and the forum set up by the Greater London Council, in effect conceded most of the community's points though they continued to criticize it.[163]

In this saga, there were two extraordinary features. One was that, in the words of the bruised leader of the official planning team, around 1968 there was 'a national nervous breakdown'.

> The whole of Great Britain was at that time involved in saving something. In the 1960s, change was considered a good thing because it improved the city, providing new facilities, open space, new housing, all the kinds of things people wanted and then profits could be made to pay for these things. Almost overnight this became a bad thing. From insensitive development to don't touch a thing . . . The whole thing went lunatic.[164]

The other point was that, even so, the community lost. As Esher put it, 'planning here becomes estate management: making the best of what one has got.'[165] But that could be very good indeed: already by 1979, the property developers had discovered that renovation cost less than half redevelopment, but could yield almost the same rents. Local shops were being replaced by boutiques and craft shops, and Covent Garden was becoming the fashionable shopping and tourist area that almost the whole world knows today.[166] Anson, writing the story years after, commented that 'a working-class shop or housing block could be destroyed by other things than a bulldozer. . . . The local baker's becomes a professional studio, the cheap cafe a chic restaurant, the dartboard is removed from the pub and gradually many more gins and tonics are sold.'[167]

Perhaps it was poetically right that this story should have happened in a country experiencing a national nervous breakdown. But, less publicized, almost the same drama was being enacted in staid Stockholm. And there, the controversy ranged over no less than the hallowed plan of 1945-6 by Sven Markelius, which had become the world's favourite textbook example

[160] Ibid. 37-8.   [161] Esher, 1981, 142.   [162] Ibid. 46-8.   [163] Ibid. 53-72.
[164] cit. Christensen, 1979, 96.   [165] Esher, 1981, 146.   [166] Ibid. 86, 133-4.
[167] Anson, 1981, 103.

of enlightened social-democratic planning. Its aim had been deliberately to concentrate the city's central business functions into a relatively small area of Lower Norrmalm, around a subway station that would be the focus of the city's planned new network. For twenty years all went ahead according to plan, Swedish-fashion; in the mid-1950s the saying was that 'it is impossible to visit Stockholm now as the town is closed for repairs.'[168] The subway lines were built; the road system was reconstructed at enormous cost around a new circus, with pedestrians circulating at lower level directly into the subway station; five uniformly massed office towers and a new pedestrian shopping mall were built.[169] All this was based quite openly on providing more space for headquarters of banks, insurance and industrial concerns, as well as department stores, hotels and entertainment.[170]

Then, in 1962, the City published a plan for the remaining area. It was not really new; really, it was a synthesis of earlier proposals that had gone through the council on the nod. It was immediately attacked in the journal *Arkitektur* by three young architects, written as 'a protest against the form which is being given to our town',[171] on the ground that it was too business-oriented and failed to give sufficient protection to residents. The attack was taken up two leading newspapers; but it failed to become an issue at the local elections, and late in 1963 the council approved it. In 1967 it produced a detailed plan for the area, based on a competition-winning design, and in 1968 approved it.[172]

At that point, just as in London, all hell broke loose. Just as there, a diverse opposition formed. It happened that a centrepiece of the plan was an Intercontinental Hotel; at the height of the Vietnam War, this became a flashpoint for anti-American feeling, then running high in Sweden. The company pulled out, leaving a huge hole in the ground. Finally, with redevelopment coming to a standstill, in 1975 the city agreed a compromise plan. Big road widenings and parking garages went; the hotel became an enclosed shopping mall; many existing buildings were preserved.[173]

Conventional urban-political analysis, especially of the Marxist kind, does not much help in these cases. In London, most of the actors agreed that the difference was not one of party politics.[174] In Stockholm, it was the Social Democrats who were committed to a scheme that displaced local residents, reduced employment opportunities, and replaced local business and small shops by big retailing, banking, financial services and consultancy.[175] Just as in London, the planners were clearly surprised and injured by the force of the attacks; they defended themselves on the ground that

[168] William-Olsson, 1961, 80.
[169] Sidenbladh, 1965, 109–10; Stockholm, 1972, 92–4; Hall, 1979, 188–93.
[170] Markelius, 1962, xxxvi.   [171] Edblom, Strömdahl and Westerman, 1962, xvi.
[172] Hall, 1979, 194–202.   [173] Ibid. 204–6; Berg, 1979, 162–3.
[174] Christensen, 1979, 101.   [175] Hall, 1979, 215, 220.

in order to attract developers, they must maintain the continuity of the
planning process and must provide the kinds of large new buildings these
developers were alleged to want.[176] What seems to have happened is that
the all-powerful technical planners made mistakes and the politicians,
obsessed by the idea that a bigger city meant more tax revenues, weakly
went along.[177] In the event, the big organizations did not even occupy the
available office space.[178]

The Battle of Paris was a more colourful affair, with a plot of enormous
length and complexity, and a huge cast of characters; everyone who
mattered in France, it seemed, had to get in on the act. In 1960, the
central government proposed that the historic wholesale food market, Les
Halles, should move out of the centre; two years after that, a decree
confirmed it; in 1963, the City Council set up an organization, SEAH
(Société Civile d'Études pour l'Aménagement du Quartier des Halles), to
plan the reconstruction of the area, and an architect was charged to prepare
a renewal plan for a huge 470-hectare strip of central Paris; four
years later, another organization, SEMAH (Société d'Économie mixte
d'Aménagement des Halles), was entrusted with carrying out the project.

This same year, 1967, the City Council invited several architects to
prepare plans for a much more modest 32-hectare site around the market
itself; a year later it turned them all down, one commissioner asking 'Are
we, twenty years later, ourselves to execute Hitler's orders?'[179] But in 1967
another body, APUR (Atelier Parisien d'Urbanisme), had approved a new
central interchange station, to form the focus of the entire Regional Express
Rail (RER); and in July 1969, a few months after Baltard's historic glass-
market pavilions had become empty, the Council accepted APUR's design
for a huge underground commercial centre and a world-trade centre on the
site, entailing their demolition. The following year, despite a proposal by
the Minister of Construction to keep them, the Council voted to raze them,
and – during the summer of 1971, when nearly all Paris was on vacation –
despite battles between conservationists and police, it did so.[180]

The future of Les Halles now became the kind of national scandal that
all French politicians love. In 1973 the council gave a permit for the world
trade centre, and work started. The next year, Valéry Giscard d'Estaing
became President and immediately annulled the permit, involving demolition
of the part-completed structure; much later, a commission determined the
damages at 65 million francs. The site became a park; the government
announced a new consultation with architects. In 1975 three projects were
displayed at the town hall; the public having indicated a pronounced
preference for one, the two others – including that by the Catalonian post-

---

[176] Westman, 1967, 421.   [177] Hall, 1979, 217, 220, 223.   [178] Ibid. 223.
[179] Paris, 1979a, 12.   [180] Paris, 1979a, 12; Paris, 1979b, 7–8.

modern architect Ricardo Bofill – were chosen. After many subsidiary sub-plots, in 1977 Bofill's plan for part of the area was exhibited, causing the President of the Syndicat des Architectes de Paris to launch an immediate campaign against it. Jacques Chirac, elected mayor in 1976, joined the campaign, referring in an unusual fit of absent-mindedness to 'Lofill? Fillbo? Ah oui! Bofill'. A few months later he dismissed Bofill, declaring 'L'architecte en chef de l'opération des Halles, c'est moi', a job he would undertake 'tranquillement et sans complexes'.

Bofill's architecture, 'greco-egyptian with Buddhist tendencies', did not appeal to Chirac. 'It has been questioned and it is questionable', he said.[181] 'These architectural Olympics have gone on long enough. Ten years is enough.' The Centre Pompidou 'was a sufficient landmark of the architectural fantasy of the end of the twentieth century.' Chirac's decision met immediate protest from every international architect of any consequence: Johnson, Venturi, Niemeyer, Stirling, Kroll, and many others. The magazine *Architecture d'aujourd'hui*, however, supported him, possibly out of exhaustion. Bofill sued for 7 million francs. In ten years, at least seventy projects had come and gone: the project had shrunk from 32 hectares, including huge skyscrapers and highways, to 15 hectares, mainly a park; Le Corbusier was truly dead, and Giscard and Chirac now began a deadly battle about whether the park should be French or Italian in character.[182]

Meanwhile, life went on. And the really significant point about Les Halles is that it then went through exactly the same process as did Covent Garden: it got gentrified. People moved out; so did local shops; boutiques and restaurants took their place. And the city did not intervene in the process. Certainly, the Battle of Les Halles did not represent any kind of triumph on the part of the local community. Indeed, it was quintessentially French in that it turned on a battle between those two traditional enemies, the French state and the city of Paris. Still less, clearly, did it represent some movement of the Paris *artisanat*, determined to take the rebuilding of the city into its own hands: in such a context, the battle was fought on different issues. But it did, like the Battles of Covent Garden and Lower Norrmalm, represent a turning-point in attitudes to large-scale urban renewal. Community activists now felt that they could fight the urban bulldozer, and win.

Community Architecture Arrives in Britain

This was nowhere more evident than in Britain. Here, the entrepreneurial approach to community architecture was certainly visible from the start.

[181] Dhuys, 1978, 9.
[182] Paris, 1978, 4–9; Paris, 1979a, 13; Paris, 1979b, 7–17.

FIGURE 8.2 *Lightmoor, Telford New Town*
The people get down to work, in the project that eventually won the accolade from
Prince Charles. On the right, Tony Gibson, Lightmoor's John Turner.

In 1971 Rod Hackney, a young architect just writing a Ph.D. at Manchester
University and short of money, paid £1,000 to buy 222 Black Road – a
small 155-year-old terrace house lacking basic amenities – in Macclesfield,
a small English industrial town south of Manchester. When he applied for
a grant to improve it, he discovered that it and its 300 neighbours were
scheduled for demolition. He organized his neighbours into a campaign
and in 1973 persuaded the local town council to change its mind: thirty-
four of the houses would be made a General Improvement Area, meaning
that the owners could receive grants to improve the houses. Hackney, who
used skills he had learned designing houses for squatters in Tripoli, could
later claim that the resulting improvement was completed in one-third of
the time, and at one-third of the cost, of the demolition and replacement
scheme. In 1975 it won a Good Design in Housing Award from the
Department of the Environment.[183]

That was just the start. Hackney soon found himself, still working from
an office in Black Road, doing similar schemes all over the country. The

[183] Knevitt, 1975, 1977.

1974 Housing Act, which switched funds into rehabilitation, was influenced by his work. By the early 1980s he was employing more than thirty people from eight area offices. Hackney gave his own views of the community architecture movement:

> Community architecture means attempting to understand the needs of a small group of residents and then working with them and under their instructions and guidance, in order to articulate their case and present it to the various organisations that hold either the purse strings or the approval/rejection powers. . . . We, the architects, got it terribly wrong in the 1960s. Community architecture will help us to bring back the integrity of the architectural profession by getting it right in this decade and subsequent decades.[184]

It was heady stuff. The media loved it because it gave them David versus Goliath stories and because Hackney, travelling from one job to another – first in his Saab, later a customized Range Rover, complete with car telephone when no one else had one – was an endless source of pithy one-liners. Younger architects loved it too, because it cocked a snook at the dreary official architecture they hated and offered them a chance of interesting private work.

They and their clients had some spectacular successes. In Liverpool, a city dominated by the insensitive slum-clearance housing built in the 1950s by the council – 25,000 of which, one-third of the total, were officially hard to let by the 1980s – a Liberal council decided to encourage the community design approach. The tenants were not asked to participate in the design; they were put in total control. They chose the architects, the site, the layout, the floor plans, the elevations, the brick colour and the landscaping; when it was all built, they ran the scheme. Their first concern, the architects soon found, was that their houses should not look like 'Corpy' housing: 'Council housing is the worst housing ever,' said the thirty-four-year-old unemployed bricklayer chairman of one co-operative, 'It's boring, pathetic, inhuman – like someone went into the architect's department and said, 'I want 400 houses – get the drawings in by half-three'. They're not houses for *people*.'[185] What emerged was small brick houses around courts, simple and almost utilitarian in style. The architects said it was hard work, but the most rewarding work they had ever done; the residents named the scheme Weller Court, after the city engineer who had been a thorn in their side.[186]

The movement gained strength. Its members founded a Community Architecture Group within the Royal Institute of British Architects, which came into increasingly bitter confrontation with the leadership. In May 1984 Prince Charles, addressing the RIBA 150th anniversary conference

[184] cit. Wates, 1982a, 43.   [185] Wates, 1982, 52.   [186] Ibid.

in Hampton Court Palace, stunned the Institute's leadership by lashing out publicly at the low quality of architectural design: the proposed extension to the National Gallery, he said, was like a monstrous carbuncle on the face of a friend. Community architecture, he declared – mentioning Hackney by name – was the answer. The architectural establishment was bitterly offended. Two and a half years later, Hackney – by then running a £4 million a year business with twenty regional offices and a staff of 200 – defeated the official candidate to become President of the RIBA: community architecture had officially arrived. It would, he confidently declared, become 'the political architecture of a post-industrial age'.

In June 1987, Hackney – just installed as President – sat on the platform at the Royal Institute of British Architects' London headquarters with Prince Charles, who presented the year's awards for outstanding community architecture. The top prize went to the Town and Country Planning Association's Lightmoor project at Telford New Town. In his speech, the Prince delivered yet another of his memorable quotes for the assembled media: he spoke of the need to overcome the 'spaghetti bolognese of red tape' that held up the efforts of ordinary people to create their own environment. As one television programme after another followed the battles of the community-builders with the entrenched bureaucracies, it seemed that Howard, Geddes, Turner and the anarchist tradition in planning had achieved ultimate respectability at last.

Few, seemingly, noticed the irony: that the accolade had come under a radical right-wing government, which now – as in Liverpool – made common cause with the anarchists against the spirit of bureaucratic socialism. That autumn, Mrs Thatcher unveiled the centrepiece of her continuing revolution of the right: following the sale of a million public housing units to their tenants, the government would now seek to turn over the remainder to tenant co-operative management, thus finally removing the dead hand of the bureaucracy. Geddes, that pupil of Bakunin and Kropotkin, who had fought so long before against its colonial manifestation, would certainly have appreciated this strange twist of history.

The City
on the Highway

This segregation of motor traffic is probably a matter that may begin even in the present decade. . . . And the quiet English citizen will, no doubt, while these things are still quite exceptional and experimental in his own land, read one day in the violently illustrated popular magazines of 1910, that there are now so many thousand miles of these roads already established in America and Germany and elsewhere. And thereupon, after some patriotic meditations, he may pull himself together.

H. G. Wells
Anticipations of the Reaction of Mechanical and Scientific Progress
upon human Life and Thought (1901)

Las Vegas takes what in other American towns is but a quixotic inflammation of the senses for some poor salary mule in the brief interval between the flagstone rambler and the automatic elevator downtown and magnifies it, foliates it, embellishes it into an institution. For example, Las Vegas is the only town in the world where the landscape is made up neither of buildings, like New York, nor trees, like Wilbraham, Massachusetts, but signs. One can look at Las Vegas from a mile away on Route 91 and see no buildings, no trees, only signs. But such signs! They tower, they revolve, they oscillate, they soar in shapes before which the existing vocabulary of art is helpless.

Tom Wolfe
The Kandy Kolored Tangerine Flake Streamline Baby (1966)

9
The City
on the Highway

The Automobile Suburb:
Long Island, Wisconsin, Los Angeles, Paris,
1920–1987

'Suburbia', a suburban child of the turn of the century later recalled, 'was
a railway state . . . a state of existence within a few minutes walk of the
railway station, a few minutes walk of the shops, and a few minutes walk
of the fields.'[1] It was the outward extension of that railway state that – as
seen in chapter 3 – brought about the growth of early-twentieth-century
London, and with it the call for urban containment. And the same was
true of the United States, where the classic early suburbs – Llewellyn Park
in New Jersey, Lake Forest and Riverside outside Chicago, Forest Hills
Gardens in New York – were planned around railway stations.[2] That
reflected stark reality: though the motor car became a technological reality
around 1900, its price restricted its ownership to a tiny minority. Only
with the revolution wrought by Henry Ford, on the magneto line at his
Highland Park works in 1913, did mass-production techniques – all
developed by others elsewhere, but here brought together – make possible
a car for the masses.[3] And even then, the car's primitive technology, and
the even more primitive state of the roads on which it ran, severely
circumscribed its use. For its first decade of life, the Model T was what
Ford had conceived it to be: a farmer's car, successor to the family horse
and buggy.[4]

A Wellsian Prophecy is Fulfilled

But one visionary had seen the future. In *Anticipations*, first published in
1901, H. G. Wells had speculated on the possibility that 'the motor omnibus

---

[1] Kenward, 1955, 74.
[2] Stern and Massingdale, 1981, 23–34; Stern, 1986, 129–35.
[3] Nevins, 1954, 471; Flink, 1975, 71–6.   [4] Flink, 1975, 80.

companies competing against the suburban railways will find themselves hampered in the speed of their longer runs by the slower horse traffic on their routes', and that they therefore would 'secure the power to form private roads of a new sort, upon which their vehicles will be free to travel up to the very limit of their possible speed.' Though Wells was wrong in many predictions in this book, this was one he got uncannily right. He said that 'almost insensibly, certainly highly profitable longer routes will be joined up', though the Americans and Germans would move much faster than the staid English. He predicted that 'they will be used only by soft-tired conveyances; the battering horseshoes, the perpetual filth of horse traffic, and the clumsy wheels of laden carts will never wear them'; that 'they will have to be very wide' and that 'their traffic in opposite directions will probably be strictly segregated'; that 'where their ways branch the streams of traffic will cross not at a level but by bridges', and that 'once they exist it will be possible to experiment with vehicles of a size and power quite beyond the dimensions prescribed by our ordinary roads – roads whose width has been entirely determined by the size of a cart a horse can pull.'[5]

Wells's remarkable prescience did not end there. For he predicted not merely the age of the motorway, but also its effect. In a chapter on the 'Probable Diffusion of Great Cities', he predicted that 'practically, by a process of confluence, the whole of Great Britain south of the Highlands seems destined to become . . . an urban region, laced all together not only by the railway and telegraph, but by novel roads such as we forecast' as well as 'a dense network of telephones, parcels delivery tubes, and the like nervous and arterial connections'. The result, he suggested, would be

> a curious and varied region, far less monotonous than our present English world, still in its thinner regions, at any rate, wooded, perhaps rather more abundantly wooded, breaking continually into park and garden, and with everywhere a scattering of houses. . . . Through the varied country the new wide roads will run, here cutting through a crest and there running like some colossal aqueduct across a valley, swarming always with a multitudinous traffic of bright, swift (and not necessarily ugly) mechanisms; and everywhere amidst the fields and trees linking wires will stretch from pole to pole.[6]

As on other occasions, Wells proved over-sanguine as to the pace of technological change. But he was uncannily right about its location. The pioneer, as he predicted, was America. That was because down to 1950, thanks to the revolution Ford had wrought, America was the only country in the world that could boast mass car ownership. By 1927, building 85 per cent of the world's cars, it could already boast one car for every five Americans: a car-ownership level of one to approximately two families.[7]

[5] Wells, 1901, 17–19.   [6] Ibid. 61–2.
[7] Flink, 1975, 142–3; Jackson, K., 1973, 212.

Thereafter, world slump and world war kept the level pegged down for more than two decades: not until the early 1950s did car ownership exceed the level of the late 1920s.

As a result, mass motorization had already begun to impinge on American cities by the mid-1920s, in a way the rest of the world would not know until the 1950s and 1960s. By 1923, traffic congestion in some cities was already so bad that there was talk of barring cars from downtown streets; by 1926, Thomas E. Pitts had closed his cigar store and soft-drink bar at a major intersection in the centre of Atlanta because congestion made it impossible to operate.[8] In the same decade, Sears Roebuck and then Montgomery Ward planned their first automobile-oriented suburban stores.[9] When the Lynds came to make their classic sociological study of 'Middletown' (actually, Muncie in Indiana), at the end of the 1920s, they found that already car ownership was allowing the ordinary worker to live farther from his work.[10] And, by that time, already in some cities – Washington, Kansas City, St Louis – downtown commuters by automobile outnumbered those coming by transit. Unsurprisingly, then, the 1920s were the first decade when the Census-takers noticed that the suburbs were growing much faster than the central cities: by 39 per cent, more than 4 million people, as against 19 per cent or 5 million in the cities. In some cities the suburbanization trend was even more marked: the relative rates of growth in New York City were 67 against 23 per cent, in Cleveland 126 against 12 per cent, in St Louis 107 against 5 per cent.[11]

The remarkable fact was that some American planners, at any rate, greeted this trend with equanimity, even with enthusiasm. At the National Conference of City Planners in 1924, Gordon Whitnall, a Los Angeles planner, proudly declared that western planners had learned from eastern mistakes, and would now lead the way to the horizontal city of the future. During the 1920s, as transit systems for the first time reported falling ridership and loss of profits, Detroit and Los Angeles considered large-scale support for transit investment in order to support their downtown areas, but found that voters would not support it.[12]

This ever-growing volume of car traffic for the most part travelled on ordinary city streets, widened and upgraded to cope with the flood. By the end of the 1920s there were few examples even of simple underpasses or overpasses on American highways.[13] The outstanding exception was New York, which during the 1920s followed a distinctive path, deriving directly from an older tradition already noticed in chapter 4: the parkway. First used by Olmsted in his design for New York's Central Park in 1858, the parkway had been widely employed by landscape architects in the planning

[8] Flink, 1975, 163, 178.   [9] Dolce, 1976, 28.   [10] Ibid. 157.
[11] Tobin, 1976, 103–4.   [12] Foster, 1981, 80–5, 88–9.
[13] Hubbard and Hubbard, 1929, 208.

of parks and new residential areas in cities as diverse as Boston, Kansas City and Chicago.[14] But, beginning with William K. Vanderbilt's Long Island Motor Parkway (1906–11), which can claim to be the world's first limited-access motor highway, and the 16-mile Bronx River Parkway (1906–23), followed by the Hutchinson River Parkway of 1928 and the Saw Mill Parkway of 1929, this distinctively American innovation was rapidly adapted to a new function: extended continuously for 10 or 20 miles into open countryside – and sometimes, as in the Bronx Parkway, used to clear up urban blight – it now gave rapid access from the congested central city both to new suburbs and to rural and coastal recreation areas.[15]

The moving spirit was New York's Master Builder, Robert Moses. Using a State Act of 1924, which he had personally drafted to give him unprecedented (and, to the hapless legislators, unappreciated) powers to appropriate land, he proceeded to drive his parkways across the cherished estates of the Long Island millionaires – the Phippses, the Whitneys, the Morgans, the Winthrops – to give New Yorkers access to the ocean beaches. It was done, like most other things Moses did, for the highest public-spirited motives; and it established the base of his unprecedented public support, which he then skilfully extended through his management of the Triborough Ridge and Tunnel Authority, tying his parkway system together and linking it to the teeming tenements of Manhattan and the Bronx.[16]

But there were limits to public spirit: deliberately, Moses built the parkway bridges too low not only for trucks, but also for buses. The magnificent bathing beaches that he created at the ends of the parkways would thus be strictly reserved for middle-class car owners; the remaining two-thirds of the population could continue to ride the subway to Coney Island. And, when in the 1930s Moses extended his system down the west side of Manhattan island to create the Henry Hudson Parkway, the world's first true urban motorway, the same applied: Moses was now consciously planning a system for car commuters.[17]

The point about Moses's gigantic public works of these years was indeed precisely this: whatever their ostensible original purpose, once linked by the Triborough Bridge they constituted a vast network of urban expressways, making it possible to commute to Manhattan offices from distances up to 20, even 30 miles: three or four times the effective radius of the subway system. There was an immediate effect: the population of Westchester and Nassau counties, served by the new roads, increased by 350,000 during the 1920s.[18] But the full implicatinos would emerge only in the suburban building boom after World War Two. It was no accident that the most

[14] Scott, 1969, 13–15, 22, 38–9; Dal Co, 1979, 177.
[15] Rae, 1971, 71–2; Dolce, 1976, 19; Jackson, K., 1985, 166; Gregg, 1986, 38–42.
[16] Caro, 1974, 143–57, 174–7, 184–5, 208–10, 386–8.
[17] Ibid. 318, 546–7.   [18] Dolce, 1976, 25.

FIGURE 9.1   *Robert Moses.*
New York's master builder and master self-publicist with a few of his projects; still,
at this point, the Moses bulldozer was unstoppable.

celebrated of all the resulting developments, the one that came almost to
symbolize the whole process, was located where it was: the original
Levittown stands just off an interchange on Moses's Wantagh State
Parkway, built nearly twenty years earlier as one of the approaches to
Jones Beach State Park.

Some planners, even then, embraced the idea of new roads as the basis
of a new urban form. One of the founding fathers of the Regional Planning
Association of America, Benton MacKaye, had – as was seen in chapter
5 – developed the idea of a townless highway, or 'motorway'. Seizing upon
the plan of Radburn – developed by two other RPAA stalwarts, Clarence
Stein and Henry Wright – he argued for its extension to the regional scale.

The townless highway is a motorway, in which the adjoining towns would
be in the same relationship to the road as the residential cul-de-sacs in
Radburn are to the main traffic avenues. What Radburn does in the local

FIGURE 9.2 *Jones Beach.*
One of the great Moses projects of the 1920s: recreation for the motorized masses, but the bridges on the parkways are built deliberately too low for buses.

community, the townless highway would do for the community at large. . . . Instead of a single roadtown slum, congealing between our big cities, the townless highway would encourage the building of real communities at definite and favorable points *off* the main road.[19]

The concept was clear and consistent:

the abolition of approaches to the main highway except at certain points; public ownership, or effective public control through rigorous zoning, of the foreground along the right-of-way . . . proper landscape development of the foreground, including the culture of shade trees and the strict regulation of telephone and electric-light lines; and finally, strict control of highway service station development.[20]

All that, of course, came to pass – but first in other places, and only long afterwards in the United States. And the other part of the prescription, the ultimate RPAA dream – 'to stimulate the growth of the distinct community, compactly planned and limited in size, like the old New

[19] MacKaye, 1930, 94.   [20] Ibid. 95.

England village or the modern Radburn'[21] – was to remain unrealized in the land of its origin.

Everywhere but in the United States, the automobile revolution had yet to come. That was undoubtedly true in Europe, where down to World War Two only a tiny minority – at most 10 per cent – of families owned cars. The first assembly line in Britain, at the Morris works in 1934, came more than twenty years after Ford's pioneering effort in Detroit, while in Germany, Adolf Hitler's promised People's Car, which began production at the huge Wolfsburg plant in 1940, was diverted into war service and became a reality in the people's garages only long after World War Two.[22] Yet Germany can dispute with America the claim to have built the world's first true motorway: the AVUS (*Automobil-Verkehrs und Übungsstrasse*), a 6-mile combined racing track and suburban commuter route, built through the Grunewald in Berlin between 1913 and 1921. Though a private company produced a plan for nearly 15,000 miles of motorways in Germany as early as 1924, and though by the end of the 1920s another company was well advanced on a plan for a 550-mile highway connecting Hamburg, Frankfurt and Basle, only one other short inter-urban motorway connecting Cologne and Bonn got built before Hitler seized power in 1933.

Originally opposed to all the plans of the Weimar Republic, the Nazis hastily reversed their position; the *Autobahnen* promised quick unemployment relief, and they had critical military importance. So they simply took over the existing plans and, using a special subsidiary of the German State Railways, turned them into concrete at epic speed. Dr Todt, Inspector-General of the Reichsautobahnen Gesellschaft, finished the first stretch from Frankfurt to Darmstadt in the summer of 1935; his name proved only too symbolic, as there was a fatal accident that very day. Thence, with a construction force that reached 250,000 workers by 1934, the completion rate was dizzying: more than 600 miles by 1936, 1,900 miles by 1938, 2,400 miles by the start of World War Two.[23]

The pace showed. By later engineering standards, these early *Autobahnen* – still seen in almost pristine form in the DDR – are strikingly primitive: they run like a roller-coaster over every undulation in the landscape, almost devoid of cut-and-fill techniques; acceleration and deceleration lanes, ill understood and probably unnecessary for the cars of those days, are conspicuous by their absence; on- and off-ramps are too tightly engineered. But, primitive though they might be, the *Autobahnen* created a new highway landscape that would later be faithfully imitated in almost every other country in the world. And, ironically, it was precisely the landscape that MacKaye – the archetypal liberal-social democrat – had imagined in that

[21] Ibid.   [22] Flink, 1975, 32; Nelson, 1967, 70–2.
[23] G.B. Admiralty, 1945, 468–70; Anon., 1979, 13–15; Petsch, 1976, 141–3.

FIGURE 9.3 *AVUS*.
The *Automobil- Verkehrs und Übungsstrasse*, built through Berlin's Grunewald and completed in 1921, can claim to be the world's first true motorway.

paper of 1930: the separated carriageways, the grade-separated interchanges, the impeccably designed and landscaped service stations, even the huge blue signs with their distinctive lower-case lettering, that became part of a new global visual symbolism. The historic irony was this: independently conceived in Weimar Germany and Coolidgean America, they were indeed part of that movement that embraced Ernst May and Benton MacKaye, Martin Wagner and Henry Wright. It was the identity of the midwife that proved so disturbingly incongruous.

For in such long-distance inter-urban highway building, during the depression decade of the 1930s the United States lagged. Though the lawyer-planner Edward M. Bassett had coined the term 'freeway' in a *New*

York Times article of 1928, the notion remained on paper.[24] Apart from a longer-distance extension of the New York Parkway system into the neighbouring state of Connecticut – the Merritt and Wilbur Cross Parkways, which were toll roads, restricted to private motor traffic – America's first true inter-city motorway, the Pennsylvania Turnpike through the Appalachians from Carlisle near Harrisburg to Irwin near Pittsburgh, opened only in 1940.[25] December of that same year marked another milestone in the automobile age: Los Angeles completed its Arroyo Seco Parkway, now part of the Pasadena Freeway. Like the early *Autobahnen*, it was under-designed; in an extraordinary re-run of the opening of the first Autobahn, the opening ceremony was marked by a multiple shunt collision involving three car-loads of dignitaries.[26] Thereafter, war intervened: at its end, Los Angeles had precisely 11 miles of freeway.[27] Its 1939 freeway plan, which had been produced by the City Engineer Lloyd Aldrich with the aid of downtown business after the City had denied the money, was implemented only over the subsequent two decades.[28] Only then did the city of freeways deserve its appellation.

But perhaps what gave Los Angeles its mythical reputation was not the extent of its network – the New York metropolitan area, with the head start Moses gave it, could always win on that score – but the total dependence of its citizens on it, revealed by the rarity of public transportation and by that telling phrase of Angelenos who talk of 'going surface' as if it were an eccentric undertaking. It was also the distinctive lifestyle that ensued: a style exemplified by the heroine of Joan Didion's novel *Play It As It Lays*, who, deserted by her husband, 'turns to the freeways for sustenance', and is finally initiated:

> Again and again she returned to an intricate stretch just south of the interchange where a successful passage from the Hollywood onto the Harbor required a diagonal move across four lanes of traffic. On the afternoon when she finally did it without once braking or once losing the beat on the radio she was exhilarated, and that night slept dreamlessly.[29]

It was also the resulting pattern of urban growth. The opening of the Arroyo Seco was followed almost immediately by higher land values in Pasadena. Thence, wherever the freeways went, the developers followed. And, unlike Moses's network in New York, this system was not radial – or at most, only partially so; it rather formed a loose trapezoidal grid, giving roughly equal accessibility from anywhere to anywhere. True, this had also been a feature of the old Big Red Cars of the Pacific Electric Railway; Los Angeles's celebrated polycentric, dispersed quality antedated

[24] Foster, 1981, 110.   [25] Rae, 1971, 79–81.   [26] Jackson, K., 1985, 167.
[27] Brodsly, 1981, 112.   [28] Rae, 1971, 82–3; Brodsly, 1981, 101–2.
[29] cit. Brodsly, 1981, 56; cf. Banham, 1971, 214–15.

the freeway era by many decades, and, as the urban area tripled in population in the 1930s and 1940s, downtown traffic stayed constant. And, ironically, as the rail system decayed under the pressure of rising car ownership from the mid-1920s, its abandoned rights of way provided ideal routes for the new freeways.[30] But the automobile revolution, coming much earlier here than in most American cities – there were already close on 800,000 cars, two to every five people, in Los Angeles County by 1930 – brought early thrombosis to the downtown area and the early spread of business activities outside it, thus contributing to the city's conscious decision in the mid-1920s not to support transit, and to the business pressures in the next decade to build a freeway system.[31]

So Wells had proved right; but it all took longer than he had imagined, and its impacts were seen on Long Island and in the Los Angeles basin long before they were observable in the English shires. The first stretch of motorway in Britain, 8 miles round Preston in Lancashire, opened in December 1958, nearly forty years after its first German equivalent and fifty years after its first American one.[32] And only in the 1960s did the car begin fundamentally to affect the ways of life, and the settlement forms, of the English countryside.

Frank Lloyd Wright and the Soviet Deurbanists

In America, long before that, automobile-oriented suburbs were being consciously planned, even on a large scale. Thus in Kansas City, George E. Kessler's great city-parks plan of 1893–1910, which included recreational parkways, provided a basis for the developer Jesse Clyde Nichols's Country Club District begun in 1907–8; influenced both by the City Beautiful movement and by a bicycle tour of European Garden Cities, designed by Kessler to integrate with his parks, it was the first garden suburb specifically based on the automobile. Nichols deliberately bought cheap land outside the range of the city's streetcar system, allowing him to build at low density – first at six houses per acre, then even less; at the centre, the brilliant Country Club Plaza (originated by the architect Edward Buhler Delle in 1923–5) was the world's first car-based shopping centre.[33] In Los Angeles both Beverly Hills (1914) and Palos Verdes Estates (1923) followed similar planning principles; though the first was originally based on a Pacific Electric Railway station, both soon became classic early automobile suburbs.[34]

[30] Fogelson, 1967, 92, 175–85; Rae, 1971, 243; Warner, 1972, 138–41; Brodsly, 1981, 4; Foster, 1981, 17; Wachs, 1984, 303; Jackson, K., 1985, 122.
[31] Fogelson, 1967, 92, 177–8.   [32] Starkie, 1982, 1.
[33] Stern and Massingdale, 1981, 76; Jackson, K., 1985, 177–8, 258.
[34] Stern and Massingdale, 1981, 78; Jackson, K., 1985, 179–80.

FIGURE 9.4 *Kansas City, Country Club District.*
J.C. Nichols' Country Club Plaza (1922), equally, can lay claim to be the first out-of-town shopping centre.

All these were private speculative developments pure and simple. They were designed to make money and they did. They owed their outstanding success to the quality of their design and to the use of private covenants to guarantee that this quality would be maintained. But there was also a highly idealized version of the automobile city, and a rationale for it. Appropriately enough, the most complete formulation of it came from America's outstanding native architect, Frank Lloyd Wright. But another, uncannily similar version came from a source as unlikely as could be imagined: the Soviet Union.

The Soviet deurbanists of the 1920s, led by Moisei Ginsburg and Moisei Okhitovich, argued – like Wright, and perhaps influenced by him – that electricity and new transportation technologies, above all the car, would allow cities to empty out.[35] They too were essentially individualistic and anti-bureaucratic; they similarly argued for new kinds of built form based

[35] Parkins, 1953, 24; Frampton, 1968, 238; Bliznakov, 1976, 250–1; Starr, 1977, 90–1; Thomas, 1978, 275.

on factory-produced materials, with individual lightweight transportable homes located in natural countryside, thus creating a 'townless, fully decentralized, and even populated country';[36] they even envisaged the eventual razing of the cities to form huge parks and urban museums.[37] But these were Soviet planners, and their version of individualism was curiously collective: all activities, save sleeping and repose, would be communal.[38] The technological imperative was identical to that of Frank Lloyd Wright; the moral order was – at least superficially – quite different.

In the event, given material conditions in the Soviet Union at the time, it was all quite fantastic. There were hardly any cars, and not much electricity. Well might Corbusier, who was of course allied to the opposite urbanist camp, parody the deurbanist vision:

> The cities will be part of the country; I shall live 30 miles from my office in one direction, under a pine tree; my secretary will live 30 miles away from it too, in the other direction, under another pine tree. We shall both have our own car. We shall use up tires, wear out road surfaces and gears, consume oil and gasoline. All of which will necessitate a great deal of work . . . enough for all.[39]

Perhaps such a vision was all conceivable in America; even in the depression-ridden America of the early 1930s. But in the Soviet Union, even given the appalling condition of Moscow's housing and infrastructure at the time, it was not. The historic 1931 Party Congress determined that anyone who denied the socialist character of existing cities was a saboteur; from 1933, a decree laid it down that city centres should be rebuilt to express 'socialist greatness'.[40] Stalin had spoken; the great Soviet urban debate was stilled for a generation.

Frank Lloyd Wright's vision, in contrast, was perfectly attuned not only to its author's personal philosophy, but also to the conditions of its time. It was, indeed, the distillation of almost everything that he felt and had expressed about the theory of built form. In the process, it managed in a rather extraordinary way to weave together almost every significant strain of American urban – more precisely, anti-urban – thinking.

Wright began to conceive of Broadacre City as early as 1924, and soon afterwards coined the title in a lecture at Princeton University.[41] The conception shares many philosophical affinities with the ideas of the Regional Planning Association of America, and some of these with Ebenezer Howard. There is the same rejection of the big city – specifically, New York – as a cancer, a 'fibrous tumour'; the same populist antipathy to finance capital and landlordism; the same anarchist rejection of big

---

[36] Bliznakov, 1976, 250.   [37] Thomas, 1978, 275.   [38] Bliznakov, 1976, 251.
[39] Le Corbusier, 1967, 74.   [40] Bliznakov, 1976, 252-4.   [41] Wright, 1945, 138.

government; the same reliance on the liberating effects of new technologies; the same belief in the homesteading principle and the return to the land; there is even that distinctively American transcendentalism that derives from writers like Emerson, Thoreau and Whitman.[42]

But there are also differences, particularly in comparison with Howard (as indeed with the Soviet deurbanists): Wright claimed to liberate men and women not in order to join in co-operation, but to live as free individuals; he desired not to marry town and country, but to merge them.[43] Above all, there is the notion that the new technological forces could recreate in America a nation of free independent farmers and proprietors: 'Edison and Ford would resurrect Jefferson.'[44] In this regard, the similarity is rather with the Greenbelt communities of Rexford Tugwell; but Tugwell shared with Mumford, Stein and Chase a belief in community planning, hard to trace in Wright. Rather, Wright shares with the RPAA a common background of experience: the slow decay of rural America, ground down between the soul-destroying drudgery of the pre-electric farm and the welcoming bright lights of the city, as poignantly recorded by Hamlin Garland in his autobiographical *A Son of the Middle Border*:

> In those few days, I perceived life without its glamor. I no longer looked upon these toiling women with the thoughtless eyes of youth. I saw no humor in the bent forms and graying hair of the men. I began to understand that my own mother had trod a similar slavish round with never a full day of leisure, with scarcely an hour of escape from the tugging hands of children, and the need of mending and washing clothes.[45]

Liberated at last by World War One and the automobile, they left the farms 'in rattle-trap automobiles, their fenders tied with springs, and curtains flapping in the breeze . . . with no funds and no prospects'.[46] And then, the migration turned into sheer necessity, as depression brought farm foreclosures and the forced conversion of proprietors into sharecroppers.[47] Yet, as Charles Abrams put it at the time, 'Not only is the frontier closed, but the city is closed'; the farmer had nowhere to go.[48] Hence the Resettlement Administration's greenbelt towns, described in chapter 4; hence Broadacre City.

[42] White and White, 1962, 193; Grabow, 1977, 116–17; Fishman, 1977, 124–7; Ciucci, 1979, 296–300, Muschamp, 1983, 75.
[43] Fishman, 1977, 92–4.   [44] Ibid. 123.   [45] Garland, 1917, 366.
[46] Fogelson, 1967, 74.   [47] Abrams, 1939, 68.   [48] Ibid.

FIGURE 9.5   *Broadacre City.*
Frank Lloyd Wright's 'Usonian Vision' of the low-density marriage of suburb and countryside; every citizen simultaneously an urbanite and a farmer. Something perilously like it happened all over the US in the 1950s, but stripped of its social and economic message.

But Broadacre would be different. The new technologies, as Kropotkin had argued more than three decades earlier, were transforming, even abolishing, the tyranny of geography. 'Given electrification, distances are all but eliminated as far as communication goes. . . . Given the steamship, airship, and the automobile, our human sphere of movement immeasurably widens by many mechanical modes, by wheel or air.'[49] Now, 'not only thought but speech and movement are volatile: the telegraph, telephone, mobilization, radio. Soon, television and safe flight.'[50] Modern mobility was available even for the poor man, 'by means of a bus or a model A Ford'.[51]

Coupled with this, new building materials – high-pressure concrete, glass and 'innumerable broad, thin, cheap sheets of wood, metal or plastics' – made a new kind of building possible: 'buildings may be made by machinery going to the building instead of the building going to machinery.'[52] And at the same time, 'machine-shop fabrication' made water and gas and electricity cheaply 'available in quantity for all instead of still more questionable luxuries for the few'.[53] So 'the congested verticality of any city is now utterly inartistic and *unscientific!*'[54]

Out of these technological ingredients, Wright constructed what he called his 'Usonian Vision':

> Imagine, now, spacious, well-landscaped highways, grade crossings eliminated by a new kind of integrated by-passing or over- or under-passing all traffic in cultivated or living areas. . . . Giant roads, themselves great architecture, pass public service stations no longer eyesores but expanded as good architecture to include all kinds of roadside service for the traveller, charm and comfort throughout. These great roads unite and separate, separate and unite, in endless series of diversified units passing by farm units, roadside markets, garden schools, dwelling places, each on its acres of individually adorned and cultivated ground, developed homes all places for pleasure in work or leisure. And imagine man-units so arranged that every citizen as he chooses may have all forms of production, distribution, self-improvement, enjoyment within the radius of, say, ten to twenty miles of his own home. And speedily available by means of his private car or public conveyance. This integrated distribution of living related to ground composes the great city that I see embracing this country. This would be the Broadacre City of tomorrow that is the nation. Democracy realized.[55]

Broadacre, of course, would be a city of individuals. Its houses would be designed

> not only in harmony with greenery and ground but intimate with the pattern of the personal life of the individual on the ground. No two homes, no two

---

[49] Wright, 1945, 34.   [50] Ibid. 36.   [51] Ibid. 86.   [52] Ibid. 37.
[53] Ibid.   [54] Ibid. 34.   [55] Ibid. 65–6.

gardens, none of the farm units on one – to two, three – to ten acres or more; no two farmsteads or factory buildings need be alike. . . . Strong but light and appropriate houses, spacious convenient workplaces to which all would be tributary, each item would be solidly and sympathetically built out of materials native to Time, Place, and Man.[56]

All this was the physical shell. But for Wright, just as for Mumford or for Howard, the built forms were merely the appropriate expression of a new kind of society. The skyscraper city, for him, represented 'the end of an epoch! The end of the plutocratic republic of America'.[57] Through another mass migration, as huge and as momentous as the original homesteading of America, the new pioneer would replace the plutocracy of the landlords and the giant corporations by 'a more simple, natural-basis right to live by and enough to live upon according to his better self'.[58] The vision is almost identical to Howard's:

> Emancipated from rent, were good ground made available to him, he – the machine worker rented by wages – paying toll to the exaggerated city in order that the city give him work to do – why should not he, the poor wage-slave, go forward, not backward, to his native birthright? Go to the good ground and grow his family in a free city?[59]

There, he would rediscover the quintessential American democracy 'the ideal of reintegrated decentralization . . . many free units developing strength as they learn by function and grow together in spacious mutual freedom.'[60] It was the vision of his Wisconsin boyhood, recaptured through the new technology.

No one liked it. For his pains, he was attacked by almost everyone: for naïvety, for architectural determinism, for encouraging suburbanization, for wasteful use of resources, for lack of urbanity, above all for being insufficiently collective in his philosophy.[61] He developed no movement to realize his ideas, received no commissions from Tugwell's Resettlement Administration, and got no moral support at all from the other powerful figures – above all the leaders of the RPAA – who were working in favour of planned decentralization.[62]

And, as Herbert Muschamp has eloquently argued, there was finally a contradiction in the whole vision: the free commonwealth of individuals would live in houses designed by the master architect:

> . . . when all the Whitmanesque windbag rhetoric extolling he pioneer spirit is swept away, what remains is a society constructed upon the strict hierarchical principle of Wright's own Taliesin Fellowship: a government of architecture, a society in which the architect is granted ultimate executive

[56] Ibid. 66.   [57] Ibid. 120.   [58] Ibid. 121.   [59] Ibid. 86.
[60] Ibid. 45–6.   [61] Grabow, 1977, 119–22.   [62] Fishman, 1977, 146–8.

power . . . It is easy, therefore, to view Broadacre as proof that within every self-styled individualist is a dictator longing to break free.[63]

The heart of the contradiction, for Muschamp, lay in the belief that the architect could control the whole process. In fact, by the early 1950s, the American actuality 'threatened to liquidate his own Romantic dream in a vista of carports, split-levels, lawn sprinklers washing away the Usonian dream to make way for the weekend barbecue.'[64] The final irony came at the end of the 1950s: Wright unsuccessfully sued the local county to remove the pylons that disfigured the view from Taliesin III, erected to carry power to new Phoenix suburbanites. Yet, in the same decade, driving Alvar Aalto around the Boston suburbs, he could claim that he had made all this possible. Muschamp comments:

> Didn't the Adventurer in Wright want to roar with laughter at the thought that the greatest architect of all time had made possible the conversion of America's natural paradise to an asphalt continent of Holiday Inns, Tastee-Freeze stands, automobile graveyards, billboards, smog, tract housing, mortgaged and franchised coast to coast?[65]

Perhaps. There was a contradiction, to be sure: Wright wanted it all architect-designed, sanitized, in uniform good taste; it came out anything but. Perhaps he did have more in common with the Soviet deurbanists than either would have admitted; they were all architects, after all. Yet Broadacre City is significant for the nature of its vision. It probably could not have occurred in just that way, when it did, in any other country. It seized the American future, embodied it in a vision. The remarkable fact is just how visionary it proved to be.

'The suburbs are coming!'

This then was the ironic outcome: after World War Two a suburban building boom created a kind of Broadacre City all over America, but entirely divorced from the economic basis or the social order Wright had so steadfastly affirmed. In the late 1940s and the 1950s, thousands of square miles of American farmland disappeared under it; one *New Yorker* cartoon showed a traditional farm family sitting on their porch with a bulldozer rearing over the brow of the near-by hill, as the wife shouts 'Pa, get your gun! The suburbs are coming.' But the people who moved into the new tract homes typically owed their living to those very mammoth corporations which Wright assailed; their homes were mortgaged to giant financial institutions; and in no sense did they constitute a society of sturdy

[63] Muschamp, 1983, 79–80.   [64] Ibid. 93.   [65] Ibid. 185.

self-sufficient proprietors. Americans had got the shell without the substance.

There were four main foundations for the suburban boom. They were new roads, to open up land outside the reach of the old trolley and commuter rail routes; zoning of land uses, to produce uniform residential tracts with stable property values; government-guaranteed mortgages, to make possible long-repayment low-interest mortgages that were affordable by families of modest incomes; and a baby boom, to produce a sudden surge in demand for family homes where young children could be raised. The first three of these were already in place, though sometimes only in embryonic form, a decade before the boom began. The fourth triggered it.

The first part, the roads, were embryonic. As already seen, they were there in one or two places: New York from the 1920s, Los Angeles from the 1940s. But, remarkably, developers do not seem to have appreciated their potential for a decade or more after they were in place. Still, in the 1930s, a majority of New Yorkers did not own cars. And many of those who did happened to work in Manhattan, to which car commuting was almost impossible; suburbanization must await the outward movement of jobs to places where the car was more convenient than the subway – which began to happen on any scale only in the 1950s. And in any event, generally the roads were not there. The Depression and the wartime years had brought a halt to the rise in car ownership; not until 1949 did registrations again exceed the level of 1929.[66] And road-building, too, had stagnated.

It was the 1956 Federal-Aid Highway Act that marked the real beginning of freeway suburbanization. But at the beginning, it does not seem to have been meant that way at all. True, Roosevelt in 1941 had appointed Rexford Tugwell, Frederic Delano and Harland Bartholomew – all known supporters of planned decentralization of people and jobs – to an Inter-Regional Highways Committee under the chairmanship of Bibb Graves of Alabama, and served by Thomas H. MacDonald, Commissioner of Public Roads – whom MacKaye had commended, in that paper of 1930, for his 'far-seeing' approach to 'broad-gauged regional and Inter-regional planning'.[67] it called for a 32,000-mile Interstate system, and Congress duly passed the Federal-Aid Highway Act of 1944. But that was to be a strictly inter-urban system, bypassing the cities; and, before it could be built, political splits emerged: between engineers who just wanted to pour concrete and city planners (like the veteran Harland Bartholomew) who wanted to use new roads to cure urban blight, between those who wanted self-financing toll roads and those who wanted federal subsidy. Truman in 1949, Eisenhower in 1954, signed Urban Renewal Acts, but kept highways out of them.

[66] Tobin, 1976, 104.   [67] MacKaye, 1930, 95.

Finally, Eisenhower – who believed that he had won the war on the German *Autobahnen* – accepted the argument that new roads were not only vital for national defence in an era of Cold War, but could also generate an economic boom. He called on a retired General, Lucius Clay, to head a committee of inquiry; most of the evidence came from the pro-roads side – including Robert Moses, who used the roads-fight-blight argument. But the fight over paying for them, which was essentially between fiscal conservatives and the highways lobby, almost killed the resulting bill. Finally, a compromise version, providing for the new roads to be built by a special fund through a tax on gasoline, oil, buses and trucks, was passed in June 1956; in the House of Representatives it went through without dissent, in the Senate one solitary vote was recorded against it.[68] The greatest public-works programme in the history of the world – $41 billion for 41,000 miles of new roads – was under way.

The critical question, still, was what sort of road system it should be. Congress in 1944 had endorsed the principle that it should bypass the cities. Planners like Bartholomew and Moses argued on the contrary that it should penetrate into their hearts, thus removing blighted areas and improving accessibility from the suburbs to downtown offices and shops. In practice, given the strength of the urban renewal lobby in the 1950s and 1960s, there was little doubt about the outcome: the system would be used to create new corridors of accessibility from city centres to potential suburbs, as Moses had tried to do thirty years earlier.[69] When the programme began in earnest, its chief Bertram D. Tallamy said that the new highways were built on principles that Moses had taught him as long ago as 1926;[70] at that time and for long after, Moses was, after all, the only really experienced urban-highway builder in the United States.

The second requirement, zoning, had originated as early as 1880 in Modesto, California, where it had been used to remove Chinese laundries: a particularly apt beginning, since thereafter one of its principal functions was to safeguard property values by excluding undesirable land uses and undesirable neighbours.[71] And – as seen in chapter 3 – the city that took the lead in the zoning movement from 1913 on, New York City, was impelled to do so by the complaints of Manhattan retailers who, complaining that industrial incursions were threatening their profits, appealed loudly to 'every man who owns a home or rents an apartment';[72] the city's Commission on Building Heights accepted their argument that zoning secured 'greater safety and security in investment'.[73] And the historic 1926 Supreme Court decision, *Euclid* v. *Ambler*, which confirmed the general validity of zoning,

[68] Davies, 1975, 13–23; Rose, 1979, 19, 26, 62–4, 70–99.
[69] Leavitt, 1970, 28–35.   [70] Caro, 1974, 11.   [71] Marcuse, 1980, 32–3.
[72] Scott, 1969, 154–5.   [73] Glaab and Brown, 1976, 266.

seems to have accepted Alfred Bettman's argument that its point was to enhance property values.[74] The point at issue, significantly, was whether land should be zoned industrial or residential.[75]

Because it was meticulously designed as part of a general police power to safeguard 'public welfare' and 'public health, safety, morals and convenience', thus to avoid all suggestion of compulsory purchase with claims for compensation, New York's comprehensive zoning resolution of 1916 deliberately avoided long-term plans; Edward Bassett, the attorney in change, proudly declared 'We have gone at it block by block', invariably confirming the status quo.[76] And most of America followed suit. Thus arose a paradox: land use control in the United States, in sharp contrast to much of Europe, came to be divorced from any kind of land-use planning; it could not be used to raise the level of design, which had to be secured – on the model of Kansas City's Country Club District and its imitators – through private restrictive covenants.[77]

The third precondition for the suburban boom was cheap long-term housing finance. In this regard, as already noticed in chapter 3, America lagged strangely behind Britain. There, the permanent building societies had developed from the turn of the century, offering twenty- or twenty-five-year mortgages with low down payments, and powerfully fuelling the great suburban spread around London in the 1920s and 1930s. In contrast, until the 1930s the typical American mortgage was only for five or ten years at 6 or 7 per cent interest: a ruinously high burden for the average family.[78] It was an early New Deal experiment – the Home Owners Loan Corporation (HOLC), introduced as an emergency measure of April 1933 to stem farm foreclosures – that introduced into America the long-term, self-amortizing mortgage. The next year, the National Housing Act established the Federal Housing Authority (FHA), with powers to insure longer-term mortgage loans by private lenders for home construction and sale, with a down payment as low as 10 per cent and a period of twenty-five or thirty years at only 2 or 3 per cent.[79] Between 1938 and 1941, it was insuring some 35 per cent of all home loans in the United States.[80]

From 1934, then, the most powerful constraint to suburban home-building had been removed. For the FHA took over from the HOLC the notion of appraising whole neighbourhoods, and thereby redlining those deemed to be undesirable; in practice, this meant the whole of America's inner cities. Further, the 'FHA exhorted racial segregation and endorsed it as a public policy'; as late as 1966, it had not insured a single mortgage in Paterson or Camden in New Jersey, two predominantly black cities.[81]

---

[74] cit. Fluck, 1986, 333.   [75] Ibid. 328; Bettman, 1946, 54.
[76] Scott, 1969, 154–6.   [77] Lubove, 1967, 14.
[78] Tunnard and Reed, 1955, 239–40; Jackson, K., 1985, 196.
[79] Jackson, K., 1985, 196, 205.   [80] Glaab and Brown, 1976, 275.
[81] Jackson, K., 1985, 213.

The central objective of the FHA was identical with that of zoning: it was to guarantee the security of residential real-estate values. And both worked through exclusion, to divert investment massively into new suburban house-building at the expense of the central city.

Some of the consequences could already be glimpsed later in that decade. The National Resources Committee's report *Our Cities*, published in 1937 (and already discussed in chapter 5), drew attention to the fact that even between 1920 and 1930, suburbs had grown twice as fast as central cities: 'the urbanite is rapidly becoming the suburbanite', as families fulfilled 'the urge to escape the obnoxious aspects of urban life without at the same time losing access to its economic and cultural advantages.'[82] During that decade, some suburbs had grown at dizzy speed: Beverly Hills by 2,500 per cent; Shaker Heights outside Cleveland by 1,000 per cent.[83] But then, the depression drastically cut new housing starts – by as much as 95 per cent between 1928 and 1933 – and brought a huge crop of mortgage foreclosures.[84] Not until after World War Two did the industry completely recover.

Given an almost complete moratorium on new construction – save for essential war-related building – between 1941 and 1945, the result at war's end was a huge accumulated shortage: an estimated 2.75–4.4 million families sharing, and another half-million in non-family quarters.[85] On top of that came the baby boom, as the servicemen returned and the delayed crop of wartime babies coincided with the regular cohorts. The industry spectacularly responded: as against a mere 515,000 starts in 1939, there were 1,466,000 by 1949, 1,554,000 by 1959.[86] And in the 1949 Housing Act – as well as initiating the urban renewal process, chronicled in chapter 7 – Congress massively increased FHA's lending powers.[87] As before, this money went into the suburbs. By 1950, the suburbs were found to be growing at ten times the rate of the central cities; by 1954, it was estimated that in the previous decade 9 million people had moved into the suburbs.[88] The 1950s, as the 1960 Census showed, was the decade of the greatest suburban growth in American history: while the central cities grew by 6 million or 11.6 per cent, the suburbs grew by a dizzy 19 million, or by 45.9 per cent. And ominously, for the first time, some of the nation's greatest cities recorded actual population decline: Boston and St Louis each lost 13 per cent of their population.[89]

This huge migration was made possible by a new breed of builder: large-scale, economy- and efficiency-conscious, capable of building houses like refrigerators or cars. The archetypal firm, which became a legend in its own time, had been founded by Abraham Levitt and his sons William and

[82] U.S. National Resources Planning Board, 1937, 35.   [83] Wright, 1981, 195.
[84] Glaab and Brown, 1976, 273.   [85] Checkoway, 1984, 154.
[86] Ibid.   [87] Ibid. 161.   [88] Jackson, K., 1985, 238.   [89] Tobin, 1976, 106.

FIGURE 9.6 *Levittown, Long Island.*
The Levitts' standard Cape Cod design, modified in countless ways by its owners; pleasant enough but ultimately bland, an *ersatz* version of the great suburbs of the American past.

Alfred, as a small family firm on Long Island outside New York City in 1929. During World War Two they learned how to build workers' housing fast, and rapidly waxed larger. In the town of Hempstead on Long Island, 23 miles from midtown Manhattan, they began in 1948 a suburb based on the techniques they had learned: flow production, division of labour, standardized designs and parts, new materials and tools, maximum use of prefabricated components, easy credit, good marketing. The people came and queued in long lines for hours to buy their houses; when the Levitts had finished, they had completed more than 17,000 homes housing some 82,000 people: the largest single housing development in history.[90] They went on to develop similar Levittowns in Pennsylvania and New Jersey.

In an afternoon peregrination down Long Island, the earnest student of planning history can progressively view Stein and Wright's pioneering Sunnyside Gardens of 1924, Atterbury's earlier model suburb at Forest Hills Gardens of 1912, and finally Levittown. The result, taken in that order, is anticlimatic. For Levittown is simply dull. It is not that there is

[90] Checkoway, 1984, 158; Jackson, K., 1985, 234–5.

anything wrong with it, considered simply as a piece of residential real estate. The Levitts' basic Cape Cod design, repeated in a limited number of variants, has since been modified by its owners in a thousand different ways, as the Levitts always intended it should. (And, if it is not sacrilegious to say, Richard Norman Shaw used a similar limited range of house types in his model London suburb at Bedford Park.) The trees have grown almost to maturity, softening the harshness of the original townscape as it appears in the old pictures.

But the residential streets are slightly too long and slightly too wide and slightly too straight, so – despite the variations – the overall result is monotonous and vapid. And the shopping centre – developed as a commercial strip along the Hempstead Turnpike that bisects the development – is a logistical and aesthetic disaster. The commuters have insufficient road access on to the main highway, so their cars back up; and once there, they come in conflict with the commercial traffic. The visual quality is the worst kind of 1950s American roadside goop; the whole area cries out for the kind of planned commercial mall that in the 1960s and 1970s the Americans did so often and so successfully. So as a piece of planning Levittown is for the most part inoffensive, only occasionally plain bad. What it lacks is any kind of imagination or visual delight, such as the best-planned suburbs in their different ways all offered. It is not bad, but it could be better.

It was, and is, also rigidly segregated by age, income and race. Those who came here were overwhelmingly young married couples in the lower-middle income range, and without exception they were white: as late as 1960, Levittown had not a single black, and in the mid-1980s it does not have conspicuously many. As the elder Levitt put it, 'We can solve a housing problem, or we can try to solve a racial problem. But we cannot combine the two.'[91] So Levittown, and all its countless imitators, were homogeneous places: like lived with like. And, as places like St Louis eloquently showed, a large part of the suburban flight from the city was white flight: here as elsewhere, the blacks were coming from the countryside to the city, the whites were simultaneously leaving the city for the suburbs.[92]

The question will be asked and should be asked: what has all this to do with planning? Does a place like Levittown belong in a history of city planning at all? Insofar as Long Island had both planners and plans, then – at least in a formal sense – it does. But Gottdiener's exhaustive analysis suggests that in practice Long Island's planners had little power: 'The decisions made by the politicians, speculators and housing developers lead to the same land-use pattern', he concludes, 'as would result from no planning or zoning.'[93] This leads him to ask: 'if planners do not implement

---

[91] Jackson, K., 1985, 241.   [92] Montgomery, 1985, 236.
[93] Gottdiener, 1977, 111.

land-use decisions nor guide directly social growth in our society, we are left with the intriguing question – what, then, do planners do?'[94] His answer is that they produce plans: 'The planning process, as it is usually practised in the society, makes planners advisory bystanders to decisions that are being carried out elsewhere – by political leaders and private businessmen';[95] their ideas – whether on physical matters, or on social – find little favour among the majority of white middle-class suburban residents, who would like yet more low-density suburban sprawl. Which, after all, is hardly surprising.

Suburbia: The Great Debate

But – here, or elsewhere – the planners had some vocal people on their side; while those who built the suburbs, and those who lived in them, were either too preoccupied or not sufficiently voluble to defend them. So, as it burgeoned, American suburbia came to be almost universally vilified in the public prints. What condemned it was the fact that it failed to conform to traditional – that is to say, European – notions of urbanity. Here are three representative critiques:

> In every department, form disintegrated: except in its heritage from the past, the city vanished as an embodiment of collective art and technics. And where, as in North America, the loss was not alleviated by the continued presence of great monuments from the past and persistent habits of social living, the result was a raw, dissolute environment and a narrow, constricted, and baffled social life.[96]

> Sprawl is bad aesthetics; it is bad economics. Five acres are being made to do the work of one, and do it very poorly. This is bad for the farmers, it is bad for communities, it is bad for industry, it is bad for utilities, it is bad for the railroads, it is bad for the recreation groups, it is bad even for the developers.[97]

> The question is, shall we have 'slurbs', or shall we plan to have attractive communities which can grow in an orderly way while showing the utmost respect for the beauty and fertility of our landscape? If present trends continue, we shall have slurbs.[98]

Many points of attack recur here: waste of land, increased commute times, higher service costs, lack of parkland. But the central criticism is that the suburbs lack *form*. As usual, Mumford puts it best, in his appreciation of the garden-city alternative: 'A modern city, no less than a medieval town

---

94 Ibid. 116.   95 Ibid. 143.   96 Mumford, 1938, 8.
97 Whyte, 1958, 117.   98 Wood and Heller, 1962, 13.

... must have a definite size, form, boundary. It was no longer to be a mere sprawl of houses along an indeterminate avenue that moved towards infinity and ended suddenly in a swamp.'[99]   Ian Nairn, similarly, criticized the suburban landscape for the fact that 'each building is treated in isolation, nothing binds it to the next one', for 'togetherness in the landscape or townscape, like the coexistence of opposites, is essential.'[100]

The interesting fact is that the intellectual counter-attack, when it finally came, originated from the American west. James E. Vance, a Berkeley geographer, argued for the San Francisco Bay Area that

> It is fashionable, if extremely trite, to refer to the urban area as a shapeless sprawl, as a cancer, as an unrelieved evil. . . . The erroneous notion that no such structure exists must result from a failure to study the dynamics of urban growth, or possibly from the desire to put forward a doctrine of what is 'right' or 'good' in urban growth.[101]

And Robert Riley similarly defended the 'new' cities of the American southwest, like Houston and Dallas and Phoenix:

> The new city has been damned simply because it is different. . . . The planning proposals made for these cities – and, largely, too, for Eastern megalopolises – are based on nothing more or less than channelling growth back into a form that we recognize as the only true city – the traditional city.[102]

Taking up the case for the defence, Melvin Webber of Berkeley argued,

> I contend that we have been searching for the wrong grail, that the values associated with the desired urban structure do not reside in the spatial structure per se. One pattern and its internal land use form is superior to another only as it better serves to accommodate ongoing spatial processes and to further the nonspatial ends of the political community. I am flatly rejecting the contention that there is an overriding universal spatial or physical aesthetic of urban form.[103]

New communications technologies, he argued, had broken down the age-old connection between community and propinquity: the urban place was being replaced by the nonplace urban realm.[104] Early the next decade, Reyner Banham wrote his appreciative essay on Los Angeles;[105] the year after that, Robert Venturi and Denise Scott Brown published their celebrated exercise in architectural iconoclasm, boldly proclaiming across its dust jacket: 'A Significance for A&P Parking Lots, or *Learning from Las Vegas* . . . Billboards are Almost All Right'.[106] The battle lines could not be more

---

[99] Mumford, 1938, 397.   [100] Nairn, 1965, 13.   [101] Vance, 1964, 68–9.
[102] Riley, 1967, 21.   [103] Webber, 1963, 52.   [104] Webber, 1964b, *passim*.
[105] Banham, 1971.   [106] Venturi, Brown and Izenour, 1972.

FIGURE 9.7   *The Las Vegas strip.*
The ultimate highway strip city; the signs are the true townscape; the buildings
are reduced to decorated sheds, surrounded by the vast spaces of the parking lots.

clearly drawn: the West Coast had at last reasserted itself against the
traditions of Europe.

The defection of Venturi, one of America's most distinguished architects,
was especially significant. For he and his colleagues were passionately
arguing that the roadside civilization of American suburbia, most exuberantly
exemplified by the great neon-lit Strip at Las Vegas, should no longer be
judged by the functionalist criteria that had ruled ever since the triumph
of the international style in the 1930s.

'Learning from the existing landscape', they began, 'is a way of being
revolutionary for an architect. Not the obvious way, which is to tear down
Paris and begin again, as Corbusier suggested in the 1920s, but another,
more tolerant way; that is, to question how we look at things.'[107] They
studied Las Vegas 'as a phenomenon of architectural communication';[108]

[107] Venturi *et al.*, 1972, 0 [*sic*].   [108] Ibid.

because people now moved in cars at high speeds and often in complex patterns, a whole new architecture of signs had arisen to guide and to persuade: 'the graphic sign in space has become the architecture of this landscape',[109] while the building itself is set back, half hidden – like most of the environment – by parked cars:

> The A&P parking lot is a current phase in the evolution of vast space since Versailles. The space that divides high-speed highway and low, sparse buildings produces no enclosure and little direction. To move through a piazza is to move through high enclosing forms. To move through this landscape is to move over vast expansive texture: the megastructure of the commercial landscape ... Because the spatial relationships are made by symbols more than by forms, architecture in this landscape becomes symbol in space rather than form in space. Architecture defines very little. The big sign and the little building is the rule of Route 66.[110]

This analysis, notice, represents the perfect analogue at the micro-, or urban-design, scale of the Berkeley geographer-planners' argument at the wider urban-structural scale: the new landscape is not worse, it is different; it cannot be appreciated and should not be judged by the traditional rules, but by its own.

The result, for international architecture, was cataclysmic: *Learning from Las Vegas* is one of the distinct breakpoints that mark the end of the modern architectural movement and its displacement by post-modernism, with its new stress on architecture as symbolic communication.[111] For the student of urbanism, it likewise marked a revolution: henceforth, the artefacts of roadside civilization were worthy of study for their own sake. So, by the mid-1980s, a scholarly treatise could trace the evolution of the 1920s motor court into the 1930s motel and finally into the 1950s motor hotel; this last mutation represented by the historic first Holiday Inn, developed by Kemmons Wilson and the prefabricated home-builder Wallace E. Johnson in Memphis, Tennessee, in 1952.[112] Or it could analyse the evolution of the fast-food outlet from the White Castle chain started by Edgard Ingram and Walter Anderson at Kansas City in 1921, via Howard Johnson's pioneering efforts in Massachusetts in 1929–30 and the historic McDonalds drive-in at San Bernardino, California, in 1948, to their standard design of 1952, first marketed nationally by Ray Kroc at Des Plaines, Illinois, in 1955.[113] Such work revealed just how long and rich this tradition of roadside architecture had been, making it the more remarkable that previously no one had possessed the sensibility or the energy to see or to analyse the landscape in front of them.

But long before this overturn in aesthetics, as early as the 1960s the

[109] Ibid. 9.   [110] Ibid. 10.   [111] Jencks, 1981, 45.   [112] Liebs, 1985, 182–5.
[113] Ibid. 185, 202, 206–8, 212–13; Langdon, 1986, 29–55, 81–109.

Figure 9.8 *The first Holiday Inn.*
Memphis, Tennessee, 1952: the birth of the roadside chain. Three years later came the first standardized, franchised McDonalds outlet, in Des Plaines, Illinois.

great intellectual reversal had begun with a whole series of studies from American social scientists, fundamentally questioning many of the basic assumptions that had underlain the previous criticisms of the suburbs and the suburban way of life. Particularly important were those from the sociologists. During the 1950s, several classic works of mainstream American urban sociology – Riesman's *The Lonely Crowd*, Whyte's *The Organization Man* – had reinforced the stereotype of the suburb as a place of boring homogeneity, in which all individuality was progressively eroded away and rich human interaction was lacking; suburbanization, the inference clearly ran, would eventually destroy most of what was valuable in the culture of cities.[114] To test these assumptions, Herbert Gans went to live in Levittown, New Jersey, for an extended period. His book, which appeared in 1967, predictably triggered critical reviews in East Coast papers. For Gans discovered that the conventional wisdom was a myth:

> The findings ... suggest that the distinction between urban and suburban ways of living postulated by the critics (and by some sociologists as well) is

[114] Riesman, 1950, 132–4; Whyte, 1956, 46–7.

more imaginary than real. Few changes can be traced to the suburban qualities of Levittown, and the sources that did cause change, like the house, the population mix, and newness, are not distinctively suburban. Moreover . . . when suburbs are compared to the large urban residential areas beyond the downtown and inner districts, culture and social structure are virtually the same among people of similar age and class. Young lower middle class people in these areas live much like their peers in the suburbs, but quite unlike older, upper middle class ones, in either urban or suburban neighborhoods.[115]

The Levittowners, Gans found, refused to fit the labels that earlier sociologists had tried to pin on them:

> Levittowners are not really members of the national society, or for that matter, of a mass society. They are not apathetic conformists ripe for takeover by a totalitarian elite or corporate merchandiser; they are not conspicuous consumers and slaves to sudden whims of fashion, they are not even organization men or particularly other-directed personalities. . . . Their culture may be less subtle and sophisticated than that of the intellectual, their family life less healthy than that advocated by psychiatrists, and their politics less thoughtful and democratic than the political philosophers' – yet all these are superior to what prevailed among the working and lower middle classes of past generations.[116]

Gans's conclusions massively reinforced those of another sociologist, Bennett Berger, of blue-collar workers in a California suburb. He too had found that these typical suburbanites did not behave as earlier investigations of suburbia had suggested they should: they were not socially or geographically mobile, they were not joiners or belongers, and their neighbours were people like themselves.[117] The fact was that these other studies had analysed relatively unusual upper-middle-class communities, or had overstressed upper-middle-class features in mixed communities. Typical suburbanites, those who inhabited the new mass-produced suburbs, simply did not share the same concerns; they would be living much the same lives, with much the same patterns of social relationships, whether they lived in areas labelled as urban or in areas labelled as suburban. Thus, sociologist-planners had hopelessly exaggerated the effect of the physical character of the urban milieu upon people's lifestyles. In Gans's conclusion:

> The planner has only limited influence over social relationships. Although the site planner can create propinquity, he can only determine which houses are to be adjacent. He can thus affect visual contacts and initial social contacts among their occupants, but he cannot determine the intensity or quality of the relationships. This depends on the characteristics of the people involved.[118]

[115] Gans, 1967a, 288.   [116] Ibid. 417.   [117] Berger, 1960, 15–25, 58–9, 65.   [118] Gans, 1961a, 139.

True, the character of an area – its social homogeneity, or otherwise – could be affected by planning. But only within very narrow limits; in a society like the American one, the market will be the main determinant and the customers will register their own preferences there. Above all, planners must beware of trying to impose their own value systems upon people with quite different ones: particularly, if they believed that long commuter trips and traffic congestion are to be avoided at all costs, and that higher densities would be better because they would cut commuter times and save land and increase urbanity, they must be aware that most suburbanites will just not agree.[119] In other words, in attacking the essential features of post-1945 American suburbia, they were simply expressing their own class prejudices.

Thus spoke the sociologist. A few years later, one of America's most distinguished land economists, Marion Clawson, made his own investigation of the costs of suburban sprawl. He gave his verdict: 'It is impossible to judge suburban land conversion simply and unequivocally – to say that it is 'good' or 'bad' or describe it by using some other single and unqualified term. The process is much too complicated for that.'[120]

On the plus side, it had been a process of extraordinary vitality, producing millions of new homes and hundreds of shopping districts, and thus contributing to national economic growth; it had produced a lot of rather good housing and of rather pleasant neighbourhoods; and the dispersed nature of the whole decision-making process had avoided big blunders.[121] On the negative side, the costs of scatteration had made house prices needlessly high; much land had simply gone to waste, needlessly, and might remain thus for a long time; and the results had been less aesthetically pleasing than many buyers might have liked, for they had little or no choice.[122] But the most serious criticism, according to Clawson, was that the whole package had proved too expensive for a full half of the population: thus the urban population had become increasingly stratified by race, income and occupation. Of course, Clawson was quick to admit, some of this segregation arose from deeper social and economic forces; but the suburban development process had certainly contributed.[123]

Thus Clawson's economic verdict put a marginal gloss on Berger's and Gans's sociological one: yes, Americans did make their free choices in the market-place, and thus got approximately what they want, more effectively and efficiently than via a centrally planned system; but no, the process was not completely efficient in doing this, and could be improved so as to generate a slightly better housing package at a slightly lower cost. There was a more-than-marginal point too: half of all Americans were shut off

[119] Gans, 1961b, 293.   [120] Clawson, 1971, 317.   [121] Ibid. 319.
[122] Ibid. 319–20.   [123] Ibid. 321.

from the process altogether because they were too poor (and, in some cases, because they were black, which amounted to being poor). But one could well retort that at bottom, this was a problem outside the province of the urban planner: the problem of the poor was that they lacked money. If they had it, Clawson affirmed, they would go and get exactly what the more fortunate half of the poupulation had: a stake in suburbia. Planning and related forms of public intervention, then, could improve the process somewhat; but fundamentally, it gave the mass of people what they wanted.

Controlling Suburban Growth in Europe

That conclusion was of more than strictly American interest. For, in varying degrees, European governments after World War Two had succeeded in controlling and regulating the suburban tide to a degree that would have been unthinkable in the United States. By the mid-1960s, that was even evident to transatlantic air travellers from their vantage point 7 miles up: travelling west, they would be bemused by the scale of the development, by the apparently endless sprawl of the suburbs in the east-coast megalopolis, by the vast network of freeways that linked them; travelling east, they would be equally surprised by the relative puniness of the development, by its toytown-like quality, by the planned precision of the almost geometrical break between town and country, by the apparent absence of agricultural decay in the fringe areas around the suburbs. And all this would be true, with slight variations, in Britain, the Netherlands, the Federal Republic of Germany, or Scandinavia.[124]

The question, of course, was what costs and what benefits these tighter, neater systems had conferred on the people who lived under them. For the perpetrators of the conventional planning wisdom, of course, the answer was self-evident; but in the light of the American questioning of that wisdom, it was worth investigating. There was no better comparison to make than America versus Britain. For, ever since 1947, Britain had operated an extremely close control over new development: the historic Town and Country Planning Act of that year (chapter 4) had effectively nationalized the right to develop land, and thereafter the local planning authorities had used the new powers to contain suburban growth around the cities, employing green-belt restrictions to divert the pressures into more distant small and medium-sized towns. So, in parallel with the Clawson study, a British team worked to analyse the operation and the impacts of this containment policy.

Their results, published in 1973, cast yet more doubt on the conventional, comfortable picture. Land-use planning in postwar England, they concluded,

---

[124] Hall, 1967, 100.

had produced three main effects. The first was *containment*: the amount of land converted from rural to urban uses has been minimized and also compacted. A second, somewhat perverse, result was what the authors called *suburbanization*: the growing spatial separation of the new residential areas from the main employment centres. A third impact was even more perverse, in that it was totally undesired by anyone except perhaps a small body of speculators: it was *the inflation of land and property values*, on a scale never previously witnessed.[125]

Containment, the first effect, worked in various ways. Green belts around the conurbations and the larger free-standing towns had effectively stopped their further peripheral growth; beyond these green belts, development had been concentrated in small towns and villages, especially in the least attractive parts of each county; typically, densities had been kept up; the conurbation authorities had responded by building public housing that was dense and high, at any rate in comparison with the kinds of housing they had built before the 1939–45 war.[126] The leapfrogging pattern of urban development, so clearly evident in Clawson's American study, had been avoided.

Suburbanization had meant that the new residential developments were nearly all farther from employment opportunities than equivalent developments of the 1930s or any earlier decade; similarly they were more distant from the higher-level shopping, entertainment, educational and cultural facilities. So journeys, especially commuter trips, had become longer. This in part reflected the preference of planners for maintaining a traditional, centralized urban structure, in part the desire of city politicians to maintain the strongest possible economic base. But sociological study showed that the new suburbanites were well satisfied with their lifestyle and particularly with the long commuter trips that this involved; their main desire, indeed, was to move out further into the country.[127]

The rise in land values had been far in excess of the general salary or price level, and this undoubtedly had made new housing more expensive in real terms than in the 1930s. The developers had adjusted by using smaller sites, building at higher densities – particularly for cheaper housing – and reducing the quality of the houses below the levels that had become mandatory in the public sector. Since many builders also responded by switching into the higher-priced end of the market, which the planning authorities preferred to see anyway, the result was less housing choice at the lower end. In this respect, the research concluded, British policies had been far less sucessful than American ones in accommodating to the demands of a more affluent, more space-using lifestyle.[128]

---

[125] Hall, Thomas, Gracey and Drewett, 1973, II. 393–4.
[126] Ibid. II. 394–7.   [127] Ibid. II. 397–9.   [128] Ibid. II. 399–405.

The interesting point, as always, was who gained and who lost. The ruralites, especially the well-heeled ones, were the clear gainers: planning, by establishing a polite English version of apartheid, simply preserved the status quo and thus their comfortable lifestyle. The more affluent new suburbanites did well enough, though at a cost; the less affluent ones did much more badly, in terms of cramped space and relatively high costs. Since they were more likely to be one-car families, the burden of commuting might also be greater for them – though on that score, the research recorded few complaints.[129]

The group that had done worst, in the view of the team, was the people left in the cities. Those who had moved into public sector housing got good-quality homes, better equipped than the poorer owner-occupiers; but they were often forced to live at high densities and in high-rise blocks, which many did not like, in comparison with their equivalents of thirty and forty years earlier. And the low-income private tenant, living in substandard accommodation, had done worst of all. Thus the overall effect of the policies, in income terms, had been perversely regressive: those with the most had gained the most, and vice versa.[130] The team's analysis concluded:

> None of this was in the minds of the founding fathers of the planning system. They cared very much for the preservation and the conservation of rural England, to be sure. But that was only part of a total package of policies, to be enforced in the interests of all by beneficent central planning. It was certainly not the intention of the founders that people should lead cramped lives in homes destined for premature slumdom, far from urban services or jobs; or that city dwellers should live in blank cliffs of flats, far from the ground, without access to playspace for their children. Somewhere along the way, a great ideal was lost, a system distorted and the great mass of the people betrayed.[131]

When the British and American researchers compared their results, they concluded that both planning systems had produced inconsistent and perverse results. The tighter British system and the looser American system had both produced urban structures which few people had actually chosen, and few would have wanted if given the choice.[132] In both countries, the rich had done well out of urban development while the poor had done badly;[133] in both, the poor were condemned to inferior housing in the older inner cities. But for the great middle group, the verdict for the two countries was almost the opposite: in Britain they were housed too densely, in small houses almost certainly destined to become slums; in America they were housed too sprawlingly, with wasted land that benefited no one, and with consequently higher servicing costs.[134] In both countries, however, land-

[129] Ibid. II. 406–7.   [130] Ibid. II. 407–8.   [131] Ibid. II. 433.
[132] Clawson and Hall, 1973, 260.   [133] Ibid. 266–7.   [134] Ibid. 269.

use controls had made land for suburban development artificially scarce and had therefore aided the land speculator. So, in both countries, ordinary people would have benefited either from a much looser land-use planning regime, or from a much tighter one; what was not satisfactory was the halfway house.[135]

Which country then did worse? Was it better to live in Britain with its rather elaborate system of urban planning, which had produced results different from those its sponsors intended, or in the United States, where city planning never really promised much, and never delivered much? The answer, the study concluded, depended on your values. If you put a high priority on giving a large section of the population the material goods they want through market mechanisms, then you must conclude that American suburbia, for all its inefficiency and its occasional ugliness, is greatly superior to the cramped and costly British equivalent. If you put a greater value on protection by society of its land and the natural resources that go with it, you will probably elect for the British system of effective land-use planning. The American policy had been populist, the British policy more elitist.[136]

In the decade and a half since that conclusion, and especially during the 1980s, the British system has moved steadily in the direction of the American: the stress there too is increasingly on setting the land market free. But the paradox remains, and is bound to do so in any advanced country where different social and income groups obtained bundles of goods and bads from collective political action. Many people in Britain are still deeply committed to the preservation of the countryside and the containment of the cities, and they continue to be well organized in their rural shires and districts. Thus, even on the right wing of the political spectrum, there is a continuing built-in contradiction between the desire to let the developer serve market needs, and the need to palliate deep-held local fears and prejudices; a contradiction well seen in the 1986 statement by Nicholas Ridley, Secretary of State for the Environment and a leading Tory free-marketeer, that the green belt was sacrosanct in his hands. In the United States this balance is different; but there, too, nothing is clearer than the rise of the anti-growth movement in certain regions such as California, with results – in higher land and property prices – very similar to those observed in Britain.[137] So, perhaps, both countries were moving slowly and hesitantly towards each other.

Squaring the Circle: Planning the European Metropolis

Long before all that, of course – as we have already seen in chapter 5 – European planners had grappled with the problem of reconciling the car

[135] Ibid. [136] Ibid. 271. [137] Dowall, 1984, 132–3, 168–70.

and the city. Over the years from 1943 to 1965, several of Europe's capital cities produced plans which, in their different ways, suggested radical alternatives to America's city on the highway. Given the very different background of the European urban experience, that perhaps was not remarkable. What was more remarkable was that the plans actually got implemented.

Already, in his London plans of 1943 and 1944, Abercrombie had sought to use new urban highways, not merely to alleviate congestion, but to help define the identity of the neighbourhoods of the giant metropolis; here, he had drawn freely on the ideas of a Scotland Yard Assistant Commissioner, Alker Tripp, who had developed the idea of the residential precinct from which extraneous through traffic – not, at that stage, all traffic – would be excluded.[138] Already, too, he had boldly used the Howard–Unwin vision of the garden city to plan new towns where the conflict between car and city would be less pervasive. For him, and for other planners of that generation, the conflict was evident, but was capable of effective and even elegant resolution.

That is well seen also in what can fairly be called the other classic metropolitan plan of that time: Sven Markelius's General Plan of 1945–52 for Stockholm.[139] Markelius, to be sure, had a far smaller metropolis and a far more tractable set of problems than Abercrombie: against a megalopolis (in Abercrombie's extended Greater London) of 10 million, he was dealing with a mere 600,000. His answer, appropriately, was the same as that of May in Frankfurt, a city of similar size, in the 1920s: satellite towns. Markelius's outer suburban units – Vällingby of 1950–4, Farsta of 1953–61, Skärholmen of 1961–8, Tensta-Rinkeby of 1964–70 – are often inaccurately called new towns; they are not, if by that is meant the pure self-contained Howardian vision. Rather, they were based on the classic assumption of a rule of halves: half the working inhabitants would commute out of them, half the workforce were to be drawn in from elsewhere. Markelius wanted to achieve that without making the city car-dependent in the process; there he showed remarkable presentiment, for Stockholm's car ownership – then a mere nine to every thousand people – was to rise twentyfold to 190 per thousand by 1964. So he proposed a balanced transportation system: a high-capacity highway network, designed especially to provide for circumferential trips, was to be supplemented by a brand-new subway system, already approved by the city council in 1941; radial in form, focusing on the redeveloped central business district, it would largely replace the then streetcar system.[140]

[138] Tripp, 1938, 1942; Forshaw and Abercrombie, 1943, 50–2.

[139] Mehr, 1972, 894–5.

[140] Sidenbladh, 1965, 114–16; Stockholm, 1972, 35, 51–72.

FIGURE 9.9 *Vällingby*.

FIGURE 9.10 *Farsta*.
Stockholm's first two 'B' level satellite town centres to be developed, with their inevitable standard features: pedestrian shopping mall, *Tunnelbana* (metro) station, **high-density high-rise apartment blocks close by.**

So the capital city of Europe's most prosperous country took off on a suburbanization path radically different from the American one. This could happen for three good reasons. First, the Stockholm city council had begun to buy land for future urban extensions decades in advance of need, as early as 1904, and by the 1940s had acquired virtually all the undeveloped land within the city boundaries.[141] Secondly, after 1934 Sweden was governed for thirty years by Social Democratic governments, committed to active intervention in the housing field; as a result, 90 per cent of dwellings built after 1946 – including virtually all built on the city's land – enjoyed some form of state subsidy, and (in stark contrast to the United States) most were built either by the city itself or by tenant-owned co-operative building societies. And thirdly, Stockholm suffered from a massive and continuing shortage of housing, which made people grateful for whatever they got; in these conditions, consumer sovereignty was a meaningless phrase.[142]

As already noticed in chapter 7, rather remarkably it all got done. During 1945–57 the first Tunnelbana line was built and, based on it, the first satellite grouping at Vällingby was completed. It took the form that was to be repeated in every subsequent case: a central, high-level shopping and service centre, roughly equal to that found in one of Abercrombie's London new towns and serving 80,000–100,000 people, was supplemented by local district centres; all were connected by the subway; residential densities were highest around the major centre, high around the local centres, progressively lower away from these centres, so as to bring the maximum number of people within walking distance of shops and services, implying that nearly everyone would be housed in apartment blocks. This standard prescription varied only slightly through the 1950s and 1960s, reflecting changes in fashion and the fruits of experience: very high high-rises around an open pedestrian mall at Farsta, with three times the car-parking that had been provided at Vällingby; a tighter, more enclosed pedestrian mall and low-rise high-density apartments at Skärholmen, with a further expansion of parking into a vast multi-storey garage for 3,000 cars, the biggest in Scandinavia; an enclosed mall, with direct access into the subway station, at Mörby.[143]

The pilgrims still come in their reverent thousands to see them, and are duly impressed: everything seems to work, everything is in place, everything is in the best of good taste; on the last subway line to be finished, they even had a separate artist to decorate each station.[144] And, a visiting American sociologist found, in the classic early satellite of Vällingby most people seemed well content: as compared with American suburbanites in

[141] Ödmann and Dahlberg, 1970, 81–4; Goldfield, 1979, 142.
[142] Stockholm, 1976, 22; Goldfield, 1979, 148–9.
[143] Stockholm, 1976, 52–71.   [144] Berg, 1979, 187–202.

Levittown the men had more time with their children, the women and teenagers found it easier to get around without a car, the children had better-planned open space and special services. Even then, polled, most said that they would prefer a house to an apartment: a conclusion that the sociologist, clearly moonstruck by the quality of Stockholm life, felt must reflect a fault in the poll.[145]

But then, in Sweden it is easy for visitors to become moonstruck; it sometimes seems as if all things vulgar and tawdry have been proscribed by Act of Parliament. Yet, on closer look, paradise is not quite gained: on the subway platforms, graffiti deface the exquisite artists' designs; on the subway trains, drunken Saturday-night gangs terrorize the passengers; press reports tell of anomie and alienation in the satellite towns, where – especially on those last to be finished, such as Tensta and Rinkeby – vast numbers of immigrant workers are concentrated. Older Stockholmers say sadly that it was not like that once; back in the 1950s, in developments like Vällingby, they believed in the possibility of a secular millennium, where liberal enlightenment and social harmony would henceforth reign for ever; but somewhere, the worm entered the bud.

In consequence, even in this holy temple of city planning, the professionals' omniscience came to be challenged. The main drama, as already retailed in chapter 7, was fought over the completion of redevelopment in the central business district of Lower Norrmalm, which from the start had been the complement to the development of the satellites. It soon extended to plans for urban renewal in the older residential districts close to the centre, where the city officialdom fought a running battle with squatters. But the criticism also came to extend to the satellites themselves; a new generation of architects and planners attacked them for being built too quickly, for sacrificing quality to quantity, for producing new slums. That was particularly because, during the 1960s, both the planning style and the sociological mix changed. The three-storey walkups and low towers of Vällingby and Farsta were replaced by six- and eight-storey elevator blocks – partly in the interests of economy, but partly in pursuit of an architectural notion of 'urbanity'. The incoming tenants included many more low-income people, working mothers, immigrants and problem groups. The combination, particularly in terms of noise, vandalism and general deterioration, proved disastrous. The volume of complaints from all sides, reported in the media, grew deafening: 'inhuman environments'; brutal destroyers of the landscape'; 'social disaster areas'; 'architectural monstrosi- ties'; 'concrete jungles'.[146] Especially, the satellite of Tensta – built in a hurry by industrialized building techniques – was execrated in the media as *ett stadsbyggande sommisslycats*: a planning disaster.[147] The question, in the

[145] Popenoe, 1977, 177–201, 236.
[146] Popenoe, 1977, 217–21. [147] Höjer et al., 1977, 19.

title of one article, became: How could it go so wrong?[148] Laying down
how people ought to live, by central edict of the planning office, came to
be seen as a form of liberal totalitarianism.

But one point, interestingly, the critics found it harder to make. All over
the world, the ecological movement was then at its height. Indeed, a central
point of conflict between the city and its critics, which in 1971 became a
national *cause célèbre*, concerned the fate of a small bunch of elm trees in
Kungsträdgården, a central Stockholm square.[149] In the aftermath of the
energy crisis, here as elsewhere, the entire automobile culture were under
attack; one early ecological movement – Alternativ Stad, founded in 1965 –
campaigned for banning cars from the city altogether.[150] But Markelius
had anticipated this conflict of affluence thirty years earlier, building a
superb public-transport system in advance of the advent of mass car
ownership. In this respect, his grand design has stood the test of time:
despite the critics, Stockholm works better, and has more effectively
reconciled the conflict between car and urban environment for a longer
period, than most other cities.

Europe's other grand historic attempt to plan a metropolis around a new
transit system came a full two decades after Markelius. In the early 1960s
Paris had been trying to limit its own growth and had been manifestly
failing. France had its own baby boom for the first time in centuries; the
young people were pouring off the land and heading for the bright lights
of the metropolis. In 1961 de Gaulle, who believed that Paris should fulfil
its historic destiny as the physical symbol of the glories of France, called
in an official who had won his spurs in the Algerian conflict, Paul
Delouvrier, and asked him to head a team to produce a new plan. They
ran the numbers and concluded that even if the national planning system
were successful in building up the biggest provincial cities as effective
métropoles d'équilibre, the Paris region would grow from 9 to between 14 and
16 million by the end of the century. Early in 1962, apparently, Delouvrier
convinced de Gaulle in a personal interview that this picture of a dynamic
Paris, 'bursting at the seams', was correct.[151] Considering alternatives –
conventional annular growth, counter-magnets 60 or more miles different,
Abercrombie-style new towns, a 'second Paris' – they rejected them all: the
magnetism of Paris was such that the people wanted to be there, not some
other place, yet if it grew as it had been growing the city would throttle.[152]

So they effectively adopted a Stockholm plan on a mega-scale, appropriate
to a metropolis ten times Stockholm's size. Paris would have new towns;
yet these would be towns not on the Howard–Abercrombie model, but
rather satellites in the May–Markelius mould. Since Paris was huge, the

[148] Lindström, 1977, 203. [149] Berg, 1979, 171–2. [150] Hertlitz, 1977, 219–20.
[151] Alduy, 1983, 75. [152] Hall, 1984, 72–6.

FIGURE 9.11   *Marne-la-Vallée.*
The Stockholm model applied on a far larger spatial scale in the new towns for Paris under the 1965 plan. The express transit system (*RER*) runs directly under the town centre deck.

satellites would be correspondingly so: against 10,000–20,000 in the Frankfurt of the 1920s, or 80,000–100,000 in the Stockholm of the 1940s, the Paris of the 1960s demanded eight units of between 300,000 and 1,000,000 each.[153] As in Stockholm, they were to be linked with the centre, and with each other, not only by circumferential highways but by a new transit system; but again with a difference. Unlike the Stockholm Tunnelbana, unlike the London Underground on which it had been based, unlike the existing Paris Métro or indeed any of the subway systems of the 1890–1910 era, this was to be an express transit system: having the characteristics of a commuter rail service, it could move people long distances in short times. Its only near equivalent, then still on the drawing board, was the Bay Area Rapid Transit System planned for San Francisco.

But BART was never seen as the agent of a coherent regional plan; presented as a solution to threatened chaos on the region's highways, in fact it promoted further suburbanization and transferred the gridlock there. The 160-mile RER, in contrast, was planned – as in Stockholm twenty

[153] Rubenstein, 1978, 107.

years earlier – integrally with the new satellites. These would be arrayed on two 'preferential axes', one on the north side of the existing agglomeration, one on the south; to link them, the RER would take the form of a letter 'H' placed sideways, with a main east–west line branching out at each end. But thus it would link not only the planned satellites, but also new inner-urban centres which would act as catalysts for urban renewal in the shabby middle ring of the Paris region and would provide badly needed sevices there. The largest such centre, at La Défense immediately outside the inner city to the west, hd already started when the plan was being prepared, and thus represented a kind of commercial *fait accompli* which the planners took in their stride.

If audacity is a criterion for merit in urban planning, then the Paris Schéma Directeur of 1965 must surely belong in some category by itself. Nothing so grandiose was ever attempted in the history of urban civilization. The total bill to the French exchequer was mind-boggling: the twelve-year plan, drawn up at the same time as the Schéma Directeur, called for a total of 29 billion francs on highways and 9 billion for public transport, not to mention 140,000 new dwellings a year.[154] Only a country led by a figure with a Messianic belief in his own destiny, only one in the middle of an economic boom almost unprecedented in history, only one with a centuries-old tradition of top–down public intervention, could even have contemplated it; maybe not even then.

It was the ultimate plan. All kinds of academic theorist, in historical retrospect, can prove anything they like from it. Marxists can represent it as a supreme instance of large-scale capital manipulating the state in its own interests, particularly to provide the social investments necessary to ensure the reproduction of labour power; not for nothing were modern urban Marxist studies born in Paris between 1965 and 1972. Believers in the resilience of national culture, contrariwise, will see in it the long tradition represented by Louis XIV and by Haussmann: Delouvrier, ironically, achieved the kind of planning to which Corbusier long aspired in vain. For theorists of the state, on the other hand, it is the classic example of a central bureaucracy entrenching its independent power. Paul Alduy, who – as a key official during its preparation and implementation, has written the definitive account of it as a conspiracy against democracy – gives them their evidence: 'it involved new methods of state intervention, that of a central State acting as an arbiter above party and their [sic] elected representatives.'[155] More than that: as he shows, large parts of the existing bureaucratic machine, and their political heads, were simply ignored in the plan's preparation: 'The purpose was obviously, not to negotiate with anybody but, above all, to develop a propaganda operation

[154] Alduy, 1983, 76.   [155] Alduy, 1983, 78.

aimed at presenting a new image of the State, a new mode of intervention and furthermore, a new relationship between the State and local authorities.'[156]

Somehow, it survived and, in a fashion, was achieved. Not of course without modification, or without pain: in 1969, economic crisis and demographic changes brought a re-write, in which three of the eight *villes nouvelles* were dropped and others reduced in scale.[157] But the others were pressed ahead; and some, indeed, proved a magnet for private construction capital which built offices, shopping centres, and homes for sale on a huge scale. That perhaps is the final moral of the Parisian story: as French planners had always argued, public plans can provide a set of clear signals to the private sector, thus enabling it in turn to make its own phased investment programmes. Audacity can work.

The Great Freeway Revolt and After

But the critical point remains: neither Stockholm in 1945, nor Paris in 1965, succeeded in weaning Europeans from their cars. The years from 1945 to 1975, indeed, were the ones in which Europe supplanted America as the main car-builder of the world; all that had happened was that the automobile revolution came to Europe forty years later.[158] In the process, it began profoundly to affect both traditional lifestyles and traditional urban structures. In Sweden, single-family homes zoomed from 32 per cent of new housing construction in 1970 to 55 per cent in 1974 and to over 70 per cent by the late 1970s, responding to individual preferences that showed as many as 90 per cent of Swedes preferring houses to flats.[159] In the Paris *villes nouvelles*, similarly, single-family homes made up the overwhelming majority of the housing completions, the supermarkets were full of barbecues and garden furniture, and – most significant sign of all – there were few restaurants to be found, let alone good ones.

So the car in Europe, as in its first homeland, was an agent of suburbanization. Which came first, the suburban chicken or the automotive egg, is impossible to say; as already noted for Los Angeles, and as earlier noted (in chapter 3) for London, suburban sprawl predated mass car ownership, but in turn the automobile allowed the suburbs to sprawl more freely, and farther, than mass transit could ever have done. What was true everywhere was that in the process, the problem of the car in the historic city became an acute one. American cities, facing the conflict from the 1920s onwards, reacted by loosening and weakening their earlier tight urban structures. European city fathers were less reluctant to see this

[156] Ibid. 78.   [157] Rubenstein, 1978, 107.   [158] Roos and Altshuler, 1984, 18–22.
[159] Popenoe, 1977, 222; Goldfield, 1979, 152–3.

happen. The crunch came over the massive construction evidently needed to accommodate the age of universal automobility in the cities.

For more than a decade from the mid-1950s onwards, a new generation of urban-traffic analysts came to dominate city planning, first in the United States, then – as they exported themselves and their techniques – in Europe also. Their computer models appeared to demonstrate the inexorable necessity to build vast networks of new urban highways in order to grapple with the rising curve of traffic. For a time, they met no resistance. In Britain at the end of 1963, the Minister of Transport published a report on *Traffic in Towns*, produced by a technical group directed by a then unknown planner-engineer, Colin Buchanan.[160] It proved a best seller; Buchanan became a public figure overnight. Buchanan's argument was a subtle one, derived from Alker Tripp's philosophy of precinctual planning a quarter-century previously: it was that the planner should set fixed standards for the urban environment, whereupon more traffic could be accommodated only through massive reconstruction; if the community were unwilling or unable to foot this bill, then it must restrain the traffic. Hardly anyone grasped the message; the public, bemused by the media pictures of vast multi-level reconstruction, became convinced that Buchanan was calling for the bulldozing of urban Britain. At first, they seemed to receive this with equanimity, even enthusiasm; this was the era of the great rebuilding of Britain, when comprehensive redevelopment was everywhere still seen as a thoroughly good thing. Behind Buchanan came the traffic engineers with their plans for urban motorways: hundreds of miles for London, similarly vast networks for every provincial city.

But in California, as usual the harbinger, the tide had already turned. San Francisco, that most European of American cities – and, therefore, the city most determined to be unlike its arch-rival Los Angeles – awoke to a plan to drive an elevated double-deck freeway along its historic waterfront, past the famous Fisherman's Wharf. In the world's first freeway revolt, the Embarcadero Freeway was stopped in its tracks. Then, dizzy with triumph, the city stopped building freeways altogether; everywhere, the bemused visitor could see elevated structures that stopped suddenly, in mid-air. It commissioned a consultants' report of 1956, and a subsequent one from the same source in 1962, calling for a $900-million new transit system, deliberately engineered to preserve San Francisco as a European-style, strong-centre city. San Franciscans voted two to one in favour; suburbanites were less enthusiastic, but the proposal scraped home and the state-of-the-art BART system started construction.[161]

The revolt spread across North America; Toronto stopped its Spadina Expressway, and later turned the right-of-way into a subway. It spawned

[160] G.B. Minister of Transport 1963.
[161] Zwerling, 1974, 22–3, 27; Hall, 1980, 114–15.

imitators in Europe: one morning in April 1973, the incoming Labour administration at the Greater London Council, fulfilling an election promise, tore up the whole of the GLC motorway plans. It was all part of the new *Zeitgeist*, in which all the popular planning slogans were suddenly stood on their heads: this was the time of the Club of Rome report, the belief that small was beautiful, the emphasis on planning for the disadvantaged, and the great OPEC energy crisis. But the revolt against the freeways came before that crisis, which merely seemed to reinforce the rightness of the policy reversal.

The logical result – not merely in Britain, but much more wholeheartedly in more affluent European economies like France and West Germany – was a massive shift of investment into urban mass transit. Now, other cities followed the pioneer trail beaten by pioneers like Stockholm and Paris. In Germany, by the early 1980s, virtually every major city was building a new or reconstructed rail-transit system.[162] The European suburb, too, was a city on the highway; but it was also a city on the subway. Its inhabitants, in particular those among them with less access to cars, were given a choice.

America, too, began to move in the European direction: by the mid-1980s, over forty major American cities had rail-transit systems either operating or building or in the planning stages, some on the BART long-distance model, some more modest light-rail systems.[163] Yet was a question not just of investing in transit, but also of structuring the suburbs around them. And that was something that American cities – driven by the market mechanism, equipped with only minimal planning powers – would be unwilling or unable to do. So the conclusion for many of these systems was likely to be the drastic one reached by Melvin Webber for BART in 1977: failure, because they simply did not fit the dispersed land use patterns and so did not offer an attractive alternative to the car.[164]

That could be changed only if Americans were suddenly willing to live like Europeans; and that would require that they accept European systems of land-use regulation. In places, to be sure, there was evidence by the 1970s that some Americans were willing to be more regulated. Californian commnities like Petaluma, faced with the outwash of suburbia from the San Francisco Bay, fought bitter battles to regulate their own growth. After huge fights between the construction lobby and the environmental lobby, the California legislature, in 1972, passed a comprehensive law that effectively stopped all development along the coastline. Such measures did affect the shape of the suburban flood: effectively, the San Francisco Bay Area is surrounded by a green belt almost as effectively protected as

[162] Hall and Hass-Klau, 1985, *passim*.
[163] McClendon, 1984, 22–3; Anon., 1985, 42–3.
[164] Webber, 1976, 34; Hall, 1980, 122–3.

London's, and the result – according to David Dowall – has been the same as that reported for London: housing-land scarcity and higher housing-land prices.[165] But it has not affected the general fact: beyond the green belt, in the corridor followed by Interstate Highway 680 from Concord to Fremont, 20 and more miles from downtown San Francisco, the suburbs continue to sprawl and the jobs are moving out too. The result, according to Dowall's colleague Robert Cervero, is that the Suburban Squeeze is followed by Suburban Gridlock: the highway system is overwhelmed by the volume of suburb-to-suburb commuter journeys, which the BART system – indeed, any conventional radial transit system – is quite unfit to serve.[166]

Not only then were Americans failing to adopt European urban lifestyles; the evidence seemed to be, if anything, that progressively just the opposite was happening. The energy crisis did not suddenly reverse, or even stem, the tide of out-migration from the cities; during the 1970s, following a pattern long familiar in the United States, more and more European countries began to report losses in their central-city populations.[167] And, though some of the European transit systems were successful in attracting passengers, they were invariably – like their American equivalents – heavily subsidized ones. On both sides of the Atlantic, it seemed, the City on the Highway was winning out over the traditionally structured transit city. The people were voting for it with their wheels; more precisely, those that had them were voting thus, and more had them every year. Wells's prophecy was coming truer every year that passed.

---

[165] Dowall, 1984.   [166] Cervero, 1986.
[167] Hall and Hay, 1980; Cheshire and Hay, 1987.

The City of Theory

Grau, teurer Freund, ist alle Theorie
Und grün das Lebens goldner Baum.

Johann Wolfgang von Goethe
Faust (1808)

Read no history; nothing but biography, for that is life without theory.

Benjamin Disraeli
Contarini Fleming (1832)

He who can, does. He who cannot, teaches.

George Bernard Shaw
Maxims for Revolutionists (*Man and Superman*) (1903)

All professions are conspiracies against the laity.

George Bernard Shaw
The Doctor's Dilemma (1913)

10
The City of Theory

Planning and the Academy:
Philadelphia, Manchester, California, Paris,
1955–1987

The chapter title might suggest total superfluity: for this book has been about nothing else than cities of theory, and attempts to bring them to actuality. And, down to about 1955, that adequately describes the main current of twentieth-century planning history; such has been the central thesis. But from then on, it will not do. Hence the need for this chapter, and the title.

The reason is paradoxical: at that point, city planning at last became legitimate; but in doing so, it began to sow the seeds of its own destruction. All too quickly, it split into two separate camps: the one, in the schools of planning, increasingly and exclusively obsessed with the theory of the subject; the other, in the offices of local authorities and consultants, concerned only with the everyday business of planning in the real world. That division was not at first evident; indeed, during the late 1950s and most of the 1960s, it seemed that at last a complete and satisfactory link had been forged between the world of theory and world of practice. But all too soon, illusion was stripped aside: honeymoon was followed in quick succession during the 1970s by tiffs and temporary reconciliations, in the 1980s by divorce. And, in the process, planning lost much of its new-found legitimacy.

The Prehistory of Academic City Planning: 1930–1955

It was not that planning was innocent of academic influence before the 1950s. On the contrary: in virtually every urbanized nation, universities and polytechnics had created courses for the professional education of planners; professional bodies had come into existence to define and protect standards, and had forged links with the academic departments. Britain

FIGURE 10.1 *Patrick Abercrombie.*
Photographed outside the Palace after receiving his knighthood in 1945, Abercrombie celebrates his two great plans for London and thirty years as a leader of British planning education.

took an early lead when in 1909 – as already retailed in chapter 5 – the soap magnate William Hesketh Lever, founder of Port Sunlight, won a libel action against a newspaper and used the proceeds to endow his local University of Liverpool with a Department of Civic Design. Stanley Adshead, the first professor, almost immediately created a new journal, the *Town Planning Review*, in which theory and good practice were to be firmly joined; its first editor was a young Faculty recruit, Patrick Abercrombie, who was later to succeed Adshead in the chair first at Liverpool, then at Britain's second school of planning: University College London, founded in 1914. The Town Planning Institute – the Royal accolade was conferred only in 1959 – was founded in 1914 on the joint initiative of the Royal Institute of British Architects, the Institution of Civil Engineers and the Royal Institution of Chartered Surveyors; by the end of the 1930s, it had recognized seven schools whose examinations provided an entry to membership.[1]

The United States was slower: though Harvard had established a planning course in 1909, neck and neck with Liverpool, it had no separate department until 1929. Nevertheless, by the 1930s America had schools also at MIT, Cornell, Columbia and Illinois, as well as courses taught in other departments at a great many universities across the country.[2] And the American City Planning Institute, founded in 1917 as a breakaway from the National Conference on City Planning, ten years later became – mainly through the insistence of Thomas Adams – a full-fledged professional body on TPI lines, a status it retained when in 1938 it broadened to include regional planning and renamed itself the American Institute of Planners.[3]

The important point about these, and other, initiatives was this: stemming as they did from professional needs, often through spin-offs from related professions like architecture and engineering, they were from the start heavily suffused with the professional styles of these design-based professions. The job of the planners was to make plans, to develop codes to enforce these plans, and then to enforce those codes; relevant planning knowledge was what was needed for that job; planning education existed to convey that knowledge together with the necessary design skills. So, by 1950, the utopian age of planning – the main theme of this book – was over; planning was now institutionalized into comprehensive land-use planning.[4] All this was strongly reflected in the curricula of the planning schools down to the mid-1950s, and often for years after that; and these in turn were reflected in the books and articles that academic planners wrote. Land-use planning, Keeble told his British audience in 1959 and Kent reminded the American counterpart in 1964, was a distinct and tightly bounded subject, quite different from social or economic planning.[5] And these texts reflected the fact that 'city planners early adopted the thoughtways and the analytical methods that engineers developed for the design of public works, and they then applied them to the design of cities.'[6]

The result, as Michael Batty has put it, was a subject that for the ordinary citizen was 'somewhat mystical' or arcane, as law or medicine were, but that was – in sharp contrast to education for these older professions – not based on any consistent body of theory; rather, in it, 'scatterings of social science bolstered the traditional architectural determinism.'[7] Planners acquired a synthetic ability not through abstract

[1] Cherry, 1974, 54, 56–60, 169, 218–22.
[2] Scott, 1969, 101, 266–7, 365–6; Wilson, 1974, 138–9.
[3] Scott, 1969, 163; Birch, 1980a, 26, 28, 31–2; Simpson, 1985, 126–7.
[4] Galloway and Mahayni, 1977, 65.
[5] Keeble, 1959, 1–2; Kent, 1964, 101.
[6] Webber, 1968, 192–3.   [7] Batty, 1979, 29.

FIGURE 10.2 *Thomas Adams.*
The ultimate transatlantic planner, Adams worked at Letchworth and became the
Town Planning Institute's first president before moving to direct the New York
Regional Plan, a job he combined with a flourishing regional planning practice in
England.

thinking, but by doing real jobs; in them, they used first creative intuition,
then reflection. Though they might draw on bits and pieces of theory about
the city – the Chicago school's sociological differentiation of the city, the
land economists' theory of urban land rent differentials, the geographers'
concepts of the natural region – these were employed simply as snippets
of useful knowledge.[8] In the important distinction later made by a number
of writers,[9] there was some theory *in* planning but there was no theory *of*
planning. The whole process was very direct, based on a single-shot
approach: survey (the Geddesian approach) was followed by analysis (an
implicit learning approach), followed immediately by design.

True, as Abercrombie's classic text of 1933 argued, the making of the
plan was only half the planner's job; the other half consisted of planning,

---

[8] Keeble, 1959, 2–2.   [9] Hightower, 1969, 326; Faludi, 1985, 27.

that is implementation;[10] but it was nowhere assumed that some kind of continuous learning process was needed. True, too, the 1947 Act provided for plans – and the surveys on which they were based – to be quinquennially updated; the assumption was still that the result would be a fixed land-use plan. And, a decade after that, though Keeble's equally classic text referred to the planning process,[11] by this he simply meant the need for a spatial hierarchy of related plans from the regional to the local, and the need at each scale for survey before plan. Nowhere is found a discussion of implementation or updating. Thus – apart from extremely generalized statements like Abercrombie's famous triad of 'beauty, health and convenience'[12] – the goals were left implicit; the planner would develop them intuitively from his own values, which by definition were 'expert' and a-political.

So, in the classic British land-use planning system created by the 1947 Town and Country Planning Act, no repeated learning process was involved, since the planner would get it right first time:[13]

> The process was therefore not characterised by explicit feedback as the search 'homed in' on the best plan, for the notion that the planner had to learn about the nature of the problem was in direct conflict with his assumed infallibility as an expert, a professional ... The assumed certainty of the process was such that possible links back to the reality in the form of new surveys were rarely if ever considered. ... This certainty, based on the infallibility of the expert, reinforced the apolitical, technical nature of the process. The political environment was regarded as totally passive, indeed subservient to the 'advice' of the planners and in practice, this was largely the case.[14]

It was, as Batty calls it, the golden age of planning: the planner, free from political interference, serenely sure of his technical capacities, was left to get on with the job. And this was appropriate to the world outside, with which planning had to deal: a world of glacially slow change – stagnant population, depressed economy – in which major planning interventions would come only seldom and for a short time, as after a major war. Abercrombie, in the plan for the West Midlands he produced with Herbert Jackson in 1948, actually wrote that a major objective of the plan should be to slow down the rate of urban change, thus reducing the rate at which built structures became obsolescent: the ideal city would be a static, stable city:

> Let us assume ... that a maximum population has been decided for a town, arrived at after consideration of all the factors appearing to be relevant. ... Allowance has been made for proper space for all conceivable purposes in

[10] Abercrombie, 1933, 139.   [11] Keeble, 1959, 2–1.
[12] Abercrombie, 1933, 104.   [13] Batty, 1979, 29–31.   [14] Ibid.

FIGURE 10.3 *T.J. Kent, Jr.*
Three waves of planning theory at the University of California, Berkeley. (1) Kent, the school's founder, wrote the classic 1962 text on the urban general plan.

the light of present facts and the town planner's experience and imagination.

Accordingly, an envelope or green belt has been prescribed, outside which the land uses will be those involving little in the way of resident population. The town planner is now in the happy position for the first time of knowing the limits of his problem. He is able to address himself to the design of the whole and the parts in the light of a basic overall figure for population. The process will be difficult enough in itself, but at least he starts with one figure to reassure him.[15]

American planning was never quite like that. Kent's text of 1964 on the urban general plan, though it deals with the same kind of land-use planning, reminds its students of 'end-directions which are continually adjusted as time passes'.[16] And, because the planner's basic understanding of the

[15] Abercrombie and Jackson, 1948, foreword.   [16] Kent, 1964, 98.

interrelationship between socio-economic forces and the physical environment was largely intuitive and speculative, Kent warned his student readers,

> In most cases it is not possible to know with any certainty what physical-
> design measures should be taken to bring about a given social or economic
> objective, or what social and economic consequences will result from a given
> physical-design proposal. Therefore, the city council and the city-planning
> commission, rather than professional city planners, should make the final
> value judgements upon which the plan is based.[17]

But even Kent was certain that, despite all this, it was still possible for the
planner to produce some kind of optimal land use plan; the problem of
objectives was just shunted off.

The Systems Revolution

It was a happy, almost dream-like, world. But increasingly, during the
1950s, it did not correspond to reality. Everything began to get out of
hand. In every industrial country, there was an unexpected baby boom, to
which the demographers reacted with surprise, the planners with alarm;
only its timing varied from one country to another, and everywhere it
created instant demands for maternity wards and child-care clinics, only
slightly delayed needs for schools and playgrounds. In every one, almost
simultaneously, the great postwar economic boom got under way, bringing
pressures for new investment in factories and offices. And, as boom
generated affluence, these countries soon passed into the realms of high
mass-consumption societies, with unprecedented demands for durable
consumer goods: most notable among these, land-hungry homes and cars.
The result everywhere – in America, in Britain, in the whole of western
Europe – was that the pace of urban development and urban change began
to accelerate to an almost superheated level. The old planning system,
geared to a static world, was overwhelmed.

These demands in themselves would force the system to change; but,
almost coincidentally, there were changes on the supply side too. In the
mid-1950s there occurred an intellectual revolution in the whole cluster of
urban and regional social studies, which provided planners with much of
their borrowed intellectual baggage. A few geographers and industrial
economists discovered the works of German theorists of location, such as
Johann Heinrich von Thünen (1826) on agriculture, Alfred Weber (1909)
on industry, Walter Christaller (1933) on central places, and August Lösch
(1940) on the general theory of location; they began to summarize and
analyse these works, and where necessary to translate them.[18] In the United

---

[17] Ibid. 104.
[18] Thünen, 1966; Weber, 1929; Christaller, 1966; Lösch, 1954.

States, academics coming from a variety of disciplines began to find regularities in many distributions, including spatial ones.[19] Geographers, beginning to espouse the tenets of logical positivism, suggested that their subject should cease to be concerned with descriptions of the detailed differentiation of the earth's surface, and should instead begin to develop general hypotheses about spatial distributions, which could then be rigorously tested against reality: the very approach which these German pioneers of location theory had adopted. These ideas, together with the relevant literature, were brilliantly synthesized by an American economist, Walter Isard, in a text that became immediately influential.[20] Between 1953 and 1957, there occurred an almost instant revolution in human geography[21] and the creation, by Isard, of a new academic discipline uniting the new geography with the German tradition of locational economics. And, with official blessing – as in the important report of Britain's Schuster Committee of 1950, which recommended a greater social-science content in planning education – the new locational analysis began to enter the curricula of the planning schools.[22]

The consequences for planning were momentous: with only a short time-lag, 'the discipline of physical planning changed more in the 10 years from 1960 to 1970, than in the previous 100, possibly even 1000 years.'[23] The subject changed from a kind of craft, based on personal knowledge of a rudimentary collection of concepts about the city, into an apparently scientific activity in which vast amounts of precise information were garnered and processed in such a way that the planner could devise very sensitive systems of guidance and control, the effects of which could be monitored and if necessary modified. More precisely, cities and regions were viewed as complex systems – they were, indeed, only a particular spatially based subset of a whole general class of systems – while planning was seen as a continuous process of control and monitoring of these systems, derived from the then new science of cybernetics developed by Norbert Wiener.[24]

There was thus, in the language later used in the celebrated work of Thomas Kuhn, a paradigm shift.[25] It affected city planning as it affected many other related areas of planning and design. Particularly, its main early applications – already in the mid-1950s – concerned defence and aerospace; for these were the Cold War years, when the United States was engaging in a crash programme to build new and complex electronically controlled missile systems. Soon, from that field, span off another application. Already in 1954, Robert Mitchell and Chester Rapkin – colleagues of Isard

[19] Zipf, 1949; Stewart, 1947, 1956; Carrothers, 1956; Stewart and Warntz, 1958, 1959; Garrison, 1959–60.
[20] Isard, 1960.   [21] Johnston, 1979.   [22] G.B. Committee, 1950.
[23] Batty, 1979, 18.   [24] Wiener, 1948; Hall, 1982, 276.   [25] Kuhn, 1962.

at the University of Pennsylvania – had published a book suggesting that urban traffic patterns were a direct and measurable function of the pattern of activities – and thus land uses – that generated them.[26] Coupled with earlier work on spatial interaction patterns, and using for the first time the data-processing powers of the computer, this produced a new science of urban transportation planning, which for the first time claimed to be able scientifically to predict future urban-traffic patterns. First applied in the historic Detroit Metropolitan Area transportation study of 1955, further developed in the Chicago study of 1956, it soon became a standardized methodology employed in literally hundreds of such studies, first across the United States, then across the world.[27]

Heavily engineering-based in its approach, it adopted a fairly standardized sequence. First, explicit goals and objectives were set for the performance of the system. Then, inventories were taken of the existing state of the system: both the traffic flows, and the activities that gave rise to them. From this, models were derived which sought to establish these relationships in precise mathematical form. Then, forecasts were made of the future state of the system, based on the relationships obtained from the models. From this, alternative solutions could be designed and evaluated in order to choose a preferred option. Finally, once implemented the network would be continually monitored and the system modified as necessary.[28]

At first, these relationships were seen as operating in one direction: activities and land uses were given; from these, the traffic patterns were derived. So the resulting methodology and techniques were part of a new field, transportation planning, which came to exist on one side of traditional city planning. Soon, however, American regional scientists suggested a crucial modification: the locational patterns of activities – commercial, industrial, residential – were in turn influenced by the available transportation opportunities; these relationships, too, could be precisely modelled and used for prediction; therefore the relationship was two-way, and there was a need to develop an interactive system of land-use–transportation planning for entire metropolitan or subregional areas. Now, for the first time, the engineering-based approach invaded the professional territory of the traditional land-use planner. Spatial interaction models, especially the Garin–Lowry model – which, given basic data about employment and transportation links, could generate a resulting pattern of activities and land uses – became part of the planner's stock in trade.[29] As put in one of the classic systems texts:

> In this general process of planning we particularise in order to deal with more specific issues: that is, a specific real world system or subsystem must be represented by a specific conceptual system or subsystem within the

[26] Mitchell and Rapkin, 1954.   [27] Bruton, 1975, 17.   [28] Ibid. 27–42.
[29] Lowry, 1964, 1965; Batty, 1976.

FIGURE 10.4 *Melvin M. Webber.*
Three waves of Berkeley planning theory continued. (2) In the 1960s Webber developed radical ideas about the nonplace urban realm and argued that planning had failed to develop a distinctive methodology.

general conceptual system. Such a particular representation of a system is called a *model*. . . . The use of models is a means whereby the high variety of the real world is reduced to a level of variety appropriate to the channel capacities of the human being.[30]

This involved more than a knowledge of computer applications – novel as that seemed to the average planner of the 1960s. It meant also a fundamentally different concept of planning. Instead of the old master-plan or blueprint approach, which assumed that the objectives were fixed from the start, the new concept was of planning as a *process*, 'whereby programmes are adapted during their implementation as and when incoming information requires such changes'.[31] And this planning process was independent of the thing that was planned;[32] as Melvin Webber put it, it was 'a special

[30] Chadwick, 1971, 63–4, 70.   [31] Faludi, 1973, 132.
[32] Galloway and Mahayni, 1977, 68.

way of deciding and acting', which involved a constantly recycled series of
logical steps: goal-setting, forecasting of change in the outside world,
assessment of chains of consequences of alternative courses of action,
appraisal of costs and benefits as a basis for action strategies, and continuous
monitoring.[33] This was the approach of the new British textbooks of systems
planning, which started to emerge at the end of the 1960s, and which were
particularly associated with a group of younger British graduates, many
teaching or studying at the University of Manchester.[34] It was also the
approach of a whole generation of subregional studies, made for fast-
growing metropolitan areas in Britain during that heroic period of
growth and change, 1965–75: Leicester–Leicestershire, Nottinghamshire–
Derbyshire, Coventry–Warwickshire–Solihull, South Hampshire. All were
heavily suffused with the new approach and the new techniques; in several,
the same key individuals – McLoughlin in Leicester, Batty in Notts.–
Derby – played a directing or a crucial consulting role.

But the revolution was less complete – at least, in its early stages – than
its supporters liked to argue: many of these 'systems' plans had a distinctly
blueprint tint, in that they soon resulted in all-too-concrete proposals for
fixed investments like freeway systems.[35] Underlying this, furthermore,
were some curious metaphysical assumptions, which the new systems
planners shared with their blueprint elders: the planning system was seen
as active, the city system as purely passive; the political system was
regarded as benign and receptive to the planner's expert advice.[36] In
practice, the systems planner was involved in two very different kinds of
activity: as a social scientist, he or she was passively observing and analysing
reality; as a designer, the same planner was acting on reality to change
it – an activity inherently less certain, and also inherently subject to
objectives that could only be set through a complex, often messy, set of
dealings between professionals, politicians and public.

The core of this problem was a logical paradox: despite the claims of
the systems planners,[37] the urban planning system was different from (say)
a weapons system. In this latter kind of system, to which the 'systems
approach' had originally and successfully been applied, the controls were
inside the system; but here, the urban-regional system was inside its own
system of control.[38] Related to this were other crucial differences: in urban
planning, there was not just one problem and one overriding objective, but
many, perhaps contradictory; it was difficult to move from general goals
to specific operational ones;[39] not all were fully perceived; the systems to
be analysed did not self-evidently exist, but had to be synthesized; most

[33] Webber, 1968, 278.   [34] McLoughlin, 1969, Chadwick, 1971.
[35] Faludi, 1973, 146.   [36] Batty, 1979, 21.   [37] Chadwick, 1971, 81.
[38] Batty, 1979, 18–21.   [39] Altshuler, 1965, 20; Catenese and Steiss, 1970, 8.

aspects were not deterministic, but probabilistic; costs and benefits were difficult to quantify. So the claims of the systems school to scientific objectivity could not readily be fulfilled. Increasingly, members of the school came to admit that in such 'open' systems, systematic analysis would need to play a subsidiary role to intuition and judgement; in other words, the traditional approach.[40] By 1975 Britton Harris, perhaps the most celebrated of all the systems planners, could write that he no longer believed that the more difficult problems of planning could be solved by optimizing methods.[41]

The Search for a New Paradigm

All this, in the late 1960s, came to focus in an attack from two very different directions, which together blew the ship of systems planning at least half out of the water. From the philosophical right came a series of theoretical and empirical studies from American political scientists, arguing that – at least in the United States – crucial urban decisions were made within a pluralist political structure in which no one individual or group had total knowledge or power, and in which, consequently, the decision-making process could best be described as 'disjointed incrementalism' or 'muddling through'. Meyerson and Banfield's classic analysis of the Chicago Housing Authority concluded that it engaged in little real planning, and failed because it did not correctly identify the real power structure in the city; its elitist view of the public interest was totally opposed to the populist view of the ward politicians, which finally prevailed. Downs theorized about such a structure, suggesting that politicians buy votes by offering bundles of policies, rather as in a market. Lindblom contrasted the whole rational-comprehensive model of planning with what he found to be the actual process of policy development, which was characterized by a mixture of values and analysis, a confusion of ends and means, a failure to analyse alternatives, and an avoidance of theory. Altshuler's analysis of Minneapolis–St Paul suggested that the professional planner carried no clout against the political machine, which backed the highway-building engineers against him; they won by stressing expertise and concentrating on narrow goals, but theirs was a political game; the conclusion was that planners should recognize their own weakness, and devise strategies appropriate to that fact.[42]

All these analyses arose from study of American urban politics, which is traditionally more populist, more pluralist, than most. Even there, Rabinowitz's study of New Jersey cities suggested that they varied greatly

---

[40] Ibid. 17, 21.   [41] Harris, 1975, 42.
[42] Meyerson and Banfield, 1955; Downs, 1957; Lindblom, 1959; Altshuler, 1965b.

in style, from the highly fragmented to the very cohesive; while Etzioni, criticizing Lindblom, suggested that recent United States history showed several important examples of non-incremental decision-making, especially in defence.[43] But, these reservations taken, the studies did at least suggest that planning in actuality was a very long way indeed from the cool, rational, Olympian style envisaged in the systems texts. Perhaps it might have been better if it had been closer; perhaps not. The worrisome point was that in practice, local democracy proved to be an infinitely messier business than the theory would have liked. Some theorists accordingly concluded that if this was the way planning was, this was the way it should be encouraged to be: partial, experimental, incremental, working on problems as they arose.[44]

That emerged even more clearly, because – as so often seems to happen – in America the left-wing criticism was reaching closely similar conclusions. By the late 1960s, fuelled by the civil-rights movement and war on poverty, the protests against the Vietnam war and the campus free-speech movement, it was this wing that was making all the running. Underlying the general current of protest were three key themes, which proved fatal to the legitimacy of the systems planners. One was a widespread distrust of expert, top–down planning generally – whether for problems of peace and war, or for problems of the cities. Another, much more specific, was an increasing paranoia about the systems approach, which in its military applications was seen as employing pseudo-science and incomprehensible jargon to create a smokescreen, behind which ethically reprehensible policies could be pursued. And a third was triggered by the riots that tore through American cities starting with Birmingham, Alabama, in 1963 and ending with Detroit, in 1967. They seemed to prove the point; systems planning had done nothing to ameliorate the condition of the cities; rather, by assisting or at least conniving in the dismemberment of inner-city comunities, it might actually have contributed to it. By 1967 one critic, Richard Bolan, could argue that systems planning was old-fashioned comprehensive planning, dressed up in fancier garb; both, alike, ignored political reality.[45]

The immediate left-wing reaction was to call on the planners themselves to turn the tables, and to practise bottom-up planning by becoming advocate-planners.[46] Particularly, in this way they would make explicit the debate about the setting of goals and objectives, which both the blueprint and systems approaches had bypassed by means of their comfortable shared assumption that this was the professional planner's job. Advocacy planners would intervene in a variety of ways, in a variety of groups; diversity should be their keynote. They would help to inform the public of alternatives; force public planning agencies to compete for support; help critics to

[43] Rabinowitz, 1969, *passim*; Etzioni, 1968, *passim*.
[44] Bolan, 1967, 239–40.   [45] Ibid. 241.   [46] Davidoff, 1965.

generate plans that were superior to official ones; compel consideration of underlying values. The resulting structure was highly American: democratic, locally grounded, pluralistic, but also legalistic in being based on institutionalized conflict. But, interestingly, while demoting the planner in one respect, it enormously advanced his or her power in another: the planner was to take many of the functions that the locally elected official had previously exercised. And, in practice, it was not entirely clear how it would all work; particularly, how the process would resolve the very real conflicts of interest that could arise within communities, or how it could avoid the risk that the planners, once again, would become manipulators.[47]

At any rate, there is more than a passing resemblance between the planner as a disjointed incrementalist, and the planner-advocate; and, indeed, between either of these and a third model set out in Bolan's paper of 1967, the planner as informal co-ordinator and catalyst, which in turn shades into a fourth: Melvin Webber's probabilistic planner, who uses new information systems to facilitate debate and improve decision-making. All are assumed to work within a pluralist world, with very many different competing groups and interests, where the planner has at most (and, further should have) only limited power or influence; all are based, at least implicitly, on continued acceptance of logical positivism. As Webber put it, at the conclusion of his long two-part paper of 1968–9:

> The burden of my argument is that city planning failed to adopt the planning method, choosing instead to impose input bundles, including regulatory constraints, on the basis of ideologically defined images of goodness. I am urging, as an alternative, that planning tries out the planning idea and the planning method.[48]

In turn, Webber's view of planning – which flatly denied the possibility of a stable predictable future or agreed goals – provided some of the philosophical underpinnings of the Social Learning or New Humanist approach of the 1970s, which stressed the importance of learning systems in helping cope with a turbulent environment.[49] But finally, this approach divorced itself from logical positivism, returning to a reliance on personal knowledge which was strangely akin to old-style blueprint planning; and, as developed by John Friedmann of the University of California at Los Angeles, it finally resulted in a demand for all political activity to be decomposed into decision by minute political groups: a return to the anarchist roots of planning, with a vengeance.

So these different approaches diverged, sometimes in detailed emphasis, sometimes more fundamentally. What they shared was the belief that – at

---

[47] Peattie, 1968, 85.
[48] Webber, 1968–9, 294–5; cf. Rittel and Webber, 1973.
[49] Schon, 1971; Friedmann, 1973.

any rate in the American political system – the planner did not have much power and did not deserve to have much either; within a decade, from 1965 to 1975, these approaches together neatly stripped the planner of whatever priestly clothing, and consequent mystique, s/he may have possessed. Needless to say, this view powerfully communicated itself to the professionals themselves. Even in countries with more centralized, top–down political systems, such as Great Britain, young graduating planners increasingly saw their roles as rather like barefoot doctors, helping the poor down on the streets of the inner city, working either for a politically acceptable local authority, or, failing that, for community organizations battling against a politically objectionable one.

Several historical factors, in addition to the demolition job on planning by the American theorists, contributed to this change: planners and politicians belatedly discovered the continued deprivation of the inner-city poor; then, it was seen that the areas where these people lived were suffering depopulation and deindustrialization; in consequence, planners progressively moved away from the merely physical, and into the social and the economic. The change can be caricatured thus: in 1955, the typical newly graduated planner was at the drawing board, producing a diagram of desired land uses; in 1965, s/he was analysing computer output of traffic patterns; in 1975, the same person was talking late into the night with community groups, in the attempt to organize against hostile forces in the world outside.

It was a remarkable inversion of roles. For what was wholly or partly lost, in that decade, was the claim to any unique and useful expertise, such as was possessed by the doctor or the lawyer. True, the planner could still offer specialized knowledge on planning laws and procedures, or on how to achieve a particular design solution; though often, given the nature of the context and the changed character of planning education, s/he might not have enough of either of these skills to be particularly useful. And, some critics were beginning to argue, this was because planning had extended so thinly over so wide an area that it became almost meaningless; in the title of Aaron Wildavsky's celebrated paper, 'If Planning is Everything, Maybe it's Nothing'.[50]

The fact was that planning, as an academic discipline, had theorized about its own role to such extent that it was denying its own claim to legitimacy. Planning, Faludi pointed out in his text of 1973, could be merely *functional*, in that the goals and objectives are taken as given; or *normative*, in that they are themselves the object of rational choice.[51] The problem was whether planning was really capable of doing that latter job. As a result, by the mid-1970s planning had reached the stage of a 'paradigm crisis';[52] it had been theoretically useful to distinguish the planning process

[50] Wildavsky, 1973, 130.   [51] Faludi, 1973, 175.
[52] Galloway and Mahayni, 1977, 66.

as something separate from what is planned, yet this had meant a neglect of substantive theory, pushing it to the periphery of the whole subject. 'Consequently, new theory is needed which attempts to bridge current planning strategies and the urban physical and social systems to which strategies are applied.'[53]

The Marxist Ascendancy

That became ever clearer in the following decade, when the logical positivists retreated from the intellectual field of battle and the Marxists took possession. As the whole world knows, the 1970s saw a remarkable resurgence – indeed a veritable explosion – of Marxist studies. This could not fail to affect the closely related worlds of urban geography, sociology, economics and planning. True, like the early neo-classical economists, Marx had been remarkably uninterested in questions of spatial location – even though Engels had made illuminating comments on the spatial distribution of classes in mid-Victorian Manchester. The disciples now reverently sought to extract from the holy texts, drop by drop, a distillation that could be used to brew the missing theoretical potion. At last, by the mid-1970s, it was ready; then came a flood of new work. It originated in various places and in various disciplines: in England and the United States the geographers David Harvey and Doreen Massey helped to explain urban growth and change in terms of the circulation of capital; in Paris, Manuel Castells and Henri Lefebvre developed sociologically based theories.[54]

In the endless debates that followed among the Marxists themselves, a critical question concerned the role of the state.[55] In France, Lokjine and others argued that it was mainly concerned, through such devices as macro-economic planning and related infrastructure investment, directly to underpin and aid the direct productive investments of private capital. Castells, in contrast, argued that its main function had been to provide collective consumption – as in public housing, or schools, or transportation – to help guarantee the reproduction of the labour force and to dampen class conflict, essential for the maintenance of the system.[56] Clearly, planning might play a very large role in both these state functions; hence, by the mid-1970s French Marxist urbanists were engaging in major studies of this role in the industrialization of such major industrial areas as Dieppe.[57]

[53] Ibid. 68.
[54] Harvey, 1973, 1982, 1985a, 1985b; Castells, 1977, 1978; Lefebvre, 1968, 1972; Massey and Meegan, 1982; Massey, 1984.
[55] Carnoy, 1984.
[56] Lokjine, 1977; Castells, 1977, 276–323; 1978, 15–36.
[57] Ibid. 62–92.

336 THE CITY OF THEORY

FIGURE 10.5   *Manuel Castells.*
Three waves of Berkeley planning theory continued. (3) Castells came in 1979 from
Paris, where his *Urban Question*, a Marxist analysis of planning's role within the
capitalist state, had become an instant international classic.

At the same time, a specifically Marxian view of planning emerged in
the English-speaking world. To describe it adequately would require a
course in Marxist theory. But, in inadequate summary, it states that the
structure of the capitalist city itself, including its land-use and activity
patterns, is the result of capital in pursuit of profit. Because capitalism is
doomed to recurrent crises, which deepen in the current stage of late
capitalism, capital calls upon the state, as its agent, to assist it by remedying
disorganization in commodity production, and by aiding the reproduction
of the labour force. It thus tries to achieve certain necessary objectives: to

facilitate continued capital accumulation, by ensuring rational allocation of resources; by assisting the reproduction of the labour force through the provision of social services, thus maintaining a delicate balance between labour and capital and preventing social disintegration; and by guaranteeing and legitimating capitalist social and property relations. As Dear and Scott put it: 'In summary, planning is an historically-specific and socially-necessary response to the self-disorganizing tendencies of *privatized* capitalist social and property relations as these appear in urban space.'[58] In particular, it seeks to guarantee collective provision of necessary infrastructure and certain basic urban services, and to reduce negative externalities whereby certain activities of capital cause losses to other parts of the system.[59]

But, since capitalism also wishes to circumscribe state planning as far as possible, there is an inbuilt contradiction: planning, because of this inherent inadequacy, always solves one problem only by creating another.[60] Thus, say the Marxists, nineteenth-century clearances in Paris created a working-class housing problem; American zoning limited the powers of industrialists to locate at the most profitable locations.[61] And planning can never do more than modify some parameters of the land development process; it cannot change its intrinsic logic, and so cannot remove the contradiction between private accumulation and collective action.[62] Further, the capitalist class is by no means homogenous; different fractions of capital may have divergent, even contradictory interests, and complex alliances may be formed in consequence; thus, latter-day Marxist explanations come close to being pluralist, albeit with a strong structural element.[63] But in the process, 'the more that the State intervenes in the urban system, the greater is the likelihood that different social groups and fractions will contest the legitimacy of its decisions. *Urban life as a whole becomes progressively invaded by political controversies and dilemmas'*.[64]

Because traditional non-Marxian planning theory has ignored this essential basis of planning, so Marxian commentators argue, it is by definition vacuous: it seeks to define what planning ideally ought to be, devoid of all context; its function has been to depoliticize planning as an activity, and thus to legitimate it.[65] It seeks to achieve this by representing itself as the force which produces the various facets of real-world planning. But in fact, its various claims – to develop abstract concepts that rationally represent real-world processes, to legitimate its own activity, to explain material processes as the outcome of ideas, to present planning goals as derived from generally shared values, and to abstract planning activity in terms of metaphors drawn from other fields like engineering – all these are

---

[58] Dear and Scott, 1981b, 13.   [59] Ibid. 11.   [60] Ibid. 14–5.
[61] Scott and Roweis, 1977, 1108.   [62] Ibid. 1107.   [63] Mollenkopf, 1983.
[64] Dear and Scott, 1981, 16.   [65] Scott and Roweis, 1977, 1098.

both very large and quite unjustified.[66] The reality, Marxists argue, is precisely the opposite: viewed objectively, planning theory is nothing other than a creation of the social forces that bring planning into existence.[67]

It makes up a disturbing body of coherent criticism: yes, of course, planning cannot simply be an independent self-legitimating activity, as scientific inquiry may claim to be; yes, of course, it is a phenomenon that – like all phenomena – represents the circumstances of its time. As Scott and Roweis put it:

> ... there is a definite mismatch between the world of current planning theory, on the one hand, and the real world of practical planning intervention on the other hand. The one is the quintessence of order and reason in relation to the other which is full of disorder and unreason. Conventional theorists then set about resolving this mismatch between theory and reality by introducing the notion that planning theory is in any case not so much an attempt to explain the world as it *is* but as it *ought* to be. Planning theory then sets itself the task of rationalizing irrationalities, and seeks to materialize itself in social and historical reality (like Hegel's World Spirit) by bringing to bear upon the world a set of abstract, independent, and transcendent norms.[68]

It was powerful criticism. But it left in turn a glaringly open question, both for the unfortunate planner – whose legitimacy is now totally torn from him, like the epaulette from the shoulder of a disgraced officer – and, equally, for the Marxist critic: what, then, is planning theory about? Has it any normative or prescriptive content whatsoever? The answer, logically, would appear to be no. One of the critics, Philip Cooke, is uncompromising:

> The main criticism that tends to have been made, justifiably, of planning is that it has remained stubbornly normative . . . in this book it will be argued that (planning theorists) should identify mechanisms which cause changes in the nature of planning to be brought about, rather than assuming such changes to be either the creative idealizations of individual minds, or mere regularities in observable events.[69]

This is at least consistent: planning theory should avoid all prescription; it should stand right outside the planning process, and seek to analyse the subject – including traditional theory – for what it is, the reflection of historical forces. Scott and Roweis, a decade earlier, seem to be saying exactly the same thing: planning theory cannot be normative, it cannot assume 'transcendent operational norms'.[70] But then, they stand their logic on its own head, saying that 'a viable theory of urban planning should not only tell us what planning is, but also what we can, and must, do as progressive planners.'[71]

---

[66] Cooke, 1983, 106–8.   [67] Scott and Roweis, 1977, 1099.   [68] Ibid. 1116.
[69] Cooke, 1983, 25, 27.   [70] Scott and Roweis, 1977, 1099.   [71] Ibid.

This, of course, is sheer rhetoric. But it nicely displays the agony of the dilemma. Either theory is about unravelling the historical logic of capitalism, or it is about prescription for action. Since the planner-theorist – however sophisticated – could never hope to divert the course of capitalist evolution by more than a millimetre or a millisecond, the logic would seem to demand that s/he sticks firmly to the first and abjures the second. In other words, the Marxian logic is strangely quietist; it suggests that the planner retreats from planning altogether into the academic ivory tower.

Some were acutely conscious of the dilemma. John Forester tried to resolve it by basing a whole theory of planning action on the work of Jürgen Habermas. Habermas, perhaps the leading German social theorist of the post-World War Two era, had argued that latter-day capitalism justified its own legitimacy by spinning around itself a complex set of distortions in communication, designed to obscure and prevent any rational understanding of its own workings.[72] Thus, he argued, individuals became powerless to understand how and why they act, and so were excluded from all power to influence their own lives,

> as they are harangued, pacified, mislead [sic], and ultimately persuaded that inequality, poverty, and ill-health are either problems for which the victim is responsible or problems so 'political' and 'complex' that they can have nothing to say about them. Habermas argues that democratic politics or planning requires the consent that grows from processes of collective criticism, not from silence or a party line.[73]

But, Forester argues, Habermas's own proposals for communicative action provide a way for planners to improve their own practice:

> By recognizing planning practice as normatively role-structured communication action which distorts, covers up, or reveals to the public the prospects and possibilities they face, a critical theory of planning aids us practically and ethically as well. This is the contribution of critical theory to planning: pragmatics with vision – to reveal true alternatives, to correct false expectations, to counter cynicism, to foster inquiry, to spread political responsibility, engagement, and action. Critical planning practice, technically skilled and politically sensitive, is an organizing and democratizing practice.[74]

Fine. The problem is that – stripped of its Germanic philosophical basis, which is necessarily a huge oversimplification of a very dense analysis – the practical prescription all comes out as good old-fashioned democratic common sense, no more and no less than Davidoff's advocacy planning of fifteen years before: cultivate community networks, listen carefully to the people, involve the less-organized groups, educate the citizens in how to join in, supply information and make sure people know how to get it,

[72] Bernstein, 1976, 1985; Held, 1980; McCarthy, 1981; Thompson and Held, 1982.
[73] Forester, 1980, 277.   [74] Ibid. 283.

develop skills in working with groups in conflict situations, emphasize the need to participate, compensate for external pressures. True, if in all this planners can sense that they have penetrated the mask of capitalism, that may help them to help others to act to change their environment and their lives; and, given the clear philosophical impasse of the late 1970s, such a massive metaphysical underpinning may be necessary.

The World Outside the Tower: Practice Retreats from Theory

Meanwhile, if the theorists were retreating in one direction, the practitioners were certainly reciprocating. Whether baffled or bored by the increasingly scholastic character of the academic debate, they lapsed into an increasingly untheoretical, unreflective, pragmatic, even visceral style of planning. That was not entirely new: planning had come under a cloud before, as during the 1950s, and had soon reappeared in a clear blue sky. What was new, strange, and seemingly unique about the 1980s was the divorce between the Marxist theoreticians of academe – essentially academic spectators, taking grandstand seats at what they saw as one of capitalism's last games – and the anti-theoretical, anti-strategic, anti-intellectual style of the players on the field down below.[75] The 1950s were never like that; then, the academics were the coaches, down there with the team.

The picture is of course exaggerated. Many academics did still try to teach real-life planning through simulation of real-world problems. The Royal Town Planning Institute enjoined them to become ever more practice-minded. The practitioners had not all shut their eyes and ears to what comes out of the academy; some even returned there for refresher courses. And if all this was true in Britain, it was even more so of America, where the divorce had never been so evident. Yet the picture does describe a clear and unmistakable trend; and it was likely to be more than a cyclical one.

The reason is simple: as professional education of any kind becomes more fully absorbed by the academy, as its teachers become more thoroughly socialized within it, as careers are seen to depend on academic peer judgements, then its norms and values – theoretical, intellectual, detached – will become ever more pervasive; and the gap between teaching and practice will progressively widen. One key illustration: of the huge output of books and papers from the planning schools in the 1980s, there were many – often, those most highly regarded within the academic community – that were simply irrelevant, even completely incomprehensible, to the average practitioner.

Perhaps, it might be argued, that was the practitioner's fault; perhaps too, we need fundamental science, with no apparent payoff, if we are later

[75] Ambrose, 1986, *passim*; Reade, 1987, *passim*.

to enjoy its technological applications. The difficulty with that argument was to find convincing evidence that – not merely here, but in the social sciences generally – such payoff eventually comes. Hence the low esteem into which the social sciences had everywhere fallen, not least in Britain and the United States: hence too the diminished level of support for them, which – at any rate in Britain – had directly redounded on the planning schools. The relationship between planning and the academy had gone sour, and that is the major unresolved question that must now be addressed.

The City of Enterprise

It is not from the benevolence of the butcher, the brewer, or the baker that we expect our dinner, but from their regard to their own interest. We address ourselves, not to their humanity but to their self-love, and never talk to them of our own necessities but of their advantages. Nobody but a beggar chooses to depend chiefly upon the benevolence of his fellow-citizens.

Adam Smith
The Wealth of Nations (1776)

But beware! The time for all this is not yet. For at least another hundred years we must pretend to ourselves and to everyone that fair is foul and foul is fair; for foul is useful and fair is not. Avarice and usury and precaution must be our gods for a little longer still. For only they can lead us out of the tunnel of economic necessity into daylight.

John Maynard Keynes
'Economic Possibilities for our Grandchildren' (Essays in Persuasion) (1930)

It is of the utmost importance to the argument of this book for the reader to keep in mind that the planning against which all our criticism is directly is solely the planning against competition – the planning that is to be substituted for competition. . . . But as in current usage 'planning' has become synonymous with the former kind of planning, it will sometimes be inevitable for the sake of brevity to refer to it simply as planning, even though this means leaving to our opponents a very good word meriting a better fate.

Friedrich von Hayek
The Road to Serfdom (1944)

11

The City of Enterprise

Planning Turned Upside Down:
Baltimore, Hong Kong, London,
1975–1987

Sometime during the 1970s, the city-planning movement began to turn upside down and inside out; during the 1980s, it seemed at times almost on the point of self-destruction. Conventional planning, the use of plans and regulations to guide the use of land, seemed more and more discredited. Instead, planning turned from regulating urban growth, to encouraging it by any and every possible means. Cities, the new message rang loud and clear, were machines for wealth creation; the first and chief aim of planning must be to oil the machinery. The planner increasingly identified with his traditional adversary, the developer; the gamekeeper turned poacher.

Nowhere was this more clearly seen than in Britain; it was poetic justice, perhaps, that the land that gave birth to the movement should also be the scene of its apparent death throes. But the origin of the whole reversal lay in the United States, where regulatory planning had never been as strong and the habit of development, the tradition of enterprise, had always been uppermost.

The root cause was economic. Conventional land-use planning had flourished in the great boom of the 1950s and 1960s, perhaps the greatest sustained period of growth the capitalist economy had ever known. That was because it had served as a means of guiding and controlling explosive physical growth. The great recession of the 1970s and 1980s was bound to change the nature of the basic perceived problem with which planning had to deal, and thus to threaten its very legitimacy. It hit the British economy with especial force, exposing deep structural weaknesses: a large part of the country's manufacturing base disappeared, bringing a loss of 2 million factory jobs between 1971 and 1981 alone.[1] A new geography emerged, with a contrast between the decaying inner cities – which now

[1] Massey and Meegan, 1982; Massey, 1984; Hudson and Williams, 1986; Hausner, 1987.

included not only old problem cases like Glasgow and Liverpool but once-proud seats of manufacture like London and Birmingham – and the still-expanding high-tech corridors of southern England.[2] In these select places, conventional regulatory planning still commanded grassroots political support. But, over wide areas of the country, the call was no longer for the control and guidance of growth; it was for the generation of growth-promoting activities by almost any means.

There was a parallel development in the United States. There, too, the traditional industrial regions – New England, the Mid Atlantic and above all the mid West – were attacked by the same virus of overseas competition, falling profits and restructuration. The nation's manufacturing belt found itself given a new media epithet: the Rustbowl. Barry Bluestone and Bennett Harrison, in their book dramatically titled *The Deindustrialization of America*, estimated that during the 1970s the combined effect of runaway plants, shutdowns and permanent physical cutbacks may have cost the country as many as 38 million jobs. And, of an estimated 35 million lost jobs between 1969 and 1976, more than half were in the so-called Frostbelt: in other words, the industrial heartland.[3]

It took planners, and their urban political leaders, by surprise. They had forgotten their history. As we noted in chapter 5, Clarence Stein, that visionary founder of the Regional Planning Association of America and designer of Radburn, had predicted the decay of the urban economy in a remarkable article in May 1925, entitled 'Dinosaur Cities'.[4] Colin Clark, that equally perspicacious economist, had correctly forecast the general contraction of manufacturing employment in his book *The Conditions of Economic Progress*, in 1940.[5] Neither had been much heeded. They had the misfortune to be too far ahead of their fellows.

Yet there was more to it than that. During the 1970s, in both Britain and the United States, neo-conservative think-tanks – the British Centre for Policy Studies, the American Heritage Foundation – began to challenge the whole cosy consensus which had produced Keynesian economic policy and welfare state social policy. Following the early arguments of classics in the genre, now elevated to the status of sacred texts – like Hayek's thirty-year-old *Road to Serfdom* – planning itself became a central part of the bundle of policies under assault. It had – so the radical right alleged –

---

[2] Boddy, Lovering and Bassett, 1986; Hall, *et al.*, 1987.
[3] Bluestone and Harrison, 1982, 26, 30.
[4] Stein, 1925.   [5] Clark, 1940.

FIGURE 11.1 *Liverpool.*
Ruins of a 1960s housing estate in the inner city; the legacy of Pruitt-Igoe comes to Britain.

distorted and inhibited the operation of market forces, forcing industrialists to take sub-optimal location decisions and even throttling entrepreneurship. It was at least partly responsible for the failure of lagging cities and regions to generate new growth industries to replace declining ones. Regional planning was especially objectionable in this respect; but – despite Hayek's own reservations as to the scope of his attack – land-use planning did not escape censure.

But the first warnings came long before this fundamental critique; they were sounded in the late 1960s. In the United States, the Johnson administration redoubled its urban anti-poverty programmes after the riots of 1964–7. The Model Cities Program and associated Community Development Program (chapter 8) were the results. Over in Britain, a series of reports – Milner Holland (1965) on London housing, Plowden (1967) on primary schools, Seebohm (1968) on social services – marked the official rediscovery of poverty by the British establishment. Perceptive academic commentators like David Eversley – brought out of academia to head strategic planning for London – began to point to the ominous decline of London's economic base.[6] Enoch Powell's notorious speech of April 1968 on the problem of racial tension in the cities, in which he recalled the Tiber flowing with blood, brought immediate panic political response from the then Wilson Labour Government: an urban programme, which was to give special aid to areas with high concentrations of immigrants – or, as the official euphemism had it, areas of special need.[7] The Community Development Projects of 1969, a carbon copy of the American programme, aimed to raise the consciousness of deprived local communities. Some of the project teams, full of youthful Marxist verve, set about their task so enthusiastically that they clashed head on with local bureaucracies, and in 1976 the whole experiment came to an abrupt end.[8]

But there was a rare historical irony. The message from the CDP teams was that the problem – of places like Saltley in Birmingham, of Benwell in Newcastle-upon-Tyne – was 'structural': a new vogue-word from academia had entered the language of planning. Major forces in the latter-day capitalist economy – in particular, the increasing concentration of capital in ever fewer monopolistic hands – were transferring control of firms and industries out of local hands and into the boardrooms of ever more distant multinational enterprises. It was that conclusion, with its implication that the solution was not to be found within the confines of the capitalist system, which made the message so unacceptable to the then political leadership of the cities or to the British Home Office. The first irony was that a decade later, a new generation of politicians in the Town

[6] Greater London Council, 1969; Donnison and Eversley, 1973.
[7] Edwards and Batley, 1978, 46.
[8] McKay and Cox, 1979, 244–5; Hall, 1981, ch. 5.

Halls would have warmly agreed. The second was that even before this happened, the notion of structural decline had became part of received establishment thinking.

The vehicle was in some ways an unlikely one. In 1972 Peter Walker, Secretary of State for the Environment in the then Tory administration, had appointed three of Britain's most senior consultancies to investigate in depth the problems of three deprived inner-city areas. Their final reports, which were published simultaneously in the summer of 1977, underlined the same conclusion: deprivation was no longer a matter of individuals or households falling below the poverty line; rather, it had become a matter of the failure of entire urban economies.[9] The government of the day, now Labour, took the message: in a White Paper of 1977,[10] and in the Inner Urban Areas Act of 1978, it switched the emphasis of inner-city policy massively to economic revival. Henceforth, inner cities would get high priority for new industrial development; central government resources were to be switched from new towns to help the cities; the urban programme would be massively expanded; and central–local government partnerships would be introduced for some of the hardest-hit areas in some of the major cities.

At first, the full extent of the shift was not apparent. Existing bureaucracies dusted down existing programmes that had been gathering dust in drawers, and these reflected traditional responsibilities and preoccupations: a leisure centre here, a piece of landscaping there. But, as the 1970s gave way to the 1980s and the inner-city economies continued to haemorrhage, the emphasis shifted. Almost all authorities by then had economic development offices under various names, staffed by a new breed of local government officer.[11] Planners sometimes took these jobs, but they then found that they must reverse their traditional roles. The guidance and control of growth, traditional concern of the British statutory planning system since 1947, had quite suddenly been replaced by an obsession with encouraging growth at almost any cost; the political issue began to centre on how best this should be done.

The Rousification of America

At that point, some British planners and politicians began to look across the Atlantic. For the message, coming loudly from the other side in these late-1970s years, was that American cities had found a magic formula. At a typical high-level Anglo-American gathering, the glum British would

[9] G.B. Department of the Environment, 1977a, 1977b, 1977c, 1977d.
[10] G.B. Secretary for the Environment, 1977.
[11] Young and Mason, 1983.

show slides of the barren desolation of inner Liverpool; the exuberant Americans would arrive with pictures of a vibrant downtown Boston, full of life and colour and excitement – plus, almost needless to say, booming sales and expanding jobs.[12] The magic recipe for urban revitalization – the American buzzword that began to circulate at such gatherings – seemed to consist in a new kind of creative partnership, a word used incessantly by the Americans, between the city government and the private sector. It would be seasoned by judicious funding from Washington, to which – in contrast with Whitehall's aid to British cities – relatively few strings were attached.

It also seemed to consist in a frank realization that the days of the urban manufacturing economy were over, and that success consisted in finding and creating a new service-sector role for the central city. Bored suburbanites would come in droves to a restored city that offered them a quality of life they could never find in the shopping mall. Yuppies, or Young Urban Professionals – the word began to circulate in the early 1980s – would gentrify the blighted Victorian residential areas close to downtown, and inject their dollars into restored boutiques, bars and restaurants. Finally, the restored city would actually become a major attraction to tourists, providing a new economic base to the city.

This was the formula that had already revived the Boston waterfront and was just then transforming the Inner Harbor of Baltimore – the two great showcases of urban revitalization in its first phase. Viewed more closely, it was of course more complex. Both cities, which began to experience urban decline as early as the 1950s, had been working on the problem since then – two decades before their British equivalents. Both, in the 1960s, had first gone for fairly conventional headquarters-type office development: a formula somewhat easier for them than for their British equivalents, since both were old-established commercial centres and Boston was a major home for financial institutions. Both had then grafted on large-scale waterfront redevelopments of their derelict inner-port areas, involving the then novel combination of restored warehouse and market buildings, boutique shopping, bars, restaurants and hotels, and restoration of old residential areas.

And, in both cities, the same key agent was at work. James Rouse was already celebrated, in the late 1960s, as a Baltimore developer who had built Columbia, one of the most ambitious of the private-enterprise new towns that were developed in the United States at that time. Through his leading role in the Greater Baltimore Committee, a business elite group founded in 1956, he had also been involved in the revitalization of downtown Baltimore from its earliest stage: the 33-acre Charles Center, a

FIGURE 11.2 *Boston, Quincy Market.*

FIGURE 11.3 *Baltimore, Inner Harbor.*
The two show pieces of American inner-city regeneration through public-private partnership, both through the Rouse Corporation: 'Rousification' enters the planner's vocabulary.

complex of offices, shop, hotel and apartments developed from the late 1950s. This, interestingly, was developed under the Urban Renewal legislation of 1949 and 1954, and in almost every respect followed the model set by Pittsburgh and Philadelphia (chapter 7): a new, radical business elite effectively took over the city, leading a pro-growth coalition which skilfully marshalled public support and combined federal and private funds to promote large-scale commercial development.[13]

There was nothing very new about that; dozens of cities were doing it, or trying to do it. But Rouse's role in the Baltimore Inner Harbor, and in the equivalent Quincy Market and Boston Waterfront schemes, marked something different. These schemes were bigger – 250 acres in Baltimore – and they incorporated a new combination of activities: recreation, culture, shopping, mixed-income housing. They also were based on the then new concept of adaptive re-use: the rehabilitation and recycling of old physical structures to new uses.[14] They involved a relatively much bigger public role and a bigger federal commitment: $180 million in the Baltimore case, against $58 million from the city and only $22 million from the private sector. So federal grantsmanship, coupled with a new view of public sector investment in speculative enterprise, and the co-operation of public and private sector entrepreneurs, were critical elements of the new formula.[15] Significantly, in both cities they were carried through by shrewd and well-established Democratic mayors who had good links with the neighbourhoods – Kevin White in Boston, William Donald Schaefer in Baltimore.

The resulting developments share much in common with London's Covent Garden, which was being recycled at much the same time (chapter 7). They are unashamedly tourist-based: Baltimore attracts 22 million visitors a year, of whom 7 million are tourists, a figure comparable with Disneyland. And this provides a critical clue to the revolutionary nature of these developments:

> The process of creating successful places is only incidentally about property development. It is much more like running a theatre, with continually changing attractions to draw people in and keep them entertained. It is no surprise that perhaps the most successful model of all, the 28,000 acre Walt Disney World in Florida, is run by a company which has divisions concerned with 'Imagineering' and 'Attractions'. It does not seem to be surveyors and planners who have the qualities needed to create major theatres, even though they may be very useful as actors or playwrights.[16]

The Rousification of Boston and Baltimore – a process now repeated in a score of older American industrial cities – thus involved the deliberate

---

[13] Lyall, 1982, 28–36; Mollenkopf, 1983, 141, 169–73; Berkowitz, 1984, 203.
[14] Hart, 1983, 19.   [15] Lyall, 1982, 51–55; Falk, 1986, 145–7.
[16] Ibid. 150.

creation of the city-as-stage. Like theatre it resembles real life, but it is not urban life as it ever actually was: the model is the Main Street America exhibit which greets entering visitors at the California Disneyland, sanitized for your protection (as the phrase goes), wholesome, undangerous, and seven-eighths real size. Around it, the charmingly-restored streets – all yuppified with a massive injection of HUD funds – have exactly the same quality: they manage to look like a Disney movie lot of an imagined urban America, but they happen incongruously to be real.

The Battle for Docklands

All this was highly relevant to the British debate. And inevitably, given the scale and the nature of the problem, that debate became politicized. For, by the late 1970s, in all the great British cities, a new phenomenon was manifest; huge tracts of vacant or semi-vacant land, marked by the gaunt ruins of derelict industrial or warehouse buildings, awaited redevelopment. Invariably, most of this land was in public or quasi-public ownership: it belonged either to the local municipalities, who had acquired it for housing or roadbuilding schemes that were now threatened by expenditure cuts (or, with the roads, public opposition), or to public corporations like Docks authorities, British Gas or British Rail, which had taken their operations elsewhere.

The most spectacular case, by far, was the London Docklands: a huge tract, some 8½ square miles in extent, beginning at the very edge of the City of London's famous square mile and stretching downstream for some 8 miles on both sides of the Thames. Once the greatest port in the world, it had been racked by labour disputes and the transfer of trade to rivals both elsewhere in southern England (Southampton, Felixstowe) and the European mainland (Rotterdam). The coming of containerization dealt the final blow. The Port of London transferred virtually all remaining operations 30 miles downstream to Tilbury, and – in a short time from 1967 to 1980 – closed down almost the entire system. Related public corporations like British Rail, and British Gas who had operated a huge coal-gas plant at Beckton near the eastern end, did the same. By 1981 employment, 30,000 in the docks' heyday in the 1950s, had plummeted to 2,000.

The problem first fell to the Tory Government of 1970–4, under Edward Heath. They gave it to a firm of engineering consultants who suggested a variety of scenarios, mostly involving a major change in the character of the area: new luxury housing, marinas, leisure activities, services. The local dockland communities, traditionally working-class and inward-looking, still reeling under the sudden loss of their livelihood, reacted vehemently; so did their overwhelmingly Labour borough councils. The London election of 1973 brought a Labour Greater London Council, the General Election in 1974 a Labour Government on the opposite side of the river in Westminster.

It was just at this time that the inner-city problem was beginning to emerge in the public consciousness. Whatever happened in London docklands would be not only important in itself, but also a model for other places. The Wilson Government could do not other than involve the local communities. But it was also aware that strong central direction and co-ordination were needed, and it was painfully aware that the GLC – the legally constituted strategic planning authority – was the logical body to provide this. It produced a compromise – masterly or shabby, depending on your view: it gave the job of producing a strategy to the Docklands Joint Committee, a GLC-borough *ad hoc* organization created in 1973 at the initiative of the GLC, with a special planning team (the Docklands Development Team) including GLC officers, but at arm's length from it.

The team, labouring mightily, produced its strategy in 1976. It reflected the then political realities. Most of the area would be redeveloped as public low-rent housing or as industry and warehousing, though it was by then evident that public-expenditure cuts were decimating the public-housing programme and that there were huge areas of vacant industrial floorspace all over the capital. Little provision was made for offices, despite the location of the area on the very fringe of the City of London financial district. As one academic observer has noticed:

> It approximates the variant . . . termed Urban Conservation – a strong emphasis on replicating and retaining present activities and structures, with their associated social and economic patterns reinforced . . . the classic mix of working-class housing, industrial and commercial jobs, and development of riverside amenity facilities and community services. . . . The style by which the planning process is conditioned is one of consultation and persuasion . . . the process must find means of gaining commitment from groups potentially in conflict . . . very wide participation and consultation makes this style cumbersome. Decisions appear to be nebulous, in that they are highly generalised.[17]

It did not have a good press. *The Times* found it 'not impressive', concluding that the DJC was 'too timidly affected by the belief that flair and grand vision are not quite compatible with democracy.'[18] The locals liked it better, but even they were disappointed by the lack of firm proposals.

The fact, which emerged soon enough, was that the strategy existed in a financial vacuum. Public expenditure was being cut, and there were no funds for major elements like an extension of the Jubilee underground line. More critically, the strategy demanded that £900 million of public money

[17] Ledgerwood, 1985, 133.   [18] Ibid. 123.

FIGURE 11.4 AND 11.5 *London Docklands: Before and After.*
The transformation of the London Docklands during the 1980s represented the
biggest piece of urban revitalization in Europe, if not the world. For some, it was
a shining example of how to do it; for others, of how not to.

be matched by £1100 million of private funds; but nowhere in the consultation process had anyone bothered to talk to the managers of pension funds, insurance companies and banks. The South East Economic Planning Council, an independent advisory body appointed by government, argued that the area required a New Town-style development corporation, reasonably free from political interference and free to get on with the job; only this, they argued, would give the private investor the necessary confidence to come in. The then Secretary of State for the Environment, Peter Shore, who happened to be Member of Parliament for a large part of the Docklands area, politely disagreed.

In May 1979 the Conservatives were swept back to power under Margaret Thatcher. Michael Heseltine became Secretary of State for the Environment, charged with inner-city policy. Almost his first act was to abolish the South East Economic Planning Council – and indeed all its regional counterparts. Almost the second was to establish an Urban Development Corporation for the London Docklands and their equally derelict Merseyside counterpart.

There was a rich historical irony here. The Development Corporation (chapter 4) was the centralist, top-down, non-democratic bureaucratic device preferred by Clement Attlee's radical Labour government of 1945 for the construction of the British new towns. Detested at that time by the solid Tory voters of the southern English shires where the eight original London new towns were built, later shunned for a decade by Tory governments of the 1950s, then reluctantly accepted as an unfortunate necessity, the Development Corporation now became the preferred Tory device for the regeneration of the inner cities, and for precisely the same reason as the Reith Committee on the new towns had argued 35 years before: bypassing the democratic niceties of local government, it could be effective and above all quick.

In its new context, it reflected two new emphases. The first was that the Conservative Party, traditionally (and recently) the party of local rights against Whitehall bureaucracy, had now become the party of the centralizers. (This was to appear ever more evident in the succeeding decade, as Westminster fought bitter battles with Labour-controlled inner-city town halls on issues like rate-support grant, rate-capping and control of local schools.) The second was something that could only be called planning as property development. The task of planning, in this view, was to facilitate the most rapid feasible recycling of derelict urban industrial or commercial land to higher and better uses. This was not of course new; witness the great property boom in Britain's city centres in the 1960s. And it directly derived from the American experience. What was nevertheless remarkable, here as elsewhere, was the style: anti-long-term strategic planning, anti-almost-any published plan at all; freewheeling, freebooting; unworried if –

as happened in Docklands – developments had to be demolished almost before they were finished, because something more profitable had come along; concerned only to exploit opportunities as they arose. It was not planning as anyone had ever understood it for the previous forty years. As the Docklands Chief Executive explained:

> The sheer scale of dereliction which the LDDC was charged with addressing was of such an order that the only way to tackle the problem without an enormous influx of public funds ... was to generate a kind of critical momentum, a development 'snowball' that would create a real credibility for Docklands early on amongst potential commercial and residential developers. Thus it was necessary to be opportunist with regard to proposals from developers.[19]

It did get a lot done. In the docks, as at Stevenage and Crawley forty years earlier, the development corporation proved its power to cut red tape. It took unprecedented powers – greater than the new towns had – away from the local authorities, and used them to welcome the private developer with open arms. In a mere five years from start, by mid-1986 it had used £279 million of public funds to attract nearly six times that amount in private investment; attracted 400 new companies and 8000 new jobs; provided sites for nearly 4000 new homes, with 10,000 under construction or planned; and had begun work on a major new light rail system.[20] The critics continued to say that the whole plan amounted to nothing more or less than the yuppification of the East End, London's traditional working-class stronghold.

The Enterprise Zone

Here, one particular notion came to play a role never imagined by its author. In an address to the Royal Town Planning Institute's conference at Chester in 1977, Peter Hall – joint author of the iconoclastic Nonplan Manifesto of 1970 (chapter 8) – addressed the emerging problem of urban decline: 'The biggest urban areas have seen their growth slow down, stop and then reverse. They are losing people and jobs.' Reviewing possible ways of rebuilding these cities' economic bases, he came to the possibility that 'none of these recipes can really perform the miracle for some areas.' Here, he suggested,

> the best may be the enemy of the good. If we really want to help inner cities, and cities generally, we may have to use highly unorthodox remedies. . . . a final possible remedy, which I would call the Freeport solution. Small, selected areas of inner cities would be simply thrown open to all kinds of

[19] Ward, 1986, 118.   [20] Ibid. 118–123.

initiative, with minimal control. In other words, we would aim to recreate the Hong Kong of the 1950s and 1960s inside inner Liverpool or inner Glasgow.[21]

This would involve three elements. Each area would be completely open to immigration of entrepreneurs and capital – meaning no immigration controls. It would be 'based on fairly shameless free enterprise'; bureaucracy would be 'kept to the absolute minimum.' And residence would be based on choice, since the area would effectively be outside the United Kingdom's normal legislation and controls. Hall concluded: 'Such an area would not conform at all to modern British conventions of the welfare state. But it could be economically vigorous on the Hong Kong model. Since it would represent an extremely drastic last-ditch solution to urban problems, it could be tried only on a very small scale.' He ended with a disclaimer, that in the event proved ironic: 'I do not expect the British government to act on this solution immediately, and I want to emphasise that I am not recommending it as a solution for our urban ills. I am saying that it is a model, and an extreme one, of a possible solution.'[22]

In some ways, as emerged from later and closer analysis, his evocation of Hong Kong was an odd one. For, in terms of Turner's campaign against third-world housing bureaucracies, Hong Kong was an outstanding example of ultimate conservatism: throughout the 1960s and 1970s, contrary to its outside-world mythical image, it had maintained what was in relative terms the largest public housing programme in the non-Communist world.[23] Jonathan Schiffer was later to suggest a ingenious explanation: the programme, by keeping the costs of mass housing to a guaranteed minimum, greatly dampened demands for wage increases and kept Hong Kong's labour costs among the lowest in the developed world.[24] Further, though by conventional British standards Hong Kong did not have a very restrictive or comprehensive British-style land-use planning system,[25] by the standards of many developing countries there was a good deal of planning intervention. Nonetheless, Hall could defend his basic point: however indirectly subsidized in this and other ways, Hong Kong had proved one of the world's most successful examples of how to move rapidly into new entrepreneurial lines in response to the state of the world market, mainly through the extraordinary adaptability of its dominant small-business sector.[26]

All this, however, was part of a rather obscure academic debate. The odd point is that, despite Hall's total scepticism as to the possibilities of action, he did not have to wait long. In 1980 the new Conservative Government in Britain introduced provision for Enterprise Zones, and the Chancellor of the Exchequer specifically cited him as the author of the

[21] Hall, 1977, 5.   [22] Ibid.   [23] Choi and Chan, 1979, 187.
[24] Schiffer, 1984, *passim*.   [25] Bristow, 1984.   [26] Sit, 1978, 92.

scheme. During 1980–1, eleven zones were designated – one of them, the Isle of Dogs, in the heart of the London Docklands. The whole notion, and its hapless author, were duly attacked by radical academics from both sides of the Atlantic.[27]

In the event, however, what emerged was something very different: a set of zones, mainly though not exclusively in derelict inner-urban areas, with especially favourable tax concessions and a simplified set of physical planning procedures.[28] Most of the other elements – the free migration of labour, the encouragement of immigrant entrepreneurs, the general freedom from mainstream legislation – were conspicuously missing: a particularly poignant example of the way that, especially in Britain, radical ideas are taken on board by the establishment, only to be sanitized into something completely harmless. What was conspicuously lacking, despite the title, was any mechanism for encouraging innovation, in the sense enunciated by Joseph Schumpeter, as a way of providing alternative industrial traditions for areas where the traditional industrial base had disappeared.[29]

It was thus a modest and unradical scheme, with modest results: at a total public cost of £132.9 million, the creation of about 8,000 new jobs, of which about three-quarters would have located in the same area anyway, zone or no zone.[30] More than one-third of the new jobs had been generated in only three of the fifteen zones, among which, interestingly, the Isle of Dogs was not one. At just about that time, though, came dramatic news: a plan by an American consortium for a huge office complex at Canary Wharf in the middle of the LDDC area, taking advantage of the Enterprise Zone status and providing an estimated 46,000 office jobs. After an extraordinary series of cliffhanger negotiations and the virtual withdrawal of the original developers, eleventh-hour agreement was finally reached with a Canadian group in July 1987. At last, six years in, an EZ had produced a real employment bonanza.

Nevertheless, the idea was in turn warmly espoused by the Reagan administration in the United States, where, interestingly, it also tended to win support from left-liberal inner-city politicians.[31] Despite this, it failed to gain enactment into federal law. The states stepped in: twenty-six legislatures adopted legislation, creating more than 1,400 local enterprise zones in 680 localities. A small sample of only ten, studied by the United States Department of Housing and Urban development in 1986, showed that 263 firms had invested over $147 million to create or keep over 7,000 jobs.[32]

The Reagan administration, however, did in an important sense implement

[27] Harrison, 1982; Massey, 1982; Goldsmith, 1982.
[28] Butler, 1981, 95–128.   [29] Hall, 1982b, 419.
[30] Tym and Partners, 1984, 144, 148.   [31] Hall, 1982, 419.
[32] U.S. Department of Housing and Urban Development, 1986.

the original notion in another way: by openly failing to police the border with Mexico, it condoned a huge illegal immigration into Sunbelt cities like Houston or Los Angeles, which – administration officials would openly boast in private – constituted working models of the pure enterprise zone idea. For the working results, of course, they were roundly condemned by left-radical urban analysts.[133]

Leveraging the Private Sector

The Docklands development followed the American models in one critical respect. This was the concept of using relatively modest public funds to generate – or, to use the quaintly ungrammatical American verb, to *leverage* – a much larger amount of private investment. In Boston, for instance, $2.7 million of federal preservation grant from the Department of Housing and Urban Development attracted private investment of more than six times that amount.[34] The Carter administration, in 1977, had enshrined this principle in legislation. The Urban Development Action Grant was posited on the notion of leveraging between 4.5 and 6.5 units of private investment for every one of public investment. A community could apply for a UDAG if it met standards of physical and economic distress or had a pocket of poverty. It had to show that it would attract at least 2.5 times as much private as public funding, and that the project could be funded no other way.

Down to the end of 1983, 929 communities had attracted over 1,900 projects and $3 billion of UDAG funds, with a median leverage ratio of 3.9; unsurprisingly, the lion's share of the funds had gone to the stricken bigger cities of the manufacturing belt, and New York City and Baltimore each had over fifty schemes. The programme had generated an expected total of some 411,000 new permanent jobs – 56 per cent of them, significantly, in commercial projects, and 55 per cent for low- or moderate-income people.[35] It was small wonder that the UDAG scheme was widely regarded as one of the few real success stories of urban regeneration policy; small wonder, either, that in 1983 the British Government's UDG scheme paid it the sincerest form of flattery.

There were, inevitably, some criticisms. Some said that too much of the money had gone on hotel projects (to which the retort was, hotels generate a lot of low-skilled employment, suitable for unemployed inner-city residents). Others posed the standard question about each and every such device: how many of the jobs would have been there anyway, scheme or

[33] Soja *et al.*, 1983.   [34] Hart, 1983, 20.
[35] Hart, 1983, 25; Gatons and Brintall, 1984, 116–17, 124, 130.

no scheme. Yet others pointed out that UDAGs could never restore lost manufacturing jobs, or even replace as many jobs as had been lost.[36] But that was part of a wider debate about the march through the sectors to the service economy. Many economists, following the pioneer analyses of A. G. B. Fisher and Colin Clark half a century before, argued that the decline in manufacturing jobs was an inevitable development of the latter-day capitalist economy, and that the only intelligent policy was to accept and anticipate it. Others argued that the service economy mainly generated low-wage fast-food-type jobs, and that – in the words of one major piece of academic polemic – Manufacturing Matters.[37]

The Attack on Planning

The point is that the real debate on both sides of the Atlantic was still all about economic development. And meanwhile, in other more traditional parts of the British planning system, during the 1980s the history increasingly resembled a movie run backwards. Progressively, after 1979, the Thatcher Government dismembered the strategic-planning system that had been painfully built up by successive governments during the 1960s and maintained during the 1970s. The Regional Economic Planning Councils were the first element to go, in 1979. The next year, when the government had to update the 1970 Strategic Plan for the South East – a plan which consisted of a main report and five large research volumes – it did so through two and a half pages of typescript; in 1986, repeating the exercise, it extended to six. The 1980 Planning Act effected a significant shift of powers from the counties to the districts, making the county structure plans less effective; a green paper of 1986 proposed doing away with them altogether, in effect removing the county level of planning. In the major urban areas, an Act of 1986 abolished the Greater London Council and the six metropolitan counties, England's unique experiment in metropolitan government.[38]

All this marked a significant change in planning style. The 1983 White Paper, which presaged the abolition of metropolitan government, declared flatly that there was no longer the same need as in the 1960s for strategic planning; the clear suggestion was that all that was needed was a residual land-use planning activity, proceeding on a case-by-case basis.[39] Local government took the hint. One county – Berkshire, one of the fastest-growing in all of England – abolished its planning department, merging it with the Surveyor's Department. Within the profession, there was a distinct

[36] Hart, 1983, 26–7.   [37] Cohen and Zysman, 1987.
[38] Breheny and Hall, 1984; Ambrose, 1986; Reade, 1987.
[39] G.B. Department of the Environment, 1983; Breheny and Hall, 1984.

weakening of the links with the university and polytechnic schools. There was a sharp reduction in the demand for planners, exacerbated by the sudden arrival on the job market of hundreds of displaced metropolitan and county planners. Simultaneously, funding organizations cut student support, precipitating the closure of several planning schools.

Perhaps, after all, in the long historical perspective it was just another turn of the cyclical screw. Planning in Britain had been rather like this in the relatively stagnant early 1950s, when – under an earlier Conservative Government – it had come under a cloud; yet after that, during the high-growth era of the 1960s, it had bounced back to register one of the most successful periods of its short life. That, in a sense, is pure grist to the academic Marxists' mill: planning changes shape as it is required to face new challenges, or old challenges come back again. What was new, as already seen in chapter 10, was the increasing detachment of the academic commentators from the whole process.

Will planning die away, then? Not entirely. Planning will survive, because in every advanced country it has a large – and in the long run, increasing – political constituency. Good environment, as the economists would say, is an income-elastic good: as people, and societies generally, get richer, they demand proportionately ever more of it. And, apart from building private estates with walls around them, the only way they are going to get it is through public action. The fact that people are willing and even anxious to spend more and more of their precious time in defending their own environment, through membership of all kinds of voluntary organizations and through attendance at public inquiries, is testimony to that fact – as also to the fact that, not seldom, my good environment is my neighbour's bad one. So, in very advanced post-industrial societies – south-east England, the San Francisco Bay Area – the politics of planning become ever more popular, ever more protracted, ever more bitter.[40]

That, ironically, became plain during the course of the 1980s. The first Thatcher Government of 1979 had been clearly determined to remove the shackles of planning from the developer. In 1983, Michael Heseltine – then Secretary of State for the Environment – shocked true-blue Tory central Berkshire by modifying the county's structure plan, allowing 4,000 extra houses to be built on green fields. There was impassioned opposition. The local district council refused to write the provision into its own district plan. Ironically, Heseltine himself had weakened the structure planners' power to control the lower-level district plans in an act of 1980; he, or shortly after his successor, was hoist with his own petard.[41]

On the other side of London, in the spring of 1984 a major consortium of the country's leading builder-developers unveiled a plan for a series of

[40] Frieden, 1979; Blowers, 1980; Hall, 1980.
[41] Short, Fleming and Witt, 1986, 240–7; Hall *et al.*, 1987, 154.

private enterprise new towns – latter-day Columbias – and, a year later, announced that the first would be built on a green-belt site at Tillingham Hall in Essex.[42] The inquiry became one of those *causes célèbres* of planning history in which the English delight. The developers lost; doubtless to their great surprise, for a whole series of well-publicized official statements, with titles like *Lifting the Burden*, had clearly led them (and almost everyone else) to believe that the government would back them.[43] Then, in 1987 – admittedly, in the runup to a general election – the government were forced to backtrack on a relatively minor policy change, which would remove the need to monitor agricultural considerations in the case of development proposals on poorer quality farmland. The radical–right government, here as elsewhere, was proving that its bark was a good deal more significant than its bite.

No, planning will not go away; no, it will never again be de-politicized, as some once hoped. Like the Abbé Sieyès in an earlier revolution, it lives. But traditional land-use planning has come under more basic attack in its country of birth than ever in its eighty years of existence. It has become determinedly reactive, artisan and anti-intellectual, while planning in the academy has retreated ever higher up its ivory tower. Meanwhile, it faces a new range of problems, with which its practitioners were never equipped by education (and perhaps by inclination) to tackle: the problem of structural economic decline of whole urban communities and of rebuilding a new economy on the ruins of the old. And, exacerbated by that fact, it faces a nightmarish return of the oldest of urban problems, which more than any other originally brought it into being and gave it its legitimacy: the problem of the urban underclass, waiting as a sullen and disaffected mass outside the gates.

---

[42] Shostak and Lock, 1984, 9–13; Consortium Developments, 1985.
[43] G.B. Minister without Portfolio, 1985.

The City
of the Permanent Underclass

The reactive mass of the industrial reserve army increases therefore with the potential energy of wealth. But the greater this reserve army in relation to the active labour-army, the greater is the mass of consolidated surplus-population, whose misery is in inverse proportion to its torment of labour. The more extensive, finally, the lazarus-layers of the working class, and the industrial reserve army, the greater is official pauperism. *This is the absolute general law of capitalist accumulation.*

Karl Marx
Capital, I (1867)

I'm bound for Black Mountain, me and my razor and my gun,
Lawd, I'm bound for Black Mountain, me and my razor and my gun;
I'm gonna shoot him if he stands still, and shoot him if he run.

. . .

There's a devil in my soul, and I'm full of bad booze,
There's a devil in my soul, and I'm full of bad booze,
I'm out here for trouble. I've got the Black Mountain Blues.

Bessie Smith
Black Mountain Blues (1930)

12

The City
of the Permanent Underclass

The Enduring Slum:
Chicago, St Louis, London,
1920–1987

There is one final enigma: for any urbanist, the greatest and least answerable of all. It was the one posed by the eighty-seven-year-old Lewis Mumford, at the start of the first volume of his autobiography, in 1982. It was the 'breakdown of law and order at the very peak of metropolitan power and prosperity', which formed for Mumford 'one of the chronic puzzles of history'.[1] Comparing the New York City of the 1980s with that of his childhood, Mumford chillingly reflected on

> the more ominous spread of violence and lawlessness, which, in the city of my youth, used to be confined, like a carbuncle, to certain self-enclosed areas, like the Bowery or Hell's Kitchen. Such quarters had not yet poured their infection into the whole bloodstream of the city.... For one thing, it was possible for men, women and children, even when alone, to walk over a great part of the city, and certainly to walk through Central Park or alongside Riverside Drive at any time of the day or evening without fear of being molested or assaulted.[2]

'There was', he continued, 'a kind of moral stability and security in the city of my youth that has now vanished even in such urban models of law and order as London.'[3] And he confessed that more than once, latter-day New York had reminded him of Pertrach's fourteenth-century account of 'the desolate, wolfish, robber-infested Provence of his maturity, in the wake of the Black Plague, with the safe, prosperous region of his youth'.[4]

Statistics, notoriously, can lie; none more so than social statistics, and none among these more so than statistics of crime. Every novice undergraduate is familiar with the multiple caveats: who reports what and when, who writes what down in the record book, who decided to prosecute and why. But no conceivable stream of qualifications and reservations will

---

[1] Mumford, 1982, 5.   [2] Ibid.   [3] Ibid.   [4] Ibid.

wash away the mountain of urban crime, and above all violent urban crime, that in the late twentieth century rose almost visibly, like some erupting volcano, to threaten the fabric of social life in every major city of the world. It was, indeed, a twentieth-century plague. And its causes were as mysterious to the afflicted, as those of the Black Death to the hapless citizenry of fourteenth-century London, Paris or Constantinople. If not to explain it, at least to understand it, some historical perspective is needed. We must go back full circle, to the origins of this story, and come forward again to the present. And, in doing so through this long chapter, somewhat whimsically, planning – the subject of the tale – will seem to disappear from view. The point, finally, must be to ask why.

For neither urban crime, nor the fear of the average urban citizen of it, is new; as Mumford reminds us, only their pervasiveness is. Indeed, twentieth-century city planning came out of the complex emotional reaction – part pity, part terror, part loathing – of the late-Victorian middle class to their discovery of the urban underclass. That reaction, as seen in chapter 2, took the form of a secular Last Judgement: the virtuous poor would be assisted to go directly via the settlement house or the municipal housing project to the garden-city heaven; the vicious would remain perpetually repressed in their own urban hell, or go to penitential labour colonies where they might at last see the light. And, in those European countries where the city-planning movement waxed strongest, that approximately is what came to pass. Half a century later, in the welfare-state era of the 1950s and 1960s, came the triumph of liberal theology: now, all – even the urban underclass – were instantly perfectible; all might gain immediate access by the strait gate to the Corbusian city of towers.

But in the United States, it was not like that at all. The established religion, whether Protestant, Catholic or Jewish, was heavily supportive of free enterprise: God helped those who helped themselves, Horatio Alger-fashion, out of the slum and into the ranks of the entrepreneurs. The main task, for public enterprise and voluntary organization alike, was therefore to socialize the immigrant and his children into knowledge of American folkways and acceptance of American values, thus to put the first foot on the ladder leading to success in the new land. Only those who stayed truly down in the pit, far out of reach of the bottom rung, might get the equivalent of poorhouse relief, in the form of public housing that carried automatic social stigma.

Chicago Discovers the Underclass

This helps to explain one significant fact: in the early twentieth century, not only American social experimentation, but also American social

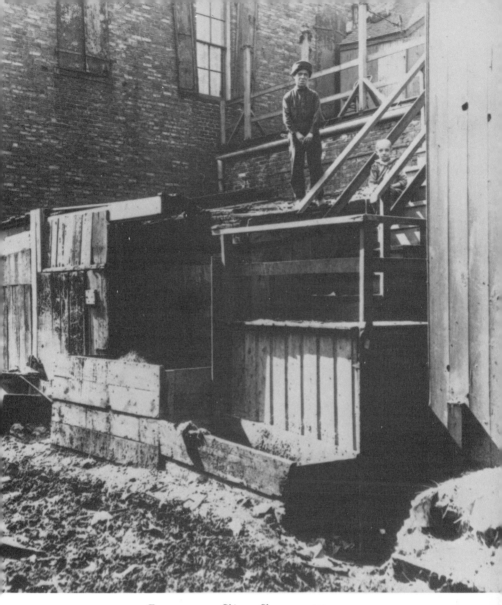

FIGURE 12.1 *Chicago Slum, ca. 1900.*
An unidentified alley at the time of the Chicago Tenement House Survey: for
hundreds of thousands of immigrants from Europe, home in America meant this.

investigation, was dominated by the central perceived problem of the
immigrant and his socialization. Since – especially after the effective closure
of the frontier in 1890 – the immigrants went overwhelmingly to the cities,
it was there that both experimentation and research focused; for there, as
observed in chapter 2, was the middle-class fear of submergence and mob

FIGURE 12.2   *Dr. Robert E. Park.*
Founder of the Chicago School of Sociology, whose studies in the 1920s first pinpointed the roots of social disintegration in the city's slums.

rule most acutely felt. And there was a certain historic justice in the fact that both activities should flower in Chicago, the quintessential immigrant city. Here, in 1889, Jane Addams founded her settlement house; here, from 1914, developed the world's first true school of urban sociology.

That last is a large claim. Booth and his collaborators, as seen in chapter 2, had pioneered modern techniques of mass social observation in London in the 1880s, and had produced a still unequalled masterpiece of empirical urban sociology. The Germans had created theoretical sociology at about that time, and Robert E. Park, one of the founders of the Chicago school, had studied under Georg Simmel in Berlin. But only in Chicago, during the 1920s, did Park, Burgess, McKenzie and Worth join these two traditions, thus to work towards a total understanding – based on theory, tested by observation – of the social structure of a great city. In 1925 they published their classic collection of essays on the sociology of the city.[5]

[5] Park *et al.*, 1925.

And in his opening essay, which laid out the school's research agenda, Park already made clear its central bundle of concerns.

The 'simplest and most elementary form of association' in the city, Park argued, was the local neighbourhood. So:

> It is important to know what are the forces which tend to break up the tensions, interests and sentiments which give neighborhoods their individual character. In general these may be said to be anything and everything that tends to render the population unstable, to divide and concentrate attentions upon widely separated objects of interest.[6]

But 'certain urban neighborhoods suffer from isolation'; here, 'to reconstruct and quicken the life of city neighborhoods and to bring them in touch with the larger interests of the community', the social settlement movement had in part sprung up.[7] And, in American cities,

> the attempt has been made to renovate evil neighborhoods by the construction of playgrounds and the introduction of supervized sports of various kinds, including municipal dances in municipal dance halls. These and other devices which are intended primarily to elevate the moral tone of the segregated populations of great cities should be studied in connection with the investigation of the neighborhood in general.[8]

But the neighbourhood essentially represented the old pre-industrial social order: industrial competition, coupled with the division of labour, was replacing it by an alternative organization of the city, based on differentiation by vocation and thus by class.[9] Through the medium of money, 'values have been rationalized and sentiments have been replaced by interests.'[10] The resulting organization, 'composed of competing individuals and of competing groups of individuals',[11] meant that

> Cities, and particularly the great cities, are in unstable equilibrium. The result is that the vast casual and mobile aggregations which constitute our urban populations are in a state of perpetual agitation, swept by every new wind of doctrine, subject to constant alarms, and in consequence the community is in a chronic condition of crisis.[12]

This suggested 'the importance of a more detailed and fundamental study of collective behavior', focusing on 'the psychology of crisis', including the extent to which 'the parliamentary system, including the electoral system, [may] be regarded as an attempt to regularize revolution and to meet and control crises.'[13]

Park went on to speculate: 'It is probably the breaking down of local attachments and the weakening of the restraints and inhibitions of the primary group, under the influence of the urban environment, which are

---

[6] Park, 1925a, 8. [7] Ibid. [8] Ibid. 9. [9] Ibid. 14. [10] Ibid. 16.
[11] Ibid. 17. [12] Ibid. 22. [13] Ibid.

FIGURE 12.3 *Chicago's 'Little Hell', 1902.*
One of the city's Italian enclaves, which became notorious as a seat of vice and crime.

largely responsible for the increase of vice and crime in great cities.'[14] In the 'immigrant colonies' which were now 'well established in every large city', foreign populations lived isolated lives, but each with an independent and vigorous political and social organization of its own:[15]

> Under these conditions the social ritual and the moral order which these immigrants brought with them from their native countries have succeeded in maintaining themselves for a considerable time under the influences of the American environment. Social control, based on the home mores, breaks down, however, in the second generation.[16]

Parallel to this erosion of primary relationships, the old informal controls, based on these family mores, were replaced by formal legal mechanisms.[17]

Part of this new and distinctive urban social organization, Park argued, was the 'moral region': 'the population tends to segregate itself, not merely in accordance with its interests, but in accordance with its tastes or its

[14] Ibid. 23.   [15] Ibid.   [16] Ibid. 27.   [17] Ibid. 28.

temperaments', producing 'detached milieus in which vagrant and sup-pressed impulses, passions, and ideals emancipate themselves from the dominant moral order.'[18] Hence 'the segregation of the poor, the vicious, the criminal, and exceptional persons generally', wherein

> Association with others of their own ilk provides . . . not merely a stimulus, but a moral support for the traits they have in common which they would not find in a less select society. In the great city the poor, the vicious, and the delinquent, crushed in an unhealthful and contagious intimacy, breed in and in, soul and body.[19]

In an essay on juvenile delinquency, later in the collection, Park developed this theme further. 'We are living', he argued, 'in . . . a period of individualization and social disorganization. Everything is in a state of agitation – everything seems to be undergoing a change. Society is, apparently, not much more than a congeries and constellation of social atoms.'[20] The automobile, the newspaper and the motion picture had contributed powerfully to this change.

> The mere movement of the population from one part of the country to another – the present migration of the Negroes northward, for example – is a disturbing influence. Such a movement may assume, from the point of view of the migrants themselves, the character of an emancipation, opening to them new economic and cultural opportunities, but it is none the less disorganizing to the communities they have left behind and to the communities into which they are now moving. It is at the same time demoralizing to the migrating people themselves, and particularly, I might add, to the younger generation.
> The enormous amount of delinquency, juvenile and adult, that exists today in the Negro communities in northern cities is due in part, though not entirely, to the fact that migrants are not able to accommodate themselves at once to a new and relatively strange environment. The same thing can be said of the immigrants from Europe, or of the younger generation of women who are just now entering in such larger numbers into the newer occupations and the freer life which the great cities offer them.[21]

As to explanation, let alone remedy, Park finally offered none: 'The thing of which we still know least is the business of carrying on an associated life.'[22] 'I have a feeling that this paper lacks a moral,' he confessed, 'and I know that every paper on a social topic should have a moral'; the fact was that 'the problem of juvenile delinquency seems to have its sources in conditions over which, in our present knowledge, we have very little control.'[23] Doubtless, were Park to return to the Chicago South Side of the 1980s, he would be an even more puzzled and worried man.

---

[18] Ibid. 43.   [19] Ibid. 45.   [20] Park, 1925b, 107.   [21] Ibid. 108.
[22] Ibid. 110.   [23] Ibid.

In a series of studies, seeking to answer the questions which Park threw out, members of the Chicago school grappled with the raw facts of social distintegration and delinquency so evident on the city's streets. Thrasher's monograph, *The Gang*, published the year after, confirmed that it was especially a phenomenon of what Burgess, in his classic social geography of the city,[24] had called the 'Zone in Transition' around the city centre:

> It is in these regions that we find deteriorating neighborhoods, great mobility, areas of immigrant first settlement, corrupt ward politics, vice, crime, and general disorder. The basic reason, however, for the development of gangs in these areas is the failure of customary social institutions to function in such a way as to organize the life of the boy.[25]

And this was a function of immigration: three-quarters of the people of Chicago, at that time, were 'foreign-born peoples and their immediate progeny':

> Chicago is a mosaic of foreign colonies with conflicting social heritages. There has not yet been time for adjustment among these diverse elements and for the development of a consistent and self-controlled social order. The gang is one symptom of this 'cultural lag'.[26]

His research showed that the great majority of gang members were immigrant children whose parents, mainly rural peasants, could no longer control them because of their inadequate English and the lack of any community code of conduct: 'the children of immigrants tend to become quickly and superficially Americanized, becoming assimilated to the more racy and more vicious aspects of American life which they encounter in the disorganized and mobile areas in which they live.'[27]

That had been the pattern of Chicago society as long as anyone had been looking at it: 'The entire history of Chicago from its birth to the First World War was characterized by the struggle, sometimes violent, of the first-comers and native whites against the later immigrants – the 'foreigners'.[28] At the time of Hull House, a settlement worker sadly observed, 'The lofty disdain with which the *Dago* regards the *Sheeny* cannot be measured except by the scornful contempt with which the *Sheeny* scans the *Dago*.[29] In this pecking order someone had to be at the bottom, and at the end of the 1920s it seemed to be the Sicilians on the North Side, where – so the Chicago newspapers told their readers – murder and mayhem were the daily rule. As one of the Chicago sociologists discovered in 1929, this Little Sicily – or Little Hell, home to 15,000 unskilled ex-peasant Sicilians – was indeed the city's main centre of bootlegging, of hijacking, of criminal gangs.[30] And in such a society,

[24] Burgess, 1925, 51, 55.   [25] Thrasher, 1926, 3.   [26] Ibid. 4.
[27] Thrasher, 1926, 4.   [28] Drake and Cayton, 1945, 17.
[29] Philpott, 1978, 68.   [30] Zorbaugh, 1929, 14.

There is an increasing amount of personal disorganization among the American-born. The second generation finds itself trying to live in two social worlds.[31]

Hence it is that the slum, particularly the foreign slum, is gangland. For gangland is but the result of the boy's creation of a social world in which he can live and find satisfaction for his wishes.[32]

More extended work from another member of the school, published that same year, confirmed that the geographical patterns of truancy, juvenile delinquency and adult crime were closely related: all were highly concentrated in the zone of transition, marked by physical deterioration and declining population, immediately around the city's central business district, occupied by European immigrants and southern blacks:

All of them come from cultural backgrounds which differ widely from the situations in the city. In the conflict of the old with the new the former social and cultural controls in these groups tend to break down. This, together with the fact that there are few constructive community forces at work to re-establish a conventional order, makes for continued social disintegration.[33]

And, in the mid-1940s, when Shaw extended this work to a wide range of other cities, he found the same patterns: in some low-income areas, delinquency was a 'social tradition'.[34]

Generalizing from the first round of Chicago studies at the end of the 1920s, Park produced a phrase that was to echo around the halls of sociology, with increasing discordance, for decades after. Migration into the cities, he argued, following the line of his earlier papers, produced a 'changed type of personality . . . Energies that were formerly controlled by custom and tradition are released. The individual is free for new adventures, but he is more or less without direction and control.'[35] The result was 'a cultural hybrid, a man living and sharing intimately in the cultural life and tradition of two different peoples . . . a man on the margin of two cultures and two societies, which never completely interpenetrated and fused',[36] whose characteristics were 'spiritual instability, intensified self-awareness, restlessness and malaise'.[37] Such a person, Park suggested, could be called the 'Marginal Man'.

Some who later inveighed against the concept of 'marginality' (chapter 8) might usefully have referred back to this original source: Park's chosen archetype of Marginal Man was the culturally cosmopolitan emancipated Jew. But, in the universal manner, the phrase proved so memorable that it became detached from its author's original meaning: increasingly, it came

---

[31] Ibid. 176.   [32] Ibid. 155.   [33] Shaw *et al.*, 1929, 205.
[34] Shaw and McKay, 1942, 437.   [35] Park, 1928, 887.
[36] Ibid. 892.   [37] Ibid. 893.

to refer to the disaffected member of Park's urban underclass, imperfectly acculturated into urban society, and sunk in what later, in another equally memorable and misunderstood phrase, Oscar Lewis was to call the culture of poverty.

The Sociologists Invade the Ghetto

Most of the delinquents who came under the Chicago school's microscope were white. That reflected the fact that in the 1920s, the children of white ethnic parents were the main inhabitants of the zone of transition and the main victims of imperfect transition from the old to the new society. It may also have reflected the difficulty which white middle-class sociologists would have experienced in penetrating Chicago's newest ghetto. They did not even recognize it by that now familiar name: in Burgess's classic typology, the 'ghetto' was Jewish, one of a number of ethnic slums – Little Sicily, Greektown, Chinatown – where old world traditions mixed with American adaptations; the Black Belt, 'with its free and disorderly life', was something quite different.[38]

But it already existed; and, labelled or not, it was already the only true ghetto in the city. Here, the founding fathers of urban sociology made one of their few mistakes. Park, Burgess and Louis Wirth taught a generation of students that all ethnic neighbourhoods were temporary ghettos; in them, voluntary segregation would eventually break down as acculturation brought assimilation. Their own research seemed to show that the black ghetto was no more ghettoized than any other. But, half a century later, researchers reanalysed their basic data to show that they had been wrong. At the level of small census tracts, no European group, at the Census of 1930, was more than 61 per cent ghettoized – and, in these so-called ghettos, the so-called ghetto population never made up more than 54 per cent of the total. But already, close on 93 per cent of the city's black population lived in ghettos; and there, they made up over 81 per cent of the total population.[39]

This segregation, other later researchers found, had come about during World War One. In 1910, no tract had been predominantly black; by 1920, ten recorded a black percentage of 75 per cent and more.[40] Between 1916 and 1918 Chicago had received 65,000 blacks from the rural areas of the Mississippi valley, most of whom poured into the city's industries.[41] Despite efforts by black community organizations and newspapers, they found it difficult to adjust to the pressures of city life. A quarter-century later, older blacks were still heard to bemoan the arrival of the newcomers,

[38] Burgess, 1925, 56.   [39] Philpott, 1978, 141.   [40] Spear, 1967, 146.
[41] Chicago Commission, 1922, 602.

which they claimed had disrupted racial integration and harmony in the city, and had 'made it hard for all of us.'[42]

When white servicemen returned from the war, there were pressures in the workplace too; for, among the city's white ethnic working class, the blacks had a reputation – inherited from the great stockyard strike of 1904 – as strikebreakers.[43] Gangs of white working-class youths from the Stockyards district, styling themselves as 'athletic clubs' and supported by a local ward politician, began to intimidate their black counterparts on the streets.[44]

Finally, on July 27, 1919, an incident involving white and black youths on a crowded bathing beach brought an open urban riot: not the first such in the twentieth century – East St Louis, in July 1917, had claimed that title – but one of the bloodiest in American history. When the militia at last brought order five days later, thirty-eight people – fifteen white, twenty-three black – were dead, and 537 injured.[45] As the Commission of Inquiry concluded – though it did not use the term – this was what later sociologists called a 'community riot', marked mainly by violence on the part of whites against blacks, whom they saw as invading their neighbourhoods and their jobs. And the Commission painted a graphic picture of the black ghetto of that time: over 40 per cent lived in grossly deteriorated housing; 90 per cent were living next to the city's segregated vice districts where children were daily exposed to vice and crime; in over a fifth of the homes children were out of control; many of the children were backward at school because they had been poorly educated in the South.[46]

Still, despite this lead, by and large the Chicago sociologists of the 1920s stayed outside the ghetto. But, by a remarkable chance – remarkable, considering the chances of black advancement in those days – two of the greatest of America's early sociologists happened to be black. And, even more remarkable, one of the founding white fathers of American sociology also devoted his early life to a study of black social life. Each of these three contributed major empirical studies, which give us a unique historical picture of late-nineteenth- and early-twentieth-century black American urban society.

What they tell us, unmistakably, is that many of the features that so much concern students of social policy in the 1980s have long antecedents. In 1899 W. E. B. DuBois used the methods of Booth's London survey to classify the black population of Philadelphia's seventh ward. There was, he told his overwhelmingly white readers, 'no surer way of misunderstanding

[42] Drake and Cayton, 1945, 73; Tuttle, 1970, 169.
[43] Tuttle, 1970, 117, 126.
[44] Chicago Commission, 1922, 12; Spear, 1967, 212; Tuttle, 1970, 199.
[45] Chicago Commission, 1922, 595–8.
[46] Ibid. 192, 264–5, 622.

FIGURE 12.4 *Murder in Chicago Race Riot, 1919.*
Unlike later riots in American cities, this was a true inter-racial conflict prompted by white resentment at black invasions of the city's housing and job markets.

the Negro or being misunderstood by him than by ignoring manifest differences of condition and power in the 40,000 black people of Philadelphia'.[47] He classified each family in his survey into one of four grades. The first, the 'very poor and semi-criminal', depending on casual labour and living in the slums, made up just under 9 per cent of the total population of the Seventh Ward; the 'poor', or 'the inefficient, unfortunate and improvident', just under 10 per cent.[48] The biggest single group, numbering nearly 48 per cent, were the 'great hard-working laboring class'; they were 'honest and good-natured' and lived in houses of three to six rooms, generally well furnished.[49] Above them were the 25 per cent described as 'comfortable', the 4 per cent in 'good circumstances' and the 4 per cent who were 'well-to-do'.

So the great majority of the blacks of Philadelphia were certainly not the degenerate, criminal, slum-dwelling underclass of the rumour mill:

> Nothing more exasperates the better class of Negroes than this tendency to ignore utterly their existence. The law-abiding, hard-working inhabitants of

[47] DuBois, 1899, 310.   [48] Ibid. 171–4.   [49] Ibid. 175.

the Thirtieth Ward are aroused to righteous indignation when they see that the word Negro carries most Philadelphians' minds to the alleys of the Fifth Ward or the police courts.[50]

The problem was that the rumour mill focused on a real enough problem: 'the increasing number of bold and daring crimes' committed by blacks in the previous decade.[51] Blacks accounted for only four per cent of the Philadelphia population but for nine per cent of the arrests.[52] The fact was that 'the illiterate fifth of the Negro population furnished a third of the worst criminals';[53] 'the more serious and revolting the crime the larger part does ignorance play as a cause.'[54] In particular, 'A crime for which Negroes of a certain class have become notorious is that of snatching pocketbooks on the streets'; and 'from pocketbook snatching to highway robbery is but a step.'[55] DuBois concluded:

> From this study we may conclude that young men are the perpetrators of serious crime among Negroes; that this crime consists mainly of stealing and assault; that ignorance, and immigration to the temptations of city life, are responsible for much of this crime but not for all; that deep social causes underlie this prevalence of crime and they have so worked as to form among Negroes since 1864 a distinct class of habitual criminals; that to this criminal class and not to the great mass of Negroes the bulk of the serious crime perpetrated by this race should be charged.[56]

When DuBois turned to 'Conjugal Condition', he found a striking anomaly:

> There is a large proportion of single men – more than in Great Britain, France or Germany; the number of married women, too, is small, while the large number of widowed and separated indicates widespread and early breaking up of family life. The number of single women is probably lessened by unfortunate girls, and increased somewhat by deserted wives who report themselves as single. The number of deserted wives, however, allowing for false reports, is astoundingly large and presents many intricate problems. A very large part of the charity given to Negroes is asked for this reason. The causes of desertion are partly laxity in morals and partly the difficulty of supporting a family. . . . The result of this large number of homes without husbands is to increase the burden of charity and benevolence, and also on account of their poor home-life to increase crime. Here is a wide field for social regeneration.[57]

DuBois's conclusions on this point are significant, since they confirm those of Howard Odum, the southern white sociologist who became the founding father of the Southern Regionalist school of the 1930s and 1940s (chapter 5). Odum's first published work was a detailed investigation of

[50] Ibid. 310.   [51] Ibid. 241.   [52] Ibid. 239.   [53] Ibid. 254.
[54] Ibid. 258.   [55] Ibid. 262, 263.   [56] Ibid. 259.   [57] Ibid. 67–8.

the lives of blacks in the towns of the South, conducted in the first decade of the twentieth century. So scathing are many of Odum's observations, that eighty years later they are almost unpublishable; were it not for his long and sympathetic subsequent record of work on black culture, it would be easy simply to dismiss him as a racist. He anticipates the criticism: 'while there is much unpleasantness and dissatisfaction in criticizing as a 'stranger' the habitations of these people, it is necessary for all concerned to paint the picture from life, to see things as they are,' he warned.[58]

On family structure, he confirmed DuBois's findings: 'The proportion of parents without legitimate children is large, in general from fifteen to twenty per cent of the families. . . . there being some ten per cent of the total number of families with a woman at the head.'[59] The average family had four persons, in two rooms: 'In such crowded quarters – not infrequently in one room – must exist the entire family with living apparatus.'[60] And, said Odum, 'with such crowded conditions habits of uncleanliness naturally grow. A glance inside the average negro cottage is most discouraging.'[61]

Additionally, since much work was done at home, and the woman of the family must go out to work,

> Throughout the day the negro home is full of haste and disorder. The mother who cooks for a white family is up and off early in the morning, leaving the children un-cared for at home; the man soon leaves also for his work. The children thus have no care and attention. . . . In the meantime the household is kept together as best it may be.[62]

As a result, 'The children rarely feel kindly towards their parents. So it is that after they have grown up the family is not united in purpose, spirit, or physical presence. . . . The one desire of the younger negroes – and it seems to be a natural one – appears to be freedom from work and parental control.'[63]

Thence, concluded Odum the moralist,

> immorality and crime, on the one hand, and disease on the other. . . . The indiscriminate mixing in the home leads to bad personal habits; the utter lack of restraint deadens any moral sensibilities that might be present. Nowhere in the home is there restraint; the contact and conduct of its members belong to the lowest classification. There is little knowledge of the sanctity of home or marital relations; consequently little regard for them. The open cohabitation of the sexes related by no ties of marriage is a very common practice; little is thought of it as it relates to the race; there is apparently no conscience in the matter.[64]

Worse than that:

> Too often every home is considered a place of debauchery; the negroes know

[58] Odum, 1910, 151.   [59] Ibid. 153.   [60] Ibid.   [61] Ibid. 154.
[62] Ibid. 155.   [63] Ibid. 162.   [64] Ibid. 163.

full well the numerous houses to which they are invited and to which they go. The 'creeper', the 'rounder-shaker', and the 'eastman' are too well known to elicit surprise among the negroes. Every home is liable to their criminal influence, when every man and every woman becomes common property. . . . Perhaps nowhere in negro life does the problem of immorality appear more stupendous than among the children. . . . The amount of knowledge of evil and evil practices possessed by small children is unthinkable. Their practices are no less appalling.[65]

With the life of immorality comes its celebration in story and song. . . . The prevailing theme of this class of songs is that of sexual relations, and there is no restraint in its expression.[66]

When it is all coupled with fears that venereal disease may compromise 'the purity of the white race', it is all too easily dismissible. All too evidently, the young Odum lacked all standard of sociological comparison; he had no comprehension that almost exactly the same results could be reported for the white underclass of Victorian London. Nor did he have much sense of historic relativity: for good or ill, much of the child behaviour he reports sounds uncannily like that of white middle-class suburban American teenagers of the 1960s – including the songs, which the Rolling Stones borrowed from his sources. It might even be said, in historical perspective, that Odum's unthinkable nightmare came true: the norms of the black southern underclass finally conquered the respectable white world. There is something eerily prophetic about his report that 'the habit of using cocaine has constantly grown, and among the better classes, with its evil results. Its extensive use in the cities brings the inevitable influence to the smaller communities.'[67]

But there is something more: something he shared with DuBois, founder of the National Association for the Advancement of Colored People. It was a sense that finally, the collapse of family structure among a section of the black community was attended by appalling consequences, which transmitted themselves from generation to generation. When Odum wrote that 'the Negro is becoming less efficient as a workman, not because of ability, but because of indisposition toward work and his persistency in idleness', he was guilty of the worst racial stereotyping. When he wrote,

the criminal ranks are increasing rather than decreasing because of these worthless negroes. From idleness to recklessness and theft, the negro easily develops from the vagrant, the bum, the hobo, the bully boy, the eastman, the rounder, the creeper, to the 'bad man' and the 'criminal'[68]

he was describing a tendency among a small black underclass that – as DuBois also too well appreciated – was a major potential problem. What

---

[65] Ibid. 165.   [66] Ibid. 166.   [67] Ibid. 173.   [68] Ibid. 221.

FIGURE 12.5   *Dr. E. Franklin Frazier.*
The great black sociologist of the Chicago school, whose work in the 1920s and
1930s meticulously detailed the breakdown of black family structures in the northern
cities.

both lacked was a clear theoretical explanation of why this might be so.
The Chicago school provided one: it was the result of the sudden transition
from a rural, traditional, society, based on primary family and neighbourhood
relationships, to the complexities of the city. And it developed in the second
generation: the first urban-born children.

That was, in the language of a later generation, the prevailing Chicago
paradigm when a black sociologist, E. Franklin Frazier, arrived there to
work on his Ph.D. in 1927. The resulting work marks a milestone in the
sociology of the black family. Frazier starts by reviewing a vast volume of
literature, from DuBois onward, on the 'Demoralization of the Negro family'.
He concludes:

> . . . we find that opinions extending over a long period had been unanimous
> concerning the widespread demoralization of Negro family life. These opinions
> arose from observers and students with diverse interests and were supported

by statistics from many sources. For all except one or two of these observers this widespread demoralization of family life was a sign of the inability of the Negro to measure up to the sex standards of Western civilization and to a few it portended the ultimate extinction of the race.[69]

Frazier's achievement was to start with the fact, and carefully to dissect the causes. He discounted the view that there were either physical or African – that is, racial – origins. Instead, he posited a double historical breakdown: first, emancipation, which had caused instant collapse of the Nego slave family and social organization, but which was followed by a return to a modified form of plantation life as a sharecropping family; secondly, urbanization, which had again led to a collapse of social structures and social control. (Much later, the fundamental research by Fogel[70] on the structure of the black family under slavery was to throw doubt on that part of the explanation; the slave-owners, it emerged, had every interest in preserving stable family structures.) And, just as Park had postulated, this was most evident in the inner city where

> Negro family life tended to disappear. This was the area of crime and vice and free relations ... the high rate of dependency was accompanied by high rates of family desertion, illegitimacy, and juvenile delinquency. The youth of the unmarried mothers indicated, as in the case of juvenile delinquency, the breakdown of family discipline as well as community organization.[71]

But these critical indices of disorganization decreased as one moved out from the 'Zone in Transition', coinciding with 'the progressive selection of the moral stable elements in the Negro population'.[72] So Frazier's work confirmed the Chicago paradigm:

> [The] customary and sympathetic bonds that had held families together in the rural communities of the South were dissolved when they were no longer supported by the neighborhood organization and institutions of the rural southern communities. ... [Thus] the widespread disorganization of Negro family life must be regarded as an aspect of the civilizational process in the Negro group. ... As the Negro is brought into contact with a larger world through increasing communication and mobility, disorganization is a natural result. The extent of the disorganization will depend on the fund of social tradition which will become the basis for the reorganization of life on a more intellectual and more efficient basis.[73]

So time might help; preserving the 'social fund' would help even more. The question was how.

From the 1930s, as professor at Howard University, Frazier extended his work into a monumental study of black social and family structure. He

---

[69] Frazier, 1932, 245.   [70] Fogel and Engermann, 1974.
[71] Frazier, 1932, 250–1.   [72] Ibid. 251.   [73] Ibid.

confirmed the pioneer work of DuBois in Philadelphia, Daniels in Boston, and others: as many as two-thirds of the entire black population of the northern cities were 'lower class', distinguished not merely by their low-skill occupations, family disorganization, illiteracy and poverty, but also by 'shiftlessness and irresponsibility . . . due partly to their lack of education and partly to the lack of economic opportunity for the great masses of Negro men'.[74] In 1930, in the larger northern cities (100,000 and more people), 30 per cent of households were female-headed; in equivalent southern cities, between one-fifth and one-third.[75] And this was only the most obvious aspect of 'the disorganized family life and unregulated sex behavior of these newcomers to the city'.[76]

Examining the causes in greater historical detail, Frazier confirmed the analysis in his dissertation. The phenomenon was of long standing: Frazier was able to show that in Washington, DC, one-fifth of black births had been illegitimate in 1881, the same rate as in 1939; most illegitimate births in northern cities were to young mothers, who were newcomers to the city, and few of whom had themselves known ordinary family life.[77] This pattern of 'fathers on leave', which was 'one of the inevitable consequences of the urbanization of the Negro population', had its origins in the matriarchal structure of the slave society. In the rural South, too, more than one-fifth of households were female-headed; early pregnancy outside marriage was simply commonplace and accepted, for it was associated with a matricentric family in which the grandmother was the key figure. But in the cities, while the female-headed household persisted, this extended family structure disintegrated; illegitimacy, not a problem in the rural areas, became one only when stripped of this supporting structure of the extended family, neighbours and institutions.[78] Thus, in Frazier's words:

> . . . social and welfare agencies have been unable to stem the tide of family disorganization that has followed as a natural consequence of the impact of modern civilization upon the folkways and mores of a simple peasant folk . . . When one views in retrospect the waste of human life, the immorality, delinquency, desertions, and broken homes which have been involved in the development of Negro family life in the United States, they appear to have been the inevitable consequences of. the attempt of a preliterate people, stripped of their cultural heritage, to adjust themselves to civilization.[79]

For the children, the consequences were dire. As Frazier went on to show, black juvenile-delinquency rates were several times higher than those for whites: three times in New York City, more than four times in Baltimore, for instance, during the 1920s.[80] But in these and other cities, delinquency

[74] Frazier, 1957, 303.   [75] Frazier, 1939, 326.   [76] Ibid. 331.
[77] Ibid. 326, 343, 346–9.   [78] Ibid. 481–4.   [79] Ibid. 485, 487.
[80] Ibid. 358–9.

was heavily concentrated in just those inner-city zones of community disorganization, where lower-class blacks, because of their poverty and cultural backwardness, were forced to live.[81] Thus it was clear that black crime rates – for adults as for children – were high; but the cause, formerly thought to represent physical or moral deficiency, was now generally ascribed to poverty, ignorance and urbanization.

Five years after Frazier's masterly work on the black family in 1939, another great social scientist made another: Gunnar Myrdal's monumental study of the American black was published in 1944. Unsurprisingly, it reached conclusions identical to Frazier's:

> ... the important thing is that the Negro lower classes, especially in the rural South, have built up a type of family organization conducive to social health, even though the practices are outside the American tradition. When these practices come into contact with white norms, as occurs when Negroes go to the cities, they tend to break down partially and to cause the demoralization of some individuals.[82]

Frazier had warned that 'the travail of civilization is not yet ended'; yet more blacks would join the road to the city, bringing with them yet new waves of disintegration. And, in the final revision of his masterpiece, finished just before his death a quarter-century later, he could report that he had proved right: 'World War 2 did not cause the Negro family to face new problems; it caused new strata of the Negro population to face the same problems of family adjustment which had been faced by former migrants to the city.'[83]

The evidence for that had been assembled on Frazier's own Chicago turf by two sociologists – one black, one white – who followed in his steps, St. Clair Drake and Horace Cayton, in 1945. They found that as blacks had continued to pour into the ghetto, it had not expanded; it had grown ever more crowded.[84] Their contribution was to dissect its class structure, a structure that had undoubtedly existed at the time of Frazier's own work and which went back to the arrival of the new migrants in World War One:[85]

> Everybody in Bronzeville recognizes the existence of social classes, whether called that or not. People with small education, small incomes and few of the social graces are always referring to the more affluent and successful as 'dicties', 'stuck-up', 'muckti-mucks', 'high-toned folks', 'tony people'. . . . People at the top of the various pyramids that we have described are apt to characterize people below them as 'low-class', 'trash', 'riff-raff', 'shiftless'.[86]

When these upper- and middle-class blacks spoke of 'advancing the Race', they meant the creation of conditions under which lower-class traits

---

[81] Ibid. 374.   [82] Myrdal, 1944, 935.   [83] Frazier, 1966, 364.
[84] Drake and Cayton, 1945, 174.   [85] Ibid. 73.   [86] Ibid. 521.

would disappear and something approaching the middle-class way of life
would prevail.[87]

Within this structure, the professional and managerial middle class made
up a scant 5 per cent of the population. About one-third constituted an
'amorphous, sandwich-like' middle class. 'Trying with difficulty to maintian
respectability, they are caught between the class above into which they (or
at least their children) wish to rise and the group below into which they
do not wish to fall.'[88] But 65 per cent of Chicago's black population fell
into the manual working class. The crucial point is that this majority fell
into two unequal halves.

> A part of this working class constitutes the backbone of Bronzeville's 'middle'
> *social* class, identified by its emphasis on the symbols of 'respectability' and
> 'success'. The largest part of this working class is in a 'lower' *social* position,
> however, characterized by less restraint and without a consuming desire for
> the symbols of higher social prestige. Desertion and illegitimacy, juvenile
> delinquency, and fighting and roistering are common in lower-class circles
> . . . the lower social class in Bronzeville have their being in a world apart
> from both white people and other Negroes.[89]

The crucial dividing line was economic. More than one out of every
three Chicago blacks, in 1940, was unemployed or on Emergency Work
Projects.[90] 'Many of these families were actually mutual-aid societies,
originated and maintained by economic necessity.'[91] Maintaining any kind
of home life was difficult, because of low and fluctuating income and poor
housing. 'Sometimes families came into being in order that the partners
could qualify for more relief. Even illegitimate babies were an asset when
confronting a case-worker. . . . In the parlance of the sociologist, Bronzeville
was suffering from social disorganization.'[92]

The result was the familiar pattern, recorded by other sociological studies
from DuBois and Odum onwards. The 'lack of economic opportunity,
coupled with denial of access to even a grade-school education, resulted
very early in a peculiar pattern of restless wandering on the part of Negro
men', which had been 'an important factor, during the eighty years since
slavery, in preventing the formation of stable, conventional family units',
and had thus 'shifted the responsibility of the maintenance of household
units to the women of the lower class, so that 'lower-class men are thus in
a weak economic position *vis-à-vis* their women and children. Male control
loosened, the woman becomes the dominant figure.'[93] Thus:

> . . . an old southern pattern is intensified and strengthened in Bronzeville.
> Unstable common-law marriages of relatively short duration alternate with
> periods of bitter disillusionment on the woman's part. The end result is often

---

[87] Ibid. 710.　　[88] Ibid. 524.　　[89] Ibid. 523.　　[90] Ibid. 214.
[91] Ibid. 581.　　[92] Ibid. 582.　　[93] Ibid. 583.

a 'widow' and her children, caused either by a husband's desertion or by a wife's impetuous dismissal of him.[94]

The inevitable results were juvenile delinquency and illegitimacy. In 1930, some 20 per cent of juvenile-court appearances were blacks; the Depression made things worse, and 'purse-snatching became general in lower-class areas and even on main thoroughfares.' And, for every one arrested, there were 'thousands of lower-class young men . . . who skirted the borderline of crime. These were the 'cats' who, clad in 'zoot-suits', stood around and 'jived' the women.'[95] Between 1928 and 1933, about one in nine of black births was illegitimate, the majority to young lower-class women who had recently come to the city; they were perpetrating an old rural trait, whereby a child is regarded as a welcome gift to help with the farm work, and no stigma attached to the fact.[96]

During the twenty years that followed that study, Chicago's black population grew mightily. Ten times as many blacks lived in the city in 1966 as in 1920; they increased from 4 per cent to 30 per cent of the population. The ghetto itself had hugely expanded; its major business artery shifted 2 miles to the south.[97] It did so only after a series of riots between 1947 and 1957, in which the retreating whites – as in 1919 – had defended their turf, but with far less bloodshed.[98]

In the process, it had also changed character: it was taken over by the Chicago Housing Authority. The resulting political battle tore the city apart and almost destroyed the Authority itself. The CHA's plan of 1949, for 40,000 additional units over six years, involved putting large numbers of blacks into white areas; as it tried to do so, there were continued riots; the city's ward politicians panicked; finally, CHA's director Elizabeth Wood was dismissed.[99] The attempt to integrate was abandoned; the CHA, in a deal with the city's political leaders, became involved in an immense scheme of *de jure* segregation.

Of thirty-three CHA projects approved between 1950 and the mid-1960s, only one when completed was in an area less than 84 per cent black; all but seven were in tracts at least 95-per-cent black; more than 98 per cent of the apartments were in all-black neighbourhoods. The CHA, as critics later charged, was building almost a solid corridor of low-rent housing along State Street and near-by streets from 22nd Street to 51st Street.[100] As it did so, the whites moved out: of 688,000 new homes built between 1945 and 1960, more than 77 per cent were built in the suburbs, where hardly any blacks were found.[101] By 1969 a judge found that CHA family housing was 99 per cent black-occupied, and that 99.5 per cent of

---

[94] Ibid. 584.   [95] Ibid. 589.   [96] Ibid. 590.   [97] Hirsch, 1983, 3.

[98] Ibid. 68–71.   [99] Bowly, 1978, 76–84.

[100] Ibid. 112; Hirsch, 1983, 243.   [101] Hirsch, 27.

its units were in black or transitional areas.[102] The city's 'second ghetto', several times larger than the first had been during the city's disastrous race riot in 1919, was also more isolated; its older, northern end was now almost solidly frozen in institutional concrete.[103]

The heart and symbol of the new ghetto was the Robert Taylor Homes, the largest public-housing project in the world: more than 4,300 units on a 95-acre site, 2 miles by one-quarter mile in extent, with twenty-eight identical sixteen-storey buildings. Of the original 27,000 residents, 20,000 were children. Almost all were black; all were poor; more than half were on public assistance. There were, in the whole project, 2,600 men: it was the equivalent of a town of more than 25,000 people, almost 90 per cent of whom were women and children.[104] One resident said: 'We live stacked on top of one another with little elbow room. Danger is all around. There's little privacy or peace and no quiet. And the world looks on all of us like project rats, living on a reservation like untouchables.'[105] A private slum had become a public one. Otherwise, in twenty years, nothing had changed.

In another mid-western public-housing ghetto, at about the same time, yet another team of sociologists was undertaking yet another investigation. This one was special, because the subject was the notorious Pruitt–Igoe development in St Louis, the life and death of which have been retold in chapter 7. What they found was virtually a carbon copy of the Robert Taylor Homes. Of the 9,952 people in the project, well over two-thirds were minors and over two-thirds of them were under twelve; women headed 62 per cent of the families; in only 45 per cent was employment the sole source of income.[106] So the story, unsurprisingly, had all the familiar ingredients of family disorganization, male marginality, delinquency and social disintegration; here, it was merely more extreme and more spectacular. Pruitt–Igeoans lived in a nightmare world in which, since moving into the project, 41 per cent had experienced theft, 35 per cent personal injury, 20 per cent serious physical assault.[107] What was significant, in Rainwater's finding, was that nevertheless the values of the people were mainstream, almost middle-class, ones: the problem was that to maintain them would have required a stability and level of income enjoyed by the upper working class, meaning 50 to 100 per cent higher than was available to most of them.[108] The result was

> the belief that respectability, conventional life, is a tenuous and unstable achievement, and that in the lower class ghetto world, the individual who is conforming to conventional expectations may fail at any time. Closely entwined with this generalized judgment about respectability is a basic

---

[102] Ibid. 265.   [103] Ibid. 265.   [104] Bowly, 1978, 124, 128.
[105] Ibid. 124.   [106] Rainwater, 1970, 13.
[107] Ibid. 104.   [108] Ibid. 50.

distrust of other persons, no matter how close they may be by blood or affection. This distrust has two focuses: others may seek to exploit a person and, more subtle but equally important, even without trying to exploit him, others may simply fail one if he depends on them . . . Relationships may just not work out, whether between lovers, spouses, relatives, or friends.[109]

Thus, 'Pruitt–Igoeans perceive a tremendous disjunction between actual behavior in their world and their norms about what behavior should be': a disjuncture that manifested itself in low self-esteem, which was a way of coping with exploitation.[110] Thus the matrifocal family, the marginal male, and the communal disintegration, were accepted as facts of life; 'men are just like that', 'naturally' irresponsible; no one could depend on anyone, even his or her spouse:[111]

> The relatively higher rate of marital disruption can be seen as a result both of the greater stress placed on the marriage by the highly developed subversion of the family by the street system and the less cohesion within the marriage resulting from the wife's lower incentive to retain her husband.[112]

And from this stemmed other curious consequences: the lack of a strong set of family attachments, or of deep psychological concern on the part of mothers for their children, which in turn appeared to contribute to a disturbingly high level of retarded behaviour on the part of the children.[113] As children entered the school years, the difficulties multiplied:

> Pruitt–Igoeans' deep pessimism about human nature, the bedrock conviction that most people will do ill when it is in their interest, that doing ill is more natural than doing good, interacts with the normal contingencies of life that make doing good very difficult. Parents feel that luck more than anything else determines whether their children grow up conforming to their ideas of goodness.[114]

The child in turn learns that he cannot depend on his family, and that unless very lucky his life will not be very different from that of the elders around him; consequently, he might as well start coping with life as it is. In adolescence, his peer group tells him that success will come not from conventional performance in school or employment, but through becoming 'the complete hustler, who gets what he wants by working on people's minds, who can produce rewards with a minimum of effort and a maximum of style.'[115]

The root causes of this tangled skein of syndromes, in Rainwater's view, are economic marginality and racial oppression. Lower-class blacks cannot find a secure niche in the economic system; racism entrenches this, while

---

[109] Ibid. 55.   [110] Ibid. 61, 75.   [111] Ibid. 165–8.   [112] Ibid. 174.
[113] Ibid. 218–20.   [114] Ibid. 222–3.   [115] Ibid. 286.

ensuring that they get poorer and dearer services, including housing and education:

> This inability to be like everyone else robs the lower-class Negro of a sense of personal meaningfulness and efficacy which is the accustomed and expected patrimony of the ordinary individual in the simpler, more 'primitive tribes' in the underdeveloped parts of the world . . . constrained to live among others who are equally marginal in economic terms, and in the community that grows up in this situation, a premium is placed on the exploitation and manipulation of peers.[116]

And the root lay in the poor economic prospects and status of the man, which gave him little status in his wife's eyes, and forced him into a self-protective role of 'going for oneself', relying on the responses of others to measure success: 'If one is successful in creating a dramatic self, a kind of security has been gained because that self can neither be taken away nor spent (at least in the short run).'[117]

The importance of this analysis lay in its policy implications: simply trying to intervene from outside, in order to teach middle-class values and aspirations through the educational system, would be foredoomed to failure, because it would not alter the life situations, within which the lower class developed their own view of the world and of their position in it. And conventional anti-poverty programmes would fail, because they required the poor to change their behaviour without the resourcs that would allow them to do so. Brutally, the first essential was to give the poor money.[118]

Moynihan Enters the Fray

In 1965, more than twenty-five years after Frazier's classic and more than twenty after Myrdal's, yet another distinguished social scientist made his contribution. Essentially, it underlined their conclusions, confirming that the problem had not gone away. But unlike their work, it caused an unprecedented political storm. The reasons were two. First, Daniel Patrick Moynihan was an academic who had entered politics as a United States senator. And second, his report, *The Negro Family: The Case for National Action*, came in the immediate wake of the most turbulent decade in American black history, exceeding even the era of emancipation, which had begun with the historic Supreme Court ruling on *Brown et al.* v. *Board of Education of Topeka et al.*. in 1954, and had culminated in President Johnson's enactment of the Civil Rights Bill in 1964.

Moynihan began as he was to go on, bluntly: 'The most difficult fact for white Americans to understand is that . . . the circumstances of the

---

[116] Ibid. 371.   [117] Ibid. 379.   [118] Ibid. 401–3.

Negro American community in recent years has [*sic*] been getting *worse*, *not better*.[19] 'The fundamental problem', he continued, echoing Frazier and Myrdal, 'is that of family structure':

> The evidence – not final, but powerfully persuasive – is that the Negro family in the urban ghettos is crumbling. A middle-class group has managed to save itself, but for vast numbers of the unskilled, poorly educated city working class the fabric of conventional social relationships has all but disintegrated . . . So long as this situation persists, the cycle of poverty and disadvantage will continue to repeat itself.[120]

The report gave the all-too-familiar evidence of family disintegration, but now the indices were much worse: nearly one-quarter of black marriages were dissolved; nearly one-quarter of black births, eight times the white rate, were illegitimate; almost one-quarter of black families were female-headed; 14 per cent of black children, against 2 per cent of white, depended on welfare.[121] So, Moynihan concluded, 'the family structure of lower class Negroes is highly unstable, and in many urban centers is approaching complete breakdown.'[122] The explanations too were identical to Frazier's: slavery, reconstruction, urbanization:

> In essence, the Negro community has been forced into a matriarchal structure which, because it is so out of line with the rest of American society, seriously retards the progress of the group as a whole, and imposes a crushing burden on the Negro male and, in consequence, on a great many Negro women as well.[123]

In particular, he asserted, matriarchal homes contributed to a psychological inability to defer gratification, and thus to a pattern of immature, neurotic behaviour in adolescent and adult life.[124]

The consequences were also familiar, at least to any reader of the earlier literature; Moynihan's report merely confirmed that there had been no change. Unemployment among blacks had 'continued at disaster levels for 35 years', with the sole exception of a few wartime years.[125] 'The combined impact of poverty, failure, and isolation among the Negro youth', Moynihan continued, 'has had the predictable outcome in a disastrous delinquency and crime rate.' It was possible that a majority of crimes against the person (rape, murder, aggravated assault) were committed by blacks, the overwhelming majority of them against other blacks.[126] Educationally, too, black youth was seriously disadvantaged: 56 per cent failed the standardized Armed Forces mental test, a basic measure of ability, and 'A grown young man who cannot pass this test is in trouble.'[127]

[119] Moynihan, 1965, n.p.   [120] Ibid., n.p.   [121] Ibid. 7–9, 12.
[122] Ibid. 5.   [123] Ibid. 29.   [124] Ibid. 39.   [125] Ibid. 20.
[126] Ibid. 38–9.   [127] Ibid. 40.

Moynihan concluded by saying that the object of his study had been to define the problem, not propose solutions: he merely urged that 'a national effort towards the problem of Negro Americans must be directed towards the question of family structure. The object should be to strengthen the Negro family so as to enable it to raise and support its members as do other families.'[129] Frazier, he reminded his readers, had said the same thing in 1950, but 'matters were left to take care of themselves, and as matters will, grew worse not better.'[129] This time, he believed, there was a crucial difference: the President backed the effort.

If he did, he soon walked away from it; the reason being not so much the subsequent controversy, but the escalating costs of the Vietnam War.[130] The controversy itself put no one in a good light, Moynihan excepted. The report was prepared for internal government circulation, but it got leaked, forcing publication. Fellow social scientists were embarrassed by Moyhnihan's open recital of uncomfortable facts; the Washington welfare establishment wanted to maintain a stance of being 'color blind'.[131] So everyone had an interest in repudiating the report, which they duly did. When the White House called a conference eight months after publication, as one participant put it, the basic assumption was that 'no such person as Daniel Patrick Moynihan exists';[132] on the basis of critiques, one at least of which had been written without reading the report, an attempt was actually made to stop the conference even discussing family structure.[133]

The Impact of the Ghetto Riots

One of the reasons for this immense controversy, without doubt, was the changed perception on the part of Americans – and above all the American media – of the black American community. But another, more important, reason was that the report came in the middle of the riots that swept through black ghettos in more than a score of American cities, starting in Birmingham, Alabama, in 1963 and culminating in Detroit in 1967.[134] In particular, its publication in March 1965 was followed the same August by the major riot in the Watts district of Los Angeles, in which thirty-four people were killed and $35 million of damage was inflicted;[135] the Moynihan report, the media suggested, 'explained' the Watts riot.[136]

In fact, later analysis suggested that perhaps it did not. The exhaustive report of the Kerner Commission, appointed by President Johnson in the

---

[128] Ibid. 47. [129] Ibid. 48. [130] Rainwater and Yancey, 1967, 294.
[131] Ibid. 299, 304–5, 310. [132] Ibid. 248. [133] Ibid. 195, 233.
[134] U.S. National Advisory Committee, 1968, 25–108.
[135] Ibid. 37–8. [136] Rainwater and Yancey, 1967, 139–40.

wake of the 1967 riots, did not look at Watts; but it concentrated on essentially similar riots that had taken place that summer in seven cities including Atlanta, Newark and Detroit. There, it concluded,

> The typical rioter in the summer of 1967 was a Negro, unmarried male between the ages of 15 and 24 in many ways different from the stereotypes. He was not a migrant. He was born in the state and was a life-long resident of the city in which the riot took place. Economically his position was about the same as his Negro neighbors who did not actively participate in the riot.
>
> Although he had not, usually, graduated from high school he was somewhat better educated than the average inner-city Negro, having at least attended high school for a time.
>
> Nevertheless, he was more likely to be working in a menial low status job as an unskilled laborer. If he was employed, he was not working full time and his employment was frequently interrupted by periods of unemployment.
>
> He feels strongly that he deserves a better job and that he is barred from achieving it, not because of lack of training, ability, or ambition, but because of discrimination by employers.
>
> He rejects the white bigot's stereotype of the Negro as ignorant and shiftless. He takes great pride in his race and believes that in some respects Negroes are superior to whites. He is extremely hostile to whites, but his hostility is more likely to be a product of social and economic class than of race; he is almost equally hostile to middle-class Negroes.[137]

In fact, this picture was not so far from the stereotype as the Commission claimed. Put another way, the typical rioter was a second-generation city-dweller, a high-school drop-out with no educational qualifications, who nevertheless believed that this was not the reason for his relative failure in the job market; he was extremely hostile to mainstream American society, white or black. Between two-thirds and nine-tenths of the rioters were young adults, one-half to three-quarters were unskilled, one-third to two-thirds were migrants to the city, one-fifth to two-fifths were unemployed and between one-third and nine-tenths had criminal records.[138] Unlike middle-class blacks, they had made little progress in jobs, housing or education. In other words, the typical rioter, if he existed, was also a fairly typical member of the underclass as Frazier had described it; the only gloss was that he belonged to the more intelligent and ambitious stratum of that underclass. And, if he did belong, he was more likely than in earlier generations to be out on the streets, especially in order to loot.[139]

Elsewhere, the Commission's report repeated the now familiar litany of the cycle of unemployment, family disintegration, and social disorganization; in ascribing family breakdown to unemployment, it in fact affirmed the

---

[137] U.S. National Advisory Committee, 1968, 128–9.
[138] Fogelson, 1971, 43, 114.
[139] Janowitz, 1969, 325; Meier and Rudwick, 1969, 312.

analysis in the Moynihan report. Between 2 and 2.5 million people, 16 to 20 per cent of the black populations of the cities, lived in squalor and depression in racial ghettos. They suffered unemployment rates more than double those for whites, and black men were three times as likely as white men to be in low-paid unskilled or service jobs; more than 40 per cent of the black population, in 1966, was below the poverty line. And another potent cause of poverty was the familiar fact that nearly 24 per cent of black families, against 9 per cent of white, were female-headed. They concluded, predictably enough:

> The culture of poverty that results from unemployment and family disorganiz-
> ation generates a system of ruthless, exploitative relationships within the
> ghetto. Prostitution, dope addiction, casual sexual affairs and crime create
> an environmental jungle characterized by personal insecurity and tension. . . .
> 1.2 million nonwhite children under 16 lived in central city families headed
> by women under 65. The great majority of these children were growing up
> in poverty under conditions that make them better candidates for crime and
> civil disorder than for jobs providing an entry into American society.[140]

This suggested a key feature of the 1960s riots, that was later underlined by Morris Janowitz: unlike the *communal riot* as in East St Louis in 1917 or Chicago in 1919, which was an interracial clash at the boundaries of expanding black ghettos, this was a *commodity riot* within the ghetto, directed at white property and based on large-scale looting.[141] White residences, and white people, were not the objects of attack; the key feature of the riots was 'shopping for free'. Whether you interpreted that as 'rioting mainly for fun and profit', as Edward Banfield did at the time, or as 'a matter of pride to many, a means of joining a national rebellion and heightening its intensity', as Kenneth Fox later did, is a matter of interpretation.[142]

It raised the question for the Kerner Commission, that for many Americans was uppermost: why then had blacks failed to follow the typical immigrant path to upward mobility? The Commission's main answer was timing. Blacks arrived in large numbers in the cities just as entry-level unskilled jobs were disappearing. Insofar as they still existed, they carried a stigma not present for earlier generations, when they constituted most jobs. Discrimination against blacks was fiercer than against earlier, white, immigrants. And the political system was no longer adjusted to serving immigrant needs.[143]

Finally, then, the Kerner Commission focused its basic explanation not on the disintegration of the black family, but on what it saw as 'white racism' which, it argued, was 'essentially responsible for the explosive

---

[140] Ibid. 262–3.   [141] Janowitz, 1969, 317.
[142] Banfield, 1968, 185–209; Fox, 1985, 160.
[143] U.S. National Advisory Committee, 1968, 278–82.

mixture which has been accumulating in our cities since the end of World War Two'.[144] Among its main features were pervasive discrimination and segregation in housing, which resulted in black ghettos; black in-migration and white exodus from the cities; and the resultant development of a ghetto culture in which 'crime, drug addiction, dependency on welfare, and bitterness and resentment against society in general and white society in particular are the result.'[145]

Thus the Kerner Commission analysis did not unearth much that was new. What was interesting, and significant, was how it made the causal connections, and thus how it placed responsibility for the riots. For Kerner, the riots were the fault of white racism. The whites were thus to blame for the fact that the blacks had rioted. A preponderantly white and conservative group had emerged with an explanation that – after thirty years of study – Frazier, the black Marxist radical, had never remotely suggested. It was an intriguing paradox; a sign of the times.

After the Riots

The Kerner report went on to recommend a series of measures aiming at 'the creation of a new union – a single society and a single American identity'.[146] Through job creation and the removal of job discrimination, better education and the removal of *de facto* discrimination in the school system, better and more uniform welfare standards, and an attack on substandard housing, it aimed to break down the invisible walls of the ghetto and finally integrate the black underclass into the mainstream of American life.

It did not succeed. There have subsequently been at least two major studies of black American progress: by William J. Wilson (1978) and by Reynolds Farley (1984). They appear to disagree, but many of their conclusions are disturbingly similar. Wilson's book is called *The Declining Significance of Race*: his thesis is that 'class has become more important than race in determining black access to privilege and power.'[147] Thus talented and educated blacks had been entering the professions as fast as, or faster than, whites with comparable qualifications; they had especially benefited from the expansion of government jobs, especially those concerned with distributing welfare.[148] So there had been a huge growth in the black middle class, from 16.4 per cent of black males in 1950 to 35.3 per cent in 1970; conversely, the lower class had fallen from 50.7 to 36.4 per cent.[149]

---

[144] Ibid. 10. [145] Ibid. [146] Ibid. 23. [147] Wilson, 1978, 2.
[148] Ibid. 103. [149] Ibid. 129.

Yet, despite these encouraging signs, 'the black underclass is in a state of hopeless stagnation, falling further behind the rest of society.'[150] The reason, Wilson suggested, was a factor called 'twist' in the demand for labour, identified by the economist Charles C. Killingworth in a study in 1968: there had been a long-term decline in the demand for low-skilled, poorly educated labour which had been faster than the decline in the supply of such labour.[151] True, such jobs still existed; but the qualifications had been raised, they were somewhat insecure, and many blacks would no longer do them because they felt that they would lose their self-respect.[152] Besides, for members of the underclass, illegal activities were more interesting and profitable; Wilson quotes a 1966 survey of residents of Harlem, where 20 per cent were so engaged.[153]

Similarly, Wilson argued, the phenomenon of the female-headed household was by then a class-based, not a race-based, phenomenon. In 1974, only 18 per cent of children in black families earning less than $4,000 lived with both parents; yet among those earning $15,000 or more, 90 per cent did.[154] The fact was that 'the situation of marginality and redundancy created by the modern industrial society deleteriously affects all the poor, regardless of race'; blacks were disproportionately represented in the underclass, and one-third of them were still there; but that was a legacy of past oppression, not of current discrimination.[155]

On that last point, Wilson's analysis agrees with Stephen Steinberg's account in his book, *The Ethnic Myth*, three years later. Steinberg too confirms the divergence between a substantial black middle class and 'the sheer existence of a vast black underclass', which to him provides 'prima facie evidence of institutionalized racism'.[156] But it turns out that what Steinberg means by this is racism in long-past generations. He argues – and in this he essentially follows Park's analysis of the 1920s – that the critical variable in the successful adaptation of different ethnic immigrant groups is whether they had previous experience of urban life. Thus the Jews, who were almost exclusively urban before they came, had been outstandingly successful; the rural southern Italians less so.[157] But the blacks, despite being one of America's oldest immigrant groups, had been deliberately kept out of the northern cities after emancipation, because of a tacit conspiracy between southern plantation owners and northern industrialists.[158] So, when they belatedly arrived, they were totally unprepared for the transition.

Farley's analysis shows much the same divergence between rich and poor blacks: the gap, he suggests, has remained about the same in a relative sense, but has markedly increased in terms of absolute incomes.[159] What

---

[150] Ibid. 2.   [151] Ibid. 95–8; Killingworth, 1968.
[152] Wilson, 1978, 104–6.   [153] Ibid. 108.   [154] Ibid. 132.   [155] Wilson, 1978, 154.
[156] Steinberg, 1981, 209.   [157] Ibid. 94–8.   [158] Ibid. 173–4, 201–2, 221.
[159] Farley, 1984, 181–3.

he does show, on the basis of more recent figures than Wilson's, is an ominous reversal in the trend of black progress: the proportion of black Americans who are poor, which declined from over 50 per cent in 1950 to a low point of 30 per cent in 1974, subsequently edged upwards again to 36 per cent in 1982.

Farley argues that his explanation contradicts Wilson; sex, not class, is now the main key to membership of the underclass. But really, his evidence does not clash with Wilson's: both demonstrate the so-called feminization of poverty, which is the product of the rapid rise in female-headed households. And here a major difference has opened up between blacks and whites: whereas in 1960 90 per cent of white children, but only 66 per cent of black ones, lived with both parents, by 1982 these figures had fallen to 81 and 42 per cent.[160] And this in turn is due to a huge rise in black illegitimacy: in 1950, the rates were 2 per cent for whites, 17 per cent for non-whites; in the late 1960s, 6 and 32 per cent; in 1980, 10 and 55 per cent.[161] Now it is true that the rise in white illegitimacy has been faster; what is disturbing about the black figure is the absolute scale of the problem. Far from getting better over time, as most observers expected and hoped, it has got spectacularly worse.

The consequences have been dire. While 19 per cent of black husband–wife families were below the official poverty line in 1982, for female-headed households the figure was 59 per cent.[162] Put another way: while in 1959 two-thirds of poor black households consisted of husband–wife families, by 1980 three in five were female-headed.[163] All this strongly supports Farley's conclusion: 'changing living arrangements help to explain persistence of high rates of poverty in the 1970s.'[164] Or, as someone has put it, poverty is no longer a matter so much of what you do, as of whom you live with.

The problem, as always, is what caused that. Farley's explanation is that higher welfare payments to families with dependent children – which rose 28 per cent in constant dollars between 1960 and 1980 – may have actually encouraged family breakup; and, in the late 1970s, some 44 per cent of recipients were black.[165] If this were so, Farley points out, it would contradict Moynihan's thesis of 1965, which was that by creating more jobs for black men, families would be encouraged to stay together; in fact many such jobs have been created, but it has not had the expected effect. Farley, rather, argued that the changes are the product of deep-seated social changes, which may well be followed by the white community.[166]

That proved prophetic. Black illegitimacy in America climbed ever higher: to 56 per cent of all births by the early 1980s, almost 40 per cent of these to teenagers; almost one in four black teenagers had illegitimate

---

[160] Ibid. 141.   [161] Ibid. 138.   [162] Ibid. 158.   [163] Ibid. 161.
[164] Ibid. 160.   [165] Ibid. 170.   [166] Ibid. 169–70.

children before the age of eighteen; 47 per cent of all black families were female-headed.[167] And the basic cause appeared to be an extraordinary drop in marriage rates, by 45 per cent in the 1970s: by the early 1980s, 86 per cent of black teenage mothers were single.[168] Further, Farley seemed to be right on another trend: a third of white teenage births, too, were by then illegitimate. The differences, though, were still startling: among unmarried girls aged seventeen and younger, the black birth rate was eight times the white.[169]

And all the time, the plight of the black underclass seemed to be getting worse. A study by Richard P. Nathan, published early in 1987, concluded that between 1970 and 1980, while the total population of the top fifty American cities fell by 5 per cent, the numbers of those in poverty rose nearly 12 per cent. Yet within this total, the number of poor whites fell by 18 per cent, from 3.2 to 2.6 million; the numbers of poor blacks rose by 18 per cent, from 2.6 to 3.1 million. Further, 84 per cent of these poor blacks lived in concentrated poverty areas. And, though data were few, indications were that these trends had continued after 1980.[170]

Something quite extraordinary was happening here; but it was not quite clear why. It could not be, as Frazier had suggested long ago, that new waves of imperfectly acculturated rural black girls were descending on the cities; during the 1970s the tide of black migration slowed and even reversed. It might be, as some suggested, that recession and unemployment were making black men reluctant to marry; but that hardly explains the virtual collapse of the institution, or the extraordinary rise in illegitimacy that accompanied it. Nor does the modest rise in welfare levels seem to provide a remotely adequate reason. The disturbing prospect was that America was seeing yet another strange socio-cultural trend among a section of the young.

But at least, in contradistinction to the original furore over Moynihan, the issue of 'children having children' was being openly aired by black community leaders, who saw in it the seeds of a real future tragedy. 'For too long, we may have been too defensive, seeing public discussion of counterproductive tendencies in our community's structure as an attack on black people,' said the President of the National Urban League, John Jacob; 'In many cases it was that. But the facts must still concern us.'[171] Indeed, as the spectre loomed of these millions of fatherless children growing up to adulthood on city streets, they did: the fire next time might beggar previous recollections.

Moynihan, it seemed, was at last rehabilitated.[172] In January 1987, he launched a major drive to replace the American welfare programme by a

[167] Hulbert, 1984, 15.   [168] Ibid. 16.   [169] Ibid.   [170] Herbers, 1987a.
[171] Ibid. 16.   [172] Moynihan, 1986.

completely new system, which would put first emphasis on earned income. Significantly, it won all-party support, from President Reagan downwards. And, a month later, Democrat and Republican state governors likewise approved a resolution demanding that the system of welfare payments be immediately turned into a 'workfare' programme. They cited in support a background paper, drawing attention to

> deep and troubling changes in the fabric of American society: huge numbers of young women and children in poverty, high rates of welfare dependency, a dramatic rise in the number of single-parent households and latchkey children, millions of adults who are functionally illiterate, a growing problem with alcohol and drug abuse, teen-agers who are bearing their second and third child, and many others who have dropped out of school.[173]

The prose was slightly purple; but not much so. Small wonder that the governors expressed widespread confidence that the administration, and Congress, would accept their proposal.

Postscript: The Underclass in Britain

Many, having reached this point in the account, might legitimately ask what it had to do with a history of planning. For planning, in any sense in which it has been used in this book, seems to have been conspicuously absent from the entire American story. There are two justifications for its inclusion. One is that a history of planning cannot be divorced from a history of the problems that give rise to planning; the relevance of the American history is precisely that, almost unbelievably, questions of city planning hardly entered into it. This suggests that in contradistinction to what might have happened in almost any other comparable country, Americans are capable of separating problems of social pathology from any discussion of design solutions. The way to the solution of the problem of the ghetto, if it existed, was by a bundle of policies – in employment, education, housing – that had very little to do with city planning, at least as Americans then understood it. This is even odder when we remember, from chapter 11, that it was just at the time of the riots that American planning theorists became convinced that planning was an approach that could be applied, suitably modified, to any problem whatsoever.

The other answer, more directly, is that other countries did not make this divorce. In particular Britain, which was also experiencing immigration of ethnic minorities into its inner cities in the 1950s and 1960s, and which in the mid-1960s also began to experience rather similar urban problems, then adopted a battery of solutions – some, such as community development,

---

[173] Herbers, 1987b.

clearly borrowed from American experience – but combined them with large-scale physical renewal of its cities. And unlike its American equivalent, which had carried the epithet of 'Negro removal' (chapter 7), this had consciously sought to provide public housing for a wide spectrum of the population, including the poorest – which, by definition, came to include many members of the minorities. By the mid-1980s, large numbers of what the Americans call blacks – that is, British people mainly of Caribbean origin – lived in public-housing projects, especially in London, where in 1981 nearly 57 per cent of all British blacks lived.

The research on them is far less rich than that on their American equivalents. Insofar as it exists, it seems to show that in some few respects the British did better. The welfare state provided a much more generous floor, especially in housing. There were lower illegitimacy rates, probably because of more effective contraception and abortion services; but figures are very hard to come by, because the British statistical services insist on being colour-blind, so this could be wrong. Forty-three per cent of all births in the London Borough of Lambeth in 1985 were illegitimate; and recent studies suggest that teenage single parenthood is indeed common among British-born black girls in London.[174] But Britain had been much more backward on questions of discrimination in employment, especially in affirmative action (or positive discrimination) programmes.

Further, Britain had probably done at least as badly in education, where the schools seemed to have produced proportionately large numbers of unqualified black school leavers, even when the figures were controlled for social class.[175] Thus, emerging from school with lower levels of qualification and skill, black British teenagers found it hard to get jobs: particularly in boroughs with high concentrations of blacks, black youth unemployment was much higher than white – though this is true only of males; black girls did about as well, or as badly, as their white sisters.[176]

It looks then as if overall, the British story is the same or worse. British blacks, like American blacks, have remained heavily concentrated in the inner and middle rings of the big cities. Relatively few have entered the ranks of the middle class. Their British-born children tend to be poorly qualified and they find it very difficult to get jobs. Though hard figures are difficult to find – those colour-blind statistics, again – the evidence suggests that they have high levels of recorded crime, or at any rate of recorded conviction.[177]

Finally, the evident fact is that the British ghettos too have rioted. In London's Brixton, Liverpool's Toxteth and Manchester's Moss Side in

---

[174] Skinner, 1986, 17–18; Coward, 1987, 29.

[175] Tomlinson, 1983, 62; Jeffcoate, 1984, 57–64; ILEA, 1987, *passim*.

[176] G.B. Manpower Services Commission, 1981, 8, D5, E5.

[177] G.B. Commons Hansard, 3 Dec 1987, col. 681.

FIGURE 12.6 *Broadwater Farm Riot, Tottenham, London, 1985.*
Like the equivalent riots of the 1960s in American cities, this was a 'commodity
riot' triggered by tensions between young blacks and police.

FIGURE 12.7 *Broadwater Farm.*
The police restore uneasy order to the indefensible spaces of the concrete jungle:
a final comment on the failure of 1960s-style urban renewal.

1981, in Birmingham's Handsworth and London's Broadwater Farm in 1985, violence, looting and widespread damage occurred. Thanks to the detailed official inquiry by Lord Justice Scarman into the Brixton riot, we have a detailed anatomy. It sounds like an uncanny re-run of the Kerner report: the same pre-history of mounting, barely controllable tension among the young ghetto blacks as they spar with police; the same small triggering incident of an arrest, followed by the spreading of rumour like wildfire; the same almost immediate conflagration.

Scarman concluded that this was not a race riot:[178] it was a clash of cultures, exacerbated by the fact that the black subculture was built on deprivation and disadvantage. And the story has some parallels with the regular outbursts of football-related violence in British cities, which stem largely from young whites. However labelled, the British riots – like their American equivalents – were the product of relatively poor, relatively under-privileged young men who had been encouraged, if not pressured, into developing an elaborate, segregated subculture very different from the mainstream society's.[129] For whatever cause, they were deeply alienated from that society. A high rate of male violence, like a high rate of female teenage illegitimate births, may be simply an expression of that profound alienation: at bottom, their hatred for society reflects self-detestation.

The latest and most spectacular of these British riots, which resulted in the hacking of a policement to death with a knife by a group of youths, took place in October 1985 at Broadwater Farm in Tottenham, north-east London. A prize-winning urban-renewal project of 1970, it had proved a case study in indefensible space (chapter 7); its medium-rise blocks, rising from a pedestrian deck above ground-level parking, provided a laboratory culture for vandalism and crime. It degenerated into a hard-to-let estate, with large numbers of problem tenants – particularly, young unmarried black mothers and their children; by 1980, the project was more than half black. A virtual no-go area for the police, it was brought back to life through a remarkable community effort led by one of the black tenants, who developed social facilities for the many unemployed teenagers. Then, her absence, and that of other key leaders, helped to precipitate a new wave of crime and thus, indirectly, the triggering of the riot.

That same year, a group appointed by the Archbishop of Canterbury published its report *Faith in the City*, triggering an immense political furore. They might have had Broadwater in mind:

> ... there is a danger of many outer estates, in particular, becoming areas which have a quite different social and economic system, operating almost at a subsistence level, dependent entirely on the public sector, where the opportunities for improvement either through self-help or through outside

[178] G. B. Home Office, 1981, 45.   [179] Ibid. 11.

intervention are minimal . . . the degeneration of many such areas has now gone so far that they are in effect 'separate territories' outside the mainstream of our social and economic life.[180]

The group's prose picture uncannily resembles those descriptions of Pruitt–Igoe before its end:

the architect-designed system-built slums of our post-war area . . . poor design, defects in construction, poor upkeep of public areas, no 'defensible space' . . . packs of dogs roaming around, filth in the stairwells, one or two shuttered shops, and main shopping centres a 20–minute expensive bus journey away . . . unemployment rates are typically 30–40 per cent, and rising . . . Bored out-of-work young people turn to vandalism, drugs, and crime – the estate takes the brunt, and the spiral of decline is given a further twist.[181]

The clerics and their lay brethren were in no doubt as to the root cause: '*It is the national decline in the number of manual jobs, and the concentration of manual workers in the UPAs that lies at the heart of the problem,*' they underlined.[182] But, given that, what astonished and depressed them was the resulting sense of fatalism. They italicized again: '*We believe that at present too much emphasis is being given to individualism, and not enough to collective obligation.*'[182] They roundly attacked the policies of the Thatcher government – on support to local authorities, on welfare – and the attitudes that underlay them: 'It is the poor who have borne the brunt of the recession, both the unemployed and the working poor. Yet it is the poor who are seen by some as 'social security scroungers', or a burden on the country, preventing economic recovery. This is a cruel example of blaming the victim.'[184] They ended with an open challenge – effectively, over the heads of the government: 'The crucial issue to be faced is whether there is any serious political will to set in motion a process which will enable those who are at present in poverty and powerlessness to rejoin the life of the nation.'[185] They were calling others to join them, to 'stand more closely alongside the risen Christ with those who are poor and powerless.'[186]

It was powerful and passionate; it was far removed from the traditional parody of the Church of England as the Tory Party at prayer. But it did curiously echo the righteous anger of Mearns and those countless other clergy, who a century before had railed against the cruelties of the Victorian slum. Here then is the final irony: in the mid-1980s the problem of the urban underclass was still as stubbornly rooted in the world's cities, and in the consciousness of its more sensitive citizens, as in the mid-1880s, when it provided the vital stimulus to the birth of modern city planning.

---

[180] Archbishop of Canterbury, 1985, 175.   [181] Ibid. 176.   [182] Ibid. 202.
[183] Ibid.   [184] Ibid. 197.   [185] Ibid. 360.   [186] Ibid.

Where, then, was planning? In that intervening century, despite its numerous errors and aberrations, city planning helped millions of relatively poor and decent people to live far better and more dignified lives than they otherwise might; for this it should be much praised in retrospect, and supported for the future. In the process, society has changed shape: it is no longer a pyramid, with few at the top and many at the bottom, but has become rather like an old-fashioned spinning-top, with a big bulge in the middle. The problem is no longer the one the first Fabians posed one hundred years ago, *Why Are The Many Poor?*,[187] but rather *Why Are The Few Poor?* Social progress – which is no myth – has left behind, as stubbornly evident as ever, a problem of what the Victorians and their American equivalents called the vicious and degenerate and semi-criminal classes, and which the more enlightened (or mealy-mouthed) late-twentieth century calls the disadvantaged and the underprivileged. Planning, and the whole twentieth-century apparatus of the welfare state, has failed to dislodge it, or even satisfactorily to explain it; as then, so now, some blame the system, others original sin.

There is this small comfort: though it is beyond precise social measurement, the locus of the problem has shifted. It is, by definition, the problem of the bottom of the social heap. A hundred years ago, contemporaries located it amongst the most desperate of those who had been driven into the slums of the giant city, and who had been least successful there in finding a foothold on the socio-economic ladder. A century later, they find it among the same groups. Meanwhile, countless numbers of the great-grandchildren of that first group have climbed out of the underclass. Doubtless, numberless progeny of the second will prove to do the same. The abiding problem is why, despite all the massive intervening economic and social improvement, the underclass should appear so steadily to recruit new members to replace those lost to it. To that question, research as yet provides no answer. Here this story ends.

[187] Fabian Society, 1884a.

References

This bibliography contains all works consulted in preparing the book. By no means all of them are actually cited in the text.

Abercrombie, P. 1910a: Modern Town Planning in England: A Comparative Review of 'Garden City' Schemes in England. *Town Planning Review*, **1**, 18–38, 111–28.

Abercrombie, P. 1910b: Some Notes on German Garden Villages. *Town Planning Review*, **1**, 246–50.

Abercrombie, P. 1911: Town Planning in Greater London: The Necessity for Co-operation. *Town Planning Review*, **2**, 261–80.

Abercrombie, P. 1914: Berlin: Its Growth and Present State. *Town Planning Review*, **4**, 219–33, 302–11.

Abercrombie, P. 1926: *The Preservation of Rural England*. Liverpool and London: University of Liverpool Press: Hodder and Stoughton.

Abercrombie, P. 1933: *Town and Country Planning*. London: Thornton Butterworth.

Abercrombie, P. 1945: *Greater London Plan 1944*. London: HMSO.

Abercrombie, P., Jackson, H. 1948: *West Midlands Plan*. Interim confidential Edition. 5 vols. London: Ministry of Town and Country Planning.

Abrams, C. 1939: *Revolution in Land*. New York and London: Harper and Brothers.

Abrams, C. 1964: *Man's Struggle for Shelter in an Urbanizing World*. Cambridge, Mass.: MIT Press.

Abrams, C. 1965: *The City is the Frontier*. New York: Harper and Row.

Abrams, C. 1971: *The Language of Cities: A Glossary of Terms*. New York: Viking.

Abu-Lughod, J. L. 1971: *Cairo: 1001 Years of the City Victorious*. Princeton: Princeton University Press.

Adams, T. 1930: The Need for a Broader Conception of Town Planning and Decentralization. In: Warren and Davidge, *op. cit.*, 135–149.

Adams, T. 1935: *Outline of Town and City Planning*. New York: Russell Sage Foundation.

Addams, J. 1910: *Twenty Years at Hull-House: with Autobiographical Notes*. New York: Macmillan.

Addams, J. 1929: A Decade of Prohibition. *Survey*; **63**, 5–10 and 54–5.

Addams, J. 1965: *The Social Thought of Jane Addams*. Edited by Christopher Lasch. Indianapolis: Bobbs–Merrill.

Adebisi, B. 1974: The Politics of Development Control in a Nigerian City: Ibadan. *Nigerian Journal of Economics and Social Studies*, **16**, 311–24.

Adejuyigbe, O. 1970: The Case for a new Federal Capital in Nigeria. *Journal of Modern African Studies*, **8**, 301–6.

Adshead, S. D. 1910: The Town Planning Conference of the Royal Institute of British Architects. *Town Planning Review*, **1**, 181.

Adshead, S. D. 1923: *Town Planning and Town Development*. London: Methuen and Co.

Agnew, J., Mercer, J. and Sopher, D. E. (eds) 1984: *The City in Cultural Context*. Boston: Allen and Unwin.

Albers, G. 1974: Ideologie und Utopie im Städtebau. In: Pehnt, R. (ed.), 1974, 453–76.

Albers, G. 1975: *Entwicklungslinien im Städtebau: Ideen, Thesen, Aussagen 1875–1945*. Berlin: Bertelesmann Fachverlag.

Albers, G. 1986: Changes in German Town Planning: A Review of the last fifty years. *Town Planning Review*, **57**, 17–34.

Albrecht, C. *et al.* (eds) 1930: *Handwörterbuch des Wohungswesens*. Jena: G. Fischer.

Albrecht, G. 1930: Gartenstadtbewegung. In: Albrecht, C. *et al.* (eds), 1930, 262–6.

Aldridge, H. R. 1915: *The Case for Town Planning; A Practical Manual for Councillors, Officers, and others engaged in the Preparation of Town Planning Schemes*. London: National Housing and Town Planning Council.

Alduy, J.-P. 1983: 40 Ans de Planification en Région Île-de-France. *Cahiers de l'Institut d'Aménagement et d'Urbanisme de la Région Île-de-France*, **70**, 11–85.

Alexander, L. A. 1981: *Winning Downtown Projects: A Photographic Case Study of Outstanding Urban Developments*. New York: Downtown Research and Development Center.

Allardice, C., Trapnell, E. R. 1974: *The Atomic Energy Commission*. New York: Praeger.

Allen, I. L. (ed.) 1977: *New Towns and the Suburban Dream: Ideology and Utopia in Planning and Development*. Port Washington: Kennikat.

Allinson, G. T. 1984: Japanese Urban Society and its Cultural Context. In: Agnew, J., Mercer, J., Sopher, D. E. (eds), 1984, 163–85.

Alonso, W. (1963) Cities and City Planners. *Daedalus*, **92**, 824–39.

Alonso, W. 1966. Cities, Planners and Urban Renewal. In: Wilson, J. Q., 1966, 437–53.

Altshuler, A. A. 1965a: The Goals of Comprehensive Planning. *Journal of the American Institute of Planners*, **31**, 186–97.

Altshuler, A. A. 1965b: *The City Planning Process*. Ithaca: Cornell UP.

Altshuler, A. A. 1983: The Intercity Freeway. In: Krueckeberg, D. A. (ed.), 1983c, 190–234.

Ambrose, P. 1986: *Whatever happened to Planning?* London: Methuen.

Anderson, M. 1964: *The Federal Bulldozer: A Critical Analysis of Urban Renewal, 1949–1962*. Cambridge, Mass.: MIT Press.

Anderson, M. 1966: The Federal Bulldozer. In: Wilson, J. Q. (ed.), 1966, 491–509.

Andrews, H. F. 1986: The early Life of Paul Vidal de la Blache and the Makings of modern Geography. *Institute of British Geographers, Transactions*, **11**, 174–82.

Anon. 1897: *Forecasts of the Coming Century, by a Decade of Writers*. Manchester: Labour Press.

(Anon.) (ed.) 1918: *Problems of Reconstruction: Lectures and Addresses delivered at the*

Summer Meeting at the Hampstead Garden Suburb, August 1917. With an Introduction by the Marquess of Crewe, KG. London: T. Fisher Unwin.

Anon. (1925) The Regional Community. *Survey*, **54**, 129.

Anon. 1937a: Prime Minister's support for Garden Cities. *Town and Country Planning*, **5**, 117.

Anon. 1937b: London Regional Planning: Notes of First Meeting of New Standing Conference. *Journal of the Town Planning Institute*, **24**, 15–16.

Anon. 1979a: *Autobahnen in Deutschland.* Bonn: Kirschbaum.

Anon. 1979b: Kvaliteten i vårt bostadsbyggande. *Plan*, **33**, 1–6 (and comments, 7–19).

Anon. 1979c: Jeu de l'Oie des Halles de Paris. *Macadam*, **8–9**, 12–13.

Anon. 1985: The Shape of North American Rail Transit. *Railway Gazette International*, **141**, 42–3.

Anson, B. 1981: *I'll fight you for it! Behind the Struggle for Covent Garden.* London: Cape.

Anthony, H. A. 1966: Le Corbusier: His Ideas for Cities. *Journal of the American Institute of Planners*, **32**, 279–88.

Applebaum, R. P. 1978: *Size, Growth, and U.S. Cities.* New York: Praeger.

Archbishop of Canterbury's Commission on Urban Priority Areas 1985: *Faith in the City: A Call for Action by Church and Nation.* London: Church House Publishing.

Architectural Review. 1957: Counter-Attack: The next stage in the fight against Subtopia. *Architectural Review*, **121**, 405–7.

Armstrong, G., Wilson, M. 1973: Delinquency and some Aspects of Housing. In: Ward, C. (ed.), 1973, 64–84.

Arnold, J. L. 1971: *The New Deal in the Suburbs: A History of the Greenbelt Town Program 1935–1954.* Columbus, Ohio: Ohio State UP.

Arnold, J. L. 1973: City Planning in America. In: Mohl, R. A., Richardson, J. F., (eds), 1973, 14–43.

Arnold, J. L. 1983: Greenbelt, Maryland, 1936–1984. *Built Environment*, **9**, 198–209.

Ashworth, W. 1954: *The Genesis of British Town Planning: A Study in Economic and Social History of the Nineteenth and Twentieth Centuries.* London: Routledge and Kegan Paul.

Aziz, S. 1978: *Rural Development: Learning from China.* New York: Holmes and Meier.

Baker, H. 1944: *Architecture and Personalities.* London: Country Life.

Baker, P. H. 1974: *Urbanization and Political Change: The Politics of Lagos, 1917–1967.* Berkeley and Los Angeles: University of California Press.

Baldwin, R. N. (ed.) (1971) (1927): *Kropotkin's Revolutionary Pamphlets: A Collection of Writings by Peter Kropotkin.* New York: Vanguard Press (repr. 1971: New York: Dover Publications).

Ballhatchet, K., Harrison, J. 1980: *The City in South Asia: Pre-Modern and Modern.* London: Curzon Press.

Banfield, E. C. 1965: *Big City Politics: A comparative Guide to the political Systems of Atlanta, Boston, Detroit, El Paso, Los Angeles, Miami, Philadelphia, St Louis, Seattle.* New York: Random House.

Banfield, E. C. 1970: *The Unheavenly City: The Nature and Future of our Urban Crisis.* Boston: Little, Brown.

Bangert, W. 1936: *Baupolitik und Stadtgestaltung in Frankfurt am Main.* Würzburg: K. Triltsch.

Banham, R. 1960: *Theory and Design in the First Machine Age.* London: Architectural Press.

Banham, R., Barker, P., Hall, P., Price, C. 1969: Non-Plan: An Experiment in Freedom. *New Society*, **26**, 435–43.

Banham, R. 1971: *Los Angeles: The Architecture of Four Ecologies*. London: Allen Lane.

Banton, M. 1971: Urbanization and the Colour Line in Africa. In: Turner, V. (ed.), 1971, 256–85.

Barber, W. J. 1967: Urbanisation and Economic Growth: The Cases of two White Settler Territories. In Miner, H. (ed.), 1967, 91–125.

Barker, T. C., Robbins, M. 1974: *A History of London Transport*. Vol. II: *The Twentieth Century to 1970*. London: George Allen and Unwin.

Barkin, W. 1978: Confronting the Separation of Town and Country in Cuba. In: Tabb, W., Sawers, L. (eds), 1978, 317–37.

Barman, C. 1979: *The Man Who Built London Transport: A Biography of Frank Pick*. Newton Abbot: David and Charles.

Barnett, H. 1918: The Garden Suburb: Its Past and Plans. In: Anon., 1918, 198–207.

Barrett, B. 1971: *The Inner Suburbs: The Evolution of an Industrial Area*. Melbourne: Melbourne UP.

Barth, G. 1980: *City People: The Rise of Modern City Culture in Nineteenth-Century America*. Oxford: Oxford UP.

Bassett, E. M. 1936: *Zoning: The Law, Administration, and Court Decisions during the first twenty Years*. New York: Russell Sage Foundation.

Bassett, E. M. 1938: *The Master Plan: With a Discussion of the Theory of Community Land Planning Legislation*. New York: Russell Sage Foundation.

Bassett, E. M. 1939: *Autobiography of Edward M. Bassett*. New York: Harbor Press.

Bastié, J. 1964: *La Croissance de la Banlieue Parisienne*. Paris: Presses Universitaires de France.

Batchelor, P. 1969: The origin of the Garden City Concept of Urban Form. *Journal of the Society of Architectural Historians*, **28**, 184–200.

Bater, J. H. 1979: The Legacy of Autocracy: Environmental Quality in St Petersburg. In: French, R. A., Hamilton, F. E. I., 1979a, 23–48.

Bater, J. H. 1984: The Soviet City: Continuity and Change in Privilege and Place. In: Agnew, J., Mercer, J., Sopher, D. E. (eds), 1984, 134–62.

Batty, M. 1976: *Urban Modelling: Algorithms, Calibrations, Predictions*. Cambridge: Cambridge UP.

Batty, M. 1979: On Planning Processes. In: Goodall, B., Kirby, A. (eds)) *Resources and Planning*. Oxford: Pergamon.

Bauer, C. 1934: *Modern Housing*. Boston and New York: Houghton Mifflin.

Bauman, J. F. 1980: Housing the Urban Poor. *Journal of Urban History*, **6**, 211–20.

Bauman, J. F. 1983: Visions of a Post-War Nation: A Perspective on Urban Planning in Philadelphia and the Nation, 1942–1945. In: Krueckeberg, D. A. (ed.), 1983c, 170–89.

Beaufoy, S. G. 1933: Regional Planning, I. The Regional Planning of South East England. *Town Planning Review*, **15**, 83–104, 188–214.

Beaujeu-Garnier, J. *et al.* 1978: *La France des villes*: 1. *Le Bassin parisien*. Paris: La Documentation Française.

Beauregard, R. A. The Occupation of Planning: A View from the Census. *Journal of the American Institute of Planners*, **42**, 187–92.

Beckinsale, R. P., Houston, J. M. (eds) 1968: *Urbanization and its Problems: Essays in Honour of E. W. Gilbert*. Oxford: Basil Blackwell.

Bell, C., Bell, R. 1969: *City Fathers: The Early History of Town Planning in Britain*. London: Cresset Press.

Bellamy, E. 1888: *Looking Backward*. New York: Ticknor.

Bellush, J., Hausknecht, M. (eds) 1967a: *Urban Renewal: People, Politics and Planning*. Garden City: Anchor.

Bellush, J., Hausknecht, M. 1967b: Urban Renewal: An Historical Overview. In: Bellush, J., Hausknecht, M. (eds), 1967a, 3–16.

Bellush, J., Hausknecht, M. 1967c: Public Housing: The contexts of Failure. In Bellush, J., Hausknecht, M. (eds), 1967a, 451–64.

Benoît-Lévy, G. 1904: *La Cité-Jardin*. Paris: Jouve.

Berg, E. 1979: *Stockholm Town Trails: From the Old Town to the New 'City'*. Stockholm: Akademilitteratur.

Berger, B. 1960: *Working Class Suburb: A Study of Auto Workers in Suburbia*. Berkeley and Los Angeles: University of California Press.

Berger, H. (ed.) 1968: *Ostafrikanische Studien: Ernst Weigt zum 60. Geburtstag*. Nürnberg: Friedrich-Alexander-Universität, Wirtschafts- und sozialgeographische Institut.

Berger-Thimme, D. 1976: *Wohnungsfrage und Sozialstaat: Untersuchen zu den Anfängen staatlicher Wohnungspolitik in Deutschland (1873–1918)*. Frankfurt: Peter Lang.

Bergmann, K. 1970: *Agrarromantik und Grossstadtfeindschaft (Marburger Abhandlungen zur Politischen Wissenschaft, 20)*. Melsenheim: Verlag Anton Heim.

Berkowitz, B. L. 1984: Economic Development really works: Baltimore, Maryland, In: Bingham, R. D. Blair, J. P. (eds) 1984, 201–21.

Berman, D. S. 1969: *Urban Renewal: Bonanza of the Real Estate Business*. Englewood Cliffs, NJ: Prentice Hall.

Bernstein, R. J. 1976: *The Restructuring of Social and Political Theory*. New York: Harcourt Brace Jovanovich.

Bernstein, R. J. 1985: *Habermas and Modernity*. Cambridge, Mass.: MIT Press.

Berton, K. 1977: *Moscow: An Architectural History*. London: Studio Vista.

Betjeman, J. 1978: *The Best of Betjeman* (selected by J. Guest). London: John Murray.

Bettman, A. 1946: *City and Regional Planning Papers*, edited by Arthur C. Comey. Cambridge, Mass.: Harvard UP.

Betts, R. F. 1985: Dakar: Ville impériale (1857–1960). In: Ross, R., Telkamp, G. J. (eds), 1985, 193–206.

Bing, A. M. 1925: Can we have Garden Cities in America? *Survey*, **54**, 172–3.

Bingham, R. D. 1975: *Public Housing and Urban Renewal: An Analysis of Federal–Local Relations*. New York: Praeger.

Bingham, R. D., Blair, J. P. (eds) 1984: *Urban Economic Development (Urban Affairs Annual Reviews, **27**)*. Beverly Hills: Sage.

Birch, A., Macmillan, D. A. (eds) 1962: *The Sydney Scene: 1788–1960*. Melbourne: Melbourne UP.

Birch, E. L. 1980a: Advancing the Art and Science of Planning. *Journal of the American Planning Association*, **46**, 22–49.

Birch, E. L. 1980b: Radburn and the American Planning Movement: The Persistence of an Idea. *Journal of the American Planning Association*, **46**, 424–39.

Birch, E. L. 1983: Radburn and the American Planning Movement: The Persistence of an Idea. In: Krueckeberg, D. A. (ed.), 1983c, 122–51.

Black, J. T., Howland, L., Rogel, S. L. 1983: *Downtown Retail Development: Conditions for Success and Project Profiles*. Washington: Urban Land Institute.

Blackwell, W. L. 1976: Modernization and Urbanization and Urbanization in Russia: A Comparative View. In: Hamm, M. F. (ed.), 1976a, 291–330.

Bliznakov, M. 1976: Urban Planning in the USSR: Integration Theories. In: Hamm, M. F. (ed.), 1976a, 243–56.

Blowers, A. 1980: *The Limits of Power: The Politics of Local Planning Policy*. Oxford: Pergamon.

Bluestone, B., Harrison, B. 1982: *The Deindustrialization of America: Plant Closures, Community Abandonment, and the Dismantling of Basic Industry*. New York: Basic Books.

Bluestone, B., Harrison, B. 1987: The Grim Truth about the Job 'Miracle'. *New York Times*, 1 February.

Boardman, P. 1944: *Patrick Geddes: Maker of the Future*. Chapel Hill: University of North Carolina Press.

Boardman, P. 1978: *The Worlds of Patrick Geddes: Biologist, Town Planner, Re-educator, Peace Warrior*. London: Routledge and Kegan Paul.

Boddy, M. 1980: *The Building Societies*. London: Macmillan.

Boddy, M., Lovering, J., Bassett, K. 1986: *Sunbelt City: A Study of Economic Change in Britain's M4 Growth Corridor*. Oxford: Oxford UP.

Bogle, J. M. L. 1929: *Town Planning: India* (India of Today, Vol. IX). Bombay: Oxford UP.

Boisier, S. 1981: Chile: Continuity and Change – Variations of Centre–Down Strategies under Different Political Regimes. In: Stöhr, W. B., Taylor, D. R. F. (eds), 1981, 401–26.

Bolan, R. S. 1967: Emerging Views of Planning. *Journal of the American Institute of Planners*, **33**, 233–45.

Bole, A. 1970: *Urbanization in India: An Inventory of source Materials*. Bombay and New Delhi: Academic Books.

Boneparth, E. (ed.) 1982: *Women Power and Policy*. New York: Pergamon.

Booth, C. 1887: The Inhabitants of Tower Hamlets (School Board Division), their Condition and Occupations. *Journal of the Royal Statistical Society*, **50**, 326–91.

Booth, C. 1888: Conditions and Occupations of the People in East London and Hackney, 1887. *Journal of the Royal Statistical Society*, **51**, 276–331.

Booth, C. (ed.) 1892: *Life and Labour of the People in London*. Vol. I: *East, Central and South London*. London: Macmillan.

Booth, C. 1901: *Improved Means of Locomotion as a First Step Towards the Cure of the Housing Difficulties of London*. London: Macmillan.

Booth, 'General' W. 1890: *In Darkest England and the Way Out*. London: Salvation Army.

Borchert, J. R. 1962: The Soviet City. In Holt, R. T., Turner, J. E. (eds), 1962, 35–61.

Borchert, J. 1980. *Alley Life in Washington: Family, Community, Religion, and Folklife in the City, 1850–1970*. Urbana: University of Illinois Press.

Bose, A. 1973: *Studies in India's Urbanization 1901–1971*. Bombay and New Delhi: Tata McGraw Hill.

Bournville Village Trust. 1941: *When We Build Again: A Study Based on Research into Conditions of Living and Working in Birmingham*. London: George Allen and Unwin.

Bowden, P. 1979: *North Rhine Westphalia: North England: Regional Development in Action*. London: Anglo-German Foundation for the Study of Industrial Society.

Bowley, M. 1945: *Housing and the State, 1919–1944*. London: George Allen and Unwin.

Bowly, D., Jun. 1978: *The Poorhouse: Subsidized Housing in Chicago, 1895–1976*. Carbondale: Southern Illinois UP.

Boyd, R. 1952: *Australia's Home: Its Origins, Builders and Occupiers*. Melbourne: Melbourne UP.

Boyd, R. 1960: *The Australian Ugliness*. Melbourne: Cheshire.

Boyer, M. C. 1983: *Dreaming the Rational City: The Myth of American City Planning.* Cambridge, Mass.: MIT Press.

Boyer, P. S. 1978: *Urban Masses and Moral Order in America, 1820–1920.* Cambridge, Mass.: Harvard UP.

Brand, R. R. 1976: The Urban Housing Challenge. In: Knight, C. G., Newman, J. L. (eds), 1976, 321–35.

Brandenburg, A., Materna, J. 1980: Zum Aufbruch in die Fabrikgesellschaft: Arbeiterkolonien. *Archiv für die Geschichte des Widerstandes und der Arbeit,* **1**, 35–48.

Branford, V. 1914: *Interpretations and Forecasts: A Study of Survivals and Tendencies in Contemporary Society.* New York and London: Mitchell Kennerley.

Branford, V., Geddes, P. 1917: *The Coming Polity: A Study in Reconstruction* (The Making of the Future). London: Williams and Norgate.

Branford, V., Geddes, P. 1919: *Our Social Inheritance.* London: Williams and Norgate.

Breese, G. (ed.) 1969: *The City in Newly Developing Countries: Readings on Urbanism and Urbanization.* Englewood Cliffs: Prentice-Hall.

Breheny, M., Hall, P. 1984: The Strange Death of Strategic Planning and the Victory of the Know-Nothing School. *Built Environment,* **10**, 95–9.

Breheny, M., Hooper, A. (eds) 1985: *Rationality in Planning: Critical Essays on the Role of Rationality in Urban and Regional Planning.* London: Pion.

Bristow, R. 1984: *Land-Use Planning in Hong Kong: History, Policies and Procedures.* Hong Kong: Oxford UP.

Brodsly, D. 1981: *L.A. Freeway: An Appreciative Essay.* Berkeley: University of California Press.

Bromley, R., Gerry, C. (eds) 1979: *Casual Work and Poverty in Third World Cities.* Chichester: John Wiley.

Brown, K. D. 1977: *John Burns.* London: Royal Historical Society.

Brownell, B. A. 1980: Urban Planning, The Planning Profession, and the Motor Vehicle in early Twentieth-Century America. In: Cherry, G. E. (ed.), 1980a, 59–77.

Brush, J. E. 1962: The Morphology of Indian Cities. In: Turner, R. (ed.), 1962, 57–70.

Brush, J. E. 1968: Spatial Patterns of Population in Indian Cities. *Geographical Review,* **58**, 362–91.

Bruton, M. 1975: *Introduction to Transportation Planning.* Second Edition. London: Hutchinson.

Bryson, L., Thompson, F. 1972: *An Australian Newtown: Life and Leadership in a Working-Class Suburb.* Harmondsworth: Penguin.

Bull, W. J. 1901: A Green Girdle round London. *Sphere,* **5**, 128–9.

Bullock, N. 1978: Housing in Frankfurt 1925 to 1931 and the New Wohnkultur. *Architectural Review,* **113**, 335–42.

Burchell, R. W., Sternlieb, G. (ed.) 1978: *Planning Theory in the 1980s: A Search for future Directions.* New Brunswick, N.J.: Rutgers University, Center for Urban Policy Research.

Burgess, E. W. 1925: The Growth of the City: An Introduction to a Research Project. In: Park, R. *et al.,* 1925, 47–62.

Burgess, R. 1978: Petty Commodity Housing or Dweller Control? A Critique of John Turner's views on Housing Policy. *World Development,* **6**, 1105–34.

Burgess, R. 1982: Self-help Housing Advocacy: A Curious Form of Radicalism. A critique of the work of J. F. C. Turner. In: Ward, P. M. (ed.), 1982, 56–97.

Burnett, J. 1978: *A Social History of Housing 1815–1970.* Newton Abbot: David and Charles.

Burnham, D. H., Bennett, E. H. 1905: *Report on a Plan for San Francisco*. San Francisco: Sunset Press. Reprinted 1971, with introduction by J. R. McCarthy. Berkeley: Urban Books.

Burnham, D. H., Bennett, E. H. 1909: *Plan of Chicago*. Chicago: Commercial Club. Reprinted 1970, New York: Da Capo Press.

Burnham, D. H., Jun., Kingery, R. 1956: *Planning the Region of Chicago*. Chicago: Chicago Regional Planning Association.

Burnley, I. H. (ed.) 1974: *Urbanization in Australia: The Post-War Experience*. London: Cambridge UP.

Burns, J. 1908: Speech on Housing, Town Planning, etc., Bill. *Commons Hansard, Fourth Series*, **188**, 947–68.

Butcher, G., Collis, P., Glen, A., Sills, P. 1980: *Community Groups in Action: Case Studies and Analysis*. London: Routledge and Kegan Paul.

Butler, C. *et al.* 1933: The Planned Community. *Architectural Forum*, **58**, 253–74.

Butler, S. M. 1981: *Enterprise Zones: Greenlining the Inner Cities*. New York: Universe Books.

Cadbury, G., Jun. 1915: *Town Planning: with Special Reference to the Birmingham Schemes*. London: Longmans, Green.

Calabi, D. 1984: Italy. In: Wynn, M. (ed.), 1984a, 37–69.

Caldenby, C., Rundberg, E. 1982: Katalog Backström & Reinius. *Arkitektur*, **82.6**, 10–32.

Callow, A. B. 1969: *American Urban History: An Interpretative Reader with Commentaries*. New York: Oxford UP.

Carnoy, M. 1984: *The State and Political Theory*. Princeton: Princeton UP.

Caro, R. A. 1974: *The Power Broker: Robert Moses and the Fall of New York*. New York: Alfred A. Knopf.

Carr, M. C. 1982: The Development and Character of a Metropolitan Suburb: Bexley, Kent. In: Thompson, F. M. L. (ed.), 1982, 212–67.

Carrothers, G. A. P. 1956: An historical Review of the Gravity and Potential Concepts of Human Interaction. *Journal of the American Institute of Planners*, **22**, 94–102.

Carver, H. 1962: *Cities in the Suburbs*. Toronto: University of Toronto Press.

Cassidy, R. 1980: *Livable Cities: A Grass-Roots Guide to Rebuilding Urban America*. New York: Holt, Rinehart and Winston.

Castells, M. 1977: *The Urban Question: A Marxist Approach*. London: Edward Arnold.

Castells, M. 1978: *City, Class and Power*. London: Macmillan.

Castells, M. 1983: *The City and the Grassroots: A Cross-Cultural Theory of Urban Social Movements*. London: Edward Arnold.

Catanese, A. J., Steiss, A. W. 1970: *Systemic Planning: Theory and Application*. Lexington: D. C. Heath.

Cederna, A. 1981: *Mussolini urbanista: Lo sventramento di Roma negli anni del Consenso*. Rome: Laterza.

Cerillo, A. Jun., 1977: The Impact of Reform Democracy: Early Twentieth Century Municipal Government in New York City. In: Ebner, M. E., Tobin, E.. M. (eds), 68–85.

Cervero, R. 1986: *Suburban Gridlock*. New Brunswick: Center for Urban Policy Studies.

Chadwick, G. 1971: *A Systems View of Planning: Towards a Theory of the Urban and Regional Planning Process*. Oxford: Pergamon.

Chapman, S. D. (ed.) 1971: *The History of Working-Class Housing*. Newton Abbot: David and Charles.

Chase, S. 1925: Coals to Newcastle. *Survey*, **54**, 143–6.

Chase, S. 1929: *Men and Machines*. New York: Macmillan.

Chase, S. 1931: *The Nemesis of American Business and other Essays*. New York: Macmillan.

Chase, S. 1932: *A New Deal*. New York: Macmillan.

Chase, S. 1934: *The Economy of Abundance*. New York: Macmillan.

Chase, S. 1936: *Rich Land Poor Land: A Study of Waste in the Natural Resources of America*. New York and London: Whittlesey House.

Cheape, C. W. 1980: *Moving the Masses: Urban Public Transit in New York, Boston, and Philadelphia, 1880–1912*. Cambridge, Mass.: Harvard UP.

Checkoway, B. 1984: Large Builders, Federal Housing Programs, and Postwar Suburbanization. In: Tabb, W., Sawers, L. (eds), 1978, 152–73.

Checkoway, B., Patton, C. V. (eds) 1985: *The Metropolitan Midwest: Policy Problems and Prospects for Change*. Urbana: University of Illinois Press.

Cherry, G. E. 1972: *Urban Change and Planning: A History of Urban Development in Britain since 1750*. Henley: Foulis.

Cherry, G. E. 1974: *The Evolution of British Town Planning*. London: Leonard Hill.

Cherry, G. E. (ed.) 1980a: *Shaping an Urban World*. London: Mansell.

Cherry, G. E. 1980b: The Place of Neville Chamberlain in British Town Planning. In: Cherry, G. E. (ed.), 1980a, 161–79.

Cherry, G. E. (ed.) 1981: *Pioneers in British Planning*. London: Architectural Press.

Cherry, G. E., Penny, L. 1986: *Holford: A Study in Architecture, Planning and Civic Design*. London: Mansell.

Cheshire, P., Hay, D. 1987: *Urban Problems in Europe*. London: Allen and Unwin.

Chicago Commission on Race Relations. 1922: *The Negro in Chicago: A Study of Race Relations and a Race Riot*. Chicago: University of Chicago Press.

Choi, C. Y., Chan, Y. K., 1979: Housing Development and Housing Policy in Hong Kong. In: Lin, T.-B. *et al.* (eds), 1979, 183–202.

Choudhuri, K., 1973: *Calcutta: Story of its Government*. New Delhi: Orient-Longman.

Christaller, W. 1966: *Central Places in Southern Germany* (translated by C. W. Baskin). Englewood Cliffs: Prentice-Hall.

Christensen, T. 1979: *Neighbourhood Survival*. Dorchester: Prism Press.

Christopher, A. J. 1977: Early Settlement and the Cadastral Framework. In: Kay, G., Smout, M. A. H. (eds), 1977, 14–25.

Chudacoff, H. P. 1975: *The Evolution of American Urban Society*. Englewood Cliffs: Prentice Hall.

Churchill, H. 1983: Henry Wright: 1878–1936. In: Krueckeberg, D. A. (ed.), 1983a, 208–24.

Cicin-Sain, B. 1980: The Costs and Benefits of Neighborhood Revitalization. In: Rosenthal, D. (ed.), 1980, 49–75.

Ciucci, G. 1979: The City in Agrarian Ideology and Frank Lloyd Wright: Origins and development of Broadacres. In: Ciucci, G. *et al.*, 1979, 293–387.

Ciucci, G., Dal Co, F., Manieri-Elia, M., Tafuri, M., 1979: *The American City: From the Civil War to the New Deal*. Cambridge, Mass.: MIT Press.

Clark, C. 1940: *The Conditions of Economic Progress*. London: Macmillan.

Clavel, P., 1986: *The Progressive City: Planning and Participation, 1969–1984*. New Brunswick, Rutgers UP.

Clavel, P., Forester, J., Goldsmith, W. W. (eds) 1980: *Urban and Regional Planning in an Age of Austerity*. New York: Pergamon.

Clawson, M. 1971: *Suburban Land Conversion in the United States: An Economic and Governmental Process*. Baltimore: Johns Hopkins UP.

Clawson, M. 1981: *New Deal Planning: the National Resources Planning Board*. Baltimore: Johns Hopkins UP.

Clawson, M., Hall, P. 1973: *Planning and Urban Growth: An Anglo-American Comparison.* Baltimore: Johns Hopkins UP.

Cloher, D. U. 1975: A Perspective on Australian Urbanization. In: Powell, J. M., Williams, M. (eds), 1975, 104–49.

Cohen, S. S., Zysman, J. 1987: *Manufacturing Matters: The Myth of the Post-Industrial Economy.* New York: Basic Books.

Coleman, A. 1985: *Utopia on Trial: Vision and Reality in Planned Housing.* London: Hilary Shipman.

Coleman, B. I. (ed.) 1973: *The Idea of the City in Nineteenth-Century Britain.* London: Routledge and Kegan Paul.

Collings, T. (ed.) 1987: *Stevenage 1946–1986: Images of the First New Town.* Stevenage: SPA Books.

Collins, J. 1969: *Lusaka: The Myth of the Garden City* (University of Zambia Institute of Social Research, *Zambian Urban Studies*, No. 2).

Collins, J. 1980: Lusaka: Urban Planning in a British Colony, 1931–64. In: Cherry, G. E. (ed.), 1980a, 227–52.

Comer, J. P. 1969: The Dynamics of Black and White Violence. In: Graham, H. D., Gurr, T. R. (eds), 1969, 341–54.

Comerio, M. C. 1984: Community Design: Idealism and Entrepreneurship. *Journal of Architectural and Planning Research*, **1**, 227–43.

Comhaire, J. 1961: Leopoldville and Lagos: Comparative Survey of Urban Condition in 1960. *Economic Bulletin for Africa*, **1.2**, 50–65.

Commonwealth of Australia Department of Home Affairs. 1913: *The Federal Capital: Report Explanatory of the Preliminary General Plan* (C. 9681). Melbourne: Albert J. Mullett, Government Printer.

Condit, C. W. 1973: *Chicago, 1910–29: Building, Planning, and Urban Technology.* Chicago and London: Chicago UP.

Condit, C. W. 1974: *Chicago, 1930–1970: Building, Planning, and Urban Technology.* Chicago and London: Chicago UP.

Conkin, P. K. 1959: *Tomorrow a New World: The New Deal Community Program.* Ithaca: Cornell UP.

Conkin, P. K. 1983: Intellectual and Political Roots. In: Hargrove, E. C. and Conkin, P. K. (eds), 1983, 3–34.

Connolly, P. 1982: Uncontrolled Settlements and Self-Build: what Kind of Solution? The Mexico City Case. In: Ward, P. M. (ed.), 1982, 141–74.

Consortium Developments. 1985: *Tillingham Hall Outline Plan.* London: Consortium Developments.

Cook, A., Gittell, M., Mack, H. (eds) 1973: *City Life, 1865–1900: Views of Urban America.* New York: Praeger.

Cook, P. 1983: Cook's Grand Tour. *Architectural Review*, **174.10**, 32–42.

Cooke, C. 1977: Activities of the Garden City Movement in Russia. *Transactions of the Martin Centre for Architectural and Urban Studies*, **1**, 225–49.

Cooke, C. 1978: Russian responses to the Garden City idea. *Architectural Review*, **163**, 354–63.

Cooke, P. N. 1983: *Theories of Planning and Spatial Development.* London: Hutchinson.

Cooley, C. H. 1909: *Social Organization: A Study of the larger Mind.* New York: Charles Scribner's Sons.

Cooley, C. H. 1918: *Social Process.* New York: Charles Scribner's Sons.

Cooney, E. W. 1974: High Flats in Local Authority Housing in England and Wales since 1945. In: Sutcliffe, A. (ed.), 1974, 151–80.

Co-Partnership Tenants' Housing Council 1906 (?): *Garden Suburbs, Villages and*

Homes: All about Co-Partnership Houses. London: The Council.

Coppock, J. T., Prince, H. (eds) 1964: *Greater London*. London: Faber and Faber.

Council for the Preservation of Rural England: Thames Valley Branch. 1929: *The Thames Valley from Cricklade to Staines* (prepared by the Earl of Mayo, S. D. Adshead and Patrick Abercrombie). London: University of London Press.

Council for the Preservation of Rural England: 'Penn Country' Branch 1933: *The Penn Country of Buckinghamshire*. London: CPRE.

Coward, J. 1987: Conceptions Outside Marriage: Regional Differences. *Population Studies*, **49**, 24–30.

Creese, W. L. 1966: *The Search for Environment: The Garden City Before and After*. New Haven: Yale UP.

Creese, W. L. (ed.) 1967: *The Legacy of Raymond Unwin: A Human Pattern for Planning*. Cambridge, Mass.: MIT Press.

Crossman, R. H. S. 1975: *The Diaries of a Cabinet Minister*. Vol. 1: *Minister of Housing 1964–66*. London: Hamish Hamilton and Jonathan Cape.

Crow, A. 1911: Town Planning in Old and Congested Areas, with special Reference to London. In: Royal Institute of British Architects, 1911, 407–26.

Cullen, G. 1953: Prairie Planning in the New Towns. *Architectural Review*, **114**, 33–6.

Cullingworth, J. B. 1979: *Environmental Planning* (Peacetime History). Vol. III: *New Towns Policy*. London: HMSO.

Culpin, E. G. 1913: *The Garden City Movement up-to-Date*. London: Garden Cities and Town Planning Association.

Cunningham, S. M. 1980: Brazilian cities old and new: Growth and Planning Experiences. In: Cherry, G. E. (ed.), 1980a, 181–202.

Curl, J. S. 1970: *European Cities and Society: A Study of the Influence of Political Change on Town Design*. London: Leonard Hill.

Dahl, R. A. 1961: *Who Governs? Democracy and Power in an American City*. New Haven and London: Yale UP.

Dakhil, F. H., Ural, O., Tewfik, M. F. 1979: *Housing Problems in Developing Countries* (Proceedings IAHS International Conference 1978), 2 vols. Chichester: John Wiley.

Dal Co, F. 1979: From Parks to the Region: Progressive Ideology and the Reform of the American City. In: Ciucci, G. *et al.*, 1979, 143–291.

Dannell, G. 1981: Planering viden skiljeväg. *Plan*, **35**, 52–6.

Darley, G. 1975: *Villages of Vision*. London: Architectural Press.

Daunton, M. J. 1983: *House and Home in the Victorian City: Working-Class Housing 1850–1914*. London: Edward Arnold.

Daunton, M. J. (ed.) 1984: *Councillors and Tenants: Local Authority Housing in English Cities, 1919–1939*. Leicester: Leicester UP.

Davidoff, P. 1965: Advocacy and Pluralism in Planning. *Journal of the American Institute of Planners*, **31**, 186–97.

Davies, J. C. 1969: The J-Curve of rising and declining Satisfactions as a Cause of some great Revolutions and a contained Rebellion. In: Graham, H. D., Gurr, T. R. (eds), 1969, 547–76.

Davies, R. O. 1975: *The Age of Asphalt: The Automobile, the Freeway, and the Condition of Metropolitan America*. Philadelphia: J. B. Lippincott.

Davis, A. F. 1967: *Spearheads for Reform: The Social Settlements and the Progressive Movement, 1890–1914*, New York: Oxford UP.

Davis, A. F. 1983: Playgrounds, Housing, and City Planning. In: Krueckeberg, D. A. (ed.), 1983c, 73–87.

Davis, D. H. 1969: *Lusaka, Zambia: some Town Planning Problems in an African City at Independence*. University of Zambia, Institute of Social Research (Zambian Urban Studies, No. 1).

Davison, G. 1979: Australian Urban History: A Progress Report. *Urban History Yearbook 1979*, 100–9. Leicester: Leicester UP.

Day, A. F. 1916: *John C. F. S. Day: His Forbears and Himself: A Biographical Study by one of his Sons*. London: Heath, Cranton.

Dear, M. S., Scott, A. J. (eds) 1981: *Urbanization and Urban Planning in Capitalist Society*. London: Methuen.

Dear, M. S., Scott, A. J. 1981b: Towards a Framework for Analysis. In: Dear, M. S., Scott, A. J. (eds), 1981a, 3–16.

De Carlo, G. 1948: The Housing Problem in Italy. *Freedom*, **9.12**, 2, and **9.13**, 2.

De Carlo, G. 1980: An Architecture of Participation. *Perspecta*, **17**, 74–9.

DeForest, R. W., Veiller, L. (eds) 1903: *The Tenement House Problem: Including the Report of the New York State Tenement House Commission of 1900*, 2 vols. New York: Macmillan.

Defries, A. 1927: *The Interpreter Geddes: The Man and his Gospel*. London: George Routledge and Sons.

Delouvrier, P. 1972: Paris. In: Robson, W. A. and Regan, D. E., 1972, II. 731–71.

Dennis, N. 1968: The Popularity of the Neighbourhood Community Idea. In: Pahl, R. E. (ed.), 1968, 74–92.

Derthick, M. 1972: *New Towns In-Town: Why a Federal Program Failed*. Washington, DC: The Urban Institute.

Dhuys, J.-F. 1978: Et si M. Chirac avait raison? *Macadam*, **4**, 9.

Diamond, S., Burke, F. G. 1966: *The Transformation of East Africa: Studies in Political Anthropology*. New York: Basic Books.

Dietrich, R. 1960: *Berlin: Neun Kapitel seiner Geschichte*. Berlin: Walter de Gruyter.

Dimaio, A. J. 1974: *Soviet Urban Housing: Problems and Politics*. New York: Praeger.

Dix, G. 1978: Little Plans and noble Diagrams. *Town Planning Review*, **49**, 329–52.

Dix, G. 1981: Patrick Abercrombie 1879–1957. In: Cherry, G. E. (ed.), 1981, 3–30.

Dobby, E. H. G. 1940: Singapore: Town and Country. *Geographical Review*, **30**, 84–109.

Dobriner, W. M. 1977: The suburban Evangel. In: Allen, I. L. (ed.), 1977, 121–40.

Dodd, K. S. 1933: Planning in the USSR. *Journal of the Town Planning Institute*, **20**, 34–53.

Dolce, P. C. (ed.) 1976: *Suburbia: The American Dream and Dilemma*. Garden City, NY: Anchor.

Donnison, D. V., Eversley, D. 1973: *London: Urban Patterns, Problems, and Policies*. London: Heinemann.

Dorsett, L. W. 1968: *The Challenge of the City, 1860–1910*. Lexington: D. C. Heath.

Dove, D. 1976: *Preserving the Urban Environment: How to Stop Destroying Cities*. Philadelphia: Dorrance and Co.

Dowall, D. 1984: *The Suburban Squeeze: Land Conversion and Regulation in the San Francisco Bay Area*. Berkeley: University of California Press.

Downs, A. 1957: *An Economic Theory of Democracy*. New York: Harper and Brothers.

Drake, S., Cayton, H. R. 1945: *Black Metropolis: A Study of Negro Life in a northern City*. New York: Harcourt, Brace.

Dreiser, T. 1947: *The Stoic*. Garden City: Doubleday.

Dubech, I., D'Espezel, P. 1931: *Histoire de Paris*, 2 vols. Paris: Les Éditions Pittoresques.

Du Bois, W. E. B. 1899: *The Philadelphia Negro: A Social Study*. Publications of the University of Pennsylvania: Series in Political Economy and Public Law. Philadelphia: The University.

Du Bois, W. E. B. 1920: *Darkwater: Voices from within the Veil*. London: Constable.

Duhl, L. J. (ed.) 1963: *The Urban Condition: People and Policy in the Metropolis*. New York: Basic Books.

Dulffer, J., Thies, J., Henke, J. 1978: *Hitlers Städte: Baupolitik im Dritten Reich*. Cologne: Bohlau.

Duncan, J. D., Duncan, N. G. 1984: A cultural Analysis of urban residential Landscapes in North America: The case of the Anglophile Elite. In: Agnew, J. A. *et al.* (eds), 1984, 255–76.

Dunkerley, H. *et al.* 1983: *Urban Land Policy: Issues and Opportunities*. New York: Oxford UP.

Dunleavy, P. 1981: *The Politics of Mass Housing in Britain, 1945–1975: A Study of Corporate Power and Professional Influence in the Welfare State*. Oxford: Clarendon Press.

Duquesne, J. 1966: *Vivre à Sarcelles? Le Grand Ensemble et ses problèmes*. Paris: Édition Cujas.

Durant, R. 1939: *Watling: A Survey of Social Life on a New Housing Estate*. London: P. S. King.

Dwyer, D. J. (ed.) 1971: *Asian Urbanization: A Hong Kong Casebook*. Hong Kong: Hong Kong University Press.

Dwyer, D. J. (ed.) 1972: *The City as a Centre of Change in Asia*. Hong Kong: Hong Kong University Press.

Dwyer, D. J. 1974a: Attitudes towards spontaneous Development in Third World Cities. In: Dwyer, D. J., 1974b, 204–18.

Dwyer, D. J. (ed.) 1974b: *The City in the Third World*. London: Macmillan.

Dyckman, J. W. 1970: Social Planning in the American Democracy. In: Erber, E. (ed.), 1970, 27–44.

Eberstadt, R. 1917 (1909) *Handbuch des Wohnungswesens und der Wohnungsfrage*. Jena: Gustav Fischer.

Eberstadt, R. 1911: Town Planning in Germany: The Greater Berlin Competition. In: Royal Institute of British Architects, 1911, 313–33.

Ebner, M. E., Tobin, E.M. (eds) 1977: *The Age of Urban Reform: New Perspectives on the Progressive Era*. Port Washington, NY: Kennikat.

Eckstein, S. 1977: *The Poverty of Revolution: The State and the Urban Poor in Mexico*. Princeton: Princeton UP.

Edblom, M., Strömdahl, J., Westerman, A. 1962: Mot en ny Miljö. *Arkitektur*, **62**, 205–24.

Editors of *Fortune* (eds) 1958: *The Exploding Metropolis*. Garden City, New York: Doubleday Anchor.

Edwards, A.M. 1981: *The Design of Suburbia: A Critical Study in Environmental History*. London: Pembridge Press.

Edwards, G. 1966. Comment: The Greenbelt Towns of the American New Deal. *Journal of the American Institute of Planners*, **32**, 225–8.

Edwards, J., Batley, R. 1978: *The Politics of Positive Discrimination: An Evaluation of the Urban Programme 1967–77*. London: Tavistock.

Edwards, S. (ed.) 1969: *Selected Writings of Pierre-Joseph Proudhon*. Garden City, NY: Anchor (Doubleday).

Eels, R., Walton, C. (eds), 1968: *Man in the City of the Future: A Symposium of Urban Philosophers*. New York: Arkville Press.

Egli, E. 1959–67: *Geschichte des Städtebaus*, 3 vols. Zurich: Rentsch.

Ehrlich, H. 1933: *Die Berliner Bauordnungen, ihre wichtigsten Bauvorschriften und deren Einfluss auf den Wohnhausbau der Stadt Berlin*. Jena: G. Neuenhahn.

Elazar, D. J. 1967: Urban Problems and the Federal Government: A Historical Inquiry. *Political Science Quarterly*, **82**, 505–25.

Ensor, R. 1936: *England 1870–1914*. Oxford: Oxford UP.

Epstein, D. G. 1973: *Brasilia, Plan and Reality: A Study of Planned and Spontaneous Urban Development*. Berkeley: University of California Press.

Erber, E. (ed.) 1970: *Urban Planning in Transition*. New York: Grossman.

Esher, L. 1981: *A Broken Wave: The Rebuilding of England 1940–1980*. London: Allen Lane.

Estall, R. C. 1977: Regional Planning in the United States: An Evaluation of Experience under the 1965 Economic Development Act. *Town Planning Review*, **48**, 341–64.

Etzioni, A. 1968: *The Active Society*. London: Collier–Macmillan.

Evenson, N. 1966: *Chandigarh*. Berkeley and Los Angeles: University of California Press.

Evenson, N. 1973: *Two Brazilian Capitals: Architecture and Urbanism in Rio de Janeiro and Brasilia*. New Haven: Yale UP.

Evenson, N. 1979: *Paris: A Century of Change, 1878–1978*. New Haven: Yale UP.

Evenson, N. 1984: Paris, 1890–1940. In: Sutcliffe, A. (ed.), 1984, 259–88.

Evers, H.-D. 1976: Urban Expansion and Land Ownership in Underdeveloped Societies. In: Walton, J., Masotti, L. H. (eds), 1976, 67–79.

Fabian Society 1884a: *Why Are The Many Poor?* (Fabian Tracts, No. 1). London: George Standring.

Fabian Society 1884b: *A Manifesto* (Fabian Tracts, No. 2). London: George Standring.

Fabian Society 1886: *What Socialism Is* (Fabian Tracts, No. 4). London: George Standring.

Fabian Society 1887: *Facts for Socialists: From the Political Economists and Statisticians* (Fabian Tracts, No. 5). London: Fabian Society.

Fabian Society 1889: *Facts for Londoners* (Fabian Tracts, No. 8). London: Fabian Society.

Fabos, J. G., Milde, G. T., Weinmayr, V. M. 1968: *Frederick Law Olmsted, Sr.: Founder of Landscape Architecture in America*. Amherst: University of Massachusetts Press.

Fainstein, N. I., Fainstein, S. S. 1983a: New Haven: The Limits of the local State. In: Fainstein, S. S. *et al.*, 1983b, 27–79.

Fainstein, N. I., Fainstein, S. S. 1983b: Regime Strategies, Communal Resistance, and Economic Forces. In: Fainstein, S. S. *et al.*, 1983b, 245–82.

Fainstein, S. S., Fainstein, N. I., Armistead, P. J. 1983a: San Francisco: Urban Transformation and the local State. In: Fainstein, S. S. *et al.*, 1983b, 202–44.

Fainstein, S. S., Fainstein, N. I., Hill, R. C., Judd, D. R., Smith, M. P. 1983b: *Restructuring the City: The Political Economy of Redevelopment*. New York: Longman.

Falk, N. 1986: Baltimore and Lowell: Two American Approaches. *Built Environment*, **12**, 145–52.

Faludi, A. 1973: *Planning Theory*. Oxford: Pergamon.

Faludi, A. 1985: The Return of Rationality. In: Breheny, M., Hooper, A. (eds), 1985, 27–47.

Farina, M. B. 1980: Urbanization, Deurbanization and Class Struggle in China 1949–79. *International Journal of Urban and Regional Research*, **4**, 485–502.

Farley, R. 1984: *Blacks and Whites: Narrowing the Gap*. Cambridge, Mass.: Harvard UP.

Fassbinder, H. 1975: *Berliner Arbeiterviertel, 1800–1918*. Berlin: Verlag für das Studium der Arbeiterbewegung.

Fava, S. F. 1956: Suburbanism as a Way of Life. *American Sociological Review*, **21**, 34–8.

Fava, S. F. 1975: Beyond Suburbia. *The Annals of the American Academy of Political and Social Sciences*, **422**, 10–24.

Fehl, G. 1983: The Niddatal Project – The Unfinished Satellite Town on the Outskirts of Frankfurt. *Built Environment*, **9**, 185–97.

Feibel, C., Walters, A. A. 1980: Ownership and Efficiency in Urban Buses (World Bank Staff Working Paper No. 371). Washington, DC: The World Bank.

Fein, A. 1967: *Landscape into Cityscape: Frederick Law Olmsted's Plans for a Greater New York City*. Ithaca: Cornell UP.

Fein, A. 1972: *Frederick Law Olmsted and the American Environmental Tradition*. New York: Braziller.

Fichter, R., Turner, J. F.C., Grenell, P. 1972: The Meaning of Autonomy. In: Turner, J. F. C., Fichter, R. (eds), 1972, 241–54.

Field, S. *et al.* 1981: *Ethnic Minorities in Britain: A Study of Trends in their Position since 1961* (Home Office Research Study, 6). London: HMSO.

Fishman, R. 1977: *Urban Utopias in the Twentieth Century: Ebenezer Howard, Frank Lloyd Wright and Le Corbusier*. New York: Basic Books.

Fishman, R. 1980: The Anti-Planners: The Contemporary Revolt against Planning and its Significance for Planning History. In: Cherry, G. E. (ed.), 1980a, 243–52.

Flink, J. J. 19175: *The Car Culture*. Cambridge, Mass.: MIT Press.

Fluck, T. A. 1986: *Euclid v. Ambler*: A Retrospective. *Journal of the American Planning Association*, **52**, 326–37.

Fogel, R. W., Engermann, S. L. 1974: *Time on the Cross: The Economics of American Negro Slavery*, 2 vols. London: Wildwood House.

Fogelson, R. M. 1967: *The Fragmented Metropolis: Los Angeles, 1850–1930*. Cambridge, Mass.: Harvard UP.

Fogelson, R. M. 1971: *Violence as Protest: A Study of Riots and Ghettos*. Garden City, NY: Anchor.

Foley, D. L. 1963: *Controlling London's growth: Planning the Great Wen, 1940–1960*. Berkeley: University of California Press.

Fonseca, R. 1969: The Walled City of Old Delhi. In: Oliver, P. H. (ed.), 1969, 103–15.

Ford, J. 1936: *Slums and Housing, with Special Reference to New York City: History, Conditions, Policy*, 2 vols. Cambridge, Mass.: Harvard UP.

Ford, C., Harrison, B. 1983: *A Hundred Years Ago: Britain in the 1880s in Words and Photographs*. London: Allen Lane.

Forester, J. 1980: Critical Theory and Planning Practice. *Journal of the American Planning Association*, **46**, 275–86.

Forshaw, J. H., Abercrombie, P. 1943: *County of London Plan*. London: Macmillan.

Fosler, R. S., Berger, R. A. 1982: *Public–Private Partnership in American Cities: Seven Case Studies*. Lexington, Mass.: Lexington Books.

Foster, M. S. 1981: *From Streetcar to Superhighway: American City Planners and Urban Transportation, 1900–1940*. Philadelphia: Temple UP.

Fox, K. 1985: *Metropolitan America: Urban Life and Urban Policy in the United States, 1940–1980*. London: Macmillan.

Frampton, K. 1968: Notes on Soviet Urbanism, 1917–32. *Architects' Yearbook*, **12**, 238–52.

Frampton, K. 1980: *Modern Architecture: A Critical History*. London: Thames and Hudson.

Frazier, E. F., 1932: *The Negro Family in Chicago*. Chicago: University of Chicago Press.

Frazier, E. F. 1939: *The Negro Family in the United States*. Chicago: University of Chicago Press.

Frazier, E. F. 1957: *The Negro in the United States*. New York: Macmillan.

Frazier, E. F. 1966: *The Negro Family in the United States*. Rev. and abridged ed. Chicago: University of Chicago Press.

French, R. A., Hamilton, F. E. I. 1979a: *The Socialist City: Spatial Structure and Urban Policy*. Chichester: John Wiley.

French, R. A., Hamilton, F. E. I. 1979b: Is there a Socialist City? In: French and Hamilton, 1979a, 1–22.

Fried, M. 1963: Grieving for a Lost Home. In: Duhl, L. J. (ed.), 1963, 151–71.

Fried, M. 1966: Grieving for a Lost Home: Psychological Costs of Relocation. In: Wilson, J. Q. (ed.), 1966, 359–79.

Fried, R. C. 1973: *Planning the Eternal City: Roman Politics and Planning since World War II*. New Haven and London: Yale UP.

Frieden, B. J. 1964: *The Future of Old Neighborhoods: Rebuilding for a Changing Population*. Cambridge, Mass.: MIT Press.

Frieden, B. J. 1965: The search for housing policy in Mexico City. *Town Planning Review*, **36**, 75–94.

Frieden, B. J., Kaplan, M. 1975: *The Politics of Neglect: Urban Aid from Model Cities to Revenue Sharing*. Cambridge, Mass.: MIT Press.

Frieden, B. J. 1979: *The Environmental Protection Hustle*. Cambridge, Mass.: MIT Press.

Friedman, L. M. 1968: *Government and Slum Housing: A Century of Frustration*. Chicago: Rand McNally.

Friedmann, J. 1955: *The Spatial Structure of Economic Development in the Tennessee Valley: A Study in Regional Planning* (Department of Geography, Research Paper No. 39). Chicago: University of Chicago Press.

Friedmann, J. 1973: *Retracking America: A Theory of Transactive Planning*. Garden City: Doubleday.

Friedmann, J., Hudson, B. 1974: Knowledge and Action: A Guide to Planning Theory. *Journal of the American Institute of Planners*, **40**, 1–16.

Friedmann, J., Wulff, R. 1976: *The Urban Transition: Comparative Studies of Newly Industrializing Societies*. London: Edward Arnold.

Friedmann, J., Weaver, C. 1979: *Territory and Function: The Evolution of Regional Planning*. London: Edward Arnold.

Fritsch, T. 1912 (1896): *Die Stadt der Zukunft*. Leipzig: Hammer Verlag.

Frolic, B. M. 1964: The Soviet City. *Town Planning Reivew*, **34**, 285–206.

Frolic, B. M. 1975: Moscow: The Socialist Alternative. In: Eldredge, H. W. (ed.) *World Capitals: Toward Guided Urbanization*. New York: Anchor Press–Doubleday.

Fry, E. C. 1972: Growth of an Australian Metropolis. In: Parker, R. S., Troy, P. N. (eds), 1972, 1–23.

Fuchs, C. J. (ed.) 1918: *Die Wohnungs- und Siedlungsfrage nach dem Kriege: Ein Programm des Kleinwohnungs- und Siedlungswesens*. Stuttgart: Wilhelm Mener-Ilschen.

Funigiello, P. A. 1983: City Planning in World War II: The Experience of the National Resources Planning Board. In: Krueckeberg, D. A. (ed.), 1983c, 152–69.

Gallion, A. B., Eisner, S. 1963: *The Urban Pattern*. Princeton: D. van Norstrand.

Galloway, T. D., Mahayni, R. G. 1977: Planning Theory in Retrospect: The Process of Paradigm Change. *Journal of the American Institute of Planners*, **43**, 62–71.

Gans, H. J. 1961a: Planning and Social Life: An Evaluation of Friendship and Neighborhood Patterns in Suburban Communities. *Journal of the American Institute of Planners*, **27**, 134–40.

Gans, H. J. 1961b: The Balanced Community: Homogeneity or Heterogeneity in Residential Areas. *Journal of the American Institute of Planners*, **27**, 176–84.

Gans, H. J. 1962: *The Urban Villagers: Group and Class in the Life of Italian–Americans*. New York: The Free Press.

Gans, H. J. 1967a: *The Levittowners: Ways of Life and Politics in a New Suburban Community*. London: Allen Lane.

Gans, H. J. 1967b: The Failure of Urban Renewal: A Critique and Some Proposals. In: Bellush, J., Hausknecht, M. (eds), 1967a, 465–84.

Gardiner, J. 1970: *Some Aspects of the Establishment of Towns in Zambia during the Nineteen Twenties and Thirties* (Zambian Urban Studies, No. 3). Lusaka: University of Zambia, Institute for African Studies (formerly Social Research).

Gardner, J. 1971: Educated Youth and Urban–Rural Inequalities, 1958–66. In: Lewis, J. W. (ed.), 1971, 235–86.

Garland, H. 1917: *A Son of the Middle Border*. London: John Lane, The Bodley Head.

Garrison, W. 1959–60: Spatial Structure of the Economy. *Annals of the Association of American Geographers*, **49**, 238–9, 471–82; **50**, 357–73.

Garside, P. L. 1984: West End, East End: London, 1890–1940. In: Sutcliffe, A. (ed.), 1984, 221–58.

Gatons, P. K., Brintall, M. 1984: Competitive Grants: The UDAG Approach. In: Bingham, R. D., Blair, J. P. (eds), 1984, 115–40.

Gauldie, E. 1974: *Cruel Habitations: A History of Working-Class Housing 1780–1918*. London: George Allen and Unwin.

G.B. Admiralty 1945: *Geographical Handbook: Germany*. Vol. IV: *Ports and Communications*. London: Naval Intelligence Division.

G.B. Commission into the Depression of Trade and Industry. 1886: *Final Report* (C. 4893), (*BPP* 1886, 23). London: HMSO.

G.B. Commission for Racial Equality 1980: *Ethnic Minorities and New or Expanding Towns*. London: The Commission.

G.B. Committee . . . Circumstances connected with the Disturbances at Featherstone. 1893: *Report* (C. 7234), (*BPP* 1893–4, 17). London: HMSO.

G.B. Committee . . . Origin and Character of the Disturbances in the Metropolis. 1886: *Report* (C. 4665), (*BPP* 1886, 34). London: HMSO.

G.B. Committee on the Qualifications of Planners. 1950: *Report* (Cmd. 8059), (*BPP* 1950, 14). London: HMSO.

G.B. Department of the Environment. 1977a: *Unequal City: Final Report of the Birmingham Inner Area Study*. London: HMSO.

G.B. Department of the Environment. 1977b: *Inner London: Proposals for Dispersal and Balance: Final Report of the Lambeth Inner Area Study*. London: HMSO.

G.B. Department of the Environment. 1977c: *Change or Decay: Final Report of the Liverpool Inner Area Study*. London: HMSO.

G.B. Department of the Environment. 1977d: *Inner Area Studies: Liverpool, Birmingham and Lambeth: Summaries of Consultants' Final Reports.* London: HMSO.

G.B. Home Office. 1981: *The Brixton Disorders, 10–12 April 1981: Report of an Inquiry by the Rt. Hon. The Lord Scarman, O.B.E.* (Cmnd. 8427), (*BPP* 1981–2). London: HMSO.

G.B. Local Government Boards for England and Wales, and Scotland. 1918: *Report of the Committee appointed by the President of the Local Government Board and the Secretary for Scotland to consider questions of Building Construction in connection with the Provision of Dwellings for the Working Classes in England and Wales, and Scotland, and report upon Methods of Securing Economy and Despatch in the Provision of such Dwellings* (Cd. 9191), (*BPP* 1918, 7). London: HMSO.

G.B. Manpower Services Commission. London Regional Manpower Intelligence Unit. 1981: *Ethnic Minority Employment in London.* 2 parts (Briefing Note No. 5). London: HMSO.

G.B. Minister without Portfolio. 1985: *Lifting the Burden* (Cmnd. 9571). London: HMSO.

G.B. Ministry of Health 1920a: *Type Plans and Elevations of Houses Designed by the Ministry of Health in Connection with State-Aided Housing Schemes.* London: HMSO.

G.B. Ministry of Health. 1920b: *Interim Report of the Committee appointed by the Minister of Health to consider and advise on the Principles to be followed in dealing with unhealthy Areas.* London: HMSO.

G.B. Ministry of Health. 1921: *Second and Final Report of the Committee appointed by the Minister of Health to consider and advise on the Principles to be followed in dealing with unhealthy Areas.* London: HMSO.

G.B. Ministry of Reconstruction Advisory Council. Women's Housing Sub-Committee. 1918: *First Interim Report* (Cd. 9166), (*BPP* 1918, 10). London: HMSO.

G.B. Ministry of Town and Country Planning. 1946: *Interim Report of the New Towns Committee* (Cmd. 6759), (*BPP* 1945–46, 14). London: HMSO.

G.B. Minister of Transport, Steering Group and Working Group. 1963: *Traffic in Towns: A Study of the long term Problems of Traffic in Urban Areas.* London: HMSO.

G.B. Ministry of Works and Planning. 1943: *Report of the Committee on Land Utilization in Rural Areas.* (Cmd. 6378). London: HMSO.

G.B. Royal Commission on the Distribution of the Industrial Population. 1940: *Report* (Cmd. 6153), (*BPP* 1939–40, 4). London: HMSO.

G.B. Royal Commission on the Geographical Distribution of the Industrial Population. 1937–9: *Minutes of Evidence,* 29 vols in 26. London: HMSO.

G.B. Royal Commission on the Housing of the Working Classes. 1885: Vol. I: *First Report,* Vol. II: *Minutes of Evidence and Appendices* (C. 4402), (*BPP* 1884–5, 30). London: Eyre and Spotiswoode.

G.B. Runnymede Trust 1982. *Ethnic Minorities in Britain: A Select Bibliography.* London: The Trust.

G.B. Secretary of State for the Environment. 1977: *Policy for the Inner Cities* (Cmnd. 6845). London: HMSO.

G.B. Select Committee on Emigration and Immigration (Foreigners) 1889. *Report* (HC 311), (*BPP* 1889, 10). London: Henry Hansard.

Geddes, P. 1904: *City Development: A Study of Parks, Gardens and Culture Institutes.* Edinburgh: Geddes and Co.

Geddes, P. 1905: Civics: as Applied Sociology. *Sociological Papers,* **1**, 101–44.

Geddes, P. 1912: The Twofold Aspect of the Industrial Age: Palaeotechnic and Neotechnic. *Town Planning Review,* **31**, 176–87.

Geddes, P. 1915: *Cities in Evolution*. London: Williams and Norgate.

Geddes, P. 1917a: *Town Planning in Lahore: A Report to the Municipal Council*. Lahore: Commercial Printing Works. Reprinted as: Geddes 1965a.

Geddes, P. 1917b: *Report on Town Planning, Dacca*. Calcutta: Bengal Secretariat Book Depot.

Geddes, P. 1917c: *Town Planning in Balrampur: A Report to the Hon'ble the Maharaja Bahadur*. Lucknow: Murray's Printing Press.

Geddes, P. 1918: *Town Planning towards City Development: A Report to the Durbar of Indore*. Indore: Holkore State Printing Press.

Geddes, P. 1925a: A Schoolboy's Bag and a City's Pageant. *Survey*, **53**, 525–29, 553.

Geddes, P. 1925b: Cities, and the Soils they grow from. *Survey*, **54**, 40–4.

Geddes, P. 1925c: The Valley Plan of Civilization. *Survey*, **54**, 288–90, 322–5.

Geddes, P. 1925d: The Valley in the Town. *Survey*, **54**, 396–400, 415–6.

Geddes, P. 1925e: Our City of Thought. *Survey*, **54**, 487–90, 504–7.

Geddes, P. 1925f: The Education of Two Boys. *Survey*, **54**, 571–5, 587–91.

Geddes, P. 1965a: *Urban Improvements: A Strategy for Urban Works* (Pt. 2: *Town Planning in Lahore*). Government of Pakistan, Planning Commission, Physical Planning and Town Planning Section.

Geddes, P. 1965b: *Reports on Re-Planning of Six Towns in Bombay Presidency, 1915*. Bombay: Government Printing and Stationery, Maharashtra State.

Geen, E., Lowe, J. R., Walker, K. 1963: *Man and the Modern City*. Pittsburgh: University of Pittsburgh Press.

Gelfand, M. I. 1975: *A Nation of Cities: The Federal Government and Urban America, 1933–1965*. New York: Oxford UP.

Gelman, T. 1924: The Planning of Moscow. *Town Planning Review*, **11**, 13–16.

George, H. 1898a: *The Complete Works of Henry George*. New York: Doubleday and McClure.

George, H. 1898b (1968): City and Country. In: George, H., 1898a, 234–40. Reprinted in: Dorsett, L. W., 1968, 4–7.

Gerckens, L. A. 1983: Bettmann and Cincinnati. In: Krueckeberg, D. A. (ed.), 1983a, 120–48.

Ghosh, M., Dutta, A. K., Ray, B. 1972: *Calcutta: A Study in Urban Growth Dynamics*. Calcutta: Firma K. L. Mukhopadhyay.

Gibb, A. 1983: *Glasgow: The Making of a City*. London: Croom Helm.

Gibberd, F. 1953: *Town Design*. London: The Architectural Press.

Gibson, A. 1979: *People Power: Community and Work Groups in Action*. Harmondsworth: Penguin.

Gibson, A. 1985: Lightmoor gives Hope for Wasted Resources. *Town and Country Planning*, **54**, 290–1.

Gilbert, A. (ed.) 1976: *Development Planning and Spatial Structure*. London: John Wiley.

Gilbert, A. (ed.) 1982: *Urbanization in Contemporary Latin America: Critical Approaches to the Analysis of Urban Issues*. Chichester: John Wiley.

Gilbert, A., Gigler, J. 1982: *Cities, Poverty and Development: Urbanization in the Third World*. New York: Oxford UP.

Gilbert, A., Ward, P. 1982: Low-income Housing and the State. In: Gilbert, A. (ed.), 1982, 79–127.

Gilbert, N., Specht, H. 1977: *Dynamics of Community Planning*. Cambridge, Mass.: Ballinger.

Gist, J. R. 1980: Urban Development Action Grants: Design and Implementation. In: Rosenthal, D. B. (ed.), 1980, 237–52.

Glaab, C. N., Brown, A. T. 1976: *A History of Urban America*. Second Edition. New York: Macmillan.

Glass, R. 1955: Urban Sociology in Great Britain: A Trend Report. *Current Sociology*, **4.4**, 5–19.

Glass, R. *et al.* 1965: *London: Aspects of Change*. (*Centre for Urban Studies, Report No. 3*). London: MacGibbon and Kee.

Glazer, N. 1968: Slums and Ethnicity. In: Sherrard, T. D. (ed.), 1968, 84–112.

Glazer, N. 1983: *Ethnic Dilemmas 1964–1982*. Cambridge, Mass.: Harvard UP.

Glazer, N., Young, K., (eds) 1983: *Ethnic Pluralism and Public Policy: Achieving Equality in the United States and Great Britain*. London: Heinemann Education.

Glynn, S. 1975: *Urbanisation in Australian History 1788–1900*. Sydney: Nelson.

Godschalk, D. R. (ed.) 1974: *Planning in America: Learning from Turbulence*. Washington, DC: American Institute of Planners.

Goetze, R., Goodman, R., Grenell, P., Linn, C., Peattie, L., Terner, D., Turner, J. 1968: Architecture of Democracy. *Architectural Design*, **38**, 354.

Goist, P. D. 1969: Lewis Mumford and 'anti-urbanism'. *Journal of the American Institute of Planners*, **35**, 340–7.

Goist, P. D. 1974: Patrick Geddes and the City. *Journal of the American Institute of Planners*, **40**, 31–37.

Goist, P. D. 1983: Seeing Things Whole: a Consideration of Lewis Mumford. In: Krueckeberg, D. A. (ed.), 1983a, 250–75.

Goldfield, D. R. 1979: Suburban Development in Stockholm and the United States: A Comparison of Form and Function. In: Hammarström, I., Hall, T. (eds), 1979, 139–56.

Goldsmith, W. W. 1982: Enterprise Zones: If they work we're in trouble. *International Journal of Urban and Regional Research*, **6**, 435–42.

Goldstein, S., Sly, D. F. (eds) 1977: *Patterns of Urbanization: Comparative Country Studies*. Dolhain (Belgium): Ordina.

Goodall, L. E., Sprengel, D. P. 1975: *The American Metropolis*. Second Edition. Columbus, Ohio: Charles E. Merrill.

Goodman, P., Goodman, P. 1960: *Communitas: Means of Livelihood and Ways of Life*. Second Edition. New York: Vintage Books.

Gottdiener, M. 1977: *Planned Sprawl: Private and Public Interests in Suburbia*. Beverly Hills: Sage.

Grabow, S. 1977: Frank Lloyd Wright and the American City: the Broadacres Debate. *Journal of the American Institute of Planners*, **43**, 115–24.

Grabow, S. 1983: *Christopher Alexander: The Search for a New Paradigm in Architecture*. Stocksfield: Oriel Press.

Gradidge, R. 1981: *Edwin Lutyens: Architect Laureate*. London: Allen and Unwin.

Graham, H. D., Gurr, T. R. (eds) 1969: *Violence in America: Historical and Comparative Perspectives*, 2 vols. Washington, DC: Government Printing Office.

Grant, J., Serle, G. (eds) 1957: *The Melbourne Scene: 1803–1956*. Melbourne: Melbourne UP.

Grava, S. 1978: Locally generated Transportation Modes of the Developing World. In: *Urban Transportation Economies: Proceedings of Five Workshops as Priority Alternatives, Economic Regulation, Labor Issues, Marketing, and Government Financing Responsibilities*, 84–95. Final Reporting March 1978. Washington, DC: Department of Transportation.

Greater London Council. 1969: *Tomorrow's London: A Background to the Greater London Development Plan*. London: GLC.

Greater London Regional Planning Committee. 1929: *First Report*. London: Knapp, Drewett.

Greater London Regional Planning Committee. 1933: *Second Report* (includes Interim Reports). London: Knapp, Drewett.

Green, C. M. 1963: *Washington: Capital City, 1879–1950*. Princeton: Princeton UP.

Green, C. M. 1965: *The Rise of Urban America*. New York: Harper and Row.

Green, H. A. 1979: Urban Planning in Nigeria. *Journal of Administration Overseas*, **18**, 22–33.

Greer, G., Hansen, A. H. 1941: *Urban Redevelopment and Housing: A Program for Post-War* (Planning Pamphlets, No. 10). Washington, DC: National Planning Association.

Greer, S. 1965: *Urban Renewal of American Cities: The Dilemma of Democratic Intervention*. Indianapolis: Bobbs-Merrill.

Gregg, D. J. 1986: The Origins and Philosophy of Parkways with particular Reference to the Contribution of Barry Parker. *Planning History Bulletin*, **8.1**, 38–50.

Grenell, P. 1972: Planning for invisible People. In: Turner and Fichter (eds), 1972, 95–121.

Griffith, E. S. 1974: *A History of American City Government: The Conspicuous Failure, 1870–1900*. New York: Praeger.

Grigsby, W. G. 1963: *Housing Markets and Public Policy*. Philadelphia: University of Pennsylvania Press.

Grindley, W. C. 1972: Owner-Builders: Survivors with a Future. In: Turner and Fichter (eds), 1972, 3–21.

Grote, L. (ed.) 1974: *Die deutsche Stadt im 19. Jahrhundert: Stadtplanung und Baugestaltung im industriellen Zeitalter*. Munich: Prestel Verlag.

Gugler, J. 1980: 'A Minimum of Urbanism and a Maximum of Ruralism': the Cuban experience. *International Journal of Urban and Regional Research*, **4**, 516–35.

Gugler, J., Flanagan, W. G. 1977: On the Political Economy of Urbanization in the Third World: The Case of West Africa. *International Journal of Urban and Regional Research*, **1**, 272–92.

Gugler, J., Flanagan, W. G. 1978: *Urbanization and Social Change in West Africa*. Cambridge: Cambridge UP.

Gupta, S. K. 1974: Chandigarh: A Study of Sociological Issues and Urban Development in India. *Architectural Design*, **44**, 362–8.

Gurley, J. G. 1975: Rural Development in China 1949–72, and the Lessons to be learned from it. *World Development*, **3**, 455–71.

Gurr, T. R. 1969: A comparative Study of civil Strife. In: Graham, H. D., Gurr, T. R. (eds), 1969, 443–86.

Gutheim, F. 1977: *Worthy of the Nation: The History of Planning for the National Capital*. Washington, DC: Smithsonian Institute Press.

Gutman, H. G. 1977: *Work, Culture, and Society in industrializing America. Essays in American Working-Class and Social History*. Oxford: Basil Blackwell.

Guttenberg, A. Z. 1978: City Encounter and Desert Encounter: Two Sources of American regional Planning Thought. *Journal of the American Institute of Planners*, **44**, 399–411.

Gwynne, R. N. 1985: *Industrialisation and Urbanisation in Latin America*. London: Croom Helm.

Haar, C. M. 1975: *Between the Idea and the Reality: A Study in the Origin, Fate and Legacy of the Model Cities Program*. Boston: Little, Brown.

Hague, C. 1984: *The Development of Planning Thought: A Critical Perspective*. London: Hutchinson.

Hake, A. 1977: *African Metropolis: Nairobi's Self-Help City*. London: Chatto and Windus (for Sussex UP).

Hall, J. M. 1982: *The Geography of Planning Decisions*. Oxford: Oxford UP.

Hall, P. 1968: The Urban Culture and the Suburban Culture. In: Eeels, R., Walton, C. (eds), 1968, 99–145.

Hall, P. 1971: Spatial Structure of Metropolitan England and Wales. In: Chisholm, M. and Manners, G., *Spatial Policy Problems of the British Economy*. Cambridge: Cambridge UP.

Hall, P. 1973: England in 1900. In: Darby, H. C. (ed.). *A New Historical Geography of England*. Cambridge: Cambridge UP.

Hall, P., Thomas, R., Gracey, H., Drewett, R. 1973: *The Containment of Urban England*, 2 vols. London: George Allen and Unwin.

Hall, P. 1977: Green Fields and Grey Areas. *Papers of the RTPI Annual Conference, Chester*. London: Royal Town Planning Institute.

Hall, P. 1978: Can Cities survive? The Potential and Limits of Action. *Ditchley Journal*, **5.2**, 33–41.

Hall, P. 1979: The European City in the Year 2000. In: Hammarström, I., Hall, T. (eds), 1979, 157–62.

Hall, P. 1980: *Great Planning Disasters*. London: Weidenfeld and Nicolson.

Hall, P. (ed.) 1981: *The Inner City in Context: The Final Report of the Social Science Research Council Inner Cities Working Party*. London: Heinemann.

Hall, P. 1982a: *Urban and Regional Planning*. Third Edition. London: George Allen and Unwin.

Hall, P. 1982b: Enterprise Zones: A Justification. *International Journal of Urban and Regional Research*, **6**, *416–21*.

Hall, P. 1984: *The World Cities*. Third Edition. London: Weidenfeld and Nicolson.

Hall, P. 1985: The People: Where will they go? *Planner*, **71.4**, 3–12.

Hall, P., Breheny, M., McQuaid, R., Hart, D. A. 1987: *Western Sunrise: The Genesis and Growth of Britain's Major High Tech Corridor*. London: Allen and Unwin.

Hall, P., Hay, D. 1980: *Growth Centres in the European Urban System*. London: Heinemann.

Hall, P., Hass-Klau, C. 1985: *Can Rail Save the City? The Impacts of Rail Rapid Transit and Pedestrianisation on British and German Cities*. Aldershot: Gower.

Hall, T. 1979: The Central Business District: Planning in Stockholm, 1928–1978. In: Hammarström, I., Hall., T. (eds), 1979, 181–232.

Halliman, D. M., Morgan, W. T. W. 1967: The City of Nairobi. In: Morgan, W. T. W. (ed.), 1967, 98–120.

Hamilton, F. E. I. 1976: *The Moscow City Region*. London: Oxford UP.

Hamm, M. F. (ed.) 1976a: *The City in Russian History*. Lexington: University of Kentucky Press.

Hamm, M. F. 1976b: The Breakdown of Urban Modernization: A Prelude to the Revolutions of 1917. In: Hamm, M. F., 1976a, 182–200.

Hamm, M. F. 1977: The modern Russian City: an historiographical analysis. *Journal of Urban History*, **4**, 39–76.

Hammarström, I., Hall, T. (eds) 1979: *Growth and Transformation of the Modern City: The Stockholm Conference September 1978*. Stockholm: Swedish Council for Building Research.

Hamzah, S. 1964: Urbanisation. In: Wang, G. (ed.) *Malaysia: A Survey*. London: Pall Mall Press.

Handlin, O., Burchard, J. (eds) 1963: *The Historian and the City*. Cambridge, Mass.: MIT Press and Harvard UP.

Hansen, A. H. 1927: *Business-Cycle Theory: Its Development and Present Status*. Boston: Gunn.

Hansen, A. M. 1932: *Economic Stabilization is an Unbalanced World*. New York: Harcourt, Brace.

Hansen, N. M. 1981: Development from Above: The Centre–Down Development Paradigm. In: Stöhr, W. B., Taylor, D. R. F. (eds), 1981, 15–38.

Hardinge of Penshurst, 1948: *My Indian Years 1910–1916*. London: John Murray.

Hardwick, P. A. 1977: The Transportation Systems. In: May, G., Smout, M. A. H. (eds), 1977, 94–112.

Hardy, C. O., Kuczynski, R. R. 1934: *The Housing Program of the City of Vienna*. Washington, DC: The Brookings Institution.

Hardy, D. 1979: *Alternative Communities in Nineteenth Century England*. London: Longman.

Hardy, D., Ward, C. 1984: *Arcadia for All: The Legacy of a Makeshift Landscape*. London: Mansell.

Hargrove, E. C., Conkin, P. K. (eds) 1983: *TVA: Fifty Years of Grass-Roots Bureaucracy*. Urbana: University of Illinois Press.

Harris, B. 1975: A Fundamental Paradigm for Planning. In: *Symposium on Planning Theory*, 1 (Planning Papers, 1). Philadelphia: Wharton School.

Harris, C. D. 1945: The Cities of the Soviet Union. *Geographical Review*, **35**, 107–21.

Harris, C. D. 1970: *Cities of the Soviet Union*. Chicago: Rand McNally.

Harris, C. D. 1970b: Population of Cities in the Soviet Union, 1897, 1926, 1939, 1959 and 1967 with Tables, Maps, and Gazetteer. *Soviet Geography: Review and Translation*, **11**, 307–444.

Harris, W. D. 1971: *The Growth of Latin American Cities*. Athens, Ohio: Ohio UP.

Harrison, B. 1982: The Politics and Economics of the urban Enterprise Zone Proposal: A Critique. *International Journal of Urban and Regional Research*, **6**, 422–8.

Harrison, J. B. 1980: Allahabad: A Sanitary History. In: Ballhatchet, K., Harrison, J., 1980, 166–95.

Harrison, P. F. 1972: Planning the Metropolis – A Case Study. In: Parker, R. S., Troy, P. N. (eds), 1972, 61–99.

Harrison, P. F. 1974: Planning the Metropolitan Areas. In: Burnley, I. H. (ed.), 203–20.

Hart, D. A. 1976: *Strategic Planning in London: The Rise and Fall of the Primary Road Network*. Oxford: Pergamon.

Hart, D. A. 1983: Urban economic Development Measures in West Germany and the United States. In: Young, K., Mason, C. (eds), 1983, 9–33.

Hartman, C. 1964: The Housing of Relocated Families. *Journal of the American Institute of Planners*, **30**, 266–86.

Hartman, C. 1966a: The Housing of Relocated Families. In: Wilson, J. Q., 1966, 293–335.

Hartman, C. 1966b: A Comment on the HHFA survey of Location. In: Wilson, J. Q., 1966, 353–8.

Hartman, C. 1984: *The Transformation of San Francisco*. Totowa: Rowman and Allanheld.

Hartman, C., Kessler, R. 1978: The Illusion and Reality of Urban Renewal: San Francisco's Yerba Buena Center. In: Tabb, W. K., Sawers, L. (eds), 1978, 153–78.

Hartmann, K. 1976: *Deutsche Gartenstadtbewegung: Kulturpolitik und Gesellschaftsreform*. Munich: Heinz Moos Verlag.

Hartog, R. 1962: *Stadterweiterungen der Zweiten Hälfte des 19. Jahrhunderts*. Darmstadt: Privately published.

Harvey, D. 1973: *Social Justice and the City*. London: Edward Arnold.

Harvey, D. 1982: *The Limits to Capital*. Oxford: Basil Blackwell.

Harvey, D. 1985: *Consciousness and the Urban Experience: Studies in the History and Theory of Capitalist Urbanization*. Baltimore: Johns Hopkins UP. Oxford: Basil Blackwell.

Harvey, D. 1985b: *The Urbanization of Capital: Studies in the History and Theory of Capitalist Urbanization*. Baltimore: Johns Hopkins UP. Oxford: Basil Blackwell.

Hausner, V. (ed.) 1987: *Critical Issues in Urban Economic Development*, 2 vols. Oxford: Oxford UP.

Hayden, D. 1976: *Seven American Utopias: The Architecture of Communitarian Socialism, 1790–1975*. Cambridge, Mass.: MIT Press.

Hayden, D. 1984: *Redesigning the American Dream: The Future of Housing, Work, and Family Life*. New York: W. W. Norton.

Hayek, F. A. 1944: *The Road to Serfdom*. London: George Routledge.

Hays, F. B. 1965: *Community Leadership: The Regional Plan Association of New York*. New York: Columbia UP.

Hearle, E. F. R., Niedercorn, J. H. 1964: *The Impact of Urban Renewal on Land-Use*. Santa Monica: The RAND Corporation (Memorandum RM-4186-RC).

Hebbert, M. 1981: Frederic Osborn 1885–1978. In: Cherry, G. E. (ed.), 1981, 177–202.

Hecker, M. 1974: *Die Berliner Mietskaserne*. In: Grote, L. (ed.), 1974, 273–94.

Hegemann, W. 1930: *Das steinerne Berlin: Geschichte der grössten Mietkasernenstadt der Welt*. Berlin: Gustav Kiepenheuer.

Hegemann, W. 1936: *City Planning: Housing, First Volume: Historical and Sociological*. New York: Architectural Book Publishing Co.

Held, D. 1980: *Introduction to Critical theory: Horkheimer to Habermas*. Berkeley: University of California Press.

Helmer, S. D. 1980: *Hitler's Berlin: Plans for reshaping the Central City developed by Albert Speer*. Ann Arbor: University Microfilms.

Herbers, J. 1987a: Poverty of Blacks spreads in Cities. *New York Times*, 26 January.

Herbers, J. 1987b: Governors urge Welfare Work Plan. *New York Times*, 22 February.

Herlitz, E. 1977: Från byalag till miljörelse. *Plan*, **31**, 216–22.

Heskin, A. D. 1980: Crisis and Response: An Historical Perspective on Advocacy Planning. *Journal of the American Planning Association*, **46**, 50–63.

Hewlett, R. G., Anderson, O. E., Jr. 1969: *The New World, 1939/1946. (A History of the United States Atomic Energy Commission*, Vol. I). University Park: Pennsylvania State UP.

Hightower, H. C. 1969: Planning Theory in Contemporary Professional Education. *Journal of the American Institute of Planners*, **35**, 326–9.

Hines, T. S. 1974: *Burnham of Chicago: Architect and Planner*. New York: Oxford UP.

Hirsch, A. R. 1983: *Making the second Ghetto: Race and Housing in Chicago, 1940–1960*. Cambridge: Cambridge UP.

Hirsch, F. 1977: *Social Limits to Growth*. London: Routledge and Kegan Paul.

Hofmeister, B. 1975: *Bundesrepublik Deutschland und Berlin* (Wissenschaftliche Länderkunde, 8). Berlin: Wissenschaftliche Buchgesellschaft.

Hogdal, L. 1981: 50-talet. *Arkitektur*, **81.5**, 14.

Höjer, J., Ljungqvist, S., Poom, J., Thörnblom, I. 1977: Vällingby, Tensta, Kista, vadå? *Arkitektur*, **77.2**, 16–21.

Holcomb, B., Beauregard, R. 1981: *Revitalizing Cities*. Washington, DC: Association of American Geographers.

Holm, L. 1977: Miljö och miljoner. *Plan*, **31**, 223–58.

Holm, L. 1981. Trettio års erfarenhet-grunden för en ny planlag. *Plan*, **35**, 57–60.

Holm, P. 1977. Det långa perspektivet – om planeringsproblem och planeringsideologie då och nu och sidan. *Plan*, **31**, 184–93.

Holt, R. T. and Turner, J. E. (eds) 1962: *Soviet Union:- Paradox and Change*. New York: Holt, Rinehart, Winston.

Hopkins, K. 1972: Public and Private Housing in Hong Kong. In: Dwyer, D. J. (ed.), 1972, 200–15.

Horowitz, D. L. 1983: Racial Violence in the United States. In: Glazer, N. and Young, K. (eds), 1983, 187–211.

Horsfall, T. C. 1904: *The Improvement of the Dwellings and Surroundings of the People: the Example of Germany*. Manchester: Manchester UP.

Howard, E. 1898: *To-morrow: A Peaceful Path to Real Reform*. London: Swan Sonnenschein.

Howe, I. 1976: *The Immigrant Jews of New York: 1881 to the Present*. London: Routledge and Kegan Paul.

Hubbard, P. J. 1961: *Origins of the TVA: The Muscle Shoals Controversy, 1920–1932*. Nashville: Vanderbilt UP.

Hubbard, T. K. 1923: *A Manual of Information on City Planning and Zoning: Including References on Regional, Rural, and National Planning*. Cambridge, Mass.: Harvard UP.

Hubbard, T. K., Hubbard, H. V. 1929: *Our Cities, Today and Tomorrow: A Study of Planning and Zoning Progress in the United States*. Cambridge, Mass.: Harvard UP.

Hudson, R., Williams, A. 1986: *The United Kingdom*. (Western Europe: Economic and Social Studies). London: Harper and Row.

Hughes, M. (ed.) 1971: *The Letters of Lewis Mumford and Frederic J. Osborn: A Transatlantic Dialogue 1938-70*. New York: Praeger.

Hulbert, J. 1984: Children as Parents. *New Republic*, 10 September, 15–23.

Hunter, R. 1901: *Tenement Conditions in Chicago: Report by the Investigating Committee of the City Homes Association*. Chicago: City Homes Association.

Hussey, C. 1953: *The Life of Sir Edwin Lutyens*. London: Country Life.

Hyndman, H. M. 1884: *The Coming Revolution in England*. London: William Reeves.

ILEA (Inner London Education Authority) 1987: *Ethnic Background and Education Results, 1985 and 1986* (RS 1120/87). London: ILEA.

Irving, R. G. 1981: *Indian Summer: Lutyens, Baker, and Imperial Delhi*. New Haven: Yale UP.

Isard, W. 1960: *Methods of Regional Analysis: An Introduction to Regional Science*. Cambridge, Mass.: MIT Press.

Jackson, A. A. 1973: *Semi-Detached London: Suburban Development, Life and Transport, 1900-39*. London: George Allen and Unwin.

Jackson, F. 1985: *Sir Raymond Unwin: Architect, Planner and Visionary*. London: Zwemmer.

Jackson, J. A. (ed.) 1969: *Migration* (Sociological Studies, 2). Cambridge: Cambridge UP.

Jackson, K. T. 1973: The Crabgrass Frontier: 150 years of suburban growth in America. In: Mohl, R. A., Richardson, J. F. (eds), 1973, 196–221.

Jackson, K. T. 1981: The Spatial Dimensions of social Control: Race, Ethnicity and Government Housing Policy in the United States, 1918–1968. In: Stave, B. M. (ed.), 1981, 79–128.

Jackson, K. T. 1984: The Capital of Capitalism: The New York Metropolitan Region, 1890–1940. In: Sutcliffe, A. (ed.), 1984, 319–54.

Jackson, K. T. 1985: *Crabgrass Frontier: The Suburbanization of the United States*. New York: Oxford UP.

Jacobs, A. B. 1976: *Making City Planning Work*. Chicago: American Society of Planning Officials.

Jacobs, A. B. 1983: 1968: Getting Going, Staffing Up, Responding to Issues. In: Krueckeberg, D. A. (ed.), 1983c, 235–57.

Jacobs, J. 1962: *The Death and Life of Great American Cities*. London: Jonathan Cape.

Jahn, M. 1982: Suburban Development in Outer West London, 1850–1900. In: Thompson, F. M. L. (ed.), 1982, 93–156.

James, H. 1907: *The American Scene*. New York: Harper and Brothers.

Janowitz, M. 1969: Patterns of collective racial Violence. In: Graham, H. D., Gurr, T. R. (eds), 1969, 317–40.

Jeffcoate, R. 1984: *Ethnic Minorities and Education*. London: Harper and Row.

Jefferys, M. 1965: Londoners in Hertfordshire. In: Glass, R. *et al.*, 1965, 207–55.

Jencks, C. 1981: *The Language of Post-Modern Architecture*. New York: Rizzoli.

Jephcott, P. 1971: *Homes in High Flats: Some of the Human Problems involved in multistorey Housing (University of Glasgow Social and Economic Studies, Occasional Papers No. 13)*. Edinburgh: Oliver and Boyd.

Joad, C. E. M. 1938: The People's Claim. In: Williams-Ellis, C., 1938, 64–85.

Johnson, C. D. 1941: *Growing Up in the Black Belt: Negro Youth in the Rural South*. New York: Shocken Books.

Johnson, J. H. 1964: The Suburban Expansion of Housing in Greater London 1918–1939. In: Coppock, J. T., Prince, H. (eds), 1964, 142–66.

Johnson, J. H. (ed.) 1974: *Suburban Growth: Geographical Processes at the Edge of the Western City*. London: John Wiley.

Johnson, D. A. 1984: Norris, Tennessee on the Occasion of its Fiftieth Anniversary. *Planning History Bulletin*, **6.1**, 32–42.

Johnson, P. B. 1968: *Land Fit for Heroes: The Planning of British Reconstruction, 1916–1919*. Chicago: University of Chicago Press.

Johnson, T. F., Morris, J. R., Butts, J. T. 1973 (1962): *Renewing America's Cities*. Westport, Conn.: Greenwood Press.

Johnston, N. J. 1983: Harland Bartholomew: Precedent for the Profession. In: Krueckeberg, D. A. (ed.), 1983a, 279–300.

Johnston, R. J. 1979: *Geography and Geographers: Anglo-American Human Geography since 1945*. London: Edward Arnold.

Jones, D. 1982: *Crime, Protest, Community and Police in Nineteenth Century Britain*. London: Routledge and Kegan Paul.

Jones, D. W., Jun. 1985: *Urban Transit Policy: An Economic and Political History*. Englewood Cliffs, NY: Prentice Hall.

Judd, D. R., Mendelson, R. E. 1973: *The Politics of Urban Planning: The East St Louis Experience*. Urbana: University of Illinois Press.

Kampffmeyer, H. 1908: Die Gartenstadtbewegung. *Jahrbücher für Nationalökonomie und Statistik*, III. Series, **36**, 577–609.

Kampffmeyer, H. 1918: Die Gartenstadtbewegung. In: Fuchs, C. J. (ed.), 1918, 331–49.

Kantor, H. A. 1973a: Charles Dyer Norton and the Origins of the Regional Plan of New York. *Journal of the American Institute of Planners*, **39**, 35–42.

Kantor, H. A. 1973b: The City Beautiful in New York. *New York Historical Society Quarterly*, **57**, 149–71.

Kantor, H. A. 1973c: Howard W. Odum: The Implications of Folk, Planning, and Regionalism. *American Journal of Sociology*, **79**, 278–95.

Kaplan, H. 1963: *Urban Renewal Politics: Slum Clearance in Newark*. New York: Columbia UP.

Karl, B. 1963: *Executive Reorganization and Reform in the New Deal: The Genesis of Administrative Management, 1900–1939.* Cambridge, Mass.: Harvard UP.

Kay, G. 1967: *A Social Geography of Zambia: A Survey of Population Patterns in a Developing Country.* London: University of London Press.

Kay, G. 1970: *Rhodesia: A Human Geography.* London: University of London Press.

Kay, G., Smout, M. A. H. (eds) 1977: *Salisbury: A Geographical Survey of the Capital of Rhodesia.* London: Hodder and Stoughton.

Keeble, L. 1959: *Principles and Practice of Town and Country Planning.* London: Estates Gazette.

Keles, R., Payne, G. 1984: Turkey. In: Wynn, M. (ed.), 1984a, 165–97.

Kemeny, J. 1981: *The Myth of Home Ownership.* London: Routledge and Kegan Paul.

Kendall, H. 1955: *Town Planning in Uganda: A Brief Description of the Efforts made by Government to control Development of Urban Areas from 1915 to 1955.* London: Crown Agents for Overseas Governments and Administrations.

Kent, T. J. 1964: *The Urban General Plan.* San Francisco: Chandler.

Kent, W. 1950: *John Burns: Labour's Lost Leader.* London: Williams and Norgate.

Kenward, J. 1955: *The Suburban Child.* Cambridge: Cambridge UP.

Kessner, T. 1977: *The Golden Door: Italian and Jewish Immigrant Mobility in New York City 1880–1915.* New York: Oxford UP.

Keynes, J. M. 1936: *The General Theory of Employment, Interest, and Money.* London: Macmillan.

Killingworth, C. M. 1968: The Continuing Labor Market Twist. *Monthly Labor Review*, **91.9**, 12–17.

Kilmartin, L. A. 1973: Urban Policy in Australia: The Case of Decentralisation. *The Australian and New Zealand Journal of Sociology*, **9.2**, 36–9.

Kilmartin, L., Thorns, D. C. 1978: *Cities Unlimited: the Sociology of Urban Development in Australia and New Zealand.* Sydney: George Allen and Unwin.

Kimble, G. H. T. 1951: The Inadequacy of the Regional Concept. In: Stamp, L. D., Wooldridge, S. W. (eds) *London Essays in Geography.* London: Longmans, Green.

King, A. D. 1974: The Language of Colonial Urbanization. *Sociology*, **8**, 81–110.

King, A. D. 1976: *Colonial Urban Development: Culture, Social Power and Environment.* London: Routledge and Kegan Paul.

King, A. D. (ed.) 1980a: *Buildings and Society: Essays on the Social Development of the Built Environment.* London: Routledge and Kegan Paul.

King, A. D. 1980b: Exporting Planning: the colonial and neo-colonial experience. In: Cherry, G. E. (ed.), 1980a, 203–26.

King, A. D. 1980c: Historical Patterns of Reaction to Urbanism: The Case of Britain 1880–1939. *International Journal of Urban and Regional Research*, **4**, 453–69.

King, A. D. 1984: *The Bungalow: The Production of a Global Culture.* London: Routledge and Kegan Paul.

Kirkby, R. J. R. 1985: *Urbanisation in China: Town and Country in a Developing Economy, 1949–2000 AD.* London: Croom Helm.

Kitchen, P. 1975: *A Most Unsettling Person: An Introduction to the Ideas and Life of Patrick Geddes.* London: Victor Gollancz.

Klapheck, R. 1930: *Siedlungswerk Krupp.* Berlin: Wasmuth.

Klein, M., Kantor, H. A. 1976: *Prisoners of Progress: American Industrial Cities 1850–1920.* New York: Macmillan.

Kleniewski, N. 1984: From Industrial to Corporate City: The Role of Urban Renewal. In: Tabb, W., Sawers, L. (eds), 1984, 205–22.

Knapp, J. M. 1895: *The Universities and the Social Problem*. London: Rivington Percival.

Knevitt, C. 1975: Macclesfield: The Self-Help G.I.A. *Architects' Journal*, **162**, 995–1002.

Knevitt, C. 1977: Down your Way: Current Projects by Rod Hackney. *Architects' Journal*, **166**, 630–4.

Knight, C. G., Newman, J. L. (eds) 1976: *Contemporary Africa: Geography and Change*. Englewood Cliffs: Prentice-Hall.

Kopp, A. 1970: *Town and Revolution: Soviet Architecture and City Planning, 1917–1935*. London: Thames and Hudson.

Krause, A. S. 1886: *Starving London*. London: Remington and Co.

Krause, R. 1958: *Der Berliner City: frühere Entwicklung/gegenwärtige Situation, mögliche Perspektiven*. Berlin: Duncker and Humblot.

Kropotkin, P. 1906: *The Conquest of Bread*, New York: Vanguard Press.

Kropotkin, P. 1908: *Modern Science and Anarchism*. New York: Mother Earth.

Kropotkin, P. 1913: *Fields, Factories and Workshops: or Industry Combined with Agriculture and Brain Work with Manual Work*. New, Revised and Enlarged Edition. New York: G.P. Putnam's Sons.

Kropotkin, P. 1920: *The State: Its Historic Role*. Fifth Edition. London: Freedom Press.

Kropotkin, P. 1971a (1927): Anarchist Morality. In: Baldwin, R. N. (ed.), 1971 (1927), 79–113.

Kropotkin, P. 1971b (1927): Modern Science and Anarchism. In: Baldwin, R. N. (ed), 1971 (1927), 146–94.

Kropotkin, P. 1971c (1927): Anarchism – Encyclopaedia Britannica Article. In: Baldwin, R. N. (ed.), 1971 (1927), 283–302.

Krueckeberg, D. A. 1980: The Story of the Planner's Journal, 1915–1980. *Journal of the American Planning Association*, **46**, 5–21.

Krueckeberg, D. A. (ed.) 1983a: *The American Planner: Biographies and Recollections*. New York and London: Methuen.

Krueckeberg, D. A. 1983b: From the Backyard Garden to the Whole U.S.A.: A Conversation with Charles W. Elliot, 2nd. In: Krueckeberg, D. A. (ed.), 1983a, 350–65.

Krueckeberg, D. A. (ed.) 1983c: *Introduction to Planning History in the United States*. New Brunswick, New Jersey: Rutgers University, Center for Urban Policy Research.

Krueckeberg, D. A. 1983d: The Culture of Planning. In: Krueckeberg, D. A. (ed.), 1983c, 1–12.

Krumholz, N. 1983: A Retrospective View of Equity Planning: Cleveland, 1969–1979. In: Krueckeberg, D. A. (ed.), 1983c, 280–94.

Kuhn, T. S. 1962: *The Structure of Scientific Revolutions*. Chicago: University of Chicago Press.

Lancaster, O. 1959: *Here, Of All Places: The Pocket Lamp of Architecture*. London: John Murray.

Lanchester, H. V. 1914: Calcutta Improvement Trust: Precis of Mr. E. P. Richard's Report on the City of Calcutta. *Town Planning Review*, **5**, 115–30.

Lanchester, H. V. 1918: *Town Planning in Madras: A Review of the Conditions and Requirements of City Improvement and Development in the Madras Presidency*. London: Constable and Co.

Lanchester, H. V. 1925: *The Art of Town Planning*. London: Chapman and Hall.

Lane, B. M. 1968: *Architecture and Politics in Germany, 1918–1945*. Cambridge, Mass.: Harvard UP.

Lang, M. H. 1982: *Gentrification amid Urban Decline: Strategies for America's Older Cities*. Cambridge, Mass.: Ballinger.

Langdon, P. 1986: *Orange Roofs, Golden Arches: The Architecture of American Chain Restaurants*. New York: Knopf.

Lange, A. 1972 (1961): *Berlin zur Zeit Bebels und Bismarcks: zwischen Reichsgründung und Jahrhundertwende*. Berlin: Das Neue Berlin.

Lappo, G. M. 1973: Trends in the Evolution of Settlement Patterns in the Moscow Region. *Soviet Geography: Review and Translation*, **14**, 13–24.

Lappo, G., Chikishev, A., Bekker, A. 1976: *Moscow – Capital of the Soviet Union*. Moscow: Progress Publishers.

Lärmer, K. 1975: *Autobahnbau in Deutschland 1933 bis 1945: zu den Hintergründen*. Berlin (East): Akademie-Verlag.

Larsson, L. O. 1978: *Die Neugestaltung der Reichshauptstadt: Albert Speers Generalbebauungsplan*. Stockholm: Almqvist and Wiksell.

Laska, S. B., Spain, D. (eds): 1980: *Back to the City: Issues in Neighborhood Revitalization*. New York: Pergamon.

Lavedan, P. 1952: *Histoire d'urbanisme. Époque contemporaine*. Paris: Henri Laurens.

Lavedan, P. 1959: *Géographie des villes*, Paris: Gaillimard.

Lavedan, P. 1960a: *Histoire de Paris*. Paris: Presses Universitaires de France.

Lavedan, P. 1960b: *Les Villes françaises*. Paris: Editions Vincent, Fréal.

Lavedan, P. 1975: *Histoire de l'urbanisme à Paris*. Paris: Hachette.

Leavitt, H. 1970: *Superhighway–Superhoax*. Garden City, N.Y.: Doubleday.

Le Corbusier 1929: *The City of Tomorrow and Its Planning*. London: John Rodher (translated by Frederick Etchells from *Urbanisme*: 8th Edition). Reprinted 1947 by Architectural Press.

Le Corbusier 1967 (1933): *The Radiant City*. London: Faber and Faber.

Le Corbusier, 1937: *Quand les Cathédrales étaient blanches: Voyage aus pays des timides*. Paris: Plon.

Le Corbusier 1948: *Concerning Town Planning*. London: Architectural Press (translated by Clive Entwistle from *Propos d'urbanisme*).

Le Corbusier, 1959: *L'Urbanisme des trois établissements humaines*. Paris: Éditions de Minuit.

Ledgerwood, G. 1985: *Urban Innovation: The Transformation of London's Docklands 1968–84*. Aldershot: Gower.

Lees, A. 1979: Critics of urban Society in Germany, 1854–1914. *Journal of the History of Ideas*, **40**, 61–83.

Lees, A. 1984: The Metropolis and the Intellectual. In: Sutcliffe, A. (ed.), 1984, 67–94.

Lees, A. 1985. *Cities Perceived: Urban Society in European and American Thought, 1820–1940*. Manchester: Manchester UP.

Lee, C. E. 1966: *Sixty Years of the Piccadilly*. London: London Transport.

Lees, R., Mayo, M. 1984: *Community Action for Change*. London: Routledge and Kegan Paul.

Lefebvre, H. 1968: *Le Droit à la ville*. Paris: Éditions Anthropos.

Lefebvre, H. 1972: *Espace et politique: Le Droit à la ville II*. Paris: Éditions Anthropos.

Lehning, A. (ed.) 1973: *Michael Bakunin: Selected Writings*. London: Jonathan Cape.

Lepawsky, A. 1976: The Planning Apparatus: a Vignette of the New Deal. *Journal of the American Institute of Planners*, **42**, 16–32.

Lerner, D. 1967: Comparative Analysis of Processes of Modernisation. In: Miner, H., 1967, 21–38.

Lewis, D. N. (ed.) 1971: *The Growth of Cities* (Architects' Year Book, XIII). London: Elek Books.

Lewis, J. W. (ed.) 1971: *The City in Communist China*. Stanford, Calif.: Stanford UP.

Lewis, N. P. 1916: *The Planning of the Modern City: A Review of the Principles Governing City Planning*. New York: John Wiley.

Lewis, O. 1952: Urbanization without Breakdown: A Case Study. *Scientific Monthly*, **75**, 31–41.

Lewis, O. 1961: *The Children of Sanchez*. New York: Random House.

Lewis, O. 1966: The Culture of Poverty. *Scientific American*, **215.4**, 19–25.

Lewis, O. 1967: *La Vida: A Puerto Rican Family in the Culture of Poverty – San Juan and New York*. London: Secker and Warburg.

Lewis, R. A., Rowland, R. H. 1976: Urbanization in Russia and the USSR, 1897–1970. In: Hamm, M. F. (ed.), 1976a, 205–21.

Liebs, C. H. 1985: *Main Street to Miracle Mile: American Roadside Architecture*. Boston: Little, Brown.

Lilienthal, D. E. 1944: *TVA: Democracy on the March*. New York and London: Harper and Brothers.

Lin, T.-B., Lee, R. P. L., Simonis, U.-E. (eds) 1979: *Hong Kong: Economic, Social and Political Studies in Development*. Folkestone: Dawson.

Lindblom, C. E. 1959: The Science of 'Muddling Through'. *Public Administration Review*, **19**, 79–88.

Lindström, J. 1977: Hur kunde det gå så illa?: Dialog fackmänallmänhet viktigast. *Plan*, **31**, 203–5.

Ling, A. 1943: *Planning and Building in USSR*. London: Todd.

Lipton, M. 1977: *Why Poor People Stay Poor: Urban Bias in World Development*. London: Temple Smith.

Little, K. L. 1974: *Urbanization as a Social Process: An Essay on Movement and Change in Contemporary Africa*. London: Routledge and Kegan Paul.

Lloyd, P. C., Mabogunje, A. L., Awe, B. (eds) 1967: *The City of Ibadan*. Cambridge: Cambridge UP.

Lloyd, P. C. 1979: *Slums of Hope? Shanty Towns of the Third World*. Manchester: Manchester UP.

Lokjine, J. 1977: *Le Marxisme, l'état et la question urbaine*. Paris: PUF.

London County Council. 1913: *Housing of the Working Classes in London: Note on the Action taken between 1855 and 1912 for the better Housing of the Working Classes in London, with special Reference to the Action taken by the London County Council between the years 1889 and 1912*. London: Odhams.

London County Council. 1928: *Housing: with particular Reference to Post-War Housing Schemes*. London: P. S. King.

Long, N. E. 1966: Local Government and Renewal Politics. In: Wilson, J. Q. (ed.), 1966, 422–34.

Lösch, A. 1954: *The Economics of Location*. Translated by W. H. Woglom and W. F. Stolper. New Haven: Yale UP.

Lowe, J. R. 1967: *Cities in a Race with Time: Progress and Poverty in America's Renewing Cities*. New York: Random House.

Lowitt, R. 1983: The TVA, 1933–45. In: Hargrove, E. C., Conkin, P. K. (eds), 1983, 35–65.

Lowry, I. S. 1964: *A Model of Metropolis*. Santa Monica: RAND Corporation (RM-4035-RC).

Lowry, I. S. 1965: A Short Course in Model Design. *Journal of the American Institute of Planners*, **31**, 158–66.

Lubetkin, B. 1932: Recent developments of Town Planning in the U.S.S.R. *Architectural Review*, **71**, 209–14.

Lubetkin, B. 1933: Town and Landscape Planning in Soviet Russia. *Journal of the*

Town Planning Institute, **18**, 69–75.

Lubove, R. 1960: Homes and 'A Few Well Placed Fruit Trees': An Object Lesson in Federal Housing. *Social Research*, **27**, 469–86.

Lubove, R. 1962a: New Cities for Old: The Urban Reconstruction Program of the 1930s. *Social Studies*, **53**, 203–13.

Lubove, R. 1962b: *The Progressives and the Slums: Tenement House Reform in New York City, 1890–1917*. Pittsburgh: University of Pittsburgh Press.

Lubove, R. 1963: *Community Planning in the 1920s: The Contribution of the Regional Planning Association of America*. Pittsburgh: Pittsburgh UP.

Lubove, R. 1967: *The Urban Community: Housing and Planning in the Progressive Era*. Englewood Cliffs: Prentice Hall.

Lubove, R. 1969: *Twentieth-Century Pittsburgh: Government, Business, and Environmental Change*. New York: John Wiley and Sons.

Lundqvist, J. 1981: Tanzania: Socialist Ideology. Bureaucratic Reality, and Development from Below. In: Stöhr, W., Taylor, D. R. F. (eds), 1981, 329–49.

Lutyens, E. (1982): *Lutyens: The Work of the English Architect Sir Edwin Lutyens (1869–1944)*. London: Arts Council of Great Britain.

Lutyens, M. 1980: *Edwin Lutyens*. London: John Murray.

Lyall, K. 1982: A Bicycle Built-for-two: Public–Private Partnership in Baltimore. In: Fosler, R. S., Berger, R. A. (eds), 1982, 17–57.

Lynch, K. 1960: *The Image of the City*. Cambridge, Mass.: MIT Press.

Lynd, H. M., 1945: *England in the Eighteen-Eighties: Toward a Social Basis for Freedom*. Oxford: Oxford UP.

Mabogunje, A. L. 1967: The Morphology of Ibadan. In: Lloyd, P. C. *et al.*, 1967, 35–56.

Mabogunje, A. L. 1968: *Urbanization in Nigeria*. London: University of London Press.

Mabogunje, A. L. 1980: *The Development Process: A Spatial Perspective*. London: Hutchinson University Library.

Mabogunje, A. L., Hardoy, J. E., Misra, R. P. 1978: *Shelter Provision in Developing Countries: The Influence of Standards and Criteria* (*Scope*, 11). Chichester: John Wiley.

McCarthy, M. P. 1970: Chicago Businessmen and the Burnham Plan. *Journal of the Illinois State Historical Society*, **63**, 228–56.

McCarthy, T. A. 1978: *The Critical Theory of Jürgen Habermas*. Cambridge, Mass.: MIT Press.

McClendon, D. 1984: Rail Transit in North America. *Planning*, **50.6**, 22–3.

McCraw, T. K. 1970: *Morgan vs. Lilienthal: The Feud within the TVA*. Chicago: Loyola UP.

McCraw, T. K. 1971: *TVA and the Power Fight, 1933–1939*. Philadelphia: Lippincott.

Macdonald, M. C. D. 1984: *America's Cities: A Report on the Myth of Urban Renaissance*. New York: Simon and Schuster.

Macfadyen, D. 1933: *Sir Ebenezer Howard and the Town Planning Movement*. Manchester: Manchester UP.

MacFarland, J. R. 1966: The Administration of the New Deal Greenbelt Towns. *Journal of the American Institute of Planners*, **32**, 217–25.

McGee, T. G. 1967: *The Southeast Asian City: A Social Geography of the Primate Cities of Southeast Asia*. London: Bell.

McGee, T. G. 1971: *The Urbanization Process in the Third World: Explorations in Search of a Theory*. London: Bell.

McGee, T. G. 1979: The Poverty Syndrome: Making out in the Southeast Asian City. In: Bromley, R., Gerry, C. (eds), 1979, 45–68.

Machler, M. 1932: Town Development in Soviet Russia. *Journal of the Town Planning Institute*, **18**, 94–7.

McKay, D. H., Cox, A. W. 1979: *The Politics of Urban Change*. London: Croom Helm.

MacKaye, B. 1925: The New Exploration. *Survey*, **54**, 153–7 and 192.

MacKaye, B. 1928: *The New Exploration*. New York: Harcourt Brace.

MacKaye, B. 1930: The Townless Highway. *New Republic*, **62**, 93–5.

McKelvey, B. 1963: *The Urbanization of America. 1860–1915*. Brunswick: Rutgers UP.

McKelvey, B. 1968: *The Emergence of Metropolitan America, 1915–1966*. New Brunswick: Rutgers UP.

McKelvey, B. 1969: *The City in American History*. London: George Allen and Unwin.

McKelvey, B. 1973: *American Urbanization: A Comparative History*. Glenview, Ill.: Scott, Foresman.

McLeod, R. 1971: *Style and Society: Architectural Ideology in Britain, 1835–1914*. London: RIBA Publications.

McLoughlin, J. B. 1969: *Urban and Regional Planning: A Systems Approach*. London: Faber and Faber.

McMaster, D. N. 1968: The Colonial District Town in Uganda. In: Beckinsale, R. P., Houston, J. M. (eds), 1968, 330–51.

McVicar, K. G. 1968: Pumwani – The Role of a Slum Community in Providing a Catalyst for Culture Change in East Africa. In: Berger, H. (ed.), 1968, 157–67.

Mairet, P. 1957: *Pioneer of Sociology: The Life and Letters of Patrick Geddes*. London: Lund Humphries.

Makielski, S. J. 1966: *The Politics of Zoning: The New York Experience*. New York: Columbia UP.

Malone, D. 1936: *Dictionary of American Biography*. Vol. XX: New York: Charles Scribner's Sons.

Mandelbaum, S. J. 1980: Urban Pasts and Urban Policies. *Journal of Urban History*, **6**, 453–83.

Mandelbaum, S. J. 1985: Thinking about Cities as Systems: Reflections on the History of an Idea. *Journal of Urban History*, **11**, 139–50.

Mangin, W. (P.) (ed.) 1970a: *Peasants in Cities: Readings in the Anthropology of Urbanization*. Boston: Houghton Mifflin.

Mangin, W. (P.) 1970b: Urbanization Case History in Peru. In: Mangin, W. (P.), 1970a, 47–54.

Mangin, W. (P.), Turner, J. C. 1969: Benavides and the Barriada Movement. In: Oliver, P. (H.) (ed.), 1969, 127–36.

Manieri-Elia, M. 1979: Toward an 'Imperial City': Daniel H. Burnham and the City Beautiful Movement. In: Ciucci, C. *et al.*, 1979, 1–142.

Mann, E. 1968: Nairobi – from Colonial to National Capital. In: Berger, H. (ed.), 1968, 141–56.

Mann, L. D. 1972: Social Science Advances and Planning Applications: 1900–1965. *Journal of the American Institute of Planners*, **38**, 346–58.

Marcuse, P. 1980: Housing Policy and City Planning: The Puzzling Split in the United States, 1893–1911. In: Cherry, G. E. (ed.), 1980a, 23–58.

Markelius, S. 1962: Stockholms City. *Arkitektur*, **62**, 274–87. (English Summary: xxxvi–xxxvii.)

Marris, P. 1961: *Family and Social Change in an African City: A Study of Rehousing in Lagos*. London: Routledge and Kegan Paul.

Marsh, J. 1982: *Back to the Land: The Pastoral Impulse in England, from 1880 to 1914*. London: Quartet.

Marshall, A. 1884: The Housing of the London Poor. I. Where to house them. *Contemporary Review*, **45**, 224–31.

Martin, R. 1982: The Formulation of a Self-Help Project in Lusaka. In: Ward, P. M. (ed.), 1982, 251–74.

Masser, I. 1980: An emerging World City. *Town and Country Planning*, **49**, 301–3.

Massey, D. 1982: Enterprise Zones: A Political Issue. *International Journal of Urban and Regional Research*, **6**, 429–34.

Massey, D. 1984: *Spatial Divisions of Labour: Social Structures and the Geography of Production*. London: Macmillan.

Massey, D., Meegan, R. 1982: *The Anatomy of Job Loss: The How, Why and Where of Employment Decline*. London: Methuen.

Masterman, C. F. G. 1909: *The Condition of England*. London: Methuen.

Masterman, C. F. G. *et al.* 1901: *The Heart of the Empire: Discussion on Problems of Modern City Life in England with an Essay on Imperialism*. London: T. Fisher Unwin.

Matzerath, H. 1978: Städtewachstum und Eingemeindungen im 19. Jahrhundert. In: Reulecke, J. (ed.), 1978, 57–89.

Matzerath, H. 1984: Berlin, 1890–1940. In: Sutcliffe, A. (ed.), 1984, 289–318.

Mawson, D. 1984: T. H. Mawson (1861–1933) – Landscape Architect and Town Planner. *Journal of the Royal Society of Arts*, **132**, 184–99.

Mawson, T. H. 1927: *The Life and Work of an English Landscape Architect*. London: Richards Press.

May, E. 1961: Cities of the Future. *Survey*, **38**, 179–85.

Mayer, H. M., Wade, R. C. 1969: *Chicago: Growth of a Metropolis*. Chicago: University of Chicago Press.

Mearns, A. 1883: *The Bitter Cry of Outcast London: An Inquiry into the Condition of the Abject Poor*. London: James Clarke.

Meehan, E. J. 1975: *Public Housing Policy: Convention versus Reality*. New Brunswick, NJ: Rutgers University, Center for Urban Policy Research.

Meehan, E. J. 1977: The Rise and Fall of Public Housing: Condemnation without Trial. In: Phares, D. (ed.), 1977, 3–42.

Meehan, E. J. 1979: *The Quality of Federal Policymaking: Programmed Failure in Public Housing*. Columbia: University of Missouri Press.

Mehr, H. 1972: Stockholm. In: Robson, W. A., Regan, D. E. (eds), 1972, II. 873–901.

Meier, A., Rudwick, E. 1969: Black Violence in the 20th Century: A Study in Rhetoric and Retaliation. In: Graham, H. D., Gurr, T. R. (eds), 1969, 307–16.

Meller, H.E. (ed.) 1979: *The Ideal City*. Leicester: University Press.

Meller, H. 1981: Patrick Geddes 1854–1932. In: Cherry, G. E. (ed.), 1981, 46–71.

Menzler, F. A. A. 1951: Lord Ashfield. *Public Administration*, **29**, 99–112.

Meyerson, M. 1961: Utopian Traditions and the Planning of Cities. *Daedalus*, **90.1**, 180–93.

Meyerson, M., Banfield, E. C. 1955: *Politics, Planning and the Public Interest*. New York: Free Press.

Miller, M. 1981: Raymond Unwin 1863–1940. In: Cherry, G. E. (ed.), 1981, 72–102.

Miller, M. 1983: Letchworth Garden City Eighty Years On. *Built Environment*, **9**, 167–84.

Miner, H. (ed.) 1967: *The City in Modern Africa*. London: Pall Mall Press.

Minney, R. J. 1958: *Viscount Addison: Leader of the Lords*. London: Odhams Press.

Mitchell, B. R. 1975: *European Historical Statistics, 1750–1970*. London: Macmillan.

Mitchell, J. C. 1969: Structural Plurality, Urbanization and Labour Circulation in Southern Rhodesia. In: Jackson, J. A. (ed.), 1969, 156–80.

Mitchell, N. 1972: *The Indian Hill Station: Kodaikanal*. University of Chicago, Department of Geography, Research Paper, No. 141.

Mitchell, R. B., Rapkin, C. 1954: *Urban Traffic: A Function of Land Use*. New York: Columbia UP.

Mohl, R. A., Richardson, J. F. (eds) 1973: *The Urban Experience: Themes in American History*. Belmont, CA: Wadsworth.

Mollenkopf, J. H. 1978: The Postwar Politics of Urban Development. In: Tabb, W. K., Sawers, L. (eds), 1978, 117–52.

Mollenkopf, J. H. 1983: *The Contested City*. Princeton: Princeton UP.

Montgomery, R. 1985: Pruitt–Igoe: Policy Failure or Societal Symptom. In: Checkoway, B., Patton, C. V. (eds), 1985, 229–43.

Moore, C. 1921: *Daniel H. Burnham: Architect, Planner of Cities*. Boston and New York: Houghton Mifflin.

Moore, C., Becker, P., Campbell, R. 1984: *The City Observed – Los Angeles: A Guide to its Architecture and Landscapes*. New York: Vintage Books.

Morgan, A. E. 1974: *The Making of TVA*. Buffalo: Prometheus Books.

Morgan, W. T. W. (eds) 1967: *Nairobi: City and Region*. Nairobi: Oxford UP.

Morizet, A. 1932: *Du vieux Paris au Paris moderne: Haussmann et ses prédécesseurs*. Paris: Hachette.

Moynihan, D. P. 1965: *The Negro Family: The Case for National Action*. Washington, DC: U.S. Department of Labor Office of Policy Planning and Research.

Moynihan, D. P. 1986: *Family and Nation: The Godkin Lectures, Harvard University*. New York: Harcourt, Brace.

Muench, L. H. and C. Z. 1968: Planning and Antiplanning in Nigeria: Lagos and Ibadan. *Journal of the American Institute of Planners*, **34**, 374–81.

Muller, T. 1976: *Economic Impacts of Land Development: Economic, Housing and Property Values*. Washington, DC: The Urban Institute.

Mullin, J. R. 1977: American Perceptions of German City Planning at the Turn of the Century. *Urbanism Past and Present*, **3**, 5–15.

Mullin, J. R. 1977: City Planning in Frankfurt, Germany, 1925–1932: A Study in Practical Utopianism. *Journal of Urban History*, **4**, 3–28.

Mumford, L. 1923: *The Story of Utopias*. London: Harrap.

Mumford, L. 1925a: The Fourth Migration. *Survey*, **54**, 130–3.

Mumford, L. 1925b: Regions – To Live In. *Survey*, **54**, 151–2.

Mumford, L. 1930: Mass-Production and the Modern House. *Architectural Record*, **67**, 13–20, 110–16.

Mumford, L. 1938: *The Culture of Cities*. London: Secker and Warburg.

Mumford, L. 1954: The Neighbourhood and the Neighbourhood Unit. *Town Planning Review*, **24**, 256–70.

Mumford, L. 1961: *The City in History: its Origins, its Transformations, and its Prospects*. New York: Harcourt, Brace.

Mumford, L. 1964: *The Highway and the City*. New York: Mentor Books.

Mumford, L. 1982: *Sketches from Life: The Autobiography of Lewis Mumford: The Early Years*. New York: Dial Press.

Murphey, R. 1977: *The Outsiders: The Western Experience in India and China*. Ann Arbor: University of Michigan Press.

Murphey, R. 1980: *The Fading of the Maoist Vision: City and Country in China's Development*. London: Methuen.

Murphey, R. 1984: City as a Mirror of Society: China, Tradition and Modernization.

In: Agnes, J. A. *et al.* (eds), 1984, 186–204.

Muschamp, H. 1983: *Man About Town: Frank Lloyd Wright in New York City*. Cambridge, Mass.: MIT Press.

Muthesius, H. 1908–11: *Das englische Haus: Entwicklung, Bedingungen, Anlage, Aufbau, Einrichtung und Innenraum*, 3 vols. Second Revised Edition. Berlin: Ernst Wasmuth.

Myhra, D. 1974: Rexford Guy Tugwell: Initiator of America's Greenbelt New Towns, 1935 to 1938. *Journal of the American Institute of Planners*, **40**, 176–88.

Myrdal, G. 1944: *An American Dilemma: The Negro Problem and Modern Democracy*. New York: Harper and Brothers.

Nairn, I. 1955: Outrage (A Special number of the Architectural Review). *Architectural Review*, **117**, 363–454.

Nairn, I. 1965: *The American Landscape: A Critical View*. New York: Random House.

Nehru, J. 1936: *An Autobiography: with Musings on Recent Events in India*. London: John Lane, The Bodley Hed.

Neild, S. M. 1979: Colonial Urbanism: The Development of Madras City in the Eighteenth and Nineteenth Centuries. *Modern Asian Studies*, **13**, 217–46.

Nelson, W. H. 1967: *Small Wonder: The Amazing Story of the Volkswagen*. London: Hutchinson.

Nettlefold, J. S. 1914: *Practical Town Planning*. London: The St. Catherine Press.

Neufang, H. 1963: Die Siedlungsverband Ruhrkohlenbezirk (1920–1963). *Die öffentliche Verwaltung*, **16**, 812–19.

Neumeyer, F. 1978: Zum Werkwohnungsbau in Deutschland um 1900. In: Siepmann, D. (ed.) *Kunst und Alltag um 1900*. Lahn–Giessen: Anabas Verlag.

Neuse, S. M. 1983: TVA at Age Fifty – Reflections and Retrospect. *Public Administration Review*, **43**, 491–9.

Neutze, G. M. 1977: *Urban Development in Australia: A Descriptive Analysis*. Sydney: George Allen and Unwin.

Neville, R. J. W. 1965: The Areal Distribution of Population in Singapore. *Journal of Tropical Geography*, **20**, 16–25.

Nevins, A. 1954: *Ford: The Times, The Man, The Company*. New York: Charles Scribner's Sons.

Newman, O. 1972: *Defensible Space: Crime Prevention and Urban Design*. New York: Macmillan.

Newman, O. 1980: *Community of Interest*. Garden City, NY: Anchor–Doubleday.

'New Townsmen' 1918: *New Towns after the War: An Argument for Garden Cities*. London: J. M. Dent.

Niethammer, L. 1981: Some Elements of the Housing Reform Debate in Nineteenth Century Europe: Or, On the Making of a new Paradigm of social Control. In: Stave, B. M. (ed.), 1981, 129–64.

Nocks, B. C. 1974: Case Studies: A Decade of Planning Education at Three Schools. In: Godschalk, D. R. (ed.), 1974, 206–26.

Nolen, J. (ed.) 1916a: *City Planning: A Series of Papers Presenting the Essential Elements of a City Plan*. New York: D. Appleton.

Nolen, J. 1916b: The Subdivision of Land. In: Nolen, J. (ed.), 1916a, 19–47.

O'Connor, A. M. 1981: *Urbanization in Tropical Africa: An Annotated Bibliography*. Boston: G. K. Hall.

O'Connor, A. 1983: *The African City*. London: Hutchinson University Library for Africa.

Ödmann, E., Dahlberg, G.-B. 1970: Urbanisation in Sweden: Means and Methods for the Planning. Stockholm: Allmanna Forlaget.

Odum, H. W. 1910: *Social and Mental Traits of the Negro: Research into the Conditions of the Negro Race in Southern Towns: A Study in Race Traits, Tendencies and Prospects* (Studies in History, Economics and Public Law, 37, No. 3). New York: Columbia University.

Odum, H. W. 1926: *An Approach to Public Welfare and Social Work.* Chapel Hill: University of North Carolina Press.

Odum, H. W. 1936: *Southern Regions of the United States.* Chapel Hill: University of North Carolina Press.

Odum, H. W., Jocher, K. (eds) 1945: *In Search of the Regional Balance of America.* Chapel Hill: University of North Carolina Press.

Odum, H. W., Johnson, G. B. 1925: *The Negro and his Songs.* Chapel Hill: University of North Carolina Press.

Odum, H. W., Moore, H. E. 1938: *American Regionalism: A Cultural-Historical Approach to National Integration.* New York: Henry Holt and Co.

Oliver, P. H. (ed.) 1969: *Shelter and Society.* London: Barrie Rokliff: The Cresset Press.

Oliver, P. (H.) (ed.) 1975: *Shelter in Africa.* London: Barrie and Jenkins.

Oliver, P. (H.), Davis, I., Bentley, I. 1981: *Dunroamin: The Suburban Semi and its Enemies.* London: Barrie and Jenkins.

Orlans, H. 1952: *Stevenage: A Sociological Study of a New Town.* London: Routledge and Kegan Paul.

Orwell, G. 1939: *Coming up for Air.* London: Secker and Warburg.

Osborn, F. J. 1934: *Transport, Town Development and Territorial Planning of Industry.* London: Fabian Society.

Osborn, F. J. 1935(?): *London's Dilemma: the Only Way Out.* London (?): Privately printed (?).

Osborn, F. J. 1937: A Lecture to London. *Journal of the Town Planning Institute,* **23**, 45–51.

Osborn, F. J. 1938: The Planning of Greater London. *Town and Country Planning,* **6**, 97–102.

Osborn, F. J. 1942: *New Towns After the War.* London: J. M. Dent.

Osborn, F. J. 1950: Sir Ebenezer Howard: The Evolution of his Ideas. *Town Planning Review,* **21**, 221–35.

Osborn, F. J. 1955: How Subsidies distort Housing Development. *Lloyds Bank Review,* **N.S. 36**, 25–38.

Osborn, F. J. 1970: *Genesis of Welwyn Garden City: Some Jubilee Memories.* London: Town and Country Planning Association.

Pahl, R. E. (ed.) 1968: *Readings in Urban Sociology.* Oxford: Pergamon.

Paris 1978: Anonymous news contributions. *Macadam,* 4, 4–9.

Paris 1979a: Anonymous news contributions. *Architecture,* 1, 7–17.

Paris 1979b: Anonymous news contributions. *Building News,* **437**, 4; **438**, 1; **456**, 8.

Paris 1979c: Jeu de l'Oie des Halles de Paris. *Macadam,* **8.9**, 12–13.

Park, R. E. 1925a: The City: Suggestions for the Investigation of Human Behavior in the Urban Environment. In: Park, R. E. *et al.,* 1925, 1–46.

Park, R. E. 1925b: Community Disorganization and Juvenile Delinquency. In: Park, R. E. *et al.,* 1925, 99–112.

Park, R. E. 1928: Human Migration and the Marginal Man. *American Journal of Sociology,* **33**, 881–93.

Park, R. E., Burgess, E. W., McKenzie, R. D. 1925: *The City,* Chicago: University of Chicago Press.

Park, R. L. 1962: The urban challenge to local and state Government: West Bengal, with special reference to Calcutta. In: Turner, R. (ed.), 1962, 382–96.

Parker, B. 1932: Highways, Parkways and Freeways: with special reference to Wythenshawe Estate, Manchester, and to Letchworth Garden City. *Town and Country Planning*, **1**, 38–43.

Parker, B., Unwin, R. 1901: *The Art of Building a Home: A Collection of Lectures and Illustrations*. London: Longmans, Green.

Parker, R. S., Troy, P. N. (eds) 1972: *The Politics of Urban Growth*. Canberra: ANU Press.

Parkin, D. J. (ed.) 1975: *Town and Country in East and Central Africa*. London: Oxford UP (for International African Institute).

Parkins, M. F. 1953: *City Planning in Soviet Russia: with an interpretative bibliography*. Chicago: University of Chicago Press.

Partners for Livable Places. 1982: *Towards Livable Communities: A Report on Partners for Livable Places, 1975–1982*. Washington, DC: Partners for Livable Places.

Patterson, O. 1982: *Slavery and Social Death: A Comparative Study*. Cambridge, Mass.: Harvard UP.

Pawlowski, C. 1967: *Tony Garnier et les débuts de l'urbanisme fonctionnel en France*. Paris: Centre de Recherche d'Urbanisme.

Payne, G. K. 1977: *Urban Housing in the Third World*. London: Leonard Hill.

Payne, G. K. 1982: Self-Help Housing: A Critique of the Gecekondus of Ankara. In: Ward, P. M. (ed.), 1982, 117–39.

Pearson, S. V. 1939: *London's Overgrowth and the Causes of Swollen Towns*. London: C. W. Daniel.

Peattie, L. 1968: Reflections on Advocacy Planning. *Journal of the American Institute of Planners*, **34**, 80–8.

Peel, J. D. Y. 1980: Urbanization and urban history in West Africa. *Journal of African History*, **21**, 269–77.

Pehnt, R. 1974: *Die Stadt in der Bundesrepublik Deutschland*. Stuttgart: Philipp Reclam.

Peil, M. 1976: African squatter settlements: A comparative study. *Urban Studies*, **3**, 155–66.

Peltz-Dreckmann, U. 1978: *Nationalsozialistischer Siedlungsbau*. Munich: Minerva.

Pepler, G. L. 1911: Greater London. In: Royal Institute of British Architects, 1911, 611–20.

Perlman, J. E. 1976: *The Myth of Marginality: Urban Poverty and Politics in Rio de Janeiro*. Berkeley: University of California Press.

Perloff, H. S. 1965: New Directions in Social Planning. *Journal of the American Institute of Planners*, **31**, 297–304.

Perloff, H. S. (with Klett, F.) 1974: The Evolution of Planning Education. In: Godschalk, D. R. (ed.), 1974, 161–80.

Perloff, H. S., Berg, T., Fountain, R., Vetter, D., Weld, J. 1975: *Modernizing the Central City: New Towns Intown . . . and Beyond*. Cambridge, Mass.: Ballinger.

Perroux, F. 1961: *L'Économie du XX^c siècle*. Paris: Presses Universitaires de France.

Perroux, F. 1965: *La Pensée économique de Joseph Schumpeter: les dynamiques du capitalisme* (Travaux de Droit, d'Économie, de Sociologie et de Sciences Politiques, 34). Geneva: Droz.

Perry, C. A. 1929: *The Neighborhood Unit: A Scheme of Arrangement for the Family-Life Community* (Regional Study of New York and its Environs, VII, Neighborhood and Community Planning, Monograph One, 2–140). New York: Regional Plan of New York and its Environs.

Perry, C.A. 1939: *Housing for the Machine Age*. New York: Russell Sage Foundation.

Peters, J. 1982: Interstates: Nearing the End of the Road. *Planning*, **47.12**, 12–15.

Petersen, W. 1977: The ideological origins of Britain's New Towns. In: Allen, I. L. (ed.), 1977, 61–81.

Peterson, J. A. 1976: The City Beautiful Movement: Forgotten Origins and Lost Meanings. *Journal of Urban History*, **2**, 415–34.

Petsch, J. 1976: *Baukunst und Stadtplanung im dritten Reich: Herleitung/ Bestandsaufnahme/ Entwicklung/ Nachfolge*. Munich: Carl Hanser.

Pfautz, H. W. 1967: *Charles Booth on the City. Physical Patterns and social Structure*. Chicago: University of Chicago Press.

Phares, D. (ed.) 1977: *A Decent Home and Environment: Housing urban America*. Cambridge, Mass.: Ballinger.

Philpott, T. L. 1978: *The Slum and the Ghetto: Neighborhood Deterioration and Middle-Class Reform, Chicago, 1880–1930*. New York: Oxford UP.

Pick, F. 1927: Growth and Form in modern Cities. *Journal of the Institute of Transport*, **8**, 156–74.

Pick, F. 1935: Some Reflections on the Administration of a Public Utility Undertaking. *Public Administration*, **13**, 135–45.

Pick, F. 1936: The Organisation of Transport: with special reference to the London Passenger Transport Board. *Journal of the Royal Society of Arts*, **84**, 207–19.

Pick, F. 1937: London Fifty Years Hence. *Journal of the Town Planning Institute*, **23**, 61–6.

Pick, F. 1938: Evidence of London Passenger Transport Board. In: G.B. R.C. Geographical Distribution, 1937–9, Day 12.

Pick, F. 1941: *Britain Must Rebuild: A Pattern for Planning* (The Democratic Order, No. 17). London: Kegan Paul, Trench, Trubner.

Piven, F. F., Cloward, R. A. 1977: *Poor People's Movements: Why They Succeed, How They Fail*. New York: Pantheon.

Piven, F. F., Cloward, R. A. 1982: *The New Class War: Reagan's Attack on the Welfare State and its Consequences*. New York: Pantheon.

Poete, M. 1931: *Une vie de cité: Paris de sa naissance à nos jours*, 3 vols. Paris: Auguste Picard.

Pollock, N. C. 1968: The Development of Urbanization in Southern Africa. In: Beckinsale, R. P. and Houston, J. M. (ed.), 1968, 304–29.

Pons, V. 1969: *Stanleyville: An African Urban Community under Belgian Administration*. London: Oxford UP.

Popenoe, D. 1977: *The Suburban Environment: Sweden and the United States*. Chicago: University of Chicago Press.

Popper, F. J. 1981: *The Politics of Land-Use Reform*. Madison: University of Wisconsin Press.

Portes, A. 1979: Housing Policy, Urban Poverty, and the State: the Favelas of Rio de Janeiro, 1972–1976. *Latin American Research Review*, **14.2**, 3–24.

Powell, J. M., Williams, M. (eds) 1975: *Australian Space, Australian Time; Geographical Perspectives*. Melbourne: Oxford UP.

Prescott, N. C. 1968: The Development of Urbanization in Southern Africa. In: Beckinsale, R. P. and Houston, J. M. (eds), 1968, 304–29.

Purdom, C. B. 1917: *The Garden City After the War*. Letchworth: Privately printed.

Purdom, C. B. (ed.) 1921: *Town Theory and Practice*. London: Benn.

Purdom, C. B. 1925: *The Building of Satellite Towns: A Contribution to the Study of Town Development and Regional Planning*. London: J. M. Dent.

Queen, S. A., Carpenter, D. B. 1953: *The American City*. New York: McGraw-Hill.

Rabinowitz, F. 1969: *City Politics and Planning*. New York: Atherton Press.

Rae, J. B. 1971: *The Road and the Car in American Life*. Cambridge, Mass.: MIT Press.

Raffe, W. G. 1936: The Reconstruction of Moscow: The Ten Year Plan. *Town and Country Planing*, **4**, 53–9.

Rainwater, L. 1967: Fear and the House-as-Haven in the Lower Class. In: Bellush, J., Hausknecht, M. (eds), 1967a, 437–50.

Rainwater, L. 1970: *Behind Ghetto Walls: Black Families in a Federal Slum.* Chicago: Aldine.

Rainwater, L., Yancey, W. L. 1967: *The Moynihan Report and the Politics of Controversy.* Cambridge, Mass.: MIT Press.

Rasmussen, S. E. 1937: *London: The Unique City.* London: Jonathan Cape.

Rave, R., Knöfel, H.-J. 1968: *Bauen seit 1900 in Berlin.* Berlin: Kiepert.

Ravetz, A. 1974: From working-class tenement to modern flat: Local Authorities and multi-storey housing between the wars. In: Sutcliffe, A. (ed.), 1974, 122–50.

Ravetz, A. 1980: *Remaking Cities: Contradictions of the Recent Urban Environment.* London: Croom Helm.

Read, J. 1978: The Garden City and the Growth of Paris. *Architectural Review,* **113**, 345–52.

Reade, E. 1987: *British Town and Country Planning.* Milton Keynes: Open University Press.

Reader, D. H. 1961: *The Black Man's Portion: History, Demography and Living Conditions in the Native Locations of East London, Cape Province.* Cape Town: Oxford UP.

Reclus, E. 1878–94: *The Earth and its Inhabitants: The Universal Geography,* edited by E. G. Ravenstein and A. H. Keane, 19 Vols. London: J. S. Virtue.

Reclus, E. 1905–8: *L'Homme et la terre,* 6 vols. Paris: Libraire Universelle.

Regional Plan of New York and its Environs (1927–31). *Regional Survey of New York and its Environs,* 8 vols. (in 10). I. Major economic Factors in Metropolitan Growth and Development. IA. Chemical, Metal, Wood, Tobacco and Printing Industries. IB. Food, Clothing & Textile Industries. Wholesale Markets and Retail Shopping & financial Districts. II. Population Land Values and Government. III. Highway Traffic. IV. Transit and Transportation. V. Public Recreation. VI. Buildings: Their Uses and the Spaces about them. VII. Neighborhoods and Community planning. VIII. Physical Conditions and Public Services. New York: The Regional Plan.

Reiner, T. A. 1963: *The Place of the Ideal Community in Urban Planning.* Philadelphia: University of Pennsylvania Press.

Reiss, R. L. 1918: *The Home I Want.* London: Hodder and Stoughton.

Reith, J. C. W. 1949: *Into the Wind.* London: Hodder and Stoughton.

Reps, J. W. 1965: *The Making of Urban America: A History of City Planning in the United States.* Princeton: Princeton UP.

Reulecke, J. (ed.) 1978: *Die deutsche Stadt im Industriezeitalter.* Wuppertal: Peter Hammer.

Rex, J. 1973: *Race, Colonialism and the City.* London: Routledge and Kegan Paul.

Richards, J. M. 1946: *The Castles on the Ground.* London: The Architectural Press.

Richards, J. M. 1953: The Failure of the New Towns. *Architectural Review,* **114**, 29–32.

Riesman, D. 1950: *The Lonely Crowd: a Study of the Changing American Character.* New Haven: Yale University Press.

Riis, J. A. 1890: *How the Other Half lives: Studies among the Tenements of New York.* New York: Scribner's Sons.

Riis, J. A. 1901: *The Making of an American.* New York: Macmillan.

Riley, R. B. 1967: Urban Myths and the New Cities of the South-West. *Landscape,* **17**, 21–3.

Rittel, H. W. J., Webber, M. M. 1973: Dilemmas in a General Theory of Planning. *Policy Sciences,* **4**, 155–69.

Roberts, S. I. 1961: Portrait of a Robber Baron, Charles T. Yerkes. *Business History Review*, **35**, 344–71.

Robinson, C. M. 1901: *The Improvement of Towns and Cities: Or, The Practical Basis of Civic Aesthetics*. New York: G. P. Putnam's Sons.

Robson, W. A. 1939: *The Government and Misgovernment of London*. London: George Allen and Unwin.

Robson, W. A. (ed.) 1954: *Great Cities of the World: Their Growth, Politics and Planning*. London: George Allen and Unwin.

Robson, W. A., Regan, D. E. (eds), 1972: *Great Cities of the World*. Third Edition, 2 vols. London: George Allen and Unwin.

Rodgers, C. 1947: *American Planning: Past, Present and Future*. New York: Harper Bros.

Rodwin, L. 1965: Ciudad Guayana: A New City. *Scientific American*, **213.3**, 122–32.

Romanos, A. G. 1969: Illegal Settlements in Athens. In: Oliver, P. (ed.), 1969, 137–55.

Roos, D., Altshuler, A. 1984: *The Future of the Automobile: The Report of MIT's International Automobile Program*. London: George Allen and Unwin.

Roosevelt, F. D. 1932: Growing up by Plan. *Survey*, **67**, 483–5, 506–7.

Roosevelt, F. D. 1938: *The Public Papers and Addresses of Franklin D. Roosevelt*. Vol. 1: *The Genesis of the New Deal 1928–1932*. New York: Random House.

Roper, L. W. 1973: *F.L.O.: A Biography of Frederick Law Olmsted*. Baltimore and London: Johns Hopkins UP.

Rose, M. H. 1979: *Interstate: Express Highway Politics, 1941–1956*. Lawrence: University of Kansas Press.

Rosenfeld, R. A. 1980: Who benefits and who decides? The Uses of Community Development Block Grants. In: Rosenthal, D. B. (ed.), 1980, 211–36.

Rosenthal, D. B. (ed.) 1980: *Urban Revitalization* (Urban Affairs Annual Reviews, No. 18). Beverly Hills: Sage.

Rosenwaike, I. 1972: *Population History of New York City*. Syracuse: Syracuse UP.

Ross, R., Telkamp, G. J. (eds) 1985: *Colonial Cities: Essays on Urbanism in a Colonial Context* (Comparative Studies in Overseas History, Vol. 5). Dordrecht: Martinus Nijhofk.

Rosser, C. 1971: Housing for the lowest income groups – the Calcutta example. *Ekistics*, **31**, 126–31.

Rosser, C. 1972: *Urbanization in India* (International Urbanization Survey. Working Papers 278). New York: Ford Foundation.

Rosser, C. 1972: Housing and Planned Urban Change: The Calcutta Experience. In: Dwyer, D. J. (ed.), 1972, 179–90.

Rossi, P. H., Dentler, R. A. 1961: *The Politics of Urban Renewal: The Chicago Findings*. New York: The Free Press of Glencoe.

Roth, G. 1967: *Paying for Roads: The Economics of Traffic Congestion*. Harmondsworth: Penguin Books.

Roth, G., Butler, E. 1982: *Private Road Ahead*. London: Adam Smith Institute.

Roth, G., Wynne, G. G. 1982: *Free Enterprise Urban Transportation* (Learning from Abroad, 5). New Brunswick and London: Transaction Books.

Rothenberg, J. 1967: *Economic Evaluation of Urban Renewal: Conceptual Foundation of Benefit–Cost Analysis*. Washington, DC: The Brookings Institution.

Royal Institute of British Architects. 1911: *Town Planning Conference – Transactions*. London: RIBA.

Rubenstein, J. M. 1978: *The French New Towns*. Baltimore: Johns Hopkins UP.

Ruskin, J. 1903–12: *The Works of John Ruskin.* Ed. by E. T. Cook and A. Wedderburn, 39 vols. (20. *Oxford Lectures on Art;* 34. *To the Clergy on the Lord's Prayer).* London: George Allen.

Ruttan, V. W. 1983: The TVA and Regional Development. In: Hargrove, E. C., Conkin, P. K. (eds), 1983, 150–63.

Sable, M. H. 1971: *Latin American Urbanization: A Guide to the Literature.* Metuchen, NJ: The Scarecrow Press.

Saint, A. 1976: *Richard Norman Shaw.* New Haven: Yale UP.

St. Clair, D. J. 1981: The Motorization and Decline of Urban Public Transit, 1935–1950. *Journal of Urban History,* **41**, 579–600.

Salau, A. T. 1977: A new capital for Nigeria: Planning, Problems and Prospects. *Africa Today,* **24.4**, 11–22.

Salisbury, H. E. 1958: *The Shook-Up Generation.* New York: Harper and Brothers.

Salisbury, R. 1964: Urban Politics: The new convergence of power. *Journal of Politics,* **26**, 775–97.

Sandercock, L. 1976: *Cities for Sale: Property, Politics and Urban Planning in Australia.* London: Heinemann.

Sanders, H. T. 1980: Urban Renewal and the revitalized city: A reconsideration of recent history. In: Rosenthal, D. B. (ed.), 1980, 103–26.

Sarin, M. 1979: Urban Planning, Petty Trading, and Squatter Settlements in Chandigarh, India. In: Bromley, R., Gerry, C. (eds), 1979, 133–60.

Sarin, M. 1982: *Urban Planning in the Third World: The Chandigarh Experience.* London: Mansell.

Saushkin, Y. G. 1966: *Moscow.* Moscow: Progress Publishers.

Sawers, L. 1978: Cities and Countryside in the Soviet Union and China. In: Tabb, W. K., Sawers, L. (eds), 1978, 338–64.

Sawers, L. 1984: The Political Economy of Urban Transportation: An interpretative essay. In: Tabb, W., Sawers, L. (eds), 1984, 223–54.

Scarpa, L. 1983: *Martin Wagner e Berlino: casa e citta nella Repubblica di Weimar 1918–1933.* Rome: Officina Edizioni.

Schaffer, D. 1982: *Garden Cities for America: The Radburn Experience.* Philadelphia: Temple UP.

Schaffer, D. 1984: The Tennessee Transplant. *Town and Country Planning,* **53**, 316–18.

Schiffer, J. 1984: *Anatomy of a Laissez-Faire Government: The Hong Kong Growth Model Reconsidered.* Hong Kong: University, Centre of Urban Studies and Urban Planning, Working Paper.

Schill, M. H., Nathan, R. P. 1983: *Revitalizing America's Cities: Neighborhood Reinvestment and Displacement.* Albany: State University of New York Press.

Schlereth, T. J. 1983: Burnham's *Plan* and Moody's *Manual*: City Planning as Progressive Reform. In: Krueckeberg, D. A. (ed.), 1983a, 75–99.

Schlesinger, A. M. 1933: *The Rise of the City, 1878–1898* (A History of American Life, Vol. X). New York: Macmillan.

Schmetzer, H., Wakely, P. 1974: Chandigarh: Twenty Years later. *Architectural Design,* **44**, 350–61.

Schmitt, P. J. 1969: *Back to Nature: The Arcadian Myth in Urban America.* New York: Oxford UP.

Schnur, R. 1970: Entwicklung der Rechtsgrundlagen und der Organisation des SVR. In: *Siedlungsverband Ruhrkohlenbezirk 1920–1970,* 29. *Schriftenreihe Siedlungsverband Ruhrkohlenbezirk.* Essen: SVR.

Schoener, A. (ed.) 1967: *Portal to America: The Lower East Side, 1870–1925.* New York: Holt.

Schon, D. A. 1971: *Beyond the Stable State*. New York: Random House.

Schon, D. A., Cremer, N. S., Osterman, P., Perry, C. 1976: Planners in Transition: Report on a Survey of Alumni of MIT's Department of Urban Studies, 1970–71. *Journal of the American Institute of Planners*, **42**, 193–202.

Schorske, C. E. 1963: The Idea of the City in European Thought: Voltaire to Spengler. In: Handlin, O., Burchard, J. (eds), 1963, 95–114.

Schultz, S. K., McShane, C. 1978: To Engineer the Metropolis: Sewers, Sanitation and City Planning in late-nineteenth-century America. *Journal of American History*, **65**, 389–411.

Schwartz, B. (ed.) 1976: *The Changing Face of the Suburbs*. Chicago: University of Chicago Press.

Scobie, J. R. 1974: *Buenos Aires: Plaza to Suburb, 1870–1910*. New York: Oxford UP.

Scott, A. J., Roweis, S. T. 1977: Urban Planning in Theory and Practice: An Appraisal. *Environment and Planning* A, **9**, 1097–1119.

Scott, A. J., Storper, M. (eds) 1986: *Production, Work, Territory: The Geographical Anatomy of Industrial Capitalism*. London: Allen and Unwin.

Scott, M. 1969: *American City Planning since 1890: A History commemorating the Fiftieth Anniversary of the American Institute of Planners*. Berkeley: University of California Press.

Scully, V. 1969: *American Architecture and Urbanism*. New York: Praeger.

Segal, H. P. 1985: *Technological Utopianism in American Culture*. Chicago: University of Chicago Press.

Sellier, H., Bruggeman, A. 1927: *Le Problème de logement: son influence sur les conditions de l'habitation et l'aménagement des villes*. Paris and New Haven: Presses Universitaires de France and Yale UP.

Selznick, P. 1949: *TVA and the Grass Roots: A Study in the Sociology of formal Organization*. Berkeley: University of California Press.

Sennett, R. 1971: *The Uses of Disorder: Personal Identity and City Life*. London: Allen Lane.

Shannon, A. H. 1930: *The Negro in Washington: A Study in Race Amalgamation*. New York: Walter Neale.

Sharp, T. 1932: *Town and Countryside: Some Aspects of Urban and Rural Development*. London: Oxford UP.

Sharp, T. 1936: *English Panorama*. London: Dent.

Shaw, C. R. *et al.* 1929: *Delinquency Areas: A Study of the Geographic Distribution of School Truants, Juvenile Delinquents, and Adult Offenders in Chicago*. Chicago: University of Chicago Press.

Shaw, C. R., McKay, H. D. 1942: *Juvenile Delinquency and Urban Areas: A Study of Rates of Delinquents in Relation to Differential Characteristics of Local Communities in American Cities*. Chicago: University of Chicago Press.

Sheail, J. 1981: *Rural Conservation in Inter-War Britain*. Oxford: Oxford UP.

Sherrard, T. D. (ed.) 1968: *Social Welfare and Social Problems*. New York: Columbia UP.

Short, J. R., Fleming, S., Witt, S. J. G. 1986: *Housebuilding, Planning and Community Action: The Production and Negotiation of the Built Environment*. London: Routledge and Kegan Paul.

Shostak, L., Lock, D. 1984: The Need for new Settlements in the South East. *Planner*, **70.11**, 9–13.

Shvidovsky, O. A. (ed.) 1970: Building in the USSR, 1917–1932. *Architectural Design*, February, 71–107.

Sidenbladh, G. 1965: Stockholm: A Planned City. *Scientific American*, **213.3**, 107–18.

Sidenbladh, G. 1969: Debat om samhällsplanering hösten – 68. *Plan*, **23**, 16–19.

Sidenbladh, G. 1977: Idedebatt och praxis i efterkrigstidens Samhällsplanering. *Plan*, **31**, 196–202.

Sigurdson, J. 1975: Rural Industrialization in China: Approaches and Results. *World Development*, **3**, 527–38.

Simmance, A. J. F. 1974: Urbanization in Zambia. *Journal of Administration Overseas*, **13**, 498–509.

Simon, E. D. *et al.* 1937a: *Moscow in the Making*. London: Longmans.

Simon, E. D. 1937b: Town Planning: Moscow or Manchester. *Journal of the Town Planning Institute*, **23**, 381–9.

Simon, R., Hookham, M. 1954: Moscow. In: Robson, W. A. (ed.), 1954, 383–41.

Simpson, M. A. 1976: Two Traditions of American Planning: Olmsted and Burnham. *Town Planning Review*, **47**, 174–9.

Simpson, M. A. 1981: Thomas Adams 1871–1940. In: Cherry, G. E. (ed.), 1981, 19–45.

Simpson, M. A. 1985: *Thomas Adams and the Modern Planning Movement: Britain, Canada and the United Statse, 1900–1940*. London: Mansell.

Sinclair, R. 1937: *Metropolitan Man: The Future of the English*. London: George Allen and Unwin.

Sinha, P. 1978: *Calcutta in Urban History*. Calcutta: Firma K. M. Private Ltd.

Sit, V. F. S. 1978: Hong Kong's approach to the development of small manufacturing enterprises. *U.N. Economic and Social Council, Small Industry Bulletin for Asia and the Pacific*, **15**, 89–98.

Skinner, C. 1986: *Illusive Mr. Right: The Social and Personal Context of a Young Woman's Use of Contraception in London*. London: Carolina Publications.

Smith, A. E. 1925: Seeing a State Whole. *The Survey*, *54*, 158–60.

Smith, D. H. 1933: *The Industries of Greater London*. London: P. S. King.

Smith, G. 1928: A Town for the Motor Age. *Survey*, **59**, 694–8.

Smith, R. 1974: Multi-dwelling Building in Scotland, 1750–1950; A Study Based on Housing in the Clyde Valley. In: Sutcliffe, A., 1974, 207–43.

Smout, M. A. H. 1977: The Townscape. In Kay, G., Smout, M. A. H. (eds), 1977, 26–40.

Snell, B. C. 1974: *American Ground Transportation: A Proposal for Restructuring the Automobile, Truck, Bus, and Rail Industries (Subcommittee on Antitrust and Monopoly, Committee on the Judiciary, U.S. Senate)*. Washington, DC: Government Printing Office.

Sociological Society. Cities Committee. 1919: Towards the Third Alternative: I. The Civic School of Applied Sociology. *Sociological Review*, **11**, 62–5.

Soja, E., Morales, R., Wolff, G. 1983: Urban Restructuring: An Analysis of Social and Spatial Change in Los Angeles. *Economic Geography*, **59**, 195–230.

Sommer, J. W. 1976: The Internal Structure of African cities. In: Knight, C. G., Newman, J. L. (eds), 1976, 306–20.

Soria y Pug, A. 1968: *Arturo Soria y la ciudad lineal*. Madrid: Revista de Occidente.

Southall, A. W. 1966: The Growth of Urban Society. In: Diamond, S., Burke, F. G. (eds), 1966, 463–92.

Southall, A. 1967: Kampala-Mengo. In: Miner, H. (ed.), 1967, 297–332.

Southall, A. 1971: The Impact of Imperialism upon Urban Development in Africa. In: Turner, V. (ed.), 1971, 216–55.

Southall, A. (ed.) 1973: *Urban Anthropology: Cross-Cultural Studies of Urbanization*. New York: Oxford UP.

Spear, A.H. 1967: *Black Chicago: The Making of a Negro Ghetto, 1890–1920*. Chicago: University of Chicago Press.

Speer, A. 1970: *Inside the Third Reich*. London: Weidenfeld and Nicolson.

Spencer, J. E., Thomas, W. L. 1948/9: The Hill Stations and Summer Resorts of the Orient. *Geographical Review*, **38**, 637–51; **39**, 671.

Spengler, J. J. 1967: Africa and the theory of optimum city size. In: Miner, H. (ed.), 1967, 55–89.

Spengler, O. 1934: *The Decline of the West*. London: George Allen and Unwin.

Stamp, G. 1982: New Delhi. In Lutyens, E. (1982), 33–43.

Stamp, L. D. 1962: *The Land of Britain: its Use and Misuse*. London: Longman.

Starkie, D. 1982: *The Motorway Age: Road and Traffic Policies in Post-War Britain*. Oxford: Pergamon.

Starr, S. F. 1971: Writings from the 1960s on the Modern Movement in Russia. *Journal of the Society of American Architectural Historians*, **30**, 170–8.

Starr, S. F. 1976: The Revival and Schism of Urban Planning in Twentieth-Century Russia. In: Hamm, M. F., 1976a, 222–42.

Starr, S. F. 1977: L'Urbanisme utopique pendant la révolution culturelle soviétique. *Annales: Économies, Sociétés, Civilizations*, **32**, 87–105.

Stave, B. M. (ed.) 1981: *Modern Industrial Cities: History, Policy, and Survival*. Beverly Hills: Sage.

Stedman Jones, G. 1971: *Outcast London: A Study in the Relationship between Classes in Victorian Society*. Oxford: Oxford UP.

Stein, C. S. 1925: Dinosaur Cities. *Survey*, **54**, 134–8.

Stein, C. 1958 (1951): *Toward New Towns for America*. Liverpool: Liverpool UP.

Steinberg, S. 1981: *The Ethnic Myth: Race, Ethnicity, and Class in America*. New York: Atheneum.

Stern, R. A. M., Massingale, J. M. (eds) 1981: The Anglo American Suburb. *Architectural Design*, **50.10–11**, entire double issue.

Stern, R. A. M. 1986: *Pride of Place: Building the American Dream*. Boston: Houghton Mifflin.

Sternlieb, G., Listokin, D. 1981: *New Tools for Economic Development: The Enterprise Zone, Development Bank, and RFC*. Piscataway, NJ: Center for Urban Policy Research, Rutgers University.

Sternlieb, G., Hughes, J. W., Hughes, C. O. 1982: *Demographic Trends and Economic Reality: Planning and Markets in the 80s*. New Brunswick: Center for Urban Policy Research.

Stewart, J. Q. 1947: Empirical mathematical rules concerning the distribution and equilibrium of population. *Geographical Review*, **37**, 461–85.

Stewart, J. Q. 1956: The Development of Social Physics. *American Journal of Physics*, **18**, 239–53.

Stewart, J. Q. 1959: Physics of Population Distribution. *Journal of Regional Science*, **1**, 99–123.

Stewart, J. Q., Warntz, W. 1958: Macrogeography and Social Science. *Geographical Review*, **48**, 167–84.

Stewman, S., Tarr, J. A. 1982: Four Decades of Public–Private Partnerships in Pittsburgh. In: Fosler, R. S., Berger, R. A. (eds), 1982, 59–128.

Stockholm Information Board 1972: *Kista, Husby, Akala: A Digest for Planners, Politicians and Critics*. Stockholm: The Board.

Stoddart, D. R. 1986: *On Geography: and its History*. Oxford: Basil Blackwell.

Stöhr, W. B. 1981: Development from Below: The Bottom–Up and Periphery–Inward Development Paradigm. In: Stöhr, W. B., Taylor, D. R. F. (eds), 1981, 39–72.

Stöhr, W. B., Taylor, D. R. F. (eds) 1981: *Development from Above or Below? The Dialectics of Regional Planning in Developing Countries*. Chichester: John Wiley.

Stokes, C. J. 1962: A Theory of Slums. *Land Economics*, **38**, 187–97.

Stone, P. A. 1959: The Economics of Housing and Urban Development. *Journal of the Royal Statistical Society*, **A, 122**, 417–76.

Stone, P. A. 1961: The Impact of Urban Development on the Use of Land and Other Resources. *Journal of the Town Planning Institute*, **47**, 128–34.

Stone, P. A. 1963: *Housing, Town Development, Land and Costs*. London: Estates Gazette.

Strauss, A. L. 1968: *The American City: A Sourcebook of Urban Imagery*. London: Allen Lane.

Stren, R. 1972: Urban Policy in Africa: A Political Analysis. *African Studies Review*, **15**, 489–516.

Strömdahl, J. 1969: Vem pląnerar du för samhällsplanerare? *Plan*, **23**, 26–8.

Sussman, C. (ed.) 1976: *Planning the Fourth Migration: The Neglected Vision of the Regional Planning Association of America*. Cambridge, Mass.: MIT Press.

Sutcliffe, A. 1970: *The Autumn of Central Paris: The Defeat of Town Planning 1850–1970*. London: Edward Arnold.

Sutcliffe, A. (ed.) 1974: *Multi-Storey Living: The British Working-Class Experience*. London: Croom Helm.

Sutcliffe, A. 1974: A Century of Flats in Birmingham, 1875–1973. In: Sutcliffe, A. (ed.), 1974, 181–206.

Sutcliffe, A. 1977: A Vision of Utopia: Optimistic Foundations of Le Corbusier's Doctrine d'Urbanisme. In: Walden, R., 1977, 216–43.

Sutcliffe, A. 1979: Environmental Control and Planning in European Capitals 1850–1914: London, Paris and Berlin. In: Hammarström, I. and Hall, T. (eds), 1979, 71–88.

Sutcliffe, A. 1981: *Towards the Planned City: Germany, Britain, the United States and France, 1780–1914*. Oxford: Blackwell.

Sutcliffe, A. (ed.) 1984: *Metropolis 1890–1940*. London: Mansell.

Svetlichny, B. 1960: Les Villes d'Avenir. *Recherches Internationales*, **20–1**, 208–29.

Swenarton, M. 1981: *Homes Fit for Heroes: The Politics and Architecture of Early State Housing in Britain*. London: Heinemann.

Swenarton, M. 1985: Sellier and Unwin. *Planning History Bulletin*, **7.2**, 50–7.

Tabb, W. K., Sawers, L. (eds) 1978: *Marxism and the Metropolis: New Perspectives in Urban Political Economy*. New York: Oxford UP.

Tabb, W. K., Sawers, L. (eds) 1984: *Marxism and the Metropolis: New Perspectives in Urban Political Economy*. Second Edition. New York: Oxford UP.

Tahmankar, D. V. 1970: *Sardar Patel*. London: Allen and Unwin.

Taneja, K. L. 1971: *Morphology of Indian Cities*. Varanasi: National Geographic Society of India.

Taper, B. 1983: Charles Abrams: Lover of Cities. In: Kreuckeberg, D. A. (ed.), 1983a, 366–95.

Tarn, J. N. 1973: *Five Per Cent Philanthropy: An Account of Housing in Urban Areas Between 1840 and 1914*. Cambridge: Cambridge UP.

Taylor, R. R. 1974: *The World in Stone: The Role of Architecture in the National Socialist Ideology*. Berkeley: University of California Press.

Teaford, J. C. 1984: *The Unheralded Triumph: City Government in America, 1870–1900*. Baltimore: Johns Hopkins UP.

Teitz, M. B. 1974: Toward a responsive Planning Methodology. In: Godschalk, D. R. (ed.), 1974, 86–110.

Teran, F. de 1978: *Planeamiento urbano en la España contemporanea: Historia de un procseso imposible*. Barcelona: Gustavo Gili.

Thernstrom, S. 1973: *The Other Bostonians: Poverty and Progress in the American*

Metropolis 1880–1970. Cambridge, Mass.: Harvard UP.

Thernstrom, S., Sennett, R. (eds) 1969: *Nineteenth-Century Cities: Essays in the New Urban History* (Yale Studies of the City, 1). New Haven: Yale UP.

Thienel, I. 1973: *Städtewachstum im Industrialisierungsprozess der 19. Jahrhundert: der Berliner Beispiel.* Berlin: de Gruyter.

Thies, J. 1978: Hitler's European building Programme. *Journal of Contemporary History,* **13**, 413–31.

Thomas, D. 1970: *London's Green Belt.* London: Faber and Faber.

Thomas, M. J. 1978: City Planning in Soviet Russia (1917–1932) *Geoforum,* **9**, 269–77.

Thomas, W. H. 1901: *The American Negro: What he was, What he is, and What he may become.* New York: Macmillan.

Thomas, W. I., Znaniecki, F. N. 1927, 1918: *The Polish Peasant in Europe and America,* 2 vols. New York: Knopf.

Thompson, F. M. L. (ed.) 1982: *The Rise of Suburbia.* Leicester: Leicester UP.

Thompson, J. B., Held, D. 1982: *Habermas: Critical Debates.* Cambridge, Mass.: MIT Press.

Thompson, R. 1975: City Planning in China. *World Development,* **3**, 595–606.

Thompson, W. S. 1947: *Population: The Growth of Metropolitan Districts in the United States: 1900–1940.* (U.S. Department of Commerce, Bureau of the Census). Washington, DC: Government Printing Office.

Thomson, J. 1880: *The City of Dreadful Night, and Other Poems.* London: Reeves and Turner.

Thorne, D. C. 1972: *Suburbia.* London: Macgibbon and Kee.

Thorne, R. 1980: *Covent Garden Market: Its History and Restoration.* London: Architectural Press.

Thornton White, L. W., Silberman, L., Anderson, P. R. 1948: *Nairobi: Master Plan for a Colonial Capital. A Report Prepared for the Municipal Council of Nairobi.* London: HMSO.

Thrasher, F. M. 1926: The Gang as a Symptom of Community Disorganization. *Journal of Applied Sociology,* **11**, 3–20.

Thünen, J. H. von 1966: *von Thünen's Isolated State.* Translated by C. M. Wartenberg, edited by P. Hall. Oxford: Pergamon Press.

Titmuss, R. M. 1950: *Problems of Social Policy* (History of the Second World War, United Kingdom Civil Series). London: HMSO and Longmans, Green.

Tobe, E. 1977: Kommunal planering 1947–77. *Plan,* **31**, 206–9.

Tobin, G. A. 1976: Suburbanization and the Development of Motor Transportation: Transportation Technology and the Suburbanization Process. In: Schwartz, B. (ed.), 1976, 95–111.

Toll, S. I. 1969: *Zoned American.* New York: Grossman.

Tomlinson, S. 1983: *Ethnic Minorities in British Schools: A Review of the Literature, 1960–82.* London: Heinemann Education.

Towers, G. 1973: City Planning in China. *Journal of the Royal Town Planning Institute,* **59**, 125–7.

Treves, A. 1980: The anti-urban policy of Fascism and a century of resistance to industrial urbanization in Italy. *International Journal of Urban and Regional Research,* **4**, 470–84.

Tripp, H. A. 1938: *Road Traffic and its Control.* London: Edward Arnold.

Tripp, H. A. 1942: *Town Planning and Road Traffic.* London: Edward Arnold.

Tuck, M., Southgate, P. 1981: *Ethnic Minorities, Crime and Policing: A Survey of the Experiences of West Indians and Whites* (Home Office Research Study, 70). London: HMSO.

Tugwell, R. G., Banfield, E. C. 1950: Grass Roots Democracy – Myth or Reality? (Review of Selznick, P. 1949), *Public Administration Review*, **10**, 47–55.

Tunnard, C. 1953: *The City of Man*. London: Architectural Press.

Tunnard, C. 1968: *The Modern American City*. Princeton: van Norstrand.

Tunnard, C., Reed, H. H. 1955: *American Skyline: The Growth and Form of our Cities and Towns*. Boston: Houghton Mifflin.

Turner, J. F. C. 1963: Village Artisan's Self-Built House. *Architectural Design*, **33**, 361–2.

Turner, J. F. C. 1965: Lima's Barriadas and Corralones: Suburbs versus Slums. *Ekistics*, **19**, 152–5.

Turner, J. F. C. 1967: Barriers and Channels for Housing Development in modernizing Countries. *Journal of the American Institute of Planners*, **33**, 167–81.

Turner, J. F. C. 1968a: *Uncontrolled Urban Settlement: Problems and Policies* (International Social Development Reviews, 1: Urbanization: Development Policies and Planning). New York: United Nations.

Turner, J. F. C. 1968b: The Squatter Settlement: Architecture that works. *Architectural Design*, **38**, 355–60.

Turner, J. F. C. 1969: Uncontrolled Urban Settlement: Problems and Policies. In: Breese, G. (ed.), 1969, 507–35.

Turner, J. F. C. 1970: Barriers and Channels for Housing Development in Modernizing Countries. In: Mangin, W. P., 1970a, 1–19.

Turner, J. C. 1971: Barriers and Channels for Housing Development in Modernizing Countries. In: Lewis, D. N. (ed.), 1971, 70–83.

Turner, J. F. C. 1972a: The Reeducation of a Professional. In: Turner and Fichter, 1972, 122–47.

Turner, J. F. C. 1972b: Housing as a Verb. In: Turner and Fichter (eds), 1972, 148–75.

Turner, J. F. C. 1976: *Housing by People: Towards Autonomy in Building Environments*. London: Marion Boyars.

Turner, J. F. C. 1982: Issues in self-help and self-managed housing. In: Ward, P. M. (ed.), 1976, 99–113.

Turner, J. F. C., Fichter, R. (eds) 1972: *Freedom to Build: Dweller Control of the Housing Process*. New York: Macmillan.

Turner, J. F. C., Roberts, B. 1975: The Self-Help Society. In: Wilsher, P., Righter, R. (eds), 1975, 126–37.

Turner, J. F. C., Turner, C., Crooke, P. 1963: Conclusions (to special section, Dwelling Resources in South America). *Architectural Design*, **33**, 389–93.

Turner, R. (ed.) 1962: *India's Urban Future*. Berkeley: University of California Press.

Turner, V. (ed.) 1971: *Colonialism in Africa 1870–1960*. Vol. 3: *Profiles of Change: African Society and Colonial Rule*. Cambridge: Cambridge UP.

Tuttle, W. M., Jun. 1970: *Race Riot: Chicago in the Red Summer of 1919*. New York: Atheneum.

Tyler, W. R. 1939: The Neighbourhood Unit Principle in Town Planning. *Town Planning Review*, **18**, 174–86.

Tym, R. and Partners 1984: *Monitoring Enterprise Zones: Year Three Report*. London: Roger Tym and Partners.

Tyrwhitt, J. (ed.) 1947: *Patrick Geddes in India*. London: Lund Humphries.

Uhlig, G. 1977: Stadtplanung in der Weimarer Republik: sozialistische Reformaspekte. In: Neue Gesellschaft für Bildende Kunst (ed.) *Wem gehört die Welt? Kunst und Gesellschaft in der Weimarer Republik*. Berlin: Neue Gesellschaft für Bildende Kunst.

Umlauf, J. 1960: Die Entwicklung der Planungsarbeit des Siedlungsverband

Ruhrkohlenbezirk. In: *Siedlungsverband Ruhrkohlenbezirk. Tätigkeitsbericht 1958–1960.* Essen: SVR.

Unikel, L. 1982: Regional Development Policies in Mexico. In: Gilbert, A. (ed.), 1982, 263–78.

Unwin, R. 1902: *Cottage Plans and Common Sense* (Fabian Tract No. 109). London: The Fabian Society.

Unwin, R. 1912: *Nothing Gained by Overcrowding!: How the Garden City Type of Development may Benefit both Owner and Occupier.* London: P. S. King.

Unwin, R. 1920 (1911): *Town Planning in Practice: An Introduction to the Art of designing Cities and Suburbs.* London: T. Fisher Unwin.

Unwin, R. 1921: Distribution. *Journal of the Town Planning Institute,* **7**, 37–45.

Unwin, R. 1930: Regional Planning with special Reference to the Greater London Regional Plan. *Journal of the Royal Institute of British Architects,* **37**, 183–93.

Urban Land Institute. Research Division 1980: *UDAG Partnerships: Nine Case Studies.* Washington, DC: Urban Land Institute.

U.S. Department of Housing and Urban Development 1986: *State-Designated Enterprise Zones: Ten Case Studies.* Washington, DC: HUD.

U.S. Housing and Home Finance Agency 1966: The Housing of Relocated Families: Summary of a Census Bureau Survey. In: Wilson, J. Q., 1966, 336–52.

U.S. Library of Congress, Congressional Research Service 1973: *The Central City Problem and Urban Renewal Policy.* Washington, DC: Government Printing Office.

U.S. National Advisory Committee on Civil Disorders 1968: *Report.* New York: Dutton.

U.S. National Resources Committee 1935: *Regional Factors in National Planning and Development.* Washington, DC: Government Printing Office.

U.S. National Resources Planning Board 1937: *Our Cities: Their Role in the National Economy.* Washington, DC: Government Printing Office.

Valladares, L. do P. 1978: Working the System: Squatter Response to the Resettlement in Rio de Janeiro. *International Journal of Urban and Regional Research,* **2**, 12–25.

Vance, J. E., Jun. 1964: *Geography and Urban Evolution in the San Francisco Bay Area.* Berkeley: Institute of Governmental Studies.

Vandervelde, E. 1903: *L'Exode rural et le retour aux champs.* Paris: Félix Alcan.

Van Velsen, J. 1975: Urban Squatters: Problem or Solution. In: Parkin, D. J. (ed.), 1975, 294–307.

Van Zwanenberg, R. M. A., King, A. 1975: *An Economic History of Kenya and Uganda: 1800–1970.* London: Macmillan.

Venturi, R., Brown, D. S., Izenour, S. 1972: *Learning from Las Vegas.* Cambridge, Mass.: MIT Press.

Vogel, I. 1959: *Bottrop: Eine Bergbaustadt in der Emscherzone des Ruhrgebietes* (Forschungen zur Deutschen Landeskunde, 114). Remagen: Bundesanstalt für Landeskunde.

Veronesi, G. 1948: *Tony Garnier.* Milan: Il Balcone.

Voigt, P. 1901: *Grundrente und Wohnungsfrage in Berlin und seinen Vororten,* Part 1. Jena: Gustav Fischer.

Wachs, M. 1984: Autos, Transit, and the Spread of Los Angeles: The 1920s. *Journal of the American Planning Association,* **5**, 297–310.

Wade, R. C. 1968: Urbanization. In: Woodward, C. V. (ed.), 1968, 187–205.

Walden, R. (ed.) 1977: *The Open Hand: Essays on Le Corbusier.* Cambridge, Mass.: MIT Press.

Walker, R. A. 1950: *The Planning Function in Urban Government* (Social Science Committee, University of Chicago, Social Science Studies, 34). Chicago:

University of Chicago Press.

Wallman, S. (ed.) 179: *Ethnicity at Work*. London: Macmillan.

Wallman, S. 1984: *Eight London Households*. London: Tavistock.

Wallman, S. *et al.* 1982: *Living in South London: Perspectives on Battersea 1971–1981*. Aldershot: Gower.

Walters, A. A. 1976: *The Outer Limits and Beyond* (Discussion Paper, No. 12). London: Foundation for Business Responsibilities.

Walters, A. A. 1979: *Costs and Scale of Bus Services* (World Bank Staff Working Paper No. 325). Washington, DC: World Bank.

Walton, J., Masotti, L. H. (eds) 1976: *The City in Comparative Perspective*. New York: Wiley.

Ward, C. 1973: *Anarchy in Action*. London: Allen and Unwin.

Ward, C. (ed.) 1973: *Vandalism*. London: Architectural Press.

Ward, C. 1976: *Housing: An Anarchist Approach*. London: Freedom Press.

Ward, D. 1971: *Cities and Immigrants*. New York: Oxford UP.

Ward, P. M. 1976: The Squatter Settlement as Slum or Housing Solution: The Evidence from Mexico City. *Land Economics*, **52**, 330–46.

Ward, P. M. (ed.) 1982: *Self-Help Housing: A Critique*. London: Mansell.

Ward, R. 1986: London: The Emerging Docklands City. *Built Environment*, **12**, 117–27.

Warner, S. B. Jun. 1972: *The Urban Wilderness: A History of the American City*. New York: Harper and Row.

Warren, H., Davidge, W. R. (eds) 1930: *Decentralisation of Population and Industry: A New Principle of Town Planning*. London: P. S. King.

Watanabe, S.-I. J. 1980: Garden City Japanese-style: The Case of the Den-en-Toshi Company Ltd., 1918–28. In: Cherry, G. (ed.), 1980a, 129–43.

Wates, N. 1982a: Community Architecture is here to stay. *Architects' Journal*, **175.23**, 42–4.

Wates, N. 1982b: The Liverpool Breakthrough: or Public Sector Housing Phase 2. *Architects' Journal*, **176.36**, 51–8.

Weaver, C. 1981: Development Theory and the Regional Question: A Critique of Spatial Planning and its Detractors. In: Stöhr, W. B., Taylor, D. R. F. (eds), 1981, 73–106.

Weaver, C. 1984a: *Regional Development and the Local Community: Planning, Politics and Social Context*. London: Wiley.

Weaver, C. 1984b: Tugwell on Morningside Heights: A Review Article. *Town Planning Review*, **55**, 228–36.

Weaver, R. C. 1964: *The Urban Complex: Human Values in Urban Life*. Garden City, New York: Doubleday.

Weaver, R. C. 1966: *Dilemmas of Urban America*. Cambridge, Mass.: Harvard UP.

Weaver, R. C. 1967. The Urban Complex. In: Bellush, J., Hausknecht, M. (eds), 1967a, 90–101.

Webb, B. 1926: *My Apprenticeship*. London: Longmans Green.

Webber, M. M. 1963: Order in Diversity: Community without Propinquity. In: Wingo, L., Jun. (ed.), 1963, 23–54.

Webber, M. M. (ed.) 1964a: *Explorations into Urban Structure*. Philadelphia: University of Pennsylvania Press.

Webber, M. M. 1964b: The Urban Place and the Nonplace Urban Realm. In: Webber 1964a, 79–153.

Webber, M. M. 1968–9: Planning in an Environment of Change. *Town Planning Review*, **39**, 179–95, 277–95.

Webber, M. M. 1976: *The BART Experience – What have we learned?* Berkeley:

University of California, Institute of Urban and Regional Development and Institute of Transportation Studies (Monograph No. 26).

Weber, A. 1929: *Alfred Weber's Theory of the Location of Industries*. Translated by C. J. Friedrich. Chicago: University of Chicago Press.

Weber, M. 1966: *The City*. London: Collier–Macmillan.

Weimer, D. R. (ed.) 1962: *City and Country in America*. New York: Appleton–Century–Crofts.

Weis, D. 1951: *Die Grossstadt Essen: Die Siedlungs-, Verkehrs- und Wirtschaftliche Entwicklung des heutigen Stadgebietes von der Stiftsgründung bis zur Gegenwart* (Bonner Geographische Abhandlungen, 7). Bonn: Geographische Institut.

Weiss, M. A. 1980: The Origins and Legacy of Urban Renewal. In: Clavel, P. *et al.* (eds), 1980, 53–80.

Welfeld, I. H., Muth, R. M., Wehner, H. G., Jun., Weicher, J. C. 1974: *Perspectives on Housing and Urban Renewal* (American Enterprise Institute Perspectives, II). New York: Praeger.

Wells, H. G. 1902: *Anticipations of the Reaction of Mechanical and Scientific Progress upon Human Life and Thought*. London: Chapman and Hall.

Werner, F. 1976: *Stadtplanung Berlin: Theorie und Realität*. Part 1: *1900–1960*. Berlin: Verlag Kiepert.

Western, J. 1984: Autonomous and directed cultural change: South Africa urbanization. In: Agnew *et al.* (eds), 1984, 205–36.

Westman, T. 1962: Cityregleringens Fortsättning. *Arkitektur*, **62**, 288–97.

Westman, T. 1967: Cityreglering – nu. *Arkitektur*, **67**, 348–9.

White, L. T., III 1971: Shanghai's Polity in Cultural Revolution. In Lewis, J. W. (ed.), 1971, 325–70.

White, M. G., White, L. 1962: *The Intellectual versus the City: From Thomas Jefferson to Frank Lloyd Wright*. Cambridge, Mass.: Harvard UP and the MIT Press.

White, P. M. 1979: *Urban Planning in Britain and the Soviet Union: A Comparative Analysis* (CURS Research Memorandum, 70). Birmingham: University, Centre for Urban and Regional Studies.

Whyte, W. H. 1956: *The Organization Man*. New York: Simon and Schuster.

Whyte, W. H. 1958: Urban Sprawl. In: Editors of *Fortune* (eds), 1958, 115–39.

Wibberley, G. P. 1959: *Agriculture and Urban Growth*. London: Michael Joseph.

Wiebenson, D. 1969: *Tony Garnier and the Cité industrielle*. London: Studio Vista.

Wiener, N. 1948: *Cybernetics*. Cambridge, Mass.: MIT Press.

Wigglesworth, J. M. 1971: The Development of New Towns. In: Dwyer, D. J. (ed.), 1971, 48–69.

Wildavsky, A. 1973: If Planning is Everything, Maybe It's Nothing. *Policy Sciences*, **4**, 127–53.

Wilde, A. (ed.) 1937: Famous Women Demand Planning for Health and Beauty. *Town and Country Planning*, **5**, 132–5.

Wilde, A. (ed.) 1938: Wanted – a National Plan for Town and Countryside. *Town and Country Plananing*, **6**, 24–30.

Williams, F. B. 1916: Public Control of Private Real Estate. In: Nolen, J. (ed.), 1916a, 48–87.

Williams, F. B. 1922: *The Law of City Planning and Zoning*. New York: Macmillan.

William-Olsson, W. 1961: *Stockholm: Structure and Development*. Stockholm: Almqvist and Wiksell.

Williams-Ellis, C. 1928: *England and the Octopus*. London: Geoffrey Bles.

Williams-Ellis, C. 1933: What's the Use? In: Council for the Preservation of Rural England, 1933, 103–86.

Williams-Ellis, C. (ed.) 1937: *Britain and the Beast*. London: J. M. Dent.

Wilsher, P., Righter, R. (eds) 1975: *The Exploding Cities*. London: André Deutsch.

Wilson, J. Q. (ed.) 1966: *Urban Renewal: The Record and the Controversy*. Cambridge, Mass.: MIT Press.

Wilson, W. H. 1974: *Coming of Age in Urban America, 1915–1945*. New York: John Wiley.

Wilson, W. H. 1983: Moses and Skylarks. In: Krueckeberg, D., 1983c, 88–121.

Wilson, W. J. 1978: *The Declining Significance of Race: Blacks and Changing American Institutions*. Chicago: University of Chicago Press.

Wingo, L., Jun. (ed.) 1963: *Cities and Space: The Future Use of Urban Land*. Baltimore: Johns Hopkins UP.

Witherspoon, R. 1982: *Codevelopment: City Rebuilding by Business and Government*. Washington: Urban Land Institute.

Wohl, A. S. (ed.) 1970: *The Bitter Cry of Outcast London*. Leicester: Leicester UP.

Wohl, A. S. (ed.) 1977: *The Eternal Slum: Housing and Social Policy in Victorian London*. London: Edward Arnold.

Wohlin, H. 1969: Plandemokrati. *Plan*, **23**, 20–6.

Wohlin, H. 1977: Arvet. *Plan*, **31**, 261–7.

Wolters, R. 1978: *Stadtmitte Berlin: Stadtbaulich Entwicklungsphasen von den Anfängen bis zur Gegenwart*. Tübingen: Wasmuth.

Wood, R. C. 1959: *Suburbia: Its People and Their Politics*. Boston: Houghton Mifflin.

Wood, S. E., Heller, A. E. 1962: *California Going, Going . . .* Sacramento: California Tomorrow.

Woodcock, G. 1962: *Anarchism: A History of Liberation Ideas and Movements*. Cleveland and New York: Meridan Books.

Woods, R. A. 1914: The Neighborhood in Social Reconstruction. *Publications of the American Sociological Society*, **8**, 14–28.

Woodward, C. V. 1968: *The Comparative Approach to American History*. New York: Basic Books.

Wright, F. L. 1916: Plan by Frank Lloyd Wright. In: Yeomans, A. B. (ed.), 1916, 96–102.

Wright, F. L. 1945: *When Democracy Builds*. Chicago: University of Chicago Press.

Wright, C. 1981: *Building the Dream: A Social History of Housing in America*. Cambridge, Mass.: MIT Press.

Wright, H. 1935: *Rehousing Urban America*. New York: Columbia UP.

Wright, H. 1925: *The Road to Good Houses*. Survey, **54**, 165–8, 189.

Wrigley, R. A. 1983: The Plan of Chicago. In: Krueckeberg, D. A. (ed.), 1983c, 58–72.

Wu, C. T., Ip, D. F. 1981: China: Rural Development – alternating combinations of top–down and bottom–up strategies. In: Stöhr, W. B., Taylor, D. R. F. (eds), 1981, 155–82.

Wu, Y. L. 1967: *The Spatial Economy of Communist China: A study on Industrial Location and Transportation*. New York: Praeger.

Wynn, M. (ed.) 1984a: *Planning and Urban Growth in Southern Europe*. London: Mansell.

Wynn, M. 1948b: Spain. In: Wynn, M. (ed.), 1984a, 111–63.

Wynn, M. (ed.) 1984c: *Housing in Europe*. London: Croom Helm.

Yago, G. 1984: *The Decline of Transit: Urban Transportation in German and U.S. Cities, 1900–1970*. Cambridge: Cambridge UP.

Yazaki, T. 1973: The History of Urbanization in Japan. In: Southall, A. (ed.), 1973, 139–61.

Yeomans, A. B. 1916: *City Residential Land Development: Studies in Planning*. Chicago: University of Chicago press.

Young, K., Mason, C. (eds) 1983: *Urban Economic Development: New Roles and Relationships*. London: Macmillan.

Young, M., Willmott, P. 1957: *Family and Kinship in East London*. London: Routledge and Kegan Paul.

Young, T. 1934: *Becontree and Dagenham: The Story of the Growth of a Housing Estate*. A Report made for the Pilgrim Trust. London: Becontree Social Survey Committee.

Zimmer, B. 1966: The Small Businessman and Location. In: Wilson, J. Q., 1966, 380–403.

Zipf, G. K. 1949: *Human Behavior and the Principle of Least Effort*. Cambridge, Mass.: Addison–Wesley.

Zorbaugh, H. W. 1929: *The Gold Coast and the Slum: A Sociological Study of Chicago's near North Side*. Chicago: University of Chicago Press.

Zwerling, S. 1974: *Mass Transit and the Politics of Technology: A Study of BART and the San Francisco Bay Area*. New York: Praeger.

Index

Notes: All cities, important suburbs and developments have been included without indications of their countries, but there are full entries under each country. Groups, government departments, reports etc. are generally British, except where otherwise indicated.

AA *see* Architectural Association
Aalto, A., 290
Abercrombie, P., 312
  background, 165, 321
  on Berlin, 33
  on bungalows, 81–2
  and garden and satellite cities, 105,
    109, 112
  on Geddes, 139, 140–1
  and Greater London Plan, 53, 134–5,
    165–6, 168–73, 220–1, 308, 310
  on planning objectives, 182–3, 323–4
Abrams, C., 35–6, 232, 252, 287, 322–3
ACRD (Allegheny Conference), 231
academic planning *see* planning
Ackerman, F., 39, 148
Adams, T., 156–9, 161, 164–6
Addams, J., 40, 41, 44, 123, 126, 366
Addison, C., 71, 74
Addison Act (1919), 71, 108, 117
Adelaide, 89
Adickes, F., 58, 117
Adshead, S. D., 165, 190–1, 321
advocate-planners, 332–3
Africa, city beautiful in, 189–92
agriculture, 285, 284, 287, 290
air, fresh *see* ventilation
alcohol, 18, 28

Aldrich, L., 282
Alduy, J. -P., 314
Alexander, C., 10, 258, 260
Alexander, L. A., 211
Allegheny Conference on Regional
  Development, 231
Alternativ Stad (Sweden), 312
Alton West, 225
Altshuler, A. A., 331
American City Planning Institute, 322
American Institute of Planners (*earlier*
  National Conference), 322
anarchism
  and regional planning, 143–4
  and roots of planning, 3, 5, 9
  triumph of *see* autonomous community
Anderson, M., 232, 233
Anderson, W., 300
Anson, B., 265–6
Anthony, H. A., 209
apartments *see* flats; garden apartments
ARCH *see* Architectural Renewal
  Committee
architects and mass transit and suburbs,
  76, 77–85
  see also individual names of architects
Architectural Association, 220–2, 225,
  248–9, 266

Index Compiled by Ann Hall